D0753499

AFRICAN HISTORICAL DICTIONARIES
Edited by Jon Woronoff

1. *Cameroon,* by Victor T. LeVine and Roger P. Nye. 1974. Out of print. See No. 48.
2. *The Congo,* 2nd ed., by Virginia Thompson and Richard Adloff. 1984
3. *Swaziland,* by John J. Grotpeter. 1975
4. *The Gambia,* 2nd ed., by Harry A. Gailey. 1987
5. *Botswana,* by Richard P. Stevens. 1975. Out of print. See No. 44.
6. *Somalia,* by Margaret F. Castagno. 1975
7. *Benin [Dahomey],* 2nd ed., by Samuel Decalo. 1987. Out of print. See No. 61.
8. *Burundi,* by Warren Weinstein. 1976
9. *Togo,* 2nd ed., by Samuel Decalo. 1987
10. *Lesotho,* by Gordon Haliburton. 1977
11. *Mali,* 2nd ed., by Pascal James Imperato. 1986
12. *Sierra Leone,* by Cyril Patrick Foray. 1977
13. *Chad,* 2nd ed., by Samuel Decalo. 1987
14. *Upper Volta,* by Daniel Miles McFarland. 1978
15. *Tanzania,* by Laura S. Kurtz. 1978
16. *Guinea,* 2nd ed., by Thomas O'Toole. 1987
17. *Sudan,* by John Voll. 1978. Out of print. See No. 53.
18. *Rhodesia / Zimbabwe,* by R. Kent Rasmussen. 1979. Out of print. See No. 46.
19. *Zambia,* by John J. Grotpeter. 1979
20. *Niger,* 2nd ed., by Samuel Decalo. 1989
21. *Equatorial Guinea,* 2nd ed., by Max Liniger-Goumaz. 1988
22. *Guinea-Bissau,* 2nd ed., by Richard Lobban and Joshua Forrest. 1988
23. *Senegal,* by Lucie G. Colvin. 1981. Out of print. See No. 65.
24. *Morocco,* by William Spencer. 1980
25. *Malawi,* by Cynthia A. Crosby. 1980. Out of print. See No. 54.
26. *Angola,* by Phyllis Martin. 1980. Out of print. See No. 52.
27. *The Central African Republic,* by Pierre Kalck. 1980. Out of print. See No. 51.
28. *Algeria,* by Alf Andrew Heggoy. 1981. Out of print. See No. 66.
29. *Kenya,* by Bethwell A. Ogot. 1981
30. *Gabon,* by David E. Gardinier. 1981. Out of print. See No. 58.
31. *Mauritania,* by Alfred G. Gerteiny. 1981
32. *Ethiopia,* by Chris Prouty and Eugene Rosenfeld. 1981. Out of print. See No. 56.
33. *Libya,* 2nd ed., by Ronald Bruce St John. 1991
34. *Mauritius,* by Lindsay Rivière. 1982. Out of print. See No. 49.
35. *Western Sahara,* by Tony Hodges. 1982. Out of print. See No. 55.

36. *Egypt,* by Joan Wucher King. 1984. Out of print. See No. 67.
37. *South Africa,* by Christopher Saunders. 1983
38. *Liberia,* by D. Elwood Dunn and Svend E. Holsoe. 1985
39. *Ghana,* by Daniel Miles McFarland. 1985. Out of print. See No. 63.
40. *Nigeria,* by Anthony Oyewole. 1987
41. *Ivory Coast,* by Robert J. Mundt. 1987
42. *Cape Verde,* 2nd ed., by Richard Lobban and Marilyn Halter. 1988. Out of print. See No. 62.
43. *Zaire,* by F. Scott Bobb. 1988
44. *Botswana,* by Fred Morton, Andrew Murray, and Jeff Ramsay. 1989
45. *Tunisia,* by Kenneth J. Perkins. 1989
46. *Zimbabwe,* 2nd ed., by R. Kent Rasmussen and Steven L. Rubert. 1990
47. *Mozambique,* by Mario Azevedo. 1991
48. *Cameroon,* 2nd ed., by Mark W. DeLancey and H. Mbella Mokeba. 1990
49. *Mauritius,* 2nd ed., by Sydney Selvon. 1991
50. *Madagascar,* by Maureen Covell. 1995
51. *The Central African Republic,* 2nd ed., by Pierre Kalck; translated by Thomas O'Toole. 1992
52. *Angola,* 2nd ed., by Susan H. Broadhead. 1992
53. *Sudan,* 2nd ed., by Carolyn Fluehr-Lobban, Richard A. Lobban, Jr., and John Obert Voll. 1992
54. *Malawi,* 2nd ed., by Cynthia A. Crosby. 1993
55. *Western Sahara,* 2nd ed., by Anthony Pazzanita and Tony Hodges. 1994
56. *Ethiopia and Eritrea,* 2nd ed., by Chris Prouty and Eugene Rosenfeld. 1994
57. *Namibia,* by John J. Grotpeter. 1994
58. *Gabon,* 2nd ed., by David Gardinier. 1994
59. *Comoro Islands,* by Martin Ottenheimer and Harriet Ottenheimer. 1994
60. *Rwanda,* by Learthen Dorsey. 1994
61. *Benin,* 3rd ed., by Samuel Decalo. 1994
62. *Republic of Cape Verde,* 3rd ed., by Richard Lobban and Marlene Lopes. 1994
63. *Ghana,* 2nd ed., by David Owusu-Ansah and Daniel Miles McFarland. 1994
64. *Uganda,* by M. Louise Pirouet. 1994
65. *Senegal,* 2nd ed., by Andrew F. Clark and Lucie Colvin Phillips. 1994
66. *Algeria,* 2nd ed., by Phillip Chiviges Naylor and Alf Andrew Heggoy. 1994
67. *Egypt,* by Arthur Goldschmidt, Jr. 1994

Historical Dictionary of EGYPT

by

ARTHUR GOLDSCHMIDT, JR.

African Historical Dictionaries, No. 67

The Scarecrow Press, Inc.
Metuchen, N.J., & London
1994

Maps on pages xi and xii are reprinted from *Atlas of the Middle East*, United States Central Intelligence Agency, Washington, DC: U.S. Government Printing Office, 1993, p. 24.

British Library Cataloguing-in-Publication data available

Library of Congress Cataloging-in-Publication Data

Goldschmidt, Arthur, 1938–
Historical dictionary of Egypt / by Arthur Goldschmidt, Jr.
p. cm. — (African historical dictionaries ; no. 67)
Includes bibliographical references (p.).
ISBN 0-8108-2949-5 (alk. paper)
1. Egypt—History—1517–1882 —Dictionaries. 2. Egypt—History—1798- —Dictionaries. 3. Egypt—History—1517–1882 —Bibliography. 4. Egypt—History—1798- —Bibliography. I. Title. II. Series.
DT75.G65 1994
962'.003—dc20 94-33856

Manufactured in the United States of America
Printed on acid-free paper

DEDICATED TO MY PARENTS

Arthur E. Goldschmidt
and
Elizabeth Wickenden Goldschmidt

TABLE OF CONTENTS

EDITOR'S FOREWORD

No country has a longer history, and few a more eventful one, than Egypt. It has generated extraordinary civilizations and passed through moments of exceptional glory, only to experience times of decline and rebirth. A vital passage from east to west and north to south, it has also figured prominently in world history from its origins to the present day. The emphasis here is on the present day. For, although less noticed than under more charismatic leaders, Egypt still plays an important role in Arab affairs and its actions are significant for the whole region and beyond.

For these reasons, it is always useful to know more about Egypt, even when it is not in the headlines. This *Historical Dictionary of Egypt* makes a serious contribution to such knowledge. Focusing on the modern and contemporary periods, it presents numerous notable Egyptians, not only rulers and politicians, but also economists, academics, entrepreneurs, and cultural and religious figures. Other entries provide information about crucial organizations, parties, institutions, events, and aspects of the political, economic, social, cultural, and religious scenes. This dictionary is rounded out by a handy chronology, which does go back to Egypt's origins, and a selective bibliography that helps readers find further literature on aspects of particular interest.

This volume was written by one of our leading authorities on Egypt, Arthur Goldschmidt, Jr. A professor of history at the Pennsylvania State University, Dr. Goldschmidt has written extensively on Egypt, including his book *Modern Egypt: The Formation of a Nation-State* and the broader *Concise History of the Middle East*. He has visited Egypt frequently, including a stint as a visiting professor at Cairo University, and closely follows the literature in English and Arabic. His experience as a teacher has certainly contributed to making this historical dictionary a useful, and very readable, guide to modern Egypt.

Jon Woronoff
Series Editor

ACKNOWLEDGMENTS

"Fools rush in where angels fear to tread" should be the motto applied to anyone who undertakes to write a historical dictionary of Egypt. Because historians of this country commonly divide themselves by period, this writer, a specialist in modern and contemporary history, chose 1760, the accession date for the first governor who tried to westernize Egypt, as the starting point, although the Introduction, Chronology, and Bibliography provide an overview of the whole span of Egypt's history. Even with the abbreviated time period for the Dictionary, rendering the title slightly inaccurate, the book threatens to overwhelm both its readers and its writer. Writing it was a challenge, forcing the author to read widely in aspects of Egypt's economic, social, cultural, and intellectual history in order to provide needed depth. Special credit is due to the previous *Historical Dictionary of Egypt*, by Joan Wucher King. Scholars have used it for a decade; this volume cannot fully replace it.

I am grateful to my wife, Louise, for encouraging me when I was most discouraged and for enduring lonely evenings and weekends when I was preoccupied with this project. I acknowledge the research assistance of Thad Merriman and of the reference staff of Penn State's Pattee Library, especially Bruce Bonta. Nicole Fedeli, Craig Fisher, Omar Imady, Robert Johnston, Kenneth Mayers, Thomas Naff, Mark Sponenburgh, Robert Tifft, and Richard Zionts helped me on specific problems. Any errors that remain in this book are my own. In this age of computerized word processing, it will be easy to correct for future editions any errors that reviewers and users call to my attention.

I have dedicated this book to my father, Arthur E. Goldschmidt, who read it in manuscript and offered helpful advice and encouragement, and my mother, Elizabeth Wickenden, whose oft-repeated insistence that historians should treat economic and social issues as well as politics, war, and diplomacy, found an echo in my writing of this *Historical Dictionary of Egypt*.

Arthur Goldschmidt, Jr.
Pennsylvania State University

CONVENTIONS

A few conventions need to be noted. All measurements are metric except for the use of "feddans" for land measurement and "cantars" for quantities of cotton, or in the rare case when English measurements were being used in a document that I paraphrased. All dates are based on the Gregorian calendar; Muslims use a 12-month lunar calendar in which the Prophet Muhammad's *hijra* ("emigration") from Mecca to Medina is the year 1, corresponding to 622 CE. Transliteration of Arabic names and terms follows the system of the *Middle East Journal*, which I find easier to read than that of the Library of Congress. The Arabic letter *ayn* is represented by an apostrophe when it appears in the middle or end of a word. No attempt is made to represent the glottal stop, or *hamza*. Such prerevolutionary titles as "pasha" and "bey" have usually been omitted, as have most contemporary titles such as "Dr." Military ranks are rendered in English only when relevant to an entry; a separate table of the old and new military ranks, adopted after the 1952 Revolution, is provided. Most organizations are given the names, whether English or Arabic, by which they are most widely known, but cross-references are provided. Personal names are alphabetized by surnames, but references in the text follow Egyptian vernacular usage, in cases when first names are most common. Arabic words commonly used in English appear in roman type; italics are used for those which have not yet been assimilated into English.

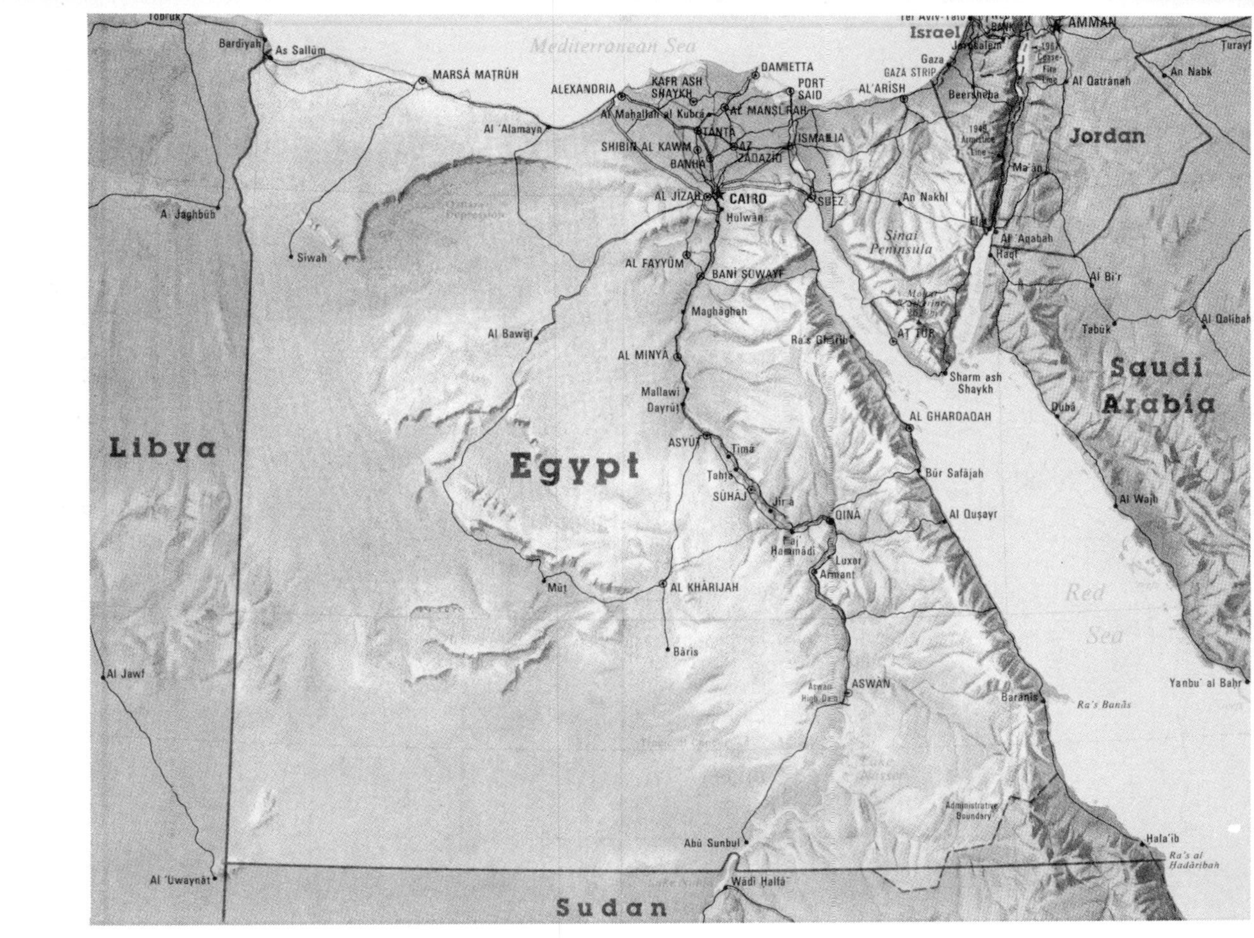
Mediterranean Sea
Libya
Egypt
Sudan
Israel
Jordan
Saudi Arabia
Red Sea
Sinai Peninsula
Bardiyah
As Sallūm
MARSĀ MAṬRŪḤ
ALEXANDRIA
KAFR ASH SHAYKH
DAMIETTA
PORT SAID
Al Maḥallah al Kubrā
AL MANṢŪRAH
ṬANṬĀ
SHIBĪN AL KAWM
BANHĀ
AZ ZAQĀZĪQ
ISMAILIA
AL 'ARĪSH
GAZA STRIP
Gaza
Beersheba
AMMAN
Al Qaṭrānah
An Nabk
Ma'ān
Al 'Alamayn
A. Jaghbūb
Siwah
AL JĪZAH
CAIRO
Ḥulwān
SUEZ
An Nakhl
Al 'Aqabah
Ḥaql
Al Bi'r
Tabūk
Al Qalībah
AL FAYYŪM
BANĪ SUWAYF
Maghāghah
Al Bawīṭi
AL MINYĀ
Mallawi
Dayrūṭ
ASYŪṬ
Ṭimā
Ṭahṭā
SŪHĀJ
Jirjā
QINĀ
Naj' Ḥammādī
Luxor
Armant
AL KHĀRIJAH
Mūṭ
Bārīs
Ra's Gharib
AT ṬŪR
Sharm ash Shaykh
Ḍubā
AL GHARDAQAH
Būr Safājah
Al Quṣayr
Al Wajh
ASWĀN
Aswan High Dam
Barānis
Ra's Banās
Yanbu' al Baḥr
Administrative Boundary
Ḥalā'ib
Ra's al Ḥaḍāribah
Abū Sunbul
Wādī Ḥalfā
Al Jawf
Al 'Uwaynāt

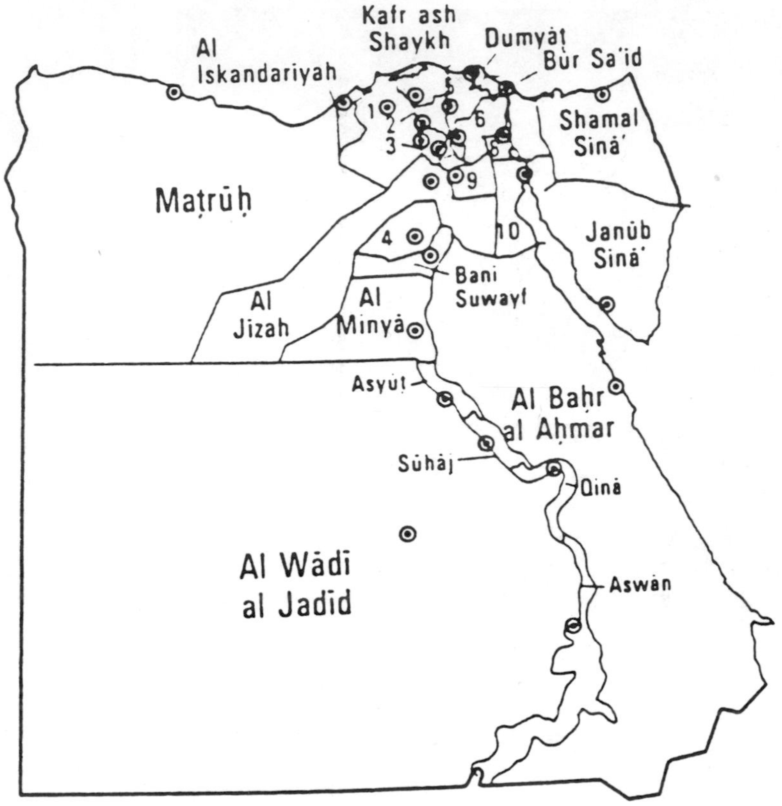

Administrative Divisions

Egypt has 26 governorates (*muḥāfaẓat*, singular *muḥāfaẓah*).

⊙ Governorate capital

1. Ad Daqahliyah
2. Al Buḥayrah
3. Al Fayyūm
4. Al Gharbīyah
5. Al Ismā'īliyah
6. Al Minūfiyah
7. Al Qāhirah
8. Al Qalyūbiyah
9. Ash Sharqiyah
10. As Suways

ABBREVIATIONS AND ACRONYMS

AID	Agency for International Development (U.S.)
ARE	Arab Republic of Egypt
ASU	Arab Socialist Union
AUC	American University in Cairo
BBC	British Broadcasting Corporation
CENTO	Central Treaty Organization ("Baghdad Pact")
CUP	Committee of Union and Progress ("Young Turks")
EEF	Egyptian Expeditionary Force
EFU	Egyptian Feminist Union
EMNL	Egyptian Movement for National Liberation
GODE	Gulf Organization for the Development of Egypt
IBRD	International Bank for Reconstruction and Development
IMF	International Monetary Fund
LE	*Livre égyptienne*, or Egyptian pound
NATO	North Atlantic Treaty Organization
NCWS	National Committee of Workers and Students
NDP	National Democratic Party
NFTUE	National Federation of Trade Unions in Egypt
NPUP	National Progressive Unionist Party (*al-Tajammu'*)
NSPO	National Service Project Organization
OAU	Organization of African Unity
PLO	Palestine Liberation Organization
RCC	Revolutionary Command Council
SCUA	Suez Canal Users Association

SLP	Socialist Labor Party
UAR	United Arab Republic
UN	United Nations
UNEF	United Nations Emergency Force
UNRWA	United Nations Relief and Works Agency
USSR	Union of Soviet Socialist Republics
YMMA	Young Men's Muslim Association (*al-Shubban al-Muslimin*)

CHRONOLOGY

3100–2700 BCE	Protodynastic Period; Upper and Lower Egypt unified; approximate dates of Dynasties I-II.
2700–2175	Old Kingdom; Dynasties III-VII.
2175–1991	First Intermediate Period; Dynasties VIII-X.
1991–1786	Middle Kingdom; Dynasties XI-XII.
1786–1575	Second Intermediate Period; Dynasties XIII-XVII.
1678–1575	Hyksos occupation; Dynasties XV-XVII.
1575–332	New Kingdom; Dynasties XVIII-XXX.
751–656	Axumite occupation (Dynasty XXV), partial overlap with Saite Period.
668–525	Saite Period (Dynasty XXVI); struggle with Assyria and Babylonia.
525–404	Persian occupation; Dynasty XXVII.
404–343	Late Egyptian Period; Dynasties XXVIII-XXX.
343–332	Second Persian occupation; Dynasty XXXI.
332–323	Reign of Alexander the Great.
323–30	Ptolemaic Period.
30 BCE-642 CE	Roman occupation.
639–642	Arab conquest of Egypt.
642–661	Rightly Guided Caliphs, ruling from Medina.
661–750	Umayyad Caliphs, ruling from Syria.
750–868	Abbasid Caliphs, ruling from Iraq.
868–905	Tulunid Dynasty in Egypt and Syria.
905–934	Abbasid Caliphs restored in Egypt.
934–969	Ikhshidid Dynasty in Egypt and Syria.

969–1171	Fatimid Caliphs in Egypt, Syria, and the Hijaz.
1171–1250	Ayyubid Dynasty in Egypt and Syria.
1250–1382	Bahri Mamluks in Egypt and Syria.
1382–1517	Burji Mamluks in Egypt and Syria.
1517–1798	Ottoman Sultans, ruling from Istanbul.
1760–1772	Ali Bey, Governor.
1772–1775	Muhammad Bey "Abu al-Dhahab," Governor.
1798	Invasion by Napoléon Bonaparte.
1798–1801	French occupation.
1801–1802	First British occupation.
1801–1914	Restored Ottoman suzerainty (nominal).
1802–1803	Khusrev, Governor (Pasha) of Egypt.
1803–1804	Power struggle in Egypt.
1804–1805	[Ahmad] Khurshid, Governor.
1805–1848	Muhammad Ali, Governor.
1831–1840	Egyptian conquest and occupation of Syria.
1840	London Convention.
1848	Ibrahim, Acting Governor.
1848–1854	Abbas Hilmi I, Governor.
1854–1863	[Muhammad] Said, Governor.
1854	Said and De Lesseps sign Suez Canal concession.
1856–1869	Construction of Suez Canal.
1863–1879	Isma'il, Governor and Khedive.
1876	Establishment of the Caisse de la Dette Publique.
1878	Establishment of the Dual Financial Control.
1879–1892	[Muhammad] Tawfiq, Khedive.
1881–1882	Nationalist movement led by Colonel Ahmad Urabi.
1882–1936	British occupation.
1883–1907	Sir Evelyn Baring, Earl of Cromer, British agent.

1892–1914	Abbas Hilmi II, Khedive.
1914	British declare Protectorate over Egypt.
1914–1917	Husayn Kamil, Sultan.
1917–1936	[Ahmad] Fuad I, Sultan and King.
1919–1922	1919 Revolution against British occupation.
1922	British declare Egypt independent.
1923–1952	Era of the 1923 Constitution.
1936–1952	Faruq, King.
1936–1954	Anglo-Egyptian Treaty limits British occupation.
1948–1949	Egypt defeated by Israel in Palestine War.
1952	Egyptian Army overthrows King Faruq.
1952–1953	[Ahmad] Fuad II, King (nominal).
1953–1954	Muhammad Najib, President.
1954–1970	Jamal Abd al-Nasir, Prime Minister and President.
1956	Egypt nationalizes Suez Canal Company, sparking Suez Crisis and War.
1958–1961	Egypt and Syria form United Arab Republic.
1962–1967	Egypt involved in Yemen Civil War.
1967	Israel defeats Egypt in June War; Israel occupies Gaza and Sinai; Arab leaders in Khartum oppose negotiations; UN Security Council passes Resolution 242, calling for Israeli withdrawal and peace.
1968–1970	Egypt and Israel fight War of Attrition.
1970	Egypt accepts Rogers Peace Plan and cease-fire with Israel; Nasir dies.
1970–1981	Anwar al-Sadat, President.
1971	Corrective Revolution.

1973	October War; Egypt crosses Suez Canal into Sinai; UN Security Council passes Resolutions 338 and 340, calling for peace negotiations.
1974	Egyptian-Israeli Separation-of-Forces Agreement.
1975	Suez Canal reopened; Egyptian-Israeli Agreement.
1977	Sadat flies to Jerusalem, addresses Knesset, and proposes peace with Israel.
1978	Camp David Accords between Egypt and Israel.
1979	Egyptian-Israeli Peace Treaty; most Arab states break diplomatic ties with Egypt; Arab League expels Egypt; Egypt and Israel begin talks on Palestinian autonomy in West Bank and Gaza Strip.
1980	Egyptian-Israeli border opened.
1980–1988	Iran-Iraq War; Egypt aids Iraq.
1981	Muslim-Coptic rioting in Zawiya al-Hamra; Anwar al-Sadat orders arrest of many political opponents; Sadat assassinated during military parade.
1981-present	Husni Mubarak, President.
1982	Israel's forces withdraw from Sinai, except for strip at Taba; Israelis invade Lebanon, causing Egypt to suspend Palestinian Autonomy Talks with Israel.
1985	*Achille Lauro* Incident harms Egypt-U.S. relations.
1986	Central Security Force riots in Cairo; Egypt and Israel submit Taba dispute to binding arbitration.
1987	Amman summit authorizes Arab states to resume diplomatic ties with Egypt.
1989	Egypt readmitted to Arab League; regains Taba.

1990–1991	Iraq-Kuwait Conflict; Egypt aids allied coalition against Iraq; Western countries forgive $14 billion of Egypt's foreign debt.
1992	Earthquake; Islamist attacks on officials, Copts, and foreigners increase.
1993	Many Egyptian Islamists arrested, tried, and executed; unrest continues in Cairo and provinces.
1994	Egypt's government facilitates PLO-Israeli negotiations.

INTRODUCTION

Egypt is the world's oldest continuous country, with a recorded past of over six thousand years. Often invaded, conquered, and occupied by foreign armies, Egypt has never lost its identity. The Egyptians of today, although they have changed their language once and their religion twice, descend mainly from the Egyptians who built the Giza Pyramids and the Temple of Karnak, who served Alexander the Great and his heirs, who submitted to Augustus Caesar and raised much of the grain that fed the Roman Empire, who started Christian monasticism and the veneration of the Virgin Mary, and who advanced and sustained Muslim learning in what is now the longest-functioning university in the world.

Located in the northeastern corner of Africa, but with a mountainous extension across the Gulf of Suez, the Sinai Peninsula, a part of Asia, Egypt is an almost square block of mostly arid land: 995,450 sq km, to be exact. Its greatest extent is 1,024 km south to north (from 22° to 32° N) and 1,240 km west to east (from 26° to 36° E. It is bounded on the north by the Mediterranean Sea, on the east by Israel and the Red Sea, on the south by the Sudan, and on the west by Libya. Most of its political borders are straight lines drawn by the European colonial powers in the twentieth century; all have been disputed before and since they were defined. All but 3.5 percent of its territory is marsh or desert, sparsely inhabited until recently by Christian monks or bedouin nomads. Almost all of Egypt's settled inhabitants depend for their sustenance on the River Nile, the longest river in Africa. The Nile has cut a troughlike valley, ranging from 3 to 15 km in width, through the plateau of northeast Africa; its silt has added the fan-shaped Delta, measuring 22,000 sq km. Through it flows the Nile's main distributary branches–the eastern one to Damietta, the western one to Rosetta; there used to be four or five smaller channels. Some of the northern Delta is occupied by freshwater lakes. In southern Egypt, the Nile was broken by a series of cascades and rapids commonly called the First Cataract, historically a barrier to navigation and the border between Upper Egypt and Nubia. The Nile Valley and Delta, home to approximately 60 million Egyptians in 1994, are bounded by the First Cataract (or, since the 1960s, by the Aswan High Dam and Lake Nasir), the mountainous Arabian desert, the sandier Libyan desert, and the Mediterranean Sea. Egypt is, in short, a well-defined country.

Egypt is also a hot and dry country. Summer temperatures may reach 43° C in Cairo and 49° C in the deserts. Winter temperatures rarely fall below 0° C, except in the higher elevations of the Sinai. Most Egyptians have never seen or felt snow. Rain occurs mainly along the Mediterranean coast, averaging 80 mm yearly, but falling sporadically in irregular amounts. Winters are mild in daytime, cold at night. Springtime may be punctuated by hot sandstorms, called *khamsin* in Arabic, that irritate humans and animals and may endanger crops. Morning fog is common in Lower Egypt and becoming so around Lake Nasir. Although air pollution is beginning to aggravate Cairo and Alexandria, Egypt's climate is generally healthful.

From the dawn of history, human habitation hinged on the Egyptian people's ability to harness the River Nile, which annually flooded its banks, depositing a fertile alluvium of silt brought down from Lakes Victoria and Albert and from the mountains of Ethiopia. The creation of a system of basin irrigation to capture the silt and to store the floodwaters, and of efficient devices to raise water from the channels and basins to the fields, was a prerequisite for the evolution of Egyptian agriculture between six and three millennia before the birth of Jesus Christ.

The Nile was not only the sustainer of people, their animals, and their crops; it was also the main means by which they transported themselves and their goods from one part of Egypt to another. In ancient times, Egyptians viewed the Nile Valley as a world unto itself. By the time of Jesus Christ, however, Egypt was also exporting its agricultural and manufactured products throughout the known world. Port cities on the Mediterranean and Red seas enabled Egyptians to buy and sell goods from China to Spain, and all the lands between, throughout the Christian and Muslim eras of their history. During the nineteenth and twentieth centuries, the rapid expansion of its export trade caused Egypt to develop perennial irrigation, facilitating the storage of greater quantities of Nile water and the production of two or three annual crops from the same fields. The construction of a maritime canal across the Isthmus of Suez enhanced Egypt's geographic and strategic location in relation to Europe, South Asia, and East Africa in the late nineteenth century. Now, in the late-twentieth century, the construction of the High Dam has extended Egypt's arable land and crop yields, while the creation of the Sumed Pipeline and new aerial and maritime port facilities has reinforced its central position in world trade.

Egypt's salubrious climate, beneficent river, and strategic location have combined to make it one of the world's best-known countries, one that most aspirants to world power have tried to master. Its history, therefore, has been marked by successive subjection to a series of non-Egyptian rulers: Nubians, Assyrians, Persians, Macedonians, Greeks, Romans, Arabs, Turks, Circassians, French, and British. Only at rare intervals did ethnic Egyptians fight in, let alone command, their armies and navies. Seldom did any Egyptians govern Egypt as a whole or serve in its highest administrative posts. They did wield power in local government, the law courts, the schools, and specific niches of the bureaucracy (as did the Coptic Christians in government accounting), but not as a people free from foreign rule. Even many aspects of Egypt's domestic economy were controlled by foreign residents: Greeks, Italians, Armenians, Syrians, and Jews. Only in 1956 could Egyptians finally claim to be masters in their own house.

How and why has Egypt seen this combination of continuous existence with recurrent subjection to outsiders? Egypt's history is long in duration and rich in detail. Ancient Egypt measured its own past by dynasties, more than 30, that ruled from around 3000 BCE, when the Upper and Lower kingdoms were united, until 332 BCE, when Alexander the Great added the Nile Valley and Delta to his expanding empire. But even ancient Egypt was subjected at interludes to invasion and conquest by Hyksos, Nubians, Assyrians, and Persians.

Alexander's conquest led to the creation of Alexandria, a great port city and intellectual center that connected the Mediterranean world with the Nile Valley, and to the Ptolemies, whose line of rulers ended with the tragic Queen Cleopatra VII (r. 51–30 BCE). Hellenistic Egypt continued under the Romans, who, as Christianity spread from Egypt westward to North Africa and Europe, evolved into Byzantines. No matter whether their masters ruled from Rome or from Constantinople, Egypt's Christians, the Copts, who traced their conversion to the evangelism of St. Mark in 40 CE, felt oppressed by high taxes and religious intolerance. Coptic Christianity broke with the Orthodox church in 451, when its Council of Chalcedon anathematized the Monophysite doctrine, held by Copts and other Middle Eastern Christians, that Christ's nature was wholly divine. For the next two centuries Orthodox and Monophysite Christianity fought a doctrinal war in Alexandria and other early Christian centers in the Middle East, unwittingly paving the way for the rise of Islam.

After another Persian interlude early in the seventh century, the Byzantines reestablished their control of Egypt until the Arab conquest of 639–642. For Egypt, the Arabs came as liberators. Early Muslim rule meant religious tolerance and lighter taxes, not forced conversion to Islam, which taught that God had spoken to a series of prophets, of whom the last was Muhammad, an unlettered Meccan merchant, to whom he had revealed the Quran, as earlier God had revealed the Torah to the Jews and the Gospels to the Christians. Muslims, therefore, respected Jews and Christians as peoples who had received scriptures and who could live within the lands of Islam without being molested, let alone converted. Coptic Christianity remained the country's majority religion until the tenth century. Conversions to Islam were discouraged at first because the state wanted the revenue generated by a special tax paid only by non-Muslims. From 642 to 868 Egypt was a province in an Arab empire, in which a tiny Muslim elite ruled a non-Muslim peasant majority. Even when Egypt escaped from Abbasid control, under Ahmad Ibn Tulun in 868, it was only to exchange distant caliphs in Baghdad for a dynasty of Turkic origin governing in Fustat, a garrison town near the site of modern Cairo. The next ruling family, the Ikhshidids, were equally foreign.

The Fatimid conquest in 969 was a watershed, not only because the new rulers espoused Isma'ili Shi'ism and hence challenged the legitimacy of the Sunni Abbasid caliphate, but also because they brought in bedouin Arabs who ravaged Nile Valley lands, then settled and later intermingled with the local inhabitants. As most Egyptians embraced Islam, they chose the Sunni sect of the Abbasid caliphate over the Shi'ism of their Fatimid rulers. Even the creation of al-Azhar as a mosque-university dedicated to training Shi'i propagandists aided the Fatimids more in other parts of the Muslim world than in Egypt itself. And few Egyptians regretted their passing from power when a Kurdish adventurer named Salah al-Din ("Saladin" to the Europeans) took control in Cairo in 1171, founded the Ayyubid dynasty, took over Syria, and captured most of Palestine from the Crusaders. The Ayyubids fended off Crusader attacks by land and sea, patronized architects and ulama ("Muslim scholars"), and developed a corps of slaves, called Mamluks (from the Arabic word, *mamluk*, meaning "owned man"), as their main fighting force.

These Mamluks, who seized control of Egypt in 1250, saved the country from the Mongol invasions that destroyed so much of Central and Southwest Asia. The early Mamluks, locally called *bahri* (referring to the Nile, which Egyptians call *al-Bahr*, "the sea," because of its size), were of Central Asian Turkic origin. Imported by Middle Eastern rulers for their skill at riding and fighting on horseback, they became a remarkable ruling caste for Egypt and Syria, continually refreshing their numbers by importing Central Asian Turkic boys and training them to become soldiers and governors. Only the ablest rose to the leadership of the state. The Bahri Mamluk era, 1250–1382, was one of commercial prosperity and cultural flowering in Egypt. The later Mamluks, called *burji* (pertaining to the *burj*, or fortress, in which some of them lived), were mainly Circassians imported from the Caucasus mountains east of the Black Sea. Their factional rivalries, exacerbated by the effects of the Black Plague, impoverished Egypt, and their exactions from European merchants trading with Asia led inadvertently to the Portuguese maritime explorations around the African continent and the Spanish voyages to the Americas, as Christian Europe sought ways to bypass the Muslim world.

The rise of the Ottoman state in Anatolia and the Balkans did not seem to threaten Mamluk rule in Egypt and Syria, for the Ottomans and the Mamluks were both Sunni Muslims and their natural enemies were the European Christians and the rising Safavid Shi'i state in Azerbaijan. But Ottoman Sultan Selim I (r. 1512–20), who defeated the Safavids in 1514 but could not conquer all of Iran, turned against the Mamluks, whom he suspected of aiding the Shi'ites, and defeated them at the north Syrian village of Marj Dabiq in 1516. Within a year, Egypt, along with Syria and the Hijaz, had become a part of the Ottoman Empire, the largest and longest-lasting Muslim state in history. From 1517 to 1798, even though nominally under governors appointed by the Ottoman sultan, the real rulers of Egypt were the Mamluks, who evolved into a hereditary caste of landowners who exploited the people. As European power began to eclipse that of the Ottomans, occasional Mamluk adventurers, such as Ali Bey and Muhammad Abu-Dhahab, defied their nominal overlords, built up strong armies, and invaded Syria and the Hijaz. They portended the westernizing reformers of the next century.

In June 1798 a French armada commanded by Napoléon Bonaparte landed at Alexandria, debouching the "Army of Egypt," a large force of soldiers, accompanied by a commission of scientists and scholars, who quickly conquered Lower Egypt from the Mamluks. For three years the French ruled in Cairo, setting in motion forces that would change Egypt and the rest of the Middle East forever. But the revolutionary forces came not from Napoléon and his savants; they were generated by Muslim military adventurers who learned from the French conquest and occupation that they must westernize their armies and governments to survive. The main agent of Egypt's transformation during the nineteenth century was an illiterate soldier of fortune, second in command of an Albanian regiment that came to Cairo as part of the Anglo-Ottoman force to replace the French occupation in 1801. By exploiting rivalries among the Mamluks and winning the support of local ulama and mystic and artisan guilds, Muhammad Ali managed to have himself named Ottoman governor of Egypt in 1805. Gradually but inexorably, he built up a mighty army and navy, buttressed by a government that seized control of most of Egypt's agricultural land. More than any other nineteenth-century Westernizing reformer, Muhammad Ali perceived the need for economic development, including cash crops that could be exported, canals to facilitate transport and irrigation, and factories to produce munitions, warships, and textiles. Although his rule was harsh and extortionate for the Egyptian people, it made Egypt a military power in its own right. Initially aiding the Ottoman Empire against Arabian and Greek rebels, Muhammad Ali later turned his army against the sultan, occupying Syria and the Hijaz in 1831. More remarkably, the soldiers who made up most of that army were Egyptian peasants, conscripted for the first time since antiquity. These peasants resisted military service, which they viewed as their death sentence, but they learned to drill and shoot well enough to defeat the Ottoman Turks. Their victories alarmed the European powers, which feared Muhammad Ali's success would undo the peace settlement that followed the Napoleonic Wars. They insisted on restoring Ottoman rule in most of the Middle East, but did leave Muhammad Ali with a governorship–one that he could pass down to his heirs–over Egypt, the Sudan, and portions of the Hijaz. Muhammad Ali, obliged to contract his army and to admit European manufactures, relinquished the state's monopoly over Egyptian agriculture and let the factories, schools, and military academies fall into desuetude. But he did not let European troops enter Egypt, allow Westerners to build railroads or canals in the country, or borrow money from foreign banks.

Muhammad Ali's heirs proved less capable. Under his grandson, Abbas Hilmi I (r. 1848–54), British entrepreneurs introduced the first railroad and telegraph lines into Egypt. His youngest son, Sa'id (r. 1854–63), signed a concession agreement with a French diplomat to form the company that built the maritime canal across the Isthmus of Suez, although Egyptians bitterly recall that they provided much of the money and nearly all the labor for its construction. His energetic grandson, Isma'il (r. 1863–79), undertook a Westernization program, more ambitious in its particulars than that of Muhammad Ali himself, which aspired to make Egypt "a part of Europe." Large areas of Cairo and Alexandria were rebuilt to resemble French cities, while the Suez Canal cities of Port Said and Ismailia were European from their inception. New law courts, libraries, learned societies, museums, schools, factories, railroads, and even schemes to explore and conquer large parts of Africa all played a part in Isma'il's efforts to make Egypt seem Western. Through diplomacy and financial inducements in Istanbul, he also acquired from the Ottoman government the title of khedive ("little lord" in Persian), the right to bequeath his position to his eldest son, and the authority to contract foreign loans without Ottoman consent. This last achievement enabled Isma'il to finance his Westernization program by borrowing money from European banks, but the state debt burden soon exceeded the ability of Egyptian taxpayers to repay it. The sale of Egypt's shares in the Suez Canal Company in 1875 was followed by the acceptance of foreign debt commissioners, the Caisse de la Dette Publique, to supervise Egypt's receipts and disbursements and, when the economy failed to improve, the admission of British and French ministers to the Egyptian cabinet in what came to be called the "Dual Control." Isma'il's efforts to engineer their overthrow led to a movement among some Egyptians to form a constitutional government and to successful efforts by the European bondholders and their governments to persuade the Ottoman sultan to dismiss Isma'il as his viceroy in Egypt.

With the accession of Tawfiq in 1879, the Europeans, especially Britain and France, became enmeshed in Egypt's economic and political crisis. When a group of Egyptian officers protested their pay-cuts and obliged the khedive to dismiss first his war minister and then his entire cabinet, their leader, Colonel Ahmad Urabi, emerged as the first champion of Egypt's resistance to foreign control. In 1881–82 the Urabist movement competed against the Europeans for mastery in Egypt, leading to riots and a devastating fire in Alexandria. Finally, a British expeditionary force invaded the country and defeated Urabi's troops at Tel-el-Kebir, occupying Cairo on 14 September 1882.

Britain's military occupation of Egypt had no legal basis and was meant to last only long enough to restore order under Khedive Tawfiq. By dissolving and reorganizing the Egyptian army, Britain restored peace and order, but it also became responsible for the Sudan, where a self-proclaimed mahdi ("rightly guided one") had risen in rebellion against Egyptian misrule. British and Egyptian forces lost the Sudan to the Mahdi by 1885, and many Englishmen believed that they could not leave Egypt until they had avenged that loss. More significantly, the British diplomatic representative in Cairo, Sir Evelyn Baring (who later became the Earl of Cromer), believed that his country's troops should remain long enough to enable a corps of British advisers to help the Egyptian ministers rebuild the economy, so that the debts that the government had contracted would no longer burden the peasants with high exactions in taxes and forced labor. Building irrigation works and taking stern measures against corruption, or "water and justice," as the British described these measures, were Cromer's policy that enabled Egypt to recover from bankruptcy. In 1896–98 British and Egyptian troops retook the Sudan from the followers of the Mahdi. The governments of the two countries agreed in 1899 to joint rule over the Sudan, which in practice became a British colony. France, which had once aspired to capture the Nile headwaters and drive the British from Egypt, where French cultural and economic interests had prevailed since Napoléon and Muhammad Ali, accepted an indefinite British occupation of Egypt in the 1904 Entente Cordiale. British control of Egypt seemed secure.

Opposition to British rule did indeed come from France and its partisans in the early days and from the Ottoman Empire, still Egypt's nominal suzerain, with the ideological fortification of pan-Islam, the idea that all the world's Muslims should unite against foreign imperialism. As long as Tawfiq was khedive, his palace staff and his ministers did not openly oppose Britain's military occupation, which was their surest protection against a resurgent Urabist movement. But Tawfiq died unexpectedly in 1892 and was succeeded by his eldest son, Abbas Hilmi II, who had been educated in Europe and was not yet 18 years old. Some of Abbas's European and Egyptian advisers pushed him into confrontation with Lord Cromer, who could easily summon more troops from London to quell any disturbances. Although Abbas eventually turned from opposing the British to making his own fortune, he spawned a new nationalist movement of lawyers and journalists demanding an end to the British occupation and the establishment of constitutional government. Its first leader, Mustafa Kamil, was able to direct his appeal simultaneously to the French, the Ottomans, and the educated Egyptian elite. The National Party that he founded became split after his early death, but the nationalist idea that Egypt should be for the Egyptians became fixed in the minds and hearts of the people.

With the outbreak of World War I, Egypt's anomalous position as a privileged Ottoman province under British military occupation, or "veiled protectorate," became untenable when the British and Turks were fighting on opposite sides. Britain pulled away the veil and proclaimed Egypt independent of Ottoman rule, with a "sultan" from the Muhammad Ali dynasty replacing Khedive Abbas, who had gone over to the Turks, and under a temporary British Protectorate. Egypt became a major base for the Allies during World War I. Although Egyptians were not asked to defend their country against the Turks and their German allies, they did suffer in other ways: rising prices for food and other necessities of life, limitations on the highly profitable cultivation of cotton, crowds of often rowdy British Empire troops in the cities, conscription for auxiliary duties when Britain's Egyptian Expeditionary Force invaded Palestine and Syria, and exactions of financial contributions and even farm animals for the Allied military effort. Discontent arose when, after the 1918 Armistice, the British Foreign Office refused to discuss the Egyptian question with either a delegation (Arabic: *wafd*) of nationalist leaders headed by Sa'd Zaghlul or even to receive a deputation of Egyptian ministers. A nationwide revolution broke out in March 1919, supported by Egyptians of every religion and class. Sa'd Zaghlul's Wafd was allowed to go to Paris, but was never granted a hearing at the Peace Conference. A British commission of inquiry led by Lord Milner was equally unable to find Egyptians who would discuss the status of their country within the framework of the British Protectorate. The Egyptian public rejected negotiations with the British by anyone other than Sa'd, even by their prime minister, Adli. Finally, the British announced in 1922 that they would end the Protectorate and grant independence to Egypt, subject to four points reserved for later negotiations: imperial communications, defense of Egypt against outside aggression, protection of foreign and minority interests, and the status of the Anglo-Egyptian Sudan.

As the British scaled down their presence as advisers in the Egyptian ministries and other areas of government and defense, the

Egyptians drew up a liberal constitution that would enable them to govern themselves as a parliamentary democracy. The 1923 Constitution provided for a bicameral legislature, to which the council of ministers would be responsible, but it also empowered Sultan (renamed King) Fuad (r. 1917–36) to undercut the elected legislators and control the government, limited somewhat by the continuing presence of British troops with a powerful high commissioner and somewhat less by Egyptian nationalism as voiced by the press, the Wafd and other political parties, and the street demonstrators. Parliamentary democracy worked poorly, given Egyptians' wide disparities of income and education, the pretensions of the king and the great landowners, and the lack of any tradition of popular participation in politics. Civil liberties were often violated by the king, his sycophants in the police and the army, the landowners and their agents, urban street gangs in the pay of powerful politicians, and mendacious journalists. Whenever free elections were held, the Wafd Party won the overwhelming majority of the parliamentary seats and Wafdist cabinets would be formed, but rarely did they last longer than two years, as the king had the power to dismiss them. Both Fuad and his son Faruq (r. 1936–52) learned to govern through minority parties, factions that had broken from the Wafd Party, and anti-democratic popular movements such as Misr al-Fatat and the Muslim Brothers. Yet no party except the Wafd could rally enough support to sign a treaty with Britain. It was only when the Italians invaded Ethiopia and threatened both Egypt and the Sudan that the Wafd, leading a delegation made up of nearly all Egypt's political parties, negotiated the Anglo-Egyptian Treaty of 1936. This pact gave Egypt the formal independence its leaders had long sought without obliging the British to withdraw their troops from the country. Egypt's government remained, until the end of the monarchy in 1952, a three-legged stool: the British, the king, and the Wafd.

Increasingly though, the loyalties of most Egyptians were alienated from all three legs and indeed from the minority parties whose politicians applied their leverage to gain power. As the country became more urbanized and industrialized and as World War II brought back many of the burdens of the British occupation that had weighed on the Egyptians during the previous war, the people flocked to other movements, either ultranationalist ones like Misr al-Fatat or such labor-oriented ones as Hadeto and the Egyptian Communist Party, but mainly to Islamist ones like the Society of Muslim Brothers. Disorders intensified after World War II, with deteriorating economic and social conditions, the frustrating quest for control of the Sudan under the slogan of "Nile Valley unity," and Egypt's humiliating defeat by Israel in the 1948–49 Palestine War. King Faruq's own corruption and debauchery symbolized to many Egyptians the disintegration of Egypt's whole political system and the need for revolutionary reforms.

Egypt's salvation came on 23 July 1952 from an unexpected source: the officer corps of the army, hitherto assumed to be loyal to King Faruq. A secret cabal of "Free Officers," intensely patriotic, became the revolutionary reformers who seized control of the barracks and the government, deposed the king, drove out the old-style politicians, locked up the Muslim Brothers, and finally negotiated (with American help) for an end to the British occupation, even of the vital Suez Canal Zone. It gave up Egypt's claims to the Sudan, allowing that country to become fully independent in 1956. If Egypt could have avoided other foreign entanglements, its political and economic development would have been impressive. The new regime limited landholdings to 200 feddans, hoping to replace the great landowners with a middle-class yeoman peasantry. It built schools and health centers in rural areas as well as the cities. Although it outlawed the political parties and terminated the 1923 Constitution, it remained committed to developing broader public participation in Egypt's government, first through the Liberation Rally and then the National Union. The officers did not aspire to a permanent military dictatorship or to squander Egypt's resources in an attempt to control the Arab world.

The Free Officers, renamed the Revolutionary Command Council (RCC) after they took power, were not initially eager to pursue a war of revenge against Israel for its earlier humiliation of Egypt. During 1953–54, they were preoccupied with securing Britain's agreement to evacuate its troops from the Suez Canal and with the power struggle between the titular leader, Muhammad Najib, who had the backing of most politically articulate civilians, and Jamal Abd al-Nasir, supported by the officer corps. These issues seemed settled in October 1954, when the Anglo-Egyptian Agreement was signed and Nasir suppressed the Muslim Brothers and others who had backed Najib. But the RCC did want to ensure that Egypt's armed forces could defend its borders, and Israel's reprisal raid in the Gaza Strip in February 1955 convinced Nasir that he needed to buy more arms. Britain, France, and the United States had an agreement not to sell weapons to the countries involved in the Arab-Israeli conflict. Although Iraq had circumvented this problem by forming an anti-Communist alliance then called the Baghdad Pact, Nasir did not want to join an alliance that could readmit Western armies into Egypt even as Britain was phasing out its 75-year occupation. While attending the Bandung Conference in April of that year, he learned that Egypt could buy from the Communist countries the weapons it needed. In September 1955 it agreed with Czechoslovakia to barter U.S.$200 million worth of Egyptian cotton for Communist arms. Britain and the United States, hoping to counteract the Communist influence that they feared would grow in Egypt, arranged a package deal to pay for building the Aswan High Dam, a public works project that the revolutionary leaders hoped would control the Nile flood, irrigate large areas of Upper Egypt, and generate enough electric power for the country's needs.

The Nasir government, suspicious of British and American intentions, did not immediately accept the offer. Anglo-Egyptian relations worsened, as Radio Cairo attacked British efforts to bring Jordan into the Baghdad Pact and inspired its dismissal of the British commander of the Jordanian Arab Legion. Egypt's ties with the United States deteriorated because of raids into Israel by Egyptian-trained Palestinian *fidaiyin* from the Gaza Strip and because of Nasir's decision to recognize China's Communist government. At the moment Egypt's ambassador in Washington was authorized to accept America's offer, U.S. Secretary of State Dulles publicly withdrew it. Angered by this rebuff, Nasir announced that Egypt was nationalizing the Suez Canal Company, a movement that electrified Egyptian and Arab opinion, for the Suez Canal had long symbolized Western imperialism, and horrified the British and the French owners of the company, as well as the Europeans who depended on imported oil shipped through the Canal itself. Diplomacy and force failed equally to dislodge the Canal from Nasir's grip. The Anglo-French attack of November 1956, coordinated with Israel's Sinai Campaign in reprisal for Egypt's *fidaiyin* raids, proved to be a military defeat but a political victory for Egypt, which got the backing of almost every other country in the world, including the United States as well as the USSR. All Israel got was the right to navigate the Gulf of Aqaba, as a United Nations Emergency Force took up positions in the Sinai and the Gaza Strip between the Egyptians and the Israelis.

During the following decade Egypt was involved more in power struggles within the Arab world between conservative and radical regimes than in the Arab-Israeli conflict. It opposed the U.S. initiative, called the Eisenhower Doctrine, to line up the Middle Eastern countries against Communism. Pressured by the Syrian government, it agreed to form an organic union with Syria in February 1958, the United Arab Republic, which all Arab states were invited to join. It backed the rebels against Lebanese President Kamil Sham'un in May and hailed the revolution of July 1958 against the Iraqi monarchy. But Iraq's new republican leaders, although they were army colonels very much like the Egyptian Free Officers, soon proved to be their rivals for influence in the Arab world; they did not join the United Arab Republic. An army coup in the Sudan also proved disappointingly resistant to Egypt's influence. In 1962, however, a military coup in San'a overthrew the Yemeni imamate. Egypt came to the aid of the new republican regime, only to become embroiled in a protracted and bitter civil war, as the imam took to the hills, gained the support of the tribal warriors and Saudi Arabia, and kept the republican officers at bay. The Yemen Civil War became the major Arab battleground between radical republics and conservative monarchies during the 1960s, costly to both but with neither side emerging as a clear victor.

Egypt also became a leader of the neutralist states in Asia and Africa, especially of those whose leaders were radical and charismatic, like Nasir himself, such as Sukarno of Indonesia, Nehru of India, and Nkrumah of Ghana. Egypt hosted the first Afro-Asian Peoples Solidarity Conference in 1957, helped to form the Casablanca group of African states in 1961, attended the summit of neutralist leaders in Belgrade in that same year, and helped to form the Organization of African Unity in 1963. Although neutralist in principle, Nasir's Egypt favored the Soviet Union, which in turn provided the capital and the engineers to build the Aswan High Dam. Egypt purchased large quantities of Soviet arms and bartered its own produce for Communist-made civilian goods, although Egypt's own Communists remained locked up until 1964.

In domestic policy, Nasir moved toward Arab socialism, which to him meant state control of economic planning and the ownership and management of major business firms; he did not believe in class warfare, the dictatorship of the proletariat, or rejection of religion as the opiate of the masses. After nationalizing companies that belonged to foreigners, Nasir's government took control of the Egyptian ones and put severe limits on landholdings, personal incomes, and the number of boards of directors any individual might sit on. These July Laws alienated Syria's capitalists and hastened the breakup of the United Arab Republic in September 1961. Egypt's capitalists either went to work for the nationalized enterprises or went into exile. Nasir convoked the National Congress of Popular Forces, which drafted the National Charter as a blueprint for Egypt's march toward Arab socialism. The government was to be the instrument of the people's interests, with decisions to be made by a legislature half of whose elected members would have to be either workers or peasants. All political participation would be funneled through a single-party organization, the Arab Socialist Union (ASU), that would convey policy commands from top to bottom and popular demands from bottom to top. The ASU would have cells in every factory, agricultural cooperative, school, government department, and place of business; these cells would become training grounds for future national leaders, who would move up to local, provincial, and national ASU councils. The government hoped also that the nationalized industries would grow according to plan and that Egypt would double its national income within ten years and enter the ranks of the industrialized world, as the Communist countries had done.

Nasir's hopes for Egypt foundered on the Arab-Israeli conflict. During the early 1960s the rivalry between Egypt and Israel could be acted out mainly in United Nations debates or in their competition to aid and hence to influence the emerging African nations. But Israel's National Water Carrier Project, taking water from the Jordan River to irrigate agricultural centers in more arid regions of the country, impinged on Jordan's water supply. Other Arab states feared that Israel's development would eventually lead to the country's expansion at their expense. Nasir convoked a summit meeting of Arab kings and presidents in Cairo, where they agreed to postpone immediate military action against Israel but to study irrigation projects that would tap the sources of the Jordan River in Syria and Lebanon. They also agreed to create the Palestine Liberation Organization (PLO) as an umbrella group for the Palestinian refugees, hitherto treated as wards of the Arab governments. The PLO itself had more bark than bite, but some of its constituent groups, notably al-Fatah, turned to terrorism. Israel made reprisal raids against Fatah's bases on the West Bank of Jordan, but its financial support and verbal encouragement were coming from Syria, where a radical regime had taken control in January 1966. Hoping to rein in its enthusiasm, Egypt made an alliance treaty with the new regime in November of the same year. The following April border incidents between Syria and Israel escalated into an aerial dogfight, in which the Israelis shot down six Syrian fighter jets. The Soviets warned Nasir that Israel was massing troops in its northeast for an attack on Syria, Damascus asked for help under the 1966 Egyptian-Syrian treaty, and Nasir mobilized his army. He called on the UN secretary-general to remove the United Nations Emergency Force from Egypt's Israeli border, massed his own troops in the Sinai, blockaded the Tiran Straits against Israeli shipping through the Gulf of Aqaba, and joined in an Arab chorus of threats against Israel's very survival. In response, Israel launched a preemptive strike against the air forces of Egypt, Syria, Jordan, and Iraq, followed by an invasion of the Gaza Strip, the Sinai Peninsula, the Arab half of Jerusalem, the West Bank, and the Golan Heights. After six days of fighting, Israel's forces stood on the banks of the Suez Canal, and Egypt's armed forces were in disarray. Nasir took responsibility for the defeat and tried to resign, but the Egyptian people demonstrated en masse for him to stay in office and continue the struggle.

With the Suez Canal closed and the Israelis in the Sinai, Egypt had to decide whether to continue leading the Arab-Israeli conflict or seek a negotiated peace. It tried to do both. At the 1967 Khartum Summit, the Arab leaders ruled out any negotiations, recognition, or peace with the Jewish state. On the other hand, the UN Security Council propounded its Resolution 242, which essentially called for the restoration of Arab lands in exchange for recognition of Israel. Nasir's government accepted the resolution, yet it also rearmed feverishly, brought in more Soviet military advisers, and began firing on the Israelis across the Suez Canal. Early in 1969 Nasir dubbed the fighting that was already going on a "War of Attrition" that would not end until Israel withdrew from the Sinai and other occupied Arab lands. In reality, though, Egypt suffered greater losses than Israel, as the fighting escalated into an air war, with Soviet pilots reportedly flying Egyptian jets. Although the oil-exporting Arab governments had agreed at Khartum to support the economies of Egypt and other "confrontation states" against Israel, their response to Nasir's pleas at the 1969 Rabat Summit disappointed him. The Egyptian government, after much soul-searching, agreed to a cease-fire proposed by U.S. Secretary of State Rogers, which should have led, through indirect negotiations, to an Israeli withdrawal from the lands occupied since June 1967. The War of Attrition ended, but the PLO continued its struggle by hijacking civilian airliners and provoking a civil war with Jordan in September 1970. Nasir convoked another Arab summit, at which a Palestinian-Jordanian truce was worked out, and died shortly thereafter.

Nasir's death occasioned an outpouring of popular grief in Egypt and elsewhere in the Arab world. He was succeeded by his vice president, Anwar al-Sadat, who seemed unlikely to survive amid the "centers of power" or cliques of Nasirites in the cabinet. But Sadat managed to secure the army's acquiescence in a purge of those powerful politicians on 15 May 1971, soon celebrated as the "Corrective Revolution." Although Sadat's government signed a friendship treaty with the USSR and promulgated a new constitution that reaffirmed Egypt's commitment to Arab socialism, he soon moved to the right. Influenced by the Saudi government, on which Egypt's economy was becoming ever more dependent, Sadat began easing out leftist politicians and journalists and restoring confiscated lands and property to Egyptians punished by Nasir. More dramatically, he burned the tapes of telephone conversations made by Nasir's secret police. When Moscow refused to sell the offensive weapons that Sadat said Egypt needed to resume fighting Israel after the Rogers Peace Plan failed to secure Israel's withdrawal from the Sinai, Sadat asked the Soviet advisers to leave Egypt in July 1972.

Sadat and his advisers hoped for a reconciliation with Washington, but decided that the U.S. government would pressure Israel to withdraw only if another Middle East crisis arose. Together with Syrian leader Hafiz al-Asad, he planned a joint attack against the Israeli troops on the Bar Lev Line facing the Suez Canal and in the Golan Heights. The coordinated attack took place on 6 October 1973, Yom Kippur for Jewish Israelis, and initially succeeded, as Egyptian troops crossed the Canal under protection from Soviet-made missiles and Syrian tanks thrust into the Golan Heights. The fighting became bitter and protracted, with both superpowers rearming their clients and maneuvering in the United Nations for a political settlement. Finally U.S. Secretary of State Kissinger flew to Moscow and negotiated with the Soviet government for a new UN resolution that called for Arab-Israeli negotiations. By this time, Israelis had broken through the Egyptian lines and crossed the Canal, occupying its west bank as far south as Suez and cutting off Egypt's Third Army in the Sinai. As the Arab states imposed an oil embargo against countries aiding Israel, especially the United States, Kissinger began working earnestly for a peace settlement, leading to a general conference in Geneva, followed by separation-of-forces agreements, first by Egypt and Israel in January 1974, then by Syria and Israel four months later. Sadat and Kissinger formed a close working relationship, and Egypt resumed diplomatic relations with the United States. The Suez Canal was dredged out with American help and reopened in June 1975. The Canal cities were rebuilt. In domestic policy, Sadat paid lip service to Arab socialism but began restoring capitalism through a policy he called *infitah* (or "open door") aimed at Arab and Western investors. Further indirect negotiations with Israel led in September 1975 to a new agreement, in which Egypt renounced war as a means to settle the Arab-Israeli conflict and Israel handed back more of the Sinai.

Sadat's policies were now diametrically opposed to those of his predecessor: capitalism took the place of socialism, creating a new Egyptian bourgeoisie; Egypt renounced its friendship pact with Moscow and began replacing its Soviet arsenal with weapons purchased from the Western countries or manufactured locally in factories financed by Arab capital; and ships bearing Israeli cargos transitted the Suez Canal and peace with Israel no longer seemed unthinkable. When a new administration in Washington tried to restart the Geneva Peace Conference, Sadat seized the initiative by offering to go to Jerusalem to speak to the Israeli Knesset. The offer raised hopes in Israel and the United States that a general Arab-Israeli peace settlement was at hand; Egyptian and Israeli negotiators soon found, however, that the goal was harder to achieve than Sadat had imagined. President Carter invited both Sadat and Israeli Premier Begin to come to his summer retreat in Maryland for an open-ended meeting to try to reach an agreement. The result was the Camp David Accords between Carter, Sadat, and Begin, the basis for the separate peace treaty signed by Egypt and Israel in March 1979, restoring the Sinai to Egypt in stages in return for the establishment of full diplomatic ties between the two countries. Egypt and Israel hoped that Jordan and other Arab governments would also make peace with Israel and that all sides would negotiate in good faith for Palestinian autonomy. Instead, the other Arab states broke diplomatic relations with Sadat's government and ended all aid and investment in Egypt because of the treaty. The U.S.

government stepped up its aid program to Egypt, whose economy fortunately benefited from rising Suez Canal tolls, tourism and oil revenues, and remittances from Egyptians working in other countries (including, ironically, the Arab states that were boycotting Egypt).

Although Egypt was at peace with Israel, its people were not at peace with their regime. President Sadat increasingly stifled attacks on his policies, passing the "Law of Shame" in 1980 and jailing many political dissidents in September 1981. Opposition came increasingly from Islamists, whom Sadat himself had encouraged to take power within the universities and the press in order to reduce the influence of the Communists, and some managed to infiltrate the army officer corps. While Sadat was reviewing a military parade on 6 October 1981, the anniversary of the crossing of the Suez Canal, he was assassinated by a group of officers who later proved to be part of an Islamist group called al-Jihad al-Jadid. Although many world leaders came to Cairo for Sadat's funeral, the occasion inspired none of the popular mourning that had occurred after Nasir's death. Sadat's vice president, Husni Mubarak, took power without opposition and promised to address Egypt's economic and social problems. While maintaining relations with Israel, Mubarak restored Egypt's ties with the Arab governments and even the PLO.

In spite of massive infusions of U.S. military and technical aid, Mubarak's Egypt has failed to solve most of the country's problems. Political opposition is permitted within narrow bounds, but the People's Assembly is dominated by the National Democratic Party, which inspires little public enthusiasm, and the election laws make it difficult for other parties to form a substantial voting bloc. Pre-revolutionary movements have been revived, including the Wafd Party, the Muslim Brothers, and even Misr al-Fatat. Genuinely popular movements, calling for the establishment of the Islamic Shari'a as the sole basis of Egypt's laws, cannot attain power legally and were, during 1992–94, heavily censored under the State of Emergency put in effect after Sadat's assassination. Disparities widen between large landowners and landless peasants, between capitalists who have benefited from the *infitah* and employees of state-owned enterprises who have not, and between Egyptians who go abroad to work and those who stay at home and see their meager salaries eroded by inflation. The population continues to rise by about 3 percent annually, land reclamation has proceeded at a slower pace and a higher cost than expected, and the Aswan High Dam has created environmental problems that offset its benefits. Many Egyptians question the value of their government's dependence on the Western countries, especially the United States, and of peace with Israel. The Iraq-Kuwait dispute, in which Mubarak joined the coalition against Saddam Husayn's invasion of Kuwait, brought economic benefits to Egypt, yet the policy was assailed by some

Egyptians. As of 1994, many Egyptians favor a more Islamic government and decry the increasingly repressive measures taken by the Mubarak regime, which they feel has made Egypt a U.S. client state.

For many Egyptians, the most significant aspect of their history as a people has been their struggle for independence from foreign occupation and domination, the "national movement" led successively by Ahmad Urabi, Mustafa Kamil and Muhammad Farid, Sa'd Zaghlul and the Wafd, and Jamal Abd al-Nasir and Anwar al-Sadat, with the ardent support of the people themselves. The foreign villains may change, and since the departure of the British, both the Soviets and the Americans have at times affronted the Egyptian people. This may be called the nationalist school of Egyptian historiography.

But Egypt's story is also one of an agrarian people who had to adapt to industrialization, first by Muhammad Ali, then by the European powers that wanted Egypt to supply raw materials and markets for their manufactures, and then by Nasir, who hoped that an industrialized Egypt would lead the Arab world toward a position of power and respect. If Egypt had heroes of economic development, they would be the peasants who gave up their lives to dig the canals, the toilers who raised and ginned the long-staple cotton that Egypt exported to Europe, the founders of Bank Misr and other companies that gave Egyptians the chance to manage their country's own industries, the workers who tried to organize trade unions to protect their dignity and raise their wages, and the economists who planned the economic growth for which Nasir and his followers yearned. This may be called Egypt's socialist historiography.

Other Egyptians view their country as the heartland of Islamic power and the center of Muslim learning since the seventh-century Arab conquest. Islam, now the religion of more than 90 percent of all Egyptians, is more than a set of beliefs about God, worship, and the afterlife; it provides a blueprint for an ideal government and a perfect society. Egypt's story is, for them, one of efforts by countless Muslims since 640 to build Islamic institutions: mosques, schools, courts of law, welfare institutions, Sufi ("mystic") societies, and trade guilds. Egyptians are a deeply religious people. Islam and indeed Coptic Christianity have assured them of survival through times of plagues, famines, foreign invaders, unjust rulers, and internal strife. There were of course the Muslim rulers: Umayyad and Abbasid caliphs, Tulunid and Ikhshidid governors, Fatimid schismatics, Kurdish Ayyubids, Turkish and Circassian Mamluks, Ottoman Turks, and the viceroys descended from Muhammad Ali, who claimed an Albanian origin. But to Muslim historians, the real heroes were not the men who sat on thrones in Cairo, but rather the ulama who compiled the Shari'a and taught it to the people of Egypt and the rest of the world. In modern times, they included Jamal al-Din al-Afghani,

Muhammad Abduh, and Rashid Rida, who showed how Islam could respond to the challenge of Europe. Most recently, they have been the leaders of the Society of Muslim Brothers and the *jama'at* ("Islamic societies"), which have united thousands of Egyptian Muslims to protect their religiously based values against Westernization. To Islamists, this is Egypt's real past.

Whether the nationalists, the socialists, or the Islamists hold the key to Egypt's future none can predict. The country's problems are daunting and the stakes are high. The Egyptian people are survivors. Whatever fate lies in store for them, however, they are confident that their country will endure.

DICTIONARY

- A -

ABBAS BRIDGE INCIDENT (1946). Political atrocity caused by an Egyptian police decision to open a drawbridge between Giza and Cairo (q.v.) during a student demonstration, causing many participants to fall into the Nile. The incident led to escalating riots and protest marches by students and workers against the Egyptian government and the British occupation (q.v.), as well as to the replacement of Premier Mahmud Fahmi al-Nuqrashi (q.v.) by Isma'il Sidqi (q.v.).

ABBAS HILMI I (1813–54). Egypt's governor from 1848 to 1854. The son of Tusun, who predeceased his father, Muhammad Ali (q.v.), Abbas was born in Jidda and reared in Cairo (q.v.). He succeeded Ibrahim (q.v.) upon his death in November 1848. Often viewed as reactionary because he dismantled some of the Westernizing reforms instituted by his grandfather, he did indeed dismiss many of the European advisers of Muhammad Ali and Ibrahim. His motives were a combination of parsimony and paranoia, but peasant taxpayers benefited from the lower imposts and rates. During his reign an English company, headed by Robert Stephenson, received the concession to build the railroad between Cairo and Alexandria (q.v.). The route from Cairo to Suez was also improved. Abbas sent troops to fight against the Russians in the Crimean War (1853–56), where they suffered heavy casualties. The circumstances of his death in Banha in 1854 have never been satisfactorily explained.

ABBAS HILMI II (1874–1944). Egypt's khedive (q.v.) from 1892 to 1914, when Britain deposed him upon severing Egypt from the Ottoman Empire (q.v.). His father, Khedive Tawfiq (q.v.), died unexpectedly in January 1892, when Abbas was a cadet at the Theresianum in Vienna, and so his reign began when he was barely 18 years old by the Muslim calendar. A high-spirited youth inclined to nationalism, he soon replaced some of the palace staff, then ran afoul of the British diplomatic agent, Lord Cromer (q.v.), when he tried in January 1893 to replace his pro-British premier, Mustafa Fahmi (q.v.), with Husayn Fakhri (q.v.) and a new cabinet without first securing Cromer's consent. Backed by his government, Cromer told the khedive that he must have prior British consent to change his ministers. Abbas again challenged the British, in particular Sir Herbert (later Lord) Kitchener (q.v.), the commander-in-chief of the Egyptian army, a year later in the Frontiers Incident (q.v.). Unable thereafter to oppose the British occupation (q.v.) openly, Abbas formed a secret organization composed of Europeans and nationalistic Egyptians, the Society for the Revival of the Nation, which became the basis for Mustafa Kamil's (q.v.) National Party (q.v.). He subsidized Mustafa's anti-British propaganda in Europe and the publication of Ali Yusuf's (q.v.) newspaper, *al-Muayyad* (q.v.).

As the Nationalists' hopes for French aid in ending the British occupation waned after the Fashoda Incident (q.v.), Abbas made peace with Britain, partly due to his friendship with the Prince of Wales, later King Edward VII. He distanced himself from the National Party after the Entente Cordiale (q.v.), although he was briefly reconciled with Mustafa Kamil and Muhammad Farid (q.v.) following the Dinshaway Incident (q.v.) and subsidized the publication of British and French editions of *al-Liwa* (q.v.). He expressed his moral support for constitutional government, one of the National Party's desiderata, but abandoned anti-British nationalism because of Cromer's retirement and the *politique d'entente* (q.v.) pursued by his successor, Sir Eldon Gorst (q.v.). To signal this new policy in 1908, he replaced the Mustafa Fahmi cabinet with a new one headed by Butros Ghali (q.v.), who opposed the Nationalists. Abbas became increasingly repressive toward the National Party and its newspapers, approving the revival of the 1881 Press Law (q.v.), the trials of Shaykh Jawish (q.v.), and the promulgation of the 1910 Exceptional Laws (q.v.), due in part to his friendship with Gorst, which he affirmed by calling on the ailing British agent shortly before his death in 1911. When Gorst was replaced by Abbas's nemesis, Kitchener, the khedive resumed his old hostility to the British, but the National Party had lost much of its influence, and its newspapers were muzzled during 1912. The elections for the new Legislative Assembly (q.v.) set up under the 1913 Organic Law (q.v.) opened new opportunities to seek political support, but much of its leadership came from the traditionally hostile Umma Party (q.v.), notably Sa'd Zaghlul (q.v.). Kitchener now hoped to replace Abbas by a more pliable relative.

While Abbas was in Istanbul in July 1914, he was shot by a deranged Egyptian student thought to be an agent of the ruling Committee of Union and Progress (CUP). Before he was well enough to leave, however, World War I (q.v.) broke out, and Britain's ambassador there warned him that he would not be allowed to return to Egypt until the war ended. The khedive decided to make peace with the CUP through War Minister Enver and with the exiled Egyptian Nationalists, notably Muhammad Farid and Shaykh Jawish. After the Ottoman Empire joined the Central Powers, he issued manifestos "dismissing" his ministers, granting a constitution to the Egyptian people, and calling on them to revolt against the British. His relations with the CUP and the Ottoman government remained troubled, however, and he left Istanbul for Vienna in December 1914. Soon afterward the British officially deposed him in favor of his uncle, Husayn Kamil (q.v.). The ex-khedive stayed away from Istanbul for three years, during which he intrigued with Germany to obtain funds, ostensibly to buy shares to subvert Paris newspapers (this became known as the Bolo Affair), and with Britain to obtain recognition of his son, Abd al-Mun'im, as the heir to the Egyptian throne. Discredited by the Bolo Affair and unable to make peace with the British, Abbas finally returned to Istanbul late in 1917 and cooperated with the Central Powers for the rest of the war. After the armistice, he moved from one European city to another, seeking until 1922 to regain control of his property in Egypt and recognition of his family's claim to its throne. He invested in real estate and various business enterprises and continued to engage in politics, notably his attempts to resolve the Palestine question, but never returned to Egypt. He backed the Axis Powers in World War II (q.v.) and died in Geneva in 1944. Though energetic and patriotic, he failed as khedive to use his powers to stem the entrenchment of the British occupation and to promote the nationalist movement. Memoirs purported to be his were published in Cairo in 1993.

ABBASIYYA BARRACKS. Major military installation in northeastern Cairo (q.v.), begun by Abbas I (q.v.) while he was governor of Egypt, then neglected by his successors. They were occupied by the British army in 1882 and later expanded into a major military installation, becoming the principal staging area of the 1952 Revolution (q.v.).

ABBUD, AHMAD (1889–1963). Wealthy industrialist. Born in Cairo, he attended the Tawfiqiyya Secondary School and the University of Glasgow, where he was trained as a civil engineer and also met his wife, who was Scottish. He worked as an engineer for a British company, then worked on an irrigation scheme in Iraq and on the Palestinian and Syrian railway system. Upon returning to Egypt in 1922, he worked on the enlargement of the Aswan Dam (q.v.) and was a supply contractor for the British army in Egypt. He was elected to the Chamber of Deputies in 1926. He became a successful entrepreneur, managed the Khedivial Mail Line (q.v.), held a near monopoly on sugar refining in Egypt, owned paper mills and fertilizer and chemical plants, had a controlling interest in several Egyptian banks, and served on the board of the Suez Canal Company (q.v.) before it was nationalized. All his enterprises, valued at more than $100 million, were nationalized by Nasir (q.v.) in July 1961.

Abbud emigrated to Switzerland in that year and continued to make money. At the time of his death in London, he was said to be one of the ten richest men in the world.

ABD AL-HADI, IBRAHIM (1898–1981). Cabinet minister, premier from 1949 to 1950, and Sa'dist Party (q.v.) leader. Trained as a lawyer, he served in the Chamber of Deputies, representing al-Zarqa (Daqahliyya) in the 1929, 1936, and 1938 sessions, then became minister of state for parliamentary affairs (1939–40), minister of commerce (1940), public works (1941–42), public health (1944–46), foreign affairs (1946), finance twice (1946–47 and 1948–49), chief of the royal cabinet (1947–48), and prime minister and interior (1948–49). Keeping Egypt under martial law, he did much to restore order following the political crisis engendered by the 1948 Palestine War (q.v.) and the assassination of his predecessor, Mahmud Fahmi al-Nuqrashi (q.v.). Owing to his repressive policies or, according to his indictment, for "corruption, terrorism, graft, and treason," Abd al-Hadi was tried after the 1952 Revolution (q.v.) and condemned to death, although this sentence was later commuted to life imprisonment, and all his property was confiscated. He was released in 1954 for health reasons but played no role in subsequent Egyptian politics. His memoirs were serialized in *al-Musawwar* (q.v.) in 1981–82.

ABD AL-HALIM (1830–94). Pretender to the khedivate of Egypt, generally known as Prince Halim. He was educated at the Khanqah School and then enrolled in a military school in France. Upon returning to Egypt, he rose through the army to the rank of lieutenant general. He became commander-in-chief of the Egyptian army, director of the war department, military commander of the Sudan (q.v.), and then member of the Ottoman Council of State in Istanbul. When Khedive Isma'il (qq.v.), changed the succession system, Prince Halim lost his primary claim to the khedivate. Accordingly, he was hostile to Isma'il and his successor, Tawfiq (q.v.), and probably backed Urabi's (q.v.) movement in 1881–82. His son, Mehmet Said Halim, joined the Committee of Union and Progress and became Ottoman grand vizir from 1913 to 1917, claiming Egypt's throne at the expense of deposed Khedive Abbas Hilmi II (q.v.).

ABD AL-MAJID, ISMAT (1923-). Diplomat and politician. He studied law at the Universities of Alexandria (q.v.) and Paris and joined the Egyptian foreign service in 1950. He became deputy foreign minister in 1970 and Egypt's United Nations (q.v.) representative from 1972 to 1983. He served from 1984 as foreign minister and deputy premier until 1991, when he was elected secretary-general of the Arab League (q.v.).

ABD AL-QUDDUS (KUDDOUS), IHSAN (1918–90). Journalist, novelist, and playwright. He was the son of the actress and pioneer woman journalist, Ruz al-Yusuf, and he began his career as a writer and editor for the popular weekly magazine that bears her name (q.v.). He achieved fame early in his career by getting to know Nasir (q.v.) before the 1952 Revolution (q.v.), thus emerging as one of the journalists close to the Revolutionary Command Council (q.v.). In 1966 he was named editor of *Akhbar al-Yawm* (q.v.) and later of *al-Ahram* (q.v.). He wrote at least 60 novels and collections of short stories, mainly psychological studies of political and social behavior, many of which were made into films. He wrote a syndicated newspaper column called "At a Cafe on Politics Street."

ABD AL-RAHMAN, UMAR (1938-). Expatriate Islamist (q.v.) leader accused of inspiring the 1993 bombings, ascribed to Muslim militants, in Cairo and at New York's World Trade Center. Blind since infancy, Umar Abd al-Rahman was educated at al-Azhar (q.v.) and began his career as a preacher in the Fayyum in 1965. His denunciations of Nasir (q.v.) as an infidel led to his imprisonment and finally to temporary exile in Saudi Arabia. He took part in al-Jihad al-Jadid (q.v.) and other *jama'at* (q.v.). Accused of conspiring against Sadat (q.v.), he was imprisoned for three years and tried with Khalid al-Islambuli (q.v.), but was acquitted. He later aided the Afghan *mujahidin* against the Soviet occupation. He left Egypt in 1990 for Saudi Arabia, the Sudan, and, finally, the United States, where he was accused of inciting militant Muslims in Jersey City and the rest of greater New York. He was arrested by U.S. authorities in July 1993.

ABD AL-RAZIQ, ALI (1888–1966). Religious judge, writer, and minister. He came from an Upper Egyptian landowning family and was educated at al-Azhar (q.v.) and in England. He became a Shari'a Court (q.v.) judge in Mansura. In 1925 he published a controversial book, *al-Islam wa usul al-hukm* (q.v.), in which he argued that the caliphate (q.v.) as a political institution was a post-Quranic innovation not essential to Islam (q.v.). Many Egyptians objected to the book because Mustafa Kemal (Atatürk) had just abolished the caliphate, because some Muslims hoped to name a new caliph in a country other than Turkey, and because King Fuad (q.v.) was seeking the office for himself. The ulama (q.v.) of al-Azhar accused Ali Abd al-Raziq of promoting atheism, took away his title of *shaykh*, and had him removed from his judgeship. Many liberal writers, including Taha Husayn (q.v.) and Muhammad Husayn Haykal (q.v.), backed him. He defended his ideas in articles written for *al-Siyasa al-usbu'iyya* (q.v.) and in lectures delivered in Cairo University's (q.v.) Faculties of Law and of Letters. He later served as *awqaf* (q.v.) minister and was elected to the Arabic Language Academy (q.v.). He published *Min athar Mustafa Abd al-Raziq*, a collection of his brother's writings.

ABDIN PALACE. Official residence of Egypt's rulers from 1874 until 1952. Located in central Cairo (q.v.), it was the site of several famous confrontations between local rulers and nationalist demonstrators, both military and civilian, and British officials, notably the 4 February Incident (q.v.). After the monarchy was overthrown in 1952, portions of Abdin were used for a time to house the state archives and a museum, but the building has been used under Sadat (q.v.) and Mubarak (q.v.) for government offices.

ABDUH, MUHAMMAD (1849–1905). Islamic reformer, author and editor, chief jurisconsult of the Maliki rite, and rector of al-Azhar (q.v.). Born in Shanra (Gharbiyya) to a family of Turkic origin, he grew up in Mahallat Nasr (Buhayra) and studied at the Ahmadi Mosque in Tanta and al-Azhar. He was attracted to philosophy and to Sufism (q.v.). He came to know Jamal al-Din al-Afghani (q.v.) during his stay in Cairo and became his most devoted disciple. He taught for a while and worked in journalism, editing *al-Waqai' al-misriyya* (q.v.) in 1880–82. He was imprisoned for three months because of his support for Urabi's (q.v.) movement, then was exiled to Syria. He later went to Paris and joined Afghani in editing an influential pan-Islamic magazine, *al-Urwa al-wuthqa* (q.v.). After it was banned, he returned to Beirut to teach and write. In 1888 he was readmitted to Egypt, where he became a judge and a chancellor in the court of appeals, and in 1899 he became the country's chief mufti (jurisconsult). Abduh's publications include an incomplete interpretation of the Quran, *Risalat al-tawhid* (translated as *The Theology of Unity*), and *al-Radd ala al-dahriyin* (translated into French as *La Réfutation des matérialistes*). He had many disciples, both religious and secular, and the Umma Party (q.v.) is sometimes called *Hizb al-Imam* ("Imam Abduh's party"). His work of Islamic reinterpretation was carried on by Muhammad Rashid Rida (q.v.), and one of his political disciples was Sa'd Zaghlul (q.v.). Although his efforts to reconcile Islam with modernism have not fully stood the test of time, and his close relationship with Lord Cromer (q.v.) rendered him suspect in the eyes of Khedive Abbas Hilmi II (qq.v.) and the National Party (q.v.), Egyptians respect him as a towering figure in their intellectual history.

ABU AL-DHAHAB, MUHAMMAD (1745?-75). Mamluk (q.v.) successor and brother-in-law of Ali Bey al-Kabir (q.v.). Originally Circassian (q.v.), he was purchased by Ali Bey around 1760, surnamed *Abu al-Dhahab* ("father of gold") for passing out gold–instead of silver–coins among the Cairo multitudes upon his elevation to the rank of bey following his pilgrimage with his master to Mecca and Medina in 1764. In 1769 he undertook a punitive expedition on behalf of Ali Bey against rebellious Mamluks in Upper Egypt. The next year Ali sent him to extend his control over the Hijaz (q.v.), while he was expanding into Palestine and Syria, and in 1771 Abu al-Dhahab led an expedition that took Damascus, but inexplicably withdrew after ten days. The two leaders became estranged during that year, ostensibly due to Abu al-Dhahab's reluctance to remain in Syria, but also to their rivalry for supremacy, and Ali exiled Abu al-Dhahab to Upper Egypt. There he organized his Mamluks to rebel against Ali while he was on campaign in Syria in 1772 and managed to take control of Cairo (q.v.). Ali tried unsuccessfully to dislodge him in May 1773, dying soon afterward. During his short reign he continued Ali's expansionist policies in Palestine and Syria and tried to loosen Egypt's ties with the Ottoman Empire (q.v.). He cultivated commercial relations with the British East India Company, hoping to revive the overland trade between the Red Sea and the Mediterranean. Like his predecessor, Abu al-Dhahab pursued policies that would later be developed by Muhammad Ali (q.v.).

ABU AL-FATH, MAHMUD (1893–1958). Leading Wafdist journalist and editor of *al-Misri* (q.v.) from 1936 to 1954. He and his brother, Ahmad, initially supported the 1952 Revolution (q.v.) but broke with the new regime because of Nasir's (q.v.) authoritarian policies. They went into exile in 1954, settling in Tunis. They were tried and sentenced in absentia for 15 years. *Al-Misri* was closed by the government and has never been allowed to reappear. His brother published a memoir, *L'Affaire Nasser* (Paris, 1962).

ABU-GHAZALA, ABD AL-HALIM (1930-). Army officer and politician. Trained at the Military Academy (q.v.), he then received four years' advanced training in the USSR. He wrote several artillery training manuals and became the commander of Egypt's artillery in October 1973. He later served as Egypt's military attaché in Washington. Appointed chief of staff in 1980, he then relinquished that post to become defense minister. He was promoted to the rank of field marshal and became a deputy prime minister in 1982. Dismissed from his position in April 1989, he is now a special assistant to Mubarak (q.v.).

ABU-KIR. Inlet east of Alexandria, commanding the main route from that city to Rosetta (q.v.) and Cairo (q.v.). It was the site of Nelson's (q.v.) naval victory over Napoléon (q.v.) in August 1798, sufficient to ensure joint Anglo-Ottoman mastery of the eastern Mediterranean, but not to end the French occupation (q.v.). In July 1799 the Ottomans dispatched a hundred ships to Abu-Kir Bay and landed about 9,000 men, but they were badly defeated by Napoléon. The British landed 17,000 troops there in March 1801 and dealt a decisive defeat to the forces of General Menou (q.v.), driving the French from Egypt. The British landed there again in 1807 en route to their defeat at Rosetta.

***ACHILLE LAURO* INCIDENT (1985)**. Palestinian hijacking of an Italian cruise ship in the Mediterranean, involving the murder of a disabled American Jew, in October 1985. Although the action was condemned by Chairman Yasir Arafat of the Palestine Liberation Organization (q.v.), the operation was conducted by PLO members, masterminded by Abu al-Abbas. Egyptian President Husni Mubarak (q.v.) arranged for the *fidaiyin* to relinquish the vessel, in return for safe passage to Tunis, where they were to be tried by the PLO. U.S. fighter jets intercepted the plane carrying Abu al-Abbas and forced it to land in Italy, but Italian authorities allowed Abu al-Abbas to go free. The incident created a strain in Egyptian-American relations and also aborted a British-sponsored initiative toward peace between the PLO and Israel.

ADLI-CURZON NEGOTIATIONS (1921). Abortive talks between Egypt's prime minister, Adli Yakan (q.v.), assisted by Husayn Rushdi (q.v.) and Isma'il Sidqi (q.v.), and the British foreign secretary, Lord Curzon, on Egypt's status. The talks were thwarted by Egyptian opposition led by Sa'd Zaghlul (q.v.) and by Britain's insistence on keeping a garrison in Egypt to protect its imperial interests. The talks failed in November, and Adli resigned a month later.

AL-AFGHANI, JAMAL AL-DIN (1838–97). Pan-Islamic agitator, philosopher, teacher, and the major inspiration of Urabi (q.v.). Born as Muhammad ibn Safdar in As'ad Abad (Persia), he later claimed to have come from a village having the same name in Afghanistan and to have been educated in Kabul, probably to disguise his Shi'i origins, and hence also changed his name. After making the hajj in 1857, he settled in Kabul and worked for the government of Dost Muhammad Khan. He then went to India, stopped briefly in Egypt, and stayed in Istanbul, where he joined the education council in 1868. Exiled two years later, he came to Egypt at the invitation of Mustafa Riyad (q.v.). After teaching briefly at al-Azhar (q.v.), he set up his own meeting place nearby and began gathering disciples who shared his views on religious reform and national resistance, notably Muhammad Abduh (q.v.) and journalists Adib Ishaq, editor of *Misr*, for which Afghani sometimes wrote, and Ya'qub Sannu' (q.v.).

Early in 1879 he helped to found a secret political society, one of whose members was Prince Tawfiq (q.v.). But when Tawfiq became khedive (q.v.) later in that year, he had Afghani banished from Egypt. He went to India and later to Paris, where he and Muhammad Abduh published *al-Urwa al-wuthqa* (q.v.). After that magazine was banned, he spent four years in St. Petersburg and then went to Munich, where he met Nasir al-Din Shah of Persia, who invited him there. He inspired the Persian Tobacco Strike of 1891–92 and is widely suspected of instigating the shah's subsequent assassination in 1896, but by then he had moved to Istanbul as the guest of Sultan Abdulhamid, who quarreled with him for receiving Abbas Hilmi II (q.v.). His death, officially ascribed to cancer, may have been due to poison administered by the sultan's agents. His fiery speeches and newspaper articles were his main legacy; some have been translated into English in *An Islamic Response to Imperialism.* He was the major inspiration for the modern revival of Islamic power.

AFRO-ASIAN PEOPLES SOLIDARITY CONFERENCE. Meeting convened in Cairo (q.v.) by Nasir's (q.v.) government from 26 December 1957 to 1 January 1958 and attended by delegations from 46 countries. The conferees condemned neoimperialism and called for concerted efforts to combat underdevelopment. Pressure to hold the conference came from Asian leftist parties, but Egypt also intended to show Dulles (q.v.) that it could not be isolated by the United States and its allies. Anwar al-Sadat (q.v.) chaired the conference, and Yusuf al-Siba'i (q.v.) was elected secretary-general of its permanent organization. Both the USSR and China were represented on its permanent secretariat. The next meeting, held in Conakry (Guinea) in April 1960, adopted a strongly anti-imperialist program. Since then, however, the organization's agenda has gradually shifted from political to social and economic issues.

AGENCY FOR INTERNATIONAL DEVELOPMENT (AID). Official U.S. government organization administering economic and technical assistance to developing countries. Founded as the Technical Cooperation Administration in 1950, it was often called "Point Four" in its early days from its place in President Truman's 1949 inaugural address. The first U.S.-Egyptian agreement was signed in May 1950, providing limited aid for Egypt in return for trade and navigation rights for the United States. Although the initial stress was on promoting trade and domestic capital formation, financial assistance later came to be viewed as a means of facilitating capital goods production and promoting political stability. In 1961 the program was incorporated into the U.S. Department of State and its present name was adopted. Because Nasir's (q.v.) policies stressed economic independence and often opposed Western political influence,

AID's activities were limited to an agricultural cooperation program called the Egyptian American Rural Improvement Service and to the sale of surplus American grain for Egyptian pounds under Public Law 480. As U.S.-Egyptian relations cooled in the mid-1960s, U.S. aid programs came under attack from anti-Communist and Zionist pressure groups, and President Johnson ended grain sales to Egypt early in 1967.

The resumption of U.S. aid accompanied the reestablishment of diplomatic ties negotiated by Sadat (q.v.) and Kissinger, beginning with the commitment of $8.5 million to clear the Suez Canal (q.v.). As Egypt moved toward peace with Israel, the aid sums allocated increased rapidly, exceeding the ability of an initially small American staff to administer them and of Egypt's economy to absorb them. By 1980 the annual amount exceeded $1 billion; in 1991 it reached $3 billion, much of which was used not only to purchase food and capital goods from the United States, but also to improve the country's infrastructure (*see* Aswan High Dam) and to aid the transition from a state-directed to a market economy. Large-scale projects included the expansion of the water and sewer system of greater Cairo (q.v.), the improvement of the telephone system, the construction of schools, the introduction of improved varieties of wheat and rice, and the extension of family planning (q.v.) services.

AGRARIAN REFORM LAW (1952), ***see*** **LAND REFORM.**

AGRICULTURE. Egypt has had, for at least six millennia, a predominantly agrarian economy, one that has depended almost entirely on irrigation (q.v.) and been market oriented rather than subsistence level. In late Ottoman times, Egypt's peasants raised cereal crops, especially millet, wheat, barley, rice, and some maize (corn); various legumes including *birsim* (clover), broad beans, lentils, and chick-peas; and cash crops such as sugar, indigo, tobacco, and some short-staple cotton. Egypt sent wheat, rice, beans, lentils, and cooking oils as tribute to Istanbul and as a Muslim gift to Mecca and Medina. It also exported cereal grains to Mediterranean ports in Christian Europe.

In Muhammad Ali's (q.v.) efforts to build a strong army, initially to protect his governorship of Egypt and later to extend his rule over the Hijaz (q.v.), the Sudan (q.v.), the eastern Mediterranean, and greater Syria, he put nearly all of Egypt's arable land under state control, began its conversion from basin (q.v.) to perennial irrigation (q.v.), and encouraged the expansion of long-staple, or Egyptian, cotton (q.v.), in part because European markets for grain were shielded by protective tariffs. The peasants resisted growing cotton because it required more man-hours of labor than other crops, and the government had to supervise every stage of production and punish shirkers harshly. Faced in addition with rising exactions in kind, corvée (q.v.), and conscription for military service or work in the factories, some peasants resorted to sabotage, self-mutilation, rebellion, and flight into the desert. The resulting labor shortages limited the growth of agrarian output. Nevertheless, government profits in 1836 reached 58 million piasters from long-staple cotton, with modest additional amounts from wheat, rice, indigo, beans, and maize.

The fall of Muhammad Ali's empire after the London Convention (q.v.) undermined state control over agriculture, and Abbas I (q.v.) relieved the peasants of burdensome tax and corvée exactions. Cotton production lost ground to wheat and flax during the 1840s but rose again in the 1850s. The abolition of the British Corn Laws in 1846 stimulated purchases of Egyptian wheat and other grains, reaching a peak in 1855, but greater still was the rising demand for Egyptian cotton in the textile mills of Lancashire. The rapid growth in Anglo-Egyptian trade was further enhanced by improvements to the port of Alexandria (q.v.) and the expansion of Egypt's railroads (q.v.). Khedive Isma'il (qq.v.) initially financed his reforms with earnings from a fivefold rise in cotton exports caused by the Civil War (1861–65), when Britain's textile mills could not import cotton from the U.S. South. Although Western demand for Egyptian cotton eased after 1865, exports rebounded in the 1870s. Maize and sugar (q.v.) gained at the expense of rice, and total cropped area increased from 2 to 4.7 million feddans (q.v.) between 1800 and 1882, but landholdings became concentrated in the khedivial family and the military and bureaucratic elites (*see* Landownership).

The British occupation (q.v.), because it was expected to be temporary, had little effect on agriculture at first. Rather, it reinforced existing trends, such as the extension of perennial irrigation, the concentration of landholdings, a shift from three-year to two-year crop rotation (leading to more cotton culture at the expense of such crops as beans), and the rising dependence on cotton as an export crop. Cotton yield per feddan, which rose during the nineteenth century, began to decline early in the twentieth because of soil depletion, mineral deposits caused by perennial irrigation, and the spread of insect pests. Maize production rose, replacing beans (higher in protein content) as the main source of nourishment for Egypt's peasants. The British were just starting to address these problems when World War I (q.v.) broke out and their relationship to Egypt changed.

Egypt's agricultural development in 1918–52 was marked by further concentration of landholdings, the spread of perennial irrigation, more stress on cotton production for export, further adoption of two-crop rotation, improved drainage, earlier sowing and closer spacing of cotton plants, increased use of artificial fertilizer (imports rose from 57,718 metric tons in 1919 to 641,838 in 1937), and some importation of farm machinery. Cropped area rose in relation to cultivated area, meaning that the land was being increasingly used for more than one crop per year. The number of water buffaloes and cattle roughly doubled between 1919 and 1937. During World War II (q.v.) the Egyptian government restricted the amount of land to be devoted to cereal grains at the expense of cotton acreage, and yields declined due to the inability to import fertilizer. After the war cotton production returned to prewar levels; sugar, *birsim*, and fruit rose markedly; maize and millet held steady; wheat and beans declined slightly; and rice and barley dropped severely. More fertilizer was imported, more land was rented for cash, and peasant conditions worsened, causing an upsurge of revolts and crime.

The 1952 Revolution (q.v.) changed Egypt's agriculture in many ways. The 1952 land reform (q.v.) and later changes reduced the number of large landholdings and increased greatly the number of small peasant proprietors. Agricultural cooperatives assumed control of the marketing of most crops. The government paid subsidies to peasants to grow food and supplied fertilizer as an additional inducement to grow food crops. As a result, more land is being used for maize, vegetables, rice, *birsim*, sugarcane, and flax, while less is allocated to cotton and wheat. Use of pesticides increased from 1,627 metric tons in 1954 to 28,344 in 1977, nitrogenous fertilizers from 569,000 metric tons in 1949 to 3,135,000 in 1978, and phosphates from 79,000 to 606,000 in the same time period. Water buffaloes and cattle doubled in number between 1949 and 1978. Importation and in recent years domestic production have led to a fivefold increase in the number of tractors in Egypt. About 300,000 additional feddans were brought under cultivation between 1952 and 1976, and the ratio of cropped to cultivated land has reached 2:1. Positive results include a marked increase in crop yields per feddan cultivated and in real wages paid to rural labor. On the downside, neglect of drainage during the Nasir (q.v.) era has had to be made up his successors. The Aswan High Dam (q.v.) has introduced new environmental hazards along with its potential for land reclamation. Badly needed farmlands have been lost to housing and urban sprawl, and some peasants deplete their topsoil by using it to make bricks. Formerly a net exporter, Egypt now imports rising amounts of foreign grain to feed its burgeoning population. Yet the numbers working in agriculture are not increasing appreciably, and many peasants have been lured to other Arab countries by higher wages paid to farm workers, depressing Egypt's agricultural yields during the 1980s.

AIDA. Opera written by Italian composer Giuseppe Verdi, under a commission from Khedive Isma'il (q.v.), ostensibly for the opening of the Suez Canal (q.v.) in 1869, but in fact first performed in Cairo (q.v.) on 24 December 1871.

AL-AHALI. Name of several newspapers, of which the most recent is the leftist weekly edited by Khalid Muhyi al-Din (q.v.). Launched in February 1978 as the organ of the National Progressive Unionist Party (q.v.), its circulation rose from 50,000 to 135,000 in 15 weeks, whereupon the government closed it because of its attacks on Sadat (q.v.) and his policies. It was allowed to reappear shortly before the 1984 election. In 1985 it reported a circulation of 100,000 copies despite its poor printing quality on the presses of *al-Jumhuriyya* (q.v.).

AL-AHRAM. Influential daily newspaper, often viewed as the semi-official organ of the Egyptian government. Originally founded in 1876 in Alexandria (q.v.) by Bishara and Salim Taqla, *al-Ahram* was moved to Cairo (q.v.) in 1898. Initially the mouthpiece of the pro-French Syrians in Egypt, it gradually became one of the country's most influential dailies, with correspondents in foreign capitals, a variety of informational material and articles, and sophisticated printing techniques. It was the first newspaper to print a photograph (1881) and it introduced the Linotype machine to Egypt in 1917. Before the 1952 Revolution (q.v.), it was independent of any political party, favored the government in power, and claimed to be Egypt's newspaper of record. It declined in the 1940s and early 1950s, as its circulation fell from 100,000 to 68,000 daily copies, but revived when Muhammad Hasanayn Haykal (q.v.) became its editor. He edited *al-Ahram* from 1957 to 1974, during which time it was eagerly read or anxiously scrutinized by everyone who needed to know what the Egyptian leaders were thinking. The newspaper was moved into an ultramodern, ten-story building with state-of-the-art typesetting and printing equipment. *Al-Ahram* had a reported circulation of 133,034 in 1962. Although officially "owned" by the National Union (q.v.) from 1960 to 1962 and then by the Arab Socialist Union (q.v.), the paper still could chart an independent editorial course on occasion. Under Sadat (q.v.), *al-Ahram* was restored to private ownership and, after Haykal ceased to be its editor, was briefly led by Ali Amin (q.v.) and by Ahmad Baha al-Din, then by Ali Hamdi al-Gammal, but it had to recover from losing its well-connected, highly articulate leader. It also publishes weekly and monthly magazines, and its Center for Strategic Studies publishes books about the Middle East. Its estimated circulation in 1982 was 400,000; in 1993 that figure had reached 900,000 on weekdays and 1.1 million on Fridays.

AL-AKHBAR. Popular Cairo (q.v.) daily newspaper, especially widely read during the early Nasir (q.v.) era under the leadership of Ali and Mustafa Amin (qq.v.), who were removed from power in 1965 on the suspicion that they were serving as agents of the U.S. Central Intelligence Agency. Its estimated circulation in 1962 was 160,000, in 1972 400,000, in 1982 700,000, and in 1993 950,000. It also publishes a weekly edition called *Akhbar al-Yawm.*

AL-ALAMAYN, BATTLE OF (1942). Decisive defeat, by the British and their allies, of the German Afrika Korps commanded by General Rommel, some 100 km west of Alexandria (q.v.). This large-scale tank battle was a major turning point in World War II (q.v.).

ALEXANDRIA. Egypt's major Mediterranean port and second-largest city. Its most glorious period was during the Hellenistic era (332 BC- 640 CE), and it suffered a decline relative to Cairo (q.v.) and other cities during the era of Muslim rule. When Napoléon (q.v.) landed his troops there in 1798, its population did not exceed 8,000. Its revival began with the French occupation (q.v.) and the reign of Muhammad Ali (q.v.), who ordered the construction both of the Mahmudiyya Canal (q.v.) to connect the city with the Nile River (q.v.) and of the naval arsenal. A railroad (q.v.) connecting Alexandria with Cairo was constructed between 1850 and 1854. Trade with Europe rose rapidly during the nineteenth century and increasingly was channeled through Alexandria. The city's rehabilitation as a port and cultural center reached a climax under Khedive Isma'il (qq.v.), when its population rose to 200,000, of whom 50,000 were foreigners. Gas lighting was introduced in 1865. The city's physical expansion tended to be eastward and southward, with the Europeans settling in al-Manshiya and al-Raml. The foreign population, including Syrians as well as Greeks (q.v.), Italians (q.v.), French, and other nationalities, enjoyed a much higher living standard than the native Egyptians, and this disparity created social tensions, as expressed in the June 1882 riots that took the lives of some 50 Europeans and 3,000 Egyptians and led to the subsequent British occupation (q.v.) of Egypt.

Alexandria grew further and prospered under the British. Public utilities, including electricity, piped water, sewer lines, tramways (q.v.), and telephones made Alexandria resemble a European city, which for many foreigners it practically was, although Lawrence Durrell's novels present a somewhat distorted picture of the city. From the early nineteenth century until the end of the monarchy, Alexandria also served as Egypt's summer capital. Its cosmopolitan character has dissipated since the 1952 Revolution (q.v.), especially with the departure of most Greeks and Italians, and of British and French nationals and most Jews (q.v.) after the Suez War (q.v.). Its population in 1900 was 320,000, in 1947 700,000, and in the 1986 census exceeded 2.7 million.

ALEXANDRIA PROTOCOL (1944). Official agreement by Arab heads of state, meeting in October 1944, to establish the Arab League (q.v.). It included a resolution stating that "Palestine constitutes an important part of the Arab world and that the rights of the [Palestinian] Arabs cannot be touched without prejudice to peace and stability in the Arab world...." It strongly opposed Zionism (q.v.), which it argued would solve the problem of the European Jews at the expense of the Palestinian Arabs of various religions. This statement helped to commit Egypt firmly to the Arab side of the Palestine question (*see* Palestine War).

ALEXANDRIA, UNIVERSITY OF. Egypt's second state institution of higher learning. It began with branches of Cairo University's (q.v.) Arts and Law Faculties in 1938. Founded in 1942, with Taha Husayn (q.v.) as its first rector and much of its faculty seconded from Cairo University, it was initially called Faruq University and took its present name in 1953. A distinctive feature is its Oceanographic Institute. It helped found Beirut's Arab University and several of the Egyptian state universities in the Delta. It had 11,000 students enrolled in 1962, more than 33,000 in 1972, and about 90,000 (and 3,610 faculty) in 1992.

ALFI BEY (1751?-1807). Mamluk (q.v.) leader, originally the protégé of Murad Bey (q.v.), who had paid 1,000 *ardabs* of wheat for him (hence his name). Alfi emerged as a leader following the French occupation (q.v.). His zeal in collecting taxes from Upper Egyptians made him a byword for cruelty, and they were greatly relieved when the British took him to England for a year to represent the Mamluks, whom the British and Ottomans were backing against the French. Upon his return, he began collecting taxes in the Delta. After Muhammad Ali (q.v.) and the Cairo ulama (q.v.) engineered the deposition of the Ottoman governor, Khurshid (q.v.), Alfi tried to make peace with Muhammad Ali, but his claims for tax farms exceeded what the new governor was prepared to grant, and he suspected Alfi of having British support. Soon after Alfi allegedly poisoned his rival, Bardisi (q.v.), he too died, presumably of cholera, on 30 January 1807. Irascible and ruthless in his treatment of Egyptian bedouin and peasants, he was the last obstacle to Muhammad Ali's taking full control of Egypt.

ALI BEY "AL-KABIR" (1728–73). Mamluk (q.v.) soldier and Egypt's de facto ruler from 1760 to 1772. Originally from the Abkhazian region of the Caucasus Mountains, Ali was brought as a slave to Egypt when he was a boy. In 1743 he was presented to Ibrahim Katkhuda, then Egypt's Mamluk leader, and given the rank of *kashif* ("local governor"). In 1753/54 he was given command of the official pilgrimage caravan from Cairo to Mecca and, for his victories over the bedouin tribes, earned the nicknames *Bulut Kapan* ("Cloud Catcher") and *Jinn Ali* ("Ali the Genie").

In 1755 he became a bey and in 1760 was named *shaykh al-balad* (q.v.), or virtual leader of Egypt's Mamluks. Thereupon he admitted into his service a younger Mamluk named Muhammad, later surnamed Abu al-Dhahab (q.v.). Muhammad Abu al-Dhahab married Ali's sister and became his trusted lieutenant in later military campaigns. Ali Bey managed to weaken the rival Mamluk factions by playing them off against one another and by poisoning or exiling their leaders. At first he was backed by Egypt's Ottoman governor, but in 1769 Ali deposed him and began building an independent Egyptian sultanate. Acting on his orders, Abu al-Dhahab occupied Mecca and Jidda in 1770. Aided by mercenary troops from the republic of Venice and the Knights of Malta, he then invaded Ottoman Palestine and Syria. Ali Bey and Abu al-Dhahab became estranged after the latter took Damascus, only to withdraw ten days later, hastening back to Cairo. When Ali Bey tried to exile his brother-in-law in 1772, the latter won the support of Ali's commanding officer and most of his troops. Ali fled to Jaffa and waged an inconclusive campaign against the Ottoman Empire (q.v.). When he returned in an attempt to resume control in Cairo, he was defeated by Abu al-Dhahab's superior forces. Captured, he was wounded while trying to resist and died of his wounds a week later.

Ali's reign marked a transition between medieval and modern Egypt, for he tried to strengthen his government by taking control of Egypt's trade, reduced his dependence on his fellow Mamluks, and made Egypt briefly independent of the Ottoman Empire. Although his expensive military campaigns led to high taxes, which alienated the people at the time, he is now viewed as a precursor to the better-known and more successful Muhammad Ali (q.v.).

ALI, KAMAL HASAN (1921-). Army officer and politician. He was trained at the Military Academy (q.v.) and commissioned in 1946. He was a battalion commander in the Palestine War (q.v.), led Egypt's expeditionary force during the Yemen Civil War (q.v.), and commanded an armored brigade in the October War (q.v.). He was an assistant to Defense Minister Jamasi (q.v.) in 1976–77 and replaced him in 1978 as minister and commander-in-chief. He took part in the peace negotiations with Israel, then became foreign minister and deputy prime minister in 1980 and premier in 1984. Ill health forced him to retire in 1985.

ALLENBY, EDMUND, FIRST VISCOUNT ALLENBY OF MEGIDDO (1861–1936). English field marshal and colonial administrator. He was educated at Haileybury and Sandhurst and saw service in South Africa, Ireland, and France. Because of his heroic victories against the Ottoman and German armies in Palestine and Syria, he was chosen by the British government to become high commissioner (q.v.) for Egypt and the Sudan following the outbreak of the 1919 Revolution (q.v.). He restored order in Egypt, in part by allowing Sa'd Zaghlul (q.v.) and his companions, who had been interned in Malta, to go to the Paris Peace Conference in April 1919. He later issued the unilateral declaration of Egypt's independence on 28 February 1922 and encouraged the drafting of the 1923 Constitution (q.v.), which became the basis of parliamentary government, though often honored in the breach, up to the 1952 Revolution (q.v.). He was deeply angered by the assassination of Sir Lee Stack (q.v.), the commander-in-chief of the Egyptian army, in 1924. Holding Premier Zaghlul and his cabinet responsible for the murder, he submitted an ultimatum demanding a large indemnity from the Egyptian government and imposing other penalties on the country, forcing the premier to resign. Estranged from the Foreign Office, Allenby resigned his post in June 1925 and retired from government service. A man of great courage and integrity, he could become irate when provoked. Some of his private papers are now in St. Antony's College, Oxford.

AMERICAN UNIVERSITY IN CAIRO (AUC). Privately owned institution of higher learning, chartered in Washington, D.C., and founded in 1919, initially with a strong Christian missionary emphasis. It began in 1920 to offer classes, starting at the upper secondary level and gradually evolving into a four-year college. Although its founders had envisaged building a campus near the Giza pyramids, it has been located in central Cairo (q.v.) since its inception. Its original building had been a palace and the first campus of the Egyptian University, which later became the University of Cairo (q.v.), and other parcels of property located nearby have gradually been purchased to facilitate its physical expansion. Plans to build on property purchased by the trustees for a larger campus had to be abandoned in 1949. At this time, AUC also phased out its preparatory section, in which most of its early students were enrolled.

Several of its constituent units have played a significant role in the life of Egypt, including its Division of Public Service, School of Oriental Studies (later renamed the Center for Arabic Studies), and Social Research Center. Its pioneer programs in education and journalism were phased out, but in recent years AUC has developed programs in management, engineering, arid-land agriculture, and mass communications. Its degrees were recognized by the People's Assembly (q.v.) as equivalent to those of the Egyptian national universities in 1976. It was accredited by the Middle States Association of Colleges and Schools in February 1982. It has placed increasing stress on research and graduate study, and in that year it opened a modern building for its library, now one of the best-equipped research libraries in Egypt. Financial support came initially from philanthropic institutions and families; more recently, from oil companies, the U.S. government, some Arab governments, and tuition fees. AUC established satellite campuses in Malta in 1977–79 for management, in Heliopolis for the Division of Public Service (adult education), and near Sadat City for desert development. Its enrollment was 668 students in 1950, 423 in 1962, 1,474 in 1972, 2,333 in 1983, and 3,682 in 1991, exclusive of adult education students.

AMIN, AHMAD (1886–1954). Arabic scholar, teacher, and editor. Born in Cairo (q.v.) to a traditional Muslim family, he received most of his education in *kuttab*s (q.v.) and at al-Azhar (q.v.). He began his career as an Arabic teacher at state primary schools in Alexandria (q.v.) and Cairo, then studied at the Shari'a (q.v.) Judges School, where he was appointed as a teaching assistant after his graduation. After a brief stint as a judge in the Kharija oasis, he returned to the school as a teacher of ethics. He also began to learn English from private tutors and formed a study group with some congenial friends. One outgrowth of this group was the Committee on Authorship, Translation, and Publication, which printed hundreds of original and translated books and produced a literary magazine, *al-Thaqafa*, of which Amin was to serve as editor from 1939 to 1953. In 1918 he began his literary career by publishing a translation of an English textbook on philosophy. Because of a change in the directorship of the Shari'a Judges School, Amin was transferred back to the judiciary in 1922, serving for two years in the country and two years in Cairo. In 1926 he became a lecturer in Arabic language and literature at Cairo University (q.v.), where he continued to teach full-time until 1946 and part-time in 1949. Working closely with Taha Husayn (q.v.) and other humanists, Amin began writing the series of volumes on Islamic history that have won him fame in the Arab world, starting with *Fajr al-Islam* ("The Dawn of Islam"), then *Duha al-Islam* ("The Forenoon of Islam"). He helped represent Egypt at the 1946 Palestine Conference in London and became director of the Arab League (q.v.) Cultural Bureau. He was awarded an honorary doctorate in 1948 and also the Fuad I Prize for his work, *Zuhr al-Islam* ("The Midday of Islam"). Hardworking but intensely shy, Ahmad Amin was an exemplar of Arabic scholarship in a time of rapid flux in Egyptian society.

AMIN, ALI (1912–76). Prominent journalist. He and his brother Mustafa (q.v.) founded a popular weekly, *Akhbar al-Yawm*, in 1944. Nominally independent but opposed to the Wafd (q.v.), the magazine was popularly believed to be close to King Faruq (q.v.). In 1952 they founded *al-Akhbar* (q.v.), which became Egypt's largest daily newspaper, with a circulation of over 700,000. They briefly published an Arabic version of the *Reader's*

Digest. Their newspapers were nationalized in 1960, but they were reappointed as editors and board chairmen in 1962. They were on poor terms with Nasir's (q.v.) government. Ali went into exile in 1965, but Sadat (q.v.) let him return in 1974 to replace Muhammad Hasanayn Haykal (q.v.) as editor of *al-Ahram* (q.v.). He later rejoined his brother at *al-Akhbar*, but Ali and Mustafa soon broke with Sadat and were dismissed in 1976. Ali died shortly thereafter.

AMIN, MUSTAFA (1912-). Influential editor of *al-Akhbar* (q.v.). He was editor-in-chief of *Akhir Sa'a* from 1938 to 1941 and of *al-Ithnayn* from 1941 to 1944. He and his brother Ali (q.v.) founded *Akhbar al-Yawm* as a weekly magazine in 1944 and purchased control of *Akhir Sa'a* in 1946. He and Ali were members of Parliament during the 1940s. In 1952 they founded *al-Ahkbar* as a popular daily. Although it was placed under the control of the National Union (q.v.) in 1960, the Amin brothers continued to manage it and were reappointed as editors in 1962. Defying efforts by the Nasir (q.v.) government to muzzle the press, they lost their positions. Mustafa was tried in 1965 for spying for the United States, convicted, and sentenced to life imprisonment. He continued writing articles in prison, succeeded in smuggling some of them out and getting them published under a pseudonym in a Beirut newspaper. Pardoned by Sadat (q.v.) in 1974 and released, Mustafa was reinstated as editor of *al-Akhbar* but was again dismissed in 1976. He has continued to work as a freelance journalist since then and published a book, *al-Kitab al-mamnu'*, on his prison experiences.

AMIN, QASIM (1863–1908). Lawyer, writer, and pioneer of Egyptian feminism (q.v.). Of Kurdish origin, he was born in Cairo (q.v.) and studied law there and in Paris. He held various judicial posts, rising to the position of chancellor of the Cairo National Court of Appeals. He wrote *Les Égyptiens*, a work defending Egypt and Islam against a critical book by a French writer, but soon came to feel that his defense of the female role in Islam was incorrect and proceeded to publish two books advocating greater rights for women, *Tahrir al-mara* ("The Liberation of Woman") and *al-Mara al-jadida* ("The New Woman"). His views were attacked by many Muslim contemporaries, including Tal'at Harb (q.v.) and Mustafa Kamil (q.v.), but have influenced later Egyptian feminists.

AMIR, ABD AL-HAKIM (1919–67). Army officer and politician. He graduated from the Military Academy (q.v.) in 1938 and served in the Palestine War (q.v.). One of the founders of the Free Officers (q.v.), he subsequently became a member of the Revolutionary Command Council (q.v.), commander-in-chief of Egypt's armed forces in June 1953, and war minister in 1954. Promoted to the rank of field marshal in 1958, he became vice president and war minister of the United Arab Republic (q.v.) in 1958. When opposition to Nasir (q.v.) grew in Syria, he went there as special commissioner to maintain the union. After Syria seceded in 1961, he became Egypt's defense minister and also a member of the Presidential Council. He was appointed first vice president and deputy commander-in-chief of the Egyptian armed forces under the 1964 Constitution (q.v.). Generally blamed for Egypt's defeat in the June War (q.v.), Amir was subsequently dismissed from all his positions. Accused of plotting a military coup, he was put under house arrest in August 1967 and committed suicide the following month, although some Egyptians believe that he was poisoned by the Mukhabarat (q.v.). Regarded as right-wing among the Free Officers, he later enriched himself from some questionable land deals and opposed the growing populism of the government and its ties to the USSR. Politically and personally loyal to Nasir, he never differed with him publicly.

ANGLO-EGYPTIAN AGREEMENT (1954). Diplomatic pact that provided for the phased evacuation, over a 20-month period, of British troops from their bases in the Suez Canal (q.v.) zone. The two countries agreed that Egypt, together with British civilian technicians, would maintain the bases in order that, in case of an armed attack on an Arab League (q.v.) member state or Turkey, a NATO member, Britain might reoccupy them during the war and withdraw upon its termination. Egypt would also provide necessary naval and air facilities in such an eventuality. The contracting parties recognized that the Suez Canal was an integral part of Egypt but also an internationally important waterway and expressed their determination to uphold the Constantinople Convention (q.v.). The agreement, initialed by the negotiators on 27 July 1954 and signed formally on 18 October, was to last for seven years. It was a labored compromise between British imperialism and Egyptian nationalism, not liked by either, and the result of diplomatic pressure from the United States, which hoped that Egypt might then agree to join a regional anti-Communist defense organization. Communist, Muslim, and nationalist groups in Egypt also attacked it. Although Britain did evacuate its last troops on 18 June 1956, the Suez War (q.v.) led to Egypt's denunciation of the agreement, which became inoperative.

ANGLO-EGYPTIAN TREATY (1936). Diplomatic pact that defined Britain's military position in Egypt and created a 20-year alliance between the two countries. It officially ended the British occupation (q.v.), provided for the exchange of ambassadors, committed Britain to support Egypt's application for League of Nations membership, created an alliance that committed the two countries not to adopt "in relation to foreign countries an attitude which is inconsistent with the alliance," provided for mutual consultations in case either party should have a dispute with a third state that might lead to a rupture of relations, committed each side to come to the aid of the other if it should become involved in a war, gave Britain the right in wartime to utilize facilities on Egyptian territory, allowed British troops to occupy a specified zone to guard the Suez Canal (q.v.), provided for the withdrawal of British troops from other parts of Egypt as soon as roads and railways were improved and new barracks constructed, postponed any change in the status of the Sudan (q.v.), renounced extraterritorial rights for British civilian subjects in Egypt, pledged Britain to work toward a prompt end to the capitulations (q.v.) and the Mixed Courts (q.v.), and provided for adjudication of disputes and ratification of the treaty by both sides.

Although Britain was limited to 10,000 land forces and 400 pilots in peacetime, plus supporting civilian personnel, the treaty permitted Britain to enlarge its occupation army in case of war, hence the burgeoning number of British Empire troops stationed in Cairo (q.v.), Alexandria (q.v.), and the Suez Canal (q.v.) zone during World War II (q.v.), an occupation many Egyptians resented. Britain felt that the Egyptians failed to see how it protected them from the Axis Powers and argued, up to the 4 February Incident (q.v.), that the Egyptian government was not fulfilling its responsibilities under the Treaty. After the war, many Egyptians demanded an end to the British occupation of Egypt and the Sudan. As the occupation became increasingly unpopular, the Egyptian government denounced the 1936 Treaty in 1951, but British troops remained in their Suez Canal base. Egyptian *fidaiyin* (q.v.) tried in vain to dislodge them by force, but an economic boycott hampered their effectiveness. After the 1952 Revolution (q.v.), the Nasir (q.v.) government negotiated a new Anglo-Egyptian agreement (q.v.) in 1954.

AQABA, GULF OF. Maritime inlet from the Red Sea, fronted by Egypt, Israel, Jordan, and Saudi Arabia. Egypt contested Israel's right of access to this waterway between 1949 and 1956 and again in May 1967, creating a casus belli for the June War (q.v.).

AL-AQQAD, ABBAS MAHMUD (1889–1964). Journalist, poet, and writer. Largely self-educated, he began his career by writing cultural and literary articles for *al-Dustur* between 1907 and 1909. He became an editor for *al-Muayyad* (q.v.) and then for *al-Ahali* and *al-Ahram* (q.v.). In 1921 he became the editor of *al-Balagh* (q.v.), the Wafd Party (q.v.) newspaper. As a Wafdist he was elected to the Chamber of Deputies in 1930, but he was imprisoned by the Sidqi (q.v.) government, allegedly for his loyalty to the 1923 Constitution (q.v.). After breaking with Nahhas (q.v.) in 1935, he joined the Sa'dist Party (q.v.) in 1937, was elected to the 1938 Parliament, and edited its newspaper, *al-Asas*. He was anti-Fascist during World War II (q.v.) and later became anti-Communist under Nasir (q.v.). He chaired the poetry committee of the Supreme Council for Arts, Literature, and Social Sciences, and in 1959 received a state prize for literature. Aqqad wrote many poems about nature, love, his own feelings, and children, but also memoirs about such public figures as Sa'd Zaghlul (q.v.), who was also the subject of one of his biographies. He also wrote biographies of the Prophet Muhammad and the first four caliphs, and many brief sketches about incidents and personalities in Egypt's modern history. One of his novels, *Sara* (1938), has been translated into English, and his literary study of Ibn al-Rumi was translated in *Four Egyptian Literary Critics*.

ARAB CONTRACTORS. Construction firm, begun in 1949 by Uthman Ahmad Uthman (q.v.), involved in building the Aswan High Dam (q.v.) and in numerous projects in the oil-rich Arab countries. Under the July Laws (q.v.), the government was supposed to assume control of 50 percent of its stock, but Uthman remained its chairman until 1973 and continued to expand its activities on behalf of Nasir's (q.v.) government. It currently employs tens of thousands of administrators, engineers, technicians, and workers, and has branches in Saudi Arabia, Kuwait, and various other Arab countries. Uthman had a high profile during the Sadat (q.v.) era, using contacts with retired Egyptian generals to siphon off cement and other scarce construction materials for his company. Mubarak (q.v.) hoped at first to curb his power by steering government contracts away from his company and by suspending some of his customary privileges. The Arab Contractors proceeded to speed up completion of projects that had languished for years, Mubarak was mollified, and the company continues to prosper.

ARAB FEDERATION PROJECTS. Independent Arab states have made many efforts to unite, ranging from the loose association of the Arab League (q.v.) to the organic union of Egypt and Syria as the United Arab Republic (q.v.) in 1958. Most common have been proposed federations of Arab countries. Egypt was involved in the proposed revival of the United Arab Republic in 1963, including both Syria and Iraq once the Ba'th Party had taken control of those countries, and the 1971 Federation of Arab Republics (q.v.), which would have included Libya (q.v.) (with which Egypt was to unite) and Syria. Libya has made other attempts to federate with Algeria, Tunisia, and Morocco, usually to oppose Egypt and never with lasting success.

ARAB LEAGUE. Political association of sovereign Arab states, founded in 1945, with its headquarters in Cairo (q.v.). Egypt played the lead role in its establishment, and for the first 33 years of its history its secretary-general was always an Egyptian. The Arab League adopted a collective security pact in 1950, but it has rarely served as a true military alliance in times when individual member states were at war, even with Israel. As a result of signing the Egyptian-Israeli Peace Treaty (q.v.) in 1979, Egypt was expelled from membership and the league's headquarters were moved to Tunis. In 1989, however, Egypt was readmitted to the league, and its headquarters returned to Cairo in 1991. The organization has disappointed the hopes of many Arabs who believed that it would pave the way for a union of all Arabic-speaking countries, but it has been a useful meeting place for otherwise disparate Arab regimes and has facilitated many economic, social, and intellectual cooperative projects.

ARAB NATIONALISM. A general term for any movement or ideology that seeks to unify all or some of the Arabic-speaking countries and that strives to ensure their independence from non-Arab control. The movement began among some of the Arabic-speaking Muslim and Christian subjects of the Ottoman Empire (q.v.) between 1880 and 1914, gaining popularity after World War I (q.v.). Despite Egypt's preponderant size, population, and cultural leadership among the Arab countries, Arab nationalism appealed more to Syrians, Palestinians, and Iraqis than to most Egyptians. However, some of the first expressions of Arab nationalism occurred in Cairo (q.v.) or Alexandria (q.v.), where Arabs were free from Ottoman censorship.

Egyptians became more interested in Arab nationalism as a result of the growing struggle against Zionism (q.v.), their disillusionment with Western liberal institutions and with Pharaonism (q.v.), and the influence of such writers as Ahmad Hasan al-Zayyat (q.v.). The growing interdependence between Egypt and the eastern Arab countries caused by the Middle East Supply Centre (q.v.) during World War II (q.v.), creation of the Arab League (q.v.) in 1945, and the mounting Palestine problem also dramatized Egypt's identity as an Arab state. Egypt was generally regarded as the leading Arab nationalist country from 1945 until 1978. Since the Egyptian-Israeli Peace Treaty (q.v.), Iraq, Syria, and Libya have at various times claimed leadership of Arab nationalism, which recently has been eclipsed by individual state nationalist movements and by Islamism (q.v.).

ARAB SOCIALISM. Ideology that calls for state control over Arab economies, or at least over their major manufacturing industries, and for a more even distribution of income among the peoples of the various Arab countries. The movement was espoused by Jamal Abd al-Nasir (q.v.), especially after 1958, and was adopted by various other Arab governments. The ideology was influenced by, but not identical with, the ideas of the Ba'th Party of Syria and Iraq. It emphasized land reform (q.v.), social insurance, nationalization of public utilities and major industries, and redistribution of wealth, but based its ideology on Islamic principles and rejected the idea of a class struggle. Its ideas are summarized in the National Charter (q.v.).

ARAB SOCIALIST UNION (ASU). Egypt's sole political party from 1962 to 1978. Founded by Nasir's (q.v.) government to replace the National Union (q.v.) and to spread Arab socialism (q.v.), it was meant to serve as a conduit of government directives from top to bottom and of popular needs and wishes from bottom to top. Organized into national, provincial, district, and village councils, its membership mushroomed to a reported 5 million Egyptians, most of whom joined to protect their rights and prestige or to attain higher positions within the bureaucracy, not to revolutionize Egyptian society and values. In 1964 Nasir proposed to create within the ASU a vanguard organization to be led by dedicated revolutionaries. He ordered the release of the Communists (q.v.) from prison, and some were given posts in the information media or in ASU branch organizations. Ali Sabri (q.v.) was given overall direction of the ASU in 1965, but his efforts to develop a vanguard foundered on the lack of committed revolutionaries within Egyptian society.

After the June War (q.v.), Egypt focused its energies on recovering from its losses, and the ASU declined as an instrument of popular mobilization. Most of Sadat's (q.v.) opposition came from the ASU, and the 1971 Corrective Revolution (q.v.) stripped the organization of its most influential leaders. By 1974 Sadat was considering ways to create an opposition movement to the ASU, as a part of his *infitah* (q.v.) policy, and during the 1976 elections for the Popular Assembly three *manabir* ("platforms") were created to permit greater diversity of opinion among the candidates. The centrist platform, which upheld the policies of Sadat's government under the leadership of Prime Minister Mamduh Salim (q.v.), became the *Misr* Party and later the National Democratic Party (q.v.), replacing the ASU formally in July 1978. It has been hard for Egyptian leaders since the 1952 Revolution (q.v.) to find ways to involve the people in the processes of political decision making, and their attempt to combine mobilization with Arab socialism has generally been viewed as a failure.

ARABIC LANGUAGE ACADEMY (1932). Scholarly organization that seeks to preserve and revive the Arabic cultural heritage by publishing an academic journal and various books, lexicons, and dictionaries.

ARCHAEOLOGY. Egypt has been a major area for the study of antiquity since the time of the ancient Greeks, when Herodotus and Plato pondered the meaning of the pyramids, obelisks, and inscriptions of the already ancient Egyptians. The development of Egyptology, however, did not begin until Champollion (q.v.) deciphered the hieroglyphic script in the early nineteenth century. Egypt contains many of the world's main sites for archaeological study, and numerous European and North American expeditions have unearthed ancient temples, sketched or photographed monuments and artifacts, and translated inscriptions. Although early Egyptology often amounted to plundering Egypt's treasures for private collections, universities, and museums in Europe, it made the country aware of its immense heritage and created the Egyptian Museum (q.v.), one of the world's greatest Egyptological collections. The discoveries made by Egyptologists, notably the excavation of Tutankhamon's Tomb (q.v.), inspired Pharaonism (q.v.) as one of the elements in Egyptian nationalism. Egyptians now play a major role in excavating, deciphering, and reporting on their country's Pharaonic heritage, due in part to the Faculty of Archaeology at Cairo University (q.v.). Other significant, if less well-known, fields of archaeology in Egypt cover the Greco-Roman period (332 BC-640 CE), the monuments of the early Copts (q.v.), and the artifacts and monuments of the first centuries of Islam (q.v.).

AL-ARISH, CONVENTION OF (1800). Abortive pact between France and Britain, which would have provided for the evacuation of the French occupation (q.v.) troops from Egypt, with their arms and baggage, in ships belonging to the Ottoman Empire (q.v.). The British government, believing that the French would soon be defeated by the Turks, refused to ratify the convention, and the fighting in Egypt continued for another year.

ARMED FORCES. From pharaonic times until the nineteenth century Egypt's defense was never entrusted to ethnic Egyptians. Under the Ottoman Empire (q.v.), military as well as political control was held by Mamluk (q.v.) princes, who purchased slave soldiers of their own and also used bedouins (q.v.) as auxiliaries. Napoléon's (q.v.) invasion discredited the Mamluk system. After the Ottomans retook Egypt in 1801, neither their appointed governors nor the Mamluk survivors could control the country, and power was seized by the commander of an Albanian regiment, Muhammad Ali (q.v.).

To remain in power and expand the lands under his control, Muhammad Ali developed a powerful army and navy, but soon realized that he could not rely on his Albanian and Turkish officers, who mutinied and almost overthrew him in 1815. He tried to recruit Sudanese soldiers from Kordofan and Sannar, but they could not withstand the rigors of

Egypt's climate or his training methods. Aided by Colonel Sève (q.v.), he established the Military Academy (q.v.), initially in Aswan, to train his own officers. By 1823 the government was also recruiting Egyptian peasants to serve as soldiers, despite their bitter resistance, and training them effectively, but they would not be admitted to the officer corps until the time of Sa'id (q.v.). At the height of Muhammad Ali's power, Egypt had about 100,000 men under arms, a high figure in relation to the country's 4.5 million inhabitants at that time. As a result of the 1840 London Convention (q.v.) and the 1841 Ottoman *firman* (q.v.), Egypt's army was cut back to 18,000. It remained small until Khedive Isma'il (qq.v.) sought to increase his power by rendering Egypt more independent of the Ottoman Empire and expanding Egyptian control over the Sudan (q.v.). During his reign new military academies were established in Abbasiyya (q.v.), the various branches of the army and navy were modernized, a general staff was established under the guidance of an American officer, General Charles Stone, and the first military newspapers were founded. These reforms proved too expensive for Egypt's economy to support, however, and the Caisse de la Dette Publique (q.v.) and the Dual Control (q.v.) demanded heavy cutbacks in the military. Their financial stringencies, which especially harmed the ethnic Egyptian officers, led to the Urabi (q.v.) revolution.

As soon as the British expeditionary force under General Wolseley (q.v.) had defeated Urabi's troops in 1882, Khedive Tawfiq (q.v.) formally dissolved the Egyptian army. A smaller force was built up under British guidance and kept strictly apolitical. Made up mainly of peasant conscripts, it performed well in retaking the Sudan in 1896–98 but played no role in the two world wars (qq.v.). Although some Egyptian individuals and units fought bravely in the 1948 Palestine War (q.v.), the army, poorly armed and led, was easily defeated by the Israelis.

Only after the 1952 Revolution (q.v.) did Egypt's armed forces gain some power and prestige, partly as a result of the Revolutionary Command Council's (q.v.) quest for legitimacy in a society accustomed to contemn military officers, but especially because of the need to build up Egypt's defenses after the Israeli raid on Gaza (q.v.) in February 1955. As a result of the Czech Arms Deal (q.v.), Egypt began to acquire large quantities of guns, tanks, airplanes, and other military equipment from Communist countries. The 1956 Suez War (q.v.) did not add to the luster of Egypt's still insufficiently trained armed forces, but Nasir (q.v.) continued to rearm and in 1962 sent troops to fight in the Yemen Civil War (q.v.). With its best fighting units in Yemen, the army was again shamed by Israel in 1967 in the June War (q.v.), which led to heavy casualties and loss of matériel in the Sinai (q.v.). Again the Communist countries rearmed Egypt, and the USSR adopted a more direct role in the training of Egypt's officers and soldiers. The performance of Egypt's troops against Israel in the War of Attrition (q.v.) remained poor, but it improved markedly under Sadat (q.v.) in the October War (q.v.). Some deterioration in the size and quality of Egypt's armed forces has occurred because of the relative decline in military expenditures since the 1979 Egyptian-Israeli Treaty (q.v.), but the United States and other Western countries have sold modern weapons and helped to upgrade training, engaging in joint exercises such as Operation Bright Star (q.v.). Egypt's army immediately after the June 1967 war was estimated at 140,000 men, of which 30,000 were serving in Yemen; this number had risen in 1972 to 275,000 and in 1989 to 320,000 (of whom 180,000 were conscripts).

Egypt's navy, although the smallest of its services, is large by Middle Eastern standards. It numbered 11,000 in 1967 and 14,000 in 1972; it now has 18,000 men (and 2,000 more in the Coast Guard). The air force had 15,000 men in 1967, 25,000 in 1972, and 30,000 in 1989; its combat aircraft numbered 225 in late 1967, 523 in 1972, and more than 500 in 1989. Expenditures on foreign arms remain high; in 1991 Egypt purchased almost $2 billion worth via the U.S. government and $990 million worth from commercial suppliers.

ARMENIANS. Indo-European Christian people who originated in the mountains of eastern Anatolia and the Caucasus. Armenian families and individuals have come to Egypt since the era of the Fatimid Caliphate, several of whose strongest *vizirs* were of Armenian origin. During the reign of Muhammad Ali (q.v.), some Armenians attained high positions in his government. An Armenian statesman prominent later in the nineteenth century was Nubar (q.v.). In modern times, Armenians have been leaders in Egyptian banking and commerce and in some of the professions, living mainly in Cairo (q.v.) and Alexandria (q.v.). They numbered about 30,000 in 1945, approximately twice the Armenian population of Egypt before World War I (q.v.), when many entered the country as refugees from the Ottoman Empire (q.v.). Under Nasir (q.v.), discrimination in Egypt caused many of its Armenian inhabitants to emigrate to Europe or North America.

ARTS, VISUAL. Since antiquity Egypt has been renowned for its monumental architecture, sculpture, and mural painting. European architectural styles, Pharaonism (q.v.) and Islam (q.v.) have combined to influence the public architecture of modern Egypt, but popular motifs have also gained prominence through the work of Hasan Fathi (q.v.). Painting, sculpture, and other representational arts used to be limited by the Muslim abhorrence of idolatry, but Muhammad Abduh (q.v.) issued a legal opinion that the Shari'a (q.v.) did not forbid artistic expression. The prominence of European architects, painters, sculptors, and photographers in Egypt in the late-nineteenth and early twentieth centuries also promoted the development of the visual arts. In 1908 Prince Yusuf Kamal founded Egypt's School of Fine Arts, one of whose early graduates, Mahmud Mukhtar (q.v.), became the pioneer sculptor of the country. Noted Egyptian painters include Mahmud Sa'id and Muhammad Naji (q.v.). Handicrafts have long been another outlet for artistic talent and expression, as Egyptian artisans excelled in textile design, glassblowing, jewelry, metalworking, turned-wood latticework (called *mashrabiyya* in Arabic), pottery, and leather-working. Although European and American tourists displaced Egyptians as the main market for some of their products, leading to some debasement of their designs, interest in authentic Egyptian handicrafts is reviving in Egypt and elsewhere in the Arab world. A well-known achievement in woven textile design derives from the pioneering work of the architect/educator Ramses Wisa-Wasif (q.v.), who encouraged peasant children in the village of Harraniyya to undertake countless variations in hand-loom weaving. Since the 1952 Revolution (q.v.), the Egyptian Ministry of Culture has facilitated development of the visual arts in the metropolitan and provincial capitals and encouraged preservation of handicrafts in such designated centers as Wikalat al-Ghuri and Bayt al-Sinnari in Cairo (q.v.). Photographic journalism, television (q.v.), museums, and international exhibitions, together with public education (q.v.) at all levels, have accentuated the visual arts and crafts, making them more accessible to popular demand and critical review.

ASHRAF. Descendants of the Prophet Muhammad, especially by his grandson, Hasan. Formerly, they enjoyed special privileges due to their high prestige among Muslims. The *ashraf* played a ceremonial role on Muslim holidays and in some cases received gifts from other Muslims. Their privileged position has declined during the twentieth century.

ASWAN DAM. Large water storage dam constructed by British and Egyptian engineers in 1898–1901 and enlarged in 1912 and 1933. The storage capacity of its reservoir reached 5.7 billion cubic meters, and its construction made it possible to convert Middle and parts of Upper Egypt to perennial irrigation (q.v.).

ASWAN HIGH DAM. Gigantic water storage and hydroelectric project undertaken by the Nasir (q.v.) regime in 1955 and constructed by Soviet and Egyptian engineers in 1960–71. The project was first conceived by a Greek Egyptian engineer, Adrian Daninos, in 1948. Although skeptical engineers feared the silting up of the reservoir that the dam would create, or high rates of surface evaporation, and the downstream erosion of the Nile River (q.v.) bed, Egyptians favored the High Dam idea over the

Century Storage Scheme (q.v.) as a means of enabling their country to control annual variations in the Nile flood, increase the area of irrigated land, and generate enough kilowatt-hours of electricity for nationwide domestic and industrial use.

After the 1952 Revolution (q.v.), the Revolutionary Command Council (q.v.) took up the project as a symbol of its resolution to modernize Egypt. The public works ministry, hitherto committed to the Century Storage Scheme, was persuaded to study the project. West Germany agreed to finance and undertake a feasibility study, and a British engineering firm was hired to review the implementation of all aspects of design and specifications with the Egyptian experts. To obtain financing, Egypt approached the International Bank for Reconstruction and Development (IBRD, or World Bank), which made its own engineering and economic studies. After political delays due to negotiations for the 1954 Anglo-Egyptian Agreement (q.v.) and the arms purchasing crisis of 1955, the IBRD recommended that the High Dam be funded. The total project cost was estimated at $1.3 billion, of which $400 million would be in foreign exchange. The IBRD agreed to lend $200 million at 5.5% interest, while the U.S. government would grant $56 million and Britain $14 million for the first stage, with an understanding that the two countries would later lend a further $130 million. Attached to the offer were several conditions: Egypt must divert one-third of its internal revenues to the project over ten years, the IBRD would periodically review relevant aspects of Egypt's economy, contracts must be awarded by open bidding–except that no bids might be accepted from a Communist country, Egypt could not assume new foreign obligations or borrow money without consulting the IBRD, and it must first reach an agreement with the Sudan (q.v.) on how the Nile waters would be allocated.

The IBRD's conditions for funding the High Dam were criticized by many Egyptians, and Nasir (q.v.) especially feared that Egypt would be pressured to make peace with Israel or to join a Western military alliance. He did not immediately accept these terms, hoping to gain Soviet support for the scheme instead. Western enthusiasm for the project waned in 1955–56 because of political differences between Egypt and the West, especially among supporters of Israel and Southerners within the U.S. Congress. Convinced that Washington would never approve the project, Nasir instructed his envoy to tell Secretary of State Dulles (q.v.) that Egypt would accept *all* conditions for financing the High Dam. Dulles withdrew the offer, hoping to punish the Nasir government for supporting the Communists. In revenge, Nasir nationalized the Suez Canal Company (q.v.), claiming that its revenues would pay for building the High Dam, which now became a symbol of Egyptian resistance against foreign imperialism.

After much hesitation, in 1958 the USSR offered Egypt a 400-million-ruble ($100 million) credit toward its construction and began making its own engineering studies. Once agreement was reached with the Sudan in 1959, Soviet and Egyptian engineers began work at the dam site in January 1960. The coffer dam was completed and was formally opened by Nasir and Khrushchev in 1964. Work on the main dam took seven years, and its official completion was in January 1971, with Soviet President Podgorny and Sadat (q.v.) presiding over the ceremonies. The dam was 3,600 meters long at its crest, which stood 111 meters above the riverbed level. Its reservoir, Lake Nasir, had a total capacity of 162 billion cubic meters and was 500 km long. Its 12 turbines could generate 10 billion kilowatt-hours of electricity annually. It was hoped that the High Dam would enable Egypt to reclaim 1.2 million feddans of cultivable land and convert some 800,000 feddans of basin-irrigated (q.v.) land in Upper Egypt to perennial irrigation (q.v.). No longer would Egypt fear the economic losses of either too high or too low an annual Nile flood.

The Aswan High Dam is one of the largest public works projects ever built. It soured Egypt's diplomatic relations with the West, but allowed no long-term political gains to the Soviet Union. The economic benefits of the High Dam seem so far to have been more than offset by its drawbacks, including the loss of fertile alluvium to Egypt's farmland and the resulting greater need for chemical fertilizers, the scouring of the Nile banks, increased mineral deposits on irrigated lands, and the loss of nutrients that formerly supported Nile river fish and marine life in the eastern Mediterranean. The costs of maintaining and repairing the dam have exceeded the government's expectations; the 12 Soviet turbines cracked and were replaced between 1985 and 1991 by the Allis Chalmers Company at a cost of $100 million, financed by the U.S. Agency for International Development (q.v.). Lake Nasir led to the displacement of many Nubians (q.v.), only some of whom have been resettled, and increased the humidity of Egypt's climate. Many Egyptians also feel that the dam made them more vulnerable to a foreign military attack. It has helped industrialize Egypt and made low-cost electric power more available. Reclamation has been started on some 900,000 feddans of desert lands, but annual costs of reclaiming this land have exceeded revenues by at least £E10 million, and no new reclamation projects have been initiated since 1972.

ASYUT. Large city in Upper Egypt, having an approximate population of 250,000 in 1986, historically important as an entrepôt in trade across the Sahara desert and with the Sudan (q.v.). It has lately been noted for its prominent Coptic (q.v.) population and for the Islamist (q.v.) riots that broke out there following Sadat's (q.v.) assassination in 1981 and again during the early 1990s. It is also the site of one of Egypt's national universities, founded in 1957 with a stress on scientific and technical subjects, and has a branch campus of al-Azhar (q.v.). One of the supplementary barrages of the first Aswan Dam (q.v.) is in Asyut.

AL-ATTAR, HASAN (1766–1835). Muslim scholar, reformer, and rector of al-Azhar (q.v.). Born in Cairo to a family of North African origin, he was educated at al-Azhar. During the French occupation (q.v.), he observed some of the work being done by French scholars. He then went to Damascus and Albania before returning to Egypt. As a teacher at al-Azhar, he introduced new teaching methods, stressing analysis in place of rote learning. His interests were wide-ranging; his essays, *al-Rasail* (first published in 1866), covered law, logic, grammar, medicine, and other sciences. Muhammad Ali (q.v.) appointed him in 1828 the first editor of Egypt's official journal, *al-Waqai al-misriyya* (q.v.), and in 1830/31 the rector of al-Azhar. He influenced such early reformers as Rifa'a Rafi' al-Tahtawi (q.v.).

ATTRITION, WAR OF. Artillery and air struggle between Egypt and Israel, following the breakdown of Gunnar Jarring's mission to negotiate a settlement between the two countries on the basis of Security Council Resolution 242 (q.v.). It began at the Suez Canal (q.v.) in September 1968, with Egyptian artillery bombardment of Israeli positions, leading to Israeli aerial attacks against civilian targets and helicopter raids deep into Egyptian territory. Israel also strengthened its position by building the Bar Lev Line (q.v.). Nasir (q.v.) had Egyptian civilians evacuated from the cities along the Suez Canal and began building, with Soviet assistance, an elaborate defense network to counteract Israel's control of the air. In March 1969 he formally launched his War of Attrition against Israeli troops at the Canal, but they soon extended the struggle over much of northern Egypt and the Red Sea coast, destroying Egyptian radar installations, attacking artillery and surface-to-air missile systems, and making deep-penetration bombing raids against Egyptian targets in the interior of the country. Nasir sought more Soviet aid, including personnel to operate the new air defense system and to fly newly supplied fighter planes. The conflict ended in August 1970, when the two countries accepted a temporary cease-fire under the Rogers Peace Plan (q.v.).

AUTONOMY TALKS, PALESTINIAN. Inconclusive negotiations between Egypt and Israel, following their 1979 peace treaty, aimed at achieving autonomous status for Gaza Strip (q.v.) and West Bank Palestinians. Egypt withdrew from the talks after Israel invaded Lebanon in June 1982, and they have not been resumed.

AVIATION, CIVIL. Egypt's first airline was founded in 1932 as Misrair, owned by Bank Misr (q.v.) but under British technical direction. In 1935 it carried 6,970 passengers, a number which tripled in 1936, when it added air service to Baghdad and Cyprus, in addition to lines between Cairo and Alexandria, Upper Egypt, Port Said, and Palestine. In 1950 it also had service to Beirut and Damascus, dropping service to Jerusalem, Haifa, and Tel Aviv. Its network has gradually expanded to include the rest of the Middle East, South and East Asia, Europe, and North America. It carried 1.6 million passengers in 1983. It was renamed United Arab Airlines in 1960 and Egyptair in 1971. There is also a state-owned airline, Air Sinai, with service from Cairo to points in the Sinai Peninsula (q.v.). Zas, Egypt's first privately owned airline, flies daily from Cairo to Aswan, Luxor, the Red Sea, and the Sinai. Egypt's airlines carried 2.6 million passengers in 1991, flying 5.2 billion passenger-km domestically.

AWQAF, ***see*** **WAQF**.

AL-AZHAR. Muslim mosque-university in Cairo (q.v.), founded in 972, initially as a center for training Fatimid Shi'i propagandists. Since the reign of Salah al-Din (1171–93), it has been Egypt's major center for training ulama (q.v.), drawing aspirants from all lands where Islam (q.v.) prevails. In the eighteenth century it was an oasis in an intellectual desert, for most *awqaf* (q.v.) that supported mosques and learning had dried up, owing to Egypt's economic decline. During the French occupation (q.v.), al-Azhar was the nerve center of Muslim resistance, despite efforts by Napoléon (q.v.) and his successors to win the support of its ulama. Muhammad Ali (q.v.) weakened al-Azhar by nationalizing many of the *awqaf* that had supported it, but started providing state subsidies, thus enabling him to appoint its rector. Some of the rectors, such as Hasan al-Attar (q.v.) and Ibrahim al-Bajuri, were leaders of Islamic reform, but major changes did not occur until after the 1858 Land Law (*see* Land Reform), which freed its *awqaf* from state control. Khedive Isma'il (qq.v.) gave money for repairs to the physical structure and encouraged its shaykhs to teach geometry, history, music, and other elective subjects. The government passed legislation that set standards for admission to the faculty. Khedives Tawfiq and Abbas Hilmi II (qq.v.) also sponsored repairs to the physical plant; the latter is honored by a new building called al-Riwaq al-Abbasiyya. Two rectors of his era, Shaykhs Muhammad al-Mahdi and Muhammad Abduh (q.v.), stand out as major reformers: establishing a general library for al-Azhar as a whole; fixing standards for the admission, registration, and examination of students; raising pay for the teachers; creating an administrative structure; placing the mosque schools of Tanta, Disuq, and Damietta under its supervision; improving the remuneration and accommodation of the students; and installing electric lighting and plumbing. A major reform law was passed in 1911 after an era of turmoil–politically as well as academically inspired–among the teachers and students. It further systemized the levels of instruction, the academic calendar, and the administration of al-Azhar and its subsidiary institutions, which included the recently formed School for Shar'ia (q.v.) Judges. The 1911 law set up the Corps of the Great Scholars (*Hayat Kibar al-Ulama*), comprising 30 leading shaykhs of whom 11 were Hanafi, nine Shafi'i, nine Maliki, and one Hanbali, with standards for admission to this august group.

Although forbidden under the 1911 law to participate in politics, the teachers and students played a major role in the 1919 Revolution (q.v.). During the constitutional period al-Azhar was often a bone of contention between Abdin Palace (q.v.) and the Wafd Party (q.v.). King Fuad (q.v.) heavily subsidized al-Azhar, seeking its shaykhs' support for his claims to the caliphate (q.v.). Reform laws were passed in 1923, providing for postgraduate studies; in 1925, placing al-Azhar under the supervision of the education ministry and bringing Dar al-Ulum (q.v.) under its control, but this law was later annulled; in 1929 replacing the students' bread dole with semiannual scholarship stipends; and in 1930, 1933, and 1936 modernizing the administrative structure to make al-Azhar more like a modern university, with specialized colleges (*kulliyyat*) for theology (*usul al-din*), law (*al-shari'a al-islamiyya*), and Arabic language (which included the liberal arts generally). Al-Azhar began sending missions to all parts of Asia and Africa to provide information about Islam and published a magazine, *Nur al-Islam*, later renamed *Majallat al-Azhar*. The 1936 law was especially comprehensive, setting up the administrative and curricular structure that survived until al-Azhar was nationalized and further modernized in 1961.

Since the 1961 reforms the University (as it has now officially become) has added modern buildings in various Cairo neighborhoods and new faculties for medicine, engineering, and other relatively secular subjects. It had an enrollment in 1950 of 2,794, with preparatory institutes in Cairo, Alexandria (q.v.), Damietta, Tanta, Zagazig, Asyut (q.v.), Minya, Shibin al-Kum, Disuq, and Suhaj. Its enrollment in 1962 was 3,798, plus 25,020 at its preparatory institutes. In that year women were admitted to al-Azhar for the first time, and in 1972 it had 16,852, including 1,208 women. Although Muslims from foreign countries had always been a component of the student body at al-Azhar, their numbers rose markedly in the early twentieth century, with the largest contingents coming from the Sudan (q.v.), the eastern Arab countries, the Maghrib, other parts of Africa, and other Asian countries. Foreign student enrollment peaked at

4,291 in 1955; it later dropped to about 2,500 in 1972. In 1992, the reported enrollment was 90,000 students, with 3,604 faculty members.

AZZAM, ABD AL-RAHMAN (1893–1976). Pan-Arab diplomat and politician. A supporter of the National Party (q.v.) in his youth, he studied medicine in London and served as a volunteer paramedic for the Ottoman army during the first Balkan War. In World War I (q.v.) he joined the Libyan (q.v.) guerrillas against the Italians in Cyrenaica, returning to Egypt after the war. He joined the Wafd (q.v.) at the time when Sa'd Zaghlul (q.v.) was prime minister and became a member of Parliament, but later left the Party and drew close to Ali Mahir (q.v.). He was Egypt's minister to Iraq, Iran, and Saudi Arabia, served as counselor to the Arab delegations to the 1939 London Conference on Palestine, and became minister of *awqaf* (q.v.) and of social affairs in Ali Mahir's government in 1939–40. A leading advocate of Arab unity from the early 1930s, Azzam took part in several all-Arab congresses. In 1945 he was chosen to be the first secretary-general of the Arab League (q.v.), but resigned after the 1952 Revolution (q.v.). He stayed away from Egypt for many years but returned in 1972. Portions of his Arabic memoirs, dictated to Jamil Arif, were published serially in Egypt and Lebanon, then in book form in 1977 as *Safahat min al-mudhakkirat al-sirriyya li awwal amin amm li al-Jami'a al-Arabiyya* ("Pages from the Secret Memoirs of the First Secretary-General of the Arab League").

- B -

BADR, OPERATION (1973). Egyptian name for its surprise attack by land, sea, and air against Israeli forces east of the Suez Canal (q.v.), launched on 6 October 1973, the 10th day of Ramadan by the Muslim calendar and hence the anniversary of Muhammad's first victory over the pagan Meccans at Badr in AH 2 (624 CE). The operation was planned over a five-year period, but mainly from 1971, when Lieutenant-General Sa'd al-Din al-Shadhili (q.v.) became the commander-in-chief of Egypt's armed forces. He tried especially to foresee military contingencies and to ensure the cooperation of Syria, so that the armies of the two countries would simultaneously attack Israeli positions in the Sinai Peninsula (q.v.) and the Golan Heights. The assaults caught the Israelis unprepared and initially drove their forces back, shattering the common belief in Israel's invincibility. Backed by surface-to-air missiles, Egyptian troops bridged the Suez Canal, crossed it in great numbers, captured most of the Israeli bunkers on the Bar Lev Line (q.v.), and penetrated the Sinai to a depth of

16 km, but failed to reach the strategic Gidi and Mitla passes (qq.v.) or to follow up on their initial gains in the ensuing October War (q.v.).

BADRAN, SHAMS AL-DIN. Powerful politician who served as office director for Abd al-Hakim Amir (q.v.) just before the June War (q.v.) and a member of the Committee to Liquidate Feudalism (*see* Kamshish Affair). He was tried and imprisoned after Egypt's defeat.

BAGHDAD PACT. Anti-Communist military alliance in the Middle East. Its name was taken from the Pact of Mutual Cooperation concluded between Iraq and Turkey in February 1955, which was preceded by bilateral agreements between Turkey and Pakistan in 1954 and between the United States and Turkey, Iraq, and Pakistan. It was joined by Britain, Iran, and Pakistan during 1955, with encouragement from the United States, and viewed as a barrier to Communist penetration. It was strongly opposed by Nasir (q.v.) for introducing great power rivalries and the Cold War into the region, and he appealed to Arabs in Jordan and other countries to oppose it. The alliance was renamed CENTO in 1959 after Iraq withdrew from membership. Following Iran's Islamic revolution in 1979, it, too, withdrew from CENTO, causing its formal dissolution.

BAGHDAD SUMMIT (1979). Meeting of Arab heads of state, called by Iraqi Vice President Saddam Husayn, to condemn Sadat's (q.v.) separate peace with Israel (*see* Egyptian-Israeli Peace Treaty). The Arab leaders agreed to break diplomatic relations with Egypt, to terminate various economic development schemes in the country, and to expel it from the Arab League (q.v.).

AL-BAGHDADI, ABD AL-LATIF (1917-). Officer and politician. A graduate of the Military Academy (q.v.), he was a leading member of the Free Officers (q.v.) and the Revolutionary Command Council (q.v.), then became inspector general of the Liberation Rally (q.v.). Defense minister under Najib (q.v.) in 1953–54, he was moved to municipal affairs when Nasir (q.v.) took power in 1954 and later assumed control of planning. He became president of the National Assembly (q.v.) in 1957 and, upon the creation of the United Arab Republic (q.v.), became its vice president for economic affairs and minister of planning. After Syria seceded, he served as Egyptian minister of finance and economic planning. In 1962 Baghdadi became one of Egypt's five vice presidents and resumed the presidency of the National Assembly. Dropped as vice president in 1964, he quit the National Assembly and has been politically inactive since. He criticized the 1971 Egyptian-Soviet Friendship Treaty (q.v.) and later the Egyptian-Israeli Peace Treaty (q.v.). His memoirs were published in 1977.

AL-BALAGH. Title of several Egyptian newspapers, of which the best-known was the Wafd Party (q.v.) organ edited by Abd al-Qadir Hamza and published in 1923–53.

BANDUNG CONFERENCE (1955). Meeting, hosted by Indonesia's Sukarno, for Asian and African leaders, at which Nasir (q.v.) met China's Zhou Enlai (Chou En-lai), who advised him to buy arms from Communist Czechoslovakia (*see* Czech Arms Deal, Non-Alignment).

BANK MISR. Egyptian bank and holding company, prominent in Egypt's industrialization in the 1920s and 1930s, founded by Tal'at Harb (q.v.) in April 1920 with a share capital of £E80,000, 92 percent of which came from large landowners interested in the availability of credit to finance their cotton (q.v.) cultivation. Its early growth was due partly to a student-led boycott, fueled by the 1919 Revolution (q.v.), against British firms, including banks. Its sustained development was fueled by growing patronage by the national, provincial, and local governments, which were encouraged to shift their deposits from the foreign-owned National Bank of Egypt (q.v.) to Bank Misr. It began its industrial activities by establishing an Arabic printing press in 1922, a paper company in 1923, a cotton-ginning mill in 1924, and a fleet of Nile transport ships and a cinema company in 1925. In 1926 came its major and most profitable investment, the Misr Cotton Spinning and Weaving Company, with its headquarters at Mahalla al-Kubra. In 1937 it had 110,000 spindles and 2,500 looms in operation and employed 15,000 workers. The Egyptian government gave funds to Bank Misr to contract loans with small industry and agricultural cooperatives and to purchase cotton for storage. It also founded Misr Airworks (*see* Aviation), an insurance firm, and a shipping company that won an Egyptian government concession to transport Muslim pilgrims to the Hijaz (q.v.). It set up branch offices in most of Egypt's provincial towns and spawned foreign subsidiaries in Syria and Lebanon and in France. In 1930 its share capital reached £E1 million.

In the 1930s it suffered from falling prices on the world cotton market but benefited from the protective tariffs imposed, especially by the Sidqi (q.v.) government, on imported goods. Bank Misr came to rely heavily on British capital and expertise in the expansion of its enterprises, and it also became involved in the cross fire between the Wafd (q.v.) and Egypt's other political parties. Depressed cotton prices caused some landowning families to petition for aid in postponing repayment of their mortgage debts, often owed to Bank Misr, and the result was a liquidity crisis for the bank, at a time when small depositors with Post Office savings accounts (which had been administered by Bank Misr since 1927) were trying to withdraw their funds. The bank appealed to the Egyptian government for financial aid, and Ali Mahir (q.v.) and Husayn Sirri (q.v.) insisted that Tal'at Harb resign his presidency in favor of Hafiz Afifi, who gradually replaced its board members and insisted that it concentrate on profiting from its existing enterprises instead of founding new ones. Of its many subsidiaries, only the textile firms were consistently profitable. When the government agreed in 1941 to guarantee the bank's deposits, it insisted that all unprofitable Misr companies go into voluntary liquidation. During World War II (q.v.), though, Egypt's inability to import European manufactures gave the bank's surviving firms new opportunities to grow, but they became ever more dependent on government support. Although Bank Misr and its subsidiaries were nationalized in 1960, most of its enterprises have survived under state ownership.

AL-BANNA, HASAN (1906–49). Founder and "Supreme Guide" of the Society of Muslim Brothers (q.v.). Born in Mahmudiyya, a village near Alexandria, he was trained as a teacher at Dar al-Ulum (q.v.). He taught principles of Islam (q.v.) in various cities, but especially Ismailia (q.v.). At first he followed the teachings of Muslim reformer Rashid Rida (q.v.). In 1928 Banna founded the Society of Muslim Brothers as an association for religious teaching, but, with the removal of its headquarters from Ismailia to Cairo (q.v.) in 1932, it evolved into a political society aiming at the purification of Islam and calling for the transformation of Egypt into an Islamic state. His simple doctrine won widespread support among urban workers and some younger intellectuals, and his charisma won him sympathy among Muslims in many Arab countries. He founded a daily newspaper, *al-Ikhwan al-Muslimun*, which became the mouthpiece for his ideas, and he reportedly tried to run candidates for election to the Chamber of Deputies. After the UN decision to partition Palestine, the Brothers were among the leading advocates of a policy of active resistance, and they formed volunteer brigades to fight against the Zionists (q.v.). As his society grew more radical and prone to terrorism, the government tried to suppress it, confiscating its funds, closing its branches, and interning some of its leaders under the state of martial law during the Palestine War (q.v.). After Prime Minister Nuqrashi (q.v.) was assassinated in December 1948 by a student attached to the Brotherhood, Banna was murdered by government agents in February 1949. Several collections of Banna's speeches and articles have been published, as have his memoirs, *Mudhakkirat al-da'wa wa al-di'aya*. A highly articulate speaker and writer, he was personally incorruptible in an era dominated by corrupt politicians, but his ideological rigidity blunted his political impact.

BAR ASSOCIATION, EGYPTIAN. Egypt's earliest lawyers' group was the Mixed Courts (q.v.) Bar Association established in 1876 by the

European advocates practicing in these new tribunals. Among the functions of the Mixed Courts Bar Association were to supervise admission of lawyers into the profession, to discipline its members, to defend their prerogatives against judges and administrators, to hear complaints against lawyers, to provide free legal aid to the needy, and to lend money to colleagues in financial trouble. It served as the model for the lawyers in the National Courts (q.v.), who formed their *niqaba* (bar association) in 1912. The lawyers in the National Courts envied the Mixed Courts lawyers and had petitioned the justice ministry under Sa'd Zaghlul (q.v.) in 1910 to be allowed to form their own syndicate with similar rights and duties. The government accepted their petition, and the lawyers met for the first time in November 1912 to elect their first president, choose a 15-member bar council, and adopt their bylaws. The Shari'a (q.v.) lawyers set up their own *niqaba* in 1916. The National Courts Bar Association played a highly visible political role between 1919 and 1952, usually within the Wafd Party (q.v.), which provided most of the association's leaders. The Mixed and Shari'a courts' *niqaba*s were absorbed by the National Courts Bar Association in 1949 and 1956, respectively, as their parent legal systems were integrated into the National Courts.

The 1952 Revolution (q.v.) led to an erosion of the Bar Association's independence, especially after it backed a return to parliamentary government and rallied to Najib (q.v.) in March 1954. When the lawyers denounced the military dictatorship and called for the dissolution of the Revolutionary Command Council (q.v.), the Nasir (q.v.) government dismissed the Bar Association officers and suspended its rules, then appointed Abd al-Rahman al-Rafi'i (q.v.) as its new president. The association did not meet again until 1958, and then only to elect new officers. It remained in conflict with the Nasir government; Ali Sabri (q.v.), as leader of the Arab Socialist Union (q.v.), even made the Bar Association admit public-sector lawyers. Law was a "receding profession" under Nasir, but Sadat (q.v.) began admitting more lawyers to the cabinet, made a symbolic visit to the Bar Association, and claimed to have restored the rule of law to Egyptian politics. It was symbolically significant that Fuad Siraj al-Din (q.v.) used the Bar Association for the site of his speech announcing his creation of the New Wafd (q.v.). In Sadat's last years, the Bar Association became a forum for opposition to his policies, including the peace treaty with Israel; he locked up half the members of its elected Bar Council in his September 1981 roundup. Under Mubarak (q.v.), the Bar Association has resisted his regime's efforts to curb its activities, and its often-reelected leader, Ahmad Khawaja, has received much press coverage for his criticisms of government policies. A slate of Muslim Brothers (q.v.) was elected to the Bar Council in 1992.

BAR LEV LINE. Fortified defense line east of the Suez Canal (q.v.), erected by the Israelis after Egypt began shelling their troops in 1968. It withstood Egyptian artillery attacks during the War of Attrition (q.v.) but was breached by Egyptian troops during Operation Badr (q.v.) in 1973.

AL-BARDISI, UTHMAN (1758–1806). Mamluk (q.v.) factional leader between the French occupation (q.v.) and the rise of Muhammad Ali (q.v.). Initially acting as a surrogate for the aging Ibrahim Bey (q.v.), he was a rival to the Alfi Bey (q.v.) faction and an ally to Muhammad Ali, who in 1802 was just taking charge of his Albanian regiment that made up the bulk of the Ottoman (q.v.) army in Egypt. He and Muhammad Ali besieged the Ottoman governor, Khusrev Pasha (q.v.) in Damietta, devastating the city in the process of capturing him. Bardisi's Mamluk factions took charge of Cairo (q.v.), where their high tax levies alienated the population to Muhammad Ali's advantage. Arrears in pay led to soldiers' demonstrations in Cairo, imposing new levies on the civilian population. Bardisi scolded the Cairo ulama (q.v.) for allowing this revolt, but Muhammad Ali openly supported the people. Muhammad Ali's forces drove Bardisi's Mamluks out of Cairo, to the delight of the ulama and the merchants. His death in October 1806 was popularly ascribed to poisoning by Alfi Bey.

AL-BARUDI, MAHMUD SAMI (1839–1904). Army officer, cabinet minister, prime minister in 1882, and neoclassical Arabic poet. He claimed descent from the brother of a Mamluk (q.v.) sultan and from a family of Buhayra tax farmers. His father was an artillery officer under Muhammad Ali (q.v.), and Mahmud was educated in one of his military schools, graduating in 1854. He then worked for the Ottoman (q.v.) government while Sa'id (q.v.) was governor of Egypt. When Isma'il (q.v.) went to Istanbul upon his succession in 1863, he brought Barudi back to command his viceregal guard and later to serve as his private secretary. Barudi also served in the Egyptian corps that aided the Ottoman army in Crete in 1865 and in the war against Russia in 1877–78, attaining the rank of brigadier general. He was named governor of Sharqiyya province in 1878. The nationalist officers around Urabi (q.v.) demanded his appointment as war minister in 1881 and as premier in 1882. He sided with the Urabist officers against the British expeditionary force. After the Battle of Tel al-Kabir (q.v.), he was tried, exiled to Ceylon, and not let back into Egypt until 1900. Weakened and blind, he played no further role in Egyptian public life. He had a gift for writing patriotic poetry, which is still read and admired for its classical Arabic allusions and motifs, and he is regarded as a leader of Egypt's literary renaissance.

BASIN IRRIGATION. System of Nile (q.v.) water utilization used extensively in Egypt up to modern times. The land is divided into basins measuring between 1,000 and 4,000 feddans (q.v.) by the construction of a longitudinal bank near the Nile with cross banks between this ridge and the desert's edge. As the Nile rises, water is let into these compartments through short canals with regulating sluices. The land is flooded to an average depth of one to two meters and the water is held there for 40–60 days. Once the Nile recedes, the water is drained back, depositing its fertile silt. The basins are usually in chains of four or five which are filled by a short canal, following a strict timetable, starting with the southern basins. In years when the Nile flood is low, water may be stored in some basins through the low Nile season. Winter crops sown in basin lands after the water recedes include wheat, beans, *birsim* (Egyptian clover), lentils, barley, and chick-peas, crops that mature and are harvested in March or April, after which the land awaits the next flood. In the twentieth century, some basin-irrigated lands in Upper Egypt were adapted to cotton (q.v.) culture by using wells and pumps.

Water-raising devices have irrigated higher grounds since antiquity: the *shaduf* (a bucket on a pole with a counterweight of mud or stone), the Archimedian screw (a wooden cylinder with a helix inside and an axis at each end), and the waterwheel or *saqiyya* (by which an animal turns a horizontal wheel that is geared to a vertical wheel carrying pots on its rim to dip into the water as it turns, dropping the water as they reach the top of their rotation). The system has enabled people to utilize the same plots of land for centuries with little expenditure of capital, but it does require a government capable of ensuring fair distribution of the waters. Starting in Muhammad Ali's (q.v.) reign, parts of the Delta were converted to perennial irrigation (q.v.); the process continued elsewhere in Egypt under Isma'il (q.v.), during the British occupation (q.v.), and especially under Nasir (q.v.), with construction of the Aswan High Dam (q.v.).

BAYT AL-UMMA. The "house of the nation," or home of Sa'd Zaghlul (q.v.) in central Cairo (q.v.), often the site of demonstrations by the Wafd (q.v.) between 1919 and 1927, later converted into a museum of the Egyptian struggle for independence from Britain.

BEDOUINS. Arab camel nomads. Traditionally, they migrated within deserts, following seasonable availability of water and forage for their camels or other animals. In modern times, the Egyptian government–and indeed most Middle Eastern states–have tried to make them settle, sometimes with the inducement of agricultural land. They are organized into tribes and clans based on patrilineal kinship, sometimes modified by adoption, and their loyalties are almost always to these extended family units rather than to a nation, region, or village. They tend to look down on Egyptians, both rural and urban, as degenerate and dishonorable, and they obey an elaborate code that defines the honor and status of their tribe. Traditional tribal honor was closely tied to martial virtues, and the Mamluk (q.v.) rulers of Egypt often used bedouin auxiliaries in their armies, but no Egyptian government has done so since the time of Muhammad Ali (q.v.). During the nineteenth century bedouins were exempt from Egyptian conscription, but about 12,000 now serve in a special frontier force equipped with remote sensors, night-vision binoculars, communications vehicles, and high-speed motorboats. Others have given up husbandry for transport and smuggling, often replacing their camels with pickup trucks and their tents with cinder-block huts. Most bedouins now buy subsidized flour and sugar through the Egyptian government and carry identity cards. Their proportion of Egypt's total population has declined during the nineteenth and twentieth centuries; their numbers are now estimated at 500,000–1 million for the entire country, including the Sinai Peninsula (q.v.).

BEVIN-SIDQI TREATY (1946). Abortive pact between the foreign ministers of Britain and Egypt, under which Britain agreed to withdraw completely from Egyptian territory by 1949 and to maintain the status quo in the Sudan (q.v.) until Britain and Egypt could reach an agreement and gain the assent of the Sudanese people. Rumors spread in Cairo, however, that Isma'il Sidqi (q.v.) had in fact extracted a British concession to unite the Sudan with Egypt. Britain's prime minister, Clement Attlee, publicly denied the rumors. Following King Faruq's (q.v.) opening speech to Parliament, stating that Egypt would be responsible for preparing the Sudanese for independence as soon as possible, the British governor-general of the Sudan issued a statement insisting that it would be up to the Sudanese themselves to choose the status of their country. Sidqi replied that the governor's statement contradicted the draft treaty that he and the British had agreed upon, whereupon he and his ministers resigned. The treaty would have given Egypt in 1946 what it eventually won in 1954; its failure underscores the Sudan's importance to Egyptian politicians before the 1952 Revolution (q.v.).

BILHARZIA. Common name in Egypt for schistosomiasis, an endemic tropical disease caused by flatworms or flukes, which live as parasites inside certain species of freshwater snails that flourish in expanses of stagnant water created by irrigation systems, such as those built in the Nile (q.v.) Valley and Delta. Their larvae enter the body of a human being or animal through the skin from the stagnant waters and become parasites of their new host. Their eggs accumulate in the blood, liver, lungs, kidneys, and other organs, obstructing blood circulation, causing tissue damage and infection, and weakening the victim, leading at times to urinary tract diseases, bladder cancer, sexual malfunctions, and even death. Some eggs leave the victim through body wastes and may reenter the water and the host snails. The disease is named after Dr. Theodor Bilharz, assistant director of Egypt's medical school from 1850 to 1862, although his discoveries were not widely disseminated and the fluke was rediscovered by an Italian researcher in the 1870s.

The incidence of the disease burgeoned with the transition from basin to perennial irrigation (qq.v.), which required peasants to stand in stagnant water for long periods of time. An American physician, writing in 1913, estimated that 30 percent of Egypt's inhabitants were infected. In 1924 an Egyptian writer raised that estimate to between 70 and 80 percent, a figure that remained constant in succeeding years despite strenuous efforts at treatment and control by both the Rockefeller Foundation and the Egyptian government. Bilharzia has spread even more since the completion of the Aswan High Dam (q.v.), with a further increase in the more pathogenic species at the expense of the one that causes milder symptoms. At first, doctors treated infected persons with such drugs as antimony tartrate, but peasants disliked losing workdays to make office visits and soon became reinfected in the irrigation ditches anyway; a more effective treatment has been to treat the waters in which the snails breed with a copper sulfate compound. Well-intended efforts to improve village sanitation, although they have reduced the incidence of other diseases, have failed to stem bilharzia, which remains, along with trachoma and diabetes, an endemic public health problem for Egypt (*see* Health Care).

BLACK BOOK **(1943)**. Scandalous revelations of political and financial misdeeds by Mustafa al-Nahhas (q.v.) and his wife, published by former Wafd Party (q.v.) Secretary-General Makram Ubayd (q.v.). Even though few of the allegations were ever proven, the book discredited the Wafdist government that had been imposed on King Faruq (q.v.) by the British.

BLACK SATURDAY. The 26 January 1952 riots, marked by burning and looting of buildings, especially those owned by Europeans or popularly associated with Western influence, in central Cairo (q.v.), following the killing by British troops of 50 Egyptian auxiliary policemen in Ismailia (q.v.) a day earlier. The heavy destruction of property and loss of European and Egyptian lives were widely construed at the time as evidence of the Egyptian government's inability to maintain order. Consequently, King Faruq (q.v.) dismissed the Wafd Party (q.v.) government of Mustafa al-Nahhas (q.v.) and appointed a series of Palace cabinets that failed to restore public confidence in the monarchy, which was toppled by a military coup exactly six months later. It has never been determined who started Black Saturday; popular theories at the time implicated the Society of Muslim Brothers (q.v.) or the Egyptian Socialist Party, formerly Misr al-Fatat (q.v.).

BLUE SHIRTS. Wafd Party (q.v.)-affiliated youth organization, formed in 1935 to counter the growing influence of the Green Shirts under Misr al-Fatat (q.v.). In 1936 there were two rival societies, one consisting mainly of students and "well-educated youth," the other mainly of non-students, but these groups and others were consolidated during 1936–37 into one organization having an estimated 30,000 members. Its participation in a demonstration near Abdin Palace (q.v.) in December 1937 led King Faruq (q.v.) to dismiss the Nahhas (q.v.) government, and Egypt banned all the "shirt" organizations in 1938.

BLUNT, WILFRID SCAWEN (1840–1922). English poet, Orientalist, horse-breeder, and supporter of Egyptian nationalism. He briefly served in the British foreign service, but after his marriage to Anne, the granddaughter of Lord Byron, he left the service and spent several years exploring the Arabian desert. He is best known for his involvement in the nationalist revolution led by Colonel Ahmad Urabi (q.v.) in 1881–82. He later wrote a memoir about that movement, entitled *The Secret History of the English Occupation of Egypt* (1907). After Urabi's defeat, Blunt hired a British attorney to defend the colonel at his treason trial and helped get the death sentences imposed by the Egyptian courts reduced to exile or imprisonment. He went on using his official connections to agitate for an early withdrawal of British forces from Egypt, about which see his *Gordon at Khartum* (1912). He also supported the later National Party (q.v.) of Mustafa Kamil (q.v.), whom he greatly admired, and Muhammad Farid (q.v.), and the 1919 Revolution (q.v.). Blunt financed the publication of a monthly magazine, *Egypt*, from 1911 to 1913. A wealthy Sussex landowner and minor poet, he often misled Egyptians by exaggerating his influence with British politicians. He published a bowdlerized version of his diaries, the originals of which are held by the Fitzwilliam Museum, Cambridge, commenting freely on politics in Egypt and elsewhere between 1888 and 1914, called *My Diaries* (1921).

BONAPARTE, *see* **NAPOLÉON BONAPARTE.**

BOURSE, ALEXANDRIA. The cotton exchange opened in 1861 as the Société Anonyme de la Bourse at Minyat al-Basal, a district of Alexandria (q.v.) harbor. Its buildings were constructed and enlarged during the decade following 1869, and each cotton exporter had its own office in the Bourse. The Société Égyptienne de la Bourse Commerciale de Minet-al-Basel was incorporated in 1884. The cotton exporters had their own professional association, the Association Cotonnière d'Alexandrie, which established standard grades for cotton in 1883; this became the Alexandria General Produce Association in 1885. Cotton futures were traded at another Bourse, the Société Anonyme de la Bourse Khédiviale d'Alexandrie. Both were nationalized under the 1961 July Laws (q.v.) and later closed.

BOUTROS-GHALI, BOUTROS (1922-). Professor, editor, and diplomat. He was educated at Cairo University (q.v.) and at the University of Paris, receiving degrees in public law, economics, and political science, as well as a Ph.D. in international law. A professor at Cairo University since 1949, he was a Fulbright research scholar at Columbia University in 1954–55. He edited *al-Ahram al-iqtisadi* and *al-Siyasa al-duwaliyya.* In 1967–69 he directed the research center of the Hague Academy of International Law. Boutros-Ghali lectured on law and international relations at Columbia, Princeton, New Delhi, Warsaw, Geneva, Algiers, Dakar, Dar as Salam, and Nairobi universities, among others, took part in various international conferences, and produced more than a hundred books, chapters, and articles in French, English, and Arabic. As secretary of state for foreign affairs, he accompanied Sadat (q.v.) on his peace mission to Jerusalem and played a key role in the Camp David (q.v.) summit. He served from 1978 to 1991 as secretary of state for foreign affairs and played an important peacemaking role within the Organization of African Unity (q.v.). Strongly Francophile, Boutros-Ghali was heading Egypt's delegation to the Francophone summit in Paris at the time he was elected secretary-general of the United Nations (q.v.) in November 1991. He has served since 1 January 1992, mediating the Cambodian crisis, the India-Pakistan dispute, and the civil wars in Bosnia and Somalia, among other issues.

BRIGHT STAR, OPERATION. Joint land and air military maneuvers of Egypt and the United States, held in 1981 and in later odd-numbered years. Similar exercises were conducted in Oman, Somalia, and the Sudan (q.v.). Their initial aims were to strengthen U.S. ties with Egypt and those other countries when President Reagan was seeking a "strategic consensus" in the Middle East against Communism and to reassure Egypt's government following Sadat's (q.v.) assassination. The largest maneuvers were held near the Suez Canal (q.v.) in 1987 and involved 9,000 ground, air, and sea personnel from each country.

BRITISH AGENCY, ***see*** **RESIDENCY.**

BRITISH OCCUPATION. Term commonly applied to Egypt's de facto subjection to control by Great Britain from September 1882, when British forces, estimated at 30,000, defeated the 10,000-man Egyptian army of Colonel Ahmad Urabi (q.v.), until June 1956, when the last British troops withdrew from their Suez Canal (q.v.) base. For most of the period between 1883 and 1914, the actual size of the British contingent in Egypt was less than 5,000. It comprised four battalions of infantry, a cavalry regiment, and two artillery batteries. When World War I (q.v.) broke out, these troops were replaced by British territorials (roughly equivalent to the U.S. National Guard), consisting of the 42nd Lancaster division and six yeomanry squadrons. They were augmented by some 50,000 imperial troops, mainly Indians, Australians, and New Zealanders, who repulsed the Ottoman (q.v.) attack on the Canal in 1915. Even larger numbers of British Empire troops were stationed in Egypt during and after the Gallipoli Campaign, angering many Egyptians by their riotous behavior.

The war's end did not immediately diminish the size of the occupying army, due to the disorders caused by the 1919 Revolution (q.v.), but most troops were withdrawn after Britain's unilateral declaration of Egypt's independence in 1922. The Wafd (q.v.) and other nationalist parties wanted Britain to evacuate Egypt completely, but Anglo-Egyptian negotiations were protracted. The 1936 Anglo-Egyptian treaty (q.v.) limited the British army of occupation to 10,000 troops during peacetime, but in 1939 55,000 British troops remained in Egypt and the Sudan (q.v.). During World War II (q.v.) burgeoning contingents from Britain and its overseas dominions occupied the Suez Canal, Cairo (q.v.), Alexandria (q.v.), and other strategic posts in defense of Allied interests.

After the war popular pressure against the British occupation intensified. The British agreed to evacuate their bases in Cairo, Alexandria, and other Egyptian towns, but retained and reinforced their installations along the Suez Canal, as a part of the Western strategy to contain Communist expansion. Successive Egyptian governments tried in vain to negotiate with Britain for complete evacuation of Egypt and the Sudan. Popular agitation turned into direct action, as Egyptian *fidaiyin* (q.v.) attacked British bases and their local employees went on strike, leading in early 1952 to armed confrontations and to Black Saturday (q.v.). The 1952 Revolution (q.v.) stilled the agitation, but the new regime resumed talks with Britain, under U.S. pressure. Britain and Egypt finally agreed to the evacuation of British troops from the Suez Canal bases, retaining only civilian technicians to reactivate them in case of an attack by any outside power against an Arab League (q.v.) member or Turkey. Inclusion of this state, a NATO member, subtly tied the Canal's strategic importance with the West's defense against the USSR, but did not draw Egypt into an alliance. The British occupation ended 20 months later. The Anglo-French attack in the 1956 Suez War (q.v.) led to a temporary reoccupation of some facilities and to Egypt's nullification of Britain's reoccupation rights under the 1954 agreement.

BULAQ. Port city for Cairo (q.v.) from Mamluk (q.v.) times until the late-nineteenth century. Under Muhammad Ali (q.v.) it became the site of the first Arabic printing press owned by the Egyptian government (*see* Press). The press was established in 1822 under the direction of Niqula al-Musabiki, of Lebanese origin. Under private ownership from 1865 to 1880, it then was restored to state control. In addition to producing printed editions of many Arabic manuscripts, it also printed military manuals, school textbooks, and administrative circulars, in addition to *al-Waqa'i al-misriyya* (q.v.). Bulaq city has lately been engulfed by Cairo, and some of its monuments and historic residences have fallen victim to urban overcrowding and the extension of the Nile Corniche (q.v.).

BUREAUCRACY. Because of its complex hydraulic economic and social organization, Egypt has the world's oldest bureaucracy, or civil service. The Egyptian government has long taken part in the provision and distribution of Nile (q.v.) floodwaters and in taxing the agricultural produce of the peasants, hence has needed a corps of trained clerks and inspectors throughout its history. Under Arab, Mamluk (q.v.), and Ottoman (q.v.) rule, Copts (q.v.) predominated in the civil service, especially in accountancy. At the time of the French occupation (q.v.), Napoléon (q.v.) announced: "All Egyptians shall be called upon to manage all posts: the wisest, the most learned, the most virtuous shall govern, and the people shall be happy." In practice, the French took the higher posts formerly reserved for Mamluks, and Copts kept their preponderant role. They, along with the Armenians (q.v.), benefited from the Westernizing reforms of Muhammad Ali (q.v.), who expanded the bureaucracy and widened its functions. He also founded the Darsakhana al-Mulkiya ("Civil Service School") in 1829 to train bureaucrats in Western methods of administration and accountancy; it was followed in 1834 by the Madrasa li-Ta'lim al-Idara al-Mulkiya ("School of Civil Administration"). Despite these schools and the government policy of sending some students on missions to study civil administration in Europe, most higher posts still went to Turks, Middle Eastern Christians, and foreigners.

Muhammad Ali's successors replaced his higher functionaries with their own appointees; Sa'id (q.v.) and Isma'il (q.v.) greatly increased the number of European civil servants. Under the financial stringencies introduced by the Law of Liquidation (1880), their number was to have been reduced, and Urabi's (q.v.) followers also objected to the fact that in 1882 Europeans, who made up 2 percent of Egypt's civil service, drew 16 percent of the total salaries. The British occupation (q.v.) led to a gradual reduction in the proportion of continental Europeans in the civil service, but Britons increased from 299 in 1886 to 455 in 1899. Under Cromer (q.v.) the Egyptian government began hiring graduates just out of Oxford and Cambridge for teaching jobs, inspectorships, and advisory posts, even where qualified Egyptians were available. The British came to dominate especially the higher government positions. World War I (q.v.) claimed many of the ablest British bureaucrats, but the Anglicization of the civil service continued and was one of the grievances leading to the 1919 Revolution (q.v.).

As a result of the Milner Mission's (q.v.) report and the 1922 declaration of Egypt's independence, the British turned over many administrative functions to Egyptians. Under the 1923 Constitution (q.v.) the Egyptian government systematically pruned its civil service of British and other foreign functionaries. Regrettably, though, government employment became snarled in partisan politics; as the Wafd Party (q.v.) and its rivals gained and lost power, their protégés benefited or suffered accordingly, and high positions became prizes for friends and relatives of the politicians. The government was considering setting up an independent civil service department responsible to the prime minister when the 1952 Revolution (q.v.) occurred.

The new regime instituted a system of regular grades and salary schedules, with promotions and raises based on merit and with definite penalties for corruption, political activity, holding outside jobs, or favoring friends or relatives. Almost half the senior bureaucrats under Faruq (q.v.) were purged. Egypt's bureaucracy ballooned from 250,000 in 1952 to 1.2 million in 1970 because of the growing state role in Egypt's economy and because of Nasir's (q.v.) 1962 commitment to offer a government post to every graduate of the national universities. Public corporations, managing most of Egypt's nationalized industries, rose from one in 1957 to 46 in 1970. Despite Sadat's *infitah* (q.v.) policy, the number of civil servants rose further to 1.9 million (3.2 million if public-sector companies are included) in 1978 and 2.6 million in 1986. Each year 100,000 new university graduates seek government jobs. With the monthly salary at the lowest civil service rank a mere $20, bureaucratic morale and performance have deteriorated. The decentralization of provincial and local government has reduced central control over the bureaucracy outside Cairo (q.v.). Short of a revolutionary change in Egypt's government, the bureaucracy will remain an obstacle to its political and economic development.

- C -

CABINET, ***see*** **COUNCIL OF MINISTERS.**

CAIRO. Egypt's capital since 969, when it was founded by the Fatimid dynasty. Located some 20 km south of the apex of the Nile Delta, Cairo's strategic location dominates the central approach axis to Upper Egypt. A major intellectual and economic center under the Mamluks (q.v.), Cairo was eclipsed when Egypt was subordinated to the Ottoman Empire (q.v.), but it began to revive under Muhammad Ali (q.v.) and was expanded and largely transformed under Isma'il (q.v.). Although under British occupation (q.v.) from 1882 to 1946, Cairo became the major center of Egyptian resistance to Western colonialism. It also became the leading center of Arab culture, including literature, journalism, the visual arts (q.v.), recording, cinema (q.v.), radio (q.v.), and television (q.v.). Its daily newspapers, weekly magazines, and literary monthlies circulate throughout the Arab world. It contains several well-known universities, including al-Azhar (q.v.), the University of Cairo (q.v.), Ayn Shams University, and the American University (q.v.), attracting students from all parts of the Arab world. Its Egyptian Museum (q.v.) and other museums are major tourist attractions, and the famous Giza pyramids and sphinx are nearby. The city served as the headquarters of the Arab League (q.v.) in 1945–79 and since 1991 and of the Afro-Asian Peoples' Solidarity Organization (q.v.). It was the site of a World War II (q.v.) meeting of Franklin D. Roosevelt, Winston Churchill, and Chiang Kai-shek, and of several summit conferences of Arab kings and heads of state since 1964. Arab leaders meeting in Cairo also effected an agreement between Jordan's King Husayn and the Palestinian *fidaiyin* (q.v.) in September 1970, ending the Jordan Civil War. Its population was approximately 250,000 in 1850, 1 million in 1930, 1.5 million in 1947, and 6 million in 1986. If Shubra al-Khayma, Giza, and Hulwan (q.v.) are included, greater Cairo had 10.9 million inhabitants in 1991 and was adding approximately 300,000 more each year. Air pollution, crowded housing, and traffic congestion are, therefore, major problems.

CAIRO TOWER. Tall structure built in the late 1950s by the Egyptian government as a tourist attraction in lands that formerly had belonged to the Gezira Sporting Club (q.v.). It is popularly believed to have been secretly financed by the U.S. Central Intelligence Agency.

CAIRO UNIVERSITY. Egypt's first secular university, founded in 1908 as the "National University" and situated in the city center, in what is now the main building of the American University in Cairo (q.v.). Credit for first proposing the University has been given to Prince Fuad (q.v.), Mustafa Kamil (q.v.), Muhammad Abduh (q.v.), Sa'd Zaghlul (q.v.), Qasim Amin (q.v.), Education Undersecretary Ya'qub Artin, and Jurji Zaydan (q.v.). The initiative was seized in 1907 by Abbas Hilmi II (q.v.), who appointed his uncle Fuad to manage the new institution, which rented the palace of tobacco magnate Nestor Gianaclis and initially offered courses in literature, philosophy, and history, all taught by European professors. It gradually added vocationally oriented courses in the social sciences, criminology, and even law, and admitted Egyptians from Dar al-Ulum (q.v.) and other schools to its faculty. Few British nationals taught at the University, but Italians and French were prominent. Student enrollment peaked at 415 in 1909–10 and–after tuition fees were raised–fell back to 107 in 1921–22; about 20 percent were Europeans, and many Egyptians tried to attend lectures without registering for degree candidacy. Many held full-time jobs and could only attend classes offered at night.

Hobbled by financial problems, the University barely survived World War I (q.v.) and the 1919 Revolution (q.v.), and the Egyptian government, together with its British advisers, began to consider establishing a state-owned university. It was reorganized as the Faculty of Arts within the University of Cairo, to which were added the Faculties of Law, Medicine, and Science in 1925. The Higher School of Commerce, the Polytechnic and Agriculture schools, and Dar al-Ulum were gradually assimilated into the new institution. Ahmad Lutfi al-Sayyid (q.v.) was its first rector. Initially housed in Za'faran Palace in Abbasiyya, it was moved in 1928 to a French-designed campus in Giza, on what then were rural lands donated by the Egyptian royal family. In its early days, Cairo University tended to be a cultural battleground between the largely Francophone faculty and those who wanted instruction in English. Gradually Egyptians replaced Europeans in the deanships and professorial chairs, making Arabic the primary language of instruction in the Arts and Law faculties; the scientific and technical subjects continued to use English mainly. Women were admitted for the first time in 1928; the first woman joined the staff in 1930. University fees remained a deterrent to the admission of poor students until 1962, when Nasir (q.v.) abolished all tuition charges. The lack of residence halls also tended to exclude poorer students with provincial backgrounds; the first men's hostel was opened in 1949 and one for women only in 1957.

Student political involvement, imitating the pattern begun by the government Law School (q.v.) students during the Mustafa Kamil (q.v.) era and in the 1919 Revolution, became endemic and vitiated the University's teaching function. The years 1935–39 and 1945–52 were especially marked by student strikes and demonstrations, as the Muslim Brothers (q.v.), Misr al-Fatat (q.v.), and the Communists (q.v.) gradually gained at the expense of the Wafd (q.v.) and other political parties. Rectors and deans were frequently changed by the government on political rather than academic grounds. Many students left their classes to become *fidaiyin* (q.v.) against the British in the Suez Canal (q.v.) zone in 1951. When Nahhas (q.v.) abrogated the 1936 Anglo-Egyptian Treaty (q.v.), all British faculty members at the University were dismissed, devastating the English and Classics departments.

The 1952 Revolution (q.v.) led to many changes in the University. Many of its students took part in the 1954 demonstrations favoring Najib (q.v.) over Nasir (q.v.) and were later subjected to purges, creating a much more repressive atmosphere. Government expenditures on higher education skyrocketed, but a growing number of universities competed for the state budget. Admissions rose rapidly, especially after the abolition of tuition fees in 1962, but faculty-to-student ratios grew steadily worse. Some faculties were able to maintain high admissions standards, notably Medicine, Engineering, and Pharmacy, but Commerce, Law, and "Arts" (humanities) became dumping grounds for students whose general secondary examination (*thanawiyya amma*) scores did not qualify them for the prestigious schools. Some faculty were siphoned off by other Egyptian universities, the new scientific research centers, and (especially after 1967) emigration to higher-paying universities in other Arab countries. Nasir made the state the employer of last resort for university graduates, but also a disturbing force in campus governance, as the minister of higher education appointed rectors and deans without regard to faculty wishes. On the other hand, professors and holders of higher degrees from the University have gained acceptance in cabinets and other high government posts since 1952; and some of the faculty autonomy that was lost early in the Revolution was later restored by Nasir and Sadat (q.v.). In student politics, the *jama'at* (q.v.) have displaced Marxist and other secular groups, and many students have adopted Islamic patterns of dress and behavior. Cairo University has spawned, at least indirectly, all the other national universities in Egypt and many in other Arab states, but its precarious independence, inadequate funding, and burgeoning student enrollments have left it weaker than its founders hoped it would be. Its reported enrollment rose from 2,027 in 1925–26, 7,021 in 1935–36, 18,246 in 1950–51, 27,973 in 1961–62, and 47,463 in 1965–66 to 76,794 students in 1992, with 4,494 faculty members.

CAISSE DE LA DETTE PUBLIQUE. The commission, comprising representatives of Britain, France, Austria-Hungary, and Italy, to which Germany and Russia were later added, that was set up to manage the Egyptian government debt in 1876 to ensure its repayment to foreign creditors. Its powers were enlarged with the appointment of the European ministry in 1878 and the promulgation of the Law of Liquidation (q.v.) in 1880. Often assailed during the early British occupation (q.v.) for obstructing financial and irrigation (q.v.) reforms, it served to represent Egypt's major creditors up to the declaration of the British Protectorate (q.v.) in 1914, but did not interfere with the government's projects after the 1904 Entente Cordiale (q.v.).

CALIPHATE. The institution of leadership of the Muslim *umma*, established after the death of Muhammad in 632 and maintained until its abolition by the Turkish government of Mustafa Kemal (Atatürk) in 1924, a move condemned by many Muslims. Egypt spearheaded several abortive attempts to revive the caliphate under Kings Fuad (q.v.) and Faruq (q.v.).

CAMP DAVID ACCORDS (1978). Agreements reached in September 1978 between President Sadat (q.v.) and Israeli Premier Menachem Begin, with the help of U.S. President Carter, aimed at establishing peace between Egypt and Israel and a framework for solving the issue of the Palestinian Arabs under Israeli occupation. The accords did lead to the Egyptian-Israeli Peace Treaty (q.v.), but the subsequent Palestinian Autonomy Talks (q.v.) between the two sides foundered on the irreconcilable differences between them.

CAPITULATIONS. Treaties granting extraterritorial immunity from local laws and taxes to subjects of Western countries living in the Ottoman Empire (q.v.) or other Muslim states, and also to Muslims living in Western countries. During the nineteenth and early twentieth centuries, Europeans who benefited from the Capitulations often exploited Egypt and other Ottoman lands, and their privileges became a focus of nationalist resentment. They were phased out in Egypt following the 1937 Montreux Convention (q.v.).

CAVE MISSION (1876). British commission of inquiry, headed by Sir Stephen Cave, a member of Parliament, and charged with determining Egypt's financial condition. The immediate cause was Khedive Isma'il's (qq.v.) sale of the Egyptian government's shares in the Suez Canal Company (q.v.) for £E4 million to the British government, which he invited to send a financial adviser. After a two-month visit, Cave reported that Egypt's finances were in a critical state, especially if Egypt contracted new loans at high rates of interest. The other European powers inferred that the Egyptian government was close to bankruptcy and that Britain was trying to take control of Egypt's finances. Egyptian stock prices fell, and Isma'il, unable to float new bonds, had to suspend payment on his treasury bills. In May 1876 he issued decrees creating the international Caisse de la Dette Publique (q.v.), with four members representing Britain, France, Austria, and Italy and issuing a new plan to fund Egypt's bonded and floating debt at £E91 million, bearing 7 percent interest. The bondholders rejected this offer and called for a new settlement, leading to the Goschen-Joubert mission (q.v.).

CENSORSHIP. State controls over written materials entering Egypt or circulating within the country have existed since ancient times. The Egyptian government promulgated press legislation as early as 1865 and enforced a stringent Press Law (q.v.) between 1881 and 1894, when publishers found that they could evade prosecution under the Capitulations (q.v.) by seeking foreign protectors. But the Press Law was revived in 1909 and strengthened following the assassination of Butros Ghali (q.v.) in 1910. The British imposed strict censorship of printed materials and letters entering Egypt during World War I (q.v.) and again during World War II (q.v.); tense political conditions after the war led to a continuation of these restrictions under Egyptian government auspices. The government imposed strict censorship on pro-Zionist materials in 1948, and unstable political conditions during and after the Palestine War (q.v.) led to a continuation of government controls until after the fall of the monarchy. Following the 1952 Revolution (q.v.), the new regime briefly lifted censorship in August but resumed it in October 1952. Muhammad Najib (q.v.) again removed restrictions in March 1954, but the widespread street disorders accompanying the power struggle between the Najib and Nasir (q.v.) factions necessitated their reimposition in April. Nasir increased surveillance of mail, films, and printed materials deemed subversive or injurious to Arab socialism. Although most forms of censorship were abolished by Sadat (q.v.) in 1974, the Egyptian government still censors some films, videos, and printed matter for political subversion, religious fanaticism, and pornography.

CENTERS OF POWER. Clique of leftist Egyptian officers and their civilian allies at the end of the Nasir (q.v.) era, informally led by Ali Sabri (q.v.) and including Interior Minister Sha'rawi Jum'a (q.v.), Presidential Affairs Minister Sami Sharaf (q.v.), War Minister Muhammad Fawzi (q.v.), and the speaker of Egypt's Parliament. They also held a majority of the executive positions within the Arab Socialist Union (q.v.) and hoped to assume power after Nasir's death. They acquiesced in Sadat's (q.v.) succession because they thought he lacked an independent power base and could easily be controlled. Sadat soon won the backing of the more conservative members of Nasir's government, appointing one of them, Mahmud Fawzi (q.v.), as his prime minister over the leftists' objections and winning the support of the senior military officers. Sadat struck at the leftists on 14 May 1971 by dismissing Ali Sabri as vice president and proceeded to purge his supporters the next day in his Corrective Revolution (q.v.). Most were tried, deprived of their posts and their property, and imprisoned. Personal rivalries and inadequate institutionalization of the Nasir regime led to their downfall.

CENTRAL AUDITING AGENCY. Office set up by Nasir (q.v.) to supervise the management of public-sector companies and government departments. It is independent of the cabinet.

CENTRAL SECURITY FORCE RIOTS (1986). Large-scale disorders in Cairo (q.v.), resulting in the total destruction of tourist hotels near the Pyramids and the Sphinx, at least 60 deaths, 300 injuries, and 2,000 damaged cars. The leaders and most of the participants were illiterate draftees whose duties in this paramilitary police force, set up after the 1977 Food Riots (q.v.) to augment the regular police, included guarding public buildings, embassies, roads, and bridges, for a monthly wage of £E6. The riots were set off by a rumor that the Egyptian government was planning to extend their three-year service by an additional year. The clashes lasted for four days before they were suppressed by loyal units of the armed forces. A ten-day curfew was imposed and 20,000 conscripts were dismissed. The Mubarak (q.v.) regime continued, however, to augment the army with the Central Security Force, which had grown to 300,000 members by 1991, for use against students, striking workers, and Islamic militants.

CENTURY STORAGE SCHEME. Elaborate system of dams proposed by various hydrologists during the early twentieth century for the several tributaries of the Nile (q.v.), as a means of increasing the amount of irrigated land in Egypt and the Sudan (q.v.), facilitating year-round water storage, and ensuring an adequate summer supply for Egypt's agriculture. A drawback to the proposal was the need to involve all the states containing those tributaries in its planning and execution, and the only action that was taken on any facet of the Century Storage Scheme was the building of the Owen Falls Dam in Uganda between 1948 and 1954. The Nasir (q.v.) government decided to scrap this proposal in favor of the construction of the Aswan High Dam (q.v.). (*See* Irrigation).

CHAMPOLLION, JEAN-FRANÇOIS (1790–1832). French Oriental scholar and the father of modern Egyptology. He was educated at home by his elder brother, at the Lycée in Grenoble, and at the Collège de France and the École Spéciale des Langues Orientales Vivantes in Paris.

He taught in at Grenoble from 1809 to 1821. As conservator of the Louvre's Egyptian collections, using his knowledge of Greek, Coptic, and other ancient languages, he gradually devised a system for translating the demotic and hieroglyphic versions of the Rosetta stone, which had been found by Napoléon's (q.v.) troops. He thus laid the groundwork for all later studies of ancient Egyptian inscriptions.

CHARTER, NATIONAL (1962). Egyptian government document stating and justifying the goals of Nasir's (q.v.) Arab socialism (q.v.). It explained the historical conditions in Egypt that made the 1952 Revolution (q.v.) necessary, noted changing political and social conditions in the world that called for socialist action, summarized the history of Egypt's struggle for independence from Western imperialism, contrasted the country's false democracy before 23 July 1952 with Nasir's truly democratic movement that stressed social justice, explained the role of Arab socialism in bettering economic conditions at home and Egypt's position in the world, laid out a socialist strategy for Egypt's agricultural and industrial development, invoked individual freedom and modern science as the means to achieve socialism, pledged Egypt to work for Arab unity, and proclaimed a foreign policy of opposition to imperialism and the pursuit of peace and international cooperation. It was a well-publicized statement of Nasir's policies up to 1967.

CHEETHAM, MILNE (1869–1938). British administrator. He served in the British Agency from 1910 to 1919 and frequently took charge of the mission on behalf of its consuls general. Born in Preston, England, he was educated at a private school and studied classics at Christ Church College, Oxford, after which he entered the diplomatic service and was posted to Madrid, Paris, Tokyo, Berlin, Rome, and Rio de Janeiro before he went to Cairo as first secretary and then as counselor. He took charge of the Agency for Gorst (q.v.) in the summers of 1910 and 1911 and likewise for Kitchener (q.v.) in subsequent summers. At the beginning of World War I (q.v.), he piloted Britain's diplomatic mission through a difficult six months of imperial mobilization at a time when Egypt was still legally a privileged province of the Ottoman Empire (q.v.), which declared war on Britain in November 1914. When the British government declared its protectorate over Egypt in December 1914, Cheetham became acting high commissioner, pending the arrival of Sir Henry McMahon (q.v.). He took charge of the Residency (q.v.) in the fall of 1915 and again during the spring and fall of 1919, hence he dealt with the political crisis brought about by the 1919 Revolution (q.v.). He also advised the Milner Mission (q.v.) during its visit to Egypt in 1919–20 and influenced the early policies of Allenby (q.v.) as high commissioner. Cheetham later served in the

British embassy in Paris and was minister in Berne, Athens, and Copenhagen, retiring from the British foreign service in 1928. He was remembered as a well-mannered, loyal, and hardworking diplomat. His unpublished memoir, "British Policy, 1910–1945," is held by the Middle East Centre, St. Antony's College, Oxford.

CHOLERA. Infectious intestinal disease caused by a bacterium usually transmitted in food or water contaminated by persons who have the disease, but sometimes also by flies. The bacteria settle in the intestines, causing diarrhea and vomiting so severe that the patient quickly becomes dehydrated, goes into shock, and dies. Treatment requires strict isolation of the patient and sterilization of utensils, burning or disinfection of all bodily wastes, and prompt replacement of body fluids. Strict sanitary measures, including quarantine, are needed to stop its spread to other people. Egypt suffered major cholera epidemics in 1831, 1848, 1865, 1883, 1902, and 1947.

CINEMA. Motion picture shows in Egypt began in 1904, if not earlier, and cinema halls were erected in Alexandria (q.v.) and Cairo (q.v.) before World War I (q.v.). The influx of British imperial troops during that war did much to introduce Egyptians to cinema productions from Europe and North America. Egyptian film production began in Alexandria in 1917. A full-length silent film, *al-Bahr byidhaq leh* ("Why Does the Nile Laugh?") soon followed, and in 1925 serious efforts at film production began, leading to the appearance of four movies two years later. The first sound film, *Awlad al-dhawat* ("Children of the Upper Class") was synchronized in Paris soon after the talking pictures began in the West. A large Arabic film company, Studio Misr, owned by Bank Misr (q.v.), was founded in 1934. Cinema halls proliferated in the cities and towns of Egypt and the rest of the Arab world, to which Egyptian films were often exported. Egyptian films and documentaries competed in the Venice Film Festival as early as 1936. There have been some objections to the motion picture industry from conservative Muslims, including al-Azhar (q.v.), the Shubban al-Muslimin (q.v.), and the Society of Muslim Brothers (q.v.). The state has censored films on moral, political, and religious grounds. In some parts of the country, women and adolescent boys have been discouraged from frequenting cinema halls.

CIRCASSIANS. Natives of the Caucasus mountain region east of the Black Sea, or their descendants living in Egypt. Many of the Mamluks (q.v.) claimed Circassian origins.

CITADEL, CAIRO. Fortress built by Salah al-Din (r. 1169–93) and augmented by later rulers of Egypt, situated on the Muqattam hills overlooking Cairo (q.v.). Muhammad Ali (q.v.) sometimes held court at the Citadel, massacred the Mamluks (q.v.) there in 1811, and destroyed many older monuments in order to build his Jawhara Palace. Its Muhammad Ali Mosque, completed by his grandson, Abbas Hilmi I (q.v.), dominates the Cairo skyline.

CLOT, AUGUSTE BARTHÉLEMY (1793–1868). French physician. Born in Grenoble, he was educated at the Hospice de la Charité, Marseilles, and Montpellier. He started a surgical practice in Marseilles, until Muhammad Ali (q.v.) invited him to serve as his chief surgeon in Egypt. Clot organized a public health service and a medical school. He and his European staff trained many Turks and Egyptians in Cairo (q.v.) to become army surgeons, taking some of his best pupils to France for specialized training there. His two-volume work, *Aperçu générale sur l'Égypte*, was published in 1840. He was an outstanding example of a French citizen who devoted himself wholeheartedly to Egypt's modernization, and a Cairo street bears his name.

COMMUNICATIONS. Given its location athwart a main international trade route, Egypt was one of the first countries involved in long-distance communications. Muhammad Ali (q.v.) established a rudimentary postal service for his own officials and officers and also commissioned the East India Company, due in part to its energetic agent, Thomas Waghorn (q.v.), to improve the road from Cairo (q.v.) to Suez, carry the mails, and erect a line of telegraph semaphores along that route. These tasks were taken over in 1840 by the Peninsular and Oriental Steamship Company. Four years later, the Egyptian government set up its own Transit Administration to manage these services. Egypt's postal service was officially established in 1865 under Khedive Isma'il (qq.v.) to carry letters and parcels within Egypt. Its functions were expanded to include transmitting money orders up to £E80 in value in 1868.

The telegraph was introduced into Egypt soon after the railroad (q.v.). In 1855 Sa'id's (q.v.) government commissioned an English firm to run lines from Alexandria (q.v.) to Cairo and from Cairo to Suez, and in the following year the Eastern Telegraph Company linked Alexandria with Crete and Istanbul by a cable under the Mediterranean. The same company began planning to lay a cable between Suez and Bombay, but technical problems in the Red Sea delayed completion of this project, so early British cable communication with India passed through Mesopotamia and Iran instead. Within Egypt a representative of the Eastern Telegraph Company got a 50-year concession to extend the lines used by the

Egyptian government. Under Khedive Isma'il, the number of lines increased from six, totaling 500 km, to 36, spanning more than 9,000 km, facilitating official, commercial, and private communication.

The telephone first appeared in Egypt in 1881 and was long managed by the American Bell Company. The number of telephones rose from 66,000 in 1940 to 122,000 in 1951 and approximately 600,000 in 1984, but the demand for commercial and home telephones exceeded the supply. Domestic service remained unreliable, despite improvements made during the 1980s, but international service improved with the introduction of direct-distance dialing. Egypt had 2.2 million telephones in 1990. The inauguration of telex facilities in the 1970s eclipsed the telegraph system, and lately fax machines have been introduced to Egyptian offices. The Arab communications satellite network, with Egypt as a focal point, opened in 1991.

COMMUNISM. Ideology calling for state or other collective ownership of the means of production, to be achieved by a workers' revolution against a dominant capitalist class. Because Egypt was under British occupation (q.v.) in the late-nineteenth and early twentieth century and because most of its capitalists were foreigners, Egyptians spent most of their political energy on such national liberation movements as the National Party (q.v.) and the Wafd (q.v.). Some did espouse socialism (q.v.), but not necessarily in its Marxist form. The Egyptian Socialist Party (q.v.) began in 1921 as an umbrella organization that included Fabians and social democrats as well as Marxists, but the next year it was recast as the Egyptian Communist Party, a member of the Comintern, having ties with at least 20 labor organizations in Egypt. In 1924 they challenged Sa'd Zaghlul's (q.v.) authority by calling workers' strikes against the Egyptian Oil Company and Alexandria textile factories, but were suppressed by the army. The leaders were arrested, their trade union confederation was disbanded, and the Communist Party, banned by the government in 1925, languished for two decades.

Egyptian Jewish intellectuals played a major role in its revival as part of their anti-Fascist efforts in the late 1930s; some Copts and Muslims took part, but in lesser numbers. The Union of Peace Supporters, formed in 1934 by Paul Jacot Descombes, was democratic-leftist, but hesitated to organize the communist movement in Egypt because its membership was mainly foreign, young, and well-off. Three Jewish Marxists, Marcel Israel, Hillel Schwartz, and Henri Curiel, founded the Democratic Union in 1939, but it soon split into factions. In 1943, the last-named formed the Egyptian Movement for National Liberation to bring Marxist ideas to the Egyptian masses. He opened a socialist bookstore in central Cairo, interviewed surviving Communists from the former party, and contacted workers in Shubra al-Khayma and al-Mahalla al-Kubra (q.v.), eventuating in the creation of the Congress of the Union of Egyptian Workers in 1946. Hillel Schwartz formed Iskra (q.v.) in 1943, appealing especially to the intelligentsia via the universities. Other factions included the group around the magazine *New Dawn* (q.v.), the Popular Vanguard for Liberation, and the Wafdist Vanguard (q.v.). After World War II (q.v.), the major student and worker groups jointly formed the National Committee of Workers and Students (q.v.), which included Communists as well as other leftists.

In 1947 the Egyptian Movement for National Liberation merged with Iskra to form the Haraka al-Dimuqratiya li al-Taharrur al-Watani ("Democratic Movement for National Liberation"), usually called Hadeto (q.v.), Egypt's main Communist movement from 1947 to 1954. Several Egyptians, notably Isma'il Sabri Abdallah and Fuad Mursi, formed the Egyptian Communist Party in 1950, aided by France's Communists. Although it based its theoretical framework on the writings of Lenin and Stalin and hoped, therefore, to organize the working class, its membership came mainly from students and intellectuals of bourgeois origin, and it practiced a tighter party discipline than Hadeto. Its tentative approaches to Misr al-Fatat (q.v.), the National Party (q.v.), and to Ihsan Abd al-Quddus (q.v.), editor of *Ruz al-Yusuf* (q.v.), proved abortive. Unlike Hadeto, it did not support the 1952 Revolution (q.v.), calling it a military dictatorship with Fascist coloring. All leftist groups opposed Nasir's (q.v.) efforts to crush the political parties, but the Communists survived underground. In 1957 Hadeto, its dissident factions, and the Egyptian Communist Party merged as the United Egyptian Communist Party, to be joined in 1958 by the Workers' Vanguard. The formation of the United Arab Republic (q.v.) and the struggle between the Arab nationalists and the Communists in postrevolutionary Iraq led to new troubles for Egypt's Communists, some 2,000 of whom were arrested and jailed in January 1959. Although Nasir moved toward scientific socialism with his July Laws (q.v.) and National Charter (q.v.), most Communists remained in jail until 1964.

Convinced of Nasir's conversion to scientific socialism, the United Egyptian Communist Party and Hadeto agreed in 1965 to dissolve their groups and to work with the Arab Socialist Union (q.v.), especially its leftist Vanguard Organization. Although they were allowed to publish a Marxist monthly, *al-Tali'a*, Nasir kept them under surveillance and prevented them from forming new organizations as a political alternative to his regime. In 1972 the Egyptian Communist Party was secretly revived and started publishing a newspaper about nine times a year called *al-Intisar*, and an internal organ on Party issues called *al-Wa'y*. It now has several splinter groups, some of them Maoist or Trotskyite; a few may be wholly fictitious. The Egyptian Communists held a congress in 1980 on

Egyptian territory, at which they called for "the liberation of the whole Arab homeland from imperialism and Zionism." Their party published reports in 1975 and 1983; they are available in English translation in Ismael and Sa'id's *Communist Movement in Egypt, 1920–1988*. The Communists held another congress in 1985. Four Communists ran as independents in the 1987 elections; all lost. The party opposed Iraq's invasion of Kuwait in 1990 and called on both Iraqi and U.S. troops to withdraw, so that the crisis could be settled peacefully.

The Communists contributed to a more sophisticated analysis of Egypt's economic and social problems and especially to the ideology of the Arab Socialist Union (q.v.), but their appeal to the Egyptian masses was blunted by their assumed ties to the USSR, their hostility to religion, their stress on class warfare, and their founders' non-Muslim background.

CONSTANTINOPLE CONVENTION (1888). Agreement reached by the European powers and the Ottoman Empire (q.v.), pledging to keep the Suez Canal (q.v.) open to ships of all nations in times of peace or war. Egypt was not a signatory to the Convention, which Britain violated in both world wars (qq.v.) by excluding Germany and its allies from the Canal. Foreign powers invoked the Convention in 1956, when Egypt nationalized the Suez Canal Company (q.v.), as did Israel when its ships and cargoes were barred from transiting the Canal.

CONSTITUTION (1882). Revised version of a constitution first proposed by Muhammad Sharif (q.v.) in 1879. Delegates to the legislature, or National Assembly (q.v.), were to be elected for five-year terms and to receive an annual salary of £E100. Its president was to be chosen by the khedive (q.v.) from among three of the delegates proposed by the Assembly. The ministers were singly and collectively responsible to the Assembly; each could be summoned to testify about his actions. Any bill initiated by the government must be read to the Assembly, debated, voted upon, and accepted by the khedive. No tax could be imposed unless it had been passed by the Assembly. Although Sharif had not wanted to let the delegates vote on the state budget, the leaders of the Assembly insisted on that right, which appears in Article 35, but they were not allowed to debate the tribute paid to the Ottoman Empire (q.v.) or the service of the public debt. The Assembly was to be in session for three months of the year; in case the cabinet had to take action at other times, the affair should be submitted to the Assembly for examination at its next session. The Assembly agreed that its delegates should in the future number 125, including 12 representatives from the Sudan and the Red Sea provinces and seven for the bedouin tribes, and that they should be elected in two stages. The Assembly, which had opened in December 1881, remained in session until 26 March 1882; many of its members, mainly rural landowners, took part in the deliberations during the subsequent political crisis, but the Assembly as a whole was never reconvened, and the 1882 Constitution was abrogated by Tawfiq (q.v.) after Urabi's (q.v.) defeat.

CONSTITUTION (1923). The most liberal of Egypt's constitutions. It guaranteed most of the civil rights and liberties enjoyed by citizens in liberal democratic countries, including freedom of expression and assembly, inviolability of domicile and property, and the right to practice any belief or religion. It made elementary education free and compulsory for both boys and girls. The king wielded executive power and shared legislative power with Parliament, consisting of the Senate and the Chamber of Deputies, judicial power being assigned to the relevant court systems. The king was the supreme head of state, his person was inviolable, he could veto laws, dissolve the Chamber of Deputies, adjourn Parliament for one month, promulgate emergency legislation between sessions, declare war or a state of siege, commission civil officials and military and naval officers, appoint and dismiss cabinet ministers and ambassadors, and name his successor with the assent of Parliament. The ministers were to conduct government policy and were responsible to the two houses of Parliament, where they were given the privilege of the floor but no vote. If Parliament took a vote of no confidence, the ministers would have to resign. In case of infractions of the Constitution and laws by the ministers, they could be tried by a special court made up of 16 members of Parliament.

Two-fifths of the Senate members were appointed by the king; the rest were elected by universal adult male suffrage. Provinces were assigned senators in proportion to their population. Minimum requirements of age, political position, social station, or property limited eligibility for appointment to the Senate, and the term was for ten years. Its session would be suspended if the Chamber of Deputies was dissolved. All members of the Chamber of Deputies were elected by universal adult male suffrage. Each province was entitled to a representative for every 60,000 of its inhabitants or fraction thereof exceeding 30,000. Each deputy had to be at least 30 years old, and terms were set at five years. If the Chamber was dissolved for a specific issue, the new one could not be dissolved over the same question. The king was to convene both houses of Parliament in Cairo on the third Saturday of November, and each session was to last for six months. Deliberations were to be public, unless ten or more members petitioned for a closed meeting, and a quorum for business was a majority of the members. Proposed laws were to be examined by the relevant committees before being passed by the houses.

Members were allowed to question the ministers and to investigate political problems, while enjoying immunity from prosecution. The Constitution guaranteed the independence of the judiciary. Provision was made for provincial and municipal councils, some of whose powers were specified. New taxes and fees could be imposed only by law. The annual budget had to be approved by both houses. Islam was the religion of the state; its language was Arabic. Any amendment to the Constitution had to be approved by a two-thirds majority of both houses and also by the king.

In practice, the provisions of the 1923 Constitution were often overridden by the king and sometimes also by the ministers and even Parliament members themselves. It was replaced for five years by the more limited 1930 Constitution (q.v.). Even after its restoration late in 1935, the Palace, the British, and the political parties often violated it, and it was abolished by the Revolutionary Command Council (q.v.) after the 1952 Revolution (q.v.).

CONSTITUTION (1930). Document promulgated by Isma'il Sidqi (q.v.) in October 1930, greatly increasing the powers of King Fuad (q.v.) at the expense of Parliament. Among its noteworthy provisions were articles giving the king sole power to propose financial legislation, increasing his ability to veto laws, enabling him to appoint three-fifths (instead of two-fifths) of the Senate members, making it harder for Parliament to pass a no-confidence vote against the ministers, and empowering the king to prorogue a parliamentary session before it had examined the government budget. The 1930 Constitution was fiercely opposed by the Wafd Party (q.v.) and the Constitutional Liberals (q.v.). Massive popular demonstrations in favor of the restoration of the 1923 Constitution (q.v.) marked the political scene in late 1935. In December the Tawfiq Nasim (q.v.) cabinet agreed to abrogate the 1930 Constitution in favor of the earlier document, which had become popularly viewed as the guardian of the people's rights.

CONSTITUTION (1956). The first set of principles for Egypt's government propounded after the 1952 Revolution (q.v.). The document included a preamble that stated the aims of the Egyptian people, a brief description of the state, a long list of articles defining the civil and property rights of members of the Egyptian community, a list of the legislative powers to be exercised by the unicameral National Assembly (q.v.) and the qualifications and limits of its members, the powers and limits of the president, the responsibilities and qualifications of the cabinet ministers, the functions of the judiciary, and methods for its revision.

Noteworthy changes from the 1923 Constitution (q.v.) include a temporary ban on political parties, the formation of the National Union (q.v.) open to all Egyptians, the enfranchisement of women, a plebiscite for the choice of the first president (who would thereafter be chosen by the National Assembly) and the adoption of this constitution, and an article giving the president "the right to initiate, to promulgate, or to veto legislation." While this document was in force, President Nasir (q.v.) wielded more power than the National Assembly, and the constitutional rights of individuals and groups who opposed government policies were often violated. It was replaced in March 1958, after the union with Syria, by a provisional constitution for the United Arab Republic (q.v.). This document was modified in 1962 by a constitutional declaration on the political organization of the higher authorities of the state and then by the 1964 Constitution (q.v.).

CONSTITUTION (1964). Often called the "Interim Constitution," this document differs from the 1956 Constitution (q.v.) mainly in its commitment to the principles of Arab socialism (q.v.). Half of the National Assembly (q.v.) members had to be workers or peasants. The president had limited legislative powers when the Assembly was adjourned or in a national emergency, but his laws were subject to the Assembly's approval. Although the Assembly chose the president, his election had to be confirmed by a nationwide plebiscite. The independence of the judiciary and the finality of its verdicts were confirmed, "except as prescribed by law." In practice, President Nasir (q.v.) exercised far more power than the Assembly, and the civil rights of dissenting individuals and groups were often violated. After the 1968 student demonstrations he promised changes, known as the 30 March Program (q.v.), which, if effected, would have strengthened civil liberties. The 1964 document was replaced by the Permanent Constitution of the Arab Republic of Egypt (*see* Constitution, 1971).

CONSTITUTION (1971). Legally called the Permanent Constitution of the Arab Republic of Egypt, it was approved by a nationwide referendum in September 1971. This document claimed to strengthen "the protection, consolidation, and preservation of the socialist gains" and enshrined the Arab Socialist Union (ASU) (q.v.) as the political organization of the state representing the alliance of the working forces of the people: farmers, workers, soldiers, intellectuals, and national capitalists. It also strengthened the people's claim to the property of the nation and the commitment of the state to economic planning and development, but also safeguarded certain individual freedoms, including rights to privacy, emigration, and public association. Amendments to the 1971 Constitution were passed in 1977 to permit the formation of political parties (*see* Party Reforms) and in 1980 to create the Consultative Council (*Majlis Shura*) to supplement the National Assembly (q.v.), to abolish the ASU, to affirm Egypt's adherence to the Shari'a (q.v.), and to forbid racial and religious discrimination.

CONSTITUTIONAL LIBERAL PARTY. Egypt's largest political rival to the Wafd Party (q.v.) between 1922 and 1952. It originated when a political organization, Jam'iyyat Misr al-mustaqilla ("Society of Independent Egypt"), was formed to back Adli Yakan (q.v.) against Sa'd Zaghlul (q.v.) during his negotiations with British Foreign Minister Curzon. The society also backed Abd al-Khaliq Tharwat (q.v.) when he succeeded Adli as premier. After one of its leaders, Hafiz Afifi, received a license to publish *al-Siyasa* (q.v.) as its journalistic organ, Adli's backers decided to transform the society into a political party, drawing heavily on surviving members of the 1913 Legislative Assembly (q.v.). The first meeting of the Constitutional Liberal Party (an exact translation of *Hizb al-Ahrar al-Dusturiyyin*) was held in October 1922. Like the prewar Umma Party (q.v.), it called for constitutional government and rejected pan-Islam, but its published principles tended to be vague.

Led by Adli Yakan, Muhammad Mahmud (q.v.), and finally Muhammad Husayn Haykal (q.v.), its main supporters were large landowners, provincial notables, and intellectuals. It cooperated with the Wafd between 1925 and 1928 in opposing the Palace and between 1930 and 1935 in rejecting the 1930 Constitution (q.v.), but at other times it formed coalition cabinets with supporters of Kings Fuad (q.v.) and Faruq (q.v.). Some of its members defected in 1930–35 to the Ittihad (q.v.) and Sha'b (q.v.) Parties, but the Constitutional Liberals regained popularity after the fall of the Isma'il Sidqi (q.v.) and Palace regimes. The Party boycotted the March 1942 elections, which were won by the Wafd. It joined the coalition government of Ahmad Mahir (q.v.) and took part in the January 1945 elections, boycotted by the Wafd and won by the Sa'dist Party (q.v.). Liberals also held cabinet posts under Nuqrashi (q.v.), Ibrahim Abd al-Hadi (q.v.), and Husayn Sirri (q.v.). The Party was dissolved and its assets seized after the 1952 Revolution (q.v.). Some of its members were later tried, and all who had held public office since 1942 were deprived of their political and civil rights for ten years. During the 1923–52 period of Egypt's history, it came closest to being a fourth force after the "power triangle" of king, Wafd, and British, but it enjoyed little popular support.

CONSTITUTIONAL REFORM PARTY. Political group, formed in 1907 by Ali Yusuf (q.v.), editor of *al-Muayyad* (q.v.), to uphold the prerogatives of Khedive Abbas Hilmi II (qq.v.) against the National and Umma parties (qq.v.). Most of its followers were individuals or groups seeking Palace favor; its vice president, Ahmad Hishmat, later became education minister.

COOPERATIVES. Egypt's organized cooperative movement began in 1908, when a Nationalist lawyer named Umar Lutfi founded an agricultural cooperative society. Other cooperatives were set up by the National Party (q.v.). In 1914 the Legislative Assembly (q.v.) discussed–but did not pass–a bill for chartering cooperative societies. Nevertheless, rising prices during 1914–18 inspired the formation of several consumer cooperatives. In 1923 a law for agricultural cooperatives was enacted; another law, passed in 1927, was applied to all types of cooperatives. When the social affairs ministry was formed in 1939, Parliament appointed a special committee and set up a department of cooperatives to supervise them. In 1944 Parliament passed a new cooperatives law that expanded the membership of the special committee and also established advisory councils in the provinces to serve as liaisons with the central department under the social affairs ministry. Cooperatives were exempted from paying the stamp duty on their contractual and other transactions, as well as from the commercial and industrial profits tax. The law set conditions for government grants to cooperative societies. Cooperatives could extend loans to their members and finance social services, using profits made from transactions with non-members earmarked for that purpose. Cooperatives were allowed to set up provincial or district syndicates to supervise the work of all local branches. The Agricultural Credit Bank, established in 1931, was transformed into the Cooperatives Bank. In 1945 Egypt had over 2,500 cooperatives, whose total membership exceeded 800,000 members, doing £E8 million worth of business annually. After the 1952 Revolution (q.v.), the government encouraged the expansion of cooperative societies and in 1961 placed them under the supervision of the agriculture ministry, and every farmer was required to join a cooperative. The number of agricultural cooperatives rose from 1,727 in 1952 to 4,897 in 1963, offering £E46 million in loans to some 920,000 borrowers.

These societies consolidate resources (such as tractors), preserve incentives (including profits), determine responsibility for planting government quotas of such crops as cotton (q.v.), and buy the state's share of procurement crops at government-fixed prices. They enhance agricultural growth by encouraging the farmers to use fertilizers and modern technology and to change from a two-year to the preferred three-year crop rotation system. A drawback is that rich farmers often take over the cooperatives, corrupting some of their managers. The Sadat (q.v.) and Mubarak (q.v.) governments have reduced somewhat their role.

COPTIC CHURCH. The national Christian church of Egypt, believed to have been founded by St. Mark in 30 CE. The Coptic church remains predominant in Ethiopia and used to be strong in Nubia. It espouses the Monophysite doctrine, declared heretical by the Orthodox Christian Council of Chalcedon in 451, which teaches that Christ had a single nature, wholly divine. In Egyptian usage, Christians who have remained loyal to the ancient Christian church call themselves Orthodox, which should not be construed as Greek Orthodox, but rather means that they have become neither Catholic nor Protestant.

The Roman Catholic Church has had ties with some Copts since 1824, if not earlier, although the formal creation of a Coptic Catholic patriarchate did not occur until 1895. Relations between the Coptic Catholic patriarch and the Vatican have often been troubled, although the current patriarch is also a cardinal of the Roman Catholic Church. In 1986 there were 200,000 Catholic Copts. The Coptic Evangelical Church was founded by Presbyterian missionaries in 1854 and now claims more than 200,000 believers.

Except for the Catholic and Evangelical groups, the ancient Coptic Orthodox Church of Alexandria commands the loyalty of Egypt's Christian population, variously estimated at 6–15 percent of the total citizenry. The church has traditionally been controlled by a hierarchy of deacons, priests, bishops, and a patriarch. The formal organization of the hierarchy is called the Holy Synod of Bishops. Since 1873 this ecclesiastical structure has been challenged by a lay-led Community Council (*majlis milli*) in matters of Coptic communal governance. Its functions were administrative, educational, financial, and judicial. At certain times, notably in the 1890s and in the 1950s, open conflict has erupted between the Council and the hierarchy over these functions. A key issue was control of the churches' *awqaf* (pious endowments), an issue finally settled by the Nasir (q.v.) government in 1960, when each Coptic *waqf* (q.v.) was limited to 200 feddans of cultivated and 200 of barren land, the rest being nationalized. The contending groups were both invited to send representatives to the Coptic Orthodox *Awqaf* Organization. The Coptic church courts, like all Egyptian religious courts, were abolished in 1955. The Coptic Museum, founded in 1908, is an important center for Coptic art and archaeology, and since 1954 there has also been a Higher Institute for Coptic Studies. A Coptic weekly newspaper, *Watani*, is published in Cairo (*see* Copts, Fundamentalism, Religion).

COPTIC CONGRESS (1911). Meeting in Asyut (q.v.) of 1,150 Copts (q.v.), mainly laymen claiming to represent 10,000 Coptic electors, protesting against alleged Egyptian government favoritism toward Muslims and demanding additional rights and privileges for Egypt's Christians. Condemned by the British, Egyptian government officials, and the church hierarchy, the Congress's demands were not met. An Egyptian Congress (q.v.) was later held in response.

COPTS. Adherents of the Coptic church (q.v.). At the time of the Arab conquest in 639–41 CE, nearly all Egyptians were Coptic Christians, but their share of the population gradually diminished as a result of conversion to Islam (q.v.) and the immigration of Arab and later Turkish and Circassian Muslims from outside Egypt. Copts have played an important role in the Egyptian government and in most professions and occupations. Some leading Copts in Egypt's national life in the past two centuries include Butros Ghali (q.v.), William Makram Ubayd (q.v.), and Salama Musa (q.v.). The 1986 Egyptian census estimated the Copts at 2 million, but Coptic authorities dispute these figures and claim that their actual number is closer to 7 million. The recent upsurge of Islamism (q.v.) in Egypt has alarmed the Copts, some of whom have responded by creating their own activist groups, others by calling for stricter enforcement of laws against discrimination and harassment (*see* Fundamentalism).

CORNICHE, ALEXANDRIA. Mediterranean shore drive linking Alexandria (q.v.) with Abu-Kir (q.v.). Once named Promenade de la Reine Nazli, it has, since the 1952 Revolution (q.v.), been officially called Tariq al-Jaysh ("Army Boulevard").

CORNICHE, CAIRO. Nile shore drive from Hulwan (q.v.) to the Delta Barrages (q.v.), built following the 1952 Revolution (q.v.), in part by taking land formerly held by the British embassy and by various palaces in Garden City.

CORRECTIVE REVOLUTION. Sadat's (q.v.) purge of his enemies on 15 May 1971, purportedly to liberalize Egypt's government by freeing it from the Centers of Power (q.v.) created in Nasir's (q.v.) last years. The purge was aided by a right-wing clique of officers and officials who opposed the pro-Nasir Centers of Power and by Sadat's ability to gain the support of senior officers in the army, the police, and the presidential guard. Rivalries within the leftist clique, especially between Ali Sabri (q.v.) and Sha'rawi Jum'a (q.v.), also hastened its downfall. As a result of the Corrective Revolution, Sadat's rule was consolidated, the Free Officers (q.v.) ceased to be a cohesive force in Egyptian politics, Egypt's orientation began to shift from Moscow toward Washington, and the government adopted a more liberal domestic policy. It showed the strength of the presidency and the bureaucratic elite, the army's reluctance to wield power, and the absence of mass participation in Egyptian politics.

CORVÉE. Obligation imposed by custom or decree on peasants to perform unremunerated labor on privately owned or government estates or to construct and repair irrigation (q.v.) works. During the early nineteenth century, the corvée could take peasants away from their plots and families for two months, if not longer, every year. No food or housing was provided by the landlord or the state. Unpaid peasant labor helped to build the Mahmudiyya Canal (q.v.), the Delta Barrages (q.v.), and the Suez Canal (q.v.). In the 1860s, in response to public pressure to abolish the corvée, Isma'il (q.v.) decreed an end to the practice. It was gradually phased out on his private estates and those of most other landlords by 1882, in part because of the growing monetization of Egypt's rural economy. The British occupation (q.v.) completed the phasing out of the corvée except in cases of emergency repairs to flood-damaged irrigation works.

COTTON, EGYPTIAN. Long-staple cotton, domesticated on a large scale for the first time by Louis Alexis Jumel, a French engineer who had been brought to Egypt by Muhammad Ali (q.v.) in 1817 to manage a textile factory in Bulaq (q.v.). Seeking a cash crop that would replace wheat, Muhammad Ali was quick to appreciate this new strain of cotton, and from 1821 ordered its large-scale cultivation in areas that would be easy to irrigate in the summer, starting on the Nile's (q.v.) Damietta branch. Although the peasants had to be taught how to nurture, harvest, and gin Egyptian cotton, the revenues that the state could realize from its sale led Muhammad Ali to extend its cultivation and to promote perennial irrigation (q.v.) to support it. All aspects of cotton growing, processing, and export were subject to a state monopoly, and it became a major revenue source financing the military and other operations of Muhammad Ali's government. By 1835 the value of Egyptian cotton exports exceeded £E1 million. Local spinning and weaving factories (*see* Textile Industry) also proliferated, but most did not withstand the competition of foreign, especially British, textile mills after the 1838 Anglo-Ottoman Tariff Convention (*see* Tariffs). Government monopolies over cotton and other agricultural produce declined or were abolished after 1841, except for a brief attempt by Abbas Hilmi I (q.v.) to revive them.

Cotton production lost ground to wheat and flax during the 1840s but revived in the 1850s, due perhaps to rising output on the estates belonging to Muhammad Ali's family. It boomed after 1861 when the naval blockade of the U.S. North against the South during the Civil War cut off the cotton supply to British and other European textile mills, causing a frantic quest for alternative sources. Cotton exports from Alexandria rose from 500,000 cantars in 1861 to five times that figure in 1865. Prices skyrocketed between 1861 and 1864, and quantities exported by Egypt quadrupled, causing a rapid expansion in the amount of Egyptian land devoted to cotton cultivation. Although cotton output and sales continued to increase in the late 1860s, prices plummeted, creating economic problems for Egyptian farmers and Khedive Isma'il's (qq.v.) government. Yet cotton remained the most profitable crop for Egyptians to raise, and production tripled between 1865 and 1879.

Cotton production mounted further during the British occupation (q.v.); exports rose from 3 million cantars to a peak of 7.5 million in 1911. British policy encouraged this growth by extending perennial irrigation and the expansion of facilities for cotton processing and marketing. The spread of the cotton maggot, poor drainage of irrigated lands, and the weakening of peasant laborers by the spread of bilharzia (q.v.) all lessened cotton yields during the early twentieth century, but measures were taken to overcome these problems. Cotton remained profitable enough so that landlords and peasants resented (and often defied) government efforts to limit the land allotted to cotton to increase food output during both world wars (qq.v.). Since the 1952 Revolution (q.v.), the Egyptian government has promoted diversification of agricultural land use. As a result, land area devoted to cotton production was halved during the next quarter century. Cotton yields rose from 1952 to 1980, as irrigation and pest control improved, but stagnated during the 1980s, as labor became more scarce. Production fell from 460,000 metric tons in 1982 to 303,000 in 1990.

COUNCIL OF JUSTICE. Advisory committee for administration and legal reform established by Muhammad Ali (q.v.). This organization, called Majlis al-Ahkam al-Misriyya ("Council of Egyptian Judicial Rulings"), reviewed petitions from Muhammad Ali's officials, who often adjudicated local disputes and interpreted his decrees. It also received judicial petitions for or against foreigners protected by the Capitulations (q.v.) and in 1849 absorbed the High Court of Justice established in 1842. Abbas Hilmi I (q.v.) established regional councils to review petitions presented to the mudirs (q.v.); these were suspended later by Sa'id (q.v.), who soon had to set up a new system of local councils. Because of the Egyptian cotton (q.v.) boom, Khedive Isma'il (qq.v.) set up five provincial courts of first instance within days of his accession. By 1870 there were courts in every province, with appeal courts for Upper and Lower Egypt, but still local officials carried judicial burdens. New village and provincial capital courts were established in 1871 to try small cases and claims. The Egyptian government set up a justice department in 1872. The Council of

Justice continued to deliberate on administrative and legislative issues, including agriculture, education, and taxes, under Sa'id and Isma'il. With the growing complexity of judicial and administrative functions, the need for systematizing the legal system became acute. Once the Mixed Courts (q.v.) were set up, the government began to develop a new judicial and legal system for Egyptians. Delayed by Urabi's (q.v.) revolution, its efforts culminated in the National Courts (q.v.) in 1883.

COUNCIL OF MINISTERS. The cabinet, or executive branch of Egypt's government, since 1878, when Isma'il (q.v.) turned over his power to a council headed by Nubar (q.v.). Earlier rulers did, however, have rudimentary councils. Muhammad Ali (q.v.) had a Ma'iyya Saniyya ("viceregal suite"), made up of sons, in-laws, Mamluks (q.v.), and selected Coptic (q.v.) and Armenian (q.v.) officials, who helped him to manage Egypt. In his later years he rewarded many of his most trusted officials with large land grants, a practice continued by his successors, in order to preserve the cabinet's loyalty to the viceregal household. In 1847 the Ma'iyya was supplanted by the Privy Council (q.v.), which received regular reports from the provinces and the various government departments and formulated state policies and laws. In form, it still served the khedive (q.v.) personally; in practice, it acted as his administration and created Egypt's bureaucracy (q.v.). Its ablest members earned high salaries and exercised vast powers. Egypt's mounting fiscal crisis led Isma'il (q.v.) to delegate many of his powers to a council of ministers, replacing his Privy Council, in a formal decree issued on 28 August 1878. The first council, headed by Nubar and including Riyad (q.v.) and Ali Mubarak (q.v.), was called the "European cabinet" because it had a British finance minister and a Frenchman holding the portfolio for public works. Although barred from his cabinet's deliberations, Isma'il soon engineered its downfall by organizing an officers' rebellion. A nominally Egyptian (but actually khedivist) cabinet, headed by Muhammad Sharif (q.v.), took power in April 1879. It fell from power when Isma'il was deposed a few months later. The cabinet's authority was eclipsed by the Dual Control (q.v.) early in Tawfiq's (q.v.) reign, but revived in 1881–82, when Barudi (q.v.) and Urabi (q.v.) led the other ministers against Tawfiq and the Europeans.

During the British occupation (q.v.), a British financial adviser was added to the cabinet, and the Egyptian ministers, although formally appointed by the khedive, actually were chosen in consultation with Lord Cromer (q.v.) and followed the instructions of British "advisers." Cabinet posts for education (q.v.) and *awqaf* (q.v.) were merged with other ministries, then reestablished. The agriculture ministry was formed in 1913. During the Protectorate (q.v.) the foreign ministry was submerged; it revived in 1922. Under the 1923 Constitution (q.v.) the cabinet grew with the addition of ministers for commerce and industry in 1934, public health in 1936, social affairs in 1939, supply in 1940, civil defense during World War II (q.v.), and a broad portfolio that included national economy and municipal and rural affairs in 1950. Several coalition governments, beginning in 1937, had ministers of state without portfolios.

The 1952 Revolution (q.v.) led to further increases in the size of the cabinet, starting with portfolios for communications and for national guidance (later called information), but its power was eclipsed by that of the Free Officers (q.v.), the Revolutionary Command Council (q.v.), and such supervisory bodies as the Central Auditing Agency (q.v.). By 1957 it had 17 members. In 1959 the central cabinet of the United Arab Republic (q.v.) had 20 members; the Egyptian Region had a 15-member executive council. In 1962 there were four vice presidents (for war, planning, social affairs, and local government) and 21 ministers, including posts for the Aswan High Dam (q.v.), economic affairs, higher education, land reform, local administration, planning, presidential affairs, and scientific research. The cabinet in 1972 included five deputy premiers and 26 ministers; in 1991 there were 32 members. Since 1952, key government decisions have been made by the president, in consultation with his closest friends, rather than by the council of ministers. Nasir (q.v.) at times presided over cabinet meetings, but not Sadat (q.v.) or Mubarak (q.v.), and internecine rivalries have blunted the effectiveness of this increasingly unwieldy body.

CROMER, SIR EVELYN BARING, EARL OF (1841–1917). Britain's agent and consul general in Cairo from 1883 to 1907 and de facto governor of Egypt during that time. He was educated as an army officer at Woolwich Academy and was commissioned in the Royal Artillery in 1858. Named secretary to the viceroy of India in 1872, he first came to Egypt in 1877 as Britain's public debt commissioner, returned in 1879 to India, and was named British agent in Cairo in 1883, with instructions to prepare for the evacuation of the British army of occupation that had defeated Urabi (q.v.) in 1882. The Mahdi's (q.v.) revolt in the Sudan (q.v.) against Egyptian rule obliged the British to delay withdrawal from Egypt, and Baring (as he was then known) undertook to reform the finances of its government. In his early years in the British Agency (q.v.), Baring had a daunting mission, because state revenues did not suffice to finance needed reforms, and the Egyptian government could not float additional loans without the approval of the European powers represented on the Caisse de la Dette Publique (q.v.). Baring, working closely with the British financial adviser, managed to balance the state budget and then, by well-chosen reforms in irrigation (q.v.), to increase agricultural output and hence land-tax revenues. Istanbul's rejection of the Drummond-Wolff

Convention (q.v.) prolonged the British occupation (q.v.). As French naval power in the Mediterranean increased and as Britain distanced itself from the Ottoman Empire (q.v.), the British navy came to need a base at Alexandria (q.v.). Baring, never eager to evacuate Egypt, began instituting the financial reforms that he believed Egypt needed, attaching British advisers to as many ministries of the government as possible and exercising discreet influence over the khedive (q.v.).

This "veiled protectorate" worked well under Khedive Tawfiq (qq.v.), but less so when his son, Abbas Hilmi II (q.v.), succeeded him. Soon after Baring was elevated to the peerage with the title of Lord Cromer in 1892, the new khedive and the old consul clashed over the choice of a prime minister to replace the ailing Mustafa Fahmi (q.v.) and then over control of the Egyptian army, leading to the Frontiers Incident (q.v.). The British government, although still opposed in principle to a prolonged occupation of Egypt, supported Cromer against the khedive and left him free to pursue the policies by which he hoped to regenerate Egypt.

In the areas of state finance and irrigation, Cromer's reforms succeeded, and his long tenure as consul-general made him increasingly impervious to criticism from either his subordinates in the Agency or from the Egyptian bureaucracy (q.v.), to which Cromer gradually added young Englishmen from Oxford and Cambridge. Cromer's annual reports on conditions in Egypt (and, after 1898, the Sudan) were published–and even translated into Arabic by *al-Muqattam* (q.v.)–and tended to become the official version of Egypt's history. As Cromer's financial successes led to Egypt's economic regeneration, European opposition to the British occupation waned, and British determination to remain grew. Rising Egyptian resistance, as expressed by Mustafa Kamil (q.v.) or by more moderate nationalists, such as Ahmad Lutfi al-Sayyid (q.v.), did not influence Cromer, who viewed this opposition as inspired by pan-Islam (q.v.). As the British distanced themselves from the Egyptian people, mutual incomprehension spread, causing such events as the 1906 Dinshaway Incident (q.v.), which occasioned so much criticism of the British occupation in both Egypt and Europe that he decided to resign. For Cromer, the only true Egyptian nationalism must include all the Europeans and other minorities living in Egypt. He believed that his veiled protectorate had benefited all classes of Egyptian society, especially the peasants. Early financial stringencies made him cut expenditures on public health and education. Neither he nor his successors ever made up for this neglect, and Egypt eventually paid a high price for their failure to invest generously in its human resources.

CURRENCY. In Ottoman Egypt the standard coin was the silver para, 40 of which made one piastre. The government's unit of account was the *kis* ("purse"), worth 25,000 paras, or, in the time of Muhammad Ali (q.v.) and his successors, about 500 piastres. Owing to the tendency of Ottoman coins to lose value, foreign merchants preferred to use European currencies, such as the Austrian thaler and the Spanish rial. From 1836 to 1885 the main unit of currency was the piastre, commonly abbreviated to PT (French: *piastre tarif*); 97.5 piastres were equivalent to one British sterling pound. The Egyptian pound (Cairene Arabic: *gineh*, from the English "guinea"), commonly abbreviated to £E (French: *livre égyptienne*), consisted of a hundred piastres. Foreign coins were also allowed to circulate and indeed often did so because of the shortage and uneven quality of Egyptian coins. Money was backed with both gold and silver until 1885, when Egypt based its currency on gold, each pound containing 8.5 grams of gold at standard fineness. In 1887 the finance minister limited foreign currencies to the English sovereign, the French 20-franc piece, and the Turkish pound; the Egyptian government issued almost no gold pounds of its own. The sterling pound, the least undervalued of these currencies, soon became Egypt's standard. The National Bank of Egypt (q.v.) began issuing paper money in 1898, but its note issue stabilized at £E2.7 million until 1914. Egyptian landowners and peasants continued to prefer gold currency for the financing of their cotton crops. With the outbreak of World War I (q.v.), the notes of the National Bank of Egypt were declared legal tender and it was no longer required to redeem them with gold. From 1916 until 1949 Egypt was on a sterling-exchange system, by which its currency was backed by British war loans and treasury bills. Since 1949 the Egyptian government has managed its own currency, which initially remained strong because of the large sterling balances it had accumulated during World War II (q.v.). In recent years, however, the Egyptian pound has depreciated in value, from U.S. $4.20 in 1949 to 30 cents in 1994.

CYRIL IV (1816–61). The "Father of Reform" and patriarch of the Coptic church (q.v.) from 1854 to 1861. He established new schools for boys and girls in Cairo (q.v.), Mansura, and St. Antony's Monastery in Bush, and purchased the first printing press for the patriarchate. Sa'id (q.v.) sent him in 1856 to negotiate with Ethiopia over its border with Egypt. He built new churches and restored the Coptic cathedral in Cairo. The circumstances of his early death have never been explained, but he is remembered as one of the church's greatest patriarchs.

CYRIL V (1824–1927). Long-living patriarch of the Coptic church (q.v.) from 1874 to 1927. Although he helped to found churches, hospitals, benevolent societies, and schools, notably the Clerical College in Cairo, he is perhaps best remembered for his quarrels with successive Coptic Community Councils (*majlis milli*) under lay leadership.

CYRIL VI (1902–71). Influential patriarch of the Coptic church (q.v.) from 1959 to 1971. He had close ties with Nasir (q.v.) and with leaders of Eastern Orthodox churches. He chaired the Oriental Orthodox Conference convened in 1965 by Ethiopian Emperor Haile Selassie in Addis Ababa, hosted the 1968 celebration of the 1,900th anniversary of the Martyrdom of St. Mark, and won membership in the World Council of Churches for the Coptic church.

CZECH ARMS DEAL. Agreement concluded on 24 September 1955 by the Nasir (q.v.) government to purchase £E200 million worth of weapons from what was then thought to be Czechoslovakia, but really from the USSR, with payment to be made in Egyptian cotton (q.v.) and other products. The U.S. and British governments strongly opposed this transaction, which they feared would tie Egypt, politically as well as economically, to the Communist bloc.

- D -

DAR AL-KUTUB. Egypt's national library, founded in 1869 by Ali Mubarak (q.v.) and endowed by Mustafa Riyad (q.v.). Located in a former palace until 1904, then near Bab al-Khalq, east of Abdin Palace (q.v.), it was moved in 1980 to a new building, which it shares with the General Egyptian Book Organization, in Bulaq (q.v.). It currently holds an estimated 1.5 million volumes and many Arabic manuscripts.

DAR AL-ULUM. Higher school established in Cairo (q.v.) by Ali Mubarak (q.v.) for the training of Arabic teachers in 1872, following a successful lecture series during the previous year. The initial students were Azharites aged 20 or older having already a sound knowledge of Arabic grammar, and classes included the sciences and Islamic *fiqh* (jurisprudence). The school became a major rival to al-Azhar (q.v.) as a source of government school teachers of Arabic and Islamic subjects. Initially its classes were held in the Darb al-Jamamiz Palace; in 1901 a special building was opened for Dar al-Ulum in the Munira district, where it remains. Up to World War I (q.v.), students at Dar al-Ulum received monthly stipends, at a time when all other higher schools charged tuition fees, so the school attracted young men whose families could not have afforded to send them to the government Law School (q.v.). By the 1920s, as the supply of teachers began to outstrip the demand, al-Azhar campaigned to have Dar al-Ulum placed under its control, which was done by the Ahmad Ziwar (q.v.) cabinet in 1925, but this action was reversed by its successor. Dar al-Ulum became a faculty within Cairo University (q.v.) in 1945 and was opened to women students in 1953. Such distinguished thinkers as Husayn al-Marsafi, Muhammad Abduh (q.v.), and Amin Sami have taught at Dar al-Ulum. Although some Azharis denounced the school as a hotbed of secularism, its graduates include such noted Islamists (q.v.) as Hasan al-Banna (q.v.) and Sayyid Qutb (q.v.).

AL-DA'WA. The weekly magazine of the Society of Muslim Brothers (q.v.), edited by Hasan al-Ashmawi, from 1951 to 1954, when it was outlawed by Nasir (q.v.). After the Society was allowed to revive, it was edited by Umar al-Tilmisani (q.v.) from 1976 until it was banned by Sadat (q.v.) in September 1981. The ban has not been lifted by Mubarak (q.v.).

DELTA BARRAGES. Two large dams, constructed 20 km north of Cairo (q.v.) where the Nile (q.v.) divides into the Rosetta (west) and Damietta (east) branches to form the Delta of Lower Egypt. Built by French engineers in 1843–61 and strengthened by the British in 1887–90, the Barrages raised the water upstream to a height of four meters above the normal Nile level, so that some of its waters could be diverted into three takeoff canals whose entrances lay above the dams, thus helping to convert Delta agricultural lands to perennial irrigation (q.v.).

DEMOCRATIC MOVEMENT FOR NATIONAL LIBERATION (1947), *see* HADETO.

***DESCRIPTION DE L'ÉGYPTE* (1808–29)**. Monumental French scholarly work, consisting of 9 volumes of text and 14 of drawings, providing detailed information about Egyptian antiquities, natural history, and social conditions at the time of the French occupation (q.v.).

DINSHAWAY INCIDENT (1906). British atrocity against Egyptian peasants accused of assaulting uniformed British officers who were hunting pigeons near the village of Dinshaway in Minufiyya Province. One officer died, probably of sunstroke. The British in Egypt feared that this assault portended a national insurrection and demanded exemplary punishment of the villagers. The accused assailants, numbering 52, were hastily arrested, tried, and sentenced to death, public flogging, or imprisonment. The sentences led to widespread protests in Europe and Egypt, and their summary public execution promoted the rise of the National Party (q.v.) and hastened the retirement of Lord Cromer (q.v.). It remains a black mark cited by Egyptians against the British occupation (q.v.).

DISENGAGEMENT OF FORCES (1974). The pressing goal of U.S. Secretary of State Kissinger's efforts to mediate an interim agreement between Egypt and Israel following the October War (q.v.), because the two sides' armies were intermingled due to the Israeli crossing of the Suez Canal (q.v.), isolating Egypt's Third Army on its east bank.

DRUMMOND WOLFF CONVENTION (1885). Abortive agreement, negotiated with Ottoman (q.v.) Sultan Abdulhamid II by Sir Henry Drummond Wolff at the behest of Britain's foreign secretary, Lord Salisbury. It would have ended the British occupation (q.v.) of Egypt following a three-year period. However, because the Convention allowed a British right of reentry under certain specified conditions, the French and Russian ambassadors in Constantinople persuaded the sultan not to sign. The Ottoman government's failure to ratify this agreement greatly prolonged Britain's occupation of Egypt and also the presence of an Ottoman high commissioner in Cairo (q.v.) from 1885 to 1914, an official with few powers but ample opportunities to foment pan-Islam (q.v.) and pro-Ottoman sentiments among Egypt's nationalists.

DUAL CONTROL. Joint Anglo-French financial administration in Egypt from 1878 to 1882, supplementing the supervision provided by the already existing Caisse de la Dette Publique (q.v.). The first controllers were in the "European cabinet" headed by Nubar (q.v.) from August 1878 to March 1879, in which an Englishman was finance minister and a Frenchman held the portfolio for public works. Four months after Khedive Isma'il (qq.v.) engineered the downfall of that cabinet, he was himself deposed by the Ottoman (q.v.) sultan in favor of his son, Tawfiq (q.v.). The British and French governments appointed their controllers, Sir Evelyn Baring (*see* Cromer) who had served on the Caisse, and de Blignières, the former works minister. They drafted what would in 1880 become the Liquidation Law (q.v.). Its strict controls on Egyptian government expenditure fomented nationalist discontent among the Egyptian army officers and government officials, leading to the rise of Urabi (q.v.) in 1881. Once the Barudi (q.v.) cabinet took control in February 1882, the controllers were no longer able to manage the budget, and the Dual Control was formally ended when the British occupied Egypt in September. The Dual Control's program for retiring the Egyptian government debt was too stringent for the country's economy and could have been imposed only by the concerted use of military force, which neither Britain nor France was willing to employ until after the Urabists had taken power.

DUFFERIN MISSION. Committee sent by the British government, just after Britain's army occupied Egypt in 1882, to study the country's administration and to recommend improvements, without committing Britain to an indefinite military occupation of Egypt. Its final report, written in 1883 by its chairman, Lord Dufferin, called for the continued presence of European advisers in the Egyptian government, especially in finance and public works. His report refuted the need for a formal constitution and argued that strong rule would be needed to restore order and confidence, but it did call for establishing a General Assembly, made up mainly of rural landowners, and a Legislative Council, but with very limited powers. This recommendation became the basis for Egypt's Organic Law of 1883 (q.v.). Although the report opposed long-term British rule over Egypt, its prescriptions implied the indefinite maintenance of Britain's paramount influence, thus laying the groundwork for Cromer's (q.v.) administration.

DULLES, JOHN FOSTER (1888–1959). U.S. secretary of state from 1953 to 1959 under President Eisenhower. He believed that the independence of the Middle Eastern countries, including Egypt, could best be safeguarded by their joining an anti-Communist defensive alliance, modeled on NATO. During a visit to Egypt in 1953 he tried to persuade Najib (q.v.) and Nasir (q.v.) to help set up a Middle East Defense Organization, but they deferred the issue until they had secured Britain's agreement to give up its Suez Canal (q.v.) base. Dulles later opposed Nasir's positive neutrality (q.v.), which he reportedly condemned as "immoral." Angered by Nasir's diplomatic recognition of Communist China in 1956, he tried to teach the Egyptians a lesson by withdrawing an American offer to help finance the building of the Aswan High Dam (q.v.). This rebuff caused Nasir to nationalize the Suez Canal Company (q.v.). When Britain and France joined forces with Israel to invade and defeat Egypt in the Suez War (q.v.), Dulles condemned their aggression against Egypt and joined the USSR in pressuring them to withdraw their forces from the Canal Zone and the Sinai Peninsula (*see* Suez War). In 1957 Dulles tried to persuade the Arab countries to subscribe to the Eisenhower Doctrine (q.v.), which seemed to be aimed at isolating Egypt politically, but most Arab governments refused to do so. His policies were widely criticized by both the Arabs (including Egypt) and Israel for their focus on Cold War issues and apparent indifference to local concerns.

- E -

EARTHQUAKE (1992). A severe earthquake, measuring 5.9 on the Richter scale, struck middle Egypt and Cairo on 12 October 1992, causing large-scale damage in Bulaq (q.v.), Shubra al-Khayma, and Heliopolis (q.v.). The quake and its numerous aftershocks left 541 dead, more than 6,000 injured, and possibly as many as 100,000 people homeless. Costs of rebuilding were estimated at £E3 billion. Government efforts to keep order and provide relief to the victims, most of whom were poor, evoked widespread criticism and protest demonstrations. Reportedly, Islamist *jama'at* (qq.v.) aided victims more than the government agencies did.

ECONOMY. From antiquity until the recent past, most Egyptians have made their living from agriculture (q.v.), with a relatively high degree of crop specialization. Cereal grains were formerly the major cash crop, but they gave way in the nineteenth century to the large-scale cultivation of Egyptian cotton (q.v.) and more recently to rice, sugar (q.v.), and edible fruits and vegetables for export. For most of its history Egypt has also been an entrepôt for international trade, with Mediterranean seaports at Alexandria (q.v.), Rosetta, Damietta, and (since 1869) Port Said (q.v.). Red Sea ports included Suez City and al-Qusayr. There was also an overland caravan trade that passed through Libya (q.v.) and Asyut (q.v.) and through the Sinai Peninsula (q.v.). The opening of the Suez Canal (q.v.) enhanced Egypt's role in international commerce. Manufacturing has played a role complementary to agriculture and commerce, with trade guilds dominating handicrafts industries until the nineteenth century.

Individual initiative (*see* Bank Misr) and government policies (*see* Planning) have both worked toward industrializing Egypt's economy in the twentieth century. Well-developed industries include textiles (q.v.), munitions (q.v.), pharmaceuticals, and food processing. Egypt's major extractive industry has been petroleum (q.v.); exploration for other minerals (q.v.) is continuing. The Egyptian economy has faced many problems, including excessive dependence on cotton, domination by foreign capitalists and creditors, government interference (*see* Bureaucracy), trade imbalances, and excessive population (q.v.). Egypt's gross domestic product rose between 1955 and 1975 at an annual rate of 4.2 percent, outstripping the rate of population growth. The annual growth rate exceeded 11 percent between 1975 and 1980 and remained high in the early 1980s, but slumped badly in 1985–87 due to the worldwide oil glut. The 1990–91 Iraq-Kuwait Conflict (q.v.) also damaged Egypt's economy because of the return of Egyptian expatriates who had been working in those two countries and the decline of tourism (q.v.). On the other hand, it led to a reduction in Egypt's indebtedness, estimated at U.S. $40 billion to foreign countries, a figure reduced as a result of Egypt's support of the allied coalition. Annual gross domestic product was estimated at U.S.$45.8 billion in 1988.

EDEN, ANTHONY (1897–1977), FIRST EARL OF AVON. English statesman, foreign minister, prime minister from 1955 to 1957, who played a major role in the Suez Crisis (q.v.). Born to an aristocratic family, Eden was educated at Eton and later, after seeing action in World War I (q.v.), at Christ Church College, Oxford, where he studied Arabic and Persian and graduated in 1922 with first-class honors. Although slated for a career in the diplomatic corps, he decided instead to run for a seat in the House of Commons. After one unsuccessful attempt, he ran in 1923 as a Conservative in the Warwick and Leamington constituency, a seat he won and retained for eight consecutive elections. He specialized in foreign and defense policy, becoming parliamentary private secretary to Austen Chamberlain, Stanley Baldwin's foreign secretary, then parliamentary undersecretary in Ramsay MacDonald's 1931 coalition government, then Lord Privy Seal in 1933. In 1935 Eden entered the cabinet as minister without portfolio for League of Nations affairs, succeeding Samuel Hoare later in that year as foreign secretary. Although mainly concerned with meeting the challenge of Hitler and Mussolini, he did negotiate the 1936 Anglo-Egyptian Treaty (q.v.), which preserved Britain's occupation of key points in Egypt and the Sudan (q.v.). He resigned from the Foreign Office in February 1938 in anger at Prime Minister Neville Chamberlain's secret negotiations with Italy, an act that later gave him the reputation of "standing up to the dictators." Excluded from the cabinet at the outbreak of World War II (q.v.), Eden became more active once Churchill became premier in 1940. He wanted to strengthen Britain's troop concentration in Egypt, but refused Churchill's offer to head the Middle East Command, holding out for the foreign secretary appointment that was offered to him in December 1940. He accompanied Churchill to all wartime Allied conferences. Seriously ill in 1945 and saddened by the loss of his eldest son (he had also lost two brothers in World War I), he accepted the Labour Party victory with equanimity. As an opposition Member of Parliament, he assailed Labour's Middle East policy and demanded strong action against Iran after Musaddiq nationalized the Anglo-Iranian Oil Company in 1951. After that year's Conservative victory, Eden reentered the cabinet as Churchill's foreign secretary and heir presumptive. He argued with Secretaries of State Acheson and Dulles (q.v.) over their pro-Iranian and pro-Egyptian policies and upheld Britain's traditional Middle East role. Only under strong U.S. pressure did he agree to evacuate the Suez Canal (q.v.) in the 1954 Anglo-Egyptian Agreement (q.v.).

Once Eden became prime minister in 1955, he became enmeshed in a power struggle with Nasir (q.v.), who once said that Eden behaved "like a prince dealing with vagabonds." Eden's efforts to set up the Baghdad Pact (q.v.) offended Nasir and did not gain American support. He worried about the Czech Arms Deal (q.v.) and agreed with the United States to form a consortium to finance the Aswan High Dam (q.v.), an offer that Nasir did not immediately accept. He was especially angered by the Egyptian agitation that blocked Jordan's adherence to the Baghdad Pact and King Husayn's decision to dismiss General Glubb as commander of Jordan's Arab Legion. He and Dulles decided to let the High Dam offer "wither on the vine." The U.S. government withdrew its offer, causing Nasir to nationalize the Suez Canal Company (q.v.).

Eden wanted to counter this act by military action, if diplomacy failed to keep the vital waterway under international control. He worked openly with France–and secretly with Israel–to plan for an attack publicly aimed at retaking the Suez Canal but actually meant to overthrow Nasir. He overlooked or underestimated U.S. and Labour Party opposition to his policies. In a secret meeting held on 22 October in Sèvres, British, French, and Israeli representatives met and agreed on plans to attack the Suez region. After Israel invaded the Sinai on the 29th, Eden (and French Premier Mollet) issued an ultimatum calling on Israel and Egypt to pull back from the Canal Zone and demanding Egypt's agreement to a temporary Anglo-French occupation of the area. Egypt rejected the ultimatum, and the British and French paratroopers landed at Port Said (q.v.) a week later. Eden was backed by his entire cabinet except for Anthony Nutting, a junior minister of state in the Foreign Office, who later assailed Eden's policies. Britain was opposed by the other Commonwealth members and by the United Nations (q.v.), where it vetoed two Security Council resolutions condemning the invasion. On 6 November Egypt and Israel accepted a cease-fire, and soon afterward Eden ordered British troops to halt their attack. Opposition from U.S. President Eisenhower probably affected him more than threats from the USSR or his Labour opposition. Britain was given no role in the subsequent UN Emergency Force (q.v.) or the clearing of the Canal, and Eden, suffering from poor health, resigned his premiership in January 1957. His name became permanently attached to the Suez "debacle." Sympathetic historians have argued that his error was to misread U.S. intentions, while critics claim that he held anachronistic views about British imperialism, Egypt, and the Arabs. His memoirs, *Full Circle*, cover the Suez Crisis.

EDUCATION. Until recently, most Egyptians were educated within the household, family farm, or workshop, or by apprenticeship; only a minority received formal schooling. In Ottoman (q.v.) Egypt, formal education was controlled by the ulama (q.v.) for Muslims, the clergy for Copts (q.v.), and the rabbinate for Jews (q.v.). For Muslim Egyptians, formal schooling came from the rural *kuttab*s (q.v.), a few urban *madrasa*s, and the mosque-university of al-Azhar (q.v.). A somewhat higher percentage of Christian and Jewish children, mainly boys, were educated, and a few mission schools were run by Franciscan and Greek Orthodox missionaries. The Mamluks (q.v.) gave military and naval training to their own recruits (*see* Military Academy). The French occupation (q.v.) disrupted rather than benefited Egyptian education.

The basis of a state-controlled, modern educational system was laid during the reign of Muhammad Ali (q.v.), who needed a cadre of military officers, engineers, and managers to carry out his Westernization program. In 1809 he sent his first mission of students abroad, choosing Italian technical institutions; larger missions began in 1826. A government school was opened at the Cairo Citadel (q.v.) in 1816, and at the same time a polytechnic institute (*muhandiskhane*) was set up nearby and later moved to Bulaq (q.v.). The first medical school was opened in 1827 at Abu Za'bal and later moved to Qasr al-Ayni. In the same year a veterinary school was opened at Rosetta and moved two years later to Abu Za'bal. Other civilian schools founded included arts and crafts (1831), irrigation (1831), translation (1836), and agriculture (1834–39, reopened in 1867). The administration of the state schools was initially centered in the Palace, moved to the war department in 1821, and entrusted to a board called the Diwan al-Madaris in 1836. The Diwan intervened vigorously to establish curricula; set salaries for teachers and stipends for students, who were subjected to military discipline; and establish boundaries between rival jurisdictions. Muhammad Ali set up some state primary and preparatory schools, but most students for the higher schools had to be drawn from army recruits or graduates of the *kuttab*s. Most of the state schools were closed after the London Convention (q.v.).

State-controlled education languished under Abbas (q.v.) and Sa'id (q.v.); even the medical school was closed briefly in 1856. The Diwan al-Madaris was closed, the school buildings were abandoned, and even the library books were stored in damp cellars, stolen, or given away. One exception was Sa'id's policy of letting missionaries found schools (*see* Frères and Jesuits). Isma'il (q.v.) found on his accession that his government had only one primary, one preparatory, one military, one naval, one medical, and one pharmaceutical school, all badly neglected. He began importing teachers from France, resumed sending student missions to Europe, strengthened the medical school, and encouraged Christian missions and other foreign educational organizations to establish schools in Egypt. Among the schools founded or revived under Isma'il were those of engineering (1866), veterinary medicine (1867), agriculture

(1868–75), and Dar al-Ulum (q.v.). The first state school for girls, later named Saniyya, was set up in 1873 under the patronage of Isma'il's wife. The Law of 10 Rajab 1284 (7 November 1867) mandated the foundation of one school for each province and for each of the major towns, specifying how they were to be financed, the qualifications and compensation for teachers, their syllabi, the school furniture, and the pupils' clothing. Many village *kuttab*s whose supporting *awqaf* (q.v.) had been depleted were placed under state control. The number of Western-style schools in Egypt reportedly rose by 1876 to 4,817, with 6,048 teachers and 140,977 pupils, although many of these schools were probably incompletely Westernized village *kuttab*s. Many of the teachers were Europeans, and French rivaled Arabic (and Turkish) as the language of instruction.

Egypt's financial crisis in 1876–82 necessitated many educational cutbacks, a policy that was continued into the British occupation (q.v.). Lord Cromer (q.v.) paid lip service to education, but in fact he limited access to state schools to the few Egyptians who could afford to pay tuition fees. English gradually supplanted both French and Arabic as the main language of instruction in the government schools. Foreign organizations (often Christian missions) set up many primary, preparatory, and secondary schools (*see* Victoria College), and some individual Egyptians founded schools that taught in Arabic and upheld Islamic or nationalist values (*see* Kamil, Mustafa). Some higher schools, notably law (*see* Law School) and medicine, flourished, but the British opposed creating a large class of educated Egyptians who were apt to oppose their rule and gave little encouragement to the establishment of the national university (*see* Cairo University). All the political parties formed in the early twentieth century called for expanded education, and the appointment in 1906 of Sa'd Zaghlul (q.v.) as education minister was widely construed as a British sop to Egyptian nationalism, although the British education adviser, Douglas Dunlop, retained control over the ministry's policies.

Following the declaration of Egypt's independence in 1922, the government began increasing the share of the budget allotted to education. The 1923 Constitution (q.v.) called for universal primary schooling, a goal not reached until later. Since the 1952 Revolution (q.v.), Egypt's leaders have all followed a concerted policy of expanding state-controlled schools both to educate and to indoctrinate the people, and nearly all Egyptian boys and a majority of girls attend elementary schools. All tuition fees for state-run schools and universities were abolished. Regrettably, academic standards have not kept pace with the growing numbers of pupils, and many school buildings and teachers are overutilized. Teachers are underpaid, and many parents pay for individual tutoring or private schools for their children. The educational system turns out far more Egyptians in liberal arts, law, and commerce than the economy can absorb. A growing proportion of secondary and higher school students enter technical and scientific curricula, but young doctors, engineers, and technicians often emigrate to the West or to other Arab countries in search of higher salaries and better working conditions. There is also a critical shortage of Egyptians trained to be plumbers, electricians, machinists, or aviation mechanics because many view these as low-status occupations. Egyptians acknowledge the need to revamp public education, but lack the means to implement the necessary reforms. In 1989 total state expenditure on education was £E4 billion, or 6.8 percent of the gross national product.

EFENDIYYA. General term used, mainly before the 1952 Revolution (q.v.), to distinguish educated or upper-class male Egyptians. Over time, the distinguishing factor has changed from landownership to education. Contemporary Egyptians often use the term *muthaqqafin* ("cultured people" or "educated people") to denote members of the elite.

EGYPTIAN CONGRESS (1911). Public assembly of Egyptian notables and intellectuals, mainly but not exclusively Muslim, held in Heliopolis (q.v.) in late April and early May 1911, as a riposte to the Coptic Congress (q.v.) held earlier in Asyut (q.v.). Participants included Nationalists (q.v.) and members of other political parties, but the dominant tone was moderate, addressing Coptic claims and Egypt's other economic and social problems. Mustafa Riyad (q.v.) chaired the Congress, whose proceedings were published in English, French, and Arabic.

EGYPTIAN EXPEDITIONARY FORCE (EEF). The British Empire force, based in Cairo, that invaded Palestine and Syria, taking them from the Ottoman Empire (q.v.) in 1917–18. Approximately 100,000 Egyptian workers and peasants volunteered or were conscripted to serve as Labor Corps and Camel Corps auxiliaries, but not as soldiers. Some of them rioted in January 1916. The EEF's heavy demand for Egyptian conscripts and farm animals angered many peasants, contributing to the 1919 Revolution (q.v.).

EGYPTIAN FEMINIST UNION (EFU). Women's rights movement founded by Huda al-Sha'rawi (q.v.) in 1923. It first signaled its existence by protesting, together with the men of the Wafd Party (q.v.), against the failure of both the 1923 Constitution (q.v.) and the electoral law to enfranchise women. In May 1923 it sent a three-woman delegation to the meeting of the International Alliance of Women in Rome. It was upon their return from this conference that Sha'rawi and one of her companions, Saiza al-Nabarawi (1897–1985), disembarked unveiled, a symbolic step toward women's liberation. The EFU, together with the Wafdist Women's Central Committee, picketed the opening session of Parliament in 1924 in protest against their exclusion from its inaugural ceremonies, then presented a list of 32 nationalist and feminist demands to members and to government officials. Nine of the EFU's ten charter members came from upper-class backgrounds, but they soon drew in women from other classes. Activities included opening a women's clubhouse, editing monthly journals in French and Arabic, running a clinic and dispensary for poor women and children, and setting up child-care facilities for working mothers. They lobbied for changes in the family laws, but their main success was in setting a minimum marriage age. They pressed for women's education (q.v.), and the government opened its first secondary school for girls in Shubra in 1924. Women were first admitted to Cairo University (q.v.) in 1928. The EFU investigated working conditions for women and pressed for women's suffrage in the 1930s. Responding to the growing conflict over Palestine, it convened an Arab women's conference in Cairo (q.v.) late in 1938. A second conference, held in 1944, founded an Arab Feminist Union and elected Sha'rawi as its first president. The EFU survived the death of its founder in 1947, but became overshadowed by other Egyptian feminist groups (*see* Feminism) that attracted younger, more politicized women. After the 1952 Revolution (q.v.), its activities were taken over by various government ministries. Renamed the "Huda al-Sha'rawi Society," the group faded away in the 1960s.

EGYPTIAN-ISRAELI AGREEMENT (1975). Diplomatic understanding, brokered by Kissinger and signed on 1 September 1975, in which Israel withdrew from the Gulf of Suez (q.v.) oil fields and from the strategic Gidi and Mitla Passes (qq.v.) in the Sinai Peninsula (q.v.), in exchange for Egypt's renunciation of war as a means to settle the Arab-Israeli conflict. U.S. civilian technicians joined the United Nations (q.v.) observer force at monitoring posts between Egypt and Israel. This was their last agreement before Sadat's (q.v.) trip to Jerusalem.

EGYPTIAN-ISRAELI PEACE TREATY (1979). Document signed in Washington, D.C., by Sadat (q.v.), Israeli Premier Menachem Begin, and U.S. President Jimmy Carter, ending the state of war between Egypt and Israel. It provided for the phased withdrawal of Israeli troops from the Sinai Peninsula (q.v.) and the reinstatement of the recognized international boundary between Egypt and the former mandated territory of Palestine as the Egyptian-Israeli border, without prejudice to the status of the Gaza Strip (q.v.). The countries agreed to refrain from the threat or use of force against each other and also to establish full diplomatic relations. Provisions were made for the stationing of United Nations (q.v.) forces and observers that could not be removed without the approval of the Security Council. Israeli ships and cargoes were allowed free right of passage through the Suez Canal (q.v.) and the Gulf of Aqaba (q.v.) and their approaches. Egypt and Israel agreed that the treaty would have precedence over such previous treaties as the Arab League (q.v.) Collective Security Pact and that they would not enter into any obligations that might conflict with this treaty. Vociferous opposition to the treaty was expressed by other Arab governments and by Egyptian Islamists (q.v.), Nasirites (q.v.), and Communists (q.v.). Many believe that Sadat was assassinated for having signed the treaty, but Egypt has continued to uphold it under Mubarak (q.v.), despite Israel's invasion of Lebanon and pressure from Palestinians and other Arab governments to denounce it.

EGYPTIAN MOVEMENT FOR NATIONAL LIBERATION (EMNL). Communist (q.v.) movement founded in 1943 by Henri Curiel, an anti-Zionist Jew from a wealthy Cairo (q.v.) family, originally an Italian citizen educated in French schools. Dedicated to creating a multiclass national front to achieve full national independence for Egypt, Curiel influenced many ethnic Egyptians. His movement merged with Iskra (q.v.) in 1947 to form the Democratic Movement for National Liberation, generally called Hadeto (q.v.).

EGYPTIAN MUSEUM. Cairo (q.v.) institution housing the world's largest collection of Egyptian antiquities. Up to the mid-nineteenth century, Egyptians were so uninterested in their country's pre-Islamic antiquities that European governments and travelers plundered them freely, thus creating the great Egyptological collections in London, Paris, Berlin, Leiden, and Turin. Champollion (q.v.) urged Muhammad Ali (q.v.) to curb the export of valuable antiquities, and in 1834 the first Egyptian museum was established in Ezbekiyya (q.v.) under Rifa'a al-Tahtawi (q.v.); that small collection was later moved to the education ministry's quarters in the Cairo Citadel (q.v.). Sa'id (q.v.) donated it to Archduke Maximilian of Austria in 1855, starting the collection now in Vienna. Auguste Mariette (q.v.) became the first director of antiquities in 1858 and opened a small museum in Bulaq (q.v.) in 1863 under the patronage of Khedive Isma'il (qq.v.). In 1878 it came under the care of the works ministry. The collection was moved to Giza Palace in 1891; the quarters, although larger, were not wholly suitable. In 1902 the present museum, designed by Marcel Dourgnon in a neoclassic style, was opened in Midan Ismailia (now Liberation Square [q.v.]). For many years the directors of antiquities and the curators of the Egyptian Museum were French, but Egyptians have taken control since the 1952 Revolution (q.v.). The present museum exhibits more than 100,000 works, ranging from prehistoric times to the beginning of the Greco-Roman period, displayed in chronological order. It is now so cramped that the culture ministry plans to build a new home for its burgeoning collection.

EGYPTIAN-SYRIAN JOINT DEFENSE AGREEMENT. Mutual defense pact, signed in Cairo on 4 November 1966, stating that any aggressive act against either state would be regarded as an attack on the other. Egypt and Syria agreed under its terms to set up a defense council and a joint military command. This pact was inspired in part by mounting border tensions between Syria and Israel, exacerbated by Israeli air and artillery attacks on a Syrian irrigation project, which if completed would have reduced the supply for Israel's national water carrier, and by Syrian shelling of Israeli settlements from the Golan Heights. A radical regime had recently come to power in Damascus and was urging the Palestinians to wage a war of national liberation against Israel, but mainly from bases on the Jordanian West Bank. The agreement may have caused Israel to retaliate for Palestinian raids later that month against al-Sammu' in Jordan rather than Syria. It also committed Nasir's (q.v.) government, which had hitherto tried to postpone war against Israel until the Arab armies were fully battleready, to come to Syria's aid in any future conflict with Israel. Far from restraining the Syrians, it let them draw Egypt further into the Arab-Israeli conflict, hence the June War (q.v.).

EISENHOWER DOCTRINE (1957). Official U.S. policy statement, issued by President Eisenhower and approved by Congress, opposing the spread of Communism in the Middle East. The Eisenhower Doctrine was interpreted by Egyptians as an attempt to limit Nasir's (q.v.) influence over other Arab countries. It was consequently condemned by Arab nationalists. Lebanon's government accepted U.S. aid under its provisions, however, leading to the 1958 civil war in that country and consequent American military intervention, to which Nasir responded by flying to Moscow to seek additional Soviet military aid.

EMERGENCY LAW (1958). Statute promulgated by the Nasir (q.v.) government, authorizing the judicial system to detain suspects without charging them or guaranteeing them due process during an investigation. After 30 days, a detainee may petition the State Security Court to review the case. If the court orders the detainee's release, the interior minister has 15 days to overrule the court, but the detainee may after 30 days petition again for release. Even if the detainee is released, however, the interior minister may rearrest the suspect. The government has often used this law against Islamists (q.v.), leftists suspected of political violence, drug smugglers, illegal currency dealers, and even striking workers, pro-

Palestinian student demonstrators, and relatives of fugitives. In mid-1989 the interior minister reported that 12,000 individuals had been detained under the Emergency Law during the preceding three years; as of 1990 the government admitted that it was holding 2,411 individuals, 813 of them on political charges. Although some civilian suspects could be tried by the military courts, in most cases detainees have been released after interrogation and without trial. The law remains in effect.

ENGINEERS. Whether viewed as a craft or a profession, engineering has long been a major occupation in Egypt, especially in matters related to irrigation (q.v.). Among Muhammad Ali's (q.v.) earliest reforms was the establishment of a polytechnic institute (*muhandiskhane*), primarily to train military engineers. It was reorganized in 1837 and provided many of the Egyptian experts who developed the perennial irrigation (q.v.) system under Isma'il (q.v.). The Polytechnic languished during the early British occupation (q.v.), but revived after another reorganization in 1903. It was integrated into Cairo University (q.v.) in 1935.

Egyptian engineers were unable to form a unified organization; one group established the Royal Society of Egyptian Engineers in 1920 to back the British irrigation projects, while another formed a professional syndicate to oppose them. King Fuad (q.v.) granted formal recognition to the former group in 1922, but it remained a staid debating society with high dues and membership requirements; the syndicate disappeared. Its revival as the Egyptian Syndicate of Engineering Professions in 1946 was due partly to the impact of wartime inflation on the salaries of younger engineers, partly to the need for an old-age pension plan for employees of the works ministry, but it never called a strike. The 1952 Revolution (q.v.), with its strong emphasis on state-directed modernization, gave engineers new opportunities for advancement, and Nasir's (q.v.) predilection for corporatism strengthened the engineers' syndicate. As engineers became more prestigious, though, they became more resistant to the egalitarian ideals of Arab socialism (q.v.). Political considerations often collided with engineering or economic realities, causing the overproduction of certain types of engineers and the promotion of some for reasons other than their skills. Setting up highly technical "prestige" industries such as steel manufacturing and automobile assembly plants increased Egyptian dependency on foreign engineers. The failure of academic engineers to keep abreast of scholarly literature in their fields suggested that Egypt was actually falling behind other modernizing countries. Nearly all Egyptian engineers work in organizations, such as government ministries, universities or technical institutes, or large corporations, such as the Arab Contractors (q.v.). Many now find higher-paying jobs in oil-exporting countries. In 1992 the Syndicate elected an Islamist (q.v.) slate of officers.

ENTENTE CORDIALE (1904). Anglo-French agreement, in which Britain promised France a free hand in Morocco, in return for which France agreed not to demand a fixed date for the evacuation of British troops from Egypt. The pact strengthened the British occupation (q.v.) and obliged its nationalist opponents to turn from France to the Ottoman Empire (q.v.) and public opinion within Egypt for support.

EVACUATION. The termination of the British occupation (q.v.) and, therefore, preponderant power over Egypt, a desideratum of Egyptian nationalism from 1882 to 1956.

EXCEPTIONAL LAWS (1910). Three laws passed, following the assassination of Prime Minister Butros Ghali (q.v.), by the Egyptian cabinet to curb agitation by the National Party (q.v.). They strengthened the limits on press freedom imposed by the 1881 Press Law (q.v.), restricted student demonstrations, and revised the Penal Code to include political conspiracy as a crime. The National Party agitated at home and abroad for their abrogation, to no avail.

EZBEKIYYA GARDENS. Public park in central Cairo (q.v.), designed in 1869 by French landscape gardener Barillet-Deschamps, often the site of political rallies.

- F -

FAHMI, ABD AL-AZIZ (1870–1951). Liberal politician, jurist, and intellectual. He was born in a Minufiyya village and came from a long line of *umda*s (q.v.). He studied at al-Azhar (q.v.), the Khedivial Secondary School, and the School of Administration (later the government Law School [q.v.]), earning his *license* in 1890. He worked for several years in the Niyaba (q.v.) before going into private practice. He headed the Egyptian Bar Association (q.v.) three times and was elected in 1913 to the Legislative Assembly (q.v.). A friend of Ahmad Lutfi al-Sayyid (q.v.), Fahmi helped found the Wafd (q.v.) but broke with Sa'd Zaghlul (q.v.) in Paris. He served on the committee that drafted the 1923 Constitution (q.v.). A founder of the Constitutional Liberal Party (q.v.), he became its president in 1924. He later became justice minister and president of the High Court of Appeals and the Court of Cassation. His memoirs were printed in *al-Hilal* (q.v.) and reissued as a book, *Hadhihi hayati* ("This Is My Life").

FAHMI, MUSTAFA (1840–1914). Politician, cabinet minister, and twice premier. He was born in Crete to a Turkish family that had earlier settled in Algeria. His father, a colonel, died in the Crimean War, and Mustafa Fahmi was adopted by an uncle who was in charge of the public works department. Fahmi was educated at the Military Academy (q.v.) and, upon being commissioned, rose through the Egyptian army to the rank of lieutenant general. He then was appointed governor of Minufiyya, followed by Cairo (q.v.), and finally Port Said (q.v.). He later became director of the khedivial estates and then master of ceremonies. He served as minister of public works in 1879, foreign affairs from 1879 to 1882, justice in 1882, finance from 1884 to 1887, interior three times (1887–88, 1891–93, and 1895–1908), and war and marine twice (1887–91 and 1894–95). He was prime minister from 1891 to 1893 and again from 1895 to 1908. His illness early in 1893 led to a crisis between Lord Cromer (q.v.) and Khedive Abbas (qq.v.), who tried to replace his cabinet with one headed by Husayn Fakhri (q.v.) without consulting the British consul. Fahmi was allowed to leave the government awhile to recover his health, but returned under Nubar (q.v.) and shortly afterward assumed the chair of what would be Egypt's longest-lasting cabinet, one in which the power of the British advisers far outweighed that of the ministers. He was pro-British for most of his active career, deferring repeatedly to Lord Cromer, but after he left office he fell under the influence of Sa'd Zaghlul (q.v.), who was married to one of his daughters. It was rumored that he might head a cabinet in 1914 after the resignation of Muhammad Sa'id (q.v.), but he was in poor health and died shortly afterward. Egyptians generally regarded him as too complaisant toward the British.

FAKHRI, HUSAYN (1843–1920). Politician, cabinet minister, and controversial premier appointed by Khedive Abbas Hilmi II (qq.v.) against the wishes of Lord Cromer (q.v.) in January 1893. Born in Cairo (q.v.) to a family of Circassian (q.v.) background, he was educated in the princely schools. In 1863 he was appointed as a *mu'awin* ("assistant") in the governorate and then transferred to foreign affairs. Sent to Paris by the Egyptian government for the 1867 exposition, he stayed there to study administrative law, returning to Egypt in 1874. He worked in the justice ministry and in the Niyaba (q.v.) of the Mixed Courts (q.v.). Fakhri became justice minister in 1879–81 under Mustafa Riyad (q.v.), in 1882–84 under Muhammad Sharif (q.v.), and in 1888–91 under Riyad again; interior minister under Mustafa Fahmi (q.v.); and after serving for three days as the khedive's prime minister, he would serve as minister of works and education under Nubar (q.v.) and Fahmi. A lover of science, he belonged to the Institut d'Égypte (q.v.), the Geographical Society (q.v.), and the Committee for the Preservation of Arab Monuments. His son, Mahmud, married Princess Fawqiyya, one of King Faruq's (q.v.) sisters. Because of the public controversy over his khedivial appointment against Cromer's wishes, Fakhri earned an undeserved reputation as a nationalist.

FALUJA. Palestinian village, the site of a lengthy siege during the 1948 Palestine war (q.v.), regarded by Egyptians as their most heroic stand against the Israeli army.

FAMILY PLANNING. Egypt's population (q.v.) has since the 1930s, if not earlier, exceeded the optimum size for its habitable area and arable land. Since the 1952 Revolution (q.v.) the Egyptian government has pursued policies intended to reduce the rate of population increase. In the mid-1950s it raised the minimum marriage age to 16 for women and 18 for men. Various efforts have been made by private organizations, the government, and UN agencies to reduce the birth rate in order to stem population growth. One private group is the Cairo Family Planning Association, founded by Aziza Husayn, who also served as president of the International Planned Parenthood Association and from 1962 to 1977 as Egypt's delegate to the UN Committee on the Status of Women. The Egyptian government formed in 1965 an interministerial body called the Supreme Council for Family Planning, but it could not fulfill its mission because it included the premier and the ministers of public health, higher education, national guidance (information), planning, religious affairs, and social affairs, as well as the ministers of state for prime minister's affairs and local administration. This body of overworked ministers could rarely meet as a group. Control over family planning was disputed between the health and social affairs ministries, and there were administrative abuses in programs for inserting intrauterine devices and dispensing birth control pills. Government spending on family planning rose from £E1.8 million in 1980 to 2.7 million in 1985. In 1988 it was reported that 30 percent of all married women of reproductive age used some form of birth control; but only one-third of that group relied on government programs. The net overall fertility rate fell from 6.5 per woman in 1965 to 4.5 in 1988, but a major cause for Egypt's burgeoning population has been the concurrent decline in infant and child mortality. As of 1991, contraceptive devices available in Egypt included condoms, diaphragms, birth control pills, intrauterine devices, injectable implants, and male and female sterilization. Abortions are legal and performed free of charge by government physicians, provided that the woman's husband approves. Egypt's inability to curb its birth rate is often blamed on Islamist (q.v.) opposition to contraception, but a more likely cause is the belief of married couples that having many children assures them of support in their old age.

FARID, MUHAMMAD (1868–1919). Nationalist leader, writer, and lawyer. The successor to Mustafa Kamil (q.v.) as the leader of Egypt's struggle for independence from Britain, Muhammad Farid came from a wealthy landowning family of Turkish origin. Trained at the School of Administration, he worked as a lawyer for the Egyptian government and the Niyaba (q.v.). Following his dismissal due to the Telegrams Incident (q.v.), he opened his own law office, one of the first Egyptians to do so. Farid was close to Mustafa Kamil, became one of his strongest political and financial supporters, and after Mustafa's premature death in 1908 was elected president of the National Party (q.v.). Farid led the party in Egypt and from March 1912 in exile until his death in November 1919 after a long illness. He adhered to the principle that the British must withdraw their forces from Egypt and that only the khedive (q.v.) could grant constitutional government to his subjects. Farid called for the spread of education and economic and social reforms. He occasionally sought the help of Egypt's suzerain, the Ottoman Empire (q.v.), especially while in exile during World War I (q.v.), but he often suspected the Turks of not backing Egyptian national aims. He sometimes espoused pan-Islam (q.v.), thus alienating the Copts (q.v.). Although the National Party became divided during Farid's presidency, Egyptians respect him for his patriotic courage and self-sacrifice. His memoirs were published as *Mudhakkirat Muhammad Farid: al-qism al-awwal, tarikh Misr min ibtida sanat 1891* (1975) and *Awraq Muhammad Farid: Mudhakkirati ba'd al-hijra (1904–1919)* (1978). The latter has been translated as *The Memoirs and Diaries of Muhammad Farid, an Egyptian Nationalist Leader (1868–1919).*

FARUQ (1920–65). King of Egypt from 1936 (under a regency up to his 18th birthday) until his abdication on 26 July 1952. Initially charismatic and highly popular, he was the first member of his family who could make a formal speech in Arabic. He occasionally led Friday congregational worship at mosques, normally a prerogative of the caliph (q.v.). Some Egyptians, notably Mustafa al-Maraghi (q.v.), hoped to revive the caliphate, which had been abolished by Mustafa Kemal (Atatürk) in 1924, so that Faruq could be elected to the position. His marriage in 1938 to Safinaz Zulfiqar, whom he renamed Farida, was welcomed by the people. He competed with the Wafd (q.v.), which controlled the government from 1936 to December 1937, when Faruq dismissed it for sponsoring a popular demonstration near Abdin Palace (q.v.) and appointed a cabinet made up of politicians from other parties. A rigged election, boycotted by the Wafd, gave these parties control of Parliament in April 1938.

When the British declared war on Germany in 1939, they asked Egypt to follow their example and sent additional troops to defend the Suez Canal (q.v.). The king and his ministers opposed going to war against Germany, which many Egyptians viewed as a potential liberator of their country from Britain. While the war was going badly for the Allies in 1940–42, Britain's ambassador to Egypt, Sir Miles Lampson (q.v.), considered deposing Faruq and began calling for the appointment of a cabinet, headed by Mustafa al-Nahhas (q.v.), that would uphold the 1936 Anglo-Egyptian Treaty (q.v.). Faruq hoped to unite Egypt's leading politicians in opposition to British interference, with Ali Mahir (q.v.) as his prime minister. Needing to secure British control of the Suez Canal, Lampson demanded that Faruq either appoint Nahhas to head a Wafdist cabinet or abdicate (*see* 4 February 1942 Incident). Faruq gave in and then withdrew from politics, devoting himself to gambling and sex. He had a car accident in 1943 and, during his prolonged convalescence in a British army hospital, medical maltreatment is thought by many Egyptians to have affected his glands, causing him to behave in eccentric ways.

After he dismissed the Wafdist ministry in October 1944, he reentered the political fray with a succession of Palace-dominated governments. Discontent spread after World War II (q.v.), as popular pressure mounted to renounce the 1936 Anglo-Egyptian Treaty, force the British troops to evacuate Egypt, and annex the Anglo-Egyptian Sudan (q.v.). Although supporting these aims, Faruq could only distract himself and the public with an enhanced enthusiasm for Arab unity. After the United Nations (q.v.) General Assembly accepted the 1947 Partition Plan for Palestine (q.v.), all the Arab governments vied to show support for the Arabs and defiance of the UN decision. Even though Faruq's ministers and his generals privately advised him that the Egyptian army was not ready for a war, he heeded the blandishments of journalist Karim Thabit (q.v.) and committed Egypt to enter the Palestine War (q.v.). Ill equipped and badly led, the Egyptians were soon thrown back. In February 1949 Egypt accepted an armistice with Israel, the first Arab state to do so. At the height of the war, Faruq announced his divorce from Queen Farida, who was beloved by the people, and he was publicly hissed for the first time at a Cairo (q.v.) cinema.

Late in 1949 Faruq finally agreed to permit free Parliamentary elections, and the Wafd returned to power. As Nahhas and his cabinet proceeded to institute some reforms, Faruq came to be seen as marginal, although the Wafd changed his title to "king of Egypt and the Sudan" when it abrogated the 1936 Treaty. His second marriage in 1951, to 16-year-old Narriman Sadiq, followed by a three-month honeymoon cruise, appalled Egyptians. On Black Saturday (q.v.), while downtown Cairo burned, Faruq was hosting a luncheon to celebrate the birth of his first son.

He dismissed the Wafdist cabinet and appointed a succession of governments, but could not restore political control. His attempt to rig the elections for the presidency of the Officers Club alienated the Egyptian army, traditionally royalist, and his appointment of his brother-in-law, Isma'il Shirrin, as war minister proved to be the last straw. On 22–23 July 1952 the Free Officers (q.v.) seized control and announced that Faruq was deposed. Unable to win support from either the British or the U.S. ambassador, he abdicated in favor of his infant son and left Egypt. He spent the rest of his life in Europe. His death in a Rome nightclub in March 1965 may have been arranged by Nasir's (q.v.) secret service.

Although intelligent and charming, Faruq lacked education and mental discipline. He could not discriminate among his would-be advisers and hence failed to lead his people to their goals of independence from Britain, constitutional government, economic development, and primacy within the Arab world. When he returned from England to succeed his father as king, he had no enemies; when he left Egypt, a failure, he had no friends.

FASHODA INCIDENT (1898). Confrontation between the 25,000-man Anglo-Egyptian army commanded by General Kitchener (q.v.), which had just reconquered the northern Sudan (q.v.) and a French expeditionary force headed by General Marchand, which had crossed Africa from west to east to take control of the upper Nile (q.v.). Although Marchand had preceded Kitchener by several months, he lacked the forces on the scene and the support back home that were available to the British. Despite a brief war scare in London and Paris, Marchand agreed to withdraw. France's concession to Britain in the Sudan started the reconciliation between the two countries that led to the Entente Cordiale (q.v.).

FATHI, HASAN (1900–89). Architect who championed traditional peasant designs. Born in Alexandria to a rich landowning family, he studied architecture at Cairo University, receiving his *license* in 1926. Although trained in the Paris beaux arts tradition, upon visiting his family's Upper Egyptian estates for the first time in 1927, he was struck by the simplicity and rightness of the local building traditions and dedicated himself to making their principles more systematic and more suitable to the housing needs of other poor people. Meanwhile, he worked in the architectural section of Cairo's (q.v.) municipal affairs department, but later went into private practice. In 1940 he got his first chance to test his ideas when the Royal Agriculture Society asked him to design an experimental farm at Bahtim. He investigated and revived Nubian techniques of building arches and domes with mud brick and also used these techniques in the construction of some private homes. Fathi's main achievement was the design and construction, begun in 1945 and only partly implemented, of the village of New Qurna ("Gourna," in Qina province, is opposite Luxor), about which he wrote a book in 1969 called *Gourna, a Tale of Two Villages*, which was republished in 1973 as *Architecture for the Poor*. He argued that the collective wisdom of a community about its use of space should guide architectural design and town planning. He also served as director of school buildings for the education ministry from 1949 to 1952, head of the architecture department of the Fine Arts faculty at Cairo University (q.v.) from 1953 to 1957, and a member of the UN Committee for Housing in South Arabia. An outstanding teacher, Fathi drew young architects and students from many parts of the world to Egypt to learn his techniques.

FAWZI, MAHMUD (1900–80). Diplomat, politician, and cabinet minister. Fawzi graduated from Cairo University's Law Faculty and did graduate studies in political science and history at the Universities of Liverpool, Columbia, and Rome, which awarded him a Ph.D. Joining the Egyptian Foreign Service, he held posts in the United States and Japan and was Egypt's consul general in Jerusalem from 1941 to 1944. He served as Egypt's chief representative to the United Nations (q.v.) from 1945 to 1952 and as foreign minister from December 1952 until 1964, deputy premier from 1964 to 1967, and Nasir's (q.v.) special adviser on foreign affairs in 1967–70. From 1968 Fawzi sat on the executive board of the Arab Socialist Union (q.v.) and reorganized it, at Nasir's behest, even though he had never been active in internal politics. He served as Sadat's (q.v.) prime minister from October 1970 to January 1972, then became once again vice president and special adviser to the president on foreign affairs until he retired in September 1974. Although Fawzi served Nasir and Sadat as a respectable spokesman to the outside world, he remained a diplomat-technician without any political influence at home. His *Suez 1956: An Egyptian Perspective* was published in London after his death.

FAWZI, MUHAMMAD (1915-). Egyptian officer and politician. He commanded Egypt's forces in the Yemen Civil War (q.v.) and succeeded Abd al-Hakim Amir (q.v.) as commander-in-chief of the armed forces after the June War (q.v.). He served as Nasir's (q.v.) defense minister from 1968 to 1971. A leftist and close political ally of Ali Sabri (q.v.), he belonged to the faction that was purged in the Corrective Revolution (q.v.), in part because he was not trusted by his chief-of-staff, let alone Sadat (q.v.). Given a 15-year sentence, he was pardoned by Sadat in 1974 because of his military record. His *Harb al-thalath sanawat, 1967–1970* ("The Three-Year War") was printed in Beirut in 1983.

FEDDAN. Egyptian land measure unit equal to 1.038 acres or 4,201 m^2.

FEDERATION OF ARAB REPUBLICS (1971). Abortive combination of Egypt, Libya (q.v.), and Syria, accepted in May 1971 by Sadat (q.v.), Mu'ammar al-Qadhafi, and Hafiz al-Asad. Sadat made his commitment to this federation a precipitating factor in his Corrective Revolution (q.v.), claiming that his enemies, the Centers of Power (q.v.), opposed it. The federation project was approved by an Egyptian, Libyan, and Syrian citizens' referendum held in September 1971, and Sadat was proposed as the first president, but it later foundered on his political differences with Qadhafi. An organic union between Egypt and Libya, scheduled to take effect on 1 September 1973, was indefinitely postponed.

FEDERATION OF EGYPTIAN INDUSTRIES. Coalition of Egyptian industrialists, formed in 1922, to represent the interests of Egyptianized capitalism, organized in more than 20 specialized branches. It led the fight to abolish excise taxes on local manufactures and to obtain protective tariffs (q.v.) on imports. It nullified union and welfare legislation that would have reduced the competitive advantage of Egypt's cheap labor force. It resisted the "nationalist" challenge of Bank Misr (q.v.), finally replacing Tal'at Harb (q.v.) in 1939 with its own board of directors. It deflected efforts to broaden the state's participation in industrialization until World War II (q.v.). Its president, Henri Naus, was a Belgian; its general secretary, Isaac Levy, was a Jew from Istanbul; and its link to native capitalists and the state was Isma'il Sidqi (q.v.), who strengthened the Federation at the expense of labor unions, political parties, and other associational groupings. After the war, the Federation reorganized itself as a semipublic body, hoping to attract investment subsidies and state support for its campaign to Egyptianize corporate management. Under Nasir (q.v.) the Federation was turned into an agency of the ministry of industry, but it emerged under Sadat (q.v.) as a spokesman for native manufacturers, including public sector managers seeking greater operational independence. Under Mubarak (q.v.) it remains, along with the chambers of commerce, a powerful voice for Egyptian industrial capitalism, although challenged now by recently founded groups of younger business leaders.

FELLAH. Peasant cultivator.

FEMINISM. The movement to attain for women (q.v.) rights equal to those enjoyed by men. The earliest voices of feminism were those of upper-class Egyptian Muslim women confined to their harems, but the best-known early advocate of women's rights was Qasim Amin (q.v.), a man who condemned female segregation and seclusion and unfair Muslim divorce laws in his two books on women's liberation, published in 1899 and 1901. In addition, women journalists, most of them Syrian Christians or Copts (q.v.), began publishing magazines for Egyptian women readers prior to World War I (q.v.). A significant opponent of polygyny was Malak Hifni Nasif (q.v.), who delivered a ten-point program for women's rights at the 1911 Egyptian Congress (q.v.) and was instrumental in the founding of the Union of Educated Egyptian Women (L'Association Intellectuelle des Dames Égyptiennes) in March 1914. Both Qasim Amin and Nasif received editorial support from Ahmad Lutfi al-Sayyid (q.v.) in the pages of *al-Jarida* (q.v.). After the war Egyptian women staged demonstrations during the 1919 Revolution (q.v.), but their demands were nationalist rather than feminist. One thousand women met at St. Mark's Cathedral in Cairo (q.v.) in 1920, to form the Wafdist Women's Central Committee. Its leader, Huda Sha'rawi (q.v.), later founded the Egyptian Feminist Union (EFU) (q.v.), which demonstrated at the opening of the Egyptian Parliament in 1924. Some members demanded the right to vote, but the EFU stressed education, welfare, and legal reforms over political issues.

A bolder program was sought by some women, among them Durriyya Shafiq [Raja'i], the first Egyptian woman to earn the *doctorat d'état* in philosophy from the University of Paris. She launched an Arabic-language magazine, *Bint al-Nil*, to champion equal rights for women. In 1948 she founded a society by that name, attracting a younger, more activist clientele than the established EFU. The two groups came together briefly in 1949 to represent Egypt within the International Council of Women, but their leaders differed on the basic issues. In 1951 Shafiq organized a mass rally that culminated in an invasion of Parliament by the 1,500 woman participants, after which she tried to transform *Bint al-Nil* into a political party. She supported the 1952 Revolution (q.v.) even when it abolished her party, but expected it to provide equal rights for women. To publicize her demands, she began a hunger strike in March 1954; it ended when President Najib (q.v.) promised to consider them. While on a lecture tour later that year, she complained that Egypt's proposed constitution, while enfranchising women, would have required them (unlike men) to pass a literacy test. Egypt's 1956 Constitution (q.v.) did give women the vote without imposing a literacy requirement. She later denounced Nasir's (q.v.) dictatorship, and when she announced another hunger strike at the Indian Embassy in February 1957, Nasir put her under house arrest, her former comrades at *Bint al-Nil* made her resign, and the other feminists condemned her as counterrevolutionary.

Another woman activist was Inji Aflatun, who became a Marxist while studying at the Lycée Français. Communist groups, especially the

House of Scientific Research under Iskra (q.v.), attracted Egyptian women members, who in 1944–45 founded the League of Women Students and Graduates from the University and Egyptian Institutes, a radical feminist group that sent representatives to the 1945 World Congress of Women in Paris but was closed down by Sidqi (q.v.) in 1946. Aflatun, who attended that congress, later formed the Egyptian Peace Movement in 1950 and the Women's Committee for Popular Resistance to back the *fidaiyin* (q.v.) against the British in the Suez Canal (q.v.) Zone. These groups were quashed by the Nasir regime, which subsumed all political activities under the state. The Arab Socialist Union (q.v.) made special provision for the election or appointment of women to positions in its organization and its committees, which included one especially for women's affairs.

Egypt's feminist movement regained some of its autonomy under Anwar al-Sadat (q.v.) due to the visibility of his wife, Jihan al-Sadat (q.v.), who pressed for legislation improving women's rights within marriage. On the other hand, the influx of foreign corporations and consumer goods that resulted from the *infitah* (q.v.) policy, tended to widen the gap between a rich minority and the middle- and lower-class majority, which sometimes reacted against the signs of upper-class Westernization by adopting ideas of Islamism (q.v.) opposed to women's rights. Employment of women in farming and manufacturing declined, but women entrepreneurs and managers increased their numbers markedly. Egyptian labor emigration, being mainly male, also opened new opportunities for women's advancement in Egypt. Nawal al-Sa'dawi (q.v.), a feminist physician, formed the Arab Women's Solidarity Conference in 1982, but its activities were hindered by the Egyptian government and it was dissolved in June 1991 by Cairo's deputy governor. In recent years, women have been admitted to all universities and technical institutes and have held positions as cabinet ministers, ambassadors, business executives, and members of the People's Assembly, yet they remain disadvantaged in issues of property inheritance, divorce, child custody, and the right to travel abroad. The male-dominated *jama'at* (q.v.) oppose feminism as an undesirable Western influence, and the recrudescence of Muslim female veiling has been accompanied by Islamist expressions of the opinion that women belong at home.

FEZ PEACE PROPOSAL (1982). Eight-point plan for Middle East peace proposed at a summit meeting of Arab leaders in Fez in September 1982. It called on Israel to withdraw from and dismantle its settlements in all lands captured in 1967 and guaranteed religious freedom in the holy shrines of Jerusalem. While reaffirming the Palestinians' right to a state led by the Palestine Liberation Organization (q.v.), with Jerusalem as its capital, it proposed to place the West Bank and Gaza Strip (q.v.) under

United Nations (q.v.) control for a brief transitional period. The Security Council would guarantee peace among all the region's countries, including the proposed Palestinian state. This plan, which resembled one offered in 1981 by Saudi Crown Prince Fahd, was in response to Reagan's Peace Plan of 1 September 1982 and Israel's invasion of Lebanon. Mubarak (q.v.) did not attend the Fez Summit. Israel rejected the proposal, which was ignored by the United States.

FIDAIYIN. Muslims who sacrifice themselves for a cause. The term was applied to Egyptians who attacked the British in the Suez Canal (q.v.) in 1951–52 and later to Palestinians fighting against Israel or its backers and to militant Shi'is.

FIRMAN. Turkish term meaning "decree," often applied in Egypt to the rescripts by the Ottoman Empire (q.v.) that defined the exercise of autonomy by Egypt's viceroys. These included the *firman*s of 1841 confirming Muhammad Ali's (q.v.) nonhereditary control over what is now known as the Sudan (q.v.) and his hereditary governorship of Egypt "within its ancient boundaries." These lands included the parts of the Sinai Peninsula (q.v.) and the Hijaz (q.v.) used by Muslim pilgrims from Egypt and North Africa to Mecca. The *firman*s sent to Khedive Tawfiq (qq.v.) in 1879 and Abbas Hilmi II (q.v.) in 1892 required some clarification over the exact boundaries of Egypt, which remained a province of the Ottoman Empire until 1914. The Ottoman sultan also modified the conditions of the 1841 *firman* to enable his viceroys to change the hereditary system to one of primogeniture, to adopt the title of khedive (q.v.), to contract foreign loans without prior permission, to conclude treaties with other countries, and to enlarge the Egyptian army. Egypt's juridical status thus evolved during the nineteenth century from that of an ordinary Ottoman provincc to virtual autonomy.

FIVE FEDDAN LAW (1912). Government statute, inspired by Lord Kitchener (q.v.), that exempted the last five feddans (q.v.) of land owned by an Egyptian peasant from being taken in case he or she defaulted on repayment of a loan. The law, which has remained in force with minor amendments in 1916 and in 1953–54, protects the peasant against seizure of land, dwelling houses, draft animals, and tools needed for cultivation. It did not help the peasants as much as its framers had hoped, as moneylenders simply refused to lend to peasants who held too little land to provide a guarantee of repayment. It weakened the Agricultural Bank of Egypt, founded in 1902 with Cromer's (q.v.) encouragement. It had no significant effect on land distribution. (*See* Landownership.)

FOOD RIOTS (1977). Mass demonstrations in Cairo (q.v.) and other Egyptian cities, the largest since the 1919 Revolution, in January 1977. The protestors, initially workers, students, and housewives, later joined by slum dwellers, were demonstrating against the Egyptian government decision, imposed by the International Monetary Fund (q.v.) as a condition for further loans to Egypt, to reduce subsidies and hence raise the retail price of basic foodstuffs. Especially sensitive was the price of *baladi* bread, which had long been fixed at one piastre per loaf. Leftist elements tried to direct the disturbances into protests against capitalism, and there were popular chants hailing Nasir (q.v.) and condemning both Anwar and Jihan al-Sadat (qq.v.). Some Islamic elements burned down nightclubs and attacked luxury stores to protest against Western cultural penetration and immorality. For the first time since 1954, the army was called out to help the police quell the riots; 79 protestors were killed, 800–1,000 wounded, and 1,500 jailed. Sadat's prestige, high since the October War (q.v.), was shaken. The government restored the subsidies, the regime became more hostile to Nasirites (q.v.) and Marxists (q.v.), and Sadat moved toward seeking peace with Israel in order to relieve Egypt's economy.

4 FEBRUARY INCIDENT (1942). As German forces advanced in the Western Desert, threatening Britain's control over Egypt, Ambassador Sir Miles Lampson (q.v.) delivered an ultimatum to King Faruq (q.v.), obliging him to appoint Mustafa al-Nahhas (q.v.) at the head of an all-Wafdist (q.v.) cabinet or to abdicate his throne, at a time when Abdin Palace (q.v.) was surrounded by British tanks. The incident showed clearly that Britain could still dominate the Egyptian government. It also weakened the Wafd's popularity and the political poise of Faruq, who became increasingly embittered against the British.

FOUR RESERVED POINTS. Britain's limitations to its unilateral declaration of Egypt's independence, issued by Allenby (q.v.) on 28 February 1922. They were (1) the security of British Imperial communications in Egypt, (2) the defense of Egypt against foreign aggression or interference, (3) the protection of foreign interests and minorities in Egypt, and (4) the [status of the] Sudan (q.v.). These points became a sensitive issue in later Anglo-Egyptian negotiations.

FREE OFFICERS. Secret Egyptian army organization, led by Colonel Jamal Abd al-Nasir (q.v.), that conspired successfully to overthrow Faruq (q.v.) in July 1952. Perhaps because it was a secret cabal that would later seize control of Egypt, conflicting stories are told about its founders and the date of its origin, but it is reasonably certain that a group of officers including Nasir was meeting regularly by 1945–46 and that it grew larger and more ambitious during and after the Palestine War (q.v.). Its founding members probably included Nasir, Hasan Ibrahim, Khalid Muhyi al-Din (q.v.), Kamal al-Din Husayn, and Abd al-Mun'im Abd al-Rauf. They were joined later by Abd al-Latif Baghdadi (q.v.), Anwar al-Sadat (q.v.), Abd al-Hakim Amir (q.v.), the brothers Jamal and Salah Salim, Husayn al-Shafi'i (q.v.), and Zakariyya Muhyi al-Din (q.v.). Their internal structure was pyramidal, with each officer responsible for developing cells within his own military unit. In addition, many served as liaisons with other political groups. Khalid had ties with Hadeto (q.v.), Kamal al-Din Husayn and Abd al-Rauf with the Muslim Brothers (q.v.), Sadat with the Palace, and Nasir with several groups. In 1949 they formulated a five-part plan to build an organization, issue propaganda, gather intelligence about the regime, contact other subversive groups, and seize power by 1954. Black Saturday (q.v.) made the Free Officers advance their timetable for seizing power to August 1952; Faruq's frenzied efforts to preserve his throne and his opposition to the election of General Najib (q.v.) as the Officers Club leader further speeded up their plans. The exact timing of their coup d'état was set when they learned of Faruq's intention to name General Husayn Sirri Amir (whom they had just tried in vain to assassinate) as his new war minister, for they expected Amir to arrest several of the conspirators. The coup was executed during the night of 22–23 July with the seizure of the army headquarters in Cairo. The Free Officers group, once it controlled the Egyptian government, reorganized itself as the Revolutionary Command Council (q.v.). It remains almost unique in Egypt's history as a cabal that succeeded.

FREEMASONRY. Masonic lodges have existed in Egypt since the French occupation (q.v.). Italian immigrants to Alexandria (q.v.) established a branch there in 1830, and a larger group of French Freemasons publicly founded a lodge in 1845. French, Italian, German, and British Freemasons set up chapters in Cairo (q.v.) and other Egyptian cities later in the nineteenth century. Between 1872 and 1878 most of these chapters were amalgamated into one Grand Orient, centered in Cairo, with Prince Abd al-Halim (q.v.) as their grand master. They played a significant role in the movement of Ya'qub Sannu' (q.v.) and Jamal al-Din al-Afghani (q.v.) in 1878–79 and in the later National Party (q.v.), especially under Muhammad Farid (q.v.), who became grand master of the Egyptian Grand Orient in 1910. The British Freemasons maintained their own lodge, apart from those attached to the National Party.

FRENCH LAW SCHOOL. The École Libre de Droit was opened in Cairo by the Frères (q.v.) in 1890. The French government soon took control of the school and put it under the direction of Gerard Pélissié de

Rausas, who served from 1892 to 1932. Most of its faculty were French, and graduates of the three-year program were awarded the *license en droit* from the authorities of metropolitan France. They could easily enter the Mixed Courts (q.v.), but had to study for an additional year to practice before the National Courts (q.v.). Almost half of its students were not Egyptians, but among those who later played a part in Egypt's national life were Mustafa Kamil (q.v.) and Sa'd Zaghlul (q.v.). In the 1920s it was graduating an average of 37 lawyers a year. It survived, despite the abolition of the Mixed Courts, until the 1956 Suez War (q.v.).

FRENCH OCCUPATION. Since the seventeenth century French rulers had wanted to occupy Egypt for strategic or commercial motives, but their country's long alliance with the Ottoman Empire (q.v.) against the Habsburgs barred their doing so. After the 1789 Revolution, France's interest in Egypt revived, mainly in order to weaken Britain by capturing the overland route to India, much of which it had gained at France's expense in the Seven Years' War (1756–63). Napoléon Bonaparte (q.v.), an ambitious general who had completed a successful campaign against Italy, threatened the ruling Directory, which hoped to channel his ambitions into the war against Britain. Estimating that France's military manpower and equipment would not adequately support an invasion across the English Channel, Napoléon organized an armada to conquer Egypt instead: a convoy of 400 ships, 34,000 soldiers and some 16,000 sailors and marines, at least 500 civilians in support roles, and (most remarkable to historians) the 167-man Commission on the Sciences and Arts. This armada managed to cross the Mediterranean in the early summer of 1798, capture Malta, evade Admiral Nelson's (q.v.) British fleet, and land in Alexandria (q.v.), which the French captured after light resistance by Mamluks (q.v.) and bedouin (q.v.) auxiliaries on 1 July 1798. Within three weeks the French crossed the Delta and defeated the Mamluks in the Battle of Imbaba (q.v.), taking Cairo (q.v.).

Napoléon proceeded to set up his headquarters in the palace of Alfi Bey (q.v.), later to become the site of Shepheard's Hotel (q.v.), and established a new government in Cairo, even as some of his forces were trying to take control of Upper Egypt. Claiming to be a Muslim, he called on the ulama (q.v.) and merchants of Cairo to support his occupation, which he claimed was intended to restore the legitimate rule of the Ottoman sultan at the expense of the rapacious Mamluks. The Muslim leaders were suspicious, having seen the French troops drinking alcohol, chasing women, and relying on Copts (q.v.) and Armenians (q.v.) as interpreters and financial administrators. Muslims did not willingly wear the revolutionary tricolor and participated reluctantly in Napoléon's new representative council. A general revolt in October 1798 was suppressed by French bombardment of al-Azhar (q.v.) from the Citadel (q.v.) and by large-scale killing, looting, and profanation of mosques. Fearing an Ottoman punitive expedition, the Egyptians dared not seem to back the French occupiers, and the failure of Napoléon's expeditionary force to capture the Ottoman fortress at Acre in April 1799 showed them that France was not invincible. Heavy exactions of taxes to support the French army of occupation guaranteed its unpopularity, although the Egyptians lacked the means to resist. The Anglo-Ottoman counterinvasion at Abu-Kir (q.v.) failed, but the French occupying forces were declining because of battle deaths, disease, and desertion, with little hope of reinforcements.

Napoléon, anxious about the rising anti-French coalition in Europe and the weakness of the Directory (according to his admirers) or ambitious for glory on a stage wider than Egypt (according to his detractors), secretly sailed back home. He left his army under the command of General Kléber (q.v.), who mainly hoped to get his men safely back to France. His attempt to do so by diplomatic means, the Convention of al-Arish (q.v.), was not ratified by the British government. He successfully defended Cairo against a superior Ottoman invading force in the Battle of Heliopolis (q.v.), only to be assassinated. He was succeeded by General Menou (q.v.). By then the French forces were so decimated and demoralized that no leader could have withstood the British and Ottoman forces that landed near Abu-Kir and besieged them at Alexandria. They finally accepted a face-saving armistice, at about the time that Napoléon, who had seized power in Paris, was ready to return Egypt to the Ottoman government. The British and French drew up a tentative treaty in London in 1801 (the definitive peace was signed at Amiens in 1802), evacuating the remaining French troops from Egypt in British warships. The British restored Ottoman and Mamluk control, leaving Egypt in 1802.

Napoléon's 1798 invasion was Egypt's first experience of conflict with a Christian power since the Crusades. The ensuing occupation was Egypt's first experience of Christian rule since the Arabs expelled the Byzantines in 640. Surrounded by romantic myths because of Napoléon's remarkable personality and ideas, his rule is often cited as starting Egypt's Westernization, although more credit is due to Ali Bey (q.v.) and to the later rule of Muhammad Ali (q.v.). France's most lasting achievements were those of its Scientific Commission, summed up in the *Description de l'Égypte* (q.v.), but some historians argue that the occupation, by weakening the Mamluks, facilitated the rise of Muhammad Ali.

FRÈRES, COLLÈGE DES. Roman Catholic missionary school in Cairo (q.v.), founded in 1854 and run by the Confraternity of the Christian Doctrine, attended by many wealthy Egyptians, including Muslims, such as Isma'il Sidqi (q.v.). The Frères also established a free school in Cairo in 1847, a school in Alexandria (q.v.), and the French Law School (q.v.).

FRONTIERS INCIDENT (1894). Confrontation between Abbas Hilmi II (q.v.) and the British commander of the Egyptian army, Colonel Herbert Kitchener (q.v.), while the young khedive (q.v.) was on an inspection tour in Upper Egypt, near the frontier of the Sudan (q.v.), then still ruled by the Mahdi's (q.v.) successors. Abbas made slighting remarks about the performance of his army's British-officered regiments, causing Kitchener to offer his resignation. Cromer (q.v.) pressured the khedive to make a public statement expressing complete satisfaction with his troops, and Kitchener withdrew his resignation. The incident widened the breach between Abbas and the British, especially Kitchener, later Britain's consul general in Egypt.

FUAD I, AHMAD (1868–1936). Prince, university leader, and sultan (later king) of Egypt from 1917 to 1936. As the youngest son of Khedive Isma'il (qq.v.), he spent most of his youth with his father in Naples and was educated in Geneva and at the military academy in Turin. He returned to Egypt after his father's death and led a dissolute youth. His first marriage, to Princess Shivékiar, failed, and he was shot (and narrowly escaped being killed) by her deranged brother. Fuad served for a time as a military attaché in Vienna and as aide-de-camp to Khedive Abbas (qq.v.). He was the nominal rector of the Egyptian University from 1908 to 1913, but his lectures were limited to marksmanship and horsemanship, at which he excelled (*see* Cairo University). Although considered in 1914 for Albania's throne, both the Albanian nationalists and the European powers preferred having a Christian ruler.

The British chose him for the sultanate in 1917, succeeding Husayn Kamil (q.v.), whose son was viewed as anti-British. Fuad secretly encouraged the agitation that led to the 1919 Revolution (q.v.). In April 1919 he married Nazli Sabri, so that he could beget an heir and thus forestall the return of ex-Khedive Abbas or his son, Abd al-Mun'im. He outwardly tolerated but privately hated the 1923 Constitution (q.v.), the Wafd Party (q.v.), and Sa'd Zaghlul (q.v.) and yearned to replace them with institutions and politicians more amenable to Palace control. He feared assassination and once told an English historian, H.A.L. Fisher, that he had ordered the construction of his coffin upon ascending the Egyptian throne. In 1930, aided by Isma'il Sidqi (q.v.), he suspended the 1923 Constitution and promulgated one that augmented his powers at the expense of Parliament. Five years later, he acceded to popular demands for the restoration of the earlier constitution and the return of the Wafd Party to power. He appointed Egypt's all-party delegation to negotiate with Britain to settle the Egyptian question but died before the Anglo-Egyptian Treaty (q.v.) was completed. Autocratic and avaricious, Fuad had no sympathy for the Egyptian people or for their elected leaders and preferred an absolutist government.

FUNDAMENTALISM. Popular term, originally connoting Protestant Christians who believed in the literal truth of the Bible, applied in recent years to Islamists (q.v.), as well as to militant adherents of other religions, including Copts (q.v.), Jews (q.v.), and Hindus, especially those who are politically active and hostile to Western political and cultural influences.

- G -

GAZA STRIP. Small sector of southwestern Palestine held by Egyptian forces at the end of the Palestine War (q.v.) and then inhabited wholly by Arabs, many of whom were refugees. The territory was administered by Egypt from 1949 to 1956, taken by Israel during the Suez War (q.v.), restored to Egypt in 1957, and recaptured by Israel in the June War (q.v.). Its status was to have been determined by the autonomy talks (q.v.) following the 1979 Egyptian-Israeli Peace Treaty (q.v.). It remained under Israeli occupation in early 1994, with a population exceeding 700,000, but was slated to come under Palestinian control, according to Israel's 1993 Statement of Principles with the Palestine Liberation Organization (q.v.).

GAZETTE, EGYPTIAN. English-language daily newspaper, published in Alexandria (q.v.) from 1881 to 1938 and since then in Cairo (q.v.). Its editorial policy was antinationalist during the British occupation (q.v.), but in recent years it has supported the policies of successive Egyptian governments. Its circulation in 1962 was around 20,000, in 1972 8,500, in 1982 19,000, and in 1993 35,000.

GENEVA CONFERENCE (1973). One-day meeting, cochaired by the United States and the USSR, including Israel, Egypt, and Jordan, held at the Palais des Nations in Geneva in December 1973. After formal speeches by the negotiating parties, the Conference was adjourned indefinitely, and U.S. Secretary of State Kissinger began his shuttle diplomacy (q.v.) that led to the Separation of Forces (q.v.) Agreements between Egypt and Israel and later in 1974 between Syria and Israel. President Carter wanted to reconvene the Conference in 1977, but the negotiators could not agree on who should represent the Palestinians. Sadat's (q.v.) trip to Jerusalem ended any plans to reopen the Conference.

GEOGRAPHICAL SOCIETY. Major Egyptian scholarly organization, founded by Georg Schweinfurth in 1875 and initially dominated by Europeans. Reorganized in 1917, it enjoyed the generous patronage of King Fuad (q.v.) and gradually came to include more Egyptians, many of whom were or became leaders in the country's intellectual life.

GEZIRA SPORTING CLUB. Athletic and social organization established on the island of Zamalek by the British in 1882, formerly notorious for excluding Egyptians from membership. The lands on which the Club was built were donated by Khedive Tawfiq (qq.v.).

GHALI, BUTROS (1846–1910). Diplomat and cabinet minister. Educated in the new Coptic school at Harat al-Saqqayin and then at the school of Prince Mustafa Fadil, he later studied at the School of Languages, but never earned a higher degree. He learned Arabic, French, English, Persian, Turkish, and Coptic. After serving as a clerk for the Alexandria Chamber of Commerce, he was appointed by Sharif (q.v.) to the head clerkship of the justice ministry in 1873. He also helped at this time to organize the Coptic (lay) Council (*see* Coptic church). When the Mixed Courts (q.v.) were being set up, he helped the justice minister prepare an Arabic translation of their law code, although he lacked any legal training. Ghali's work brought him to the attention of Prime Minister Nubar (q.v.), who appointed him to represent Egypt on the Caisse de la Dette Publique (q.v.); he thus became an intermediary between the Egyptian government and its European creditors. In 1879 he became deputy justice minister. Following the Urabi (q.v.) revolution he mediated between Khedive Tawfiq (qq.v.) and the Nationalists, securing trials that saved many of them from execution.

Butros Ghali's first ministerial appointment was within the 1893 Husayn Fakhri (q.v.) cabinet that pitted Abbas Hilmi II (q.v.) against Lord Cromer (q.v.), but he was able to retain the finance portfolio in the compromise cabinet of Riyad (q.v.). Ghali served as foreign minister from 1894 to 1910 under Nubar and Mustafa Fahmi (q.v.), and finally in his own cabinet. He continued to play a mediating role between power centers, signing the 1899 Sudan Convention (q.v.). He represented the cabinet on the bench in the 1906 Dinshaway (q.v.) trial, concurring in the death sentences that angered the National Party (q.v.). Abbas recommended him to Gorst (q.v.) to replace Fahmi as prime minister in 1908, overriding Gorst's concerns about letting a Copt head Egypt's government. As prime minister he further angered politically articulate Egyptians by reviving the Press Law (q.v.) and publicly advocating the extension of the Suez Canal Company's (q.v.) concession, policies that he is said to have privately opposed. He was assassinated by a Nationalist pharmacist in February 1910; his death set off a wave of Muslim-Christian polemics and more government repression against the National Party (q.v.). A subtle and conciliatory politician who stayed in office to uphold unpopular policies, Ghali believed that he served Egypt's best interests and fell victim to others who were less willing to compromise than he.

GHALI, BUTROS BUTROS, ***see*** **BOUTROS-GHALI, BOUTROS.**

GIDI PASS. Strategic point in the western Sinai Peninsula (q.v.), taken from Egypt by Israel in 1956 and 1967, relinquished to a United Nations (q.v.) force under the 1975 Egyptian-Israeli Agreement (q.v.), and restored to Egypt's control in 1979 by the Egyptian-Israeli Peace Treaty (q.v.).

GORDON, CHARLES "CHINESE" (1833–85). British general noted for his valiant defense of Khartum. The son of an artillery officer at Woolwich, he was educated there and commissioned in the Royal Engineers in 1852. He fought in the Crimean War, the French expedition against the Chinese emperor in Peking, and the suppression on behalf of that emperor (hence his nickname) of the Taiping rebellion. He then supervised Thames River defenses at Gravesend and represented Britain during 1871–73 on the commission to improve Danube River navigation. Visiting Istanbul in 1872, Gordon met Nubar (q.v.), who urged him to become governor of Egypt's equatorial province in the Sudan (q.v.). He was appointed to the position at the end of 1873, refusing to take more than £E2,000 of the £E10,000 annual salary that Khedive Isma'il (qq.v.) offered to pay. He restored security to that war-torn province, moved its capital from Gondokoro to Lado, and tried in vain to suppress the slave trade. He resigned in 1876 and returned to England, but Isma'il induced him to return by naming him governor of the Sudan, the equatorial provinces, Darfur, and the Red Sea coast. After quelling uprisings in several parts of the Sudan, Gordon managed to destroy the slave trade. He resigned soon after Tawfiq (q.v.) replaced his father, but not before he was imprisoned briefly by the Ethiopian emperor. After working in Switzerland, India, China, and the Cape Colony, he made a pilgrimage to the Holy Land in 1883. Meanwhile, Britain's defeat of Urabi (q.v.) had strengthened the Mahdi's (q.v.) uprising against Egypt's rule in the Sudan.

After a British expeditionary force sent there in 1883 was defeated, the cabinet asked Gordon–who was preparing to serve King Leopold in the Congo–to go to Khartum to help the Egyptian government evacuate its garrisons from the country. He was given the position of governor-general of the Sudan, but in Cairo he received additional instructions to organize an independent government in Khartum. He hoped, upon arriving there, to negotiate directly with the Mahdi and asked for Turkish and Indian reinforcements, requests that were denied. He managed to evacuate more than 2,500 people and used his remaining forces to organize the defense of Khartum against the Mahdists besieging the city. The British government was slow to send a rescue mission, which arrived at Khartum two days too late to save the city or its chief defender, who had been killed near the gate of his palace. Gordon's death led to widespread British mourning and attacks on Prime Minister Gladstone's government for its dilatory rescue efforts. Modest and retiring, yet fierce, temperamental, and deeply imbued with Christian ideals, he threw himself into any work he was called on to do.

GORST, [JOHN] ELDON (1861–1911). British Foreign Office official and colonial administrator, who served as British agent and consul general in Egypt from 1907 to 1911. Born in New Zealand but reared in London, he attended Eton and Trinity College, Cambridge. In 1885 he became both a barrister and a member of the diplomatic corps, going to Egypt the following year to serve in various capacities under Lord Cromer (q.v.). He was financial adviser from 1898 to 1904 and then returned to London, where, in effect, he represented Cromer in the Foreign Office until his retirement in 1907, following the Dinshaway Incident (q.v.).

With a new Liberal Party government in power, Gorst was sent to replace Cromer in Cairo with instructions to give Egyptians greater responsibility to manage their internal affairs. As British agent, Gorst quickly improved relations with Khedive Abbas Hilmi II (qq.v.) with his *politique d'entente* (q.v.), brought more Egyptians into responsible government positions, and weakened the National Party (q.v.). However, his efforts to rein in the burgeoning corps of Anglo-Egyptian officials antagonized many old Egypt hands. The appointment of Butros Ghali (q.v.) as prime minister, popularly ascribed to Gorst, angered the Nationalists and many other Muslims, leading to press attacks and eventually to his assassination. The revival of the Press Law (q.v.) alienated Europeans as well as Egyptians and proved unenforceable. His attempt to extend the Suez Canal Company's (q.v.) concession in 1909–10 to raise additional funds for development in Egypt and the Sudan (q.v.) was unpopular among Egyptians; when Gorst put the issue to the General Assembly, vehement opposition from the Nationalist press led to its rejection. This act, combined with the assassination of Butros Ghali, caused Gorst to abandon his lenient policy in favor of a harsher one, using the Exceptional Laws (q.v.) and various penal measures to silence the Nationalists. He had almost restored British control when he became stricken with cancer and went back to England to die. An unprepossessing but egotistical man, disliked by the older British colonial administrators in Egypt and distrusted by Egyptians as sphinxlike, he never was accorded the respect that his intelligence and strong will warranted. His diaries are held by St Antony's College, Oxford.

GOSCHEN-JOUBERT MISSION (1876). Committee sent to Egypt at the behest of Khedive Isma'il's (qq.v.) French and British creditors, following his proposal to refinance Egypt's bonded and floating government debt, then £E92 million, at 7 percent interest, which they had rejected. Arriving in 1876 to negotiate with Isma'il, Goschen and Joubert obtained the unification of the funded Egyptian government debt, the appointment of French and English controllers, and the creation of the Caisse de la Dette Publique (q.v.) to ensure the service of the debt. What they could not have foreseen, however, was that some of the European creditors would use the newly formed Mixed Courts (q.v.) to suc thc Egyptian government for the fulfillment of the terms under which it had originally contracted its debts. A low Nile and large military outlays caused by Egypt's participation in the 1877 Russo-Turkish war ensured that the government would not be able to carry out the Goschen-Joubert mission's recommendations, leading eventually to the formation of the European ministry and the Dual Control (q.v.).

GREEKS. Greeks have colonized Egypt since antiquity. Under the Ottoman Empire (q.v.), Egypt experienced periodic infusions of Greek subjects, mainly merchants. Greece's War for Independence increased Egypt's Greek population, as some war captives were brought in, and Greeks came in from other Ottoman lands where they felt less secure. Rising immigration in the late-nineteenth century was partly due to the declining opportunities for artisans and peasants in mainland Greece and its islands; it would have been greater if North America had not drawn so many Greeks. Although most immigrants settled in Cairo (q.v.) or Alexandria (q.v.), some went to the Suez Canal (q.v.) cities and the rural villages; usually, they retained Greek nationality to benefit from the Capitulations (q.v.). Religious identification with the Greek Orthodox church, a legacy of the *millet* (q.v.) system, gradually gave way to an ethnicity influenced by nationalism, and the Greek consulates gained influence at the expense of the religious hierarchy.

Greeks ran their own schools, hospitals, welfare institutions, newspapers, literary journals (viewed as avant-garde by mainland Greek intellectuals), publishing houses, social clubs, and athletic teams. They saw themselves as an extension of European culture into an African land. They held a major role in the sale and export of Egyptian cotton (q.v.), banking and finance, shipping, retail commerce, skilled trades, and some white-collar occupations. Greeks owned only 1 percent of Egypt's agricultural land in the early twentieth century, mostly through land companies, and this share later declined. Greeks owned about one-third of Egypt's cotton gins in the 1870s, a share that also declined later. Some were industrial entrepreneurs; the Gianaclis family pioneered cigarette manufacturing, one of Egypt's major export industries, and also introduced viticulture to Egypt. Other Egyptian industries in which Greeks played a major role included soft drinks, chocolates, pasta, paper, ironworks, alcohol, textiles, fertilizers, and building materials. Greek grocers, who often served as moneylenders, were popularly thought to be ubiquitous, but in fact they lost ground to Egyptian competitors after World War I (q.v.). Greek industrial workers took the lead in organizing unions (q.v.). A few labor leaders also espoused Communism (q.v.) or socialism (q.v.). Many Greeks cooperated with Egyptians in their quest for independence; Greek marble was used in the Sa'd Zaghlul (q.v.) mausoleum, even though some Greeks were killed or injured during the 1919 Revolution (q.v.). Overall, Egypt's Greek population peaked at 99,793 in the 1927 census. The rise of Egyptian nationalism and phasing out of the Capitulations caused some Greeks to emigrate in the 1930s, a trend that accelerated after the 1952 Revolution (q.v.), which reduced the professional and commercial opportunities formerly available to Greeks and other minorities. Although Greek names of some business firms and restaurants survive in Cairo and Alexandria and Egyptian colloquial Arabic words suggest the Greek origins of certain cheeses, poultry, and vegetables, the Greek presence in Egypt today is much diminished.

GREEN SHIRTS, ***see*** **MISR AL-FATAT.**

GULF ORGANIZATION FOR THE DEVELOPMENT OF EGYPT. Association of Arab countries formed in 1976 to aid in Egypt's industrialization. Its initial capital of almost $2 billion was supplied by Saudi Arabia (40 percent), Kuwait (35 percent), the United Arab Emirates (15 percent), and Qatar (10 percent). The fund was to be used to set up industrial and agricultural investment projects and to finance imports of capital goods. Its secondary purpose was to help solve Egypt's liquidity problem and to improve its balance of payments. By May 1978 Egypt had exhausted the entire amount in obtaining loans and credit facilities from Chase Manhattan and other banks to pay back debts and to meet its balance-of-payments deficit. No moneys were used in any productive investments. The Organization also guaranteed a $250-million loan to Egypt by a syndicate of Western and Japanese banks. Following the Camp David Accords (q.v.), financial aid to Egypt from other Arab countries was cut off. The U.S. Agency for International Development (q.v.) has helped make up the difference.

- H -

HADETO. Acronym for *al-Haraka al-Dimuqratiya li al-Taharrur al-Watani* ("Democratic Movement for National Liberation"), Egypt's largest Communist faction (*see* Communism), formed in 1947 as a coalition of the Egyptian Movement for National Liberation (q.v.), Iskra (q.v.), and the smaller People's Liberation movement. It published *al-Jamahir* and later *al-Malayin*. Its members, approximately 1,700 in 1947, were mainly upper- or middle-class intellectuals, but some skilled workers and trade unionists joined. Hadeto aided textile workers' strikes in Mahalla al-Kubra and Shubra al-Khayma in 1947. It tried to appeal to peasants by advocating land reform (q.v.) and to pacifists by opposing Egypt's involvement in the Palestine War (q.v.). Hadeto, like the Egyptian Communist Party (q.v.), officially supported the partition of Palestine in 1947 and opposed intervention in the war (q.v.), and many of its leaders were jailed by the Nuqrashi (q.v.) and Abd al-Hadi (q.v.) governments. Dissident groups, such as the Revolutionary Faction and the Voice of the Opposition, emerged briefly in protest against the leadership's acceptance of Jewish statehood in Palestine. Hadeto aided the *fidaiyin* (q.v.) against the British in the Suez Canal (q.v.) Zone in 1951–52.

Some discontented Egyptian army officers had ties with Hadeto, although the Free Officers (q.v.) were independent of all other political parties or movements, and it welcomed the 1952 Revolution (q.v.) as a step toward altering Egyptian society. Khalid Muhyi al-Din (q.v.) was the main contact between the Revolutionary Command Council (q.v.) and Hadeto, although he was never a member of the organization. Hadeto had also helped the Free Officers publish their propaganda before the revolution and continued to support them once they held power, even after the Kafr al-Dawwar Incident (q.v.). Less surprisingly, Hadeto backed the officers on their land reform program against their first premier, Ali Mahir (q.v.). When the Revolutionary Command Council banned all political parties in January 1953, however, Hadeto joined the Egyptian Communist Party, the Muslim Brothers (q.v.), the Wafdist Vanguard (q.v.), and other leftists in opposing its policy, forming the National Democratic Front (q.v.). The new organization won the backing of Muhammad Najib (q.v.) as well as Khalid Muhyi al-Din, but the triumph of Nasir's (q.v.) faction sealed the fate of all Communist groups. Most Hadeto members were jailed and later released. The Suez War (q.v.) led to better relations between the Nasir regime and the Communists. Left-wing publishing houses and even their newspaper, *al-Masa*, flourished, and in 1958 Hadeto reunited with the Egyptian Communist Party.

AL-HAKIM, TAWFIQ (1898–1987). Playwright, novelist, and essayist. Born in Alexandria (q.v.) to an Egyptian landowning father and an aristocratic Turkish mother, his family moved frequently because of his father's work as a district magistrate. His earliest exposure to drama came from seeing an Arabic adaptation of *Romeo and Juliet*, allegedly by Salama al-Hijazi's (q.v.) troupe, in Disuq. He attended many dramatic productions in Cairo (q.v.), began studying classical Greek and French drama, and was already writing plays while still in secondary school. He spent four years at the government Law School (q.v.), graduating third from the bottom of his class in 1925. His parents, hoping to distract him from writing for the stage, sent him to Paris for more legal studies, but he failed to earn his doctorate and returned to Egypt in 1928. Hakim then worked for the Niyaba (q.v.) of the Alexandria Mixed Courts (q.v.) and soon was promoted to deputy public prosecutor. His legal experiences were immortalized in a novel, *Yawmiyyat naib fi al-aryaf* ("Diaries of a Prosecutor in the Countryside"), published in 1937 and later translated into English as *The Maze of Justice*. During this period he also wrote *Ahl al-kahf* ("The Sleepers in the Cave"), *Rasasa fi al-qalb* ("A Bullet in the Heart"), and *Shahrazad* ("Sheherazade"). His plays scandalized his Niyaba colleagues, and he was obliged to resign.

In 1933 Hakim published a novel, *Awdat al-ruh* ("Return of the Spirit"), an allegory of Egypt's modern renaissance that inspired many Egyptians, including Nasir (q.v.). He became director of the education ministry's research department in 1934 and of the social affairs ministry's information service in 1939, but retired from the government in 1943. In 1951 Taha Husayn (q.v.) named him director of Dar al-Kutub (q.v.). He was elected to membership in the Arabic Language Academy (q.v.) in 1954, Nasir appointed him to the Supreme Council on the Arts in 1956, and he later represented Egypt at UNESCO in Paris, where he was exposed to the "theater of the absurd." He received the first State Prize for Literature in 1961 and was also honored by a government theater named for him, which opened in 1963. Among his plays produced in the Nasir era are *al-Sultan al-hair* ("The Perplexed Sultan"), a historical drama about the Mamluks (q.v.) with contemporary implications, and *Ya tali' al-shajara* ("The Tree Climber"), influenced by the theater of the absurd. Although he had written regularly for *al-Ahram* (q.v.) throughout the Nasir era, Hakim denounced Nasir's policies in 1975 in a controversial manifesto, *Awdat al-wa'y*, translated as *The Return of Consciousness* (1985). He was one of the first Egyptian writers to call for a peace treaty with Israel, due perhaps to his disillusionment with Nasir, but he later recanted. In 1983 he published a biting attack on Egypt's religious leaders called *Ahadith ma'a Allah* ("Conversations with God"), arousing debates throughout the Arab world. He wrote an autobiography, *Sijn al-umr* ("Prison of the Life

Span"). A controversial writer, he was respected by Arabs generally even when they disagreed with him.

HALIM, ABBAS (1897-1978). *Nabil* ("Prince") of the Muhammad Ali (q.v.) dynasty who became a labor leader (*see* Unions). Educated in Germany, he served as an aide-de-camp to Kaiser Wilhelm II, became a fighter pilot for that country in World War I (q.v.), and later joined the Ottoman (q.v.) army. After the war, he spent several years traveling before he was readmitted to Egypt. A patron of athletics (including sports for the poor), Halim headed the Royal Automobile Club and the Royal Flying Club. Having quarreled with King Fuad (q.v.), his cousin, he backed the Wafd (q.v.) in 1930 against Isma'il Sidqi's (q.v.) efforts to changc Egypt's constitution. In that December he was elected president of the pro-Wafdist National Federation of Trade Unions in Egypt. He ensured that the Federation's leaders were actual workers and that its goals furthered their class interests regarding wages, working conditions, housing, education, and unemployment compensation. However, his leading associates were skilled, semiautonomous workers and small proprietors, not industrial laborers. His attempt to establish a workers' party in 1931 alarmed his Wafdist allies, but he and Nahhas (q.v.) agreed that the National Federation would leave politics to the Wafd. Eclipsed for several years due to Sidqi's repressive policies, the National Federation resumed its efforts to organize workers in 1934, after he had been replaced by Abd al-Fattah Yahya (q.v.). The police barred Abbas Halim's Cairo (q.v.) palace to the workers, setting off demonstrations in which one worker was killed and others injured. Another demonstration ensued at the slain worker's funeral. Abbas Halim was arrested but released after his well-publicized hunger strike. As thc National Federation grew, the Wafd tried to draw it away from Halim, who was forming ties with Misr al-Fatat (q.v.). The labor movement became split between the Wafd and the prince. When the Wafd regained power in 1936, he left labor politics, and the National Federation died out. He tried again in 1937 to lead a labor group, the Committee to Organize the Workers' Movement, but it allowed him only nominal leadership. He reappeared in 1939 as "supreme president" of the Cairo Tramway Workers' Union, which hoped to exploit his ties with King Faruq (q.v.) and enmity to the Wafd. He negotiated on behalf of the transport workers with the tramway company, gaining some benefits for them in July 1940. He also combined the transport workers' organizations into the Joint Transport Federation and, when this new group struck in September 1941, he negotiated on its behalf for higher wages, but failed to fulfill his promises to the workers. This failure, along with the Wafd's return to power in 1942, undermined Halim; Britain interned him and a few friends for two years. Once he was free to resume his activities, the workers distrusted him for his ties with Faruq, who was no longer popular. As Marxist ideas of working-class solidarity spread among the workers, his influence waned in the late 1940s.

HARB, [MUHAMMAD] TAL'AT (1867–1941). Financier, founder of Bank Misr (q.v.), and "father of Egypt's economic independence." Born in Cairo to a family that claimed tribal Arab origins, he graduated from the government Law School (q.v.), worked for the state domains administration from 1888 to 1905, and became a financial manager for a few large landowners and the director of several companies. He was an ardent patriot and devout Muslim who wrote books glorifying Islamic civilization, defending the veiling of women, and opposing the proposed extension of the Suez Canal Company (q.v.) concession. While arguing against that project, he called for the establishment of a purely Egyptian bank, a portent of his later efforts. Visiting Germany shortly before World War I (q.v.), he was impressed by its banking system.

In April 1920 Harb and his associates established Bank Misr, which became a holding company for many other business enterprises spawned by his intelligence and efforts. He was remarkably open to new ideas; in 1937 he was making his business trips to Syria, Iraq, and the Hijaz by airplane. On Anglo-Egyptian relations, he said: "For good or for ill, our two countries are wedded to one another, and there is little prospect of a divorce, even if we should wish it. For God's sake, then, let us make our married life as tolerable and mutually profitable as possible." He also pioneered in strengthening economic ties between Egypt and other Arab countries, making him an influential figure among early Arab nationalists. Regrettably, Bank Misr was overextended financially, suffered a liquidity crisis in 1939, and needed financial assistance from the Egyptian government to survive. Harb resigned from the presidency of Bank Misr and personally chose his successor, but some feel that he was the victim of a political conspiracy by Ahmad Mahir (q.v.) and Husayn Sirri (q.v.).

HASANAYN, MUHAMMAD AHMAD (1889–1946). Arab explorer, sportsman, and close associate of the Egyptian royal family. Hasanayn was born in Bulaq (q.v.) and educated at Oxford. An avid adventurer, he was sent by King Fuad (q.v.) to explore Egypt's Western Desert from the Mediterranean to Darfur, discovered several hitherto unknown oases, and published an account of his finds, *Fi Sahra Libya*, translated into English as *The Lost Oases* (1925). The Egyptian government appointed him to negotiate with Italy over Egypt's border with Libya (q.v.) in 1924. King Fuad then appointed him as a royal adviser. Some believe that he secretly married or had a sexual relationship with Queen Nazli, Fuad's widow and the mother of Faruq (q.v.), over whom he exercised great influence during the first ten years of his reign. His death in an automobile accident deprived the king of a capable mentor at a critical time.

HATIM, ABD AL-QADIR (1917-). Officer and politician. Dr. Hatim graduated from the Military Academy (q.v.) in 1939 and from Staff College in 1952. He also earned a B.A. in political economy at the London School of Economics in 1947 and an M.A. in political science and a Ph.D. in information from Cairo University (q.v.). One of the Free Officers (q.v.) who staged the 1952 Revolution (q.v.), he served as Nasir's (q.v.) assistant for press relations. He became a member of the National Assembly in 1957, then minister of state for information in 1959, and was minister of information, national guidance, and culture from 1962 to 1966. He also served as deputy prime minister from 1964. Out of the government from 1966 to 1971, he rejoined when Sadat (q.v.) ousted his rivals, again serving as deputy prime minister and information minister until 1974. He chaired the board of *al-Ahram* (q.v.) in 1974–75 and also served as an adviser to Sadat. He is the author of *Information and the Arab Cause* (1974) and other works about information and propaganda.

HAYKAL, MUHAMMAD HASANAYN (1923-). Political journalist, writer, and editor. Originally from a Cairo (q.v.) middle-class family, he graduated from a public secondary school and attended classes at Cairo University (q.v.) and the American University in Cairo (q.v.), but did not graduate. He began his journalistic career as an unpaid reporter for the *Egyptian Gazette* (q.v.) and *Ruz al-Yusuf* (q.v.), covering the Battle of al-Alamayn (q.v.) and Egypt's Parliamentary debates. He then became a reporter for *Akhir Sa'a*, winning a King Faruq (q.v.) prize for investigative journalism for his coverage of the 1947 cholera (q.v.) epidemic. He covered the Palestine struggle from 1946 to 1949 for *Akhbar al-Yawm*, interviewing David Ben-Gurion and King Abdallah, also meeting Major Jamal Abd al-Nasir (q.v.) for the first time. Traveling widely, he also covered the Greek Civil War, the Musaddiq crisis in Iran, and the 1952 U.S. presidential campaign (supported at the time by a State Department "Leader Grant"). He claims to have been intimately involved with the Free Officers (q.v.), especially Nasir, at the time of the 1952 Revolution (q.v.); whether this is true, Haykal certainly was closer to Nasir throughout his period in power than any other journalist. He edited *Akhir Sa'a* in the early 1950s and then *al-Akhbar* (q.v.), of which he became editor-in-chief in 1956, but he became estranged from Ali and Mustafa Amin (qq.v.). After numerous attempts by *al-Ahram* (q.v.) to lure him, he finally agreed to be its editor in 1957. He built up this newspaper into the most prestigious and influential one in Egypt and arguably the whole Arab world. Haykal also became an adviser, confidant, and spokesman for

Nasir, and is widely credited with ghostwriting his *Falsafat al-thawra* ("The Philosophy of the Revolution"). A strong believer in press freedom and scientific management, he made the physical facilities of *al-Ahram* among the most modern anywhere in the world, and the newspaper spawned various influential periodicals, ranging from the Marxist *al-Tali'a* to the conservative *al-Ahram al-iqtisadi*. His weekly column, *Bi al-saraha* ("Speaking Frankly"), was read throughout the Arab world as an indicator of the direction of Nasir's thinking. He served briefly in 1970 as his minister of information and national guidance.

A loyal Nasirist (q.v.), he soon broke with Sadat (q.v.) because of his growing ties with the United States and his willingness to make peace with Israel. In 1974 Haykal was dismissed as editor and chairman of *al-Ahram* and barred from publishing articles in the Egyptian press, although he continued to publish in Arabic newspapers in Lebanon, as well as in books and articles written in English and directed at an American audience. Among his publications of that period were his *Nasser: The Cairo Documents* (1973) and *The Sphinx and the Commissar* (1978). He was interrogated by the Egyptian police and the state prosecutor in 1977–78, forbidden to travel abroad, and imprisoned during Sadat's purge in September 1981. Under Mubarak (q.v.) he has not regained his former influence on policy decisions or his editorial power, but he is respected as an intellectual, writer, and journalist. He wrote a scathing attack on his erstwhile friend and sponsor, Anwar al-Sadat, *Autumn of Fury* (1983), and a memoir of the 1956 Suez War (q.v.), *Twisting the Lion's Tail* (1986). He has been mentioned as a possible mediator between Egypt and other Arab countries, such as Libya (q.v.). His memoirs of the June War (q.v.) were published in 1990 as *1967: al-Infijar* ("1967: The Explosion"). Haykal's memories of events in which he was an observer or participant are historically valuable but sometimes self-serving.

HAYKAL, MUHAMMAD HUSAYN (1888–1956). Writer, politician, and lawyer. Born to a landowning family in Daqahliyya, he was educated at the government Law School (q.v.) and the University of Paris, where he wrote his doctoral dissertation on the Egyptian public debt. Homesick while he was living there for his native village, Kafr Ghannam, he also wrote a bucolic fiction piece called *Zaynab* (q.v.), published anonymously in 1913. Upon returning to Egypt in 1914, he practiced law, wrote for *al-Jarida* (q.v.), published a magazine called *al-Sufur* during World War I (q.v.), and taught at the Law School. When the 1919 Revolution (q.v.) broke out, he backed the Wafd (q.v.) and Sa'd Zaghlul (q.v.), but broke with them over the Adli-Curzon Negotiations (q.v.) in 1921. At this time Adli Yakan (q.v.), Haykal, and some other educated Egyptians formed the Constitutional Liberal Party (q.v.). In 1922 Haykal became editor of its newspaper, *al-Siyasa* (q.v.), for which he later founded an influential weekly edition, *al-Siyasa al-usbu'iyya*. He kept up his literary production with *Fi awqat al-faragh* ("In Moments of Leisure"), *Tarajim misriyya wa gharbiyya* ("Egyptian and Western Biographies"), and a touching eulogy of his son, who died in childhood, called *Waladi*. In 1934, at a time when the Constitutional Liberals were vying for popular favor with the Wafd, the Palace, and the rising Muslim groups, he published *Hayat Muhammad* ("The Life of Muhammad"), an attempt to apply modern scholarship to the biography of the Prophet and to reconcile the principles of personal freedom, which he had long espoused, with the teachings of Islam (q.v.). Increasingly pious, he made the hajj in 1936 and published *Fi manzal al-wahy* ("In the Dwelling Place of Conscience"), relating his experience as a pilgrim. He served as education minister in seven cabinets during the late 1930s and 1940s and as president of the Senate from 1945 to 1950. He published an additional novel, *Hakadha khuliqat* ("Thus Was She Created"), shortly before his death and also his memoirs, *Mudhakkirat fi al-siyasa al-misriyya* ("Memories of Egyptian Politics"), of which two volumes appeared during his lifetime and one posthumously. An ambitious man with many talents, Haykal felt torn between secularism and Islam, freedom and authority, and his party's democratic principles and his belief that Egypt should be governed by its most educated citizens.

HEALTH CARE. Medicine has been an important science in Egypt since pharaonic times, a role reinforced by Islam's positive attitude toward hygiene and medical care. Hospitals, public baths, free medical education, and guilds of medical practitioners (female as well as male) promoted public and individual health in medieval Egyptian society. Although medical practice had deteriorated in Egypt by the time of Napoléon (q.v.), European doctors during the French occupation (q.v.) noted the success of native healers in treating typhus and smallpox. Napoléon's army had military hospitals, and the Institut d'Égypte (q.v.) planned to found a civil counterpart in Cairo large enough to accommodate 300–400 patients, to be staffed by French doctors and nurses.

As a part of his Westernizing reform program, Muhammad Ali (q.v.) set up a medical school at Qasr al-Ayni under the leadership of Clot Bey (q.v.) in 1827, by which time there were already some 50 European doctors attending his troops. Frequent plague and cholera (q.v.) epidemics, as well as such endemic diseases as ophthalmia and diabetes, and the appearance, with perennial irrigation (q.v.), of bilharzia (q.v.), ensured that civilian Egyptians as well as soldiers would need the attention of these emerging practitioners. Regrettably for Egypt, its new health care system imitated the European pattern, although there was an ephemeral attempt under Muhammad Ali to train "barefoot doctors" to work in the Egyptian countryside. Egyptians trained in European medicine ministered mainly to the troops or to the Westernized bureaucratic elite; Egypt's peasants looked to midwives, barber-surgeons, faith healers, Sufis (*see* Sufism), and other traditional healers who often lacked adequate training. Likewise, in the area of public health, Egypt adopted the quarantine practices of Mediterranean Europe, even when they failed to halt the periodic influx of cholera. Later reformers, including Isma'il (q.v.) and the British occupation (q.v.), reinforced this tendency to imitate Western health-care models to the detriment of public health in the countryside and the growing cities. The last Wafd Party (q.v.) cabinet began to redress the problem by establishing rural health centers, which later were expanded under Nasir (q.v.). Only after the 1952 Revolution (q.v.) did the Egyptian government take a sustained interest in bringing health care to poor people, promoting public health, and stressing preventive measures. The Islamist (q.v.) societies have lately outstripped the government in delivering health care to the people, and it is noteworthy that their candidates were elected as the officers of the Egyptian Medical Association at its 1992 meeting.

HELIOPOLIS. Garden suburb of Cairo (q.v.) begun by tramway magnate Baron Empain in 1906; it was also the site of an Ottoman (q.v.) defeat by the French under Kléber (q.v.) in 1800.

HIGH COMMISSIONER. Title of Britain's political representative in Egypt from its declaration of the protectorate (q.v.) in 1914 until the signing of the 1936 Anglo-Egyptian Treaty (q.v.). His office was called the Residency (q.v.).

HIJAZ. Mountainous area of western Arabia ruled by Muhammad Ali (q.v.) following his 1811–18 military campaign against the Wahhabis (q.v.). Some portions of the coastal pilgrimage route to Mecca remained under de facto Egyptian control until 1892.

HIJAZI, SALAMA (1855–1917). Egypt's first great Muslim singer, actor, and stage director. Born into a poor Alexandria (q.v.) family, he was trained as a Quran reciter. He was exposed to performances by European theatrical troupes as a youth and had contacts with Syrian actors. He organized his own troupe, in which he was a frequent actor and singer, at a theater that he founded in Cairo (q.v.) near the Ezbekiyya Gardens (q.v.) called Dar al-Tamthil al-Arabi ("House of Arabic Acting") in 1905. His troupe toured Syria and North Africa and helped to make music and theater (q.v.) seem respectable to Arabic-speaking Muslims.

AL-HILAL. Popular monthly magazine founded in Cairo (q.v.) by Jurji Zaydan in 1892. Its contributors have included Khalil Jibran, Amin al-Rayhani, Taha Husayn (q.v.), Ahmad Amin (q.v.), and Salama Musa (q.v.), who was its editor from 1923 to 1929. It set up a major publishing house, printing Arabic books for general readers and such popular periodicals as *al-Musawwar* (q.v.).

AL-HILALI, AHMAD NAJIB (1891–1958). Lawyer, politician, and prime minister. He served as education minister in Tawfiq Nasim's (q.v.) cabinet from 1934 to 1936, but joined the Wafd Party (q.v.) in 1937 and held the education portfolio in Mustafa al-Nahhas's (q.v.) wartime government. In 1943 he published *A Report on Educational Reform in Egypt*. Estranged from the Wafdist leaders, Hilali criticized them for corruption and was expelled from the Party. He headed independent cabinets for three months in 1952 after Black Saturday (q.v.) and again for one day prior to the 1952 Revolution (q.v.). Imprisoned briefly by the Revolutionary Command Council (q.v.), he was one of the old regime politicians deprived of their civil and political rights, but he died before his rights were restored and his reputation could be rehabilitated.

AL-HUDAYBI, HASAN ISMA'IL (1895?-1973). Successor to Hasan al-Banna (q.v.) as supreme guide of the Society of Muslim Brothers (q.v.). Born in a village near Shibin to worker parents, he began his education at its *kuttab* (q.v.). Although his father wanted to send him to al-Azhar (q.v.), he chose to become a lawyer, graduated from the government Law School (q.v.) in 1915 and served his apprenticeship in Hafiz Ramadan's (q.v.) office. He practiced law in Cairo (q.v.) and Suhaj and became a judge in 1924, but quit the bench when he joined the Brothers. Following the assassination of Supreme Guide al-Banna, Hudaybi was named his successor in 1951, partly because he was not associated with terrorism or the secret apparatus within the Society. He cultivated Faruq (q.v.) as an ally against the Wafd (q.v.). Arrested on Black Saturday (q.v.), he was immediately released for lack of evidence that he or the Society planned the burning of Cairo. He backed the abortive reform efforts of Ahmad Najib al-Hilali (q.v.) and also the Free Officers (q.v.), especially Nasir (q.v.).

Although he welcomed the 1952 Revolution (q.v.), Hudaybi's relations with Nasir soon cooled when he rejected the officers' offer to admit three leading brothers to the new cabinet. Nasir's creation of the Liberation Rally (q.v.) also antagonized Hudaybi, who feared that it would eclipse the Society. His call for an end to martial law and the lifting of government censorship (q.v.) angered Nasir, as did his secret meetings with the British Oriental secretary during the Suez Canal (q.v.)

negotiations. Former Banna supporters within the Society objected to Hudaybi's tendency to bypass its governing council. The Egyptian government dissolved the Society in January 1954 and arrested many of its leaders, including Hudaybi. After massive demonstrations supporting the nominal president, Muhammad Najib (q.v.), Nasir agreed in March 1954 to release Hudaybi, end martial law, lift all censorship, and allow freedom of expression to all viewpoints; in fact Nasir was laying a trap to expose his opponents, who engaged in mass demonstrations. Hudaybi, however, backed Nasir's government, which soon suppressed all political movements except the Brothers. The government went on arresting officers associated with the Brothers, especially their secret branch, and Hudaybi wrote to Nasir, accusing the Revolutionary Command Council (q.v.) of breaking promises. Ignoring a summons to meet with Nasir, he set out on a tour of eastern Arab countries. When Britain and Egypt announced their 1954 Agreement (q.v.), Hudaybi publicly criticized it in a Beirut newspaper. Upon returning to Egypt, he went into hiding, but sent Nasir another letter, calling for an open debate on the outstanding issues. The government instead stepped up its campaign against the Society. The secret branch remained in existence–but outside Hudaybi's control–and plotted to kill Nasir. When the attempt failed, the plotters were arrested, as were thousands of Brothers, including Hudaybi. He was subjected to a show trial and given a death sentence, which was later commuted to penal servitude because of his age. His *Sab'at asila fi al-aqida wa al-radd alayha: takhatti al-su'ubat wa al-aqabat* ("Seven Questions and Answers about Doctrine: Surmounting Difficulties and Obstacles") was published in 1978. Cautious and rather conservative, he tried but failed to moderate the Society's emotionalism and violence.

HULWAN. Health resort and industrial center located 25 km south of Cairo (q.v.), to which it is connected by railroads (q.v.) and the Cairo Corniche (q.v.). During the reign of Abbas Hilmi I (q.v.), its hot springs were uncovered, and it became a center for the treatment of soldiers suffering from skin diseases and rheumatism; these were later opened for civilian use, and several palaces were constructed there. Since 1954 it has been the center of Egypt's iron and steel industry (q.v.) and later of assembly plants for motor vehicles and munitions (q.v.). Large-scale workers' demonstrations took place there in February 1968 against Nasir's (q.v.) policies, leading to the 30 March Program (q.v.).

HUSAYN, AHMAD (1911–82). Leader of Misr al-Fatat (q.v.). Born in Cairo (q.v.), he graduated from the Cairo University (q.v.) Faculty of Law in 1931, then worked as a lawyer and journalist, writing for *al-Siyasa* (q.v.). He and Fathi Ridwan founded Misr al-Fatat ("Young Egypt") in the early 1930s in the belief that the existing political parties had abandoned their patriotic ideals. They also inaugurated the "Piastre Plan," inviting all Egyptians to invest one piastre (then worth 5 U.S. cents) in locally owned and managed manufacturing firms. He became a strong and charismatic leader, especially of Egyptian Muslim youth, and was thought to enjoy King Faruq's (q.v.) support against the Wafd Party (q.v.). Accused of insulting the monarchy, he was arrested several times. His disciples included Nasir (q.v.) and Sadat (q.v.), who later put many of his ideas into practice. He became totally paralyzed in 1969 and died in relative obscurity. His memoirs appeared in *al-Sha'b* in August 1981.

HUSAYN, AHMAD (1902-). Landowner, agronomist, and politician. He was minister of social affairs in the last Wafd Party (q.v.) government and Egypt's ambassador to the United States when Dulles (q.v.) withdrew the American offer to help build the Aswan High Dam (q.v.).

HUSAYN, TAHA (1889–1973). Writer, educational administrator, and minister, sometimes called "the dean of Arab letters." Blind from early childhood, he studied at a *kuttab* (q.v.) in his native town, Maghagha, and had memorized the Quran by the age of nine. He entered al-Azhar (q.v.) in 1902 and came under the influence of Muhammad Abduh (q.v.) and his circle of Muslim modernists. Disappointed in al-Azhar, he began attending lectures at the Egyptian University (*see* Cairo University) and in 1913 was the first student to earn a Ph.D. there. Taha Husayn went to Paris in 1915 and earned a *doctorat d'état* at the Sorbonne in 1919 on his thesis *La Philosophie sociale d'Ibn Khaldoun.* After his return to Egypt he became a lecturer in ancient history at the Egyptian University and in 1925 was given the chair of Arabic literature. He published a book in 1926, *Fi al-shi'r al-jahili* ("On Pre-Islamic Poetry"), in which he questioned the authenticity of pre-Islamic Arabic poetry and of some narrative chapters of the Quran, arousing protests at al-Azhar and in Parliament. He withdrew the book, replacing it in 1927 with a revised version, *Fi al-adab al-jahili* ("On Pre-Islamic Literature"). He served in 1930–31 as dean of the Faculty of Arts at Cairo University, but was dismissed after a year by the education minister. He joined the Wafd Party (q.v.) and became an editor of its newspapers.

In 1938 Husayn published one of his best-known books, *Mustaqbil al-thaqafa fi Misr*, later translated into English as *The Future of Education in Egypt*, arguing that Egypt was more a Mediterranean country than an Arabic or Islamic one. He was appointed acting rector of Faruq (Alexandria) University in 1944 and was education minister from 1950 to 1952. He abstained from politics after the 1952 Revolution (q.v.) but continued to publish books and articles that were widely read in Egypt and the rest of the Arab world, including memoirs, three volumes of which have been translated into English as *An Egyptian Childhood* (1932; reprinted 1990), *The Stream of Days* (1943; revised 1948), and *A Passage to France* (1976). A strong Westernizer, Taha Husayn's personality was more influential than the ideas he espoused.

HUSAYN KAMIL (1853–1917). Sultan of Egypt from 19 December 1914 until his death in October 1917. Born and educated in Cairo (q.v.), he was the son of Isma'il (q.v.) and hence a younger brother of Khedive Tawfiq (qq.v.). He completed his studies in Paris. Public works director under Isma'il, he is said to have ordered the construction of the railroad (q.v.) from central Cairo to Hulwan (q.v.). When Isma'il was exiled in 1879, Husayn Kamil accompanied him for three years, then returned to Egypt and supervised the farming of his lands, also serving on the boards of several Egyptian and foreign companies. He organized the first agricultural fair and inaugurated a flower show in the Ezbekiyya Gardens (q.v.) in 1896. One of the leaders of the Islamic Benevolent Society, he was sympathetic to Egypt's peasants and hostile to the National Party (q.v.). He chaired the Legislative Council in 1909–10 and, when Abbas Hilmi II (q.v.) was deposed in 1914, the British named him the first "sultan" of an Egypt severed from the Ottoman Empire (q.v.). Two attempts were made on his life while he was sultan, but he died from natural causes. The British Protectorate (q.v.) and wartime conditions did not permit him to use his organizational abilities.

- I -

IBRAHIM (1789–1848). General and acting viceroy. The presumed eldest son of Muhammad Ali (q.v.), he was born near Qavalla (Macedonia) and first came to Egypt in 1805 with his brother, Tusun. He was sent by Muhammad Ali on the campaign to the Hijaz (q.v.) and Najd in 1813 and took command of the Sudan (q.v.) expedition in 1823. In 1831 he led the Syrian campaign, taking Acre, Damascus, Homs, and Aleppo. The Ottoman Empire (q.v.) sent an expeditionary force against him, but Ibrahim defeated it at Alexandretta and invaded Anatolia. When his forces crossed the Taurus Mountains and threatened to take Istanbul, the European powers threatened to intervene to protect the Ottoman sultan, and so Ibrahim signed the Convention of Kütahya (q.v.), giving Egypt suzerainty over Syria. Ibrahim became governor of the new province, with his capital at Antioch, and introduced many of his father's reforms. Another Ottoman effort to dislodge him from Syria failed in 1838. After Abdulmejid became sultan in 1839, he made an alliance with the British to expel Ibrahim's forces from Syria. Ibrahim was defeated and obliged to return to Egypt in 1840, but Muhammad Ali was permitted under the Convention of London (q.v.) to pass control of Egypt down to his heirs. He did so in 1848, naming Ibrahim governor of Egypt with the concurrence of the Ottoman government. Ibrahim went to Istanbul to receive his decree of investiture, became ill, and died shortly after his return to Cairo (q.v.). He is popularly believed to have espoused Arab nationalist ideals during his governorship of Syria, presumably to stress its ties with Egypt. His relationship with Muhammad Ali was clouded over by the latter's suspicion that he was not truly Ibrahim's father, but he was an able military commander and governor.

IBRAHIM, MUHAMMAD HAFIZ (1871?-1932). Egyptian nationalist poet, often called *Sha'ir al-Nil* ("Poet of the Nile"). Born in a Nile houseboat near Dayrut, he lost his father at an early age. His mother brought him to Cairo (q.v.), where he was educated. He began as a boy to write poetry, influenced by classical poets and also by Barudi (q.v.). He began practicing law, without formal training, with some lawyers in Tanta and Cairo, and then entered the Military Academy (q.v.), graduating in 1891 with a commission in the artillery. He served under Kitchener (q.v.) in the Sudan (q.v.) campaign, spending time in Sawakin and Khartum, where he formed a secret nationalist society with some fellow officers. Apprehended by the British, he was court-martialed and transferred to the reserves. Hafiz then sought the protection of Muhammad Abduh (q.v.) and obtained a police post at a monthly salary of £E4 until he was pensioned off. He became an editor of *al-Ahram* (q.v.), winning fame for his poetry and prose as he came under the inspiration of Mustafa Kamil (q.v.). He was appointed head of the literary section of Dar al-Kutub (q.v.) in 1911, remaining there until shortly before his death.

His poetry, neoclassical in style, excelled in expressing popular feelings and humor in terms that ordinary people could understand. Hafiz often recited his poetry publicly to large groups of listeners and freely contributed his verses to the Egyptian press. He often addressed social problems or political events in his verse, thus affirming his political support for Egyptian national aspirations. Especially famous are his attacks on the British for the Dinshaway Incident (q.v.) and for suppressing a women's demonstration during the 1919 Revolution (q.v.). He also wrote elegies and poems about natural disasters. In addition to his two-volume *diwan* ("collection of poems"), he translated Victor Hugo's *Les Misérables* and a book on political economy from French into Arabic. Hafiz was closer to the Egyptian people than his famous rival Ahmad Shawqi (q.v.), but the two were reconciled before they died and are now equally revered throughout the Arab world.

IBRAHIM, YAHYA (1861–1936). Politician, cabinet minister, and last premier before the 1923 Constitution (q.v.). Born in a village near Bani Suwayf, he was educated at the main Coptic college in Cairo (q.v.) and the government Law School (q.v.), where he later taught. He served as president of the National Court of Appeals, education minister (1919–20 and 1922–23), prime minister and interior minister (1923–24), and finance minister (1925–26). While he was prime minister the 1923 Constitution and the Election Law were promulgated and Sa'd Zaghlul (q.v.) was allowed to return from exile. He was the first president of the Ittihad Party (q.v.) in 1925. Although well-intentioned, he could not resist pressure from either King Fuad (q.v.) or the British residency (q.v.) to execute policies in their favor.

IBRAHIM BEY MUHAMMAD. Mamluk (q.v.) leader of Egypt, successor of Muhammad Abu al-Dhahab (q.v.), and rival to Murad Bey Muhammad (q.v.) as Egypt's ruler from 1775 to 1798. A rapacious and tyrannical ruler, he escaped to Syria when Napoléon (q.v.) invaded Egypt. He returned after the French occupation (q.v.) and opposed the Ottoman (q.v.) governor, Khusrev (q.v.), but he played no further role in the country's history. He and his followers encamped near present-day Dongola, thus evading Muhammad Ali's (q.v.) massacre of the Mamluks in 1811. News of his death reached Cairo in March 1816.

ID AL-ADHA. Feast of the sacrifice, also called Id al-Kabir and Qurban Bayram, the annual Muslim holiday commemorating Abraham's obedience to God's command by offering his son, Ishmael (Isma'il), as a sacrifice. It is also the tenth day of the pilgrimage month and is traditionally observed by butchering a sheep and sharing its meat with the poor.

ID AL-FITR. Feast of the fast-breaking, also called Ramadan Bayram, the annual Muslim holiday ending the month of daytime fasting, Ramadan.

IDRIS, YUSUF (1927–91). Doctor, journalist, and playwright. Originally from Sharqiyya province, he earned his M.D. at Cairo University (q.v.) in 1951. He worked briefly as a physician and health inspector, but drifted into journalism, writing on social problems. His first collection of short stories, *Arkhas layali* ("The Cheapest of Nights"), published in 1954, gained widespread public attention. His first play, "The Farhat Republic," was produced in 1957. He began introducing Western experimental techniques into his work during the 1960s. In 1966 he was awarded the medal of the republic after he had refused a prize from *al-Hiwar*. He hoped to create an indigenous Arab drama derived from the shadow and puppet plays that have been a staple of Arabic Islamic culture for centuries, as in *al-Farafir* ("The Small Birds") produced in 1966 and *al-Mukhattatun* ("The Striped Ones") in 1969. The latter play criticized the Nasir (q.v.) regime's restrictions on intellectual freedoms. Idris later wrote psychological plays and theater of the absurd and tried to develop an Arabic style that could express the most subtle and tender nuances of the mind and spirit.

AL-IKHWAN AL-MUSLIMUN, *see* **MUSLIM BROTHERS.**

IMBABA, BATTLE OF (1798). Often misnamed the "Battle of the Pyramids," this was the major triumph of Napoléon Bonaparte's (q.v.) army over the Mamluks (q.v.). His decisive victory, due to greater numbers and more effective use of artillery, paved the way for his conquest of Cairo (q.v.) and the French occupation (q.v.) of Egypt.

INFITAH. Sadat's (q.v.) open door policy of restoring free enterprise capitalism in Egypt, a reaction against Nasir's (q.v.) Arab socialism (q.v.). Officially launched with the October Paper (q.v.), relaxation of government controls on business had begun in 1971, when Egypt was declining economically. The acceleration of this policy after the October War (q.v.) was designed to attract foreign funds to help finance the importation of materials and parts needed to restore Egypt's economy to full production, to convert the short-term foreign debt to longer and less onerous terms, and to implement investments that would provide future income, jobs, and foreign exchange. Law 43 (1974) activated the *infitah* policy by giving incentives to Arab and foreign investors in industry, land reclamation, tourism, and banking, with reduced taxes and import tariffs (q.v.) and guarantees against nationalization. Some of Sadat's advisers wanted to limit the policy to encouraging foreigners to invest in Egypt's economy; others called for the application of capitalist norms to domestic firms, whether publicly or privately owned. The latter view prevailed, undermining state planning (q.v.) and labor laws and stimulating the growth of corruption, profiteering, and conspicuous consumption of foreign-made goods, especially by the new entrepreneurial class, often called *munfatihin* ("those who operate the open door"). Sadat's attempt, encouraged by American advisers, to remove exchange controls and reduce subsidies on basic foodstuffs, led to the 1977 Food Riots (q.v.), but liberalization continued. In recent years, the *munfatihin* have become an interest group in their own right, resisting efforts by Mubarak's (q.v.) government to reduce their opportunities for enrichment or to trim their level of consumption. The *infitah* policy has increased Egypt's economic dependency on the richer Arab countries, Europe, and the United States.

It has also widened the gap between rich and poor Egyptians, with potentially explosive social implications.

INSTITUT D'ÉGYPTE. Scholarly organization, founded in Egypt by Napoléon Bonaparte (q.v.) in 1798, to work for the advancement of knowledge in Egypt; to study the natural, industrial, and historical sciences relevant to the country; and to advise the government on specific matters related to policy. The Institute impressed some Egyptians such as Abd al-Rahman al-Jabarti (q.v.), who visited it and witnessed some of its scientific experiments. Its findings laid the basis for many scholarly monographs as well as the monumental *Description de l'Égypte* (q.v.). Closed after the French withdrew from Egypt, it was revived in 1859.

INTERNATIONAL MONETARY FUND. Organization established by the 1944 Bretton Woods Conference to stabilize the national currencies of the world. It has played a prominent role in advising the Egyptian government, during and since the *infitah* (q.v.), on its transition to a market economy. The January 1977 Food Riots (q.v.). are commonly ascribed to its recommendation to remove the subsidies that kept down the price of basic foodstuffs.

IRAQ-KUWAIT CONFLICT. Iraq, created by the victorious World War I (q.v.) allies out of three provinces of the Ottoman Empire (q.v.), was a British mandate under the League of Nations from 1922 to 1932, when it became an independent state. It has long claimed that all or part of the neighboring Emirate of Kuwait belonged to Iraq. When Kuwait became independent in 1961, Iraqi troops occupied that oil-rich country but withdrew under heavy pressure from Britain and the other Arab states, including Egypt, which sent a peacekeeping force to occupy Kuwait long enough to forestall an Iraqi annexation. In 1963 Iraq signed a treaty with Kuwait recognizing its independence, but political disputes between them continued to arise periodically. During the reconstruction period following its eight-year war with Iran, Iraq accused Kuwait of stealing its oil by slant-drilling into the Rumayla oil field that they share and rejected Kuwaiti demands for repayment of the $50 billion in loans it had made during the war, arguing that it had saved Kuwait and the other Gulf states from an Islamic revolution. Iraq's relations with Egypt also worsened, as returning Iraqi soldiers tried to reclaim jobs that had been taken by expatriate Egyptian workers during the war. Some Egyptians were killed, maimed, or deported, angering the people of Egypt against Iraq and its president, Saddam Husayn.

Mubarak (q.v.) offered to mediate between Iraq and Kuwait, acting in the interests of Arab solidarity. Saddam, however, violated an agreement brokered by Mubarak and invaded Kuwait on 2 August 1990, declaring Iraq's annexation of the emirate. Egypt initially tried to remain a mediator, proposing and hosting an Arab summit, but several key leaders did not attend. The summit condemned the annexation, and 12 Arab League member states voted to send an Arab deterrent force to the Gulf in support of U.S. efforts, code-named "Operation Desert Shield," to deter an Iraqi invasion of Saudi Arabia, and 5,000 Egyptian troops were reportedly there by the end of August. Egypt had about 800,000 workers in Iraq and 100,000 in Kuwait prior to the invasion; nearly all of them left the region and returned to Egypt, often suffering extreme privation and loss of all their savings. Mubarak emerged as a leader of the "moderate" Arab states that supported the allied coalition against Iraq, both diplomatically in the Arab League (q.v.) and the United Nations (q.v.), and militarily in "Operation Desert Storm," which took place in January and February 1991. Egypt's contingent in the multinational force reached 38,500 men–two armored divisions with 250 tanks–but their casualties were light. Iraqi troops were driven from Kuwait, and Egypt was rewarded by the other Arab "moderates" with additional jobs for expatriate Egyptian workers, replacing the Palestinians and Yemenis (whose leaders had supported Iraq), and by the Western and Gulf governments by the cancellation of almost $14 billion in debts owed to them. An additional $10 billion owed to Western creditors was rescheduled after the war, and the remaining $10 billion owed was to be canceled over a three-year period. After the war, Egypt and seven other Arab states that had taken part in "Operation Desert Storm" met in Damascus to set up an Arab regional security force, made up mainly of Egyptian and Syrian troops, for the Gulf states. However, Egypt, piqued by Kuwait's failure to award enough reconstruction contracts to Egyptian firms, suddenly withdrew its troops in May 1991.

Egypt's prominent support for Kuwait in the war against Iraq was due to its renewed attempts to become the leader of the Arab countries, its economic dependence on the oil-exporting Arab states of the Gulf region, and its close ties with the U.S. and other Western governments. Opposing Mubarak's involvement in the war were Egypt's Islamists (q.v.), Nasirists (q.v.), and Communists (q.v.), notably at the national universities, but the press and the streets were so controlled during the crisis that no one knows for certain what the average Egyptian felt.

IRON AND STEEL INDUSTRY. The state-owned Egyptian Iron and Steel Company was founded in 1954 at Hulwan (q.v.), using low-grade iron ore deposits found near Aswan. In the 1970s additional iron ore deposits, of a higher quality, were found near Bahriyya oasis. The Hulwan factory, built by the Soviets between 1955 and 1973, grew rapidly up to

1967, and total Egyptian production of reinforced iron rose from 50,000 metric tons in 1952 to 347,000 in 1977. Production of cast-iron parts, steel sections, and steel sheets also increased, but more gradually. Lately, the industry has reduced its per-unit costs of production. The government has let out contracts to upgrade the Hulwan plant, a Japanese firm is building a new plant at al-Dukhayla, near Alexandria (q.v.), and another is projected at Abu-Za'bal, near Cairo (q.v.).

IRRIGATION. Egypt, with the retreat of the glaciers after the last Ice Age, became mainly a desert country unable to support a substantial population without the Nile River (q.v.). Thanks to the annual flood, the Nile is beneficent to human habitation and the cultivation of crops, but only if its waters are harnessed. Egypt receives little or no rainfall, except along portions of the Mediterranean coast, and the Nile has no tributaries that originate within the country. Even before the dynastic period of ancient Egyptian history (3000 BCE), the peoples of Egypt were building basins and channels to utilize the Nile waters. The major method used since antiquity is called basin irrigation (q.v.), a system of water utilization that produces one annual crop. Since the early nineteenth century, however, Egypt's rulers have converted first the Delta and later the middle and upper Nile valley to perennial irrigation (q.v.), a system that produces two or three crops per year, by constructing larger canals, barrages, and dams. But since floods varied, and either a high Nile or a low one could devastate Egypt's harvests, the Egyptian government studied programs that would provide year-long water storage, such as the Century Storage Scheme (q.v.), but ultimately opted for the construction of the Aswan High Dam (q.v.), which was completed in 1971. So great is Egypt's dependence on irrigation that some hydrologists have proposed tapping underground water sources, building large seaside desalinization plants, or opening a channel to conduct seawater from the Mediterranean to one of the inland oases in the Western Desert.

ISKRA. Communist splinter group. Founded in 1943 by Hillel Schwartz, it appealed mainly to wealthy, cosmopolitan Jews. Many of its members were women. It established the House of Scientific Research (*Dar al-Abhath al-Ilmiyya*) as a front organization to acquaint Egyptians with Communist ideas under the guise of scientific and cultural research and discussion. It was closed by Sidqi's (q.v.) government in 1946. Iskra also reached students in Cairo University's (q.v.) Faculties of Law, Medicine, and Science. Some ethnic Egyptian intellectuals such as Anwar Abd al-Malik, Shuhdi Atiya al-Shafi'i, and Sharif Hatata became Marxists through exposure to Iskra. Essentially a marginal group in Egyptian society, it merged in 1947 with the Egyptian Movement for National Liberation (q.v.) to form Hadeto (q.v.).

ISLAM. The religion, now prevalent in Egypt and in many other African and Asian countries, that believes in one all-powerful God who has been revealed through scriptures to a series of prophets ending with Muhammad, to whom the Quran was revealed between 610 and 632. Islam stresses the idea that its believers constitute a single community (Arabic: *umma*) and that their religious solidarity should take precedence over family, tribal, or racial loyalties. Many Muslims, therefore, think that Islamic loyalty should supersede nationalism (*see* Islamism).

AL-ISLAM WA USUL AL-HUKM. Title of a controversial book, written by Ali Abd al-Raziq (q.v.) and published in 1925, arguing that the caliphate (q.v.) is not a necessary institution in Islam (q.v.). The treatise deeply offended many ulama (q.v.) and also King Fuad (q.v.), who was trying to secure international Muslim support to become the new caliph, after the Turkish government of Mustafa Kemal (Atatürk) had abolished the Ottoman caliphate in 1924.

AL-ISLAMBULI, KHALID (1957?-1982). Egyptian army lieutenant convicted of assassinating Sadat (q.v.). Born in Mallawi (near Minya), his father was a legal adviser to the nationalized sugar refinery in Naj' Hammadi. Khalid graduated from the Military Academy (q.v.), and was commissioned in the artillery corps. His immediate motive was to avenge the arrest of his brother, Mahmud, leader of the student *jama'a* (q.v.) at Asyut University in the sweeping round-up of Sadat's opposition in September 1981. He was also inspired by *al-Farida al-ghaiba* by Abd al-Salam Faraj, ideological spokesman for al-Jihad al-Jadid (q.v.), advocating the replacement of the Sadat regime by an Islamic state. Khalid had charge of an armored transport vehicle in the 6 October military parade and managed to replace the soldiers assigned to ride with him by three accomplices and to conceal the grenades and ammunition gathered by his accomplices in his duffel bag, which was not searched. When his vehicle reached the reviewing stand, it stopped, the conspirators pretended to salute Sadat, and then opened fire. As Sadat collapsed, Khalid shouted: "I have killed the Pharaoh!" Although several of the conspirators were killed by Sadat's security forces, Khalid and some of his confederates, although wounded, were eventually able to stand trial. He was one of five (out of the 24) defendants who were sentenced to death. His execution occurred on 15 April 1982.

ISLAMIC ALLIANCE. Coalition of the Muslim Brothers (q.v.) with the Liberal (q.v.) and Socialist Labor (q.v.) parties, formed to run a common slate of candidates in the 1987 elections. It won 60 seats, against 390 for the ruling National Democratic Party (q.v.). The Alliance parties boycotted the 1990 elections, protesting what they felt were unfair electoral laws.

ISLAMIC CONGRESS. Muslim organization founded by Egypt in 1954, joined later by Pakistan and Saudi Arabia, and initially led by Anwar al-Sadat (q.v.). Established in part to compensate for the Nasir (q.v.) government's suppression of the Muslim Brothers (q.v.), it hoped to use the organization to spread Islamic culture, to coordinate the economic policies of the Muslim countries, and to promote administrative and financial reforms. Its first congress was convened in Mecca in 1955. Sadat told an interviewer in 1958 that the regime hoped that the Congress would replace all of Egypt's existing agencies as a religious guide, because it was better attuned to the needs of modern Muslims. The Congress focused special attention on the newly independent Black African countries, and scholarships at Egypt's universities were offered to African Muslim students. Kamal al-Din Husayn replaced Sadat as president of the Islamic Congress in 1961. After convening an international meeting of ulama (q.v.) in 1966, the Congress became dormant. Its relative obscurity, partially due to the establishment of a Muslim League (including Saudi Arabia, Pakistan, and Iran) hostile to Nasir, also reflects the lack of Islamic focus in his political program. It has been superseded by the Organization of the Islamic Conference, founded in 1972 after the Rabat Islamic Summit Conference of September 1969 and three preparatory meetings of foreign ministers from the Muslim countries.

ISLAMIC GROUP, *see* ABD AL-RAHMAN, UMAR; ISLAMISM; JAMA'AT; AL-JIHAD AL-JADID; and AL-TAKFIR WA AL-HIJRA.

ISLAMIC GUIDANCE, SOCIETY OF. Rival organization to the Muslim Brothers (q.v.). Organized by Hafiz Salama, formerly a member of Shabab Muhammad (q.v.), his society set up centers of Quranic teaching at the Martyrs Mosque in Suez and the Nur Mosque in Cairo's (q.v.) Abbasiyya (q.v.) district. The organization openly opposed Sadat's (q.v.) peace policies in the 1970s and agitated strongly in 1985 for the immediate application of the Shari'a (q.v.) to Egypt. The Egyptian government responded by putting all private (*ahli*) mosques under the *awqaf* (q.v.) ministry's supervision, hoping to curb Islamism (q.v.).

ISLAMISM. Preferred term for the ideology, popular among many Muslims in Egypt and other countries, that the Shari'a (q.v.) should be the basis for the government and laws of all Muslim states. This doctrine is often called "Islamic Fundamentalism" in the Western press and even by some Muslims themselves. Islamist groups in Egypt include al-Shubban al-Muslimin (q.v.), the Muslim Brothers (q.v.), Shabab Muhammad (q.v.), the Society of Islamic Guidance (q.v.), al-Jihad al-Jadid (q.v.), al-Takfir wa al-Hijra (q.v.), and other *jama'at* (q.v.). Islamism has always appealed to Egyptian Muslims, but its ideas were eclipsed somewhat by the Westernization policies of Muhammad Ali (q.v.), Isma'il (q.v.), and their successors, and by the Arab socialism (q.v.) of Jamal Abd al-Nasir (q.v.). The revival of this ideology was inspired by the successful Islamic revolution in Iran, the Muslim resistance (in which some Egyptians took part) against the Soviet occupation of Afghanistan, and the formal reestablishment of the Shari'a in the Sudan (q.v.) and Pakistan. In the 1990s Egypt's Islamists have assailed their government for overreliance on U.S. support and failure to meet popular needs. Growing in strength and numbers, they are believed to get training and material support from Iran and the Sudan.

ISMA'IL (1830–95). Modernizing governor, later khedive (q.v.), of Egypt from 1863 to 1879. Born in Cairo (q.v.) and educated at the princes' school founded by his grandfather at Qasr al-Ayni and at France's military academy in St.-Cyr, he then went to Istanbul to serve on the sultan's council. Upon returning to Cairo, he chaired the corresponding council there. Upon succeeding his uncle, Sa'id (q.v.), in 1863, he undertook to modernize Egypt by ordering the construction of factories, irrigation works, and public buildings. Many cultural institutions also began during his reign, including the Cairo Opera House (q.v.), Dar al-Kutub (q.v.), the Geographical Society (q.v.), the Egyptian Museum (q.v.), and various primary, secondary, and higher schools, such as Dar al-Ulum (q.v.). The Suez Canal (q.v.) was completed while he was viceroy. Isma'il established the system of provincial (q.v.) and local administration and convoked the first representative assembly in 1866. Other developments included the organization of the National, Mixed, and Shari'a courts (qq.v.), the creation of a postal service, and the extension of rail and telegraph lines throughout Egypt. He sent explorers to the African interior and armies to conquer most of the Sudan (q.v.).

Isma'il tried to make Egypt more independent of the Ottoman Empire (q.v.), obtaining the title of *khedive*, the authority to pass down his khedivate to his eldest son, and the right to contract loans without obtaining prior permission from the sultan. His industrial, military, and construction projects proved expensive, and he also sponsored many other extravagant schemes having no long-term value to Egypt, such as his many palaces and expensive luxuries that he purchased for his wives and mistresses. Initially he financed his reforms by revenues from the expanded production of Egyptian cotton (q.v.), demand for which soared during the American Civil War, but when textile manufacturers were able to buy cotton from other sources, Isma'il resorted to higher taxes and loans obtained from European bankers on ever less favorable terms. Increasingly hard-pressed to repay them, he resorted to unorthodox fiscal measures such as the 1871 Muqabala (q.v.), the sale of the Egyptian government's shares in the Suez Canal Company (q.v.), and finally accepting European financial control through the Caisse de la Dette Publique (q.v.). In 1878, after a low Nile, poor harvests, and rising military outlays, he surrendered much of his authority to a "European cabinet," headed by Nubar (q.v.) with English and French ministers. In March 1879 a riot by officers who had been put on half-pay led to the resignation of the European cabinet and its replacement by one headed by Sharif (q.v.). The European bondholders and their governments suspected that Isma'il had engineered the uprising to regain his absolute rule. In June their envoys in Istanbul called on Sultan Abdulhamid II to dismiss Isma'il in favor of his son, Tawfiq (q.v.). Isma'il left Egypt and lived out his years in Naples. A willful and visionary man, ambitious for Egypt's development and his own aggrandizement, his achievements were eclipsed by his fiscal mismanagement, which led to Egypt's subjection to Britain.

ISMAILIA. Egyptian city that has contained the headquarters of the Suez Canal Company (q.v.) until the latter was nationalized in 1956 and, since then, of the Suez Canal Authority. The Society of Muslim Brothers (q.v.) was founded there, and it was the site of several meetings between Sadat (q.v.) and other national leaders.

ITALIANS. Italians were, after the Greeks (q.v.), Egypt's second-largest ethnic minority. Italian immigrants came in the nineteenth century for mainly political reasons and tended to be army officers, professionals, and technicians. Italians staffed a silk factory under Muhammad Ali (q.v.), who also was attended by Italian physicians. Others came to be closely associated with the khedivial family and held many high posts in Egypt's government. Later immigration comprised merchants, artisans, and unskilled workers, most notably in construction. During the British occupation (q.v.), the Italian presence in the Egyptian government declined, but they remained important in retail commerce, skilled trades, and nascent industries. Their numbers peaked in the 1927 census at 51,175, concentrated mainly in Cairo (q.v.), Alexandria (q.v.), and Port Said (q.v.). Their communal organization was less close-knit than the

Greeks'; with the rise of fascism they came under intense Italian government supervision, and many were expelled in 1940. Most have left the country since the 1952 Revolution (q.v.).

ITTIHAD PARTY. The organization set up in January 1925 by followers of King Fuad (q.v.) to counter the influence of the Wafd (q.v.). Its chief organizer, Hasan Nashat, was a wily and ambitious operator, whom the British later pressured the king to send abroad as Egypt's ambassador to Spain and later to England. This "palace party" formed a coalition government with the Constitutional Liberals (q.v.) but did not win seats in the 1926 Parliamentary elections. Its first president was Yahya Ibrahim (q.v.), with Ali Mahir (q.v.) as vice president; it had an administrative board and an executive committee. Its program resembled that of the Constitutional Liberals, with whom it competed for members among the landowning notables. It merged with the Sha'b Party (q.v.) in 1938 and the combined group remained in existence as late as the 4 February Incident (q.v.) but never gained any popular support.

- J -

AL-JABARTI, ABD AL-RAHMAN (1754–1822). Historian, biographer, and chronicler of events in Egypt in the late-eighteenth and early nineteenth centuries. Born in Cairo (q.v.) and educated at al-Azhar (q.v.), he served as a clerk in Napoléon's (q.v.) council during the French occupation (q.v.). During the reign of Muhammad Ali (q.v.), he became the chief Hanafi mufti ("jurisconsult"). When one of his sons was killed, he became blind from crying, and soon afterward was himself executed by hanging. His best-known work is a chronicle of events from AH 1100 to 1236 (1685–1821), called *Ajaib al-athar fi al-tarajim wa al-akhbar* ("Amazing Records from Biographies and History"), parts of which have been translated into English.

JALLABIYYA. The standard, gownlike garment worn by male Egyptian peasants and laborers. The Nasir (q.v.) government tried to discourage its use in factories for safety reasons and perhaps because it was viewed as "backward," but it remains popular because it is inexpensive, modest, and comfortable in a hot climate. Islamists (q.v.) have tried to persuade men to readopt it, just as they have called for the reveiling of women.

JAMA'AT. Generic term for Islamist (q.v.) societies formed under Sadat (q.v.), initially in 1972 with his blessing in order to combat communist (q.v.) and Nasirist (q.v.) groups, especially in the national universities.

The leading *jama'at*, such as al-Takfir wa al-Hijra (q.v.), attacked his regime for what they viewed as his secularizing tendencies, failure to address Egypt's social problems, and movement toward peace with Israel. Increasingly popular among young, urban Muslims of all classes, they often provide to poor people better social and medical services than what the government provides, notably during the 1992 earthquake (q.v.). They dissociate themselves from the revived Muslim Brothers (q.v.), to which most are hostile. One of these societies kidnapped and murdered Sadat's former minister of *awqaf* (q.v.) in July 1977. Another, al-Jihad al-Jadid (q.v.), was implicated in Sadat's assassination in October 1981. A related group, al-Jama'a al-Islamiyya ("Islamic Group"), has killed security officials and made attempts on the lives of high officials, Copts (q.v.), and even foreign tourists, hoping to discredit and overthrow Mubarak's (q.v.) regime during 1992–94. In response, the government has jailed many members of the *jama'at* and even sentenced some to death, making strenuous (but largely unsuccessful) efforts to limit the appeal of these revolutionary societies.

AL-JAMASI, MUHAMMAD ABD AL-GHANI (1921-). Army general and government official. Born in al-Batanun (Minufiyya), he was educated at the Military Academy (q.v.), Staff College, and Nasir (q.v.) High Military Academy. He held a series of staff positions in the 1950s and took charge of the Armor School in 1961–66. At the time of the June 1967 War (q.v.) he was chief of the Army Operational Branch. He then rose through the ranks from chief of staff for the Eastern Military Zone, to deputy director of the Reconnaissance and Intelligence Department from 1968 to 1970, to commander of the Egyptian operational group on the Syrian front in 1970–71, to chief of the Armed Forces Training Department in 1971–72, to chief of the Operations Department and deputy chief-of-staff of the Egyptian Armed Forces in 1972–73, finally becoming chief-of-staff in 1973–74. From 1974 to 1978 Jamasi was minister of war and war production and also commander-in-chief of the armed forces, also becoming a deputy prime minister in 1975. In 1978 he became military adviser to President Sadat (q.v.) and then left public life. His memoirs, *Mudhakkirat al-Jamasi* (1990), have been translated into English as *The October War: Memoirs of Field Marshall El-Gamasy of Egypt.*

***AL-JARIDA*.** Daily newspaper founded in 1907 by the Umma Party (q.v.) and edited by Ahmad Lutfi al-Sayyid (q.v.) until 1914. A pioneer in literary criticism, feminism (q.v.), and social reform, *al-Jarida* included among its contributors Muhammad Husayn Haykal (q.v.), Malak Hifni Nasif (q.v.), and Taha Husayn (q.v.). It was read by many Egyptian intellectuals. Less popular than *al-Liwa* (q.v.), this journal tried to articulate purely Egyptian interests, independent of British, Ottoman, or khedivial influences. Its editorial offices were frequented by students in the government Law School (q.v.) and the Egyptian University (q.v.). It closed in 1915 because of wartime censorship.

JAWISH, ABD AL-AZIZ (1872–1929). Journalist and educator. Born in Alexandria (q.v.) to a Tunisian father and a Turkish mother, he attended al-Azhar (q.v.) and later Borough Road Teacher's Training College in London. Upon returning to Egypt, he worked as an inspector for the education ministry, but resigned in 1908 to become editor of the National Party (q.v.) daily newspaper, *al-Liwa* (q.v.). He soon became famous for his attacks on British administration and also on the Coptic editors of a rival newspaper, *al-Watan*, causing many Egyptians and foreigners to assume that he was hostile to Copts (q.v.) generally. He was tried four times for his anti-British articles, served two prison sentences, and eventually went into exile. He served as editor of the Arabic-language publications of the Committee of Union and Progress in Istanbul and during World War I (q.v.) of *Die islamische Welt* and *al-Alam al-islami*, published in Berlin by the German Foreign Office. After the war Jawish worked for Mustafa Kemal (Atatürk) but broke with him on the abolition of the caliphate (q.v.) and returned to Cairo in 1924, where he resumed work in the education ministry. He was elected vice president of Jam'iyyat al-Shubban al-Muslimin (q.v.). Admired by young Egyptians as a speaker and writer, his bombastic style alienated more conservative supporters of the National Party.

JEEP CASE. Trial of Muslim Brothers (q.v.) who were officers in the Egyptian army. The incident takes its name from the discovery in November 1948 of an army jeep filled with papers that provided the first proof that the brothers had a secret apparatus using terrorism to undermine public order, giving the government grounds to dissolve the Society on 6 December 1948. The trial of the arrested brothers was delayed for two years; some of the evidence proved to be tainted, and half of the defendants were acquitted.

JESUITS. Roman Catholic missionaries who established influential schools in Egypt, such as the Collège de la Sainte Famille in Cairo's (q.v.) Fajjala district. Its graduates included conservative politician Ahmad Ziwar (q.v.) and a Jewish Communist (q.v.), Henri Curiel.

JEWS. Egypt has had a significant Jewish community since antiquity. In early Islamic, Mamluk (q.v.), and Ottoman (q.v.) times, Jews played a major role in the economic life of the country. Egyptian Jewry was not a unified community, but included Karaite as well as rabbinic Jews, who in turn were divided between Ashkenazim (Jews of East European origin), Sephardim (Jews of Spanish and Portuguese origin), North Africans, and Egyptians. Their communal leadership was, however, mostly Sephardic. During the nineteenth century many Jews migrated into Egypt from other parts of the Ottoman Empire (q.v.), North Africa, Italy, and Eastern Europe, usually for economic reasons but sometimes to escape persecution, for the general policy of Egypt's rulers was to tolerate and encourage the Jewish *millet* (q.v.). Jewish immigrants, both Sephardi and Ashkenazi, settled in Cairo (q.v.), Tanta, and the new cities along the Suez Canal (q.v.). Their overall number rose from 25,000 in 1897 to more than 60,000 in 1919.

During World War I (q.v.) more than 10,000 Jews, mainly of East European background and strongly Zionist (q.v.) in orientation, took temporary refuge in Egypt from Palestine. Egyptian Jews gradually grew more Westernized, often adopting Italian and later French as their lingua franca. They had their own schools, charities, hospitals, clubs, sports teams, newspapers, and political organizations. Although most Jews supported the British occupation (q.v.), a few worked for closer relations with the Wafd (q.v.) and other secular nationalist movements. Very few contemplated going to Palestine, but many were interested in the work of the Zionist settlers there. Jews played a major role in such professions as medicine, in banking, in retail sales, and in the marketing of Egyptian cotton (q.v.). Most regarded Egypt as their permanent home, although up to the 1940s many claimed a foreign nationality to enjoy protection under the Capitulations (q.v.). There was always at least one Jew in the Senate, and one community leader was finance minister in the 1920s (his wife was a lady-in-waiting to Queen Nazli). The richer and more educated Jews were, like the Copts (q.v.), active in their Community Council (*majlis milli*), as opposed to the rabbinate. Egyptian Jews also led boycotts against Nazi Germany, opposed fascism, and helped launch the nascent Communist (q.v.) movement.

The rise of political Zionism and the State of Israel eroded the Jews' secure position in Egypt, especially during and after the 1936–39 Palestinian Arab revolution, which made Egyptians more aware of Zionism. Although the Egyptian government continued to protect the Jews, generalized attacks against them appeared in nationalist newspapers and in speeches of some of the leaders of Misr al-Fatat (q.v.) and the Muslim Brothers (q.v.). Unscrupulous leaders stirred up urban mobs against both Christians and Jews after World War II (q.v.), especially during the Palestine War (q.v.), even though Egypt's Jewish leaders repeatedly denied any support for Zionism. Between 1948 and 1956, most Jews tried to remain in Egypt, but rising nationalism threatened the autonomy of their schools and other institutions, undermined their business firms, and hampered their role in the professions. The 1956 Suez War (q.v.) led to a general policy of repression against Jews, and the vast majority of the community left Egypt, many for France or Canada, others for Israel. Those who remained faced further discrimination under Nasir (q.v.) and were interned in concentration camps during and after the June War (q.v.). Since Sadat's (q.v.) peace initiative, conditions have ameliorated for Egypt's Jews, but most of those who remain are elderly and politically passive. Barring some new Jewish influx, the community in Egypt will soon vanish, an unwilling victim of Israel's victories.

JIHAD. Although the word literally means "struggle" in the sense of defending Islam (q.v.) against attackers, to both Muslims and non-Muslims it now connotes "holy war" by Muslims against unbelievers or even all non-Muslims. Egypt's Muslim *jama'at* (q.v.) have stressed this militant aspect of jihad, which some Muslims regard as the sixth pillar of Islam.

AL-JIHAD AL-JADID. Islamist (q.v.) revolutionary group (*see jama'at*) credited with plotting the assassination of Sadat (q.v.) in 1981. It had strong support among Muslim students coming from Upper Egypt, such as the brother of the leading assassin, Khalid al-Islambuli (q.v.). Following the assassination, members of the group seized control of Asyut (q.v.) for four days. Most of its leaders were arrested and tried during 1982, some were executed, and many received long prison terms. Its ideology is expressed in *al-Farida al-ghaiba* (translated into English as *The Hidden Imperative*), written by Abd al-Salam Faraj, who was executed with Islambuli. An offshoot of *al-Jihad*, commonly called "the Islamic Group," has been linked to the bombing of the World Trade Center in New York and to miscellaneous bombing incidents in Egypt in 1993–94.

JOINT NOTE (1882). Letter written by the French and British foreign ministers to the Egyptian government in January 1882, upholding the authority of Khedive Tawfiq (qq.v.) against Urabi's (q.v.) followers and implicitly threatening military intervention. The note strengthened the extremists within the National Party (q.v.) against the moderates and the khedive (q.v.), however, because the Egyptians did not believe that France and Britain would actually intervene.

JULY LAWS (1961). Nasir's (q.v.) decrees instituting Arab socialism (q.v.) and nationalizing many Egyptian firms. Actually, these "laws" were one step in a larger process by which the Egyptian government took control of the country's major economic assets, starting with the Suez Canal Company (q.v.), British-, French-, and Jewish-owned firms that

Nasir nationalized after the Suez War (q.v.), Bank Misr (q.v.) and the National Bank of Egypt (q.v.) in 1960, and Belgian-owned firms nationalized during the 1960–61 Congo crisis. Under the July Laws, technically Laws 117–119 for 1961, the state nationalized all remaining banks and insurance companies, 50 shipping companies and firms in heavy and basic industries, obliged 83 other companies to sell at least 50 percent of their shares to public agencies, and stipulated in the case of 147 medium-sized companies that the state would acquire all shares in excess of a limit of £E10,000 in shares per shareholder. Additional laws nationalized privately owned utilities, all foreign trade, and the Alexandria cotton exchange. It is estimated that Egypt acquired £E124 million in assets as a result of these acts. In 1963–64, privately owned shares of the affected companies were nationalized, and in addition pharmaceutical companies and large construction firms were also brought under state ownership. Law 127 (1961) lowered the limit on individual landownership to 100 feddans (q.v.), or 300 per family. Other properties belonging to "reactionary capitalists" were placed under sequestration. These laws also attempted to remove gross disparities in income distribution. All gross incomes exceeding £E10,000 per year were to be taxed at 90 percent, and owners of sequestered property received no compensation beyond £E5,000 annually for a "living allowance" and £E15,000 in compensation for seized property. The July Laws turned many Syrian capitalists against the United Arab Republic (q.v.), probably causing Syria's secession in September 1961. For Egypt, they strengthened state power against the landed aristocracy and industrial bourgeoisie.

JUM'A, SHA'RAWI (1920-). Arab Socialist Union (q.v.) leader and interior minister, widely regarded as Nasir's (q.v.) most influential companion in his last years. He was a leading member of the faction favorable to Ali Sabri (q.v.) and one of the leaders purged by Sadat (q.v.) in his 1971 Corrective Revolution (q.v.). Tried for conspiracy and sentenced to life imprisonment, he was released in 1976 for health reasons.

***AL-JUMHURIYYA*.** Government-owned daily newspaper set up by the Revolutionary Command Council (q.v.) after the 1952 Revolution (q.v.). Its first editor was Anwar al-Sadat (q.v.). Usually leaning to the left, it has rarely competed successfully against *al-Ahram* (q.v.) or *al-Akhbar* (q.v.). Its estimated circulation in 1972 was 80,000; in 1993 it reached 650,000.

JUNE WAR (1967). Conflict in which Israel inflicted a major defeat against Egypt, taking the Gaza Strip (q.v.) and the Sinai Peninsula (q.v.), as well as against Jordan and Syria. The war took most experts by surprise, because Israel was in an economic recession and Egypt's best troops were committed to the Yemen Civil War (q.v.). Its root causes included the rise of the Palestine Liberation Organization (q.v.) and especially of its *fidaiyin* (q.v.) raids, which caused Israeli retaliation against their bases in Jordan; the mounting conflict over the utilization of the waters of the Jordan River and its tributaries; and the Egyptian-Syrian Joint Defense Agreement (q.v.). More immediate causes were a dogfight between Syrian and Israel aircraft in April 1967 and the subsequent report by Soviet intelligence that Israel was massing troops on the Syrian border. Accused by other Arab governments of "hiding behind the UN's skirts," Nasir (q.v.) ordered the withdrawal of the United Nations Emergency Force (q.v.) that had been posted in the Sinai Peninsula and the Gaza Strip since the Suez War (q.v.). Secretary General U Thant promptly complied, and Nasir proceeded to move large numbers of troops through Cairo (q.v.) and into the Sinai, as his newspapers, radio, and television threatened the infliction of immense losses on Israel if it attacked Egypt or Syria. Egypt raised the stakes on 21 May by closing the Straits of Tiran (q.v.) and proclaiming a blockade against Israeli shipping in the Gulf of Aqaba (q.v.). Some writers, notably Muhammad Hasanayn Haykal (q.v.), argue that Israel was laying a trap for Egypt, but most accounts stress the incautious threats made by Egypt and other Arab governments against Israel. On 30 May Egypt and Jordan settled their long-standing differences with a military pact that effectively placed Jordan's army under Egyptian command. Israel, unable to obtain what it viewed as adequate backing from the United States and other Western nations, mobilized its armed forces, prepared for all-out war, and formed a "wall-to-wall" coalition cabinet that included Moshe Dayan as defense minister.

On 5 June Israel launched a preemptive attack against the air bases of Egypt, Jordan, Syria, and Iraq, catching them off-guard and destroying most of their fighter planes. Without air support, the Arab armies were easily defeated on the ground; Egypt's forces were driven from the Sinai within 72 hours. The Egyptian public, having been told by the state broadcasting and print media that its forces were winning the war, was shocked when it learned that they had been defeated, although official sources blamed this defeat on clandestine U.S. military aid to Israel. In a nationally televised speech on 9 June, Nasir took full responsibility for Egypt's humiliating setback and offered to resign. Mass demonstrations ensued throughout Egypt, pleading with him to retain the presidency. After 24 hours, he relented.

Egypt suffered severe military and economic losses as a result of the June War; these included 356 of its 431 fighter aircraft, about 700 of its 1,300 tanks, and some 3,000 men killed, 5,000 wounded, and 4,980 prisoners or missing. Although the USSR quickly replaced equipment lost in the war, it took direct charge of Egypt's military reconstruction. The oil-exporting Arab countries pressed Egypt to withdraw from Yemen and later to modify its economic policies. The Khartum summit (q.v.) ruled out negotiations with Israel, but Egypt later accepted UN Security Council Resolution 242 (q.v.) as a basis to end the conflict.

- K -

KAFR AL-DAWWAR INCIDENT. Suppression by the Egyptian army just after the 1952 Revolution (q.v.) of a workers' uprising at a textile manufacturing center 25 km south of Alexandria (q.v.) in August 1952. The mill was owned by Bank Misr (q.v.), its director had been closely connected with King Faruq (q.v.), and workers' efforts to unionize had been stymied. The workers at the Dyers Company struck on 9 August, declaring their support for Muhammad Najib (q.v.) and asking for the right to form a union. The workers' demands were met. The workers at the other Misr factories in Kafr al-Dawwar then struck, too, locking themselves into their factories, and some suspicious fires started. Soldiers were dispatched from Alexandria, unknown snipers shot at them, and the army returned fire. Two soldiers, a policeman, and four workers were killed and many others were wounded. The army arrested 545 workers, court-martialed some of them hastily, and eventually executed two of the convicted ringleaders. Left-wing sources questioned the fairness of the proceedings and aver that the management started both the fires and the firing. The incident underscored the determination of the Revolutionary Command Council (q.v.) to oppose any workers' efforts at unionization and to combat any labor groups associated with Communism (q.v.).

KAMIL, MUSTAFA (1874–1908). Nationalist leader, orator, and editor. The son of an army officer from an ethnic Egyptian family, Mustafa Kamil was educated in government schools, the French Law School (q.v.), and the University of Toulouse, where he received his law degree in 1894. An ardent opponent of the British occupation (q.v.), he drew close to Khedive Abbas Hilmi II (qq.v.) and Sultan Abdulhamid II, both of whom supported him materially as well as morally in his campaigns to persuade European governments and peoples to demand the evacuation of Egypt promised by successive British governments. Together with Muhammad Farid (q.v.), Ahmad Lutfi al-Sayyid (q.v.), and other Egyptians, he formed a secret society called the "Society for the Revival of the Nation," initially under the aegis of the khedive. The society soon became known as the National Party (q.v.), for which Mustafa founded a daily Arabic newspaper, *al-Liwa* (q.v.), and a boys' school that bore his own name. As the likelihood of

French support waned after the Fashoda Incident (q.v.), he gradually distanced himself from Abbas, publicly breaking with him in 1904. He continued to court the support of the Ottoman Empire (q.v.) and to promote pan-Islam (q.v.), but he also hailed Japan's rising power in a book called *al-Shams al-mushriqa* ("The Rising Sun"). He backed Ottoman claims to part of the Sinai Peninsula (q.v.) during the 1906 Taba Incident (q.v.) and condemned the atrocities of British rule in Egypt following that year's Dinshaway Incident (q.v.). In October 1906 he became reconciled with the khedive, who offered him financial assistance to found *The Egyptian Standard* and *L'Étendard égyptien* as Nationalist dailies to influence European opinion. In December 1907 he formally established the National Party, which elected him as its first president. Stricken with tuberculosis (although some people thought that he was poisoned), he took to his bed and died on 10 February 1908. His funeral occasioned a massive demonstration of popular grief. Mustafa Kamil is remembered as a fervent patriot, demanding the British evacuation of Egypt and constitutional government, and as an occasional supporter of the Ottoman Empire and pan-Islam. A museum bearing his name, near the Cairo Citadel (q.v.), memorializes his contribution to the Egyptian nationalist movement and contains his tomb, together with those of Muhammad Farid (q.v.) and Abd al-Rahman al-Rafi'i (q.v.).

KAMSHISH INCIDENT (1986). Murder of a village-level Arab Socialist Union (q.v.) official by a powerful rural landowner. The incident, which raised intense debates in the National Assembly, pitted socialists who resented the local power retained by "feudalists" (large landowners) against those who opposed the high-handed activities of the Committee for the Liquidation of Feudalism, which was chaired by Abd al-Hakim Amir (q.v.), himself a landowner. The debate, which took place in May 1966, marked the apogee for Arab socialism (q.v.) in Egypt.

KHALIL, MUSTAFA (1920-). Egypt's prime minister from 1978 to 1980. He graduated from Cairo University's (q.v.) Faculty of Engineering and received a doctorate in 1951 from the University of Illinois. He was Nasir's (q.v.) minister of communications and housing from 1956 to 1965 and of industry and energy from 1965 to 1966, also serving as deputy prime minister in 1964. Opposed to the leftward drift of the Egyptian government, he resigned in 1966 and did not return to political life until after Sadat's (q.v.) Corrective Revolution (q.v.) of May 1971. He became the last secretary-general of the Arab Socialist Union (q.v.) in 1976 and presided over its division into three *manabir* ("pulpits," or "platforms") that evolved into separate political parties in 1978. He accompanied Sadat to Jerusalem in 1977 and took part in the negotiations with Israel. In addition to being premier from October 1978 to May 1980, he served as foreign minister from May 1979. When Sadat assumed the premiership in 1980, Khalil became deputy chairman of his National Democratic Party (q.v.). Although less influential under Mubarak (q.v.) than under Sadat, he retains his party post, is a respected member of the president's inner circle, and maintains relations with Israeli leaders. He serves on the Board of Trustees of the American University in Cairo (q.v.) and chairs the board of the Arab International Bank.

KHARTUM SUMMIT MEETING (1967). Conference of Arab heads of state held on 31 August and 1 September 1967, eventuating in a declaration rejecting recognition of or peace negotiations with Israel. The meeting also facilitated the reconciliation between Nasir (q.v.) and Saudi King Faysal, ending the Yemen Civil War (q.v.) and ensuring that the oil-rich Arab countries would aid Egypt and other states that were directly confronting Israel.

KHEDIVE. French rendition of a Turkish title, taken from a Persian word meaning "little lord," used by Egypt's viceroys from 1867 to 1914. Although the khedive was legally the viceroy for the sultan of the Ottoman Empire (q.v.) and was appointed and dismissed by an imperial *firman* (q.v.), he actually exercised some sovereign powers, including the appointment of his council of ministers (q.v.), the rector of al-Azhar (q.v.), and high-ranking military and naval officers. He could sign treaties with foreign powers and borrow money for the state treasury. The succession to the khedivate went to the eldest son rather than the senior male relative as in other Muslim states. The khedive also administered (and allegedly misappropriated) *waqf* (q.v.) monies up to 1913. After 1882 the khedive's exercise of power was limited by the advice of Britain's agent and consul-general in Egypt.

KHEDIVIAL MAIL LINE. Egypt's passenger and mercantile shipping firm, founded by Bank Misr (q.v.) under the aegis of the Misr Maritime Navigation Company in 1934. It used to play an important role in transporting Muslim pilgrims to the Hijaz (q.v.).

KHURSHID, AHMAD. Ottoman (q.v.) official. Appointed mayor of Alexandria (q.v.) immediately after the French evacuated Egypt in 1801, he was named Egypt's governor in 1804 at Muhammad Ali's (q.v.) behest. Allied with Britain's diplomatic representative, he tried to get Muhammad Ali and his Albanians removed from Egypt, bringing in the *Delhi* ("madmen") troops from Syria. Muhammad Ali managed to win the *Delhi*s to his side and, backed by a demonstration of ulama (q.v.) and guild leaders in Cairo (q.v.), had himself named governor of Egypt in May 1805. Abandoned by his troops, Khurshid was besieged in the Cairo Citadel (q.v.), from which he agreed to depart only after he saw the Ottoman decree investing Muhammad Ali as governor of Egypt. His brief rule in Egypt was totally ineffectual.

KHUSREV PASHA. Ottoman (q.v.) official and first governor of Egypt after the expulsion of the French. A singularly incompetent administrator, he commanded a weak Ottoman force that could not compete against the Mamluks (q.v.) or the Albanian troops of Muhammad Ali (q.v.). After he tried to repatriate the latter with false promises to pay them, they deposed him in 1803, igniting a protracted power struggle in Cairo (q.v.).

KILLEARN, ***see*** **LAMPSON, MILES.**

KILOMETER 101 TALKS (1973). Negotiations between Egyptian General Jamasi (q.v.) and Israeli General Aharon Yariv, held in a tent on the road between Cairo and Suez, following the October War (q.v.), the first publicly known talks between an Israeli and an Arab officer since 1949. Their purposes were to implement the cease-fire called for in Security Council Resolution 338 (q.v.), to return to the positions each side had occupied on 22 October, to ensure that food, water, and medicine could cross Israeli lines to the town of Suez, to end the Israeli blockade of nonmilitary supplies to the Egyptian Third Army entrapped on the Suez Canal's (q.v.) east bank, to replace Israeli checkpoints on the Cairo-Suez road with United Nations (q.v.) ones, and to exchange prisoners of war. The talks reportedly broke down because of differences between the official positions of Israel, which demanded a return to the prewar lines, and of Egypt, which wanted the Israelis to give up nearly half the Sinai (q.v.). In fact, the negotiating generals were close to an agreement. Some Israelis allege that U.S. Secretary of State Kissinger sabotaged it because he wanted to mediate any talks between the two sides, as he would later do in the first Separation of Forces (q.v.) Agreement in January 1974. Indeed, its technical details were worked out by the Egyptian and Israeli generals at precisely the same spot as before.

KITCHENER, [HORATIO] HERBERT (1850–1916). British general, colonial administrator, and agent and consul general in Egypt from 1911 to 1914. Born to an Anglo-Irish landowning family, he studied in Switzerland and at the Royal Military Academy in Woolwich. Commissioned into the Royal Engineers in 1871, he conducted land surveys in Palestine, Cyprus, and the Sinai from 1874 to 1883. He then joined the Egyptian army and took part in the unsuccessful Gordon (q.v.)

rescue mission in 1884–85. He served in Zanzibar and the Eastern Sudan (q.v.) before becoming adjutant general to the Egyptian army in 1888. Soon after his accession, Khedive Abbas Hilmi II (qq.v.) chose Kitchener, with the concurrence of the British government, to become commander-in-chief of the Egyptian army, but their relations soured due to the 1894 Frontiers Incident (q.v.). He brilliantly organized and led the Anglo-Egyptian campaign to regain the Sudan from the Mahdi's (q.v.) successors in 1896–98 and repulsed France's effort to gain control of the Nile (q.v.) headwaters at Fashoda (q.v.).

Kitchener played a major role in Britain's victory over the Boers in South Africa in 1899–1902, then became commander of the Indian army. After Gorst's (q.v.) death, Kitchener was sent to Egypt by the Liberal cabinet to keep the country quiet and to improve its economic condition. While serving as Britain's chief diplomatic representative and de facto colonial administrator, he subdued the Nationalists, improved the irrigation system, persuaded the Egyptian government to pass the Five Feddan Law (q.v.), established the agriculture ministry, and revised the Organic Law (q.v.). He pressured National Party (q.v.) leaders to go into exile and banned most of their newspapers. Twice he narrowly escaped assassination. He kept Egypt out of the Ottoman Empire's (q.v.) wars in Libya (q.v.) and the Balkans. His relations with Abbas deteriorated to the point where he was thinking of deposing him just prior to the outbreak of World War I (q.v.). At that time, Kitchener was importuned by Prime Minister Asquith to enter the cabinet as his war minister. Although popular and often perceptive, Kitchener never enjoyed being a wartime mobilizer in London as much as he had cared about managing Egypt, to which he always hoped someday to return.

KLÉBER, JEAN-BAPTISTE (1753–1800). General in Napoléon's (q.v.) army and his successor as commander of the French forces in Egypt. The son of a Strasbourg mason, he joined the Bavarian army in 1777 but returned to Alsace in 1785 to become an inspector of public buildings. He joined the local national guard in 1789 and saw action in the struggle for Mainz in 1793. For distinguished service against the Vendée rebels, he was promoted to the rank of general and took part in the French occupation of the Rhineland. Napoléon invited him to command a division in his Army of Egypt, where he saw action in most of the major battles against the Ottoman Empire (q.v.). When Napoléon returned to France in 1799, Kléber took over his command. Early in 1800 he signed the abortive Convention of al-Arish (q.v.). He successfully secured Cairo (q.v.) from an Ottoman attack by winning the Battle of Heliopolis (q.v.). Shortly afterward, he was stabbed to death at his Cairo headquarters. He was a soldier's soldier, lacking in charisma and self-confidence, but intelligent and capable.

KÜTAHYA, CONVENTION OF (1833). Treaty ending Ibrahim's (q.v.) first campaign against the Ottoman Empire (q.v.), confirming Egypt's control over geographic Syria, Adana, and the Hijaz (q.v.). Only military and naval intervention by Russia, which became the Ottomans' main protector, kept Egypt from taking more of Anatolia.

KUTTAB. Muslim elementary school, usually located near or in a mosque and supported by a waqf (q.v.), stressing Quran recitation and memorization. Traditionally, attendance was limited to boys, although Islam (q.v.) does not oppose women's education, and a few girls were admitted to *kuttab*s or were tutored at home. The *kuttab* teacher was called a *fiqi* (Egyptian colloquial Arabic for the classical word *faqih*, meaning "legal expert"); he would sometimes be assisted by an *arif*. Up to the reign of Muhammad Ali (q.v.), the *kuttab* was the main means of primary education in Egypt, but in the nineteenth century the Egyptian government began to set up competing secular schools that prepared pupils for the new professional schools. Under the educational reforms passed in 1867, the *kuttab*s were subject to government inspection. Starting in 1907, they were integrated into the state-controlled educational system.

- L -

LABOR LEGISLATION. Government regulation of working conditions began late in Egypt, partly because so many business firms were controlled by foreign nationals protected from Egyptian legislation by the Capitulations (q.v.). Licensing of factories did not begin until 1904, and five years later employment of children under nine years old in cotton ginning, tobacco, and textile factories was banned, a prohibition extended to 20 other industries in 1931. A statutory limit of nine hours per day was applied to women workers in 1933 and men in 1935, although they were permitted two additional hours of overtime. Enforcement of these rules was lax. No legal liability for industrial accidents existed until 1936, no compulsory insurance until 1942, and no required contracts for workers until 1944. Unions (q.v.) were officially recognized only in 1942. A 1948 law set up an arbitration procedure for labor disputes, and in 1950 collective agreements between employers and labor unions were regulated. The 1952 Revolution (q.v.) had no immediate effect on workers, except that the government banned strikes after the Kafr al-Dawwar Incident (q.v.) and unions were soon placed under state control.

Nasir (q.v.) often spoke out for the welfare of workers and committed his government to bettering their conditions. Public Law 91 of 1959 recodified all existing labor legislation. It fixed maximum work hours for adults and juveniles; raised sick pay, indemnities for termination of employment, and the length of paid vacations; banned child labor; and set minimum wages. Public Law 92 extended insurance to employees of all industrial firms in Egypt. The July Laws (q.v.) increased workers' rights, including profit-sharing and compulsory social insurance. New legislation in 1971 and 1972 further extended paid vacations and limited workweeks, but restricted sick leaves. The minimum wage was applied to private employers. The government also committed itself to find employment for all secondary school and university graduates, accelerating the growth of the bureaucracy (q.v.). The enforcement of labor laws was weakened by the *infitah* (q.v.), but Egyptian wages and working conditions have recently improved because of competition for skilled labor from other, more munificent, Arab countries.

LAMPSON, MILES WEDDERBURN, FIRST BARON KILLEARN (1880–1964). British diplomat. Originally from Killearn (Stirlingshire) and educated at Eton, he entered the Foreign Office, serving in Japan and China and then briefly in Siberia after World War I (q.v.). He went to the Washington Naval Conference, headed the Foreign Office's Central European department, and was Britain's minister to Peking from 1926 to 1933. Lampson was appointed high commissioner for Egypt and the Sudan (q.v.) in December 1933. His early diplomatic achievement was the signing of the 1936 Anglo-Egyptian Treaty (q.v.), after which his title changed to ambassador. His firm stance ensured that Egypt would remain a base for Britain's Eighth Army and Mediterranean Fleet during World War II (q.v.), although Egypt remained a nonbelligerent for most of the war. Suspecting King Faruq (q.v.) and his advisers of favoring the Axis Powers, Lampson precipitated the 4 February 1942 Incident (q.v.), forcing the king to accept a Wafdist (q.v.) cabinet to carry out the 1936 Treaty. Although Lampson's behavior has often been assailed, especially by Egyptians, others argue that the British Empire could not have survived World War II without firm action in Egypt before its victory at al-Alamayn (q.v.). He was elevated to the peerage as Baron Killearn in 1943. As Egyptian agitation grew for the British evacuation (q.v.) after the war, the Labour government removed him from Cairo (q.v.), naming him high commissioner for Southeast Asia. Some of his Egyptian diaries were published as *The Killearn Diaries, 1934–46*, parts of which were translated into Arabic and printed in *al-Ahram* (q.v.); the full text can be found at the Middle East Centre, St. Antony's College, Oxford. A tough negotiator, Lampson cared little about rising nationalism in Egypt, where more subtle diplomacy would have averted ill feeling toward Britain.

LAND REFORM. Unequal agricultural land distribution (*see* Landownership) was a major problem for Egypt, but few people, except the Communists (q.v.), proposed reforms until the 1940s. The peasants were proverbially apathetic, all legislative bodies were dominated by landowners, and the royal family owned about one-fifth of all Egypt's arable land. The first public discussion of land redistribution occurred when a Senate member proposed a bill in 1944 to limit agricultural landholdings to 50 feddans (q.v.); the bill was formally rejected in 1945. A few social reformers raised the issue at that time, but the general attitude of the political parties, all of which were led by landowners, remained hostile. Egyptian leaders aware of the problem argued that portions of the state domains should be given to Egypt's landless peasants. Some interest in redistribution was expressed by leaders of the Muslim Brothers (q.v.) and Misr al-Fatat (q.v.), but neither group stressed the issue before the 1952 Revolution (q.v.).

An issue more widely discussed in prerevolutionary Egypt was the abuse of the *waqf ahli* system, which had enabled some landowners to evade Islamic inheritance laws (*see waqf*). Proposals to abolish or modify the system were first made in 1927, revived in 1936, and finally passed in a 1946 act that restricted the right of property owners to set up new *awqaf* by bequest, but existing ones were not abolished. The party leaders differed on whether the system needed further reforms. Many Muslim modernists perceived the need for *waqf* reform, and fewer leading families viewed such changes as harming their interests.

One of the first major acts of the 1952 Revolution was to enact major land reform legislation, nationalizing all lands held by the deposed King Faruq (q.v.) and his relatives and limiting the total amount of agricultural land that could be owned by an individual to 200 feddans (with an additional 100 for each dependent). The *waqf ahli* system was abolished five days later. Motives for these measures include the non-landowner origins of most of the Free Officers (q.v.), the previous system's tendency to impede industrialization by overvaluing land as a store of value, the contribution of the poor health of the landless peasant soldiers to Egypt's defeat in the Palestine War (q.v.), and the need for measures to restore order after the 1951 peasant revolts. In practice, these reforms were less radical than they sounded, because many large landowners were allowed to sell their excess landholdings, usually to peasants who already owned some land, before they could be confiscated by the state. In addition, owners of land that was confiscated were reimbursed with government bonds. The limits were reduced to 100 feddans per individual in 1961 and 50 in 1969. The 1952 Land Reform law led to the redistribution of 365,247 feddans to 146,496 families; later laws brought the total up to almost 800,000 feddans going to 334,727 families. The growth of farm cooperatives (q.v.) helped to maintain high output levels and to spread modern methods of cultivation, but richer peasants still wielded great power, and about 40 percent of the rural population in 1980 owned no land at all.

LANDOWNERSHIP. When Egypt was a part of the Ottoman Empire (q.v.), its lands, except those set aside as *waqf* (q.v.), were theoretically the property of the sultan, who had the authority to delegate its exploitation to his subjects. The peasants were supposed to use the land and to enjoy a portion of its produce, but other shares were to go to their supervisors and tax collectors, who initially were salaried state officials expected to remit all taxes in money or in kind to the imperial treasury. By the eighteenth century, however, tax collectors were frequently assigned portions of land as tax farms (*iltizam*), for which they paid a fixed sum to the Ottoman treasury and were entitled to keep whatever they could collect, an obvious incentive to extortion. Many peasants fled from their farms. Tax payments were often not assessed on households, but rather on villages, imposing hardships on those peasants who continued to cultivate their lands. The tax farmers (*multazim*) were often Mamluks (q.v.), Egypt's military aristocracy; however, some were ulama (q.v.) or wealthy peasants. At times tax farms were converted into hereditary property (*malikane*), and one-fifth of all cultivated land had become Muslim or Coptic *awqaf*.

The French occupation (q.v.) was too brief to affect the land tenure system. However, Muhammad Ali (q.v.) reasserted state control over the land, first by establishing a government monopoly over grain trade in 1808, then by ordering a cadastral survey in 1813–14, and then by abolishing the *iltizam* system. New cadastral surveys in the 1820s increased the state's ability to tax lands and to control their use. At the height of his power, Muhammad Ali enjoyed in fact full rights of ownership over most of Egypt's arable lands. He began to make large land grants to family members, high-ranking army officers, and his most trusted officials. His successors, Ibrahim (q.v.), Abbas (q.v.), Sa'id (q.v.), and Isma'il (q.v.), continued this devolution, creating most of Egypt's landholding aristocracy.

In 1855 Sa'id promulgated a land law that established the rights of private ownership, including inheritance and sale to other subjects or even to foreigners. Some lands were classified as *ushriyya*, subject to an annual tithe; most lands were *kharajiyya*, subject to the higher land tax called the *kharaj*. Peasants could establish ownership rights by cultivating a land parcel for five years and by obtaining a registration certificate from the *mudir* (q.v.). Islamic inheritance laws, which require equal shares to all sons, with half-shares to all daughters, usually fragment landholdings. Many peasants owned parcels that were too small, or too scattered among others' lands, to support a household. By the early twentieth century most of Egypt's arable land was concentrated in the possession of members of the khedivial (later royal) family, or absentee landowners who lived in Cairo (q.v.) or Alexandria (q.v.), or foreign-owned land management companies (whose share of privately owned land peaked at 13.2 percent in 1910). Other lands, usually uncultivated, became part of the state domains. In the early twentieth century, the Egyptian government distributed parts of these domains to graduates of the Agricultural College, but in general private landholdings became ever more concentrated in the royal household and a few wealthy families. Most peasants owned too little land to support their families; tenant farmers or wage laborers predominated in Egypt.

Many articulate Egyptians called for agrarian redistribution, but legislation was impossible as long as the parliament was dominated by large landowners. Soon after the 1952 Revolution (q.v.), the Revolutionary Command Council (q.v.) promulgated its famous land reform (q.v.) that limited the maximum holding to 200 feddans (q.v.) per individual. Strenuous efforts were made by the Nasir (q.v.) government to redistribute large estates to landless peasants, but it was never possible to equalize landholdings or to break completely the power of the large landowners. The trend under Sadat (q.v.) was to restore many of the estates that had been taken from their owners for political reasons. Egypt today remains a country characterized by wide disparities in the quantity and quality of the land owned by its citizens.

LANE, EDWARD WILLIAM (1801–76). British Arabic scholar. Although trained as an engraver, he was fascinated by Egypt and went there in 1825 to explore the country and to write a book on its ancient monuments. He became increasingly interested in the modern inhabitants of the country, settled in Cairo (q.v.) for three years, and wrote a pioneer ethnographic study entitled *An Account of the Manners and Customs of the Modern Egyptians*. He later translated the *Thousand and One Nights* from Arabic into English and compiled an Arabic-English dictionary in eight volumes, a project that he did not live to complete.

LAVON AFFAIR. Israeli political scandal that originated in a botched attempt in 1954 to damage Egypt's relations with the United States by hiring Egyptian Jews to plant explosives in the U.S. Information Agency Library in Cairo. The Jewish agents were arrested, tried, and sentenced to death or imprisonment early in 1955. The sentences were one cause of

Israel's raid on Gaza that February, starting the building of tensions that eventuated in the Suez War (q.v.).

LAW SCHOOL, GOVERNMENT. Main law school in Cairo (q.v.), which has had during its history several names, locations, and affiliations. The parent institutions were the School of Languages and Translation, formed in 1836 by Rifa'a Rafi' al-Tahtawi (q.v.), and the short-lived School of Administration. These institutions lapsed and were revived under Isma'il (q.v.) in 1868, officially becoming the Khedivial School of Law in 1886. Up to 1907 the school stayed under French administration, a redoubt of France's educational influence–and a nationalist hotbed–even as English language instruction came to prevail in the primary and secondary schools. The replacement of its able French director by a mediocre English one became a nationalist and diplomatic cause célèbre, but the school had British directors until 1923, during which time it taught in English, even though Egyptian courts used mainly French and Arabic.

Ali Mahir (q.v.) became its first Egyptian director, the school was assimilated in 1925 into Cairo University (q.v.), and French and Arabic became its languages of instruction. European, especially French, professors dominated the Law Faculty until after World War II (q.v.), although French-trained Egyptians also entered the faculty. The Cairo school also spawned satellite educational institutions in Alexandria (q.v.) in 1938 and in Heliopolis (q.v.), which would later be incorporated respectively into the Universities of Alexandria and Ayn Shams. Following the French system, the social sciences were taught under the aegis of law, and legal studies were highly theoretical. New graduates learned the practical side of the legal profession by working as *stagiaires* in the offices of established attorneys. Students tended to come from upper-class backgrounds, and many had the advantage of graduating from French-language lycées, equipping them better intellectually and linguistically for their studies than graduates of government schools. Law students played a central role in the national movement from the inception of the National Party (q.v.); they organized the first great student strike in 1906, helped to lead the 1919 Revolution (q.v.), and participated in every major demonstration thereafter. Although the 1952 Revolution (q.v.) suspended parliamentary democracy for a while and hence reduced the political role of lawyers, the number of students enrolled in law faculties of Egypt's national universities continued to increase far beyond the market for their services. In modern times Egyptian law graduates, notably Abd al-Razzaq al-Sanhuri (q.v.), have greatly influenced the development of secular law and legal education in other Arab countries.

LEAGUE OF ARAB STATES, *see* ARAB LEAGUE.

LEGISLATIVE ASSEMBLY. Legislature set up under the 1913 Organic Law (q.v.). During its brief existence in 1914, its elected vice president, Sa'd Zaghlul (q.v.), emerged as a leading critic of the Egyptian government, a portent of his role in the 1919 Revolution (q.v.).

LESSEPS, FERDINAND DE (1805-94). French diplomat and entrepreneur, the creator of the Suez Canal (q.v.). Born in Versailles, the son of a French consul who had earlier served in Egypt, he was reared in Pisa and Paris and educated at the Lycée Napoléon (Collège Henri IV). After briefly studying law, he took a job in the army commissariat and then became an apprentice consul, working for his uncle in Lisbon and later with his father in Tunis. In 1832 he was appointed vice-consul in Alexandria (q.v.), where he got to know most of the leading European and Muslim inhabitants, learned Arabic, and explored the countryside on horseback. During this time he met Prince Sa'id (q.v.), then an adolescent under strict orders from his father, Muhammad Ali (q.v.), to lose weight. Lesseps befriended the boy, fed him macaroni, taught him French, and took him riding; years later the friendship would serve Lesseps well. In 1838 he was transferred to Holland and then to various consulates in Spain. During the 1840s he became attracted to the doctrines of Saint-Simon (q.v.), including the idea of building a canal across the Isthmus of Suez. Betrayed by the government of Louis Napoléon's Second Republic while he was consul in Rome, Lesseps suffered public disgrace and resigned from the French foreign service. Soon afterward, he returned to his pursuit of the Suez Canal.

The violent death of Abbas I (q.v.) and succession of Lesseps's friend Sa'id to the governorship of Egypt caused him to hasten back to Alexandria. He renewed his friendship with the new ruler and wrote him a memorandum on the advantages of a maritime canal joining the Mediterranean to the Red Sea. Easily convinced of the merits of the project, Sa'id announced the Suez Canal as his own decision to an assemblage of foreign consuls. It took just five days for Lesseps to draft a formal agreement, by which Sa'id granted the Suez Canal Company (q.v.) a 99-year concession to build and operate the projected waterway. Permission from the Ottoman (q.v.) sultan, which Sa'id had set as a prerequisite, proved hard to get, and although merchants in London (as elsewhere) saw the advantages of the canal project to world shipping, the British government opposed the Suez Canal. French Emperor Napoléon III, allied with Britain in the Crimean War, also resisted the project at first. For a while even Sa'id turned against the project and refused to meet with Lesseps. Only belatedly did those governments support the project, well after the work had begun. Although Lesseps persuaded many capitalists to invest in his company, the capital requirements of building the canal exceeded his estimates, and Sa'id had to commit large sums from his own pocket, shares that were assumed by the Egyptian government when Sa'id died and was succeeded by his nephew, Isma'il (q.v.).

As construction began, British and other hostile observers noted the heavy use of Egyptian corvée (q.v.) labor and persuaded the Ottoman government to pressure Egypt to pay the workers, further raising construction costs. Fortunately for Lesseps, the excavating machine had just become economically feasible. He also had ties through his wife to the French Empress Eugénie, who influenced her husband to back him. Napoléon III arbitrated the corvée issue between the Canal Company and the Egyptian government, arranging a settlement by which Egypt paid 84 million francs ($17 million) as compensation for the loss of corvée labor, just as Lesseps was finding new machinery less costly than his lost conscripts. British efforts to obtain Ottoman intervention to block this settlement failed after the grand vezir was suddenly relieved of a personal debt to a Paris bank. Construction went on despite Anglo-French diplomatic rivalry and a cholera (q.v.) epidemic in Egypt. Once the French National Assembly passed an act authorizing the Company to issue preferred shares, Lesseps could assure everyone that the Suez Canal would be opened by 1869. The khedive (q.v.) planned an elaborate celebration that included visits from many European heads of state, much development in Cairo (q.v.), and several months of feasting and ceremonies.

The Canal began operation, with Lesseps heading the company that he had founded. His hope that the governments of the world would buy shares, making his enterprise truly international, was never realized, but the Egyptian government's slide into near bankruptcy in 1875 enabled Britain to buy its shares at a bargain rate, with Lesseps's blessing. But his own power waned, especially after Tawfiq (q.v.) replaced Isma'il in 1879. His inability to keep British troops from invading Egypt via the Canal in 1882 to quell Urabi (q.v.) underscored his declining influence. His efforts to recapture some of his earlier glory by organizing the construction of a canal across Panama led to financial scandals in Paris and further disgrace. A man of boundless energy and vision, Ferdinand de Lesseps's hope that the Suez Canal would benefit Egypt was never realized, and most Egyptians now view him as the archetypal exploiter of their country.

LIBERAL CONSTITUTIONALIST PARTY, *see* **CONSTITUTIONAL LIBERAL PARTY.**

LIBERAL PARTY. Right-wing group formed in 1978 as the Socialist Liberal Organization, following Sadat's (q.v.) Party Reforms (q.v.). Led by Mustafa Kamil Murad, a rich cotton broker who had led the Federation of Chambers of Commerce during the 1970s, it appealed to the *munfatihin*, the beneficiaries of Sadat's *infitah* (q.v.), and won 12 seats in the 1976 elections. Backed by large landowners and a few professionals, its platform called for selling off state-owned companies, ending subsidies, and unrestricted foreign investment. Recently it has moved closer to the Muslim Brothers (q.v.) and the Socialist Labor Party (q.v.), forming the Islamic Alliance (q.v.) that won 60 seats in the 1987 elections. It boycotted the 1990 elections. It has a weekly newspaper, *al-Ahrar*.

LIBERATION PROVINCE. Experimental land-reclamation area, near Alexandria (q.v.), started in 1953 under the leadership of one of the Free Officers (q.v.), Majdi Hasanayn, who hoped to make it a socialist showcase, using resettled peasants organized into cooperative work teams and living in 12 model villages. The government hoped to reclaim 1.2 million feddans (q.v.), financing the initial stages from the sale of confiscated royal properties. In practice, of the first 25,000 people settled there by the government, all but 2,000 worked in construction and manufacturing, industry being favored over agriculture.

In 1957 the project was absorbed by the agriculture ministry, where Sayyid Mar'i (q.v.) began redistributing its lands to small peasant proprietors between 1957 and 1961. Of the 800,000 feddans of sandy desert soil to be reclaimed, only some 25,000 were under cultivation in 1959, at a reported government expenditure of £E25–30 million, due in part to faulty planning and mismanagement, and only 389 families had been accepted as settlers. Another Free Officer, Abd al-Muhsin Abd al-Nur, took charge of the project in 1961 and resumed the policy of collective ownership of reclaimed land, mainly in the northern sector, up to 1967. Meanwhile, an American company reclaimed 14,000 and an Italian consulting/engineering firm reclaimed 37,600 feddans in the southern sector, whose management was entrusted to a state authority. The Soviets agreed to reclaim large parts of the Western Desert and to build a 10,000-feddan model farm in the northern sector. Peasant settlers were organized into cooperatives (q.v.), but nearly all administrative direction came from the state. Shortly before his death, Nasir (q.v.) acknowledged that the project had failed.

Under Sadat (q.v.), 20 to 30 feddan lots of the reclaimed lands were assigned to graduates from the agriculture faculties of the various national universities, and smaller lots were given to former employees of the state authority. The state farms were privatized, starting in 1976, and the government also tried in 1984 to bring agribusiness firms in to manage part of the southern sector. Three such firms, all capitalized by oil-exporting Arab countries, were reported in operation as of 1987. Egypt's high investment in land reclamation, infrastructure, and employees has not yet been justified by the amount of land reclaimed or the number of peasants resettled.

LIBERATION RALLY. Organization formed in 1953 by Nasir (q.v.) to mobilize Egyptian supporters for his policies and to replace the outlawed political parties. It managed to co-opt a few labor groups, such as the Cairo Transport Workers Union, which aided Nasir's 1954 struggle against Najib (q.v.). Its most visible activity was to organize "popular" demonstrations for the regime; it played no role in formulating major government policies. Under the 1956 Constitution (q.v.), it was replaced by the National Union (q.v.).

LIBERATION SQUARE (MIDAN AL-TAHRIR). Major open area in Cairo (q.v.), east of the Nile (q.v.), used by Nasir's (q.v.) government as a showpiece for its modernization projects after the removal of the Qasr al-Nil Barracks (q.v.). It was officially renamed for Anwar al-Sadat (q.v.) immediately after his assassination in 1981, but the change never gained popular acceptance.

LIBYA. Egypt's relations with its western neighbor have often been troubled. The first attempt to set Egypt's western border appears in the *firman* (q.v.) sent to Muhammad Ali (q.v.) by the Ottoman Empire (q.v.) in 1841. Its demarcation excluded both the coastal village of Sollum and the Siwa Oasis from Egyptian territory; in fact, however, both were treated as parts of Egypt in the nineteenth century. The Italian invasion of Tripoli in 1911 and subsequently of Cyrenaica angered many Muslim Egyptians, but Lord Kitchener (q.v.) barred transit of Ottoman soldiers and matériel across Egypt. Italy could not quell the resistance of the Sanusi Sufis (q.v.), who enjoyed some Egyptian support. During World War I (q.v.) the Sanusis invaded Egypt's Western Desert, but were repelled by the British. In 1922 the Sanusi leader, Idris (who would later become king of independent Libya), took refuge in Egypt and stayed there until 1951, but the Sanusi rebellion against the Italians continued through the 1920s. At Italy's insistence, Egypt agreed in December 1925 to cede the Jaghbub Oasis (a Sanusi stronghold) to Libya and to form a joint boundary commission, which fixed the Egyptian-Libyan border during 1926. During World War II (q.v.) the British, as well as the Egyptians, encouraged the Sanusiyya to rebel against Italian rule. Libya served as a base for the Italians in 1941 and then the German Afrikakorps to invade Egypt, but the Allies successfully stopped the Axis at al-Alamayn (q.v.) in October 1942. British forces subsequently captured Libya and established a temporary government there; it was later placed under United Nations (q.v.) trusteeship, leading to formal independence in 1951. Egypt's relations with the Kingdom of Libya under Idris (r. 1951–69) were correct but not friendly, due mainly to Nasir's (q.v.) policy of Arab nationalism (q.v.).

The major turning point was the 1 September 1969 revolution that ousted King Idris and brought Colonel Mu'ammar al-Qadhafi to power. An ardent Arab nationalist, Qadhafi pledged his support for Nasir and for the struggle against Israel. Soon after Sadat (q.v.) succeeded to the presidency, he entered into unity talks with Libya, leading in 1971 to the Federation of Arab Republics (q.v.), which would have provided for an organic Egyptian-Libyan union. Due to Qadhafi's nationalist zeal, however, the federation and union were postponed and finally canceled in 1973, shortly before the October War (q.v.), about which Qadhafi received no advance warning. By July 1977 Egyptian-Libyan relations had so deteriorated that border warfare broke out. Border skirmishes escalated to air raids and attacks by Egyptian paratroopers on Jaghbub oasis. Both sides claimed victory and neither one published its casualty figures, but the brief war may have hastened Sadat's peace initiative toward Israel. An added factor in Egyptian-Libyan relations has been the presence of many Egyptian professional and manual workers in Libya due to its oil industry; some were expelled due to the border war or the Egyptian-Israeli Peace Treaty (q.v.), but many Egyptians have continued to migrate to Libya, which needs their skills but uses their presence as a means of putting pressure on the Egyptian government. Libya has assailed Egypt's close ties with the United States, especially after the latter bombarded Tripoli in April 1986, and the Egyptian government has accused Libya of harboring terrorist movements and of concealing its role in the bombing of an American passenger jet over Lockerbie (Scotland) in December 1988.

LIQUIDATION, LAW OF (1880). Egyptian government statute, formally proposed by Riyad's (q.v.) cabinet but actually sought by the main European creditor governments and drafted by the Dual Control (q.v.). The controllers reorganized the Egyptian public debt, setting a budget that would balance the demands of Egypt's creditors against the country's needs and creating a sinking fund for the eventual liquidation of the debt, assuming that the controllers would have indefinite responsibility for managing Egyptian state finances. They lacked the means to enforce their plans, however, and the rise of Urabi (q.v.) and the Egyptian nationalist army officers in 1881–82 proved to the Europeans that only some form of military intervention would ensure that the Egyptian government paid its debts. During the British occupation (q.v.) the Caisse de la Dette Publique (q.v.) tried to enforce portions of the Liquidation Law, blocking British attempts to institute irrigation (q.v.) or other economic reforms.

LITERACY. The ability to read and write, although highly prized by Islamic culture, has traditionally lagged in Egypt, especially in the countryside and among girls and women. This regrettable situation is due in part to the neglect of basic education under Muhammad Ali (q.v.) and his successors, who aimed at creating a technocratic elite (*see* Education), and to the inadequate attention to state-controlled education under the British occupation (q.v.). At the time of the 1952 Revolution (q.v.), fewer than 50 percent of all primary-school-aged children were enrolled, and nearly 75 percent of the population over ten years of age was illiterate. The Free Officers (q.v.) abolished all school fees and greatly expanded government spending on education, but as recently as 1990 only 45 percent of Egypt's population over 15 could read and write.

AL-LIWA. Daily newspaper founded in 1900 by Mustafa Kamil (q.v.), becoming the National Party (q.v.) organ in 1907. Its sharp attacks on British rule in Egypt won widespread backing from Egyptian students and young intellectuals, and it attained a daily circulation of 15,000 by 1908, the highest in Egypt at the time. Edited by Mustafa Kamil until his death in 1908, it was then briefly taken over by Ali Fahmi Kamil, but the National Party's executive board named Abd al-Aziz Jawish (q.v.) as its editor. His attacks on the Egyptian ministers and their British advisers soon led to legal actions and then to the revival of the 1881 Press Law (q.v.), under which it received two warnings. The party's control of *al-Liwa* was challenged in the Mixed Courts (q.v.) by Mustafa Kamil's heirs, who won their case in February 1910. It was placed under judicial sequestration and, although it continued to appear, it was superseded for two years by *al-Alam*. Restored to the National Party in March 1912, it was suppressed by the Egyptian government in September of that year under the amended Press Law. The Nationalists then used *al-Sha'b*, another Arabic daily, as their journalistic organ up to World War I (q.v.).

LIWA AL-ISLAM. Name of two Egyptian Muslim magazines, of which the more recent is the government-approved weekly published since 1982. Its 1992 circulation was 30,000.

LLOYD, GEORGE AMBROSE, FIRST BARON LLOYD (1879–1941). British high commissioner from 1925 to 1929. He was educated at Eton and at Trinity College, Cambridge, but did not complete his degree due to the death of his parents. After a few years in his father's steel tubing business, he embarked on a career of public service. He became an honorary attaché in Istanbul and then headed a commission to inquire into future British trade with the Ottoman Empire (q.v.) and the Persian Gulf. He was elected to the House of Commons as a Conservative in 1910 and traveled during recesses to Europe and the Middle East. He held various staff positions during World War I (q.v.), serving briefly at Gallipoli in 1915 and Basra in 1916. He was later attached to the Arab Bureau, where he came to know many of the Arab leaders. He then served for five years as governor of the Bombay presidency, improving housing and irrigation, but also curbing nationalist agitation. He again won a seat in the 1924 parliamentary elections, but in the following year he accepted the post of high commissioner for Egypt and the Sudan (q.v.), replacing Allenby (q.v.). Lloyd tried to establish firm control over Egyptian affairs, but the Foreign Office criticized his policies and undermined his position by negotiating with Abd al-Khaliq Tharwat (q.v.) for a treaty in 1927. When a Labour government took power in 1929, the new foreign secretary obliged him to resign. He then served on the boards of several companies, spoke out strongly in favor of imperial causes, and took charge of the British Council in 1937. His views on rearmament, collective security, and Indian policy agreed with those of Winston Churchill, hence his return to official life in 1940, when he became colonial secretary and then leader of the House of Lords. Although sustained by idealism and resolution, his devotion to British imperialism made him unsympathetic to Egyptian national aspirations.

LONDON, CONVENTION OF (1840). Treaty between Austria, Great Britain, Prussia, and Russia, with the Ottoman Empire (q.v.), in which they offered to Muhammad Ali (q.v.) and his heirs control over Egypt and the province of Acre (roughly what is now Israel), provided that he agreed within ten days to withdraw from the rest of Syria and returned to the sultan the Ottoman fleet, which had defected to Alexandria (q.v.). The European powers agreed to use all possible means of persuasion to effect this agreement, but Muhammad Ali, backed by France, refused. British and Austrian forces then intervened militarily, defeating his troops late in 1840. Muhammad Ali finally accepted the terms of the Convention and the *firmans* (q.v.) issued by the Ottoman sultan, confirming his rule over Egypt and the Sudan (q.v.). He withdrew from Syria and Crete and sent back the Ottoman fleet. The London Convention and the *firmans* were the legal basis for Egypt's status as a privileged Ottoman province. Later nationalists cited them to discredit claims for the British Occupation (q.v.).

LORAINE, PERCY (1880–1961). British high commissioner from 1929 to 1933. Educated at Eton and New College, Oxford, he fought in the Boer War. He entered the diplomatic corps in 1904 and served in Istanbul and Tehran, then in Rome, Peking, Paris, and Madrid. He attended the Paris Peace Conference and later served as Britain's minister in Tehran and then in Athens. He became high commissioner for Egypt and the

Sudan (q.v.) in 1929, but his policy of letting King Fuad (q.v.) control his ministers led the Foreign Office to remove him in 1933. Loraine was sent to Ankara, where he developed close ties with Kemal Atatürk and strengthened Anglo-Turkish relations. He served as Britain's last ambassador to Italy in 1939–40. Churchill made no use of his Middle East knowledge during World War II (q.v.), and he retired from public life.

- M -

MAHDI. For educated Muslims, the mahdi is the divinely guided leader who will come to restore justice on earth shortly before the Day of Judgment; in popular Islam, the mahdi is viewed as a messiah. For Egyptians and Sudanese, "the Mahdi" usually connotes Muhammad Ahmad (1848–85), who became convinced that he had a mission to purify the world of the immorality that he ascribed to the rulers of the day. He led a rebellion against Egyptian rule in the Sudan (q.v.) from 1881, gaining popular support throughout the country and defeating British expeditions headed by William Hicks in 1883 and by "Chinese" Gordon (q.v.) in 1884–85. He tried to organize a government modeled after that of the early Islamic community but died in Omdurman soon after he and his followers captured Khartum in 1885. Some of his descendants became leaders in the Sudanese political party that opposed union with Egypt.

MAHFUZ, NAJIB (1911-). Cairene novelist and playwright, winner of the 1988 Nobel prize for literature. He graduated from Cairo University's (q.v.) Faculty of Arts in 1934 with a degree in philosophy, worked as a secretary in the University from 1936 to 1939, then at the ministry of *awqaf* (q.v.) from 1939 to 1954, when he was appointed director of technical supervision at the ministry of culture; and, finally, served as director of the cinema organization. Mahfuz published his first story in 1932, his first collection of stories in 1938, and his first novel in 1939. After writing three historical novels on pharaonic subjects that were disguised attacks on Egyptian politicians ruling under British tutelage, he published a number of novels about life in Cairo (q.v.), notably *al-Qahira al-jadida* ("New Cairo"), *Khan al-Khalili*, and *Zuqaq al-midaqq* (published in English translation as *Midaq Alley* in 1966). He then wrote several other novels and film scripts followed in 1956–57 by his famous Cairo trilogy: *Bayn al-Qasrayn* (translated into English as *Palace Walk*), *Qasr al-Shawq* (*Palace of Desire*), and *al-Sukkariyya* (*Sugar Street*), portraying three generations of a Cairo family and the evolution of Egyptian politics, society, and culture during the twentieth century. In 1959 he published a controversial novel, *Awlad haratina* (translated as *Children of Gebelawi*), which treats Judaism, Christianity, and Islam in allegorical terms offensive to strict Muslims. His novel *Miramar*, written just before the June War (q.v.), assailed the pretensions and shortcomings of the Nasir (q.v.) regime. A later work, *al-Maraya* (translated as *Mirrors*), presents 55 autobiographical sketches representing multiple viewpoints. His *al-Hubb taht al-matar* ("Love in the Rain") shows the 1967 war's impact on Egypt's younger generation. Following the October War (q.v.), Mahfuz was one of the first Egyptian writers to call for peace with Israel, and his books were boycotted–but still read–by Arabs outside Egypt. His Nobel prize, the first to be awarded to an Arab writer, recognized his success in expressing the hopes and fears of the Egyptian people and in shaping classical Arabic into a vehicle of popular speech.

MAHIR, AHMAD (1885–1945). Lawyer, minister, and party leader. The son of a prominent landowning family known for its nationalism, he earned his *license en droit* from Montpellier and taught at the government Law School (q.v.). He joined the Wafd (q.v.) during the 1919 Revolution (q.v.) and was elected as a Wafdist to Parliament in 1924, briefly serving as education minister under Sa'd Zaghlul (q.v.). Accused of backing a terrorist group involved in assassinating Sir Lee Stack (q.v.), he left the government. He served as speaker of Parliament in 1936. His efforts to effect a reconciliation between young King Faruq (q.v.) and the Wafd led to his expulsion from the Party. He and Nuqrashi (q.v.) proceeded to set up the Sa'dist Party (q.v.), which claimed to represent the principles of the Wafd's late founder, but their new movement soon sided with the king against the Wafd. Following the 1938 election, which the Wafd boycotted, the Sa'dists formed a coalition government with the Constitutional Liberals (q.v.), and Ahmad Mahir became finance minister. In 1940 he was again elected speaker of Parliament. After Faruq dismissed the Wafdist cabinet, led by Mustafa al-Nahhas (q.v.), that had been forced on him by the British, Ahmad Mahir headed a coalition government from October 1944 until February 1945, when he was assassinated by a young nationalist (probably a member of Misr al-Fatat) just after he had obtained parliamentary endorsement for the Egyptian government's declaration of war against the Axis Powers. An honest and patriotic statesman, he was not politically close to his brother Ali (q.v.).

MAHIR, ALI (1883–1960). Prominent politician, cabinet minister, and prime minister on four separate occasions. From a landowning family famous for its opposition to the British, he graduated from the government Law School (q.v.) and worked for a time in the Niyaba (q.v.) in Cairo. He joined the Wafd (q.v.) in 1919 but soon drifted into the court party surrounding Sultan (later King) Fuad (q.v.). Ali Mahir administered the

Law School, chaired the assembly that drafted the 1923 Constitution (q.v.), and was elected to Parliament, as an independent, in 1924. At times when the Wafd Party (q.v.) was out of power, he held many cabinet portfolios, including education (1925–26), finance (1928–29), and justice (1930–32). He served as prime minister in early 1936 during the period when Egypt was resuming parliamentary government, as office director for both King Fuad (in 1935) and his son (in 1937), and as a member of the regency council in 1936–37, until King Faruq (q.v.) attained his majority. He formed a royalist government in August 1939, serving as both foreign and interior minister. Although he acquiesced in the expulsion of German and Austrian nationals from Egypt and the increase of the British garrison after the outbreak of World War II (q.v.), he became increasingly anti-British and appointed nationalists to cabinet positions, causing the British to suspect him of secret contacts with Nazi Germany and Fascist Italy. He resigned in favor of Hasan Sabri (q.v.) in June 1940. When the British suspected that Faruq was about to reappoint him to head a neutralist cabinet, they forced the king to appoint a Wafdist cabinet (*see* 4 February 1942 Incident). Ali Mahir was kept under house arrest for the rest of the war. In January 1952 when "Black Saturday" (q.v.) led to Nahhas's fall from power, he headed another royalist government. When the Free Officers (q.v.) ousted Faruq in July of that year, they asked him to form a civilian government, but he soon resigned because he opposed their land reform (q.v.) law and other revolutionary ideas. He played no further role in Egyptian politics.

MAHMAL. Muslim ceremony marking the start of the annual procession carrying the *kiswa*, the embroidered cloth covering fabricated in Egypt for the Ka'ba, from Cairo to Mecca.

MAHMUD, MUHAMMAD (1877–1941). Politician and cabinet minister. Born in a village near Asyut (q.v.) to a wealthy, Upper Egyptian family, he was educated in Asyut, Cairo, and at Balliol College, Oxford. He held various administrative positions, becoming governor of Fayyum, the Suez Canal (q.v.) district, and Buhayra. He joined the Wafd (q.v.) during the 1919 Revolution (q.v.) but soon broke with Sa'd Zaghlul (q.v.) and became one of the founders of the Constitutional Liberal Party (q.v.) in 1922, serving as its vice president and becoming its president in 1929. He first joined the cabinet in 1926, became finance minister in 1927, and premier in 1928–29. During his term of office, he negotiated a tentative agreement with the Foreign Office, but the British insisted on getting the approval of the Wafd Party (q.v.), which demanded the restoration of parliamentary democracy under the 1923 Constitution (q.v.), so Mahmud resigned. He was a member of the coalition of politicians that negotiated the 1936

Anglo-Egyptian Treaty (q.v.). After King Faruq (q.v.) dismissed the Wafdist government in 1937, he formed a caretaker coalition cabinet. His Constitutional Liberal Party regained power in the 1938 parliamentary elections that were boycotted by the Wafd, and he became prime minister in 1938–39. Intelligent, patriotic, but rather nervous, a British observer remarked in 1927 that "he is at times held back by the fact that he does not consider any Egyptian but himself clever enough to run the country without the English, and so wants to keep them here till he has maneuvered himself to the head of affairs."

MAHMUDIYYA CANAL. Artificial waterway, built at Muhammad Ali's (q.v.) command in 1817–20, as a navigation canal connecting Alexandria (q.v.) to Bulaq (q.v.). Muhammad Ali relied on corvée labor to build the canal, peasants often arrived for work with ropes around their necks, and its construction took the lives of 12,000 to 100,000 laborers. In addition to promoting river transport (q.v.), the canal irrigated about 10,000 feddans (q.v.) of Delta land and brought additional drinking water to Alexandria. It has been dredged often and substantially improved.

MAJLIS AL-SHA'B, *see* PEOPLE'S ASSEMBLY.

MAJLIS AL-SHURA. Consultative council or advisory body established by Sadat (q.v.), backed by a plebiscite in 1980, as the upper house of Egypt's Parliament. It was meant to counter opposition to Sadat's policies by the Socialist Labor Party (q.v.) in the lower house. Replacing the Central Committee of the Arab Socialist Union (q.v.), it was also given 51 percent ownership of Egypt's main newspapers, the remaining shares being reserved for their employees. A third of its 210 members were presidential appointees; the rest were popularly elected. All its elected members have so far come from the National Democratic Party (q.v.).

MAJLIS AL-UMMA, *see* NATIONAL ASSEMBLY.

MAKRAM, UMAR (1755?-1811). Popular leader and *naqib al-ashraf* (q.v.) at the time of the French occupation (q.v.). Born in Asyut and educated at al-Azhar (q.v.), he led a crowd of Cairo (q.v.) residents against Napoléon's (q.v.) invasion. When their resistance failed, he escaped to al-Arish and then Jaffa, but after Napoléon captured these cities, Makram returned to Cairo. When the Ottoman (q.v.) army invaded Egypt from Syria in 1800 and threatened to oust the French, he led another popular uprising that lasted 37 days but finally collapsed after the Battle of Heliopolis (q.v.). Umar escaped again and did not return until the British and Ottoman armies had expelled the French from Egypt. Upon returning to Cairo and resuming his duties as *naqib*, he backed Muhammad Ali's (q.v.) rise to power but, when he demanded a voice in Egypt's affairs, was expelled to Damietta and four years later to Tanta. He petitioned Muhammad Ali for permission to make the hajj to Mecca and, upon his return, resumed living in Cairo. Soon afterward, a small rebellion broke out. Muhammad Ali, suspecting Umar's involvement, expelled him again to Tanta, where he died. Egyptians remember him as an early hero of their independence struggle.

MALET, SIR EDWARD (1837–1908). English diplomat and Britain's agent and consul general in Egypt from 1879 to 1883. He came from a family of diplomats and, after three years at Eton, entered the foreign service at the age of 17. He served as attaché to his father in Frankfurt, then in Brussels. He saw service in Argentina, Brazil, the United States, France, China, Athens, and Rome. He served as minister plenipotentiary in Istanbul during 1878, the year of the San Stefano and Berlin treaties, forming close ties with Ottoman (q.v.) Sultan Abdulhamid. In October 1879 Malet was sent to Egypt, shortly after Khedive Tawfiq (qq.v.) had succeeded his father, and negotiated for financial and administrative reforms. Initially sympathetic to Urabi's (q.v.) demand for constitutional government, he insisted that Egypt must repay its public debts and sought Ottoman military intervention under European supervision; otherwise, he believed that joint Anglo-French action would be needed. When riots broke out in Alexandria (q.v.) in May 1882, he refused asylum on a British warship and stayed in the city to try to restore confidence among the Europeans. He suddenly became gravely ill and had to leave to regain his health, but returned in time to accompany General Wolseley (q.v.) on his entry into Cairo (q.v.) in September 1882. He opposed executing Urabi and his associates. Malet then collaborated with Lord Dufferin (q.v.) in making plans for the reorganization of Egypt's government, but his health remained poor and he was replaced later in 1883 by Sir Evelyn Baring, later Lord Cromer (q.v.). His incomplete memoirs were edited by Lord Sanderson after his death and published as *Egypt, 1879–1883*. There is also a section on his Egyptian experiences in his general memoirs, *Shifting Scenes*. Ambitious and capable of influencing Tawfiq, he lacked the necessary self-assurance and familiarity with Egypt to uphold Britain's interests effectively.

MAMLUKS. Turkish or Circassian (q.v.) slave soldiers, originally imported by the Ayyubid dynasty (1171–1250). They became a military oligarchy ruling over Egypt (1250–1517) and Syria (1260–1516) and retained power during the era of Ottoman rule (q.v.) in most of Egypt. Their factionalism and failure to resist Napoléon's (q.v.) invasion in 1798 discredited them among Egyptians and, although restored to power by the British in 1802, they were weakened and finally exterminated by Muhammad Ali (q.v.) in 1811.

AL-MANAR. Influential monthly magazine founded by Muhammad Abduh (q.v.) and edited by Rashid Rida (q.v.). Published in Cairo (q.v.) from 1898 to 1940, it advocated Islamic reform.

AL-MARAGHI, [MUHAMMAD] MUSTAFA (1881–1945). Islamic scholar, reformer, and rector of al-Azhar (q.v.). Born in Maragha (near Jirja), he was educated in Cairo and became a disciple of Muhammad Abduh (q.v.). He entered the Shari'a Court (q.v.) judiciary, and served from 1908 to 1919 as the chief judge in the Sudan (q.v.). He was named rector of al-Azhar in 1928–29 and from 1935 until his death. He influenced young King Faruq (q.v.), encouraging his campaign for the caliphate. Maraghi wrote several books of Quranic interpretation and a famous book on translating the Quran into foreign languages.

30 MARCH PROGRAM (1968). Promises made by Nasir (q.v.) to reassure restive students and workers who demonstrated against the government in February 1968. While affirming Egypt's continuing commitment to Arabism and socialism, it called for a restructuring of the Arab Socialist Union (q.v.) through a system of successive, multilevel elections and for the drafting of a permanent constitution that would ensure workers' rights to political participation, guarantee individual freedom and security, define the branches of the government and their functions, stress the independence of the judiciary and the right to seek justice, and guarantee the protection of public, cooperative, and private property. Although these reforms were not fully implemented in Nasir's lifetime, some liberalization of the legal system, curbing of the Mukhabarat (q.v.), and work on what became the 1971 Constitution (q.v.) did ensue.

MAR'I, SAYYID (1913-). Politician, landowner, and economist. Originally from Sharqiyya province, he studied agricultural engineering at Cairo University (q.v.), graduating in 1937. He became keenly interested in agrarian reforms, planning, and development and was first elected to Parliament in 1944 as a Sa'dist (q.v.). After the 1952 Revolution (q.v.) he began advising Nasir's (q.v.) government about land reform (q.v.) and played a major role in formulating the program, becoming minister of state for agrarian reform in 1956. During the union with Syria, Mar'i was minister of agriculture and land reform. He was also on the executive committee of the National Union (q.v.) in 1956–61 and of the Arab Socialist Union (q.v.) from 1962, serving also as its secretary-general in

1971–73. He was agriculture and land reform minister from June 1967 and also deputy prime minister from November 1970 until December 1971. He was one of Sadat's (q.v.) most trusted advisers and had close ties to his family through his son's marriage to Sadat's daughter. He was nominated to head the UN Food and Agriculture Organization but was not elected. He chaired the People's Assembly (q.v.) from 1974 to 1978 and then assisted and advised Sadat until the latter's assassination. Mar'i has been a political survivor, a large landowner dedicated to agrarian reform, and a man highly gifted in adjusting to the changing tides of power in the Egyptian government. His memoirs, entitled *Awraq siyasiyya* ("Political Papers"), were published in three volumes in 1978–79.

MARIETTE, AUGUSTE (1821–81). French founder of Egypt's Antiquities Service, excavator of many archaeological sites, and organizer of the Egyptian Museum (q.v.). Born in Boulogne-sur-Mer, he was educated at the Collège de Boulogne. Unable to complete his education, he went to England to work as a teacher and model designer, then returned to France to earn his *baccalauréat-ès-lettres* at Douai. Supporting himself as a French teacher, he became interested in ancient Egyptian hieroglyphics, which he taught himself. In 1849 he took a position at the Louvre Museum, where he transcribed all its inscriptions. Sent to Egypt to acquire Coptic manuscripts in 1850, he began excavating the Memphis Serapeum, where his discoveries made him famous. In 1855 he became assistant curator of the Louvre's Egyptian department. He campaigned vigorously for the preservation of Egyptian monuments, which were rapidly being destroyed. At the same time he began many excavations of sites in the Nile (q.v.) valley, eventually numbering 35 sites with more than 2,780 workers, maintaining high standards of archaeological workmanship. Mariette's numerous and prodigious publications could not encompass all of his discoveries, and many of his notes were destroyed when his Cairo (q.v.) house was flooded in 1878. He also helped to compose the libretto for *Aida* (q.v.). After his death, his remains were interred in a sarcophagus now set in front of the Egyptian Museum.

MARXISM. Any socialist ideology that follows closely the teachings of Karl Marx. Due in part to the great inequality of incomes and living standards in Egypt, Marxist ideas appealed to an articulate minority of Egyptians during the 1940s and later exerted some influence on Nasir's (q.v.) government, but never dominated Arab socialism (q.v.), which sought to combine nationalist and Islamic ideas with a quest for economic equality and social justice (*see* Communism, Hadeto, Iskra, Socialism).

AL-MAZINI, IBRAHIM ABD AL-QADIR (1889–1949). Humorous writer, literary critic, and modernist poet. Born in Cairo (q.v.), his family traced its origins to the Minufiyya village of Kum Mazin. Trained as a teacher, he soon left pedagogy for journalism. He was especially gifted at translation from English to Arabic. He wrote Arabic poetry for a while, then shifted to prose after reading widely in English and Arabic literature. He worked for *al-Akhbar*, *al-Balagh* (q.v.), and other daily newspapers; wrote articles for weekly and monthly magazines; and briefly published his own review, *al-Usbu'*. Mazini belonged to the Arabic Language Academies of both Damascus and Cairo. Of his many published books, *Ibrahim al-Katib* has been translated by Majdi Wahba into English as *Ibrahim the Writer* (1976). William Hutchins translated several of his short stories, with an introduction, in *Al-Mazini's Egypt* (1983). His poetry was deeply subjective, sometimes heavily derivative from classical Arabic or from English models, but often quite moving and humorous.

MCMAHON, [ARTHUR] HENRY (1862–1949). British officer, imperial administrator, and first high commissioner for Egypt and the Sudan (q.v.). Born in Simla (India) to a military family, he was educated at Haileybury and the Royal Military College at Sandhurst, where he was the top 1882 graduate. He served on the Punjab Frontier Force, then in the Indian Political Department from 1890 to 1914, rising to the position of foreign secretary of the government of India in 1911. He was responsible for demarcating the boundaries between Baluchistan and Pakistan and between India and China. At the start of World War I (q.v.), when Kitchener (q.v.) took charge of the War Office and Britain proclaimed a protectorate (q.v.) over Egypt and the Sudan, McMahon was named the first British high commissioner. He managed to maintain order in a troubled time, as two attempts were made on the life of Sultan Husayn Kamil (q.v.), the reservists rioted, and thousands of troops from all parts of the British Empire occupied Egypt. He is best-known for the Husayn-McMahon Correspondence, his exchange of letters with Sharif Husayn of Mecca, in which he is thought to have guaranteed that the sharif's family, the Hashimites, would rule over Palestine, Syria, and Iraq once they had overthrown Ottoman (q.v.) rule there in World War I. He was recalled suddenly at the end of 1916. An enthusiastic sportsman and a great conversationalist, McMahon knew little about Egypt and its needs.

MENOU, JACQUES "ABDALLAH" (1750–1810). French general and successor to Napoléon (q.v.) and Kléber (q.v.) as commander of France's Army of Egypt. The son of an officer, he had served the Comte de Provence and the Legion of Flanders. Chosen by the nobility to represent them in the 1789 Estates-General, he returned to military life, commanding a regiment in the Army of the Rhine. In 1798 he joined the Army of the Orient (Egypt) and became governor of Rosetta and then Alexandria (q.v.). He believed strongly in France's imperial mission in Egypt. He acquired notoriety by marrying a Muslim Egyptian woman and converting to Islam (q.v.). Upon succeeding Kléber in 1800, Menou was defeated by the British. After his return to France, he held several political and military posts in Napoléon's empire. He was widely ridiculed for his stout, unmartial appearance and character, his conversion to Islam, and his belief in a permanent French occupation (q.v.).

METRO, CAIRO. High-speed light railway, using some existing tracks and partly constructed by a French company, connecting al-Marg, central Cairo (q.v.), Ma'adi, and Hulwan (q.v.), with 33 stations, five of them underground. The 42.5-km project was begun in 1982. The southern leg was opened in July 1987 (18 months later than originally planned), the northeastern leg in 1989. The original cost estimate of $197 million has doubled. The city plans to build a western extension from Shubra to Giza. Construction of the Metro is intended to reduce the congestion of Cairo streets, buses, and trains.

MIDDLE EAST NEWS AGENCY. Press service founded in 1956 and controlled by the Egyptian government.

MIDDLE EAST SUPPLY CENTRE. Cairo-based organization, formed in 1941 by the British government and later joined by U.S. representatives, which coordinated manufacturing and transport in the Arab states and Iran during World War II (q.v.), when imports from Europe were unavailable. It stimulated the development of manufacturing industry in Egypt and strengthened economic ties among the Middle Eastern countries, but it was dissolved in 1945, because no foreign or local government was willing to sustain it.

MIG. Any one of several types of Soviet-made fighter airplanes, which formed the backbone of Egypt's air force from the Czech Arms Deal (q.v.) until the late 1970s, when Sadat (q.v.) started buying French Mirage fighter jets and U.S.-made F-4's. Some upgraded MiGs remained in the air force in 1990, including Chinese versions assembled in Egypt.

MILITARY ACADEMY. Institution for training Egyptian army officers since the early nineteenth century. The Mamluks (q.v.) had only informal methods for training their soldiers and officers, derived from the Ottoman (q.v.) system. The French occupation (q.v.) exposed their weakness and also led to the training of some young Mamluks–and Copts (q.v.) and

Turks–in European fighting methods. Muhammad Ali (q.v.) established his first military training school, patterned after the Ottoman *nizam-i-jedid* (q.v.), in the Cairo Citadel (q.v.) in 1815, relying heavily on Christian trainers. Fierce Muslim opposition obliged Muhammad Ali to move his academy out of Cairo (q.v.), first to Isna in 1820 and then to Aswan in the following year, aided by Colonel Sève (q.v.) and other Europeans. Unable to fill the cadet ranks with his personal slaves, Muhammad Ali imported Black Africans from the Sudan (q.v.) and, when they could not survive Egypt's climate, began recruiting Egyptian peasants, but the majority of his officer corps continued to be Turks and other Muslims from outside Egypt. Initially, the Academy trained infantry officers, but artillery, cavalry, and naval sections were soon added. A military preparatory school was founded in Bulaq (q.v.) but moved in 1825 to Qasr al-Ayni and was renamed Madrasat al-Tajhiziyya al-Harbiyya, moved again to Abu-Za'bal in 1836, and closed in 1842. The first staff college, organized wholly on French lines, was opened in 1826. Other schools taught military music, veterinary science, and munitions manufacturing.

Military cutbacks shut down most of the schools in 1841; Abbas Hilmi I (q.v.) closed the remaining ones for the training of naval, cavalry, and artillery officers (the one for infantry officers had almost no students). During his reign a consolidated military academy, al-Madrasa al-Mafruza, was founded in the new suburb of al-Abbasiyya (q.v.); its enrollment, nearly 1,700 students in 1849, was greater than those of all the abolished schools combined. Sa'id (q.v.) dealt harshly with this school, changing its director several times and abolishing it in 1861. Earlier, he had set up a new military school, located in the Citadel and directed by Rifa'a al-Tahtawi (q.v.). It, too, closed in 1861, and in the following year a new academy was opened at the Delta Barrages (q.v.), near an ephemeral military engineering school. Isma'il (q.v.) completely revamped the military educational system, consolidating the schools at the Abbasiyya Barracks in 1865, with branches for infantry, cavalry, artillery and military engineering, staff (an innovation often credited to General Stone, an American Civil War veteran), and noncommissioned officers training. Schools for naval officers and architects, located in Alexandria (q.v.), were revamped. Egypt's campaigns to conquer the Sudan (q.v.) and other parts of Africa together with the Ottoman demand for Egyptian forces caused these military schools to grow rapidly in the 1870s, but the ensuing financial crisis threatened their survival. After the British quelled Urabi's (q.v.) movement, the Egyptian army was dissolved and its training schools closed. The Military Academy was reopened in 1887 with a set two-year training program. During most of the British occupation (q.v.), its size and importance lagged behind the professional schools, as British officers dominated the higher ranks of the Egyptian army. As late as 1937 the army had only 600 officers and 18,000 other ranks.

A turning point was the 1936 Anglo-Egyptian Treaty (q.v.), which enabled the government to expand its armed forces. In what would prove a fateful move, the Wafd (q.v.) government opened admittance into the Military Academy to secondary school graduates who could pass a competitive examination. Formerly limited to sons of wealthy landowners who could furnish letters of introduction to secure admittance, the Academy now included ambitious sons of peasants, lower and middle-class bureaucrats, and merchants, including the core of the Free Officers (q.v.). As World War II (q.v.) began, the Egyptian armed services grew, and the Army Staff College was founded in 1939. The 1952 Revolution (q.v.) enhanced the prestige of the military academies in proportion to the increased power of the officers in Egyptian politics, and admissions and academic standards have risen accordingly. In many areas of Egyptian life, graduation from the Military Academy or one of the related schools has become a prerequisite for political or business advancement. Other military schools include the Naval Academy at Ras al-Tin (Alexandria), the Air Force Academy at Bilbays, the Military Technical Academy in Heliopolis (q.v.), the Higher War College and the National Defense College (combined in 1965 to become the Nasir High Military Academy), and the Air Defense Academy in Alexandria.

MILLET. Religious association for Jews (q.v.), Orthodox Christians, and Armenians (q.v.) living in the Ottoman Empire (q.v.), including Egypt. The rabbis and clergy within each *millet* took charge of justice, education, welfare institutions, and maintenance of local order. Reforms in the Ottoman *millet* system in the nineteenth century led to the establishment of a lay-led communal council, called *majlis milli* in Arabic, in each religious community. In Egypt, the Coptic *majlis milli*, founded in 1873, often clashed with the clergy; there was also some tension between the Jewish council and the rabbinate. The *millet* system gave considerable autonomy, but not full equality with Muslims, to Jews and Christians living under Islam (q.v.).

MILNER MISSION (1919). Official British commission sent by the Foreign Office in 1919 to ascertain Egyptian political aspirations "within the framework of the Protectorate." Its formation was announced eight months before it actually arrived on the scene, diminishing its ability to address the causes of the 1919 Revolution (q.v.). The Wafd (q.v.) and its supporters organized a nationwide boycott of the Milner Mission, showing widespread opposition among the Egyptian people to any continuation of the British protectorate (q.v.). The members did meet with King Fuad (q.v.), the current and some former ministers, and a few notables. Muslim ulama (q.v.), Coptic (q.v.) priests, women (q.v.), and students all played a part in the popular boycott, which was coordinated by the Wafd's central committee. Milner's final report, published in 1920, admitted strong Egyptian support for independence and greatly influenced British policy. Ironically, Milner had begun his own career in Cairo (q.v.), under Lord Cromer (q.v.), and his book, *England in Egypt* (1892), had persuaded European public opinion to accept the British occupation (q.v.) at that time. His papers are held by Oxford's Bodleian Library.

MINING AND MINERALS. Mining has occurred in Egypt since antiquity, but the country is not well endowed with mineral resources. Other than petroleum, the main minerals currently exploited in Egypt are natural gas (*see* Petroleum Industry) and iron ore (*see* Iron and Steel Industry). As of 1989, Egypt mined 1.3 million metric tons of iron ore (this figure is based on the metallic content of the ore), 1.1 million tons of salt, 1.35 million tons of phosphate, and 1.3 million tons of gypsum. Egypt also has small quantities of manganese, kaolin (clay), talc and steatite, asbestos, natron, sulphur, coal, and limestone.

MISR AL-FATAT. Egyptian nationalist youth movement, popular in the 1930s, often called pro-Fascist. Its founder and first president was Ahmad Husayn (q.v.); Fathi Ridwan, later active in the National Party (q.v.), was its general secretary. Both were 22 years old when they founded the original movement, Jam'iyyat Misr al-Fatat, in October 1933. The movement grew out of an industrialization project called the "Piastre Plan" that the two young men began while still in law school; this project collected money nationally to start factories to make goods commonly imported by Egyptians. Its first campaign (1932) raised £E17,000, which was eventually used to start a tarbush (q.v.) factory. The factory proved to be quite profitable, in part because every educated male Egyptian had to wear one. Later fund-raising efforts and factories were less successful economically. The society began as an ultranationalist youth movement, consisting of "members" and "fighters" (*mujahidin*), whose elite status was shown by their uniforms, which included the dark green shirts for which Misr al-Fatat became well-known, and their nationalistic rallies. The society called on the Egyptian youth to help build a mighty empire composed of Egypt and the Sudan (q.v.), allied with the Arab states, and leading the Muslim world. It adopted as its motto "God, Fatherland, King"; denounced the privileged position of foreigners in Egypt; promoted the expansion of agriculture and industry; sought the improvement of education, of rural and urban living conditions, and of family life; called for the elimination of "immorality, alcoholic beverages, and effeminacy";

and inspired a "martial spirit" among young men. Misr al-Fatat did not endorse any of the existing political parties, but soon turned against the Wafd (q.v.) and supported the monarchy and Ali Mahir (q.v.), who may have subsidized it. It adopted *al-Sarkha* as its mouthpiece and briefly also used a Nationalist daily, *Wadi al-Nil*, before establishing its own journal, *Misr al-Fatat*. Accused of Fascist leanings, Ahmad Husayn was publicly hostile to Mussolini's Italy and was even rebuffed by the German Embassy, which he visited. The rallies, uniforms, and well-publicized boycotts of foreign manufactures were the society's best-known activities. In 1936 it became a party, but it could not run for parliamentary elections because its members were almost all under 30, the minimum candidacy age. Hizb Misr al-Fatat did gain influence in 1937 through its "Green Shirt" clashes against the Wafd's "Blue Shirts" (q.v.), its publication of pamphlets and a "Book of the Month" (for Egypt a novelty that would later be imitated by other publishing houses, movements, and eventually the government), and its support for the Palestine Arabs. Later, it engaged in anti-Zionist (q.v.) propaganda that soon turned into activity against Egyptian Jews (q.v.), as well as campaigns against taverns, pornography, and prostitution. Still unable to win broad Egyptian support, it contemplated uniting with the more popular Muslim Brothers (q.v.).

In 1940 Ahmad Husayn renamed his group the Islamic National Party, but the government's wartime censorship severely hampered its activities. It reemerged, again as Misr al-Fatat, in 1944, but its ideology seemed increasingly anachronistic and unrelated to Egypt's needs. In 1946 it reorganized itself as the Egyptian Socialist Party, winning one seat in the 1950 Parliamentary elections. Nasir (q.v.) and other Free Officers (q.v.) may have belonged to this organization, but they did not try to preserve it when they made all the parties disband in 1953. A party bearing the same name was reportedly founded in 1990.

AL-MISRI. The influential daily newspaper of the Wafd Party (q.v.), edited by Mahmud Abu al-Fath (q.v.). It survived the 1952 Revolution (q.v.) and the later abolition of the Wafd, and Mahmud's brother, Ahmad Abu al-Fath, was initially close to the Free Officers (q.v.). It was banned, however, following its April 1954 attacks on Nasir (q.v.) and the Revolutionary Command Council (q.v.) in editorials headed "Back to your Barracks." Its estimated circulation of 150,000 was the largest of any newspaper in the Arab world at the time.

AL-MISRI, AZIZ ALI (1879–1965). Arab nationalist officer and politician. Of mixed Arab and Circassian (q.v.) background, Aziz Ali studied at Istanbul's military academy and was commissioned into the Ottoman (q.v.) army in 1901. He became a member of the Committee of

Union and Progress (CUP), but after it restored the Ottoman Constitution, he turned against the CUP and began to advocate Arab nationalism (q.v.), founding a secret society called Qahtaniyya (named for Qahtan, legendary ancestor of the southern Arabs) in 1909 and an Arab officers' group called Ahd ("Covenant") in 1913. Arrested, tried for treason, and sentenced to death early in 1914, Aziz Ali was freed by the Ottoman government and allowed to go to Egypt. When the Arab revolt began in 1916, he served briefly as Sharif Husayn's chief of staff.

In the interwar years he joined a few fringe groups dedicated to reorienting Egypt toward Arab nationalism (q.v.) and then some pro-Nazi organizations. In 1939 Premier Ali Mahir (q.v.) named him chief of staff of the Egyptian army, but the British accused him of sabotaging Egypt's participation in World War II (q.v.), as mandated by the 1936 Anglo-Egyptian Treaty (q.v.), and insisted on his dismissal in February 1940. He deserted the Egyptian army and tried to reach the Axis forces in the Western Desert, but was caught in 1941 and put on trial. Due to legal technicalities, he was released by the Nahhas (q.v.) government in 1942. Aziz Ali helped the Free Officers (q.v.) prepare for the 1952 Revolution (q.v.). They named him Egypt's ambassador to Moscow in 1953 and wanted to make him president in place of Muhammad Najib (q.v.), but he retired in 1954. Fiercely nationalistic, his enthusiasm often exceeded his political judgment.

MITLA PASS. Strategic mountain pass in the western Sinai Peninsula (q.v.), captured by Israel in 1956 and 1967, relinquished to a UN buffer force under the 1975 Egyptian-Israeli Agreement (q.v.), and restored to Egypt's control under the 1979 Egyptian-Israeli Peace Treaty (q.v.).

MIXED COURTS. Egyptian tribunals, organized by Nubar (q.v.) and set up in 1876 by the Egyptian government by agreements with the Western countries, to try civil cases involving foreign nationals protected by the Capitulations (q.v.). In his efforts to persuade foreign governments to accept his proposed judicial system, Nubar won early backing from Germany and Britain and eventually overcame Ottoman (q.v.) fears that the Mixed Courts would detach Egypt from Istanbul. France long resisted the projected Courts, even though they would use mainly the Code Napoléon, because it preferred the older system by which all cases between Egyptians and foreign nationals were tried in the consular courts of the latter. The Mixed Courts later served as a model for the National Courts (q.v.) and the Egyptian legal profession generally. In their heyday, the Mixed Courts conferred great privileges on foreign residents and businesses in Egypt, and yet the Egyptian nationalists defended them as a bulwark against the British occupation (q.v.). As an Egyptian capitalist class emerged in the 1920s, and especially once Egypt's government adopted a policy of protecting infant industries in 1930, needing permission from foreign governments to raise import tariffs (q.v.) rendered the Mixed Courts anachronistic to most politically articulate Egyptians. They were gradually phased out after the 1937 Montreux Convention (q.v.), closing altogether in 1949.

MONITEUR ÉGYPTIEN. Egypt's French-language official newspaper, founded in 1832.

MONTREUX CONVENTION (1937). International negotiations by the Egyptian government, supported by Britain, with the countries having capitulatory treaties, leading to an agreement by the signatories to phase out the Capitulations (q.v.) and the Mixed Courts (q.v.) by 1949.

AL-MUAYYAD. Daily Arabic newspaper, originally founded by Mustafa Riyad (q.v.) in 1889 to counter the pro-French *al-Ahram* (q.v.) and pro-British *al-Muqattam* (q.v.) and edited by Shaykh Ali Yusuf (q.v.) until his death in 1913. Its growth as a popular newspaper was a giant step in the development of vernacular journalism in Egypt, but its uncritical backing of Khedive Abbas (qq.v.) led eventually to its eclipse by *al-Liwa* (q.v.).

MUBARAK, ALI (1823–93). Official, cabinet minister, and writer. Born in Birinbal (Daqahliyya province) to a family of ulama (q.v.), Ali decided at an early age to enter government service. Educated at the Cairo (q.v.) and Paris polytechnics and at an artillery school at Metz, he served a year in the French army before returning to Egypt in 1849. He attracted Abbas I's (q.v.) attention by developing an economical method of facilitating the passage of boats through the Delta Barrages (q.v.) and was promoted from teaching in the artillery school to managing all the government primary and preparatory schools and the Muhandiskhana (polytechnic). Dismissed from government service by Sa'id (q.v.), he served in the Crimean War. He held various low-paying positions and was repeatedly dismissed from government service. Isma'il's (q.v.) accession enabled Ali Mubarak to move up through a series of government posts, becoming director of education and public works and then of communications and railways in 1868, of *awqaf* (q.v.) and again of communications in 1869, of education again in 1870 and 1872, and of public works again in 1871–72. He served on the Privy Council (q.v.) in 1873–74, became head of the office of engineering and adviser of the public works department in 1875, and served again on the cabinet as director of education in August 1878. He would later serve in three cabinets under Tawfiq (q.v.). Ali often was dismissed from government posts because he lacked protection, even within the village elite, and depended wholly on his ruler's patronage. Strongly patriotic, he urged Egyptians to view government work as an opportunity to serve the people, not merely to enrich themselves. He did benefit materially from his posts, but less than other officials. He was proud of his ethnic Egyptian background, cared about the students and peasants under his care, and advanced the careers of several notable Egyptians. He wrote a patriotic story inspired by the traditional *maqamat* (a genre of Arabic literature, written in rhymed prose), *Alam al-Din*, and a detailed description of nineteenth-century Egypt still used by historians, *al-Khitat al-Tawfiqiyya*.

MUBARAK, [MUHAMMAD] HUSNI (1928-). Officer, politician, and Egypt's president since Sadat's (q.v.) assassination. Born in Minufiyya province to a peasant family, Husni Mubarak graduated from the Military Academy (q.v.) in 1949 and the Air Force Academy in 1950. After a brief stint as a fighter pilot, he was an instructor at the Air Force Academy in 1954–61 and spent the following academic year at the Soviet General Staff Academy. He was commandant of the Air Force Academy in 1967–69, chief of staff of the air force in 1969–71, and then became commander-in-chief of the air force, where he spearheaded Egypt's preparations for the October War (q.v.). Because of the air force's stellar performance in the war, he was promoted to the rank of air marshal in 1974. The following year Mubarak was appointed vice president by Sadat (q.v.), whom he served loyally for the rest of Sadat's life. He assumed the presidency after the assassination, was nominated within a week by the National Democratic Party (q.v.), and was confirmed by a referendum without opposition. His policies have included maintaining close relations with the United States, on whose economic aid Egypt has become ever more dependent; strengthening state control over the economy to promote efficiency, raise general living standards, and curb government corruption; reestablishing diplomatic and economic ties with the Arab states without breaking Egypt's relations with Israel; and curbing the resurgent Islamists (q.v.). More self-effacing than his predecessors, Mubarak inspires neither strong loyalty nor aversion among the Egyptian people.

MUDIR. Governor of a rural province (called a *mudiriyya*), before 1960.

MUFATTISH. A financial or irrigation inspector; more specifically, Khedive Isma'il's (qq.v.) powerful financial official, Isma'il Siddiq (q.v.).

MUHAFAZA. Formerly, the term used for the governorates of Cairo (q.v.) and Alexandria (q.v.), used since 1960 to denote all Egyptian provinces (*see* Provincial Government).

MUHAMMAD ALI (1769–1849). Ottoman (q.v.) officer, reforming viceroy from 1805 to 1848, and founder of the dynasty that ruled Egypt until 1952. Born in Qavalla (Macedonia), he was the son of a tobacco merchant who was also a soldier. His military (and possibly naval) experience was gleaned from fighting bandits and pirates in his province, and he became an officer in the Ottoman army despite his lack of formal education; he did not learn to read until he was 45. He came to Egypt in 1801 as second in command of a 300-man Albanian regiment in the Ottoman army, allied with the British, to end the French occupation (q.v.). He persuaded the Mamluks (q.v.) to aid the Ottomans and his Albanians against the French. He then maneuvered the ulama (q.v.) and Mamluk factions to oust the Ottoman-appointed governors Khusrev (q.v.) and then Khurshid (q.v.), so that he could himself be named governor in 1805. He went on contending with the remaining Mamluks, until he had them massacred in 1811.

Acting as a loyal vassal of the Ottoman sultan, Muhammad Ali sent troops to suppress the Wahhabi (q.v.) rebellion in Arabia, thus conquering the Hijaz (q.v.) for Egypt. Constructing a Nile (q.v.) river fleet, he also sent forces to conquer the eastern Sudan (q.v.) in 1822, hoping to staff his armies with Blacks, but most could not survive Egypt's climate. He replaced them with Egyptian peasants, who had not been conscripted since antiquity. He ordered dams, dikes, canals, and catch basins built to improve Nile irrigation (q.v.), and many cash crops were introduced, including long-staple Egyptian cotton (q.v.). By putting all agricultural land under a state monopoly, he controlled the output and price of cash crops, thus raising the money needed to pay for his other reforms.

Muhammad Ali was the first non-Western ruler who tried to industrialize his country on a Western model. He sent student missions to European universities, military academies, and technical institutes; he also imported Western instructors to staff the academies and schools that he founded in Egypt to train officers, engineers, physicians, and administrators. He set up factories to spin and weave textiles and to manufacture munitions, staffing them with Egyptian peasant conscripts. He created an arsenal in Alexandria (q.v.) for naval ship construction, enabling Egypt to take part in the Morean campaign against the Greek war for independence, but most of the Egyptian fleet was sunk at Navarino (q.v.) and the Ottomans eventually lost that war. When they reneged on their promise to award Crete to Muhammad Ali, his son Ibrahim (q.v.) invaded Syria in 1831 and governed that region for eight years. When the Ottomans tried to retake Syria, Ibrahim defeated them at Nezib (q.v.), the reigning sultan died, and the Ottoman fleet deserted Istanbul for Alexandria. Britain and Austria intervened against the victors, eventually making Ibrahim withdraw from Syria but promising that Muhammad Ali could pass down his governorship of Egypt to his heirs. Once Egypt accepted the 1840 London Convention (q.v.), it had to abide by the 1838 Anglo-Ottoman trade agreement, which caused most of the state-run factories to close because they could not compete against British manufactures, and also had to limit its army to 18,000 active soldiers.

Muhammad Ali then lost interest in his Westernizing reforms. He let his factories and schools decay and gave away many state-controlled lands to family members or to favored officers and officials of his government. Treated with silver nitrate for a bowel complaint, the cure affected his mental powers, and in 1848 he agreed to relinquish his governorship to Ibrahim, who died soon afterward of tuberculosis, leaving the post to Abbas Hilmi I (q.v.). Muhammad Ali was one of the ablest men ever to govern Egypt and did much to increase the country's power and wealth, but he showed no concern for his subjects' welfare and established a system of personal rule that, in the hands of less capable descendants, would prove ruinous to his dynasty and injurious to Egypt.

MUHAMMAD ALI (1876–1955). Younger brother of Abbas Hilmi II (q.v.), horse breeder, art collector, owner of Manyal Palace on the island of Rawda, world traveler, and writer, he served on Faruq's (q.v.) regency council in 1936–37 and was heir apparent until the king's son was born in 1952. A handsome, cosmopolitan bachelor, aloof from politics, he wrote Arabic and French memoirs, portions of which appear in Emine Foat Tugay's *Three Centuries* (1963).

MUHAMMAD ALI CLUB. Upper-class men's social organization. Located in central Cairo (q.v.), it has in recent years been converted into a club for foreign diplomats.

MUHYI AL-DIN, KHALID (1923-). Officer, leftist politician, and close friend of Nasir (q.v.). Born to a middle-income landowning family in Daqahliyya province, he graduated in 1940 from the Military Academy (q.v.) and also earned a B.A. in economics at Cairo University (q.v.) in 1951. He was associated with Hadeto (q.v.), but probably never joined that communist group. A member of the Free Officers (q.v.) and the Revolutionary Command Council (RCC) (q.v.), he backed Najib (q.v.) against Nasir, leading to his expulsion and brief arrest. Khalid led the left wing of the officers' group, served on the central committee of the National Union (q.v.), became a member of the National Assembly (q.v.) in 1957, chaired the Egyptian Peace Council, and hence became a member of the World Peace Movement's presidential council in 1958, and edited *al-Masa* (a leftist newspaper) in 1955–59. He briefly chaired the board of *al-Akhbar* (q.v.) in 1964 and the Press Council in 1965. He became a member of the eight-man executive committee of the Arab Socialist Union (ASU) (q.v.) in 1964, chaired the Aswan High Dam (q.v.) Committee, and was awarded the Lenin Peace Prize in 1970. Under Sadat (q.v.) Khalid's power diminished. Within the ASU he took the leadership of the leftist platform that evolved into the National Progressive Union Party (q.v.) and was one of the three delegates elected to the People's Assembly in 1976. In 1978 he founded its party organ, *al-Ahali* (q.v.). In 1979 he was charged with antistate activities but was never tried. As a former RCC member, he was spared when Sadat jailed other dissidents in 1981. Now a leftist "loyal opposition" to Mubarak (q.v.), he published *Li-hadha nu'aridu Mubarak* in 1987. Khalid won a parliamentary seat in 1990, after three earlier defeats, and has emerged as an elder statesman.

MUHYI AL-DIN, ZAKARIYYA (1918-). Officer, politician, and vice president from 1961 to 1968. Like his cousin, Khalid (q.v.), Zakariyya studied at the Military Academy (q.v.), graduating with Nasir (q.v.) and Sadat (q.v.) in 1938. He joined the Free Officers (q.v.) on the eve of 1952 Revolution (q.v.) and became a member of the Revolutionary Command Council (q.v.) He was interior minister from 1953 to 1962; his responsibilities also covered state security and the secret service. He became vice president one month before the United Arab Republic (q.v.) broke up. He also was premier and interior minister from October 1965 to September 1966. When Nasir resigned at the end of the June War (q.v.), he designated Zakariyya as his successor, but this nomination was withdrawn after massive protest demonstrations. He continued to serve as vice president and also as deputy prime minister until he left the cabinet in February 1968. He has held no government post since that time, although he was considered as a possible successor to Nasir in 1970. He publicly opposed Sadat's peace initiative with Israel. Zakariyya is thought to have opposed the extension of Arab socialism (q.v.) and of close ties with the USSR, but he could not persuade Nasir to adopt his policies.

MUKHABARAT. Secret police under Nasir (q.v.) and his successors.

MUKHTAR, MAHMUD (1883–1934). Egypt's best-known sculptor. Born in a village near al-Mahalla al-Kubra, he attended his village *kuttab* (q.v.), then studied in Prince Yusuf Kamal's School of Fine Arts in Cairo (q.v.), graduating in 1911, and was sent to complete his studies at the École Supérieure des Beaux Arts in Paris. During his stay there, he was attracted to the heroic interpretations of the sculptor Antoine Bourdelle and to the Art Deco movement. In addition, he was strongly influenced by his teacher Guillaume Laplagne and by his early exposure to Egyptian Arab folk epics. Although he enjoyed fully the bohemian life of a Paris artist, he remained strongly nationalistic. Upon returning to Cairo, he sculpted the statue called *Nahdat Misr* ("The Awakening of Egypt"), which was featured in a modern Egyptian art exhibit in France in 1930. It was then placed in front of Cairo's main railway station and later on the mall leading to the University of Cairo (q.v.). Upon returning to Egypt, he began a statue of Sa'd Zaghlul (q.v.) but died of tuberculosis before he could finish it. Mukhtar's best work combines pharaonic formalism with a romantic celebration of Egypt's folklore and environment. His sculptures are well-known and loved by the Egyptian people and many are housed in the Mukhtar Museum in Zamalek.

MUNITIONS INDUSTRY. The manufacture in modern Egypt of firearms and warships began under Muhammad Ali (q.v.), who set up production complexes in the Cairo Citadel (q.v.), the Bulaq (q.v.) arsenal, and the Alexandria (q.v.) shipyard, but these early factories were closed following the 1840 London Convention (q.v.). Munitions production resumed under Isma'il (q.v.), but high production costs and insufficient domestic demand soon ended his program. During World War II (q.v.), when German submarines throttled Allied shipping, Egyptian capitalists such as Ahmad Abbud (q.v.) set up factories to produce bullets, bombs, torpedoes, and guns. The 1948 Palestine War (q.v.) stimulated the industry, and the Egyptian government later contracted with European firms to assemble warplanes, arms, and ammunition.

Following the 1952 Revolution (q.v.), the government tried to strengthen its military, setting up three new ammunition factories in 1954. Pressures to rearm mounted along with border tensions with Israel in 1955 and especially after the Czech Arms Deal (q.v.). Five major military factories were established in the late 1950s and early 1960s, producing HA-200 trainer aircraft, surface-to-surface missiles, spare parts for imported Soviet fighter planes, and armored personnel carriers. The missile program, advised by a team of privately contracted German engineers, alarmed many backers of Israel, which allegedly tried to assassinate the experts and sabotage the program. Nasir's (q.v.) government tried to take control of munitions industries and to avoid joint-venture programs with European firms. It tried to develop all areas of arms production, relying heavily on West European engineers and technicians. The missile program, for example, was crippled by U.S. and Israeli pressure on the West German government, causing the German engineers to leave before they had perfected the guidance systems. Egypt allegedly manufactured chemical weapons used in the Yemen Civil War (q.v.). Unable to attract foreign buyers, Egypt's munitions factories also began making consumer products, such as sewing machines, radios, and telephones, for the local market. The aircraft factories were converted into maintenance workshops, and the locally manufactured rifles and armored vehicles were deemed unfit for field combat. Personal rivalries among directors of the munitions factories also rendered them inefficient and unprofitable, and defeat in the June War (q.v.) revealed the shortcomings of Egypt's armament policy. In his last years, Nasir negotiated with the Soviets to bolster his country's military industries.

Shortly after Nasir's death, the USSR agreed to license the production of helicopters, radar systems, and heavy ammunition, but Sadat (q.v.) was already looking to the Western countries to revitalize the munitions industry. In 1971 he revived the ministry of military production, through which he began negotiating with France and Britain to license new munitions factories. After the October War (q.v.) he followed a strategy that combined Arab petrodollar financing, Western technology, and Egyptian facilities and labor, manufacturing parts instead of whole weapons systems and preferring weapons systems that were highly destructive relative to their production costs. Egypt also used reverse engineering to produce missiles and bombs suited to the MiG-21 fighter jet and the Soviet BMP armored vehicle. In 1975 several governments set up an industrial consortium (*see* Gulf Organization for the Industrialization of Egypt), but its program was aborted by the 1979 Egyptian-Israeli Peace Treaty (q.v.).

Unlike other production sectors, the munitions industry is now wholly state controlled. The government sponsors domestic research and development in order to reduce its dependence on foreign scientists and engineers. Egypt sells arms to other Arab and African countries; Egyptian arms sales played a major role in aiding Iraq in its war against Iran. In 1988 29 Egyptian firms were producing weapons worth $1.5 billion. Egypt also signed an agreement with the United States to assemble the M1A1 main battle tank. Due to the National Service Project Organization (q.v.), a growing share of the production of Egypt's munitions factories is entering the civilian market. Items thus manufactured include clothing, doors, window frames, stationery, microscopes, and many food items. Military contractors have built many of Egypt's new roads, bridges, sewer lines, and other infrastructure projects, and the military seems to be ever more involved in Egypt's economic life, with portentous consequences for future relations between the armed forces and the citizenry.

MURAD BEY MUHAMMAD (-1801). Mamluk (q.v.) leader, successor to Muhammad Bey Abu al-Dhahab (q.v.), and rival to Ibrahim Bey Muhammad (q.v.) as leader of Egypt from 1775 to 1798. A cruel and extortionate ruler, he commanded the Mamluk cavalry that was defeated by Napoléon's (q.v.) army in the Battle of Imbaba (q.v.). As Napoléon occupied Cairo (q.v.) and tried to open negotiations with him, he fled to

Upper Egypt. Murad Bey spurned his offer of the governorship of Jirja province and tried to offer money to the French forces to leave Egypt. He repeatedly evaded French attempts to capture him and later offered to make an alliance with the British, whom he would have allowed to occupy Alexandria (q.v.), Damietta, and Rosetta. The Mamluks would also have paid the Ottomans (q.v.) an annual tribute and a war indemnity. He died of the plague before he could conclude this agreement.

MUQABALA (1871). Law, promulgated by the Mufattish (q.v.) for Isma'il (q.v.), that invited landowners to pay in advance six times the annual land tax in return for a perpetual 50 percent tax reduction. The measure benefited mainly large landowners, bringing into the treasury only half the revenue expected by the government. It was abolished in May 1876 but reinstated in November, although without the previous land tax reductions. This law came to be viewed by Egyptian landlords as a privilege to be shielded from the foreign financial advisers, who called in 1879 for its abrogation. It was repealed in January 1880 by Riyad's (q.v.) cabinet at the behest of Tawfiq (q.v.) and the Dual Control (q.v.), causing landowners to back Urabi (q.v.).

AL-MUQATTAM. Pro-British Arabic daily newspaper, founded in 1889 by two Syrian Protestant College graduates, Ya'qub Sarruf and Dr. Faris Nimr. It was widely believed by Egyptians to enjoy moral and probably material support from the British Agency (q.v.) before World War I (q.v.), but later became more independent. Unable to compete against *al-Misri* (q.v.) and *al-Akhbar* (q.v.) for a mass audience, it closed in 1952.

AL-MUQTATAF. Scientific monthly published by the editors of *al-Muqattam* (q.v.) between 1876 and 1952, at first in Beirut and later in Cairo (q.v.). It long competed for influence with *al-Hilal* (q.v.).

MUSA, SALAMA (1887–1958). Journalist, writer, and socialist. Born in Kafr al-Afi, near Zaqaziq, to a Coptic (q.v.) family, he attended a Muslim *kuttab* (q.v.), a Coptic school, and then a government primary school. He studied at the Khedivial Secondary School from 1903 to 1907, but his intellectual formation owed more to the influence of Farah Antun, a secularist writer, and to Ahmad Lutfi al-Sayyid (q.v.). Drawing on a monthly pension that he had inherited from his father, he traveled in 1907 to Istanbul and then to Europe, spending a year in France to improve his knowledge of the French language and culture, for which he had a lifelong predilection. Musa lived in London for four years, initially studying law, and came under the influence of the Fabian Society. Returning to Egypt in 1912, he tried to found a socialist magazine, *al-Mustaqbal* ("The

Future"), but the government ordered him to suspend publication. He spent most of World War I (q.v.) living in a village near Zagazig and observing peasant living conditions. He taught briefly and then became an editor for *al-Hilal* (q.v.) and *Kull shay*. In 1927 he published attacks on the Lebanese press in Egypt and later opposed Isma'il Sidqi's (q.v.) cabinet. An avowed secularist, he introduced the writings of Darwin, Nietzsche, and Freud to Egyptian readers and scandalized public opinion by calling for writing Arabic in the Roman alphabet. Musa wanted Egypt to embrace European thought and civilization, espoused the theory of evolution by natural selection, and advocated an egalitarian socialism influenced to some degree by Marxism (q.v.), although he was never an avowed Communist. He was imprisoned in 1946 on trumped-up charges of sabotage, but really for attacking the monarchy. He authored or translated more than 40 published books, including his autobiography, *Tarbiyat Salama Musa*, translated as *The Education of Salama Musa*.

AL-MUSAWWAR. Popular weekly illustrated magazine published by *al-Hilal* (q.v.) since 1924. Its reported circulation in 1993 was 130,423.

MUSLIM BROTHERS, SOCIETY OF. Political group, founded in Ismailia (q.v.) by Hasan al-Banna (q.v.) in 1928 and moved to Cairo (q.v.) in 1932, especially strong in Egypt between 1936 and 1954 and later revived during Sadat's (q.v.) presidency, that called for an Islamic political and social system in place of the secular constitution. Many Egyptians, especially lower- and middle-class city dwellers, joined the Society, which is believed to have had about 500,000 members and an equal number of sympathizers at its apogee in 1948–49. It contained a secret wing, al-Jihaz al-Sirri, that was often accused of using terrorist methods against its enemies (*see* Jeep Case) and of assassinating political leaders such as Mahmud Fahmi al-Nuqrashi (q.v.) in 1948. After Banna was killed by government agents in February 1949, Hasan al-Hudaybi (q.v.) was chosen to succeed him as supreme guide. Some Free Officers (q.v.) had ties with the Society, which remained influential just after the 1952 Revolution (q.v.), but its support for Najib (q.v.) in 1954 estranged it from Nasir (q.v.). Its secret wing's attempt to kill him in November 1954 led to its suppression. Some of its leaders were put to death, and many served long prison terms at hard labor. Nasir briefly relaxed his repression of the Society in 1964, only to revert to further arrests, trials, incarcerations, and executions, notably of Sayyid Qutb (q.v.).

The Society revived after Sadat veered away from Arab socialism (q.v.). Led by Umar al-Tilmisani (q.v.), it was able to resume publishing its weekly journal, *al-Da'wa* (q.v.), and to contest student elections in the national universities. Suppression resumed, however, when Sadat arrested his political opponents in September 1981. Although the Society has stressed its peaceful character, distancing itself from more violent groups such as al-Takfir wa al-Hijra (q.v.), it has been severely restrained by Mubarak (q.v.). For example, publication of *al-Da'wa*, banned in 1981, has not yet been allowed to resume. It ran candidates for the 1984 elections to the Popular Assembly in conjunction with the New Wafd (q.v.), and in 1987 in a coalition with the Liberal (q.v.) and Socialist Labor (q.v.) parties, called the "Islamic Alliance" (q.v.), winning 60 seats. It boycotted the 1990 elections, but remains influential in Egyptian public life. Its supporters won control of the lawyers', physicians', and engineers' syndicates in 1992 elections.

Its female affiliate, the Muslim Women's Association, taught lessons on Islam (q.v.) to women, ran an orphanage, offered assistance to poor families, and helped to reconcile estranged couples. From 1936 to 1965 it was led by Zaynab al-Ghazali. The Society's youth group, the Rover Scouts (q.v.), often accused of terrorism, has not been revived.

- N -

NADIM, ABDALLAH (1845–96). Nationalist editor, poet and speaker, sometimes called "the Orator of the Urabi (q.v.) Revolution." Born and educated in Alexandria (q.v.), he worked as a telegraph clerk in Banha and at al-Qasr al-Ali Palace in Cairo (q.v.), as a tutor and farmer in Badawa (Daqahliyya), and as a shopkeeper in Mansura. He drifted into journalism, writing articles for the newspapers *al-Mahrusa* and *al-Asr al-jadid*, and for *Misr* and *al-Tijara*, published by Adib Ishaq, a disciple of Afghani (q.v.). In 1881 he began publishing his own weekly paper, *al-Tankit wa al-tabkit*, followed shortly by *al-Taif*, in which he first proclaimed his nationalist struggle. He was one of the leading proponents of Urabi and his movement. After the British occupied Egypt, Nadim went into hiding for nine years. Once discovered and arrested, he was expelled from Egypt, so he lived in Jaffa for a year until he was invited to return by Abbas Hilmi II (q.v.). He published *al-Ustadh*, a Cairo weekly, in 1892–93, thus becoming one of the few human links between the Urabist movement and Mustafa Kamil (q.v.), then a law student editing his own journal, *al-Madrasa*. Exiled again from Egypt in 1893, he went to Istanbul, where the Ottoman (q.v.) government employed him in its education department and then as an inspector for printed matter, and he died there. Nadim was an inspiring, often humorous, speaker and writer. Some of his writings were collected by his son and published as *Sulafat al-Nadim* (1901).

AL-NAHHAS, MUSTAFA (1879–1965). Judge, politician, cabinet minister, five-time premier, and Wafd Party (q.v.) leader. Born to a poor family in Samanud (Gharbiyya), he graduated from the government Law School (q.v.) in 1900, practiced law in Mansura, and in 1914 was appointed a judge in the Tanta National Court (q.v.). He was dismissed in 1919 when he joined the Wafd (q.v.) to represent the National Party (q.v.), which he had quietly backed. Exiled with Sa'd Zaghlul (q.v.) to the Seychelles from 1921 to 1923, Nahhas was chosen upon his repatriation to represent Samanud in the first Chamber of Deputies elected under the 1923 Constitution (q.v.). He became communications minister in 1924. Reelected to the 1926 Chamber as a deputy from Abu Sir Banna (Gharbiyya) and barred by the British from a cabinet post, he was elected one of its two vice presidents and, in the following year, its president.

After Sa'd Zaghlul died in August 1927, he defeated Sa'd's nephew in the contest to lead the Wafd Party (q.v.). Nahhas would become prime minister on five different occasions: 1928, 1930, 1936–37, 1942–44, and 1950–52. In most of these cabinets he was also the interior minister; in 1942–44 he was foreign minister. He headed the Egyptian delegation to the talks with Britain that produced the 1936 Anglo-Egyptian Treaty (q.v.). The popularly elected Nahhas government of 1936–37 also negotiated at Montreux (q.v.) to end the Capitulations (q.v.) and the Mixed Courts (q.v.). His government also persuaded the Suez Canal Company (q.v.) to admit two Egyptians to its governing board, set up Egypt's military schools for aviators and mechanics, and expanded the Military Academy (q.v.) by opening it to secondary school graduates who could pass a competitive examination, thus admitting many of the future Free Officers (q.v.). However, Nahhas's hastily formed youth group, the "Blue Shirts" (q.v.), broke into the Sa'dist Party (q.v.) clubhouse to intimidate its members and staged a noisy demonstration in front of Abdin Palace (q.v.), alienating King Faruq (q.v.) and giving him a pretext to dismiss the Wafdist cabinet. The king installed a caretaker coalition government of the rival parties and called an election, held in 1938, that was boycotted by the Wafd.

World War II (q.v.) drove Nahhas into an alliance with his erstwhile foes, the British, who made Faruq appoint Nahhas at the head of an all-Wafdist cabinet (*see* 4 February Incident). Soon after this incident, which tarnished his nationalist credentials for many Egyptians, Nahhas was further discredited by the defection of the Wafdist secretary-general, Makram Ubayd (q.v.), who denounced his policies and exposed his corruption in his *Black Book* (q.v.). Nahhas's wartime cabinet tried to solve several social issues by raising the farm workers' minimum daily wage, abolishing fees for the government elementary schools, lowering the taxes on small landowners, and legalizing labor unions (q.v.). His greatest accomplishment, however, was to initiate the Arab League (q.v.) by convoking the Arab leaders' conference that produced the Alexandria Protocol (q.v.). On the day after it was signed, Faruq asked Nahhas to resign. Nahhas played a major role, therefore, in committing Egypt to Arab nationalism (q.v.).

By the time Nahhas resumed the leadership of Egypt's politics, the country's ties to the Arab world had been confirmed by its involvement in the Palestine War (q.v.). Its defeat had discredited both the king and the constitutional system generally, but the old order made a final bid for popularity by calling a general election for January 1950. The Wafd won most of the parliamentary seats (although less than half of the total votes cast), and Nahhas managed to form a Wafdist government that lasted for almost two years. It passed new laws to benefit poor people, notably one that distributed a million acres to landless peasants; but his main aim was to get Britain to renounce its 1936 treaty, leave its Suez Canal (q.v.) base, and hand the Sudan (q.v.) over to Egypt. He failed. After 19 months of fruitless talks, Nahhas unilaterally abrogated the treaty that he had signed on Egypt's behalf in 1936 and also the 1899 Sudan Convention (q.v.). The British troops did not leave, but 100,000 Egyptians stopped working for them in the Canal Zone, the remaining British civil servants and teachers in Egypt were summarily dismissed, and extremist youths, or *fidaiyin* (q.v.), began harassing British forces. A shooting incident on 25 January 1952 led to the death of more than 50 Egyptian auxiliary policemen in Ismailia (q.v.), setting off protest demonstrations that led the next day to the burning of much of downtown Cairo (q.v.) (*see* Black Saturday). Faruq gave Nahhas emergency powers to quell the riots, but dismissed him the next day for failing to maintain order.

The fires of Black Saturday illumined the breakdown of Egypt's political institutions, and six months later the Free Officers (q.v.) seized control of the government. Nahhas, vacationing in Europe, hastened back to Egypt, expecting to be invited to head a new cabinet. Najib (q.v.) and Nasir (q.v.) met with him at length before deciding that the powers that he sought for the Wafd were more than they cared to give. In September 1952 the officers ordered all parties to purge themselves of their leaders. Nahhas defied the order, but the officers managed to split the Wafd. In January 1953 they abolished all political parties and seized their assets. The officers arrested Nahhas and, assuming that his wife had taken control of the party, took her into custody as well. Both were put on trial. He was censured for condoning corruption and she was fined for rigging the Alexandria (q.v.) cotton market. Both were deprived of their political and civil rights from 1954 to 1960 and confined to their Cairo villa, where they lived in relative obscurity. Nahhas's death in 1965 occasioned a larger funeral than Nasir's government had wanted. Personally honest but easily influenced by less scrupulous colleagues, sometimes jealous of people richer or better connected than himself, principled to the point of obstinacy, Nahhas remained popular because of his solicitude for poor people and his unflinching patriotism.

NAJI, MUHAMMAD (1888–1956). Painter. Born in Alexandria (q.v.) and educated at the University of Lyons, he worked briefly in the foreign service. Always drawn to an artistic career, he resigned in 1930. He was influenced by the Mexican muralists who stressed art's social mission, and his best-known work, "The Renaissance of Egypt," graces the wall of the Egyptian Senate.

NAJIB, MUHAMMAD (1901–84). Officer, politician, and titular leader of the 1952 Revolution (q.v.). He was born in Khartum and educated at Gordon College and the Military Academy (q.v.), which commissioned him as an artillery officer in 1921. He rose through the ranks slowly, becoming a brigade commander in the Palestine War (q.v.). He later commanded the Frontier Force in 1950 and became director general of the Infantry Corps in 1951. Admired by other officers for his integrity and his opposition to corruption, the Free Officers (q.v.) wanted to elect him president of the Officers' Club early in 1952. King Faruq (q.v.) rigged the vote against him, occasioning a political crisis. The Free Officers made him nominal leader of their revolution against Faruq (although Najib insisted in his memoirs that he had actually been given control earlier). He became premier, war and naval minister, commander-in-chief of the army, and governor-general of Egypt from 1952 to 1953. He was its president from 1953 to 1954, but with diminishing power, as Nasir (q.v.) used his control over the army and organized labor to counter Najib's backing from the Wafd (q.v.), Muslim Brothers (q.v.), Communists (q.v.), and many liberal Egyptians. He was placed under house arrest from 1954 to 1971 and his supporters were purged. Released by Sadat (q.v.), he attacked Nasir in subsequent articles and interviews and backed his benefactor, but was never given an influential government post. His publications include *Kalimati li al-tarikh* ("My Word to History") in 1975 and *Kuntu ra'isan: mudhakkirat Muhammad Najib* ("I Was President: The Memoirs of Muhammad Najib") in 1984. Modest and gentle, he was more a father figure than a revolutionary leader.

NAPOLÉON BONAPARTE (1769–1821). Conqueror of Egypt and Emperor of the French. Napoléone Buonaparte (his original name) was born in Corsica, the son of a lawyer with aristocratic connections. He was sent in 1778 to learn French at a preparatory school in Autun and then to boarding school in Brienne, followed by the Paris Military Academy. After spending several years fighting the French for Corsican independence, he quarreled with his patron and returned to France, where he established his reputation by besieging Toulon and taking it from British control, then campaigned in northern Italy. Arrested after the overthrow of Robespierre, a politician of the French Directory employed him to quash a royalist demonstration. Napoléon went on to command the Army of Italy, capturing most of the peninsula. The Directory wanted him to conquer England, but he realized that the Royal Navy would keep his troops from crossing the English Channel. He chose instead to strike at Britain's Levant trade and possibly its hold on India by occupying Egypt. He easily defeated the Mamluks (q.v.) at Alexandria (q.v.) and in the Battle of Imbaba (q.v.), but the British landed at Abu-Kir (q.v.) and destroyed many of his ships. Napoléon launched a counterassault into Palestine in 1799, but failed to capture Acre, whence the Anglo-Ottoman alliance and the bubonic plague forced him to retreat. He decided to return to France, of which he soon took control. His greatest achievement in Egypt was his introduction of a large corps of scientists and artists who recorded and illustrated the condition of the country (*see Description de l'Égypte*). His claim to be a Muslim and his support for the ulama (q.v.) against the Mamluks earned him no local backing. Instead, popular resistance was fierce and could only be quelled by force. His conquest of Egypt and his reforms profoundly disrupted its politics and society, accelerating changes that would lead to the rise of Muhammad Ali (q.v.) and his Westernization program (*see* French Occupation).

NAQIB AL-ASHRAF. Leader, or marshal, of the descendants of the Prophet Muhammad's grandson, Hasan, commonly called *ashraf* (q.v.). This position in Egypt was regularized during the Ottoman (q.v.) period and enjoyed great prestige by the time of the French occupation (q.v.), because the *naqib* was authorized to check the credentials of claimants to descent from Muhammad and to discipline those accused of crimes against the Shari'a (q.v.). One of the best-known *naqib*s was Umar Makram (q.v.), who held the post in the early reign of Muhammad Ali (q.v.), who later curtailed the powers of the *ashraf* by depriving them of their judicial authority and their private *awqaf* (q.v.) and tax farms (*see* Landownership). During the nineteenth century the position became hereditary within the Bakri family, often overlapped with that of *Shaykh al-Sadat* (q.v.), and was tied closely with Egypt's Sufi (q.v.) orders. As the privileges of the *ashraf* declined in the twentieth century, the position of *naqib* has fallen into desuetude.

NASIF, MALAK HIFNI (1886–1918). Woman poet, writer, and orator, often called *Bahithat al-Badiya* ("Searcher in the Desert"). Born in Cairo (q.v.), she was educated at home and in Egyptian government schools.

She taught at the Khedivial School for Girls, then married Abd al-Sattar Basil, a bedouin (q.v.) tribal leader. Her many articles for *al-Jarida* (q.v.) were collected into a two-volume book, *al-Nisaiyat*, of which only the first was printed. She was the only woman to speak at the 1911 Egyptian Congress (q.v.) and was writing a book on women's rights at the time of her death (*see* Feminism).

NASIM, MUHAMMAD TAWFIQ (1875–1938). Politician, minister, and premier. Of Anatolian Turkish origin, he was born and educated in Cairo (q.v.), graduating from the government Law School (q.v.). He served as minister of *awqaf* (q.v.), then finance, and twice held the post of premier at the behest of King Fuad (q.v.). He also served as the director of his office and president of the Senate. Nasim had a calm temperament and loved literature. His marriage to an Austrian in his last years set off press attacks, based on the public fear that his wife would take his vast wealth out of the country.

AL-NASIR, JAMAL ABD (1918–1970). Army officer, leader of the 1952 Revolution (q.v.), premier, and president of Egypt. Born in Alexandria (q.v.), the son of a postal clerk with family roots in Bani Murr, near Asyut (q.v.), he was educated at al-Nahda Secondary School in Cairo (q.v.), the government Law School (q.v.), and the Military Academy (q.v.). After being commissioned in 1938, he served in the Sudan (q.v.). From 1941 he taught at the Academy, also receiving advanced training at the Staff College. In the Palestine War (q.v.) he commanded a battalion that was besieged for six months at Faluja (q.v.), earning respect from both Israelis and Egyptians for its steadfastness. Promoted to colonel in 1951, he became a lecturer at the Staff College. Much of his energy went into organizing the Free Officers (q.v.) group that conspired to oust King Faruq (q.v.) and the other governing powers that it believed had led Egypt to defeat in Palestine and fostered corruption and backwardness in the country.

They executed a successful coup on the night of 22–23 July and took power, forming a 12-member Revolutionary Command Council (RCC) (q.v.) headed by General Muhammad Najib (q.v.). After the officers decided that they could not relinquish control to civilian politicians, Nasir began a power struggle with Najib, who wanted to restore the multiparty, parliamentary government. Nasir, who favored a one-party regime led by the army, prevailed, and in January 1953 the RCC abolished all political parties, except the Muslim Brothers (q.v.), and set up a single organization, the Liberation Rally (q.v.). Nasir also became deputy secretary-general of the RCC and in May 1953 deputy premier and interior minister. He had many leaders of the old regime put on trial and imprisoned. The power struggle with Najib came to a head in February and March 1954, when Nasir tried to use his position to oust his rival, who enjoyed the conspicuous support of the Muslim Brothers, backers of the outlawed political parties, Communists (q.v.), and other liberal Egyptians. Although Najib seemed to triumph at first, Nasir rallied his officers and some labor leaders and finally maneuvered him out of power. After the Muslim Brothers tried to assassinate Nasir in October, he banned their Society, executed or jailed its leaders, ousted Najib, and put him under house arrest.

During the early Nasir era, the revolutionary officers made major gains in domestic and foreign policy, land reform (q.v.), expansion of educational and health services, and elimination of much government corruption. They relinquished Egypt's claims on the Sudan and signed the 1954 Anglo-Egyptian agreement (q.v.), providing for the evacuation of Britain's forces from the Suez Canal (q.v.). Nasir even put out clandestine peace feelers to Israel, but they were negated by secret Israeli attempts to sabotage U.S.-Egyptian relations (*see* Lavon Affair). His evenhanded execution of both Muslim Brothers implicated in the attempt on his life and Egyptian Jews in the Lavon Affair was meant to placate domestic opinion, but antagonized Israel. In February 1955 Israel raided the Egyptian-administered Gaza Strip (q.v.), causing many casualties and revealing the Egyptian army's weakness. Nasir sought additional arms from the West, but his refusal to join the British-sponsored Baghdad Pact (q.v.) caused Britain and the United States to block any sales, invoking their tripartite declaration (q.v.). Influenced by Indian Premier Nehru, Nasir attended the Bandung Conference (q.v.), where he was persuaded to seek arms from Communist countries. As a consequence, Egypt concluded the Czech Arms Deal (q.v.) in September 1955. Anxious to prevent Egypt from falling to Communism, the United States and Britain, together with the World Bank, offered aid to help finance construction of the Aswan High Dam (q.v.), one of the regime's desiderata. Once Egypt accepted their terms, however, U.S. Secretary of State Dulles (q.v.) retracted the offer in July 1956. In retaliation, Nasir nationalized the Suez Canal Company (q.v.), a risky move that won widespread support in Egypt and the Arab world. The West's failure to restore international control over the Canal, either by diplomacy or by the Suez War (q.v.), enhanced Nasir's prestige. When Egypt promulgated its 1956 Constitution (q.v.), he was elected president for a six-year term.

As Nasir's leadership became entrenched, he began promoting state-sponsored economic development, including the nationalization of public utilities and basic industries, a policy which he called Arab socialism (q.v.). Nasir took up a conspicuous role in inter-Arab politics, generally backing Syria and Saudi Arabia against the Hashimite kingdoms of Jordan and Iraq. His idea of Arab nationalism (q.v.), appealing to the people against their rulers, became a *leitmotif* of Egyptian foreign policy, as did his policy of positive neutrality (q.v.), by which Egypt avoided forming Cold War alliances while seeking military and economic aid from both sides. Nasir opposed both the Baghdad Pact and the Eisenhower Doctrine (q.v.) and appealed to workers and students (and, at times, Palestinian refugees) to undercut pro-Western regimes. In 1958, at Syria's behest, Nasir agreed to an organic union of Egypt and Syria, to be called the United Arab Republic (UAR) (q.v.), which they hoped other Arab countries would eventually join. Egypt also hosted a non-governmental Afro-Asian Peoples Solidarity Conference (q.v.) in 1957 and in 1961 formed an alliance of non-aligned African states called the Casablanca Bloc (*see* Pan-Africanism) and attended a neutralist summit in Belgrade.

Iraq's refusal, after its July 1958 revolution, to join the UAR was a setback, and several other Arab countries that sympathized with Nasir's neutralism also remained aloof. In 1961, after he promulgated the July Laws (q.v.), Syria seceded from the UAR. Although chagrined, Nasir cultivated new allies, especially Algeria, and strongly backed Yemen's 1962 military coup, precipitating the costly Yemen Civil War (q.v.). At home Nasir convoked the National Congress of Popular Forces (q.v.), drew up the National Charter (q.v.), and established the Arab Socialist Union (q.v.) as the new single political party. The appointment of Ali Sabri (q.v.) as prime minister of a cabinet that included a worker and a female member for the first time, signaled Nasir's leftward drift. Although he continued to influence other Arab governments and rejoiced when Ba'thist officers overthrew hostile regimes in Iraq and Syria early in 1963, leading to new Arab unity talks, his regime was acquiescing in the continuation of separate Arab states. Responding to the draining of the Arabs' fresh water supply by Israel's irrigation projects in the Jordan River valley, Egypt convened two summits of Arab kings and heads of state in 1964, proclaiming plans to divert the sources of the Jordan and creating the Palestine Liberation Organization (q.v.). His ostensible aim was to satisfy Arab demands to harm Israel; the result was to postpone armed confrontation with the Jewish state.

In 1966, however, a radical Ba'thist regime took power in Syria and began provoking Israel by backing raids by Palestinian *fidaiyin* (q.v.). The Egyptian-Syrian Joint Defense Agreement (q.v.) failed to restrain Syria, which lost six fighter planes in a dogfight with Israel in April 1967. Advised by Soviet sources that Israel was massing troops to invade Syria, Nasir cast off all caution to build up Egypt's forces in the Sinai Peninsula (q.v.). He demanded the withdrawal of the United Nations Emergency Force (q.v.) and then blockaded the Tiran Straits (q.v.) against Israeli shipping in the Gulf of Aqaba (q.v.). Egypt's press, radio, and television competed with the mass media of other Arab states in issuing threats against Israel. Israeli jet fighters attacked Egypt and other Arab powers, starting the June War (q.v.). Within six days Israel had tripled the land area under its control, including the Gaza Strip (q.v.) and the Sinai, and Nasir had to accept a UN cease-fire. He addressed the nation on television, took responsibility for the defeat (although he accused the United States of aiding Israel), and offered to resign. Mass demonstrations, seemingly spontaneous but probably officially orchestrated, persuaded him to withdraw his resignation.

Nasir's postwar policies were more subdued. At the Khartum Summit (q.v.), the Arab leaders rejected any negotiations with Israel, but Nasir made peace with Saudi Arabia and withdrew his troops from Yemen in return for Saudi financial support. He later accepted UN Security Council Resolution 242 (q.v.), but waged a costly War of Attrition (q.v.) against Israel, only to end it abruptly by agreeing to the Rogers Peace Plan (q.v.) in July 1970. He seemingly was moving toward a settlement with Israel at the time of his sudden death in September 1970, just after he had mediated a Jordanian-Palestinian civil war.

His successor, Anwar al-Sadat (q.v.), changed many domestic and foreign policies, enabling Egyptians to assail the oppressive character of Nasir's regime and the failure of his economic policies. Nevertheless, his personal integrity, commitment to Arab unity, concern for the welfare of poor workers and peasants, and ability to stand up to the West are honored by many Egyptians. When Sadat's policies worked, Nasir's reputation suffered, but to the degree that Sadat, too, failed, Nasir's memory has continued to be revered by many Arabs.

NASIRISM. Western term for Nasir's (q.v.) political philosophy and program, which included nationalism, neutralism, and Arab socialism (q.v.). After his death, the term was applied to the political views of Egyptians and other Arabs who opposed Sadat's (q.v.) policies. A Nasirite Arab Democratic Party was formally licensed in April 1992.

NATIONAL ASSEMBLY. Term used for Egypt's short-lived representative assembly under the 1882 Constitution (q.v.), the larger parliament set up under the 1956 Constitution (q.v.), and the representative body, having restricted legislative powers, set up under the 1964 Constitution (q.v.) and initially limited to Arab Socialist Union (q.v.) members. The 1971 Constitution (q.v.) renamed it Majlis al-Sha'b, or "People's Assembly" (q.v.), and expanded its power to initiate and vote on legislation. Under Sadat (q.v.), it held spirited debates on many issues, even though it could not determine defense or foreign policy, nor could it revise the government's budget. It served as a sounding board for the

Egyptian bourgeoisie, Sadat's natural constituency, and as a place for politicians temporarily out of power. It sometimes blocked government initiatives, such as a tax on fruit trees, or checked abuses of power, as in attempts to build a resort on the lands surrounding the Pyramids. In 1976 its members were allowed to form alternative pulpits (*manabir*) to express dissident viewpoints and, from 1978, separate political parties. Sadat bypassed the Assembly by resort to plebiscites, e.g., in obtaining popular assent for the "Law of Shame" (q.v.). Mubarak (q.v.) has not continued this practice, but the electoral laws have so far ensured that most Assembly members come from the National Democratic Party (q.v.), which supports the government's policies.

NATIONAL BANK OF EGYPT. Privately owned bank, founded by Sir Ernest Cassel, Raphael Suarès, and C. M. Salvago, in 1898. It was an Egyptian company, founded in Egypt by a khedivial decree and having its board meetings in Cairo (q.v.), and its purposes were to serve as the government bank and the bank of issue for Egypt's currency. The timing of its creation was partly due to the concurrent need to finance the building of the Aswan Dam (q.v.) and the barrage at Asyut (q.v.) at a cost of £E2 million and also to sell the state domain (*daira saniyya*) lands to Egyptian buyers. In another sense, it was foreign, in that half the shares were subscribed in the City of London and that the London directors for many years had special rights. The Egyptian government was represented by two controllers paid by the bank. It soon established as subsidiaries the Agricultural Bank of Egypt and the Bank of Abyssinia. It helped other banks and businesses to weather the panic of 1907, the removal of the gold cover from banknotes during World War I (q.v.), and the Great Depression of 1929–39. During World War II (q.v.) the National Bank played a crucial role in retiring and refunding the existing government debt and in administering exchange controls. Upon the renewal of the bank's charter in 1940 for an additional 40 years, its role as a bank of issue was further defined and provisions were made for the further Egyptianization of its board of directors, but its conversion to the status of Egypt's central bank was postponed due to the war. Nationalized by the Nasir (q.v.) government in 1960, its national bank functions were turned over to the newly created Central Bank of Egypt. In 1971 it became the primary bank for financing Egypt's foreign trade.

NATIONAL CHARTER (1962), ***see*** **CHARTER, NATIONAL.**

NATIONAL COMMITTEE OF WORKERS AND STUDENTS (NCWS). Coalition of mainly leftist organizations set up after the Abbas Bridge Incident (q.v.) to oppose Sidqi's (q.v.) government. Joined by members of Iskra (q.v.), the Egyptian Movement of National Liberation (q.v.), and the Wafdist Vanguard (q.v.), it organized the Cairo (q.v.) demonstration by students and workers of 21 February 1946. Orderly at first, it turned violent in Midan Ismailia (now Liberation Square [q.v.]) because of aggressive behavior by British troops, leading first to small fights and then to massive violence as demonstrators attacked foreign shops, clubs, and the British Qasr al-Nil (q.v.) barracks. The reported toll was 23 dead and 121 wounded. The National Committee declared 4 March as a day of mourning. It became a general strike, provoking clashes in Alexandria (q.v.) between demonstrators and police, causing 28 deaths and 342 injuries. Britain's announcement four days later that it was evacuating its barracks in Cairo, Alexandria, and the Delta was interpreted as an NCWS victory. However, the group was loosely organized, and the Sidqi ministry managed to crush it in July 1946 as part of its general suppression of leftist organizations.

NATIONAL CONGRESS OF POPULAR FORCES (1962). Assembly made up of 1,500 popularly elected delegates, representing intellectuals, workers, peasants, national capitalists, and soldiers, and an appointed preparatory committee of 250 delegates charged by the Nasir (q.v.) government with debating and approving the National Charter (q.v.).

NATIONAL COURTS. The tribunals set up in 1883 to try civil and criminal cases involving Egyptian nationals. The procedures and many of the laws originally reflected those already incorporated into the Mixed Courts (q.v.) and were mainly influenced by the Code Napoléon, but also included aspects of Egypt's existing administrative (*see* Council of Justice) and Shari'a Courts (q.v.). Because of Egypt's political and historical evolution during the twentieth century, the national tribunals have absorbed the Mixed Courts and those of the Muslims and other religious communities. Nasir's (q.v.) government sapped the independence of the judiciary, but under Sadat (q.v.) and Mubarak (q.v.) the National Courts have occasionally resisted government attempts to violate civil liberties and to manipulate parliamentary elections.

NATIONAL DEMOCRATIC FRONT. Coalition of Muslim Brothers (q.v.), Wafdists (q.v.), Communists (q.v.), and other Egyptian political groups that backed Najib (q.v.) in 1953–54 against Nasir's (q.v.) efforts to ban all parties other than the government-sanctioned Liberation Rally (q.v.). Highly articulate in their condemnation of military dictatorship, the National Democratic Front's leaders were divided on their methods and goals. They failed to persuade enough Egyptians to support democratic government, which many believed had failed to benefit them between 1923 and 1952. The army crushed the Front in April 1954, and hundreds of its members were sentenced to penal servitude as Nasir took power.

NATIONAL DEMOCRATIC PARTY (NDP). Political organization founded by Sadat (q.v.) in 1978 to replace the Arab Socialist Union (ASU) (q.v.). The drive to create this party began within the People's Assembly (q.v.) in 1976, when Mahmud Abu Wafia assumed the leadership of the ASU's central platform (*minbar*), taking the name of "the Arab Socialist Party of Egypt," often abbreviated to Misr Party, and led by the prime minister, Mamduh Salim (q.v.). In 1978 Sadat abolished the ASU and designated the Misr Party as the official organization, renamed it the National Democratic Party, and made himself its president. He later turned the leadership over to Husni Mubarak (q.v.) in 1980. The party's proclaimed policies, such as the preservation of the Arab socialist gains made under Nasir (q.v.), the defense of the Arab cause, and positive neutrality, were generally the opposite of the government ones that it supported in fact. It served more as an instrument of indoctrination from above than of recruitment from below. The NDP was heavily subservient to Sadat's person and policies during his lifetime. Mubarak sought a middle ground between identifying with the party and distancing himself from it. The government has appointed its leaders; only in 1986 did the NDP finally hold a congress. Party membership is viewed as necessary for holding public office, but does not necessarily imply active involvement, and the interior ministry often intervenes to decide who runs for the People's Assembly as an NDP candidate. Egypt's people care little about the party and its candidates; candidates enter–and leave–NDP election lists often. Opposition parties stir greater public interest, but the electoral system ensures that NDP candidates will retain the majority. The interests articulated by the NDP are those of the bureaucracy (q.v.) and the bourgeoisie, rather than the workers and peasants of the ASU under Nasir (q.v.). In the 1990 elections it received 79.8 percent of the popular vote, winning 348 of the 437 People's Assembly seats.

NATIONAL FRONT (1935). Coalition of political parties and associations formed to oppose the Palace-dominated government and to restore the 1923 Constitution (q.v.).

NATIONAL ISLAMIC PARTY, *see* MISR AL-FATAT.

NATIONAL PARTY. Name generally applied by Egyptians and foreigners to several political organizations involved in the movement, led by Colonel Ahmad Urabi (q.v.), opposing foreign control of Egypt in 1881–82. It also denotes the political organization founded initially in

1895 as a secret society under Khedive Abbas Hilmi II (qq.v.), later as a public movement led by Mustafa Kamil (q.v.) and open to all Egyptians desiring the evacuation of British troops from Egypt and the Sudan (q.v.). The National Party also called on the khedive (q.v.) to grant a constitution that would introduce parliamentary government and ministerial responsibility to Egypt. After Mustafa's death in 1908, Muhammad Farid (q.v.) led the Party in a more radical direction, espousing pan-Islam (q.v.) and far-reaching economic and social reforms. However, British repressive measures such as the 1909 Press Law (q.v.) and later the Exceptional Laws (q.v.) and internal divisions weakened the Nationalists in Egypt. The assassination of Prime Minister Butros Ghali (q.v.) by a Nationalist alienated many moderate backers of the movement. Most Nationalist leaders sought refuge in Europe, where they aided the Ottoman Empire (q.v.) and Germany during World War I (q.v.). After the armistice, the National Party in Egypt helped the Wafd (q.v.) in organizing what became the 1919 Revolution (q.v.), but gradually lost most of its members to Sa'd Zaghlul (q.v.). Led by Hafiz Ramadan (q.v.), the Party survived until 1952, when it voluntarily disbanded itself to support the revolutionary officers.

NATIONAL PROGRESSIVE UNIONIST PARTY (NPUP). The leftist offshoot of the Arab Socialist Union (ASU) (q.v.). Headed by Khalid Muhyi al-Din (q.v.), the NPUP, often called the Tajammu' ("coalition") Party in Arabic, sought to preserve the socialist gains of the 1952 Revolution (q.v.). Feared by Sadat (q.v.) as a Nasirite (q.v.) front, he tried to weaken it by instigating the formation of the Socialist Labor Party (q.v.) in 1978. The NPUP has survived, however, because of Khalid's political acumen and its appeal to the groups that had benefited from Nasir's (q.v.) reforms. Marxists (q.v.) and journalists are strong within the party; there are few army officers, bureaucrats, or ASU operatives, except for backers of the Vanguard group once led by Ali Sabri (q.v.). It claimed 150,000 members in 1978, and its mouthpiece, *al-Ahali* (q.v.), attracted 100,000 readers before it was suppressed, at the time when Sadat tried, unsuccessfully, to disband the NPUP in May 1978. It won five parliamentary seats in 1976 and fared poorly in subsequent elections, due to government harassment and to the exclusion of parties earning less than 8 percent of the popular vote from representation in the People's Assembly (q.v.). In 1990 the Supreme Constitutional Court voided the amendments to the 1972 election law, which discriminated against small parties and independent candidates. In the subsequent election for the People's Assembly the NPUP received 1.8 percent of the vote and won six seats. Other opposition parties boycotted the election.

NATIONAL SERVICE PROJECT ORGANIZATION (NSPO) (1978). Group created in 1978 by the government to manage the Egyptian armed forces' enterprises that produce goods for military and civilian use. In 1985 NSPO production included £E488 million in agriculture, £E347 million in nonmilitary manufactured goods, £E174 million in construction, and £E144 million in other goods and services. The military accounted for 18 percent of Egypt's total food production in that year. Egyptians disagree on the desirability of the military's involvement in competition against private enterprise and the diversion of its energies from national defense. Its activities have been more restricted since Abd al-Hamid Abu-Ghazala (q.v.) was dismissed as defense minister in 1989.

NATIONAL UNION. Nasir's (q.v.) organization, established by the 1956 Constitution (q.v.), to mobilize the Egyptians to support his regime, replacing the Liberation Rally (q.v.). Its executive committee, containing three members of the abolished Revolutionary Command Council (q.v.), screened 2,500 candidates for the National Assembly (q.v.), approving 1,188 for the 1957 election. The National Union had a comprehensive pyramidal structure based on villages, quarters, district centers, provincial capitals, and a national congress, with an executive committee at the top. Established local elites soon took control of the rural committees, and Nasir came to view the National Union as a haven for reactionaries. When the United Arab Republic (UAR) (q.v.) was formed in 1958, membership was extended to Syrians as well, but the National Union did not adapt well to the UAR. After Syria's secession, Nasir abolished the National Union in October 1961 during his crackdown on the bourgeoisie and replaced it in 1962 by the Arab Socialist Union (q.v.). The government never involved National Union members in debating any policy issues; its role was limited to rallying the people behind the regime.

NAVARINO, BATTLE OF (1827). Defeat and destruction of the Ottoman (q.v.) and Egyptian fleets by the British, French, and Russians, during the Greek War of Independence.

NELSON, HORATIO, VISCOUNT NELSON (1758–1805). British admiral and victor over Napoléon (q.v.) in Egypt. In 1770 he entered the navy, where he was trained by his maternal uncle. He saw service in the West Indies, the North Sea, Canada, and France. In 1793 he took command of a 64-gun ship, the *Agamemnon*, occupying the port of Toulon and then the island of Corsica. In 1797 he defeated the Spanish fleet, for which he was knighted and promoted to the rank of rear admiral, and the next summer he pursued Napoléon's fleet across the Mediterranean, reaching Alexandria (q.v.) on 1 August. He attacked the 13 French ships moored in Abu-Kir Bay (q.v.), overwhelmed their greater size and numbers with superior strategy and tactics, and scored a devastating victory. Although he could not drive the French from Egypt, Nelson's victory assured Britain of mastery in the Mediterranean. He continued to fight against the French and their allies until his death at Cape Trafalgar.

NEUTRALISM, *see* **NON-ALIGNMENT** and **POSITIVE NEUTRALITY**.

NEW DAWN. Informal association of leftist intellectuals who published a magazine by that name, also called *al-Fajr al-Jadid*, and who cooperated with the Wafdist Vanguard (q.v.) in combating British imperialism and local conservatism. It also had ties with the Workers' Committee for National Liberation, which was influential among the textile workers of Shubra al-Khayma and Mahalla al-Kubra. After Sidqi's (q.v.) government cracked down on the Left in July 1946, it formed an underground party called al-Tali'a al-Sha'biyya li al-Taharrur ("Popular Vanguard for Liberation"), which helped to radicalize some labor union (q.v.) leaders and promote women's (q.v.) liberation. Despite its small membership, its journalistic activities gave it influence. It merged with Hadeto (q.v.) and the Egyptian Communist Party (q.v.) in 1958.

NEW TOWNS. Satellite cities established by the Sadat (q.v.) and Mubarak (q.v.) governments to ease population pressure on Cairo (q.v.) and Alexandria (q.v.). In 1956 the government published its first master plan for Cairo's development, estimating that by 2000 it would have approximately 5.5 million inhabitants, a figure that was exceeded during the 1980s. A second master plan was released in 1971, calling for the construction of "New Cities" in lands reclaimed from the desert in order to decentralize Cairo's burgeoning population. Among the new towns founded during the 1970s were Tenth of Ramadan City located 60 km from Cairo toward Ismailia (q.v.), Sadat City located 75 km from Cairo on the Desert Road to Alexandria, and New Amiriyya City located 55 km southwest of Alexandria. These were originally planned to have 500,000 inhabitants apiece, a figure subsequently cut back to 250,000, and the costs of construction were estimated in 1982 at £E3.5 billion to be spread out over a 20-year period. Hoping to promote the growth of the desert cities, the government offered doubled salaries for its employees, rent subsidies for both industrial and residential units, and ten-year tax exemptions for new industries. However, it has been hard to persuade families to relocate to these cities. In addition, Cairo has new satellite suburbs, called Sixth of October City and Fifteenth of May City, which have been made relatively attractive by accessible public transportation.

NEW WAFD PARTY, *see* **WAFD, NEW.**

NEZIB, BATTLE OF (1839). Triumph of the Egyptian army, commanded by Ibrahim (q.v.), over the Prussian-trained troops of the Ottoman (q.v.) army. If Muhammad Ali (q.v.) had not ordered Ibrahim to refrain from pursuing them, his forces probably could have crossed the Taurus mountains, traversed Anatolia, and seized control of Istanbul.

NILE, BATTLE OF THE, *see* **ABU-KIR, BATTLE OF.**

NILE RIVER. Longest river in Africa, second longest in the world, and the dominant natural feature of northeastern Africa. Measured from its most remote source in Tanzania to the Mediterranean Sea, the Nile is 6,600 km long and its waters serve a basin of more than 2.6 million square km. For Egypt, it is almost the sole source of drinking water and irrigation (q.v.), and Egyptians have always been concerned about how its waters are used. About twelve billion cubic meters of water flow through the Nile annually. Most of this water comes from the Ethiopian highlands, but some comes from the lakes of central Africa. Much of the rainfall in the southern Sudan (q.v.) is absorbed by its swamps, and of course much is lost to evaporation. The water entering Egypt from Central Africa, via the White Nile, is relatively constant throughout the year, but that coming from Ethiopia, via the Atbara and the Blue Nile, fluctuates, increasing when the mountain snows melt. Consequently, the Nile rises in the summertime and reaches its peak in Egypt in September.

Ever since human beings have tried to raise crops in order to control their food supply, they have made efforts to channel the Nile flood, using methods of basin irrigation (q.v.) or, more recently, perennial irrigation (q.v.) made possible by building such large-scale public works as the Delta Barrages (q.v.), the Aswan Dam (q.v.), and the Aswan High Dam (q.v.). The Nile Valley's soaring population in modern times has created problems of pollution, waterborne diseases such as bilharzia (q.v.), and depletion of animal life.

NIYABA. The institution of Egypt's legal system that represents the state's interests and that investigates cases and prepares them for trial. Often called the parquet, it resembles that institution within the French legal system and has some of the functions of the prosecution or the attorney general's office in English-speaking countries. In the Egyptian system, the Niyaba is subject to the interior ministry, whereas the judges are under the justice ministry. It guards its independence and its reputation for impartiality.

NIZAM-I-JEDID. "New Order," or the Ottoman (q.v.) military and political reform program, promulgated by Sultan Selim III (r. 1789–1807). Although stifled by a Janissary revolt in 1807, it served as the initial basis for Muhammad Ali's (q.v.) reforms in Egypt.

NON-ALIGNMENT. Preferred term for "neutralism" or the policy that Nasir (q.v.) called "Positive Neutrality" (q.v.), meaning abstention by governments from military pacts sponsored by Communist or Western countries. Egypt became interested in non-alignment in reaction to pressures from the U.S. government in the early 1950s to join an anti-Soviet Middle East Defense Organization and as a result of the personal influence on Nasir of Indian Prime Minister Nehru and Yugoslav President Tito. Although not billed as such, the Bandung Conference (q.v.) marked the rise of non-alignment as a basis for relations between governments. It took concrete form in September 1961 with the Belgrade Non-Aligned Summit, for which the three leaders held a preparatory conference in Cairo (q.v.) three months earlier. The non-aligned leaders reached the understanding that they would not abstain from all military alliances (in Egypt's case, the Arab League Collective Security Pact of 1950), but only those related to the Cold War between the USSR and the West. Cairo hosted the 1964 Non-Aligned Summit. Under Sadat (q.v.) Egypt's alienation from the USSR strained its ties with the non-aligned movement.

NORTHBROOK MISSION (1884). Unsuccessful British government initiative to reform Egypt's finances at a time when tax revenues were falling, due in part to the low Nile (q.v.) flood and the cholera (q.v.) epidemic of 1883, and disbursements were rising, due to military expenses, the Sudan (q.v.) campaigns, and indemnities awarded in compensation for damages resulting from the Alexandria (q.v.) massacre and fire. Seeking to relieve Egypt's treasury, Northbrook advised its government to defy the 1880 Law of Liquidation (q.v.) by paying the treasury some of the money earmarked for the service of the debt, causing the Caisse de la Dette Publique (q.v.) to sue the Egyptian government in the Mixed Courts (q.v.). In 1885 Britain convened a conference that modified some parts of the Liquidation Law, in return for admitting German and Russian commissioners to the Caisse. Egypt was permitted to float an internationally guaranteed loan for £E9 million to cover the Alexandria indemnities and to rehabilitate some of its irrigation works. The principle of international control over Egyptian finance was upheld, to protect the foreign bondholders, at some cost to the Egyptian taxpayer.

NUBAR NUBARIAN (1825–99). Armenian (q.v.) official, legal reformer, cabinet minister, and three-time premier. Educated in France and

Switzerland, he was brought to Egypt by an uncle, Boghos Yusufiyan, who was Muhammad Ali's (q.v.) chief translator. He worked at his uncle's side for some time and, after his death in 1844, was employed by his successor, Khusrev Bey. He soon became translator and unofficial adviser to Ibrahim (q.v.). He married into a rich Istanbul Armenian family, whose Ottoman (q.v.) connections would later enable him to serve his patrons, notably Khedive Isma'il (qq.v.). Abbas Hilmi I (q.v.) used Nubar as his chief negotiator with the British to build Egypt's first railway (q.v.). Having lived in Europe as a boy, he spoke 11 foreign languages, had read widely in Western literature, and knew how to charm Europeans. After seeking permission to leave the government service in 1853, he nevertheless acceded to Abbas's request to be his chargé d'affaires in Vienna. Recalled by Sa'id (q.v.) when he closed Egypt's agencies abroad, Nubar organized the growing transit traffic between Cairo and Suez, was named secretary to his cabinet, and in 1858 became director of the communications and railways department. He was dismissed 15 months later, ostensibly because of the delayed delivery of two guns ordered by the viceroy but due in fact to Nubar's dependence on the British consul general, one of several occasions when Nubar sought British backing.

Isma'il sent Nubar to Istanbul and to Paris to represent his views on the Suez Canal (q.v.) concession. In 1864 he assumed almost total control over public works and railways, becoming in European eyes the mastermind of Egypt's administration, but Isma'il's suspicion that Nubar was abusing his powers led in 1866 to his transfer to foreign affairs. Meanwhile, his rapid accumulation of land and money was making him one of the richest men in Egypt. He helped obtain loans for Isma'il, negotiated with the Ottoman government for the decrees that increased Egypt's autonomy, and worked between 1867 and 1875 to create the Mixed Courts (q.v.). Nubar served from 1875 to 1878 as director of the commerce department. When Isma'il agreed in August 1878 to turn his powers over to a cabinet modeled after those of Europe, he named Nubar as his prime minister. This "European cabinet," which included an Englishman as finance minister and a French public works minister, was dismissed by Isma'il in March 1879, following an officers' mutiny. Nubar returned to power in 1884, when Egypt was being pressed to evacuate the Sudan (q.v.), and served until 1888, a period when the power of the British occupation (q.v.) was expanding. He served as premier a third time in 1894–95, following the Frontiers Incident (q.v.). Adaptable, clever, and diplomatic, he is remembered by Egyptians for using his foreign connections to enrich himself at their expense. Mirrit Boutros Ghali annotated and published his *Mémoires de Nubar Pacha* in Beirut.

NUBIANS. Dark-skinned inhabitants of the Nile (q.v.) Valley between the First Cataract and the northern Sudan (q.v.). Until the 1960s most Nubians lived in small, almost isolated, villages strung out along the banks of the upper Nile. The men often migrated to Cairo (q.v.) or other cities to take jobs as household or hotel servants, leaving their wives behind. Often the sons of these servants would become educated and advance to middle-class status. Because the Nubians have been Muslim since the seventeenth century, there has been no barrier to their intermarriage with other Muslim Egyptians. The Nubians who lived in Upper Egypt were displaced by the various Nile irrigation (q.v.) projects, especially the Aswan High Dam (q.v.) in 1962–65. Energetic and adaptable, they are assimilating to Egyptian ways and speaking Arabic instead of their vernacular languages. Estimated Nubian population in 1990 was 160,000.

NUCLEAR ENERGY. Egypt acquired its first nuclear equipment, a 2-megawatt research reactor, in 1961 as a gift from the USSR and considered developing nuclear weapons in competition with Israel during the 1960s, an idea subsequently abandoned because of the cost. It signed the Nuclear Non-Proliferation Treaty in 1968 but did not actually ratify it until 1981, a delay that hindered Egypt's efforts to buy nuclear technology from the United States, Canada, Britain, and even the USSR during the 1970s. Soon after the Egyptian government ratified the treaty, however, it signed an agreement with the United States to build two nuclear power stations, but no action has ensued. In 1984, working initially with France, the Italian government began feasibility studies for a nuclear power station west of Alexandria (q.v.). Concerned about generating electric power, the Egyptian government has proposed to build eight (later reduced to three) 1,000-megawatt nuclear power plants by 2005, but financial problems have delayed implementation of this program. Egypt reportedly has deposits of uranium in the Western Desert 500 km southwest of Cairo (q.v.), in the Sinai Peninsula (q.v.), and in phosphate rock found among the beach sands of the Nile (q.v.) Delta.

AL-NUQRASHI, MAHMUD FAHMI (1888–1948). Educator, politician, and minister. Born in Alexandria (q.v.), he received his higher education in Nottingham (England). Upon returning to Egypt, he taught school, then rose in the administration until he became director of public instruction for Asyut (q.v.). A supporter of the Wafd (q.v.), he became the vice governor of Cairo (q.v.) and then deputy interior minister under Sa'd Zaghlul (q.v.). Implicated in the murder of Sir Lee Stack (q.v.), Nuqrashi was imprisoned briefly but then cleared. He held ministerial posts in the Wafdist cabinets of 1930 and 1936, but broke with Mustafa al-Nahhas (q.v.) in 1937. Together with Ahmad Mahir (q.v.), he formed the Sa'dist Party (q.v.), which joined several Palace-led coalition governments. After Ahmad Mahir was assassinated in 1945, he became the Party leader and headed cabinets in 1945–46 and 1947–48. He led the 1947 Egyptian delegation to the UN Security Council to demand that Britain withdraw from the Sudan (q.v.) and allow it to unite with Egypt, but did not gain its support. When fighting broke out between Jews and Arabs in Palestine, Nuqrashi reportedly tried to avoid committing Egyptian troops, but was overridden by King Faruq (q.v.) in May 1948. As defeats in Palestine stirred up discontent within Egypt, he tried to outlaw the Muslim Brothers (q.v.). He was assassinated by a student on 28 February 1948. Conscientious and patriotic, he was neither as charismatic as his rival Nahhas, nor as flamboyant as his royal patron.

- O -

OCTOBER PAPER. Programmatic statement issued by Sadat (q.v.) in April 1974. On first glance, it reaffirmed Nasir's (q.v.) commitments to strengthen Egypt, confront Israel, unite the Arabs, and lead the movement for non-alignment (q.v.). It paid lip service to maintaining socialism and the public-sector industries. In reality, the document muted these goals and stressed Egypt's need for foreign resources and, more specifically, Arab and Western investment capital and Western technology. As Egypt reverted to a market economy, the October Paper came to be seen as Sadat's first statement of his *infitah* (q.v.) policy.

OCTOBER WAR (1973). Large-scale war started by Egypt and Syria to regain lands occupied by Israel since 1967, also called the "Yom Kippur War" or "Ramadan War." Concerted planning began in 1971, following the breakdown in the indirect Egyptian-Israeli negotiations conducted under the Rogers Peace Plan (q.v.). Israel's rejection of a peace proposal involving an interim pullback from the Suez Canal (q.v.) and an eventual settlement based on Security Council Resolution 242 (q.v.) convinced Sadat (q.v.) that only by fighting could Egypt regain the lands it had lost in the June War (q.v.). He opened secret talks with Syrian President Hafiz al-Asad under the aegis of the proposed Federation of Arab Republics (q.v.), and both leaders agreed that a two-front war would be needed to defeat Israel. They decided to exclude the Libyan (q.v.) leader, Mu'ammar al-Qadhafi, from their planning, even though his oil wealth was helping to pay for their rearmament, but Jordan's King Husayn and Saudi King Faysal were informed. Sadat's ousting of the Soviet advisers from Egypt in July 1972 seemed to weaken his war-making potential, but actually it accelerated USSR arms deliveries to Egypt, and not all advisers actually left. By November 1972, Sadat felt that Egypt was ready militarily to go to war, but rearmament, training, and diplomatic efforts went on for most of 1973, leading Israel and the United States to disregard Sadat's public warnings of a renewed Arab war.

The coordinated Egyptian and Syrian attacks, code-named Operation Badr (q.v.), began at 2:05 PM on 6 October, which was the Jewish Day of Atonement (Yom Kippur) and the 10th of Ramadan. Using rubber dinghies, ferries, and hastily erected bridges, Egypt managed to get 90,000 officers and men across the Suez Canal within 18 hours. Their high-pressure hoses scoured 60 breaks in the earthen embankments of the Bar Lev line (q.v.). Egyptian artillery and missiles also downed dozens of Israeli airplanes and destroyed hundreds of tanks. Israel's forces had to retreat from the Canal, letting Egypt establish defensive beachheads along its east bank. But Egypt did not use its victory to capture the Gidi and Mitla Passes (qq.v.) and cross the Sinai Peninsula (q.v.), enabling Israel to shift most of its men and matériel to its northern front against Syria. Finally, at Syria's insistence, Sadat ignored his generals' advice and ordered an offensive to capture the strategic passes, leading to the fiercest tank battle since World War II (q.v.). On 15 October an Israeli unit pierced a gap in Egypt's defenses, crossing the Suez Canal under heavy fire. After two days of bitter fighting, larger numbers of Israeli men and tanks poured across the Canal and drove southward toward Suez City, placing Egypt in grave danger.

As Arabs and Israelis were receiving immense arms shipments from the USSR and the United States, respectively, U.S. Secretary of State Kissinger flew to Moscow to confer with the Soviet government about drafting a cease-fire resolution that could be passed by the UN Security Council. The draft became Resolution 338 (q.v.), which Sadat promptly accepted, to Syria's dismay. Syria hoped to regain some of the lands it had lost during the Israeli counteroffensive, and Israel also did not want the cease-fire to take effect until it had encircled Suez City. The fighting went on for two more days before it stopped, with the Israelis surrounding Suez City and Egypt's Third Army cut off from relief supplies. Egypt wanted the superpowers to intervene by sending a joint peacekeeping force to police the cease-fire, a move so threatening to the Nixon administration that it put U.S. forces on red alert. Nixon's drastic response may also have been due to an unconfirmed report that the Soviets were shipping nuclear-tipped missiles to Egypt through the Dardanelles. Fearing a confrontation with Washington, Moscow withdrew its peacekeeping proposal, and the danger of a superpower nuclear war receded.

Egypt's October War losses included 1,100 tanks and 450 armored personnel carriers, 44 jet fighters and 223 helicopters, 42 warships, and about 5,000 men killed, 12,000 injured, and 8,031 prisoners or missing.

The postwar resolution included visits by Kissinger and the Soviet leaders to the area, the Kilometer 101 talks (q.v.), the Geneva Peace Conference (q.v.), Kissinger's Shuttle Diplomacy (q.v.), and Separation-of-Forces agreements (q.v.) between the contending parties. The October War shattered the myths of Israeli invincibility and Arab military incompetence, proved the Arabs' ability to unsheathe their oil weapon against the West, enabled Sadat to restore Egypt's political and economic ties with the United States, and prepared the path for later steps toward peace with Israel: the Egyptian-Israeli Agreement (q.v.), Sadat's trip to Jerusalem, the Camp David Accords (q.v.), and the Egyptian-Israeli Peace Treaty (q.v.).

OPEN DOOR, ***see*** **INFITAH.**

OPERA HOUSE. Large theater in central Cairo (q.v.) built in five months during 1869 for the Suez Canal (q.v.) inaugural ceremonies. It was the scene of major speeches, ceremonies, and other public events for the following century. Destroyed by a fire in 1971, it has been replaced by a new opera house built in Zamalek by a Japanese construction firm.

ORGANIC LAW (1883). Based on the report of the Dufferin Mission (q.v.), this document provided for the limited participation of some Egyptians in their government during the early years of the British occupation (q.v.). It set up two quasi-parliamentary institutions having limited powers. One was the Legislative Council (*Majlis Shura al-Qawanin*) having 30 members, of whom 14 permanent ones, including the president and one of the vice presidents, were to be nominated by the khedive (q.v.) and his cabinet. The remaining 16, including the second vice president, were to be elected for six-year terms by the provincial councils and by elector-delegates from Cairo (q.v.) and Alexandria (q.v.). It was to meet five times a year to discuss legislation and the state budget. The government could spurn its advice but had to justify doing so, and Council members could question the ministers about their policies. The other was the General Assembly (*al-Jam'iyya al-Umumiyya*) with 82 members, including the ministers, the Legislative Council members, and 46 delegates chosen for six-year terms by electors throughout Egypt. Its members had to be over 30, literate, and paying at least £E50 in annual taxes. It was to meet at least once every other year and had mainly advisory powers. The government had to seek its advice on public loans, building of canals and railways, and classification of lands. If it rejected the Assembly's advice, it had to give reasons for doing so. The General Assembly was free to discuss any topic and to offer advice thereon. All members were remunerated for travel and for the cost of living in Cairo.

The president of the Legislative Council also chaired meetings of the General Assembly.

As of 1883, less than one-seventh of Egypt's population could vote for representatives, and only a small percentage of those eligible commonly exercised their franchise. Timid at first, the members of the two bodies gradually learned parliamentary procedure and methods of opposing unpopular policies, such as expenditures on the British army of occupation (q.v.) and the neglect of public education (q.v.). Muhammad Abduh (q.v.), appointed to the Legislative Council in 1899, played an influential role in its proceedings up to his death in 1905. The General Assembly was enlivened in 1909–10 by the decision of Butros Ghali's (q.v.) cabinet to let it vote on the Suez Canal Company's (q.v.) concession extension agreement. Rising Egyptian demands for popular participation in the country's affairs inspired much debate about enlarging the role of these bodies, and a formal committee went to London in 1908 to present its demands to the British government. Kitchener (q.v.), sensitive to these demands and hoping to divert nationalist attacks from the British onto Abbas Hilmi II (q.v.), called for revising the 1883 Organic Law to widen the powers of its representative bodies.

ORGANIC LAW (1913). Statutes promulgated by the Egyptian government, under Kitchener's (q.v.) supervision, that provided for a Legislative Assembly (q.v.), to be elected in two stages, with limited lawmaking powers. This Assembly included the ministers, 17 other members nominated by the government, and 66 elected members. Nomination of some members ensured a minimum representation of the communities and the professions: four members for the Copts (q.v.), three bedouins (q.v.), two merchants, two physicians, one engineer (q.v.), two representing educational groups, and one representing municipal interests. The government appointed the Assembly president and senior vice president. It could not promulgate any new laws without an Assembly debate, and no tax could be imposed without its prior approval. It could express its opinion on governmental measures, formulate its own projects, and could accept, amend, or reject any proposal of the government. If the government and the legislature differed, the matter was to be postponed for 15 days, and if no agreement could be reached in that interim, the government might either prorogue the Legislative Assembly or publish its law, provided that it explained its reasons for doing so. Excluded from debate were the civil list, the tribute to the Ottoman Empire (q.v.), the public debt, and all obligations toward foreign powers. The 1913 Organic Law fell short of the National Party's (q.v.) constitutional demands but did lead to two-stage elections late in 1913 for the Legislative Assembly. The Organic Law and Assembly were suspended during World War I (q.v.).

ORGANIZATION OF AFRICAN UNITY (OAU). Association of sovereign African states (including Egypt), formed at Addis Ababa in 1963 to concert their policies (*see* Pan-Africanism).

OTTOMAN EMPIRE. A multinational Islamic state that began in northwestern Anatolia in 1299 and spread across the Balkans, most of southwestern Asia, and the North African coast, including Egypt from 1517 to 1798. Following the French occupation (q.v.), formal Ottoman suzerainty was reestablished, but with the emergence of Muhammad Ali (q.v.) Egypt became increasingly independent de facto. Muhammad Ali's son Ibrahim (q.v.) invaded Ottoman Syria in 1831. Forced by the European powers to withdraw in 1840, the viceroy of Egypt received from the Convention of London (q.v.) the right to bequeath his position to his heirs, subject to an Ottoman *firman* (q.v.). During Isma'il's (q.v.) reign, his envoys negotiated with the Ottoman government to empower Egypt to contract foreign loans without prior consent from Istanbul, to change the succession to the viceroyalty to a system based on primogeniture, and to give the viceroy the title, already in current use, of khedive (q.v.). Each of these privileges accorded to Egypt increased the annual tribute that it had to pay to the Ottoman Empire, a figure that would reach £E500 million by 1914. The Ottoman sultan issued the *firman* deposing Isma'il in 1879 and replacing him with Tawfiq (q.v.). The investiture *firman* for Tawfiq's successor, Abbas Hilmi II (q.v.), caused a brief Anglo-Ottoman crisis in 1892 because it seemed to deny Egypt's control over the Sinai Peninsula (q.v.), an issue also raised by the 1906 Taba Incident (q.v.). Egypt remained de jure an Ottoman province until Britain severed its ties with the Empire in December 1914. During World War I (q.v.), the Ottoman government aided the deposed Khedive Abbas and the exiled Egyptian Nationalists, invaded the Sinai (q.v.), and reached the Suez Canal (q.v.) in February 1915, but its forces were repulsed. Late in 1916 the British-officered Egyptian Expeditionary Force (q.v.) led a counterattack that advanced into Palestine, taking Jerusalem in December 1917. Cooperating with Arab forces advised by T. E. Lawrence, the British drove the Ottomans from what now are Syria and Lebanon. Surrendering at Mudros in late 1918, the Ottoman government renounced all claims to Egypt in the 1920 Sèvres Treaty and again at Lausanne in 1923.

- P -

PALESTINE LIBERATION ORGANIZATION (PLO). Group formed in 1964 by the Arab heads of state to serve the needs of Palestinian Arabs and, in principle, to work for Israel's replacement by a secular state of

Palestine. It became the umbrella for most Palestinian military, political, economic, and social organizations and has, since 1969, been led by Yasir Arafat. Its relations with Egypt were close under Nasir (q.v.) and increasingly bitter under Sadat (q.v.), especially when he made peace with Israel. In 1983 Arafat made peace with Mubarak (q.v.) after the Israeli invasion of Lebanon and military defeat of Palestinian forces under his control, but PLO-Egyptian relations worsened during the Iraq-Kuwait dispute (q.v.). Since then the PLO has made peace with Egypt and sought negotiations with and territorial concessions from Israel. In 1992–93 its representatives negotiated secretly in Norway with Israel's foreign minister, leading to a Declaration of Principles signed in Washington on 13 September 1993 and subsequent negotiations, often held in Cairo, intended to create a PLO self-governing authority in the Gaza Strip (q.v.) and Jericho, eventually including the entire West Bank. This shift in PLO policy, if it succeeds, may vindicate Egypt's peace policies under Sadat (q.v.), once assailed by the PLO and other Arabs.

PALESTINE WAR (1948–49). Arab name for the war in which the armies of Egypt, Syria, Lebanon, Jordan, and Iraq were defeated by the newly proclaimed state of Israel, the end result of the Arab-Jewish struggle for control over the British mandate of Palestine. Individual Egyptians had backed Arab claims to Palestine throughout this struggle, and the Muslim Brothers (q.v.) and al-Shubban al-Muslimin (q.v.) became involved in the early 1930s, but the Egyptian government had not taken up the issue until after 1936. It was invited to send representatives to the 1939 London Round Table Conference. Egypt's delegation was headed by Ali Mahir (q.v.), a leading adviser to King Faruq (q.v.); he used his position to curry favor with both the delegations from the other Arab countries and the Zionists (q.v.). Indeed, up until 1942, it was common for Egyptians to seek a mediating role between Arabs and Jews in Palestine and to prefer Nile Valley unity over Arab nationalism (q.v.).

The premiership of Mustafa al-Nahhas (q.v.) marked the turning point, after he rejected Iraqi Premier Nuri al-Sa'id's proposal, backed by the wartime British government, for a Fertile Crescent union. Nahhas adopted Arab nationalism also to distract Egyptians from the damaging revelations of *The Black Book* (q.v.) and to win support from Muslim activists. Nahhas was the main organizer of the conference that produced the Alexandria Protocol (q.v.), calling for the creation of the Arab League (q.v.) and refuting Zionist claims to Palestine. King Faruq (q.v.), Ahmad Mahir (q.v.), and Mahmud al-Nuqrashi (q.v.), not wishing to be outdone by the Wafd Party (q.v.), completed Nahhas's work of creating the Arab League under Egypt's leadership. After the League was set up and World War II (q.v.) ended, Egypt's government and people reacted against Zionist and international pressures to admit more Jewish refugees to Palestine. Popular demonstrations on Balfour Day (2 November) 1945 led to widespread rioting and looting against Jews (q.v.) and other religious minorities. Egypt's interest in the Palestine issue was distracted by the movement to revise the 1936 Anglo-Egyptian treaty (q.v.), especially regarding the Sudan (q.v.), but the presence of the Arab League and pressures from other Arab countries and the Muslim Brothers meant that no Egyptian government could ignore it.

The UN General Assembly's Partition Plan for Palestine (q.v.), which Egypt had wrongly assumed would not pass, galvanized the government into taking action. Driven by fear of the Muslim Brothers and calls for jihad emanating from al-Azhar (q.v.) and believing that the other Arab states would go to war anyway, Egypt mobilized its army. Faruq was popularly thought to have been inspired by Karim Thabit (q.v.), but the British ambassador also assured Nuqrashi that his government would not hamper Egypt's intervention in Palestine. They ignored warnings from high-ranking Egyptian officers that the army was unprepared for war. The withdrawal of Britain's last high commissioner for Palestine and the Jewish Agency's declaration of Israel's independence on 14 May 1948 marked the start of the Palestine War for Egypt and the other Arab countries, as their armies attacked the new Jewish state on the 15th. Egypt's forces crossed the Sinai (q.v.) and occupied most of the Negev desert, but their drive on Tel Aviv was stalled by Jewish forces for six days. All the combatants accepted a cease-fire proposed by UN mediator Folke Bernadotte in late May. Israel used the respite to acquire more weapons from abroad; the Arab armies failed to do likewise. They lacked a unified command or even a common strategy. When Bernadotte's mediation efforts broke down and the fighting resumed, Israel drove back the Arabs on all fronts. Another cease-fire followed, one broken by both Israel and Egypt in October 1948, but Israel had succeeded in isolating the Egyptians from their Arab allies and drove them out of the Negev Desert, even briefly crossing the international boundary in the Sinai. Only Britain's threat to defend Egypt under the 1936 Anglo-Egyptian Treaty (q.v.) ended this Israeli invasion, and Egypt, embarrassed at the prospect of using a British protection it was trying to terminate, agreed to indirect armistice negotiations (*see* Rhodes Proximity Talks).

The Palestine War affected Egypt in various ways: it severed its overland connections with the eastern Arab countries, it revealed the corruption and incompetence of the Egyptian government and thus helped spark the 1952 Revolution (q.v.), it gave Egypt stewardship over the Gaza Strip (q.v.), and it committed all Egyptian leaders to advancing the claims of the Palestinian refugees and to issuing calls for revenge against Israel (*see* Suez War).

PAN-AFRICANISM. Movement calling for political unification, economic cooperation, or cultural unity of all Africans, often including persons of African descent. African-Americans and West Indians first developed the ideas and organization of pan-Africanism in the early twentieth century. One lesser-known advocate, Duse Muhammad Ali (1866–1945), son of an Egyptian father and a Sudanese mother, edited *The African Times and Orient Review*, the first pan-African monthly, in London from 1912 to 1914. He opened its pages to Muhammad Farid (q.v.) and other Egyptian nationalists and also wrote a book, *In the Land of the Pharaohs* (1910), supporting their independence struggle.

Historically, Egypt's interests in Africa were limited to trading with the peoples of the Sahara and the western Sudan and to claiming control over the Nile Sudan (q.v.). After the 1952 Revolution (q.v.), these interests broadened. Nasir (q.v.) included Africa among the three spheres of Egyptian activity in his *Philosophy of the Revolution* (1954). Following his participation in the 1955 Bandung Conference (q.v.), which confirmed his anti-imperialism, Nasir set up a committee of high-ranking government officials to develop Egypt's political, economic, social, and cultural policy toward sub-Saharan Africa and later created an African Association to lead the struggle to liberate the continent from Western imperialism. A more visible step was the convening in Cairo (q.v.) of the first Afro-Asian Peoples Solidarity Conference (q.v.) in December 1957, followed by an Afro-Asian Youth Conference in January 1959. Angered at the West's manipulation of the Congo's independence from Belgium in 1960, Egypt joined in 1961 with Ghana, Guinea, and other radical and neutralist African states to form what came to be called the Casablanca Bloc, opposing the more moderate Monrovia group of mainly French-speaking African states. When Egypt hosted the third All-Africa Peoples' Conference in March 1961, Nasir addressed the opening session and affirmed his government's "principles and responsibility" to promote the liberation of Africa. The division between the Casablanca and Monrovia blocs troubled most African leaders, including Nasir. On reexamining his policy, he decided that the radical demand, pressed by Ghana's Kwame Nkrumah, for an immediate political federation of all African states was impractical; economic cooperation must come first. Egypt also muted its demand that other African states end their ties with Israel, a concession welcomed by those countries in which Israel had a flourishing technical assistance program. Egypt joined with the other African countries in the Addis Ababa conference that established the Organization of African Unity (q.v.) in May 1963. Since then Egypt has offered scholarships to African students, promoted economic and cultural cooperation, denounced white settler regimes and other forms of colonialism, opposed racism, and generally cooperated with existing African states. However, the idea of African political unity has been largely abandoned.

PAN-ARABISM, ***see*** **ARAB NATIONALISM.**

PAN-ISLAM. Movement calling for the political unity of all Muslims, popularized by Jamal al-Din al-Afghani (q.v.) and promoted by the Ottoman Empire (q.v.) during the late-nineteenth and early twentieth centuries. At times, the term has also been applied to patriotic or nationalist movements in individual Muslim countries ruled by non-Muslims, especially if they sought the support of outside Muslim governments, groups, or individuals. Although Europeans suspected Urabi (q.v.) of pan-Islamic inspiration, recent findings show that the Ottoman government tried to use Islam (q.v.) to make him more obedient to the sultan's viceroy, Khedive Tawfiq (qq.v.). Early in his nationalist career, Mustafa Kamil (q.v.) sought ties to Sultan Abdulhamid II and used pan-Islamic appeals in his speeches and writings. Many Egyptians, including Khedive Abbas (q.v.) and Ali Yusuf (q.v.) joined him in backing Ottoman claims to the Sinai Peninsula (q.v.) in the 1906 Taba Incident (q.v.), even at Egypt's expense. Mustafa's successor, Muhammad Farid (q.v.), sought support from the sultan and the Young Turks against the British occupation (q.v.), taking refuge in Istanbul in 1912. In January 1913 he founded a pan-Islamic society in Geneva; it published a monthly bulletin detailing conditions of Muslims under the rule of the World War I (q.v.) Allies. Abd al-Aziz Jawish (q.v.), former editor of *al-Liwa* (q.v.) and other Egyptian nationalist newspapers, wrote a pan-Islamic manifesto for the Ottoman government when it entered the war and later edited a monthly magazine, *al-Alam al-islami*, also published as *Die islamische Welt*, in Berlin from 1916 to 1918. The work of these expatriate leaders of the National Party (q.v.), had little influence in Egypt because of the strict British censorship.

After the war, Egyptian nationalism promoted unity between Muslims and Copts (q.v.) during the 1919 Revolution (q.v.) and within the Wafd Party (q.v.), consciously rejecting pan-Islam. Rashid Rida (q.v.) expressed fear about the effect of the Turkish abolition of the caliphate (q.v.) on Muslims, and there was some debate among Egyptians, notably Ali Abd al-Raziq (q.v.) and Abd al-Razzaq al-Sanhuri (q.v.), about the caliphate, but neither of these liberals favored pan-Islam. Hasan al-Banna (q.v.), the supreme guide of the Muslim Brothers (q.v.), favored an association of Muslim nations, effectively advocating both nationalism and Islamic unity. Other Egyptian groups, such as al-Shubban al-Muslimin (q.v.) and the Society of Islamic Guidance (q.v.) espoused pan-Islamic views, and individual Egyptians organized or took part in international

Muslim conferences held in Jerusalem (1931) and Geneva (1935). Although Egypt's lead role in Arab nationalism (q.v.) after World War II (q.v.) eclipsed pan-Islam, some Egyptians, such as Sayyid Qutb (q.v.) and Ahmad Hasan al-Zayyat (q.v.), continued to advocate it, and Nasir (q.v.) founded the Islamic Congress (q.v.) in 1954. Egypt opposed the Muslim World League, organized by Saudi Arabia and other countries in 1962, but has taken part in the Organization of the Islamic Conference, established after the 1969 Muslim Summit at Rabat. Although expelled after the Egyptian-Israeli Treaty (q.v.), Egypt has since been reinstated and is now active in the Organization. Pan-Islam now stresses social and cultural cooperation among Muslim peoples rather than formal unity.

PARIS PEACE CONFERENCE (1919). Meeting of the victorious countries after World War I (q.v.) to restore peace in Europe and the Middle East. Egyptians led by Sa'd Zaghlul (q.v.) formed a delegation or *wafd* (q.v.) to attend the conference and to advocate Egypt's independence, but it was not admitted. Britain persuaded its allies, notably U.S. President Wilson, not to raise the Egyptian question, thus prolonging the 1919 Revolution (q.v.).

PARTITION PLAN FOR PALESTINE. The United Nations (q.v.) General Assembly's proposed division of Britain's Palestine mandate into Jewish and Arab states, with an international zone for Jerusalem and Bethlehem. The plan was approved by a two-thirds majority in November 1947, despite the opposition of Egypt and the other Arab states. The proposed Jewish area became the basis for the State of Israel, which expanded its territory as a result of the Palestine War (q.v.) and the subsequent June War (q.v.).

PARTY REFORMS. Sadat's (q.v.) policy of forming *manabir* ("pulpits," or "platforms") within the dominant Arab Socialist Union (ASU) (q.v.), a step toward Egypt's democratization. Many Egyptians felt that the ASU did not adequately provide for political participation or the articulation of popular needs. The ASU role in the "Centers of Power" (q.v.) opposing Sadat in 1971 and the inauguration of the *infitah* (q.v.) in 1974 turned him against one-party socialism. A parliamentary committee first studied a return to multiparty politics in 1974, but the "popular" organizations representing workers, peasants, and other ASU-empowered groups feared that such a change would subvert the achievements of the 1952 Revolution (q.v.). Sadat and the People's Assembly (q.v.) agreed to put off debate, reopening the issue in January 1976 and suggesting that left, center, and right "platforms" be set up within the ASU by October for the Assembly elections. Khalid Muhyi al-Din (q.v.) headed the left, Premier Mamduh

Salim (q.v.) the center, and Mustafa Kamil Murad the right, winning 2, 280, and 12 seats, respectively. Political parties were formally legalized in June 1977. The left *minbar* evolved into the National Progressive Unionist Party (q.v.). The center became the Egyptian Arab Socialist Union, or Misr platform, later the National Democratic Party (q.v.). The right later called itself the Socialist Liberal Organization and eventually the Liberal Party (q.v.). Muslim Brothers (q.v.) and Communists (q.v.) were not allowed to participate, and the debates among the legal parties were restricted to domestic policies. Although unforeseen by Sadat, the party reforms also inspired the rise of the New Wafd (q.v.) and of extralegal parties. State controls limit the range of difference among the parties and their ability to articulate popular needs, but these reforms have invigorated the press (q.v.) and parliamentary elections under Sadat and Mubarak (q.v.).

PEOPLE'S ASSEMBLY. Since 1971 the official name for the lower house of Parliament, formerly called the National Assembly (q.v.).

PERENNIAL IRRIGATION. System for distributing Nile (q.v.) waters to the Valley and Delta in modern times, replacing basin irrigation (q.v.). The basic distinction is that smaller quantities of water are applied to the land at two- to three-week intervals throughout the year, using larger canals deep enough to take in water from a low Nile. These canals need extensive dredging, formerly supplied by corvée (q.v.) labor, to keep them clear. To raise the level of the Nile, Muhammad Ali (q.v.) ordered the construction of the Delta Barrages (q.v.). Consequently, three channels were cut to irrigate the Delta: the Buhayra, Minufiyya, and Tawfiqiyya canals. In addition, the Ismailia canal, built under Lesseps's (q.v.) supervision, carried Nile waters from Cairo to the Suez Canal (q.v.). During the twentieth century British and Egyptian engineers extended perennial irrigation into Middle Egypt through the construction of barrages at Asyut (q.v.) (1902), Zifta (1903), Isna (1909), Naj' Hammadi (1930), and Edfina (1951). In addition, they twice enlarged the Aswan Dam (q.v.). Soviet and Egyptian engineers extended perennial irrigation to the rest of Upper Egypt by building the Aswan High Dam (q.v.). Perennial irrigation has made it possible to grow three crops a year on some irrigated land and has facilitated the cultivation of rice, which requires large quantities of water. Most Egyptian cotton (q.v.) is raised on land under perennial irrigation. This system has caused problems, such as the buildup of mineral deposits, which must be drained or flushed away; the loss of fertile alluvium that must be replaced by applying artificial fertilizers; and waterborne diseases, especially bilharzia (q.v.), that afflict workers who stand in stagnant waters.

PETROLEUM INDUSTRY. Exploration for petroleum oil in Egypt began during the reign of Khedive Isma'il (qq.v.), earlier than anywhere else in the Middle East. However, production only began in 1911 in the Sinai Peninsula (q.v.) and near Suez. The Anglo-Egyptian Oilfields Company was set up to manage oil production in 1912 and continued to do so until after the 1952 Revolution (q.v.), when the Egyptian government formed the state-run General Petroleum Company, although private concerns and joint ventures were allowed to continue work. Exploration in the Western Desert began in the 1950s, but the first discoveries, by the Western Desert Petroleum Operating Company, jointly run by Phillips Petroleum and the Egyptian government, were not made until 1966. Israel captured the Sinai oil fields in the June War (q.v.) and exploited them up to their retrocession under the 1975 Egyptian-Israeli Agreement (q.v.). In 1976 Egypt had a surplus of oil exports over imports for the first time in its history, but nearly three-quarters of Egypt's oil output came from the Sinai and Suez area. During the oil crisis engendered by the Islamic Revolution in Iran, more than 30 companies began exploring for petroleum in Egypt's deserts, and output rose from 400,000 barrels (2.5 million metric tons) per day in 1977 to 925,000 (6 million metric tons) in 1990 (about one-fifth of this was exported). Petroleum revenues peaked at $3.4 billion in 1981 and were reported to be $1.65 billion in 1989 due to falling prices. Reserves are not abundant and are likely to be exhausted within 30 years, but later if natural gas is taken into account. The first natural gas project at Abu Madi went on line in 1974. Egypt's proven reserves amount to 325 billion cubic meters, with a daily capacity of 240 million cubic meters. Egypt's seven oil refineries, concentrated around Suez City, had a combined daily output of 448,000 barrels in 1987.

PHARAONISM. Idea tracing Egypt's main identity to its own ancient civilization, as opposed to stressing its ties to Arab nationalism (q.v.) or pan-Islam (q.v.). Pharaonism was the prevalent expression of Egyptian nationalism during the 1920s and has retained support among many Copts (q.v.) up to now. It found expression in some architectural works, such as the campus of Cairo University (q.v.) and the tomb of Sa'd Zaghlul (q.v.), and its ideas have sometimes been adopted by Egyptians wishing to oppose the Muslim Brothers (q.v.), the Arab nationalism (q.v.) espoused by Nasir (q.v.), or ties with other Arab countries when Sadat (q.v.) sought peace with Israel in 1978–79. For most Egyptians, however, ties with the Arabs and Islam (q.v.) are too vital for them to identify with a long-dead, pagan civilization.

PLANNING, GOVERNMENT. Although the Egyptian government always influenced the national economy (q.v.) by investing in irrigation (q.v.), it rarely intervened in industry, except during the reforms of Muhammad Ali (q.v.), until after World War II (q.v.). Price controls, a few labor laws, the development of public transport, and a few munitions industries (q.v.) were the limit of government involvement in Egypt's economy before the 1952 Revolution (q.v.). The 1956 nationalization of the Suez Canal Company (q.v.), other British and French enterprises in Egypt, and foreign banks led to the expansion of the government's economic role, and the first Industrial Plan was promulgated for 1957–60. It called for a total investment of £E114 million (of which the government's share was to be £E24 million) in some 115 projects, especially in engineering, metals, machinery, transport equipment, and chemicals. The largest growth was, however, in textiles (q.v.), and the government's overall share in investment probably exceeded 30 percent. The government assumed the main share of investment under its First Five-Year General Plan (1960–65). A newly formed National Planning Committee proposed investing in chemicals, rubber, paper, petroleum (q.v.), and basic metals. Although impressive gains were made, the government's political needs and especially Nasir's (q.v.) claimed objective of doubling Egypt's national income within ten years often undermined rational economic decision making. Showcase projects, such as factories for assembling automobiles, jet aircraft, and rockets, often took precedence over others better suited to Egypt's natural and human resources. The first plan also stressed land reclamation (*see* Liberation Province). A second plan, to cover 1965–72, was effectively annulled by Egypt's defeat in the June War (q.v.). Emphasis shifted to rationalizing existing industries and offering incentives to improve performance.

Although less interested in economic management than Nasir, Sadat (q.v.) offered a ten-year plan (1971–80), which soon had to be replaced by an 18-month transitional plan. A new Five-Year Plan for 1976–80, which envisaged spending £E12 billion, was postponed in 1976 due to financial problems and hence was rescheduled to cover 1978–82. It was replaced by his 1980–84 "Peace Plan," with a planned investment of £E25 billion.

In a speech delivered on 20 February 1982, Mubarak proposed a more rational economic policy, featuring another First Five-Year Plan for 1982–86, emphasizing heavy industry and electrification, with £E27 billion in public and £E8 billion in private investment, but it fell short of its goals, due in part to the cost of servicing Egypt's large external debt. A new Second Five-Year Plan (1987–92) called on the private sector to play a larger role in industrialization (39 percent of the targeted investment, up from 23 percent in the earlier plan), mainly in electricity and power, industry, public utilities, irrigation and land reclamation. Specifically, it called for the reclamation of 627,000 feddans (q.v.), mainly east and west of the Delta, at an estimated cost of £E2,500 to £E5,000 per feddan, mainly at state expense. It also hoped to raise Egypt's gross domestic product by 5.8 percent annually, a goal that it failed to meet. Certain government policies, such as paying subsidies to hold down prices of wheat, cooking oil, sugar, kerosene, and electric power, have distorted supply and demand, hampering any rational economic planning. Such external events as wars and falling oil prices have also disrupted Egypt's economic development. The plan for 1992–97 calls for a total investment of £E154 billion, of which 58 percent is to come from the private sector.

POLITIQUE D'ENTENTE. Policy instituted in 1907 by Sir Eldon Gorst (q.v.), promoting closer ties between the British Agency (q.v.) and Abbas Hilmi II (q.v.), in an effort to win him away from the National Party (q.v.). Although the policy succeeded, it aborted a possible alliance between the British and the more moderate Umma (q.v.) Party, thus delaying the process by which Britain conferred more authority on such qualified Egyptians as Sa'd Zaghlul (q.v.).

POPULATION. In the eighteenth and nineteenth centuries Egypt's population was well below the optimum level for the size of the country, and measures were taken to encourage large families. There was immigration from other parts of the Arab world as well as from Europe. Overpopulation did not become acute until the 1930s, and efforts by the Egyptian government, foreign governments, private groups, and individuals to solve the problem date only from the 1950s (*see* Family Planning). One cause of the problem is that the death rate for infants fell from 183 per 1,000 in 1960 to 85 in 1988 and for children aged 1 to 5 from 155 to 42 in the same period. The overall death rate dropped from 10.5 in 1978 to 9.5 in 1987. Although the birth rate, too, has fallen, due in part to the later age of marriage and the spread of contraception, it was still 38.8 per 1,000 in 1987. Egypt's population is relatively young; 43 percent of the population in 1984 was under 15 years old. The number reaching marriageable age annually will probably augment its population faster than the number that the land can support. The total is likely to pass 60 million in 1994, the year in which Cairo hosts an international conference on the population problem.

PORT SAID. Egyptian city, founded in 1869, located where the Suez Canal (q.v.) meets the Mediterranean, hence a major entrepôt. Invaded by British and French troops during the 1956 Suez War (q.v.), it became for Egyptians a symbol of resistance to Western imperialism. Under the *infitah* (q.v.) policy, it became a free trade zone. Its 1986 population was nearly 400,000.

POSITIVE NEUTRALITY. Nasir's (q.v.) policy of not aligning Egypt with either the Communist countries or the West (*see* Non-Alignment).

PRESS. Although some Muslims resisted the introduction of the printing press, Arabic printed materials have entered Egypt since the seventeenth century, due in part to the development of Arabic presses in Europe for the propagation of Christianity. The French occupation (q.v.) led to large-scale printing in Arabic and French. Muhammad Ali (q.v.) founded a government press in Bulaq (q.v.) in 1822; it began translating European technical and military books into Turkish and Arabic. Later, it reissued many works of the classical Arabic heritage. Egypt has always led the Arab world in book printing and publishing.

Egypt has had a periodical press since Napoléon (q.v.) founded *Le Courrier de l'Égypte* and *La Décade égyptienne* in 1798. The official journal, *al-Waqai' al-misriyya* (q.v.), began publication in 1828. The first privately published Arabic newspaper was Abdallah Abu al-Su'ud's *Wadi al-Nil* (1866). Many daily, weekly, and monthly journals, both in Arabic and in European languages, followed, reaching an early peak during the Urabi (q.v.) revolution. The British occupation (q.v.) briefly halted the growth of the press, but by 1890 Arabic newspapers and magazines were burgeoning. Mustafa Kamil (q.v.) showed that journalism could inspire nationalism (*see al-Liwa*), and periodicals also appeared that espoused the spread of science (*see al-Hilal* and *al-Muqtataf*), feminism (q.v.), moderate reform (*see al-Jarida*), and support for the khedive (q.v.) (*see al-Muayyad*) and for the British (*see al-Muqattam*). Martial law in World War I (q.v.) closed many newspapers and magazines. After the lifting of censorship (q.v.) in 1919 journalistic activity resumed, aided in part by the introduction of the linotype typesetter and wireless telegraphy. Political parties played a major role in the growth of newspapers, with *al-Akhbar* and later *al-Misri* (q.v.) serving as organs for the Wafd Party (q.v.) and *al-Siyasa* (q.v.) for the Constitutional Liberals (q.v.).

After the 1952 Revolution (q.v.), Nasir's (q.v.) government promoted the growth of the press as a means of educating or indoctrinating the people, both through mass-circulation newspapers and magazines and by publishing inexpensive editions of books. Some partisan dailies were closed down when their sponsors were outlawed, but *al-Akhbar* (q.v.) and then *al-Ahram* (q.v.) expanded their circulation and influence, despite the restraints of government censorship and of part ownership by the National Union (q.v.) in 1960–62 and of the Arab Socialist Union (q.v.) in 1962–76. These controls were relaxed under Sadat (q.v.), especially after the party reforms (q.v.), but new limitations were introduced in the 1980 Law of Shame (q.v.) and during the state of emergency imposed since Sadat's assassination. Communist (q.v.) and Islamist (q.v.) papers have been accorded less freedom than the rest of the press under Mubarak (q.v.). Due in part to these press controls in Egypt, much printing and publishing have recently shifted from Cairo (q.v.) to other Arab capitals or cultural centers.

PRESS LAW (1881). Government statute permitting the suppression of an Egyptian newspaper or periodical "in the interests of order, morality, and religion" on the interior minister's orders after two previous reprimands or on a decision by the cabinet without any prior warning, in which case the offending paper could also be fined £E5 to £E20. The law was rigorously enforced at first, but newspapers discovered that foreign owners or editors could claim immunity from the law under the Capitulations (q.v.), and so the government stopped trying to enforce it in 1894. Its revival in 1909, directed against the excesses of the nationalist press, occasioned protests by Egyptians and foreigners, who again utilized the Capitulations to impede its enforcement. The cabinet passed a stiffer press law as part of the Exceptional Laws (q.v.) after the assassination of Butros Ghali (q.v.) in 1910. Severe limitations on press freedom were established during the martial law in World War I (q.v.) and lifted slightly after the 1919 Revolution (q.v.). The Press Law was reactivated by Abd al-Khaliq Tharwat (q.v.) in 1922, by Sa'd Zaghlul (q.v.) in 1924, and by Muhammad Mahmud (q.v.) in 1929, often in an effort to curb press criticism from rival parties (*see* Censorship).

PRISONS. Penal institutions have always existed in Egypt, especially when the central government was strong. The French occupation (q.v.) exiled or jailed Muslim resistance leaders (*see* Makram, Umar), and Muhammad Ali (q.v.) often executed or locked up opponents of his reform policies, using the Cairo Citadel (q.v.) or the rock quarries at Tura and Abu-Za'bal. The colonization of the Sudan (q.v.) afforded Muhammad Ali and his successors new means of getting rid of criminals and political foes. With the establishment of the Mixed Courts (q.v.) and the reformed National Courts (q.v.), Egypt needed a more orderly penal system. The prisons were placed under the interior ministry and administered by the provincial *mudirs* (q.v.), hence were separated from the justice ministry and the Niyaba (q.v.). In the early days of the British occupation (q.v.), budgetary stringencies blocked any reforms: overcrowding and disease were rife, food rations inadequate (relatives were expected to bring food to the prisoners), and clothing nonexistent. Many prisoners died. Criminals and delinquents were housed together, and suspects awaiting trial were often not separated from convicts. The public works ministry (especially public health) tended to regard jails as its dominion. With the appointment of a British inspector general of prisons in 1897, major reforms, notably in the quantity and quality of prisons constructed, were implemented. The provision of food, clothing, and better living and working conditions so improved the prisons that many Egyptians called them "hotels." Special provisions were made for juvenile and adult reformatories. A system of national, provincial, district, and village prisons developed and remains essentially intact.

After the 1952 Revolution (q.v.), the regime added hospitals to some of the prisons and built separate women's facilities. More emphasis was placed on rehabilitation and on reform schools for juveniles. Regrettably, prison overcrowding has led to wretched conditions, at times exacerbated by vindictive actions by the government, the judicial system, or prison wardens. It was reported in 1988 that six new prisons were under construction in nonresidential areas, with space available for farming and dairying by convict laborers. Amnesty International has reported cases of physical and mental torture, prolonged confinement, and inhuman treatment, especially of political prisoners, who in recent years have been mainly Islamists (q.v.) or Communists (q.v.). Descriptions of Egyptian prison conditions can be found in the writings of Anwar al-Sadat (q.v.), Sayyid Qutb (q.v.), Muhammad Hasanayn Haykal (q.v.), and Nawal al-Sa'dawi (q.v.), among others.

PRIVY COUNCIL. Founded in January 1847, this Council (Arabic: *Majlis Khususi*) was Egypt's most important conclave until the creation of the Council of Ministers (q.v.) in 1878. Except during the two times when Sa'id (q.v.) abolished it, it outranked the Council of Justice (q.v.) and dealt with problems arising within the administration of Egypt. It began with five high-ranking officials, mainly members of Muhammad Ali's (q.v.) family, and expanded to 12 by 1849. Khedive Isma'il (qq.v.) regularized it, decreeing that it should meet at least once weekly, with the directors of the finance and war departments, the head of his cabinet, the governor of Cairo (q.v.), the president of the Council of Justice, and one of his close friends. New members were added during the 1870s, including the directors of foreign affairs and interior. They were expected both to advise the khedive and to make laws, even sometimes to serve as a supreme court, and they occasionally advised him against policies he wished to adopt. The growing complexity of Egypt's administration and finances placed heavy burdens on the Privy Council, and the 1876–82 economic crisis led to the adoption of a cabinet system of government (*see* Council of Ministers).

***PROGRÈS ÉGYPTIEN, LE*.** Egypt's French-language daily newspaper. It began in 1890, one of the many French journals published in Egypt. It has been owned by the Egyptian government since 1956. Its reported circulation in 1972 was 14,500, increasing to 21,000 in 1992.

PROTECTORATE. The system of quasi-colonial government imposed on Egypt by the British government in December 1914, following the entry of the Ottoman Empire (q.v.), Egypt's nominal suzerain, into World War I (q.v.) on the side of the Central Powers. It was modified by the unilateral British declaration of Egypt's independence in 1922 but was not formally terminated until the 1936 Anglo-Egyptian Treaty (q.v.).

PROVINCIAL GOVERNMENT. For provincial and local administration, Egypt is currently divided into 26 governorates (Arabic: *muhafazat*), most of which are further subdivided into *marakiz* (singular: *markaz*). At the time of the French occupation (q.v.), *Description de l'Égypte* (q.v.) records the following *wilayat* ("provinces"), listed south to north: I: Thebes (Luxor), Jirja, Asyut, Minya, Bani Suwayf, al-Fayyum, Iftih, and Giza; and II: Qalyub, al-Sharqiyya, al-Mansura, Damietta (Dumyat), al-Gharbiyya, Minuf, Rosetta (Rashid), and al-Buhayra. Muhammad Ali (q.v.) divided the provinces into *khutt*s (districts), each consisting of several villages under a local governor. In 1826 he replaced the term *wilaya* with *mamuriyya* ("district governed by a police superintendent") and in 1833 with *mudiriyya* (q.v.), with 14 in Lower and ten in Upper Egypt, as had been done under the pre-Ottoman rulers. The term *markaz* was revived in 1871, under Khedive Isma'il (qq.v.). In 1890 the capital of each *mudiriyya* was separated into a city that was administratively independent of the smaller towns and villages. The Nasir (q.v.) government promulgated extensive reforms in provincial and local government in 1960. Since then the term *muhafaza* (q.v.), initially used for Alexandria (q.v.) and Cairo (q.v.), has replaced the term *mudiriyya*. As of 1991 the *muhafazat*, or "governorates," numbered 26, of which four were city governorates: Alexandria, Cairo, Port Said (q.v.), and Suez City; nine were in the Nile (q.v.) Delta or Lower Egypt: Ismailia (q.v.), Buhayra, Dumyat, Kafr al-Shaykh, Gharbiyya, Daqahliyya, Sharqiyya, Minufiyya, and Qalyubiyya; eight were in Upper Egypt: Giza, Fayyum, Bani Suwayf, Minya, Asyut (q.v.), Suhaj, Qina, and Aswan; and five were frontier governorates: Red Sea, New Valley, Matruh, North Sinai, and South Sinai. Under the monarchy and Nasir, the provincial and local units were subordinated to the central government, but Sadat (q.v.) and Mubarak (q.v.), have made a concerted attempt to promote their autonomy.

PYRAMIDS, BATTLE OF THE, *see* **IMBABA.**

- Q -

QASR AL-DUBARA. Square in central Cairo (q.v.) near the location of the British Embassy, hence formerly the term often used to denote the British Agency or Residency (q.v.).

QASR AL-NIL BARRACKS. Originally built by the Egyptian government during the reign of Sa'id (q.v.) to house his troops, these buildings became the site of Urabi's (q.v.) rebellion against Uthman Rifqi (q.v.) in February 1881. During the British occupation (q.v.), they were the main headquarters for the British army in central Cairo (q.v.), adjacent to Midan Ismailia, now Liberation Square (q.v.). They were razed after the British left Cairo, and their site is now occupied by the Nile Hilton Hotel and the headquarters of the Arab League (q.v.). Both the barracks and the nearby bridge took their name from a nearby palace used by Ibrahim (q.v.), Sa'id (q.v.), and Isma'il (q.v.), but later demolished.

AL-QAYSUNI, ABD AL-MUN'IM (1916–87). Egyptian economist. Educated at the University of Cairo (q.v.) and the London School of Economics, he worked for Barclay's Bank in England from 1942 to 1943, was a lecturer and assistant professor of economics at Cairo University from 1944 to 1946, directed the Middle East department of the International Monetary Fund (q.v.) in Washington from 1946 to 1950, and then served with the National Bank of Egypt (q.v.) in 1950–54. He was finance minister in 1954–66 and again in 1968, also serving for part of that time as deputy prime minister. He was influential in formulating Nasir's (q.v.) economic policies. He chaired the Arab International Bank in 1971–76 and again in 1978, but also returned to the Egyptian government as minister for economic and financial affairs in 1976–78, because of which he was criticized for the 1977 Food Riots (q.v.). He served also as minister of planning in 1977–78 and later served as adviser to the finance ministry under Mubarak (q.v.). A patriotic technocrat, his economic views were conservative for the era of Arab socialism (q.v.), but well suited to Sadat's (q.v.) policy of *infitah* (q.v.).

QUTB, SAYYID (1903–66). Muslim thinker and writer. Born in Musha (near Asyut [q.v.]), the son of a respected farmer who belonged to the National Party (q.v.), he was educated at his village *kuttab* (q.v.), where he memorized the Quran by the age of ten; at a Cairo secondary school; and at Dar al-Ulum (q.v.), where he came under the influence of Aqqad (q.v.) and became interested in English literature. After graduating in 1934, he worked for *al-Ahram* (q.v.) and wrote literary articles for *al-Risala* and *al-Thaqafa*, taught Arabic, and served as an education ministry inspector in Qina. He was sent to study educational administration in the United States from 1948 to 1951, during which time he grew disenchanted with the West as he observed the moral corruption of American society and its strong anti-Arab bias caused by the Palestine War (q.v.).

Upon returning, he criticized Egypt's educational programs for their British influence and called for a more Islamic curriculum. He developed close ties to some of the Free Officers (q.v.), notably Kamal al-Din Husayn, who wanted to make him education minister, and he served as the first secretary-general of the Liberation Rally (q.v.). He resigned from the government in 1953 and joined the Muslim Brothers (q.v.), taking charge of their instructional program and editing their newspaper. Imprisoned with the others after their failed attempt to assassinate Nasir (q.v.), he began writing books that were smuggled out of Egypt and published abroad, notably *al-Adala al-ijtima'iyya fi al-Islam* (translated into English as *Social Justice in Islam*), *Fi zalal al-Quran* (translated as *In the Shade of the Quran*), and *Ma'alim fi al-tariq*. He became bitterly disillusioned with the Nasir government and argued that every person is an arena in the battle between godly and satanic forces. He called for a small community of good people to expel evil and establish righteousness in the world. Drawing on Quranic passages, he taught that Jews and Christians will always be implacably opposed to Islam (q.v.) and that Muslims must be prepared to combat Zionism (q.v.), "crusaderism," and Communism (q.v.) to protect their community and its values. His 30-volume interpretation of the Quran has become a standard reference work in mosques and homes throughout the Muslim world. Released in 1964, he was imprisoned again in 1965 and subjected to press vilification before being hanged for treason in September 1966. Since his death his ideas have inspired many Muslim individuals and groups, notably al-Takfir wa al-Hijra (q.v.) and al-Jihad al-Jadid (q.v.) in Egypt (*see* Islamism).

- R -

RABAT CONFERENCE. Summit meeting of Arab heads of state, held in December 1969, which withheld aid sought by Nasir (q.v.) for the War of Attrition (q.v.). During this meeting the United States announced a hitherto secret Arab-Israeli peace proposal (*see* Rogers Peace Plan).

RABAT SUMMIT (1974). Meeting of 20 Arab heads of state, unanimously designating the Palestine Liberation Organization (PLO) (q.v.) as the "sole legitimate representative for the Palestinian people." This statement delayed Egypt's progress toward a reconciliation with Israel, which refused to negotiate with the PLO as a precondition for a comprehensive settlement.

RADIO. Wireless telegraphy was introduced into Egypt by the British armed forces during World War I (q.v.). By the late 1920s, some private citizens in Alexandria (q.v.) and Cairo (q.v.) had radio receivers and even transmitters, but the government closed all private stations in 1931 and in 1932 chartered its own system. In 1934 the Cairo studios of the Egyptian Broadcasting Service, built by the Marconi Company with the BBC's help, were formally opened. Because foreigners owned a large percentage of the radio receivers in Egypt, the initial formula of 70 percent Arabic and 30 percent foreign-language programs did not work well, and special stations were set aside for European broadcasts. The early Arabic broadcasting stressed Quran reading and Arab music, European shows were mainly BBC relays, and all programs were kept free from politics and advertising. By 1937 Egyptian broadcasts could be heard in Palestine, Syria, and Iraq. The Egyptian government took over the ownership and management of the service in 1947. By 1950 Egyptian State Broadcasting was transmitting programs in Arabic, English, Greek, and Italian, and there were 260,000 radios in the country. This number increased by 1975 to 4.9 million radio sets and to an estimated 16.4 million in 1990. In 1982 Egypt's home service was broadcasting in Arabic, English, French, Armenian, German, Greek, Italian, and Hebrew; its foreign service included broadcasts in 28 languages, 32 in 1991. Egyptian state radio was well-known during the Nasir (q.v.) era for its tendentious broadcasts, inspiring Arabs in other countries to oppose their own governments. Although radio retains some of this propaganda function, the government stations now broadcast mainly Arabic music, some situation comedies, informational programs, and hourly news. There are regional programs designed for specific areas of the country. Egypt also has a new commercial radio service provided by the Société Égyptienne de Publicité.

RAFAH. Border village divided between the Gaza Strip (q.v.) and Egypt.

AL-RAFI'I, ABD AL-RAHMAN (1889–1966). Lawyer, member of Parliament, cabinet minister, and leading historian of Egypt's nationalist movement. He was born in Cairo (q.v.) to a family originally from Tripoli (now in Lebanon) and educated in the government Law School (q.v.), from which he graduated in 1907. He practiced law for a time in Tanta and then in Cairo. He sometimes worked with his brother, Amin al-Rafi'i, a leading journalist. He wrote articles regularly for the National Party (q.v.) press and served on its administrative board from 1911. He was arrested and his papers seized at the outbreak of World War I (q.v.). He played an important role in the early organization of the 1919 Revolution (q.v.) but did not join the Wafd (q.v.). Elected as a Nationalist to many sessions of the Chamber of Deputies and in 1939 to the Senate, he led a coalition of young Nationalists who objected to Hafiz Ramadan's (q.v.) joining the cabinet, arguing that party members should abstain from participation in any government as long as the British occupation (q.v.) continued, but he later served as minister of supply in the caretaker government of Husayn Sirri (q.v.) in 1949. The Nasir (q.v.) regime appointed him to head the Egyptian Bar Association (q.v.) in 1954. He was the most prolific chronicler of Egypt's political history, with books on the French occupation (q.v.), Muhammad Ali (q.v.), Isma'il (q.v.), the Urabi (q.v.) Revolution, Mustafa Kamil (q.v.), Muhammad Farid (q.v.), the 1919 Revolution (q.v.), its aftermath, and the 1952 Revolution (q.v.). His memoirs, *Mudhakkirati*, appeared in 1949. He remains a towering figure in Egyptian historiography.

RAILROADS. Rail lines and steam-driven land transport were introduced into Egypt soon after the death of Muhammad Ali (q.v.), when Abbas I (q.v.) gave an English company headed by Robert Stephenson a concession to construct a railroad between Cairo (q.v.) and Alexandria (q.v.) in 1851. This line, the first built on the African continent, was opened in stages between 1853 and 1856, and the Cairo-Suez line was built in 1856–57, but it took several years to reduce freight-carrying costs to those of river transport (q.v.). Branch lines to Samanud and Zagazig were opened before 1860, and the booming demand for Egyptian cotton (q.v.) caused by the U.S. Civil War accelerated the growth of rail transport. Additional lines had to be laid down, at government expense, to facilitate building the Suez Canal (q.v.). Khedive Isma'il (qq.v.) invested at least £E10 million in railroads during his reign. Especially noteworthy was the rail line from Bulaq al-Dakrur, across the Nile from Cairo, to Upper Egypt, reaching Asyut (q.v.) and Fayyum in 1874 and Aswan by 1877, when Egyptian standard-gauge railways amounted to 1,519 km. During the British occupation (q.v.) the government let various foreign and Egyptian companies build light agricultural railways in the Delta, and investment in railroad construction and improvement peaked in 1906–8. In 1913 total trackage amounted to 2,953 km of standard-gauge and 1,376 km of light railways. Including its canal network, Egypt's transport system was comparable to that of many European countries.

During World War I (q.v.) a military railroad was built across the Sinai Peninsula (q.v.) and Egypt's network was later linked to that of Palestine, but few other additions were made until World War II (q.v.). The Egyptian state railways grew from 5,766 km in 1939 to 7,102 in 1949, not counting 1,400 km of light railways. Portions of the system were destroyed during the June War (q.v.) and others have fallen into disuse, but in 1989 4,800 km of track, mainly standard gauge, were in use, covering the Nile Valley and Delta and the coastal regions. Problems included the deterioration of some rolling stock, roadbeds, signaling equipment, passenger and freight depots, and passenger cars, but the government has made improvements (*see* Planning) when its financial resources permit. Egypt still depends on rail transport of both passengers and goods; in 1991 its railroads carried 3.045 billion metric ton-kilometers of freight and 28.6 billion passenger-kilometers.

RAMADAN, MUHAMMAD HAFIZ (1879–1955). Lawyer, successor to Muhammad Farid (q.v.) as president of the National Party (q.v.), member of Parliament, and cabinet minister. Born and educated in Cairo, he had a successful law practice, was elected to almost every session of Parliament, and served in several anti-Wafd (q.v.) coalition governments, but his party leadership was challenged in 1940 by younger Nationalists who objected to his participation in governing Egypt while British troops continued to occupy the country. He published memoirs, entitled *Qala li Abu al-Hawl* ("The Sphinx Told Me").

RAMADAN WAR (1973), ***see*** **OCTOBER WAR.**

RAS AL-TIN PALACE. The main summer residence of Egypt's rulers in Alexandria (q.v.) and the site of King Faruq's (q.v.) abdication on 26 July 1952. Ras al-Tin Palace has since been a museum.

RELIGION. For most Egyptians, religion is the main badge of their identity and social status as well as a system of beliefs and moral laws. Egypt's state religion is Islam (q.v.), and some 55 million Egyptians are Sunni Muslims, observing mainly the Shafi'i and Maliki rites of Shari'a (q.v.) jurisprudence. The number of "orthodox" Copts (q.v.) in Egypt is disputed: the 1986 census reported 2 million, but the Copts themselves claim a figure closer to 7 million. There also were in 1986 350,000 Greek Orthodox, about 225,000 Catholics (mainly Copts, but also some Armenians, Chaldeans, Latins, Maronites, Melkites, and Syrians in communion with Rome), 10,000 Armenians, 200,000 Protestants (mainly of the Coptic Evangelical Church), and a dwindling number of Jews (1,631 were counted in 1976). At most times Egyptians of differing religions have enjoyed good relations, but the upsurge of fundamentalism (q.v.) in recent years has frayed the ties between Copts and Muslims.

RESIDENCY. The office of the British high commissioner for Egypt and the Sudan (q.v.) from the proclamation of the Protectorate (q.v.) until the signing of the 1936 Anglo-Egyptian Treaty (q.v.). Prior to 1914, it was called the British Agency (*see* Qasr al-Dubara).

REVOLUTION (1919). Nationwide movement of popular resistance, sometimes violent, directed against the British Protectorate (q.v.) and supporting the Egyptian *wafd* ("delegation") (q.v.) that wished to attend the Paris Peace Conference (q.v.). When Sa'd Zaghlul (q.v.) warned Sultan Fuad (q.v.) against helping the British by forming a new cabinet, Milne Cheetham (q.v.) called for his arrest. Two days later he and three of his associates, Isma'il Sidqi (q.v.), Muhammad Mahmud (q.v.), and bedouin (q.v.) leader Hamad al-Basil, were deported to Malta. Far from daunting the Egyptians, this action ignited nationalist passions. Students, transport workers, Azharites, lawyers, and even judges and government clerks went out on strike, and violence escalated. By mid-March 1919 all telephone, telegraph, and rail lines between Cairo (q.v.) and the rest of Egypt had been cut. Contemporary observers noted the participation of all classes of Egyptian society, of Copts (q.v.) as well as Muslims, and of women as well as men, in the popular demonstrations. The revolution continued with the nationwide boycott in 1919–20 of the Milner mission (q.v.) and resumed in 1921 in opposition to the Adli-Curzon talks (q.v.). Most Egyptian intellectuals regard the 1919 Revolution as the most truly nationwide uprising in their country's modern history, but some believe that it should have put forward a program of economic and social reform to benefit the Egyptian masses and complement Zaghlul's demand for Egypt's complete independence from Britain.

REVOLUTION (1952). The military coup that overthrew King Faruq (q.v.) and brought the Free Officers (q.v.) to power in Egypt. In popular usage, the term is often used to connote the transition from a hereditary monarchy dominated by the landowning aristocracy to a populist republic, headed by Jamal Abd al-Nasir (q.v.) and instituting many political, economic, and social reforms (*see* Agrarian Reform, Arab Socialism, Aswàn High Dam, Najib, and Nasir).

REVOLUTIONARY COMMAND COUNCIL (RCC). The governing board for Egypt set up by the Free Officers (q.v.) after they seized power in July 1952, although some say that it was not officially formed until January 1953. The officers, meeting secretly after the 1952 Revolution (q.v.), decided to let Faruq (q.v.) go into exile, retained his infant son as the king under a regency, and offered the post of prime minister to Ali Mahir (q.v.). The RCC, although strongly patriotic, had no fixed program for governing Egypt, and would have gladly let a civilian cabinet reestablish order under the 1923 Constitution (q.v.), if a strong and dedicated leader could be found. Some considered restoring the Wafd Party (q.v.) to power; others favored collaboration with the Muslim Brothers (q.v.). Some leaders, including Nasir (q.v.), who directed the RCC behind the facade of the genuinely popular General Najib (q.v.), had been influenced by Hadeto (q.v.). The Kafr al-Dawwar Incident (q.v.), however, soon alienated the Communists (q.v.) from the RCC. On the other hand, the officers' commitment to land reform (q.v.) estranged Ali Mahir, who would not accept a limit of less than 500 feddans (q.v.) per landowner. In September 1952 the RCC named Najib as the new premier but retained a predominantly civilian cabinet (with officers serving as "advisers" behind the scenes). The RCC called on the political parties to purge their dishonest politicians, as a prerequisite to new parliamentary elections. When the Wafd and other parties failed to comply, the RCC dissolved them and confiscated their property and funds. Many prerevolutionary politicians were arrested and tried for corruption; most of those convicted were fined, confined to prison or house arrest, and deprived of their civil and political rights, but none was executed.

RCC members gradually took charge of the major cabinet posts; in June 1953 Nasir became deputy prime minister and also interior minister, a key post in any Egyptian government because of its control over the police and local government. During 1953 the RCC, while disclaiming any desire to establish a dictatorship, maneuvered both the Communist groups and the Muslim Brothers out of positions of power within the Egyptian government. In 1954 the RCC became the main arena for the power struggle between Najib, who enjoyed support from the Brothers and the outlawed political parties, and Nasir, backed by his security forces and some labor groups within the Liberation Rally (q.v.). When Nasir emerged victorious and assumed the premiership of the Egyptian government and the presidency of the RCC in April 1954, the importance of the latter group started to wane. Although debates continued within the RCC in 1954–55 over policy issues, such as the suppression of the Muslim Brothers, the Anglo-Egyptian Agreement (q.v.), and the restoration of parliamentary government, Nasir increasingly bypassed the Council. After he unilaterally named the committee that drafted the 1956 Constitution (q.v.), which was approved by a popular referendum in July 1956, the RCC was quietly terminated.

RHODES PROXIMITY TALKS (1949). Negotiations, mainly indirect and mediated by United Nations (q.v.) envoy Ralph Bunche, leading to an armistice between Egypt and Israel on 25 February 1949, and subsequently between other Arab states and Israel, held in a hotel on the island of Rhodes. The armistice lines accepted there remained Israel's boundaries up to June 1967, except during the Suez War (q.v.) and its aftermath, but the state of war between the Arab states and Israel remained in effect. Later UN efforts to convene a general Arab-Israeli peace conference at Lausanne failed. The Rhodes Talks were favored by Israel's backers as a model for negotiations because they kept the Arab states from acting in unison, but Egypt's governments prefer general peace conferences.

RIDA, MUHAMMAD RASHID (1865–1935). Writer, editor, and Muslim reformer. Baghdad-born but of Syrian extraction, educated in *kuttab*s (q.v.) and Ottoman (q.v.) government schools, Rida became the chief disciple of the Islamic scholar and rector of al-Azhar (q.v.), Muhammad Abduh (q.v.), continuing and developing his reformist teachings. They founded an influential Arabic monthly, *al-Manar* (q.v.), which disseminated their ideas throughout the Muslim world. He also wrote a commentary on the Quran and a three-volume biography of Abduh. From 1912 to 1914 he directed a school for the training of Muslim preachers. His reformism was influenced by Wahhabi (q.v.) puritanism, calling for a return to the pristine Islam of Muhammad and his associates, hence its name, Salafiyya ("way of the righteous ancestors"). He was also one of the founders of the Decentralization Party, which advocated loyalty to the Ottoman sultanate within a loose state that would extend greater freedom to the Arabs, the nation which he saw as the core of the Islamic community. He was actively involved during World War I (q.v.) with the Arab nationalists in Cairo (q.v.) who worked for future independence. He chaired the first Syrian Arab Congress in 1920 and served on a Syrian-Palestinian delegation in Geneva. He opposed both Zionism (q.v.) in Palestine and French colonialism in Syria. Hoping to revive the caliphate (q.v.), he took part in Islamic conferences in Mecca in 1926 and Jerusalem in 1931. Unattached to specific political parties and movements, Rida wielded much moral influence in his later years but was basically a marginal figure in the history of Arab nationalism and increasingly outside the mainstream of Islamism (q.v.) in Egypt.

RIFQI, UTHMAN (1839–86). War minister from 1879 to 1881, his alleged favoritism to Turks and Circassians (q.v.) over native Egyptians in the army officer corps sparked a mutiny led by Ahmad Urabi (q.v.) in February 1881, and he was dismissed by Riyad (q.v.).

RIVER TRANSPORT. From the dawn of history to the spread of the railroad (q.v.), the Nile River (q.v.) was the main avenue of transport for people and goods in Egypt. Early travelers and shippers between Europe and Asia often used a navigation route that included the Nile Delta and River to Bulaq (q.v.) and across the desert, sometimes by canal to Suez City, or even to Qina and then overland to Qusayr on the Red Sea.

African trade also entered the Nile by way of the river ports of Asyut (q.v.) and Isna, but river transport was often hindered by piracy, which weak governments could not keep in check. The French occupation (q.v.) was too brief to affect Nile river transport.

In the early nineteenth century, Muhammad Ali (q.v.) enhanced river navigation between Alexandria (q.v.) and Bulaq by ordering the construction of the Mahmudiyya Canal (q.v.) between 1817 and 1820. Other navigation canals were built in the Delta region, turning Rosetta and Bulaq into boat-building centers. Steam navigation facilitated travel and transport not only to Egypt, but also within its riverways and canals; by 1841 steam tugs were being used to draw passenger barges. Muhammad Ali set up the Egyptian Transit Administration in 1844 to control and operate the transit of passengers and goods across Egypt, making it a major center of international trade even before the Suez Canal (q.v.) was built. The rise of cotton (q.v.) cultivation greatly expanded river transport up to the 1870s, when railroads (q.v.) became extensive and more economical for bulk freight movement. Under Khedive Isma'il (qq.v.) 14,000 km of canals were constructed and many existing ones dredged. During the British occupation (q.v.), river transport received less attention than the extension of railroads and later the development of motor roads. Consequently, its importance declined.

In 1958 Egypt had altogether 3,100 km of navigable waterways, including the Nile River and its Rosetta branch, with a river fleet of 12,000 units, including barges, passenger steamers, and the traditional sailboats called feluccas (Arabic: *faluka*). The average annual volume of freight carried between 1948 and 1956 was 5.1 million metric tons, and passenger traffic per year averaged 12.4 million in 1947–56. Nasir's (q.v.) government promoted Nile use by improving navigation canals, river harbors, and loading facilities, and by slightly lengthening inland waterways. The Aswan High Dam (q.v.) spurred the use of ferries and freight ships on Lake Nasir, linking Aswan with the Sudan (q.v.).

One aspect of river transport familiar to generations of European and North American travelers was the Nile boat tour. Intrepid foreigners had sailed up the Nile earlier in the nineteenth century, but Thomas Cook organized his first guided tour of Egypt, which included a Nile boat journey, in 1869. By 1871 his company ran regular Nile tours, using steamers that it owned, facilitating greatly the development of tourism (q.v.) in Egypt. So impressed was Isma'il by the enterprise that he authorized Cook's ships to carry the Egyptian mails to Upper Egypt, starting in 1875. Cook's boats helped to evacuate wounded British soldiers during the 1882 campaign against Urabi (q.v.) and transported the abortive Gordon (q.v.) rescue expedition in 1884–85. Cook's Nile tours remained popular for generations and have been immortalized in countless travel memoirs and works of fiction, notably Agatha Christie's *Death on the Nile*. Other firms, including one owned by Bank Misr (q.v.), have also run Nile boat tours, as did the Egyptian government in the early 1960s. Cook's Egyptian tours were suspended due to the Suez War (q.v.), but were revived on a grand scale in 1989.

RIYAD, MAHMUD (1917–92). Officer, diplomat, and Arab League (q.v.) secretary-general. He graduated from the Military Academy (q.v.) in 1939 and later from the Staff College. He represented Egypt on the Egyptian-Israeli Mixed Armistice Commission from 1949 to 1952 and then served from 1954 to 1955 as director of the Arab affairs department within the Egyptian foreign ministry. He served as ambassador to Syria from 1955 up to the creation of the United Arab Republic (q.v.) in February 1958, whereupon he became a presidential adviser on foreign affairs. In 1961 he was named deputy head of Egypt's permanent mission to the United Nations (q.v.) and became its head in the following year. He was foreign minister from 1964 to 1972, also holding the rank of deputy premier from 1970. Sadat removed him from his cabinet in January 1972 and gave him the essentially honorific title of special adviser to the president. In 1974 he became secretary-general of the Arab League and held that position until April 1979, when Egypt's membership in that organization was suspended as a result of its separate treaty with Israel, a policy that Riyad opposed. Since his resignation from the Arab League he has not been active in politics. His political memoirs include *The Struggle for Peace in the Middle East* (1981) and *Mudhakkirat Mahmud Riyad* (three volumes published as of 1986). He was more a diplomat-technician than a shaper of Egypt's foreign policies.

RIYAD, MUSTAFA (1834–1911). Government official, agronomist, cabinet minister, and three-time premier. His origins are obscure; he spoke Turkish as his first language but was widely believed to have really been a Jew (q.v.) from Smyrna. He began his career as a clerk in the finance ministry and then joined the officer corps of the Egyptian army as a clerk and then as a musician. Around 1850 Riyad became an aide-de-camp to Abbas I (q.v.), who in 1851 promoted him in rank; he then became governor of Giza province from 1853 to 1856. Sa'id (q.v.) made him administrative chief of Fayyum and then governor of Qina province. Isma'il (q.v.) promoted him again upon his accession, named him keeper of the seal, admitted him to the Council of Justice (q.v.), and, in 1864, made him director of the khedive's (q.v.) private estates. A personal clash with Isma'il caused his sudden dismissal from all his posts in 1868.

Riyad was soon recalled as Isma'il's chief treasurer, perhaps because the khedive needed an honest official who knew both Arabic and

Turkish. In 1872 he was named adviser to the crown prince, Tawfiq (q.v.). From 1873 to 1874 he was director of education (q.v.), building on the foundations laid by Ali Mubarak (q.v.). He was responsible for bringing Jamal al-Din al-Afghani (q.v.) and the founders of *al-Muqtataf* (q.v.) to Egypt. He endowed the revenue from some 1,800 acres of Delta farm land to support the newly created Dar al-Kutub (q.v.). After serving briefly in 1874 as adviser to the director of interior, he held the portfolios for foreign affairs (1874–75), agriculture (1875, 1877–78), justice (1875–76 and 1877), education again (1876–77), and commerce (1877–78). Riyad headed the 1878 commission of inquiry empowered to look into Egypt's financial situation, collaborating with the European creditors against Isma'il. He was minister of both interior and justice in Prince Tawfiq's short-lived cabinet of March 1879, but did not serve in the "Egyptian" (i.e., pro-Isma'il) cabinet of Sharif (q.v.), but went to Europe until he was recalled by Tawfiq after his accession later that year to serve as his interior minister. A month later the new khedive asked Riyad to head a cabinet, in which he also held portfolios for interior and finance. His main efforts were directed at reorganizing Egyptian government finances, which were close to bankruptcy. This he achieved, working with the European commissioners, with the 1880 Law of Liquidation (q.v.). He ignored the Assembly of Delegates, neutralized most of his opponents, including Nubar (q.v.) and Sharif, and co-opted Afghani's remaining supporters by naming his disciple Muhammad Abduh (q.v.) editor of *al-Waqai' al-misriyya* (q.v.). He underestimated the Egyptian army officers, however, ignoring their petition for the dismissal of Uthman Rifqi (q.v.) as war minister until they mutinied and he had to accede to their demands in February 1881. Riyad then tried to improve the officers' conditions, but they made further demands on the government in August. Finally they massed at Abdin Palace on 9 September, demanding that Tawfiq convoke the Assembly of Delegates, enlarge his army, and dismiss Riyad. He stayed in Europe during the year in which Urabi (q.v.) was in power.

During the early years of the British occupation (q.v.), his opposition was noted by many nationalists, and he backed the creation of *al-Muayyad* (q.v.) in 1889 as a Muslim-owned daily newspaper to compete against the Syrian-owned *al-Muqattam* (q.v.) and *al-Ahram* (q.v.). Riyad served as premier from 1888 to 1891 and again in 1893–94, resigning after having failed to back Abbas Hilmi II (q.v.) in the Frontiers Incident (q.v.). He played no further role in the Egyptian government. In 1911 he chaired the Egyptian Congress (q.v.) that was convened to oppose the demands of the Coptic Congress (q.v.), held earlier that year in Asyut (q.v.). Capable but often tactless, he favored the introduction of European science and technology but fiercely resisted Europe's growing power over Egyptian finance, justice, and government.

ROGERS PEACE PLAN. U.S. proposal, first announced by Secretary of State William Rogers on 9 December 1969, to end the War of Attrition (q.v.). The plan coupled a nearly full Israeli withdrawal from the lands it had taken in the June 1967 war (q.v.) in return for a binding peace treaty signed by the Arabs. In this form, the plan was rejected immediately by Israel and then by the USSR; Egypt's response was cool but not categorically negative. The timing of Rogers's announcement may have reflected bureaucratic infighting in Washington, but it also coincided with Nasir's (q.v.) disappointment with the Rabat Conference (q.v.), which denied Egypt the Arab backing it needed for its war against Israel. Rogers was stating publicly proposals that the United States had already discussed privately with the USSR, Egypt, and Israel. The 9 December plan specifically concerned an Israeli-Egyptian settlement; a parallel proposal for an Israeli-Jordanian peace was made nine days later. The plan failed because the USSR refused to pressure its Arab allies, the White House staff–especially Kissinger–had not been involved in its formulation, and Israel could withstand U.S. diplomatic pressure.

The War of Attrition escalated early in 1970, as the USSR introduced new surface-to-air missiles, accompanied by more than 10,000 military advisers, into Egypt. Israel's deep-penetration bombing attacks near Cairo (q.v.) seemed aimed at overthrowing Nasir. The U.S. government decided to delay selling more Phantom jet fighter planes to Israel and to send a high-ranking official to Cairo in April 1970. In a public speech on May Day, Nasir called on Washington to take a new political initiative. After secretly conferring with Israel and the USSR, Rogers announced a modified plan on 25 June, calling for a 90-day cease-fire tied to Israel's withdrawal from lands taken in 1967. Israel rejected this plan, too, but Nasir accepted the cease-fire on 23 July, followed by Jordan. Israel halted its attacks upon receiving President Nixon's assurances of political and economic support, and the cease-fire took effect on 7 August. Its terms differed from those of the Rogers Plan, in that Israel made no prior commitment to withdraw. When Egypt moved its missiles closer to the Suez Canal (q.v.) in violation of the cease-fire, the talks proposed by the U.S. government were canceled. After civil war broke out in Jordan, the Rogers Peace Plan was shelved.

ROOSEVELT, KERMIT (1916-). U.S. intelligence officer, businessman, and writer. Born in Buenos Aires (Argentina), a grandson of Theodore Roosevelt, he studied at the Groton School and Harvard College. During World War II (q.v.) he worked in the Office of Strategic Services, becoming assistant to the director of secret intelligence in the Near East. After the war he joined the Central Intelligence Agency and became a special assistant for political operations to the head of its clandestine service. Living in Cairo in 1951–53, he is widely (but probably incorrectly) believed to have aided the Free Officers (q.v.) in the 1952 Revolution (q.v.). He later engineered the countercoup in Iran against Musaddiq that helped restore the shah to power.

ROSETTA, BATTLE OF (1807). Muhammad Ali's (q.v.) defeat of a 7,000-man British expeditionary force sent to capture Egypt, probably to overthrow him and restore the Mamluks (q.v.) to power. After the British occupied Alexandria (q.v.), Muhammad Ali tried to settle with them but was rebuffed. They marched on Rosetta, apparently hoping to forestall a new French occupation, but their two attacks were repulsed with heavy casualties. After the Russian czar's treaty with Napoléon drove the Ottoman Empire (q.v.) to Britain's side, the expeditionary force became pointless, and it withdrew from Alexandria in September 1807. This Egyptian victory over the British later became a source of national pride.

ROVER SCOUTS. Paramilitary youth organization, founded by Hasan al-Banna (q.v.) while the Muslim Brothers (q.v.) were still in Ismailia (q.v.) (i.e., before 1932). In 1935 the Society formally attached it to its headquarters by naming a leader to supervise and unify its local units, which were called Rovers (Arabic: *jawwala*). Unable to affiliate with the Egyptian Boy Scouts, they stressed athletic activity, physical training, community service, and (when needed) defense for the Muslim Brothers. Graduates of the Rover section included volunteers in the Palestine War (q.v.) and Nuqrashi's (q.v.) assassin. In 1948 the Muslim Brothers claimed to have 40,000 Rovers; government repression of the Society reduced that number to about 7,000 in 1953, and it was subsequently absorbed into the general Egyptian scouting movement.

RUSHDI, HUSAYN (1863–1928). Lawyer, cabinet minister, and four-time premier. Born in Cairo (q.v.) to a Turkish family named Topuzzadeh, he studied law in Cairo and Paris. He became justice minister in the Butros Ghali (q.v.) cabinet from 1908 to 1910, then served as foreign minister up to the resignation of Sa'd Zaghlul (q.v.) in 1912, whereupon he resumed the justice portfolio.

After Muhammad Sa'id (q.v.) resigned in April 1914, Abbas Hilmi II (q.v.) named him the new premier (and interior minister). He served as regent while the khedive (q.v.) was in Istanbul, hence was acting head of state when World War I (q.v.) began and when the Ottoman Empire (q.v.), Egypt's nominal suzerain, declared war on Britain. When the Protectorate (q.v.) was declared on 19 December 1914, Rushdi agreed to remain as premier, but on the understanding that it would end after the war. Following the Armistice, he encouraged Sa'd and others to speak to High

Commissioner Wingate (q.v.) about sending a delegation to the Foreign Office to discuss Egypt's future. When the British refused to receive any delegation, Rushdi resigned as premier, although he did stay on as education minister until November 1919. Serving later as deputy premier, he accompanied Adli Yakan (q.v.) to negotiate with the Foreign Office in 1921. He was later appointed to the Senate by King Fuad (q.v.) and chaired that body until his death. He played a thankless role in Egyptian politics with great courage and integrity.

RUZ AL-YUSUF. Popular weekly magazine, anti-Wafdist in the time of the monarchy, pro-Najib (q.v.) in 1954, and turned over to the National Union (q.v.) in 1960. From a leftist perspective, it criticized Sadat (q.v.) during the student demonstrations of the early 1970s and following the 1977 Food Riots (q.v.). Its name was taken from that of its founder, the Egyptian actress Ruz al-Yusuf; it was later edited by her son Ihsan Abd al-Quddus (q.v.). Its circulation in 1993 was 35,000.

- S -

SABRI, ALI (1920–91). Officer and politician, widely regarded as Nasir's most pro-Communist associate, and prime minister from 1962 to 1965. He graduated from the Military Academy (q.v.) in 1939. Although not one of the original Free Officers (q.v.), Sabri was close to them and may have been their liaison with the U.S. embassy before the 1952 Revolution (q.v.). He served as director of the president's office from 1957 up to the formation of the United Arab Republic (q.v.) in 1958, when he became minister for presidential affairs. Nasir (q.v.) appointed him prime minister and a member of the presidential council in 1962. He was then vice president until 1967 and chairman of the Arab Socialist Union (q.v.), which he tried to pattern after the Soviet Communist Party, from 1965 to 1969, although his influence was weakened by Egypt's defeat in the June War (q.v.). Upon Nasir's death in 1970, the USSR hoped that Sabri would succeed him. He did become one of Sadat's (q.v.) two vice presidents and a leader of the so-called Centers of Power (q.v.). As one of the Nasirist (q.v.) politicians whom Sadat accused of plotting against his regime, he was ousted from all his posts in the 1971 Corrective Revolution (q.v.). Tried and condemned to death, his sentence was commuted to life imprisonment. Eventually he was pardoned and released by Sadat in May 1981. Sabri's reputation for favoring the USSR and Communism (q.v.) aided his rise to power in the early 1960s, but Egyptians were aware of his ties to several major landowning families. The more conservative Arab regimes, on which Egypt came to depend after the June War, disliked him and may have turned Sadat against him. His memoirs, *Ali Sabri yatadhakkir* ("Ali Sabri Remembers"), were published in Beirut in 1988.

SABRI, HASAN (1875–1940). Politician, cabinet minister, and premier. He was trained at the Teachers College and the government Law School (q.v.) and then was appointed headmaster of the Muhammad Ali School in Cairo (q.v.). He later taught mathematics, history, and geography at al-Azhar (q.v.). He was elected to represent Shirbin (Gharbiyya) in the Chamber of Deputies in 1926 and in the Senate in 1931, later becoming the vice president of this body. In 1933 Abd al-Fattah Yahya (q.v.) appointed him finance minister. In 1934 he became Egypt's last minister to London before its legation was raised to embassy status. Upon returning to Egypt he became Ali Mahir's (q.v.) commerce and communications minister and later served in that post and then as war minister under Muhammad Mahmud (q.v.). Upon taking charge of the cabinet in 1940, Sabri took the office of foreign minister and later added the interior portfolio. His sudden death while reading the annual speech from the throne before Parliament on 14 November has not been fully explained. A non-partisan technocrat, he was committed to carrying out the letter of the 1936 Anglo-Egyptian Treaty (q.v.).

AL-SADAT, [MUHAMMAD] ANWAR (1918–81). Officer, writer, politician, and president from 1970 to 1981. Born in Mit Abu al-Kum (Minufiyya) to an Egyptian father, who was an army clerk, and a Sudanese mother, he was reared in Cairo (q.v.) and trained at the Military Academy (q.v.), graduating in 1938. He backed Misr al-Fatat (q.v.) and the Muslim Brothers (q.v.) in his youth and had secret contact with German agents early in World War II (q.v.). Expelled from the army, he was jailed but managed to escape in 1944. He was arrested again in 1946 on suspicion of conspiring to assassinate Amin Uthman (q.v.) and Nahhas (q.v.). Imprisoned during the two-year trial, he was acquitted and released in 1948. After working for a year as a journalist, he managed to regain his military commission. He joined the Free Officers (q.v.), playing a major role in the 1952 Revolution (q.v.). Close to Nasir (q.v.), he joined the Revolutionary Command Council (q.v.) that headed the new regime, serving as its liaison with the Muslim Brothers (q.v.) and other right-wing groups. He was minister of state from 1954 to 1956, edited the government newspaper, *al-Jumhuriyya* (q.v.), wrote books about Nasir and the revolution, chaired the National Assembly (q.v.), and served as secretary-general of the Islamic Congress (q.v.). Nasir named him vice president in 1969 to halt the rise of Ali Sabri's (q.v.) left wing within his ruling circle, but Nasir allegedly planned to replace him. Upon Nasir's death, Sadat was chosen as his successor as Egypt's president and chairman of the Arab Socialist Union (q.v.). Egypt's leaders hoped by choosing him to avert a power struggle between the right wing, led by Zakariyya Muhyi al-Din (q.v.), and the leftists, although the latter group expected Sadat to fall from power, enabling them to take control of Egypt.

Sadat proved to have his own policies and powerful backers. In May 1971 he quashed a leftist conspiracy by his Corrective Revolution (q.v.), purging Sabri and his allies. While signing the Soviet-Egyptian Treaty (q.v.) in May 1971 and visiting Moscow in October 1971 and May 1972, he actually moved closer to the conservative Arab states, notably Saudi Arabia. He called for the Federation of Arab Republics (q.v.) but resisted organic union with Libya (q.v.). He hoped to gain U.S. support in 1972 by ousting some 20,000 Soviet experts, mainly military ones, although some historians argue that Moscow approved this measure and that key advisers remained to help Sadat's army before and during the October War (q.v.). Early in his presidency, he sought peace talks with Israel, but demanded its prior commitment to withdraw from the Sinai Peninsula (q.v.) and settle the Palestine refugee problem. When Israel rejected these terms in 1971, Sadat warned that he would take military action. He and Syria's Hafiz al-Asad planned a joint attack on the Israeli-occupied Sinai and Golan Heights for 6 October 1973. Caught by surprise, the Israelis were driven back as the Egyptian army crossed the Suez Canal (q.v.). Although Israel soon counterattacked against both Egypt and Syria and drove their forces back, the October War (q.v.) was widely viewed in the Arab world as restoring Egypt's honor and enhancing Sadat's reputation at Nasir's posthumous expense.

Sadat used his hard-won prestige to extricate Egypt from the war against Israel and to regain control of the Sinai. Kissinger's Shuttle Diplomacy (q.v.) helped Egypt recover portions of the Sinai, including the oil wells and the Gidi and Mitla passes (qq.v.), in two interim agreements reached in 1974 and 1975. The peace negotiations became deadlocked, however, on the issue of Palestinian participation. Sadat broke the deadlock in November 1977 by his dramatic flight to Jerusalem. Addressing the Israeli Knesset, he offered peaceful coexistence between the Arabs and Israel, provided that Israel agreed first to withdraw from all the lands it had occupied in June 1967 and negotiated a solution to the Palestinian Arab problem. He tried to negotiate directly with Israeli Premier Menachem Begin, but talks soon faltered. U.S. President Carter invited both leaders to an open-ended summit at his summer retreat, where the three men and their advisers hammered out a set of agreements known as the Camp David Accords (q.v.), which after further negotiations led to the Egyptian-Israeli Peace Treaty (q.v.). The other Arab states condemned these accords and tried with inducements and threats to persuade Sadat not to sign the treaty. When he dismissed their appeals, they broke diplomatic ties, cut off financial support, and expelled Egypt from the Arab League (q.v.). Sadat preferred greater political and economic dependence on the United States over submitting to the other Arab states' demands, but the Autonomy Talks (q.v.) that Egypt and Israel had agreed to conduct for the Palestinians stalled and were suspended in 1982.

Sadat's foreign policies, partly a reaction against Nasir's Arab and pro-Soviet orientation, also reflected Egypt's deteriorating economy (q.v.). His solution was to renounce Arab socialism (q.v.) by gradually restoring capitalism, a policy which he called *infitah* (q.v.), and luring foreigners to invest in Egyptian manufacturing industries. From 1974 to 1978 the oil-rich Arab states invested heavily, notably in the Gulf Organization for the Development of Egypt (q.v.), but American and European investment fell short of Sadat's expectations. The reopening of the Suez Canal, revival of tourism (q.v.), and rising remittances from Egyptians working abroad (mainly in other Arab countries) helped Egypt's economy. Regrettably, investors preferred Egyptian real estate, consumer goods, and luxury hotels to manufacturing firms,. The state-owned industries developed under Nasir languished, as did state-provided services in health (q.v.), education (q.v.), welfare, and transport. Income inequalities widened. The 1977 Food Riots (q.v.) expressed the dissatisfaction felt by many Egyptians, and Sadat used his Israeli peace initiative to distract the public. When attacks on his policies intensified, he censored the press (q.v.), passed the Law of Shame (q.v.), and in September 1981 jailed many of his suspected opponents.

Sadat gradually gave up his simple lifestyle, moved into palaces, befriended rich and powerful Egyptians and foreigners, and let some of his friends and relatives use their connections for personal gain. Islamist (q.v.) opposition, which he had at first used to fight communism (q.v.) and Nasirism (q.v.), then tried to curb, attacked his abuse of power. His peace with Israel, economic and social issues, his opulent lifestyle, and his perceived opposition to Islam (q.v.) all helped cause his assassination in 1981 while reviewing a parade on the anniversary of the October War. Many foreign leaders, including three former U.S. presidents and Menachem Begin, flew to Cairo to attend his funeral, but most Egyptians were barred from the procession, and few mourned his death. A superb actor and a shrewd diplomat, often highly patriotic, he lost his popular touch and tied Egypt's position too closely to American policies. Two of his books, *Revolt on the Nile* (1957) and *In Search of Identity: An Autobiography* (1978), serve as partial memoirs; portions of his diaries have been published as *The Public Diaries of Anwar al-Sadat.*

AL-SADAT, JIHAN (1933-). Second wife of Anwar al-Sadat (q.v.), organizer of a private charitable organization to teach women marketable skills, and prominent advocate of women's rights. Her role was evident in the 1979 divorce legislation called "Jihan's Law," which required the husband to register his divorce and to inform his wife and gave the wife a claim to larger alimony and child support payments, also lengthening the period when she may retain custody of her children. Although polygyny (which is rare in Egypt) was not outlawed, the first wife's consent was made a prerequisite for a man's taking a second wife. Many Muslims opposed these changes as contrary to the Shari'a (q.v.), and parts of the 1979 legislation were changed in 1985. She was often criticized by conservative Muslims for playing too prominent a role in Egypt's public life during her husband's presidency, and since his assassination she has spent much of her time outside the country. She published her memoirs, *A Woman of Egypt*, in 1986.

AL-SA'DAWI, NAWAL (1930-). Physician, author, and feminist. Born in the Delta village of Kafr Tahla, she was trained at Cairo University's (q.v.) Medical Faculty and Columbia University Medical School and began her practice in 1955. Two years later she published in *Ruz al-Yusuf* (q.v.) a memoir, based on her early life and training, part of which appears in her *Memoirs of a Woman Doctor*. She taught for some years in the medical faculty and became the editor of *al-Sihha* ("Health") magazine and the director of education in the ministry of health, but she was dismissed in 1972 for publishing *Women and Sex*. She later was a consultant for the United Nations (q.v.) and published in 1980 an exposé of women's conditions in the Arab world, *The Hidden Face of Eve*. Arrested by Sadat (q.v.) for alleged "crimes against the state" in 1981, Sa'dawi later described her experiences in *Memoirs from the Women's Prison*, published in English in 1988. She has also written many novels, some of which have been translated. In 1982 she founded the Arab Women's Solidarity Organization, which was barred by the Egyptian government in 1991 (*see* Feminism).

SA'DIST PARTY. Breakaway faction from the Wafd Party (q.v.) in 1937–38, led by Ahmad Mahir (q.v.) and Mahmud Fahmi al-Nuqrashi (q.v.). Claiming to be the true heir to Sa'd Zaghlul's (q.v.) principles, it ran candidates in the 1938 elections, which the Wafd boycotted, and joined in Muhammad Mahmud's (q.v.) coalition government. It led anti-Wafdist coalition governments between 1944 and 1949. Its constituency was heavily upper- and middle-class and was well represented in the Federation of Egyptian Industries (q.v.). After the 1952 Revolution (q.v.), it was dissolved. It never attained the popularity of the Wafd.

SA'ID (1822–63). Governor of Egypt from 1854 to 1863. The fourth surviving son of Muhammad Ali (q.v.), he was educated by Palace tutors.

A bright pupil but painfully shy, perhaps because he was overweight, Muhammad Ali required him to make daily calls on the various European consuls and address them in French. Thus he overcame his shyness, became fluent in French, and was befriended by the young French consul, Ferdinand de Lesseps (q.v.), with fateful consequences for Egypt's later history. He became an ensign in the Egyptian navy when he was 13, and Muhammad Ali made him its commander, a position that he retained through the reign of Abbas I (q.v.), despite the bad relations between them. Upon succeeding him as Egypt's governor, he quickly improved ties with France and with some of the Turks and Egyptians whom Abbas had exiled. Most historical accounts commend Sa'id's reign for granting the concession to build the Suez Canal (q.v.), his friendly relations with Europeans, his promulgation of the 1855 Land Law (*see* Landownership), phasing out remnants of Muhammad Ali's monopolies, admitting peasants to the officer corps of the Egyptian army, and improving the systems of irrigation (q.v.), transport, and communications. His reign led to massive European immigration, foreign indebtedness, and political interference by Western consuls. The deindustrialization of Egypt, popularly ascribed to Abbas but really due to the changing policies of Muhammad Ali after 1841, continued under Sa'id. He also granted more power to the rural notables and their sons in the administration and the army, but the emergence of ethnic Egyptians into political prominence occurred only after his death. Sa'id was a weak ruler and his reign was an era of quiescence in Egypt's modernization, yet also a portent of the changes to come under Khedive Isma'il (qq.v.) and the British occupation (q.v.).

SA'ID, MUHAMMAD (1863–1928). Politician, cabinet minister, and two-time premier. Born in Alexandria (q.v.) to a family of Turkish origin, he was educated at the government Law School (q.v.) and rose up through the judiciary, becoming interior minister under Butros Ghali (q.v.) from 1908 to 1910, then succeeding him as premier upon his assassination. Although widely assumed to be a Nationalist, he opposed the National Party (q.v.) while in power. He resigned in 1914 and held no government post during World War I (q.v.), but during the 1919 Revolution (q.v.) he chaired the cabinet again and also held the interior portfolio. Elected to the first and second sessions of the Chamber of Deputies, he served as education and justice minister in Sa'd Zaghlul's (q.v.) cabinets and briefly held the agriculture portfolio after his resignation. He was widely viewed in his lifetime as a political manipulator without fixed principles.

SA'IDIS. Inhabitants of Upper Egypt, popularly assumed to be physically stronger but less intelligent than other Egyptians. Until the construction of the Aswan High Dam (q.v.), they were less apt to suffer from waterborne diseases such as bilharzia (q.v.) than Delta peasants. Nasir (q.v.) was of Sa'idi extraction, which may have made him more sensitive to criticism.

SAINT-SIMON, CLAUDE-HENRI (1760–1825). French Utopian socialist. He was one of the first advocates of a maritime canal connecting the Mediterranean to the Red Sea. Some of his supporters tried unsuccessfully to gain Muhammad Ali's (q.v.) support for such a project, which later inspired the construction of the Suez Canal (q.v.).

SALAFIYYA. Movement for gradual Islamic reform, advocated by Muhammad Abduh (q.v.) and Muhammad Rashid Rida (q.v.), especially in *al-Manar* (q.v.).

SALIM, MAMDUH MUHAMMAD (1918–88). Police general, administrator, and premier. Born in Alexandria (q.v.), he was educated at the Police Academy. He served as commander of the Alexandria police from 1964 to 1968, governor of Asyut (q.v.) province from 1968 to 1970, and governor of Alexandria in 1970–71. Joining Sadat's (q.v.) cabinet following the Corrective Revolution (q.v.), he was interior minister and deputy premier in 1971–75, then prime minister from 1975 to 1978 (also serving briefly as interior minister in 1977). He was the leader of the Arab Socialist Union (q.v.) during those years. He was named special assistant to Sadat (q.v.) in October 1978, after Sadat's foreign minister resigned in protest against his signing the Camp David Accords (q.v.), and continued to serve in this capacity under Mubarak (q.v.). He was also a member of the Higher Council for Nuclear Energy. He played an important role in modernizing Egypt's security forces, abolishing exit visas for Egyptians, and instituting democratic reforms within the government.

AL-SANHURI, ABD AL-RAZZAQ (1895–1971). Expert in Egyptian law. Born in Alexandria (q.v.), he began his official life by working in its customhouse. He graduated from the government Law School (q.v.) in 1917 and was sent on an educational mission to France, earning his doctorate in political economy and law under the supervision of Édouard Lambert, former Law School director. Sanhuri joined the Niyaba (q.v.) upon his return and was appointed deputy public prosecutor in 1926. He also became a professor of civil law at Cairo University (q.v.), represented Egypt at the Congress of Comparative Law held in Paris in 1932, and was appointed dean of the Law Faculty in 1936, a position that he soon lost because of his political and personal hostility to Nahhas (q.v.). He was also a judge in the Mixed Courts (q.v.) and drafted revisions to Egypt's civil code during intervals when the Wafd Party (q.v.) was out of power.

He served as education minister in 1939 and 1945 and justice minister in 1944. In 1946 he was elected to membership in the Arabic Language Academy (q.v.) and in 1949 to the presidency of the Council of State, an advisory judicial body, where he directed the revision of Egypt's civil code. Because Sanhuri backed Najib (q.v.) in 1954, Nasir's (q.v.) government forced him into early retirement. He then helped revise the civil codes of Syria, Iraq, and Libya (q.v.), and also Kuwait's commercial code. He received Egypt's state prize for social sciences in 1970.

SANNU', YA'QUB "ABU NADDARA" (1839–1912). Humorous writer, journalist, playwright, and early Egyptian nationalist. Born in Cairo (q.v.) to a Jewish family of Italian origin, Sannu' was taught the rudiments of Islam (q.v.) as well as of Judaism and in 1852 was sent to Leghorn to study at the expense of a generous nephew of Muhammad Ali (q.v.). He spent three years studying political economy, international law, natural science, and the fine arts, also gaining exposure to the theater and to nascent Italian nationalism. He returned to the court of Sa'id (q.v.), whom he admired, and worked as a tutor, then began teaching in the Cairo polytechnic school in 1862. His classroom duties were outweighed by his extracurricular meetings with students who would later become supporters of Urabi's (q.v.) movement.

Because Khedive Isma'il (qq.v.) included among his reforms the opening of an opera house (q.v.) and a comic theater in Cairo, Egyptians, among them Sannu', came to know European drama. He began writing and producing comic plays, using Cairo colloquial Arabic, for Egyptian audiences. He was the first director to put women actors on the Egyptian stage. After meeting Jamal al-Din al-Afghani (q.v.) in 1871, he also began composing political satires. His first plays were performed in a small theater in Cairo's old city, but he soon moved to one near the Ezbekiyya Gardens (q.v.) and eventually to Qasr al-Nil (q.v.) Palace, where he performed before the khedive, who called him "Egypt's Molière." As his Arabic plays and his adaptation of French plays became better known, his satires grew bolder, and the British convinced Isma'il that Sannu's influence was subversive. The khedive forbade him to write or produce further plays. Sannu' formed two secret literary societies, both noteworthy for including members from all the major religions, but they were closed in 1875; he would later claim them to have been precursors of the first National Party (q.v.). Sannu' made peace with Isma'il in 1876 and was named "court poet," but they soon quarreled again. He became involved in the Freemasonic (q.v.) movement and lampooned the court and its hangers-on ever more stridently. Afghani and Abduh (q.v.) encouraged him to publish a comic newspaper, partly written in colloquial Arabic, called *Abu Naddara Zarqa* ("The Wearer of Blue Spectacles"), in which he satirized both the khedive and the sultan, but hailed Prince Abd al-Halim (q.v.) as Egypt's potential savior. This newspaper was the first in Egypt to print cartoons. Threats against the editor and even his printer did not deter him, so Isma'il banished him from Egypt in 1878. He went to Paris, where he met many other Middle Eastern émigrés and continued to publish papers attacking Isma'il and his successors, gleaning financial support from various sources, possibly including Prince Halim. A pioneer of both drama and journalism in Egypt, Sannu' now stands out for having been at the same time a Jew (q.v.) and an Egyptian nationalist, but in his own time he was hailed for his witty social comedies and his satires against native and foreign rulers.

AL-SAYYID, AHMAD LUTFI (1872–1963). Writer, editor, and educational leader, often called *Ustadh al-jil* ("Professor of the Generation") because of his influence on younger men. Born to an Egyptian landowning family, he was supposed to study at al-Azhar (q.v.), but instead ended up at the government Law School (q.v.). While studying there, he founded a law review called *al-Tashri'* ("Legislation"), together with Abd al-Aziz Fahmi (q.v.) and Abd al-Khaliq Tharwat (q.v.). After graduating in 1894, he worked as a deputy public prosecutor. In 1896 he joined the secret society that became the basis for the National Party (q.v.) and was advised by Abbas Hilmi II (q.v.) to live in Switzerland for a year in order to acquire its nationality, so that he could edit a nationalist newspaper, protected by the Capitulations (q.v.) from prosecution under the 1881 Press Law (q.v.). While there, Lutfi came under the influence of Muhammad Abduh (q.v.) and decided to distance himself from the khedive (q.v.). Returning to Egypt, he worked in the Niyaba (q.v.), but his growing estrangement from the British led him to resign in 1905. He opened his own law firm and defended the peasants in the Dinshaway (q.v.) trial.

Early in 1907, a group of Egyptian liberals established *al-Jarida* (q.v.) and named Lutfi as its editor, a post he held from 1907 to 1914. Its shareholders formed the Umma Party (q.v.) as a middle force between the khedive and the Nationalists. Because Lutfi believed strongly in individual rights and constitutional liberties, his editorials opposed Abbas's autocratic pretensions and rejected ties with the Ottoman Empire (q.v.) and pan-Islam (q.v.). He focused on promoting a sound Egyptian patriotism based on education and a sense of self-worth. Although he opposed the National Party's extremism, he admired Mustafa Kamil (q.v.) personally and cooperated with Muhammad Farid (q.v.) during Britain's *politique d'entente* (q.v.) with Abbas. After Britain declared the Protectorate (q.v.), *al-Jarida* ceased publication.

In 1919 Lutfi was one of the first to join the Wafd (q.v.), but he gradually distanced himself from party politics. From 1923 to 1941 he was the rector of Cairo University (q.v.). He translated Aristotle's *Nichomachean Ethics* and other writings into Arabic. Some of his *al-Jarida* editorials were reprinted in 1937 and 1949 as *al-Muntakhabat* ("Selected Passages"), *Safahat matwiya min tarikh al-haraka al-istiqlaliyya fi Misr* ("Unwritten Pages from the History of the Independence Movement in Egypt") in 1946, and *Taammulat fi al-falsafa wa al-adab wa al-siyasa wa al-ijtima'* ("Meditations in Philosophy, Literature, Politics, and Society") in 1946 and reprinted in 1965. His memoirs, published in *al-Musawwar* in 1950, were reissued in book form as *Qissat hayati* ("The Story of My Life") in 1963. An advocate of reason who preferred a life of scholarship to a political career, he could not inspire the Egyptian masses, but his influence on Egypt's intellectuals was immense.

SECURITY COUNCIL RESOLUTION 242 (1967). United Nations statement of principles for achieving peace between the Arab states and Israel, adopted by the Security Council on 22 November 1967. The resolution called for a just and lasting peace so that every state in the Middle East would have the right "to live in peace within secure and recognized borders." It called on Israel to withdraw its troops from "territories occupied in the recent conflict." Egypt and the other Arab countries interpreted this passage to mean withdrawal from *all* occupied lands, including the Sinai Peninsula (q.v.) and Gaza Strip (q.v.); Israel argued that it meant *some* territories. It also called for freedom of navigation through international waterways in the Middle East, a just solution to the refugee problem, and measures including demilitarized zones to guarantee the territorial inviolability and political independence of every state in the area. Resolution 242 was accepted in 1967 by Egypt and Israel (but with differing interpretations) and has since been reaffirmed (but not implemented, so far) as a basis for Arab-Israeli peace.

SECURITY COUNCIL RESOLUTION 338 (1973). United Nations resolution, prepared by the United States and the USSR, calling for a cease-fire between Israel and the Arab states involved in the October War (q.v.), prompt implementation of Security Council Resolution 242 (q.v.) in all of its parts, and immediate negotiations, concurrent with the cease-fire, among the parties concerned under appropriate auspices to establish a just and durable peace in the Middle East. It was followed by Resolutions 339, asking the secretary-general to send UN observers to supervise the cease-fire, and 340, demanding that all parties return to the positions that they occupied on 22 October 1973, implying Israel's withdrawal from its position surrounding Suez. It is often cited as a basis for Arab-Israeli peace negotiations.

SEPARATION OF FORCES (1974). Term used by U.S. Secretary of State Kissinger for the realignment of Egyptian and Israeli troops near the Suez Canal (q.v.), culminating in the first Egyptian-Israeli agreement, signed on 18 January 1974. Israel agreed to withdraw its troops from the west side of the Canal, and Egypt reduced its forces east of it. Both sides agreed to meet again at Kilometer 101 (q.v.) to work out the details to implement the troop movements. The signatories stated that this agreement was the first step toward a final, just, and durable peace under the provisions of Security Council Resolution 338 (q.v.) and within the framework of the Geneva Conference (q.v.). Kissinger later mediated a similar accord between Syria and Israel.

SÈVE, OCTAVE-JOSEPH-ANTHELME, "SULAYMAN PASHA" (1787–1860). French army officer in Egyptian service. Born in Lyons, he showed strong aptitude for a military profession and excelled in the study of mathematics as an aspiring naval officer, but his early involvement in a duel made him quit the French navy. Joining Napoléon's (q.v.) army, he saw action in Italy, in Russia, and in the hundred-day attempt to regain power. His career derailed by the restoration of the Bourbon monarchy, he left France in 1816 for Persia. On reaching Egypt, Muhammad Ali (q.v.) offered to make him an instructor in his new army. Sève managed to assert his authority over a corps of young Georgian and Circassian Mamluks (qq.v.) by arresting some of their cadets who had tried to shoot him during their target practice. He even taught European military techniques to Ibrahim (q.v.), just back from his war against the Wahhabis (q.v.) in Arabia. In a few years he managed to weld a polyglot group of Turks, Circassians, and Arabs, to which were added Egyptian peasants, into a 130,000-man army that could be doubled, in case of need, by bedouin (q.v.) irregulars, auxiliaries, and cadets. Sève married into Muhammad Ali's family; converted to Islam (q.v.), taking the name Sulayman; and was promoted to the rank of colonel. He aided Ibrahim in the Morean war against the Greeks and later in Egypt's Syrian campaign against the Ottoman Empire (q.v.). Although his role was diminished by the Convention of London (q.v.), he remained in the Egyptian army, helping it to take part in the Crimean War.

SHA'B PARTY. Small clique organized in November 1930 by Isma'il Sidqi (q.v.) as a counterpoise to King Fuad's Ittihad Party (q.v.), so that he would not depend wholly on Palace support. In the May-June 1931 Parliamentary elections, which were boycotted by the Wafd (q.v.) and the

Constitutional Liberals (q.v.), 83 Sha'b deputies were elected. When Sidqi turned his premiership over to Abd al-Fattah Yahya (q.v.) in 1933, the latter also assumed the presidency of the Sha'b Party. Dominated by large landowners, with a scattering of urban middle-class backers, it declined after 1936. It merged in November 1938 with the Ittihad Party; together they played a marginal role in Egyptian politics.

SHABAB MUHAMMAD. Revolutionary Muslim youth movement, formed in 1939 as a splinter group from the Muslim Brothers (q.v.), active in the Palestine War (q.v.) and the anti-British struggle in the Suez Canal (q.v.) Zone in 1951, implicated in Black Saturday (q.v.), and later banned by the Revolutionary Command Council (q.v.). Later, one of its members, Hafiz Salama, formed the Society of Islamic Guidance (q.v.).

AL-SHADHILI (SHAZLY), SA'D AL-DIN (1922-). Army officer, diplomat, and writer. Born in Cairo (q.v.), he was educated in government schools, Cairo University (q.v.), the Military Academy (q.v.), and the USSR. After five years' service in the Guards Regiment, he was a platoon commander in the Palestine War (q.v.). He was commander of the Parachute School from 1954 to 1956, of a paratroop battalion from 1956 to 1958, and of the United Arab Republic (q.v.) contingent of the UN forces in the Congo in 1960–61. He served as defense attaché of the Egyptian Embassy in London from 1961 to 1963. He then became brigadier commander of the Egyptian forces in the Yemen Civil War (q.v.) from 1965 to 1966, of the Shadhili Group in the June War (q.v.), of the Special Forces in 1967–69, and of the Red Sea district from 1970 to 1971. Shadhili was commander-in-chief of the Egyptian armed forces from 1971 to 1973 and is generally credited with having led the Egyptians' successful crossing of the Suez Canal (q.v.) in Operation Badr (q.v.). He later quarreled with Sadat (q.v.) and was sent as Egypt's ambassador to Britain in 1974–75, then Portugal in 1975–78. An expatriate critic of Sadat's policies, he founded the Egyptian National Front in 1980 and began publishing *al-Jabha* magazine. He also published books on the October War, notably *The Crossing of the Suez* in 1980.

AL-SHAFI'I, HUSAYN (1918-). Officer and politician. A Military Academy (q.v.) graduate, he was one of the Free Officers (q.v.) who carried out the 1952 Revolution (q.v.), after which he joined the Revolutionary Command Council (q.v.). Shafi'i became minister of war and marine briefly in 1954, then minister for social affairs up to 1958. During the union with Syria, he served as minister of labor and social affairs and briefly held one of the vice presidential positions. Following the breakup of the United Arab Republic (q.v.), he was minister of social affairs with the rank of deputy premier. In 1962 he joined the Presidential Council and was a vice president in 1964–67. He again became minister of social affairs and *awqaf* (q.v.) in 1967–68, and during that time he also chaired the revolutionary court that tried 55 officers accused of plotting against Nasir (q.v.). He served again as vice president under Sadat (q.v.) from 1970 to 1975. He opposed Sadat's peace initiative and denounced the Camp David Accords (q.v.) in October 1978. Since then Shafi'i has not been active in politics.

SHAME, LAW OF (1980). Authoritarian decree by Sadat (q.v.), approved by 98 percent of all Egyptian voters in a national plebiscite, that severely restricted public criticism of his person and policies. Also punishable were "advocating any doctrinc that implies negation of divine teaching," "causing children or youth to go astray by advocating the repudiation of popular, religious, moral, or national values or by setting a bad example in a public place," and "broadcasting gross or scurrilous words or pictures that could offend public sensibilities or undermine the dignity of the state." Offenders could be barred from public life, conducting business, managing their own property, living in their own homes, or leaving Egypt. Although many lawyers and journalists have criticized the Law of Shame, it has not been repealed.

SHAMM AL-NASIM. Egyptian spring holiday, coinciding with Coptic (q.v.) Easter Monday, celebrated by most Muslims as well as Christians.

SHARAF, SAMI (1929-). Intelligence operative and close associate of Jamal Abd al-Nasir (q.v.), especially following the June 1967 War (q.v.). He was the cousin of General Muhammad Fawzi (q.v.), whom he urged Nasir to appoint as his defense minister. Sharaf was minister of presidential affairs under both Nasir and Sadat (q.v.), who purged him in the Corrective Revolution (q.v.) despite his personal friendship with the commander of the presidential guard. Convicted of plotting against Sadat, he was given a long prison sentence, but was released in the summer of 1981. He has played no further role in politics.

AL-SHA'RAWI, HUDA (1879–1947). Pioneer leader of Egyptian feminism (q.v.). She was a daughter of Muhammad Sultan, a wealthy Egyptian landowner, and the wife of Ali al-Sha'rawi, the first treasurer of the Wafd (q.v.). She helped to organize Mubarrat Muhammad Ali, a women's social service organization, in 1909 and the Union of Educated Egyptian Women in 1914, which was also the first time she traveled to Europe. She took part in the first women's street demonstration during the 1919 Revolution (q.v.) and was elected president of the Wafdist Women's

Central Committee. In 1923 Sha'rawi founded and became the first president of the Egyptian Feminist Union (q.v.), which sent her to an international feminist meeting in Rome. Upon her return, she took off her face veil in public for the first time. Under her leadership Egyptian women picketed the opening of Parliament in January 1924 and submitted a list of nationalist and feminist demands. She resigned later from the Wafdist Women's Central Committee but continued to lead the Egyptian Feminist Union until her death. Sha'rawi was instrumental in forming an Arab feminist organization in 1944. Her memoirs of her secluded early life have been translated into English and published as *Harem Years: The Memoirs of an Egyptian Feminist*; regrettably, they do not cover her later years as a feminist leader.

SHARI'A. The comprehensive code of Muslim behavior, or the rules and laws of Islam (q.v.). The Shari'a has been derived by generations of Muslim legal experts from the Quran and the recorded sayings and acts of Muhammad, augmented by analogy, consensus of the Islamic community, and previous judicial decisions. Although the Shari'a purports to cover all aspects of Muslim behavior, for most of Islamic history it has coexisted with other legal systems, including rulers' edicts, or *qanuns*, commercial law administered by *muhtasibs* ("market inspectors"), and *mazalim* courts that investigated bureaucratic injustices. Learned Muslims, or ulama (q.v.), developed and administered the Shari'a. Westernizing reforms in nineteenth-century Egypt gradually limited the ulama's judicial authority to issues of worship and personal relationships between Muslims, including marriage, divorce, and inheritance of property. With the rise of Islamism (q.v.) in the 1970s, some National Assembly (q.v.) members argued that the Shari'a should become the basis of Egypt's laws. An amendment to the 1971 Constitution (q.v.) identifies the Shari'a as the main basis of Egyptian legislation.

SHARI'A COURTS. Egypt's Muslim tribunals up to 1956. In Ottoman (q.v.) times, the judicial system included courts headed by an appointed *qadi-asker*, handling cases involving Mamluks (q.v.) or other soldiers in Egypt, and courts headed by *qadi*s ("judges"), who heard cases involving civilian Muslims. Under Muhammad Ali (q.v.), the jurisdiction of these courts was further limited by the Ottoman Nizam-i-Jedid (q.v.). A rudimentary secular court system was established under Muhammad Ali and Isma'il (q.v.), leading to comprehensive National Courts (q.v.) in 1883, but the Shari'a Courts continued to hear cases involving marriage, divorce, child custody, administration of family *awqaf* (q.v.), and other matters most likely to affect the daily lives of most Egyptian Muslims; the Copts (q.v.), other Christian sects, and Jews (q.v.) had similar courts.

Although most of the Shari'a Court personnel were trained by al-Azhar (q.v.), the Egyptian government tried to bypass that conservative institution. When he was education minister, Sa'd Zaghlul (q.v.) founded a School for Muslim Qadis in 1907 to train clerks, judges, and even lawyers (who had played no role in traditional Muslim practice). Azharite complaints led to the closing of this school in 1928. The Shari'a lawyers formed their own bar association in 1916, but regarded themselves as underprivileged relative to National and Mixed Court (qq.v.) attorneys. Indeed, Shari'a court judges, lawyers, and clerks wielded less power, enjoyed less prestige, and earned lower wages than their counterparts in Egypt's other tribunals. Piecemeal reforms were made in marriage and divorce laws in the 1920s, but the *awqaf* remained subject to many abuses, and Sanhuri's (q.v.) efforts at civil law reform did not affect the Shari'a courts. Nasir's (q.v.) government abolished all religious courts in January 1956, and the Shari'a court judges were incorporated into the National Court system. In recent years, Egypt's Islamists (q.v.) have called for reinstitution of the Shari'a (q.v.) as the law of the land. If they succeed, the Shari'a courts will probably be revived.

SHARIF, MUHAMMAD (1826–87). Army officer, cabinet minister, and three-time premier. Born in Istanbul, he accompanied his father when he was sent by the Ottoman (q.v.) sultan to be a judge in Mecca. Muhammad Ali (q.v.) saw him as a boy, took a fancy to him, and offered to rear him as one of his own sons. He was enrolled in the Princes' School (*Maktab al-Khanqa*) and accompanied them on the 1844 education mission to Paris. Sharif spent two years at St.-Cyr Military Academy and became the captain of a French regiment. He returned to Cairo (q.v.) in 1849 to become a captain under Colonel Sève (q.v.), or "Sulayman Pasha," whose daughter he married, and may have been a clerk to Prince Abd al-Halim (q.v.). He was in Istanbul during Abbas Hilmi I's (q.v.) last year as viceroy, but returned after the accession of Sa'id (q.v.), who promoted him to colonel and put him in command of an infantry regiment.

Sharif entered the civil administration as director of the foreign affairs department in 1858. He mixed well with Europeans and was scrupulously honest, but was extremely proud of his Turkish background, contemptuous toward Armenians (q.v.) and Egyptians, and somewhat lazy. He chaired the Council of Justice (q.v.) from 1861 to 1863 and later in 1867. He briefly directed education, then returned to foreign affairs in 1863; took charge of interior in 1866, adding public works for a time; served on four occasions as acting viceroy when Isma'il (q.v.) was away from Egypt; and headed the department of justice from 1872 to 1875, adding commerce in 1874–and again from 1876. As prime minister in 1879, then in 1881–82, and in 1882–84, Sharif acquired an undeserved reputation for favoring constitutional government and Urabi's (q.v.) movement. He was well liked by Europeans and Turco-Egyptian aristocrats and built up substantial landholdings in Egypt. Dominated by Khedives Isma'il and Tawfiq (q.v.), he rarely tried to assert his convictions, except when he resigned in 1884 rather than countenance surrendering Egyptian control over the Sudan (q.v.).

SHARIF, OMAR (1932-). Cinema (q.v.) actor. Originally named Michel Shalhub, he was educated at Cairo's Victoria College. He worked briefly as a salesman for a lumber export firm and began acting in films in 1953. His first film was called *The Blazing Sun.* He starred in 24 Egyptian and two French coproduction films in the following five years. He began his international career with a supporting role in *Lawrence of Arabia* and has starred in other British and American movies, including *Behold a Pale Horse*, *Doctor Zhivago*, and *Funny Girl.* He published an autobiography, *The Eternal Male*, in 1978.

SHARM AL-SHAYKH. Fortified point on the shore of the Sinai Peninsula (q.v.) near the Straits of Tiran (q.v.) used by Egypt from 1949 to 1956 and in 1967 to block the passage of Israeli shipping between the Gulf of Aqaba (q.v.) and the Red Sea, on the claim that Israel was not entitled to use either waterway.

AL-SHARQAWI, ABD AL-RAHMAN (1920–87). Leftist novelist and journalist. Sharqawi's first novel, *al-Ard* (translated as *Egyptian Earth*), depicted the privations of the Egyptian peasants before the 1952 Revolution (q.v.). He became chairman of the Afro-Asian Peoples Solidarity Conference (q.v.) and of the political weekly magazine, *Ruz al-Yusuf* (q.v.). He became secretary-general of the Supreme Council for the Arts and wrote a weekly column for *al-Ahram* (q.v.) under Nasir (q.v.). He broke with Sadat (q.v.) after he formed the Supreme Press Council in 1975. Sharqawi's manifesto, *Muhammad rasul al-hurriyya* ("Muhammad, Messenger of Freedom"), preached a form of Islamic socialism.

SHAWQI, AHMAD (1868–1932). Distinguished Arabic poet and playwright, often called *amir al-shu'ara* ("prince of poets"). He came from a wealthy family of mixed Turkish, Arab, Kurdish, and Greek origin with close connections to the khedivial family. Born in Cairo (q.v.), he was educated at the Khedivial Secondary School, then the School of Languages (later the government Law School [q.v.]) in Cairo from 1885 to 1889, and studied in Montpellier and Paris in 1891–93. He was fascinated by France and equally impressed by the beautiful monuments and the "great commercial and industrial developments" in London, which he visited during his stay. Upon returning to Egypt, he went to work in the court of Abbas Hilmi II (q.v.) and began writing poetry, often glorifying his patron. He read one of his poems at the 1894 International Congress of Orientalists in Geneva. Shawqi wrote poems attacking Riyad (q.v.) for praising the British occupation (q.v.) in 1904 and Cromer (q.v.) on the occasion of his departure in 1907. He bitterly mourned the deposition of Ottoman Sultan Abdulhamid in 1909 and would later pen an elegy to the caliphate (q.v.) when it was abolished by Kemal Atatürk. When Abbas was deposed in 1914, Shawqi was exiled to Barcelona, Spain. After returning to Egypt in 1919, he managed to win public recognition as the greatest living Arabic poet. He was elected to the Senate in 1923 and was formally named "Prince of the Arab Poets" by his colleagues, including Hafiz (q.v.), at a ceremony in Cairo in 1927. His enemies called him the "poet of Arab princes" because of his close ties with Abdin Palace (q.v.), but his work remains a model for neoclassical Arabic poetry. He is still widely read and admired throughout the Arab world, and his elegant home in Giza has been converted into a museum.

SHAYKH AL-BALAD. Assistant to the umda (q.v.) as village magistrate.

SHAYKH AL-SADAT. Prestigious Egyptian leader of the descendants of the Prophet Muhammad, especially via his grandson Husayn. In the nineteenth century, this position became tied to the leadership of the Wafa'iyya family and Sufi (q.v.) order, then was held for a while by members of the Bakri family (*see* Naqib al-Ashraf). The marriage of journalist Shaykh Ali Yusuf (q.v.) to the daughter of the shaykh al-sadat became a public issue in 1904. The position has lost power and prestige during the twentieth century.

SHEPHEARD'S HOTEL. Famous Cairo (q.v.) inn, opened in 1841 as the British Hotel, near what was to become the Ezbekiyya Gardens (q.v.). It soon developed a reputation as a comfortable oasis for travelers on the arduous overland route between Europe and India. Partly destroyed by fire in 1869, it was rebuilt in time to help accommodate the crowds attending the inauguration of the Suez Canal (q.v.). Its popularity increased with the development of Cook's Tours in the 1870s (*see* River Transport). It was enlarged in 1888 and then completely rebuilt in 1890, when it became the first hotel in the Middle East to have electric lighting. In World Wars I and II (qq.v.) it was host to thousands of British Empire troops, and its Long Bar became famous for its libations. The first ball of Cairo's social season was always held at Shepheard's. In part because it was frequented by wealthy foreigners, Shepheard's was the prime target for demonstrators on Black Saturday (q.v.), when it was totally destroyed by fire. Its name was later given to a new hotel built in another location, near the Cairo Corniche (q.v.), but it has not been as successful.

AL-SHUBBAN AL-MUSLIMIN. Often called the "Young Men's Muslim Association" in English, this educational society was founded in November 1927 by Abd al-Hamid Sa'id, Abd al-Aziz Jawish (q.v.), and Muhibb al-Din al-Khatib to counter the Westernizing influence of the YMCA and other foreign groups. Its aims were to teach Islamic morals and ethics, to spread that knowledge best suited to the modern way of life, to discourage dissension and abuses among Muslims, and to utilize what is best in both Eastern and Western cultures while rejecting all that is bad in them. The Association forswore all political activity, but its leaders were involved with either the National Party (q.v.) or the Salafiyya (q.v.) movement. It was in fact a highly militant, politicized, and pan-Islamic group, which formed branches throughout Egypt and in other Muslim countries. It was influential under the government of Ali Mahir (q.v.), tended to back anti-imperialist movements (some of them pro-Nazi) during World War II (q.v.), and sent volunteers to fight in the Palestine War (q.v.), but it never achieved as much popular support as the Muslim Brothers (q.v.).

SHUTTLE DIPLOMACY. U.S. Secretary of State Kissinger's method of mediating between individual Arab countries and Israel during 1974–75, by which he moved frequently between Arab and Israeli leaders to forge Separation of Forces Agreements (q.v.) in 1974 and the Egyptian-Israeli Agreement (q.v.) in the following year. This method, influenced by the Rhodes Proximity Talks (q.v.), has since been imitated by other U.S. mediators between Israel and the Arabs.

AL-SIBA'I, YUSUF (1917–78). Army officer, politician, journalist, and writer. Born in Cairo (q.v.), he graduated from the Military Academy (q.v.) in 1937. In 1952 he became director of the Military Museum, then general secretary of the Council for Literature and Art, chairman of the Writers' Association and of the Cinema Critics' Association, and subsequently secretary-general of the Afro-Asian Peoples Solidarity Conference (q.v.). He became editor of *Akhar Sa'a*, a weekly, in 1966 and later chairman of the board of directors for *Dar al-Hilal* and editor of *al-Musawwar* (q.v.). Siba'i was minister of culture and information in 1973–76 and he was elected chairman of the Journalists' Syndicate in 1977. The author of many novels and short stories that were popular among Egyptians, he was killed in February 1978 by Palestinian *fidaiyin* (q.v.) during an attack on an Afro-Asian Solidarity Conference meeting in Cyprus, angering many Egyptians against the Palestinians.

SIDDIQ, ISMA'IL (1821–76). Major Egyptian official under Khedive Isma'il (qq.v.), often called the Mufattish (q.v.). The son of a poor peasant, Siddiq's mother was the wet nurse to Isma'il, and hence the two boys grew up together. He got little schooling, spoke no language other than Arabic, and rarely dealt with Europeans, yet he became one of Egypt's richest and most powerful officials. Starting as a local inspector for the khedivial estates under Abbas Hilmi I (q.v.) and Sa'id (q.v.), he eventually became their inspector general. Upon his accession, Isma'il raised his salary and made him director general of all khedivial properties. Siddiq gradually advanced in his responsibilities until he became in 1866 inspector general for all Egypt, the position that made him famous. In 1867 he joined the Regency Council that governed Egypt while Isma'il was visiting Paris; the next year he took charge of the finance department. He married a freed slave of Ibrahim (q.v.), Isma'il's father, and his son later married an adopted daughter of the khedive. Although he had no formal training in finance, Siddiq had a flexible mind that enabled him to adapt to new situations and to understand his patron's wishes. He became adept at bargaining with Egypt's creditors, devising new stratagems to collect taxes, and supervising provincial officials. He accumulated agricultural lands, several palaces in Cairo (q.v.), and immense sums of money. Despite his ties to Isma'il, his patron watched him closely and grew increasingly suspicious about his fortune, gained mostly by graft and extortion. Consequently, he was dismissed from all his positions in 1876. Siddiq "vanished" suddenly in November 1876; in fact, he was being pursued by the new Caisse (q.v.) and was arrested by the khedive's (q.v.) Privy Council (q.v.), tried, found guilty, and secretly murdered–allegedly by Mustafa Fahmi (q.v.). In a critical era of Egypt's history, he was an official with unparalleled power, extraordinary wealth, strong patronage, few scruples, and no education.

SIDQI, AZIZ (1920-). Engineer, politician, cabinet minister, and premier. Educated at Cairo University (q.v.), the University of Oregon, and Harvard, he served as minister of industry from 1956 to 1963, then deputy prime minister for industry and mineral wealth in 1964–65, later becoming adviser to President Nasir (q.v.) for production in 1966–67, and finally minister of industry, petroleum, and mineral wealth from 1968 to 1971. After Sadat (q.v.) succeeded Nasir, he became a deputy prime minister in 1971 and prime minister in 1972–73. When Sadat took charge of the cabinet shortly before the October War (q.v.), Sidqi became a special assistant to the president. He represented Egypt at numerous international conferences on industrial affairs.

SIDQI, ISMA'IL (1875–1950). Lawyer, cabinet minister, and two-time premier. Born in Alexandria (q.v.), he was educated at the Collège des Frères (q.v.) and the government Law School (q.v.). Sidqi advanced rapidly through the judiciary and became agriculture minister from 1914 to 1917, when he resigned because of a compromising scandal. A member of the original Wafd (q.v.) in 1918, he was interned in Malta with Sa'd Zaghlul (q.v.) in March 1919. Sidqi later broke with Sa'd and helped to establish the Constitutional Liberal Party (q.v.) in 1922. He served as interior minister in 1924–25, worked closely with King Fuad (q.v.), and founded the Sha'b Party (q.v.), to back his campaign for prime minister under the 1930 Constitution (q.v.). He headed a strong cabinet in 1930–33, but Fuad dismissed him for being too powerful in his own right. He served on the Egyptian delegation that negotiated for the 1936 Anglo-Egyptian Treaty (q.v.). He chaired another cabinet from February to December 1946, concluding the abortive Bevin-Sidqi Agreement (q.v.). He returned to the Senate and opposed Egypt's involvement in the Palestine War (q.v.). Sidqi was one of the cleverest politicians of his time, devoted to the monarchy, and disliked by nationalists. His memoirs, *Mudhakkirati*, were published in 1950.

SINAI CAMPAIGN, *see* SUEZ WAR.

SINAI PENINSULA. Mountainous Egyptian territory between the Suez Canal (q.v.) and the Israeli border, invaded by Israel in 1949, 1956, and 1967, then occupied by Israel continuously until 1973, when Egyptian forces retook portions nearest the Canal during the October War (q.v.). Israel relinquished portions of the Sinai to Egypt as part of the first Disengagement of Forces (q.v.) Agreement of 1974, the 1975 Interim Accord (q.v.), and the 1979 Egyptian-Israeli Peace Treaty (q.v.). The rest of the Sinai was restored in April 1982, except for Taba (q.v.), which was awarded to Egypt following international arbitration in 1989.

SIRAJ AL-DIN, FUAD (1910-). Landowning politician, lawyer, and leader of the old and New Wafd Party (q.v.). Born in Kafr al-Garayda (Gharbiyya), his father and grandfather were umdas (q.v.) and landowners. His mother came from the Badrawi Ashur landowning family, into which Fuad later married. He attended the government Law School (q.v.), graduating in 1931. He worked in the Niyaba (q.v.) until his father died in 1934, then went home to manage the family estates, but ran successfully in the 1936 parliamentary elections as a Wafd Party (q.v.) candidate, partly due to his prior ties with Makram Ubayd (q.v.). He soon came to know Nahhas (q.v.) and became a financial adviser to his young wife. When Nahhas returned to power in February 1942, he named Fuad, despite his youth, his agriculture minister. He remained loyal to Nahhas when Makram left the Wafd, becoming interior minister in 1943.

After the fall of the Wafd cabinet, Fuad went back to managing his estates and serving on several corporate boards, including the Egyptian Coca-Cola Company. Although he won a Senate seat in 1946, he strove to become his party's secretary-general, a post that he gained in 1948 and used to maneuver the left-wing Wafdists out of influential positions. In 1949 he joined Sirri's (q.v.) coalition cabinet as communications minister. He campaigned in the general elections that led to the Wafd's return to power in 1950 and assumed the portfolio for interior, later adding those of finance and even, for a while, education. He and other members of his faction used their positions to engage in questionable business deals on the side. The aging Premier Nahhas became suspicious of Fuad, who also faced a rival clique loyal to Ahmad Najib al-Hilali (q.v.). He tried to both co-opt and coerce the leftists, and resisted attempts to limit maximum landholdings; significantly, one of the 1951 peasant revolts was against his Badrawi relatives. The high-living Wafdists were also making their peace with King Faruq (q.v.), but the rumors of manipulating the Alexandria cotton market, buying titles, and European sprees served to discredit both sides. He ordered a poorly armed police force in Ismailia (q.v.) to resist the British, leading to heavy casualties and to Black Saturday (q.v.). The Wafd cabinet was dismissed the next day, and he was briefly detained for smuggling arms. Abroad when the 1952 Revolution (q.v.) occurred, he hastened back, hoping to be appointed by the Free Officers (q.v.), but he balked at their land reform (q.v.) program. Fuad resigned from the Wafd, but was arrested twice and released each time. Tried for rigging the cotton market, granting favors to the king, inadequately planning the abrogation of the Anglo-Egyptian Treaty (q.v.), and negligence during the burning of Cairo (q.v.), he received a 15-year prison sentence. Quietly released later, he remained under house arrest.

Only in 1975 was his family able to regain some of its confiscated lands. In 1977 he revived the Wafd Party as a vehicle for regaining power at the expense of Sadat (q.v.), who promptly banned it. Although jailed on Sadat's orders in 1981, he managed to resume his political activities under Mubarak (q.v.). His New Wafd, in alliance with the Muslim Brothers (q.v.), finished second to the National Democratic Party (q.v.) in the 1984 parliamentary elections, and Fuad remains a significant, now elderly, figure on the Egyptian political stage.

SIRRI, HUSAYN (1892–1961). Engineer, politician, and three-time premier. Born in Cairo, his father was Isma'il Sirri, also an engineer, who served as public works minister for many years. Husayn Sirri studied engineering in Cairo and then earned a diploma at the École Centrale in Paris during World War I (q.v.). Upon returning to Egypt, he worked for the public works ministry and developed a reputation as an expert on irrigation, publishing treatises on the Nile defense works, irrigation, the Qattara depression, water policy, and state finances. In 1937 he was appointed to the Senate and also became undersecretary of state for public works, After the fall of the Wafd (q.v.) government, he became public works minister, serving in three cabinets until 1939, when he assumed the portfolio for war and marine. He was finance minister in 1939–40, public works minister again in 1940, and communications later in that year. After the sudden death of Hasan Sabri (q.v.), Sirri became premier and interior minister from November 1940 to 1942 (serving also as foreign minister for part of that time), but resigned just before the 4 February 1942 incident (q.v.) and went into business for several years. He was again called on to serve as premier and interior and foreign minister in 1949–50, until free elections restored the Wafd Party to power. He then served as director of the royal cabinet, but resigned after a year, intimating disapproval of some of King Faruq's (q.v.) policies. He headed a short-lived cabinet, with portfolios for foreign affairs and war and marine, in July 1952, just before the 1952 Revolution (q.v.). A non-partisan politician, Sirri was a reputable administrator.

AL-SIYASA. Organ for the Constitutional Liberal Party (q.v.) from 1922 to 1951, founded by Muhammad Husayn Haykal (q.v.) and Mahmud Abd al-Raziq. It also had a weekly magazine, *al-Siyasa al-Usbu'iyya*, from 1926 to 1949. Contributors included Mahmud Azmi, Taha Husayn (q.v.), Mustafa Abd al-Raziq (q.v.), Ibrahim Naji, Ali Mahmud Taha, Salama Musa (q.v.), and Ibrahim Abd al-Qadir al-Mazini (q.v.), making it the leading Arabic literary review of its day. The daily and weekly newspapers were never financially viable and were subsidized by the Abd al-Raziq family and by Muhammad Mahmud (q.v.).

SOCIALISM. Ideas of collective property ownership have influenced some Egyptians since Saint-Simon's (q.v.) disciples visited Muhammad Ali (q.v.). A Syrian Christian physician, Shibli Shumayyil (1860–1917), wrote in favor of socialism in the Egyptian press before World War I (q.v.). An Egyptian teacher named Mustafa Hasanayn al-Mansuri reportedly tried to establish a socialist party in 1909 and in 1915 published a study of socialism, drawing on translations from European literature. He was arrested, denounced by al-Azhar (q.v.), and later dismissed as a teacher.

Niqula Haddad (1878–1954), a Syrian who had lived for a while in New York, wrote many articles and books to popularize socialist ideas in Egypt. The best-known pioneer of Egyptian socialism, however, was Salama Musa (q.v.), who founded the first socialist magazine, *al-Mustaqbil*, which was promptly banned by the Egyptian government.

The 1917 Bolshevik revolution and the formation of the Third International in 1919 made socialism better known in Egypt. In 1921 an Egyptian Jew, Joseph Rosenthal, founded an Egyptian socialist party, including Salama Musa among its charter members. Its political program opposed imperialism, militarism, dictatorship, the arms race, offensive wars, and secret treaties. It advocated an end to capitalist exploitation, integration of natural resources into the public means of production, and just distribution of the products of labor. It called for universal education, higher wages, better working conditions, and the liberation of "Eastern women." The party proposed to form agricultural syndicates for peasants, workers, and consumers, to run socialist deputies for Parliament, and to disseminate its program by publications and speeches (*see* Communism).

A non-Communist "Socialist Party" was founded by Ahmad Husayn (q.v.) in 1946; it was actually the renamed Misr al-Fatat (q.v.). The Arab Socialist Union (ASU) (q.v.), a mobilizational movement that replaced the National Union (q.v.) in 1962, espoused socialist principles but adhered closely to the policies of Nasir (q.v.) and later Sadat (q.v.). When the 1976 Party Reforms (q.v.) opened the ASU to competing pulpits (*manabir*), the leftist group, made up of Nasirists (q.v.) and Marxists (q.v.) opposed to the regime's move toward capitalism and rapprochement with the West, became the National Progressive Unionist Party (q.v.), which now serves as Egypt's major socialist party.

Some socialist ideas, such as state ownership of major industries and better working conditions, have become generally accepted in Egypt, but democratic socialist parties failed to develop ideologically rigorous programs that most Egyptians could understood and accept.

SOCIALIST LABOR PARTY (SLP). Loyalist opposition group formed in 1978, at Sadat's (q.v.) behest, to weaken the National Progressive Union Party (q.v.). Led by Ibrahim Shukri, formerly of Misr al-Fatat (q.v.) and an early advocate of land reform (q.v.), its founders tended to be upper- and middle-class educated people, much like members of the dominant National Democratic Party (q.v.). The SLP won 29 seats in the 1979 parliamentary elections and claimed 180,000 members in 1980. Its weekly paper, *al-Sha'b*, had a circulation of 60,000. Initially hesitant to criticize Sadat's *infitah* (q.v.) and peace policies, it later assailed government corruption and Sadat's proposal to channel Nile water to Israel's Negev Desert. Some of its leaders were jailed when Sadat arrested his opponents in September 1981. Under Mubarak (q.v.), the SLP worked closely with the Muslim Brothers (q.v.), and the two groups joined with the Liberal Party (q.v.) in a coalition for the 1987 parliamentary elections, winning 1.1 million votes. The SLP refused to participate in the 1990 elections. Thanks to its leader, the SLP is the heir to Egypt's national-socialist heritage, but the voters do not seem to know what it represents.

SOCIALIST PARTY, ***see*** **MISR AL-FATAT.**

SOVIET-EGYPTIAN TREATY OF FRIENDSHIP AND COOPERATION (1971). Pact pledging eternal friendship between the USSR and Egypt, signed in Cairo (q.v.) on 28 May 1971, shortly after Sadat's (q.v.) Corrective Revolution (q.v.). This event seems to have alarmed Moscow, since his purge included Ali Sabri (q.v.) and other leaders friendly to the Soviets. The pact pledged the two parties to concert their international policies and "to regularly consult . . . at different levels on all important questions affecting the interests of both sides." This wording was stronger than that used by Soviet treaties with other non-Communist states and implied heavier commitment of Soviet military support to Egypt against Israel, in the wake of the failed Rogers Peace Plan (q.v.). Actually, Sadat's government was disappointed at the quantity and quality of arms that it was able to buy from the USSR, which seemed more intent on promoting détente with the West than liberation of Israeli-occupied Arab lands. A year later Sadat asked most Soviet military advisers to leave Egypt. Some remained, however, and during the October War (q.v.), Moscow resupplied arms–even, it was rumored, nuclear-tipped missiles–to Egypt as well as Syria on a massive scale. Sadat later aligned Egypt's policies with the United States to regain control of the Sinai Peninsula (q.v.), ceased buying weapons from the USSR, annulled Egypt's $6-billion debt to Moscow, and in 1976 renounced the treaty.

STACK, LEE (1868–1924). British commander-in-chief of the Egyptian Army and governor-general of the Sudan (q.v.) from 1919 to November 1924. His assassination by Egyptian terrorists caused Allenby (q.v.) to issue an extremely strong ultimatum to the Egyptian government, leading to the resignation of the Wafd (q.v.) cabinet headed by Zaghlul (q.v.).

STUDENTS' DAY. Annual holiday commemorating the students' (and workers') uprising of 21 February 1946 against the British occupation (q.v.).

SUDAN. The country south of Egypt that corresponds approximately to the areas of the Upper Nile (q.v.) valley captured by Turco-Egyptian forces during the reigns of Muhammad Ali (q.v.) and Isma'il (q.v.). Inspired by the Mahdi (q.v.) between 1881 and 1885, the Sudanese Muslims rebelled against Egyptian rule and established an independent state, which British and Egyptian forces failed to subdue in 1884–85. Under the leadership of the British commander of the Egyptian army, Sir Herbert Kitchener (q.v.), British and Egyptian forces defeated the Sudanese rebels between 1896 and 1898 and restored control over the former Egyptian provinces. Following the Sudan Convention (q.v.), it came under joint Anglo-Egyptian control. In reality, Egyptian officials and officers were subordinate to the British, even though the Egyptian government bore most of the occupation costs, £E19 million from 1899 to 1940. The murder of Sir Lee Stack (q.v.) in 1924 caused Britain to expel Egyptian troops and officials from the country and also to expand use of Nile waters to irrigate the Sudanese *jazira* to raise cotton in competition with Egypt. Egypt's population growth and increasing independence from Britain led to more strident claims to rule the Sudan, in part because all Egypt's irrigation (q.v.) water comes from that country, but also because of its ties with some northern Sudanese Muslims. The British seemed to stir up separatist feelings among the Sudanese, especially the Mahdi's descendants and the Christians and animists in the south.

The Sudan issue was shelved during the negotiations for the 1936 Anglo-Egyptian Treaty (q.v.) but revived after World War II (q.v.). The 1946 Bevin-Sidqi Agreement (q.v.) was popularly believed in Egypt to ensure Egyptian rule over the Sudan, but the British denied any such concession. Egypt brought its claims to the Sudan before the UN Security Council in 1947, but failed to win its case. When Nahhas (q.v.) abrogated the 1936 Treaty in 1951, he proclaimed Faruq (q.v.) king of Egypt and the Sudan, and in the last days of the monarchy much Egyptian agitation centered on the issue of Nile Valley unity. After the 1952 Revolution (q.v.), Najib (q.v.) and the Free Officers (q.v.) agreed to let the Sudanese vote on whether they wanted to join with Egypt after independence from Britain. The 1954 plebiscite went against Egypt, however, and the Sudan became fully independent in 1956.

Egypt's relations with the independent Sudan have varied. Nasir's government disputed its border with the Sudan in 1958, and the two states had to reach agreement on sharing the Nile waters before construction of the Aswan High Dam (q.v.) could begin. Ja'far al-Numayri's government, initially socialist and revolutionary but later pro-Western, was on good terms with Egypt under Sadat (q.v.) and Mubarak (q.v.). Since a 1985 revolution led by Sudanese army officers, the government in Khartum has not been friendly to Egypt and is, as of 1993, strongly committed to Islamism (q.v.) and close ties with Iran. Since 1982, both Egypt and the Sudan have belonged to the UNDUGU group, together with Zaire, Uganda,

Central Africa, Rwanda, Burundi, and Tanzania, to consider and coordinate interstate projects involving Nile River waters.

SUDAN CONVENTION (1899). Agreement signed by Butros Ghali (q.v.) for the Egyptian government and Lord Cromer (q.v.) on behalf of Britain, setting up a condominium over the Sudan (q.v.), which had been reconquered between 1896 and 1898 by a joint Anglo-Egyptian force. The convention defined the Sudan's borders; provided for the joint use of the two countries' flags; vested military and civil authority in the governor-general of the Sudan, a British official who was to be appointed by the khedive (q.v.) on the British government's recommendation; gave legislative authority for the Sudan to the governor-general; excluded capitulatory privileges for foreigners and the jurisdiction of the Mixed Courts (q.v.) from the Sudan; provided for customs duties on imports into the Sudan from countries other than Egypt; and barred the importation of slaves into the Sudan. Egyptian nationalists attacked the resulting Anglo-Egyptian Condominium (q.v.) for giving too much power to Britain, even though the cost of conquering and administering the Sudan was largely borne by Egyptian taxpayers, and Butros Ghali was also attacked for having assented to the Convention.

SUEZ AFFAIR (1956). Political dispute precipitated by Nasir's (q.v.) unilateral nationalization of the Suez Canal Company (q.v.) on 26 July 1956, an act decried by Britain and France because of their shareholders' interest in the company and their strategic concern for safe passage of Western shipping, especially oil, through that waterway. Egypt claimed the right to nationalize the canal, as it had repeatedly been recognized as an Egyptian waterway and the Suez Canal Company had been chartered as an Egyptian corporation. It promised to pay compensation to owners based on the value of their shares on the Paris Bourse (financial market) as of 26 July 1956. Many Arabs hailed Nasir's audacious act as a blow to Western imperialism and a first step toward a war of revenge against Israel, and his popularity soared throughout the Arab world. Western countries feared that Egypt would not be able to manage the canal, especially after most of the foreign pilots quit their jobs. To their surprise, Egyptian pilots kept it open. The West also feared that Egypt might close the international waterway to blackmail oil-importing nations, although Nasir's public vow to build the Aswan High Dam (q.v.) from the proceeds of the canal tolls suggests that Egypt needed to keep it open. Zionists (q.v.) protected the exclusion of Israeli ships and even cargoes from using the Canal, but this practice had preceded its nationalization.

At the insistence of the Western countries, an international conference met in London in August 1956, and Australian Premier

Menzies was deputized to talk to Nasir about a plan to place the canal under international control. Nasir rejected the plan, as well as a U.S. proposal for a Suez Canal Users Association (q.v.). Although the Egyptian people adamantly backed Nasir, Egyptian diplomats were conciliatory in the United Nations (q.v.) Security Council and agreed to meet with American, British, and French diplomats in Geneva to devise a compromise. But the Israelis had already joined the British and French in planning the attack that would become the Suez War (q.v.), and the Geneva meetings were aborted.

SUEZ CANAL. Human-made channel, initially 9 meters deep and 30 meters wide, built in 1856–69 by the Universal Maritime Suez Canal Company (q.v.) to connect the Mediterranean and Red seas. The construction costs, estimated at more than 450 million francs (approximately $100 million at that time) were borne mainly by the Egyptian government, not to mention the unpaid thousands of Egyptian peasants who had to do the manual labor until the European powers and the Ottoman (q.v.) government enjoined the Company and the Egyptian government to end the corvée (q.v.). It is estimated that 20,000 peasants died during the Canal's construction. After its formal inauguration in 1869, it was administered by the Company until it was nationalized by the Egyptian government in 1956. Since then it has been managed by the Egyptian-owned Suez Canal Authority. It was closed in 1956–57 and 1967–75 due to Arab-Israeli fighting. It has been enlarged since 1975 to accommodate larger oil tankers.

SUEZ CANAL COMPANY. Limited-liability corporation, organized by French entrepreneur Ferdinand de Lesseps (q.v.) and chartered by the Egyptian government in 1854, that constructed the Suez Canal (q.v.) between 1856 and 1869 and managed it under a 99-year concession, which would have expired in 1968. It was nationalized by the Egyptian government on 26 July 1956.

SUEZ CANAL USERS' ASSOCIATION (SCUA). Group proposed by U.S. Secretary of State Dulles (q.v.) in September 1956 to collect tolls from ships transiting the Canal after Nasir (q.v.) had nationalized the Suez Canal Company (q.v.) and rejected international control.

SUEZ, GULF OF. Maritime inlet dividing Egypt from the Sinai Peninsula (q.v.). This gulf is shallower than the Gulf of Aqaba (q.v.) or the Red Sea and is rich in oil deposits.

SUEZ WAR (1956). The coordinated attack by Israel, Britain, and France, against Egypt in October-November 1956, also called the "Tripartite Aggression" in Egypt and the "Sinai Campaign" in Israel. Military planning by Britain and France began soon after Nasir (q.v.) nationalized the Suez Canal Company (q.v.) on 26 July, threatening British and French interests as Company owners and Canal users. The U.S. government would not countenance an attack and called for a negotiated settlement, but President Eisenhower and Secretary of State Dulles (q.v.) did not state clearly whether they would block military action. Israel, hoping to stop border raids by Palestinian *fidaiyin* (q.v.) trained by Egypt, initiated secret talks with Britain and France. Israel agreed to invade the Gaza Strip (q.v.) and the Sinai Peninsula (q.v.), seemingly threatening the Canal. Under the 1954 Anglo-Egyptian Agreement (q.v.), Britain would then invade and reoccupy the military bases that it had only recently evacuated.

The Israel Defense Force attacked on 29 October, invading the Gaza Strip (q.v.) and dropping paratroops near the Mitla Pass (q.v.). The joint Anglo-French ultimatum of the next day called on the Israelis and Egyptians to withdraw to positions ten miles away from the Canal, even though the fighting between Egypt and Israel was mainly in the Sinai. Obeying the ultimatum would have obliged Egypt to withdraw its 30,000 troops who were fighting in the peninsula, and so Nasir refused, although he did order his forces to pull back to protect the Canal if the British and French attacked. As British and French air forces bombed Egyptian air fields on 31 October, destroying many of Egypt's fighter planes, the Egyptians evacuated the Sinai, which the Israelis managed to capture by 5 November. On that day Anglo-French ground troops occupied Port Said (q.v.) and portions of the Canal, but stiff civilian resistance delayed their advance. Heavy United Nations (q.v.) pressure, led by the United States and the USSR, was placed on Britain, France, and Israel to stop their attack on Egypt. Britain accepted the United Nations cease-fire resolution on 6–7 November; France and Israel soon followed suit. Britain and France evacuated Egypt on 23 December. Only Israel achieved its military aims; although its forces also had to evacuate the Sinai and Gaza Strip, it gained the right to send ships through the Gulf of Aqaba (q.v.). The war, a military defeat but a political victory for Nasir, ended British and French influence in Egypt and weakened their ties with other Arab states.

SUFISM. Organized Islamic (q.v.) mysticism. Sufi organizations (*turuq*), often associated with particular saints and shrines, played a large role in the daily lives of most Egyptian Muslims in the nineteenth century. In an effort to curb some of the excesses of the Sufis, khedivial decrees regulating their behavior were promulgated in 1895 and in 1903. The spread of education and Western culture have eclipsed some of the Sufi orders, but many still survive.

SUGAR. Sugarcane, probably introduced in early Islamic times, has long been cultivated in Egypt, especially since the development of perennial irrigation (q.v.). It is now a major summer crop, one that is likely to increase because of its high government price supports and despite its heavy water requirements. Total sugarcane production amounted to more than 11 million metric tons in 1990, plus 700 thousand metric tons of sugar beets, yielding a total of 977 thousand metric tons of raw sugar.

SULAYMAN PASHA, ***see*** **SÈVE**.

SUMED PIPELINE. Oil pipeline linking Ayn Sukhna on the Gulf of Suez (q.v.) to Sidi Khayr, a Mediterranean coastal village 30 km west of Alexandria (q.v.). Although the Bechtel Corporation had contracted shortly before the October War (q.v.) to build it, the company could not raise the necessary capital. The pipeline was built instead by Italian contractors between 1974 and 1977 at a cost of $348 million, financed by the Arab Company for Oil Pipelines-SUMED. Egypt owns 50 percent of its shares; the other half is owned by Saudi Arabia, Kuwait, Qatar, and Abu Dhabi. It was linked to offshore facilities for supertankers in 1981. Contracts were signed in 1991 to raise its annual carrying capacity from 80 to 120 million tons, at an estimated cost of $120 million.

- T -

TABA DISPUTE (1981–89). Diplomatic quarrel between Egypt and Israel for possession of 2.5 km^2 of the Sinai Peninsula (q.v.) at Taba. Egypt argued that the 1906 international boundary had placed Taba within its territory and that the Israelis had removed the markers when they occupied the Sinai between 1967 and 1982. Israel claimed that the original border had not been clearly drawn and that it had commissioned the construction in Taba of a resort hotel patronized mainly by Israelis. After years of fruitless debate, Israel agreed in 1986 to submit the dispute to binding arbitration. Taba was awarded to Egypt in 1989.

TABA INCIDENT (1906). Diplomatic dispute between Britain, acting in Egypt's behalf, and the Ottoman Empire (q.v.) over the demarcation of the Turco-Egyptian border in the Sinai Peninsula (q.v.). The issue grew out of the vague definition of Egypt's borders in the original 1841 *firman* (q.v.) from Sultan Abdulmejid to Muhammad Ali (q.v.), referring to a map that was lost because of a fire in the Egyptian archives and long mislaid in their Ottoman counterpart. From 1841 to 1892, Egypt administered not only the Sinai's southern coast but also the eastern shores of the Gulf of Aqaba (q.v.) and the Red Sea as part of the pilgrimage route to Mecca. In 1892 a dispute arose over the wording of the *firman* of investiture to Khedive Abbas Hilmi II (qq.v.); it was resolved, after some British pressure, by maintaining the vague definition, although the khedive (q.v.) did cede control of the Arabian coast between Aqaba and Yanbu' to the sultan. The subsequent Ottoman effort to strengthen control over its territory and especially the building of the Hijaz Railway collided with Britain's defense of the Suez Canal (q.v.), and a dispute arose in 1906 at the border outpost of Taba, near Aqaba, between British-officered Egyptians and Ottoman troops. The British government threatened military action against the Ottoman Empire and did actually augment its troops in Egypt. The Ottoman government, which claimed the right to control the Sinai as far west as Suez, gave in to British pressure and agreed to a joint Turco-Egyptian demarcation commission, which drew up the international boundary in October 1906. This border, seemingly favorable to Egypt, did place several crucial tribal watering holes on the Ottoman side. Although Britain seemed to be upholding Egyptian geopolitical interests, Khedive Abbas and the National Party (q.v.) supported the Ottoman claims, a policy widely construed at the time to tie Egyptian nationalism to pan-Islam (q.v.).

AL-TAHTAWI, RIFA'A RAFI' (1801–73). Writer and educational reformer. Originally from a family of ulama (q.v.), Tahtawi was educated at al-Azhar (q.v.) and in Paris, to which he was sent as the imam for the first student mission in 1826. His observations there were published as *Takhlis al-ibriz fi ṭarkhis Bariz*. He became a translator for the School of Medicine in 1832 and director of the new School of Languages set up in 1836. In 1841 he headed Muhammad Ali's (q.v.) translation bureau, which was closed in 1851. Exiled to the Sudan (q.v.) under Abbas Hilmi I (q.v.), he became director of the Egyptian School of Khartum. Under Sa'id (q.v.) he was deputy director of the Military Academy (q.v.). Tahtawi then directed the revived translation bureau under Isma'il (q.v.) from 1863 to 1873 and worked to expand the Bulaq (q.v.) press. He wrote several original works, including two volumes of a projected complete history of Egypt, a book on education entitled *al-Murshid al-amin li al-banat wa al-banin*, and a general work on Egypt's political and social development called *Manahij al-albab al-misriyya fi mabahij al-adab al-asriyya*. This work advocated benevolent autocracy, limited by the Shari'a (q.v.) but modified to meet the needs of the modern world, stressing agricultural development, the education of girls as well as boys, and the development of a national community (*watan*, or "homeland"). Tahtawi's ideas facilitated the growth of Egyptian nationalism and the harmonization of European social concepts with Islam (q.v.).

AL-TAKFIR WA AL-HIJRA. Journalistic name for a popular Muslim organization that opposes Western influence in Egypt. It was founded about 1967 by a group of already imprisoned Muslim Brothers (q.v.) who had mutinied after the execution of Sayyid Qutb (q.v.). Led by Shukri Mustafa (b. 1942), it called for a purification of Muslims as individuals, just as Muhammad and his associates had moved away from the evil of pagan Meccan society in the original *Hijra*. Their transformation was to lead to a revolutionary purification of Egypt's government and society. In 1971 Shukri was released from prison and began spreading his doctrines in Asyut (q.v.) and other Egyptian cities. The group was accused of kidnapping and assassinating a former minister of *awqaf* (q.v.) in 1977 and of complicity in Sadat's (q.v.) murder in 1981. It has been subjected to severe repression during the state of emergency under Mubarak (q.v.). Its journalistic title can best be translated as "Identifying Unbelief and Leaving Evil Behind." Many of its members back the Islamic Group (q.v.) and Shaykh Umar Abd al-Rahman (q.v.) (*see* Fundamentalism, Islamism, and *Jama'at*).

TANZIMAT. The reforms instituted by the Ottoman Empire (q.v.) in 1839–76. Some parts were applied to Egypt up to the reign of Khedive Isma'il (qq.v.).

TARBUSH. Maroon cylindrical headcovering, also called a fez, having a distinctive black tassel, worn by Egyptian male officials and officers before the 1952 Revolution (q.v.).

TARIFFS. As long as Egypt was an Ottoman (q.v.) province, its import duties were set by Istanbul. Under the 1838 Anglo-Ottoman Tariff Convention, duties on goods imported from abroad were limited to 8 percent ad valorem. Once this agreement was applied to Egypt, following the 1840 London Convention (q.v.), the Egyptian government could not use tariff policies to protect the infant industries founded by Muhammad Ali (q.v.), and nearly all of them succumbed to European competition. Khedive Isma'il (qq.v.), too, was hampered in nurturing his infant industries, although a new tariff convention had been reached in 1861–62. During the British occupation (q.v.), tariff and excise taxes were set in ways that blocked industrialization. Even agricultural products were subjected to a 1 percent export tax (except for alcohol, sugar, timber, petroleum, and live animals, which were subjected to a higher rate). Any attempt to raise tariff imposts had to be approved by the Western powers under the Capitulations (q.v.).

Only in 1930 did Egypt gain the right to set its own tariffs. In an effort to encourage industrialization, Sidqi's (q.v.) government raised rates to 4 percent for raw materials, 6–10 percent for semi-manufactured goods, and 15 percent for most manufactures. Higher tariffs were imposed on countries that subsidized exports, such as Japan and China, and there were additional wharfage and ad valorem duties on products other than tobacco. The government enacted further tariff protection for sugar (q.v.), coarse yarn, low-grade textiles, rubber shoes, and cast-iron products in the late 1930s. All specific duties were multiplied by a factor of 1.5 in October 1941, increased to 1.75 and later to 2.0 during World War II (q.v.). An additional ad valorem tax was imposed on luxury goods in 1949. Import licensing fees were imposed on most foreign products following the 1952 Revolution (q.v.). Tariff protection increased further during the industrialization drive by the Nasir (q.v.) government. From 1961 to 1974, all Egyptian imports were administered by a state-owned company, partly to promote the growth of national industries. Tariff protection was especially high for wearing apparel, including leather shoes, electrical appliances and machinery, rubber, and basic metals; it was lower for food, wood, furniture, petroleum, and tobacco. Although import restrictions were relaxed during the *infitah* (q.v.), Mubarak (q.v.) has raised tariffs.

TAWFIQ (1852–92). Khedive (q.v.) of Egypt from 1879 until his death in January 1892. The eldest son of Isma'il (q.v.), he was born and educated in Cairo (q.v.), studying in Manyal and then at the Tajhiziyya School. Unlike most members of his dynasty, he never studied outside Egypt. Starting at age 19, he held various administrative posts under his father, including the presidency of his privy council, director of the interior and of public works, and president of the Council of Ministers (q.v.) in 1879. Pressured by Egypt's European creditors, the Ottoman (q.v.) government named Tawfiq to succeed his father in June 1879, and he took steps to placate the Europeans, exiling Jamal al-Din al-Afghani (q.v.) and enforcing the financial stringencies caused by the 1880 Law of Liquidation (q.v.). These measures alienated many army officers and civil officials, leading to mutinies against War Minister Rifqi (q.v.) in February 1881 and Premier Riyad (q.v.) in September of that year. Historians disagree as to whether Tawfiq himself encouraged the rebels; it is certain, though, that by 1882 Urabi's (q.v.) followers had taken over the cabinet and were plotting to depose him. Following the Alexandria (q.v.) riots in June 1882, when Britain threatened to bombard the port's fortifications, Tawfiq turned against the Egyptian cabinet, and Urabi's movement was defeated by a British invasion.

He believed for the rest of his life that he owed his throne to this intervention, which led to Urabi's defeat, the dismissal of his government, the dissolution of the army, and the British occupation (q.v.) of Egypt. He accordingly accepted the "advice" he received from Britain's diplomatic representatives in Cairo, Sir Edward Malet (q.v.) and especially Sir Evelyn Baring, who later became Lord Cromer (q.v.). Among the reforms instituted later in Tawfiq's reign were the reorganization of the National Courts (q.v.), the establishment of the Legislative Council and General Assembly under the Organic Law (q.v.), various irrigation (q.v.) projects, the improvement of mosques and other religious buildings, and the reform of the benevolent *awqaf* (q.v.). He died unexpectedly in Hulwan (q.v.) in January 1892. Although reputedly devoted to the people's welfare, most Egyptians recall him as a weak viceroy who acquiesced in the British occupation and the loss of the Sudan (q.v.).

TAX FARMING. System, technically called *iltizam*, of collecting government imposts that allows the collector to pocket a share of the proceeds, common in Egypt up to the nineteenth century, when Muhammad Ali (q.v.) abolished the practice (*see* Landownership).

TAYMUR, MAHMUD (1894–1973). Writer of essays, plays, and short stories. Born in Cairo (q.v.), he was a son of Ahmad Taymur, a well-known writer and scholar, and the younger brother of Muhammad, a playwright. He studied in Egyptian schools and in Switzerland, where he went for his health. His first stories, published in 1919, were written in the colloquial dialect, but he later advocated using classical Arabic. He was invited to conferences in Beirut, the University of Peshawar, and Damascus. In 1947 he was awarded the first prize for fiction by the Arabic Language Academy (q.v.), of which he became a member in 1949. He wrote many stories, plays, and research articles. Some of his works have been translated, such as *Hakamat al-Mahkama* ("The Court Rules") in Ali al-Manzalawi's *Arabic Writing Today: Drama*.

TEL EL-KEBIR, BATTLE OF (1882). Decisive defeat of the Egyptian army under Ahmad Urabi (q.v.) by a British expeditionary force, leading to the British occupation (q.v.).

TELEGRAMS INCIDENT (1896). Courtroom episode in which Muhammad Farid (q.v.), a lawyer for the Niyaba (q.v.), openly hailed the acquittal of Ali Yusuf (q.v.), the editor of *al-Muayyad* (q.v.), accused of printing a stolen telegram from Kitchener (q.v.) describing a cholera (q.v.)

outbreak among Egyptian soldiers during the Sudan (q.v.) campaign. Obliged to resign from his post, Farid opened his own law office and became more involved in the National Party (q.v.) under Mustafa Kamil (q.v.), whom he later succeeded as president.

TELEVISION. In 1960 Egypt became the third Arab country to begin television broadcasting. Nasir (q.v.) used television as well as radio (q.v.) to appeal directly to the people. The culture ministry installed public television receivers in cities and villages, although Egyptians flocked to buy private sets as soon as they became available. It is estimated that 550,000 television receivers were in use in 1970, 1.1 million in 1978, and 5 million in 1990. In 1991, the Egyptian television organization had two main and three regional channels, presenting 42 hours of programming daily. News, music, educational programs, and situation comedies (American as well as Egyptian) predominate, but religious programs are growing more popular. State-owned television faces competition from videocassettes and from rooftop dishes capable of receiving signals from satellites transmitting other countries' programs.

TEXTILE INDUSTRY. Egypt has been a leader in spinning, weaving, and sewing textiles throughout its history. In the eighteenth century, textile manufacturing was mainly a domestic handicraft industry. At the time of the French occupation (q.v.), Upper Egypt was the center for cotton spinning and weaving, using short-staple cotton grown around Isna or imported from Syria. Linen was woven in Fayyum and the Delta; silk in Damietta, Mahalla, and Cairo; and wool in all of Egypt's towns and villages. Weaving was a male occupation, but women did the spinning in their homes. Textile handicrafts continued through the nineteenth century, but cotton gained at the expense of wool. The silk cloth of Damietta retained a high prestige in the Egyptian market, enjoyed some foreign demand, and was featured at trade expositions. As late as 1930, it was estimated that Egypt had 20,000 hand looms, capable of producing each year 30 million square meters of cloth, but textile handicrafts could not compete against the cheap manufactured imports from Japan, Italy, and India during the 1930s.

Mechanized textile manufacturing began under Muhammad Ali (q.v.), who imported European engineers and machinery for the spinning and weaving of wool, silk, and cotton. The first factories were opened in 1820, and by 1830–31 the income from their production was sufficiently important for Muhammad Ali to ban all domestic textile production. The textile monopoly reached its height in 1837, but the costs of the Syrian campaign, followed by the application of the 1838 Anglo-Ottoman Tariff Convention to Egypt following the Convention of London (q.v.), destroyed its first mechanized textile industry. Cheap imported textiles from Britain and later from other European countries, even with an 8 percent tariff ad valorem, easily undercut the Egyptian products, except in the specialized handicrafts industry, and Khedive Isma'il (qq.v.) did not compete in textile manufacturing as he did in other industries.

Although Egyptian cotton (q.v.) output soared during the nineteenth century, few entrepreneurs set up spinning and weaving factories. In the 1890s two foreign residents founded joint-stock companies for textile manufacture, but Lord Cromer (q.v.), fearful of creating competition for British manufacturers, advised the Egyptian government to impose an 8 percent excise on domestic textiles. A more successful venture was the Filature Nationale d'Égypte, which bought the factory and machinery of one of the earlier textile companies. It expanded its spinning and weaving operations during World War I (q.v.), which cut Egypt off from former suppliers. In the 1920s high capitalization and low labor costs enabled the company to provide cheap textiles for the domestic market. Bank Misr (q.v.) entered the textile industry with its Misr Cotton Spinning and Weaving Company, founded at Mahalla al-Kubra in 1926. The rise of these domestic industries was aided by Egypt's higher protective tariff (q.v.) after 1930. The Calico Printers Association, a British firm, reached an agreement with Filature Nationale in 1934, increasing the number of its spindles, sales, and dividends to investors. Bank Misr was slower to seek affiliation with a British company, partly due to Tal'at Harb's (q.v.) devotion to Egypt's economic independence. Finally, however, Misr Cotton Spinning and Weaving signed an agreement with the Bradford Dyers Association in 1938. Total output of mechanically woven cloth in Egypt rose from 9 million square meters in 1917 to 20 million in 1931 and 159 million in 1939.

World War II (q.v.) again cut Egypt off from Europe and also led to the creation of the Middle East Supply Centre (q.v.), which accelerated the industrialization of the region. Cotton yarn output, for example, quintupled between 1938 and 1951; cloth production rose almost as rapidly. The number of cotton spindles in Egypt increased from 500,000 in 1950 to 1.3 million in 1960; corresponding figures for weaving looms indicate a 50 percent increase during the same period. Nasir's (q.v.) industrialization plans called for further growth in the Egyptian textile industry, most of which was nationalized in 1961 (*see* July Laws), but the rate of gain decelerated during the 1960s and 1970s. Textiles remain Egypt's largest manufacturing industry, but their share has declined as Egyptian industrial output has become more diversified and as foreign buyers of Egyptian textiles are increasingly manufacturing their own.

THABIT, KARIM (1902–64). Journalist and press adviser to King Faruq (q.v.). The son of an editor of *al-Muqattam* (q.v.) of Lebanese origin, he attended the American University in Cairo (q.v.). He worked as a reporter for *al-Siyasa* (q.v.), *al-Alam*, and then *al-Dunya*, of which he became the editor when it merged with *al-Hilal* (q.v.). During World War II (q.v.) he worked for *al-Muqattam* (q.v.). He met Faruq in 1946 and soon became his press adviser, gaining influence over the king and his entourage. He is popularly believed to have influenced Faruq's decision to enter the 1948 Palestine War (q.v.) as a means of reviving his popularity. Thabit wrote various biographies and histories, and his memoirs were serialized in *al-Jumhuriyya* in 1955. He is remembered as a sycophant partly responsible for corrupting the king.

THARWAT, ABD AL-KHALIQ (1873–1928). Judge, cabinet minister, and two-time premier. Of Turco-Egyptian extraction, he attended the government Law School (q.v.), where he joined Ahmad Lutfi al-Sayyid (q.v.) and Abd al-Aziz Fahmi (q.v.) in founding Egypt's first law review. Tharwat worked for the State Domains (*Daira Saniyya*) administration after his graduation, then for the justice ministry. He was deputy chairman of Qina's National Court (q.v.) and then became director of administration for the National Courts as a whole. In 1907 he served briefly as chancellor of the National Court of Appeals, then became governor of Asyut (q.v.) province (1907–8), head of the Niyaba (q.v.) (1908–14), minister of justice (1914–19), interior (1921, 1922, and 1927–28), and foreign affairs (1922 and 1926–27), deputy premier, and prime minister from 1922 to 1923 and from 1927 to 1928, when ill health forced him to retire. Tharwat was elected to the Chamber of Deputies in 1924 and appointed to the Senate in 1925. He served on the boards of the Islamic Benevolent Society and the Egyptian University until his death (*see* Cairo University) and was respected by his colleagues for his legal expertise. A British diplomat described him in 1926 as "probably the most capable man and the nearest approach to a statesman among Egyptians. . . . He is a genuine believer in Egyptian independence, but appreciates British power and capacity and is anxious to use them." Some Egyptians, though, accused him of corruption and resented his opposing the Wafd.

THEATER. Drama in Muslim Egypt was long constrained by religious opposition to figural representation and to women performing as actors and musicians. Nevertheless, Egypt has had a long tradition of mimicry and popular farce. Shadow plays, popularly named Karagöz, after their best-known character, have been performed since at least Mamluk (q.v.) times. Dramatic theater is said to have been introduced during the French occupation (q.v.); it was reintroduced in the 1830s by Italians (q.v.) living in Alexandria (q.v.), and other European residents soon afterward began performing plays in Cairo (q.v.). Syrian refugees from the Ottoman Empire (q.v.) helped to establish Arabic theater in Cairo in the 1870s, but the most successful playwright at that time was Ya'qub Sannu' (q.v.). Theaters offering plays in Arabic or in European languages proliferated during the British occupation (q.v.); pioneers of Egyptian drama in Arabic before 1914 included George Abyad and Salama al-Hijazi (q.v.). Arabic drama had to overcome Muslim prejudice against acting, especially by women, and struggled to raise the level of popular taste, which preferred musicals, farces, and burlesques in the vernacular dialect to tragedies and comedies in classical Arabic. Arabic drama in Egypt advanced farther than in other Arabic-speaking countries, and many Egyptian troupes have performed on stages elsewhere in the Arab world. Notable playwrights include Ahmad Shawqi (q.v.), Mahmud Taymur (q.v.), and Tawfiq al-Hakim (q.v.). In recent years, cinema (q.v.), television (q.v.), and videocassettes have all competed heavily with Arabic drama.

AL-TILMISANI, UMAR (1902?-86). Supreme guide of the revived Society of Muslim Brothers (q.v.) and editor of its weekly magazine, *al-Da'wa* (q.v.). A graduate of the government Law School (q.v.) in 1931, he joined the Society two years later. He was one of the Brothers jailed following the abortive assassination attempt on Nasir (q.v.) in 1954, serving a 15-year term. Tilmisani began publishing *al-Da'wa* in 1976; in it he inveighed against secularism and the power of the Jews (q.v.), even ascribing Atatürk's reforms to his alleged Jewish background, and the "Crusaders," alluding to both the predominantly Christian West and Egypt's Copts (q.v.). He blamed the riots in al-Zawiya al-Hamra (q.v.) on a "Crusader conspiracy" against Islam (q.v.). He was one of the 1,600 political and religious leaders jailed by Sadat (q.v.) in September 1981, but was freed by Mubarak (q.v.) three months later. Tilmisani called for the gradual application of the Shari'a (q.v.) to Egypt's laws, but opposed violence and terrorism. He wrote *Dhikrayat la mudhakkirat* ("Recollections, not Memoirs").

TIRAN. Straits linking the Gulf of Aqaba (q.v.) to the Red Sea, blockaded by Egypt to impede Israeli shipping between 1949 and 1956 and again in May 1967, sparking the June War (q.v.).

TOBACCO INDUSTRY. Although tobacco became one of Egypt's main cash crops during the nineteenth century, its cultivation was banned in 1890, apparently to generate tariff (q.v.) income for the government. Cigarette manufacturing, using imported tobacco, grew in the late-nineteenth century; it was one of the first in which the workers organized unions (q.v.) and has long been a major Egyptian industry. Egypt produced 39.8 billion cigarettes in 1990.

TOURISM. Foreigners have traveled to Egypt since antiquity, and the first guide in English was published by Murray as early as 1836, but organized visits by groups of foreigners began in the late 1860s, following the extension of steam-driven railways (q.v.) and river transport (q.v.), the establishment of such hotels as Shepheard's (q.v.), and the extension of Thomas Cook's tours from Europe to the Holy Land and the Nile (q.v.) Valley. Early tourists to Egypt were mainly upper- and middle-class Europeans who came for the winter social season, from November to May. Popular tourist sites included the Giza Pyramids and Sphinx, the Saqqara Pyramids, the Egyptian Museum (q.v.), the bazaars of Cairo (q.v.), and the pharaonic tombs and temples near Luxor and Aswan. Many Egyptians depended economically on tourism, working for travel agencies, hotels, and restaurants, selling souvenirs, or serving as guides and translators (the dragoman, or *tarjuman* ["translator," in Arabic], was a familiar companion to many a foreign tourist). Since the 1952 Revolution (q.v.), the Egyptian government has striven to stimulate tourism as a source of foreign exchange, taking control of most popular hotels, restaurants, and travel agencies, and has had a tourism ministry since the 1960s. Group tourism from western and eastern Europe has spurred the development of the Red Sea and Mediterranean beaches. Increasing numbers of visitors to Egypt come from other Arab countries. Although foreign tourism has become one of Egypt's foreign exchange earners (Egypt reportedly earned $3 billion in hard currencies in 1991–92), it is highly sensitive to political conditions, declining during and after such crises as the Suez War (q.v.), the June War (q.v.), the assassination of Sadat (q.v.), the Iraq-Kuwait Conflict (q.v.), and the rise of Islamist (q.v.) violence against Copts (q.v.) and foreigners in 1992–94.

TRAMWAYS. Street electric railways, introduced in 1897, long played an important part in the public transportation system of Cairo (q.v.) and Alexandria (q.v.). The first tramway concession in Cairo was granted in December 1894 to Baron Empain, a Belgian magnate, who assigned it to a joint stock company. The agreement called for eight tram lines, of which six were to radiate from a central terminal at Midan al-Ataba al-Khadra at the southeast corner of the Ezbekiyya Gardens (q.v.). Nine additional lines were constructed between 1899 and 1907, including one to the Giza Pyramids, and 13 more between 1908 and 1917. Two lines were added in 1931. In 1930 bus routes began to supplement the tramways, which continued, however, to play a primary role in determining the pattern of Cairo's expansion. Alexandria's electric tramway network began to develop between 1899 and 1907. Centered on Muhammad Ali Square, they accelerated the city's expansion both eastward and westward along the shoreline. Although some tracks have been removed to improve traffic circulation, Egypt's tramways, nationalized since 1960, have not been wholly replaced by buses and taxis.

TRIPARTITE AGGRESSION (1956), *see* **SUEZ WAR.**

TRIPARTITE DECLARATION (1950). Agreement by Britain, France, and the United States not to sell arms to the countries involved in the Arab-Israeli conflict. Angered at Egypt's support for the Algerian rebels, France secretly began arming Israel. Nasir (q.v.) believed that Britain also was secretly supplying Israel with weapons in violation of this agreement, and his Czech Arms Deal (q.v.) effectively undercut it.

TURCO-CIRCASSIANS. Term popularly applied to members of Egypt's military or civilian elite who descended from Turkish and/or Circassian Mamluks (qq.v.), as distinct from those who descended from native Egyptians. The term became significant in 1881–82 during the movement of the Egyptian officers led by Ahmad Urabi (q.v.), who alleged that Turks and Circassians received preferential treatment within the Egyptian army. It has often been noted that nearly all the Egyptian ministers during the British occupation (q.v.) were of Turkish or Circassian descent. Many spoke French or English better than Arabic. They have become less prominent since World War I (q.v.), and most have now assimilated with Arabic-speaking Muslims.

TUTANKHAMON'S TOMB. The 1923 discovery of this fully-intact pharaonic tomb, located in the Valley of the Kings near Qurna, brought worldwide attention to Egypt, influencing styles in architecture, furniture, clothing, and coiffure in some Western countries at the time. It also stimulated national pride among Egyptian advocates of Pharaonism (q.v.).

- U -

UBAYD, WILLIAM MAKRAM (1889–1961). Coptic (q.v.) politician and longtime secretary-general of the Wafd Party (q.v.). Born in Qina to a family originally from Asyut (q.v.), his father developed the railway from Naj' Hammadi to Luxor, enabling him to buy land from the royal estates. Makram attended the American College in Asyut and New College, Oxford, where he studied law, graduating in 1908. He then spent two years studying Egyptology in France before returning to Egypt. He married the daughter of Murqus Hanna, an early supporter of the National Party (q.v.). After World War I (q.v.), Makram joined the Wafd (q.v.) and became the political "son" of Sa'd Zaghlul (q.v.), with whom he was associated until Sa'd died in 1927. He represented Qina in every Parliament in which the early Wafd Party won a majority of the seats in free elections and served as communications minister briefly in 1928 and as finance minister in the Wafdist cabinets of 1930, 1936–37, and 1942. Increasingly alarmed at the Wafd's corruption and possibly encouraged by King Faruq (q.v.), he left the government in 1942 and then published the *Black Book* (q.v.), attacking Wafdist leader Nahhas (q.v.). Makram founded a rival party called the Wafdist Bloc (q.v.) and later served in several coalition governments from which the Wafd was excluded. Some of his speeches and writings were collected posthumously and published in 1990 as *Kalimat wa mawaqif* ("Words and Positions"). His other writings include a pamphlet denouncing the Milner mission (q.v.) and articles in *al-Hilal* (q.v.). His heroic role in the national movement has not yet been fully appreciated.

ULAMA. Muslim learned men, now usually denoting those who have been educated in religious schools, such as al-Azhar (q.v.), and who serve as Shari'a (q.v.) judges, mosque preachers, or teachers. In the eighteenth century, the ulama served as the main intermediaries between the Egyptian people and their rulers and exercised great economic power as managers of *awqaf* (q.v.) and sometimes as tax farmers (q.v.). They spearheaded the opposition to the French occupation (q.v.) and to the attempts by the Mamluks (q.v.) to regain their power after the French and British left Egypt. Many were staunch supporters of Muhammad Ali (q.v.) and welcomed his destruction of the Mamluks in 1811. However, the ulama soon lost much of their economic power, as the new regime took control of many *awqaf* and abolished the tax farms. Their power and prestige were undermined by Muhammad Ali's schools and other Westernizing reforms. Nevertheless, the ulama retained their strong hold over Egypt's Muslims through the village *kuttab*s (q.v.) and mosques. Some ulama supported Urabi (q.v.) in 1882 and many took part in later resistance movements against the British occupation (q.v.). In the twentieth century their power has diminished further, especially when Nasir (q.v.) closed the Shari'a Courts (q.v.). Many have become apologists for any group that controls the Egyptian government, but others have supported the Muslim Brothers (q.v.) and lately the *jama'at* (q.v.).

UMDA. Chief village magistrate, responsible to the government for maintaining security and public order.

UMM KULTHUM (1908?-75). Popular female vocalist, arguably the most famous in the Arab world. Born in Tammay, a Delta village near Sinbalawin, her father was a village shaykh who called villagers to prayer, led Friday worship, and recited the Quran at *mawlid*s (birthdays of revered Muslims) and other religious occasions. Her father soon recognized her exceptional musical gifts and brought her with him to sing at *mawlid*s and public concerts. Eventually her talents came to the attention of the best-known musicians of the day, and she broadened her repertoire and began singing in Cairo (q.v.) cabarets. Because entertainers were still not respected by many Egyptians, her father continued to chaperon her, but she increasingly became her own business manager, and by the late 1920s she was earning large royalties for her recorded songs, both religious and popular. She learned to sing secular as well as religious poems, some of which were written especially for her by well-known writers. She sang regularly on the first Thursday of each month at a small theater near the Ezbekiyya Gardens (q.v.) and later at Cinema Radio. She was invited to sing at the weddings of many notables and at the behest of King Faruq (q.v.), later under the patronage of Nasir's (q.v.) government, and at the invitation of Jihan Sadat (q.v.). Umm Kulthum's funeral in 1975 occasioned a large popular turnout almost equal to the record numbers who had followed Nasir's procession. Her singing did much to raise the status and fame of female entertainers in the Arab world. Her memoirs appear in translation in *Middle Eastern Muslim Women Speak.*

UMMA PARTY. The "People's Party," made up mainly of landowners and intelligentsia, having as its house organ the Arabic daily newspaper *al-Jarida* (q.v.) between 1907 and 1915. Ostensibly the rival of the National Party (q.v.), it differed little in its devotion to political independence and parliamentary government, except that it argued that these goals could be attained only gradually, and it tended to distance itself more from Khedive Abbas Hilmi II (qq.v.) and the Ottoman Empire (q.v.). Its leaders were Hasan Abd al-Raziq and Mahmud Sulayman; Sa'd Zaghlul (q.v.), if not officially a member, was a supporter. Many Umma Party members later ran for the 1914 Legislative Assembly (q.v.) or joined the Wafd (q.v.) in 1919. Some became founders of the Constitutional Liberal Party (q.v.) in 1922.

UNIONS, LABOR. Egypt has long had city-based artisans and apprentices, and in Ottoman (q.v.) times they were incorporated into a highly articulated system of trade guilds (*asnaf*). With the rise of capitalism in the nineteenth century, many of the guilds fell into desuetude, but some survived into the twentieth century. For most of the new urban occupations, there were at first no organizations that enabled workers to bargain over their wages and working conditions with their employers, who often were foreign companies or individuals. Egyptian workers were slow to view themselves as a class, because many hoped to make enough money to buy plots of farmland and return to rural life. Often peasants took seasonal jobs in sugar refineries, cotton ginning mills, or local industries, returning to agriculture during the sowing and harvesting seasons. Although some strikes occurred during Urabi's (q.v.) movement in 1882, the first example of an organized labor movement took place among the Greek workers in the cigarette industry in 1899. In the early twentieth century, textile workers, tram operators, coalheavers, and sugar refinery workers formed ephemeral unions and struck against their employers for higher wages.

Most Egyptians only belatedly realized the need for labor organization, but the National Party (q.v.) did inspire some workers through its organization of night schools, consumer cooperatives, and the Manual Trade Workers' Union (*Niqabat Ummal al-Sanai' al-Yadawiyya).* The example set by foreign workers, most of them skilled or semiskilled, was equally instructive to the Egyptian laborers. Workers' strikes and sabotage played an important role in the 1919 Revolution (q.v.). The attempt of the Wafd (q.v.) to make the independence struggle a national one, obliterating distinctions of family, religion, and class, delayed the growth of a working-class consciousness. However, the industrialization of Egypt before and during World War II (q.v.) spawned new factories and workshops hiring far more laborers than ever before. Wages were low, hours long, and working conditions poor and sometimes dangerous. Many foremen routinely abused workers physically and psychologically. Egypt's pioneer socialists (q.v.) tried to organize unions, as did the Wafd Party (q.v.), Prince Abbas Halim (q.v.), and even King Faruq (q.v.). The greatest successes were the unionization of the workers in public transport, the Egyptian state railways (q.v.), and the textile industry (q.v.), but not until November 1942 did Parliament pass legislation making it legal for workers to organize. The Egyptian Communists (q.v.) organized some industrial workers after the war, especially in the textile industry. Although most Egyptians still lived in the countryside and worked in agriculture, early attempts to unionize the peasants failed.

The 1952 Revolution (q.v.) raised great hopes, but the Free Officers' (q.v.) suppression of the Kafr al-Dawwar (q.v.) workers showed that the new regime did not favor organized labor. Although paying lip service to social justice and workers' rights, Najib (q.v.) and Nasir (q.v.) undermined the independent labor unions and subordinated them to the Liberation Rally (q.v.) and the National Union (q.v.). The Arab Socialist Union (q.v.) later co-opted the labor movement. Some workers rose to powerful government posts, but most remained disorganized and alienated from the state-run factories that employed them, even though workers' representatives sat on their boards of directors. The Sadat (q.v.) government allowed more freedom of speech, but its *infitah* (q.v.) policy effectively turned ownership of state-run enterprises over to foreign-owned multinational corporations that barred workers' representatives from their managing boards. Their wages sapped by price inflation, some workers went on strike, only to face fines and arrest, but under Mubarak (q.v.) the courts have overturned jail sentences imposed against some strikers. As long as unemployment remains above 10 percent and opportunities for workers to go to the oil-exporting countries contract, the ability of Egyptian labor to organize itself to raise wages and improve working conditions will be severely limited.

UNITED ARAB REPUBLIC (UAR) (1958–61). Union of Egypt and Syria during the presidency of Jamal Abd al-Nasir (q.v.). Widely hailed as the first step toward the goals of Arab nationalism (q.v.), the integration of the two countries proved harder than their leaders had foreseen. The July Laws (q.v.) alienated many Syrian capitalists and may have sparked the military mutiny that led to Syria's secession in September 1961. Although Nasir believed that conservative Arab regimes and agents of Israel and Western imperialism inspired the breakup of the union, he acquiesced in Syria's secession, but continued to call Egypt the UAR, hoping that Syria or other Arab states would rejoin. Its name was changed to the "Arab Republic of Egypt" in 1971.

UNITED NATIONS (UN). Although coined by Churchill and Roosevelt to denote the World War II (q.v.) allied coalition that fought against the Axis powers–Nazi Germany, Fascist Italy, and Imperial Japan–the term later came to be used for the United Nations Organization founded at San Francisco in 1945. In order to be represented at the founding conference, Egypt had to declare war on the Axis before 1 March 1945. Parliament voted to do so on 26 February, causing the assassination of Premier Ahmad Mahir (q.v.). Egypt's delegation, led by Abd al-Hamid Badawi, a distinguished jurist, hoped that the UN Charter would provide for readjustment of the 1936 Anglo-Egyptian Treaty (q.v.), lest the British occupation (q.v.) be made permanent. It sought to strengthen the authority of the General Assembly, proposed to expand the Security Council from 11 to 14 members, with a representative system of nine regional constituencies for the various parts of the world, and sought to limit the use of the veto by the five permanent members. It wanted to raise the Economic and Social Council to the level of the other UN organs and to admit more members to that group. It also hoped to increase the obligations of the countries governing trust territories. Almost none of its suggestions were adopted. Egypt ratified the Charter after a lengthy parliamentary debate, hoping that the new collective security measures would lessen Britain's need to station troops on Egyptian soil.

Elected to membership in the first Security Council, Egypt often raised the issue of revising the Anglo-Egyptian Treaty, most notably under Nuqrashi (q.v.) in 1947, but without success. Egypt opposed the recommendation of the Special Committee on Palestine to partition the former British mandate between the Jews and the Arabs, who constituted two-thirds of Palestine's population, but failed to persuade enough General Assembly members to reject its Partition Plan (q.v.) in November 1947, leading to the Palestine War (q.v.) in 1948. The UN helped end the fighting in January 1949 and sponsored the Rhodes Proximity Talks (q.v.). Egypt became disillusioned with the UN, especially when it admitted Israel to full membership in May 1949, even though the Jewish state had not adhered to all its existing resolutions.

Egypt remained an active participant, however, pushing for the establishment of the UN Relief and Works Agency to benefit the Palestinian Arab refugees and for annual resolutions by the General Assembly, calling on Israel to readmit them. Egypt encouraged the extension of membership to newly independent states and called on the UN specialized agencies to promote economic development and international cooperation. Following the 1956 Suez War (q.v.), Egypt agreed to the stationing of the United Nations Emergency Force (q.v.) on its territory, despite reservations about a new foreign occupation so soon after the British evacuation, and it also took part in peacekeeping operations in the Congo in 1960–61. Nasir's (q.v.) demand that the UN withdraw its forces from Egyptian territory in May 1967 led to lengthy Security Council debates and contributed to the escalation of tensions preceding the June War (q.v.). Following its defeat, Egypt tried to draw on support from other member nations that supported its cause to force an Israeli withdrawal from all Arab territories captured during the fighting, leading to Security Council Resolution 242 (q.v.). The UN again served as the main debating forum during the October War (q.v.), when Egypt and its backers tried to parlay the Arabs' early gains into a resolution that would oblige Israel to withdraw from all occupied territories and recognize the rights of the Palestinian people. Egypt did, however, accept Resolutions 338–340 (q.v.) that ended the war. It later backed General Assembly resolutions that declared the Palestine Liberation Organization (q.v.) to be the sole representative of the Palestinian people, denounced Zionism (q.v.) as "a form of racism," and set up a committee to work for implementing the "inalienable rights of the Palestinian people." Egypt worked with the world organization in condemning Israel's invasions of Lebanon in 1978 and 1982 and Iraq's 1990 invasion of Kuwait (*see* Iraq-Kuwait Conflict).

Many Egyptians have held important posts within the UN organization, most notably Secretary-General Boutros Boutros-Ghali (q.v.).

UNITED NATIONS EMERGENCY FORCE (UNEF). International army stationed in the Gaza Strip (q.v.) and the Sinai Peninsula (q.v.) between Egypt and Israel in 1957–67, then withdrawn at the demand of Egypt's government, an action that led to its blockade of the Gulf of Aqaba (q.v.) and, in the opinion of many, the June War (q.v.). A new UNEF was established, as a result of Kissinger's shuttle diplomacy (q.v.), by the first Separation of Forces Agreement (q.v.) of 1974, serving as a buffer between Egypt and Israel. Since 1979 that role has been played by a multinational force, because of Israel's distrust of the UN.

URABI, AHMAD (1841–1911). Egyptian nationalist leader and army officer. Urabi was the son of a village shaykh of Iraqi Arab origin. He studied for two years at al-Azhar (q.v.) and then entered the Military Academy (q.v.) at Sa'id's (q.v.) behest in 1854–55 and soon earned his commission. He rose rapidly through the ranks under Sa'id, but his career was stalled under Isma'il (q.v.), who favored army officers of Turkish or Circassian (q.v.) origin. After Isma'il's deposition in 1879, Urabi is said to have backed the emerging National Party (q.v.), but his first known act was to represent a group of discontented ethnic Egyptian officers who were protesting in February 1881 against War Minister Rifqi's (q.v.) favoritism to their Turco-Circassian (q.v.) colleagues. Khedive Tawfiq (qq.v.) and Premier Riyad (q.v.) planned to cashier Urabi and his followers for insubordination, but other Egyptian officers seized control of the ministry, rescuing them. The khedive then agreed to replace Rifqi with Mahmud Sami al-Barudi (q.v.) as war minister. On 9 September, fearing a khedivial counterplot, the Nationalist officers surrounded Abdin Palace (q.v.), confronted Tawfiq, and obliged him to set up a constitutional government headed by Muhammad Sharif (q.v.) and to enlarge the Egyptian army. Britain and France (especially the latter), concerned about the safety of the Suez Canal (q.v.) and their investments and citizens in Egypt, became increasingly hostile to the Urabist movement, expressing their views in the Joint Note (q.v.) of January 1882. The Nationalists countered by replacing Sharif with Barudi as premier in February, making Urabi the new war minister. Still fearing a khedivial counterplot, the Nationalists took steps to weaken the Turks and Circassians within the officer corps, also stirring up popular feeling against the European powers, and in some cases threatened the Europeans living in Egypt as well. Riots broke out in Alexandria (q.v.) in June 1882, and many European residents fled for safety, sometimes to the English and French warships that were gathering near its harbor. Britain and France threatened military intervention to back the khedive and to protect their citizens, demanding that the Egyptian army dismantle its fortifications at Alexandria harbor. When Urabi refused, British ships bombarded them. In Alexandria fires broke out, caused either by the bombardment (as the Egyptians claimed) or by Egyptian officials (according to the British).

British troops–unaided by France, which had pulled out due to a ministerial crisis in Paris–landed at Alexandria and later at Ismailia (q.v.) to restore order. Urabi and the Egyptian army continued to resist the British invaders, even after the khedive had gone over to their side and declared him a rebel, but they were defeated at Tel el-Kebir (q.v.) on 13 September. Once the British entered Cairo (q.v.) the next day, Urabi surrendered, was tried for treason against the khedive, and ultimately was spared execution. He and his followers were exiled to Ceylon. Abbas Hilmi II (q.v.) let him return to Egypt in 1901, but he did not join the later National Party of Mustafa Kamil (q.v.), died in obscurity, and was scorned by most educated Egyptians up to the 1952 Revolution (q.v.). Afterward he was rehabilitated by Nasir (q.v.) and his fellow officers, whose occupational and class backgrounds paralleled his own. Now he is viewed as a patriot who resisted the British, the khedive, and the large landowners to promote constitutional government and the people's welfare.

***AL-URWA AL-WUTHQA* (1884)**. Influential Arabic fortnightly journal published in Paris by Jamal al-Din al-Afghani (q.v.) and Muhammad Abduh (q.v.), advocating Islamic solidarity against Western imperialism.

UTHMAN, AMIN (1900–46). Pro-British minister. Educated at Victoria College (q.v.) in Alexandria (q.v.) and at Brasenose College, Oxford, he was called to the bar at the Inner Temple in London and later received his *licence* and doctorate in law from Paris. Uthman taught briefly at Victoria after his return to Egypt, then worked as a lawyer within the government's legal department. Later he became a financial inspector, director of imports for the Alexandria municipality, director of the direct tax department, deputy minister of finance, head of the accounts council, and in 1942 finance minister in Nahhas's (q.v.) cabinet. He instituted a national bond drive and set up the government employees' pension system. After the ministry fell, he went into business. He was a member of the Senate and served on the boards of many companies and banks. Although he belonged to the Wafd Party (q.v.), in 1945 he founded a non-political movement called Rabitat al-Nahda ("Renaissance League"). Uthman was knighted by King George VI into the Order of the British Empire, had an English wife, and raised over £E100,000 for a memorial at al-Alamayn (q.v.). His assassination in Cairo in January 1946, probably by Muslim

Brothers (q.v.) with help from Anwar al-Sadat (q.v.), signaled Egypt's growing anger against Britain.

UTHMAN, UTHMAN AHMAD (1916-). Civil engineer, construction magnate, and cabinet minister. He was educated at Cairo University (q.v.) and founded the Civil Engineering Company in 1941, with its headquarters at Ismailia (q.v.). An early member of the Muslim Brothers (q.v.), he resented the discrimination that Egyptians suffered in that city at the hands of Europeans. In 1950 Uthman moved the main center of operations of his firm, now renamed the Arab Contractors (q.v.), to Saudi Arabia, where his business flourished with the growth of the oil industry, soon moving into other Arab countries as well. Uthman did not neglect Egypt; his firm spearheaded the reconstruction of Port Said (q.v.) following the Suez War (q.v.) and won a $48-million contract for part of the building of the Aswan High Dam (q.v.). His enthusiasm for working with the Soviets palled, however, when they denied him access to one of their bases after he had won a contract to build shelters for their fighter planes. Uthman and members of his family held most of the shares in the Engineering Company for Industries and Contracts and in many other firms, such as the Nasr Company for Pencils and Graphite Products. From 1949 to 1973 he was president of the Arab Contractors and of its Saudi, Kuwaiti, and Libyan (q.v.) affiliate organizations. An advocate of Sadat's (q.v.) *infitah* (q.v.) policy, he became minister for reconstruction in 1973 and of housing and reconstruction from 1974 to 1976. He has represented Ismailia in the People's Assembly (q.v.) since 1976 and has chaired the Engineers Syndicate, the National Democratic Party (q.v.), the Committee for Popular Development, and the Ismailia Football Club. Uthman holds an honorary LL.D. from Ricker College and decorations from the Egyptian and Soviet governments. His construction projects include the Aswan High Dam, the deepening of the Suez Canal (q.v.), the Cairo International Airport, the Dhahran Airport, the Kuwait Municipality Centre, the Benghazi sewer system, the Kirkuk Feeder Canal, dams and tunnels on Jordan's Yarmuk River, and a first-class hotel in Khartum. Under Sadat he accumulated power and wealth in ways that many people questioned, being at the same time a minister who could issue tenders for contracts and a contractor who could bid on them; he has had less power under Mubarak (q.v.). Uthman published memoirs in 1981.

- V -

VANGUARD, WAFDIST. The Wafd Party's (q.v.) radical branch that flourished in the late 1940s, often in alliance with such pro-Communist groups as New Dawn (q.v.). It published a newspaper, *Sawt al-Umma*, edited by Muhammad Mandur, and such journals as *al-Ba'th* and *al-Fajr al-Jadid*. Critical of traditional institutions, it demanded radical reforms. Its members, mainly young intellectuals, clashed with Nahhas (q.v.) and Fuad Siraj al-Din (q.v.).

VICTORIA COLLEGE. Private boys' boarding school in Alexandria (q.v.), founded in 1902, following an English curriculum, and attended by sons of wealthy Egyptian and foreign families. It was nationalized after the Suez War (q.v.) by the Egyptian government and renamed "Victory College." Amin Uthman (q.v.), Jordan's King Husayn, and Edward Said were among the many famous Middle Easterners who studied there.

VIRGIN MARY, APPARITION OF THE. Many Egyptians, both Christian and Muslim, believe that the Virgin Mary appeared in February 1968 in the night sky above a Coptic (q.v.) church in Matariyya, to reassure them following their country's defeat in the June War (q.v.).

VOICE OF THE ARABS. Influential Egyptian radio (q.v.) station that spread Nasir's (q.v.) policies and ideology during the 1960s, especially among Palestinians and Arabs living in countries deemed unsympathetic to Arab nationalism (q.v.).

- W -

WAFD. Egypt's unofficial delegation to the 1919 Paris Peace Conference. The idea of sending Egyptian representatives to the postwar talks arose during World War I (q.v.) and may have originated with Fuad (q.v.). The charter members were Sa'd Zaghlul (q.v.), Ali Sha'rawi, Abd al-Aziz Fahmi (q.v.), Ahmad Lutfi al-Sayyid (q.v.), Abd al-Latif al-Makabbati, Muhammad Ali Alluba, Hamad al-Basil, and Sinut Hanna. Their first overt action was a visit by Zaghlul, Fahmi, and Sha'rawi to Sir Reginald Wingate (q.v.) at the Residency (q.v.) in November 1918, two days after the armistice, expressing their desire to go to London to negotiate with the Foreign Office for an end to the British Protectorate. A similar request was made the same day by Premier Husayn Rushdi (q.v.) and Adli Yakan (q.v.). Wingate wired home for instructions, but was advised that the Foreign Office was too busy preparing for the Paris Peace Conference (q.v.) to meet even an official Egyptian delegation, let alone Sa'd, who was convening meetings of Legislative Assembly (q.v.) members, demanding Egypt's complete independence, and proposing to lead a delegation to the Peace Conference. When the British government questioned the credentials of Sa'd and his friends to represent Egypt, his followers set up a central committee to gather financial contributions and circulate petitions on which Egyptians could sign their names (or press their seal-rings), authorizing Sa'd and his *wafd* ("delegation") to speak on their behalf. Wingate tried to discourage these meetings, and the interior ministry confiscated some of the petitions. But even Rushdi and Adli resigned from the cabinet when the Foreign Office refused to receive them. Sa'd and his backers kept on writing memoranda to Clemenceau as president of the Peace Conference, President Wilson, the representatives of the Western powers in Egypt, and foreign residents.

Although the Wafd's main aim was to achieve Egypt's complete independence by peaceful means, the British failure to perceive the depth of popular support for the Wafd led to repressive measures in March, including the internment in Malta of Sa'd and three of his associates, causing the nationwide 1919 Revolution (q.v.). The violence subsided only after the British government appointed a war hero, General Edmund Allenby (q.v.), to replace Wingate as high commissioner and authorized him to take whatever measures he deemed necessary to restore order. Allenby firmly suppressed the violence but also declared Sa'd free to go to Paris. The other Wafdists drew up a covenant that listed the Wafd's founding members and pledged them to secrecy. They chose a president to direct the Wafd and supervise the work of its committees and the other officers, a secretary to control its written communications and archives, and a treasurer to keep its accounts and take responsibility for its funds. Members of the Wafd were required to have the president's permission to negotiate in its name with persons of political standing. They had to report their conversations to the president in writing. Formally organized like a European political party, the Wafd delegated many powers to its president, Sa'd Zaghlul. Once he was free to go to the Peace Conference, the other 17 members of the Egyptian delegation still in Egypt met before their departure to form the Central Committee, whose vital function was to gather funds and information on the situation in Egypt. It soon became the nerve center of Egyptian resistance to British rule. When Britain dispatched the Milner Mission (q.v.) to Egypt, it was the Central Committee that organized the boycott and demonstrations against it, the main focus of the 1919 Revolution after Sa'd's release from Malta.

The Wafd's hopes of presenting its case to the Conference were dashed when, on the day Sa'd reached Paris, the U.S. government announced that it recognized the British Protectorate over Egypt. The Wafd was not invited to address the Conference, and its members spent their time issuing manifestos and making informal contacts with members of the other delegations, hoping to persuade officials to back Egypt's independence. Some members resigned, and others joined. In 1920 Lord

Milner (q.v.) and Sa'd Zaghlul held informal talks about the Egyptian question without reaching an agreement. New disturbances broke out in 1921 in protest against the Adli-Curzon negotiations (q.v.), and many of the Wafd's leaders, including Sa'd, were exiled. Some of the estranged supporters of the Wafd helped create the Constitutional Liberal Party (q.v.) and took part in drafting the 1923 Constitution (q.v.). Once the new constitution took effect, the Wafd, which had insisted that only an elected constituent assembly could write it, voted to reconstitute itself as a party in order to run candidates in the elections for the first session of Parliament. From 1918 to 1923, the Wafd had viewed itself not as a distinct party, but as spokesman to the world for the whole Egyptian nation, which in 1919 it almost was.

WAFD PARTY. Egypt's main nationalist political party from 1923 until after the 1952 Revolution (q.v.). From the start it considered itself to be the representative of the Egyptian people, while at the same time conferring much power on its leader: Sa'd Zaghlul (q.v.) until his death in 1927 and then Mustafa al-Nahhas (q.v.) until 1952. Although the Wafd contended that a nationally chosen constituent assembly should have drafted the 1923 Constitution (q.v.), it voted to reconstitute itself as a party to run candidates for both the Chamber of Deputies and the Senate. Its central leadership in 1923 was made up of large and medium-size landowners, with a few members of the urban middle class, but it sought to reach all social classes. Wafdists ran for all Chamber of Deputies seats during the 1923 elections, winning 183 against 27 for all the other parties; in the Senate it fared less well because it was harder to find qualified candidates to run for its constituencies. Wafdist voters included the medium and small landowners, urban professionals, merchants and industrialists, shopkeepers, workers, and peasants.

The Wafd Party also won in the 1925 elections, after Sir Lee Stack's (q.v.) assassination, but by a smaller margin because of massive Palace interference. The Stack murder also revealed the existence of a "secret apparatus" within the Wafd, led by Ahmad Mahir (q.v.) and Mustafa Fahmi al-Nuqrashi (q.v.), both relative newcomers to the party. Although the Wafd continued to dominate the Chamber of Deputies, which Sa'd chaired in 1926–27, it could not form a cabinet because King Fuad (q.v.) used his power under the 1923 Constitution to appoint non-Wafdist ministries. In the 1929 elections, the Wafd Party won 205 seats, and Nahhas briefly headed a government. At this time the party was strongly organized at the constituency and provincial as well as the national level, but its central committee tended to assume power at the expense of the local groups, especially after the formation in 1924 of the Wafdist Parliamentary Organization, which required Wafdist deputies to obey the decisions of the central executive committee and became the connecting link between local committees and the central leadership. Its leaders were not popularly chosen, but picked by Sa'd or Nahhas. However, the Wafd Party usually secured the consent of the Parliamentary Organization for its major decisions. Its program stressed Egypt's attainment of complete independence from Britain, but also encouraged local industry and Bank Misr (q.v.), public education (q.v.), and agriculture (q.v.), as well as the development of cooperatives (q.v.) and labor unions (q.v.).

The Great Depression and the repressive policies of the Palace and Isma'il Sidqi (q.v.) hamstrung the Wafd Party. It opposed the prorogation of the 1929 Parliament and the imposition of the 1930 Constitution (q.v.), some factions even resorting to terrorism. Divisions hampered the Wafd in combating Fuad's policies, and the British opposed restoring the 1923 Constitution, which they believed would ensure the Wafd's return to power. All parties except the Wafd met in November 1935 to demand that Tawfiq Nasim (q.v.) restore the 1923 Constitution. Massive demonstrations, resulting in several deaths and arrests, dramatized popular opposition to the 1930 Constitution, and finally Nahhas agreed to join a National Front (q.v.) with all the other parties to petition the king to restore the 1923 Constitution and the high commissioner to reopen Anglo-Egyptian negotiations. While the Wafd continued to appeal to its traditional constituencies, it adopted confrontational tactics such as boycotting foreign manufactures and organizing industrial workers. In 1935 the Wafd held a national congress that showed its ongoing mass support, including villagers, women, and youth. After Nasim restored the earlier constitution, the Wafd decided not to join a coalition cabinet, but rather to accept a caretaker government that would hold free elections in which it could take part.

In the 1936 elections, the Wafd won 179 of the 232 seats in the Chamber of Deputies and 65 out of 79 elected Senate seats. Nahhas formed an all-Wafdist cabinet. Hoping to increase Parliament's power, he appointed members as undersecretaries of state for health, interior, justice, and foreign affairs. That summer Egypt successfully concluded the 1936 Anglo-Egyptian Treaty (q.v.), laying the groundwork for the Montreux Convention (q.v.). The Party became distracted by its power struggle with King Faruq (q.v.) and internal dissensions, as Nuqrashi left the cabinet and then the Wafd's high command. He was followed in January 1938 by Ahmad Mahir, with whom he formed the Sa'dist Party (q.v.). By this time, Faruq had dissolved the government, after an escalating quarrel with Nahhas and a crescendo of demonstrations by the Green Shirts (*see* Misr al-Fatat) for the king and the Blue Shirts (q.v.) for the Wafd, replacing it with a coalition of anti-Wafd politicians. They decided to dissolve Parliament and hold new elections, but the government used pressure tactics to help its candidates and to prevent known Wafdists from voting. The result was a victory for the Sa'dists and the Constitutional Liberals (q.v.); the Wafd won only 12 seats. Out of power, the Wafd scored gains among university students and government employees. The ministers were united only by their desire to keep the Wafd out of power. A series of weak cabinets that were either ultranationalist or subservient to Faruq persuaded the British to bring back the Wafd to ensure Egypt's cooperation with the Allies during World War II (q.v.). This policy led to the 4 February Incident (q.v.), which restored Nahhas to power with an all-Wafdist cabinet.

This incident marked the beginning of the Wafd's downfall, for it had attained power by neither popular election, parliamentary support, nor royal command, but by the power of British tanks. The Wafd's leaders began amassing fortunes from their public offices and especially from war profiteering. Makram Ubayd (q.v.), the Wafd's secretary-general, quit his position as finance minister and was expelled in July 1942 from the party. He proceeded to document Wafdist corruption in his *Black Book* (q.v.) and formed his own splinter group. Youth groups became alienated from the party leaders, the leadership atrophied, and Nahhas fell under the influence of Fuad Siraj al-Din (q.v.). As soon as Allied victory in World War II (q.v.) seemed certain, the British let Faruq replace Nahhas with another non-Wafdist coalition. Only after the Palestine War (q.v.), when the king had a reconciliation with Nahhas, united perhaps by the specter of a revolution by the outlawed Muslim Brothers (q.v.), did Faruq call new elections. The Wafd returned to power in 1950 with less than half the votes cast but a respectable majority of deputies elected. The last Wafdist cabinet, made up mainly of old party leaders but including respected figures such as Ahmad Husayn (q.v.) in social affairs and Taha Husayn (q.v.) in education, proposed an ambitious social reform program, which was eclipsed by the inconclusive negotiations with Britain over the Sudan (q.v.) and the evacuation of the Suez Canal (q.v.). Nahhas made a dramatic gesture by unilaterally abrogating the 1936 Treaty on the floor of the Parliament in October 1951, causing street demonstrations and the dispatch of *fidaiyin* (q.v.) to attack the British troops in the Canal Zone. The climax was Black Saturday (q.v.), when fires destroyed much of central Cairo (q.v.), and the Wafdist cabinet was dismissed.

The Wafd never again held power. After six months of fitful efforts to solve Egypt's political and social problems, using four different appointed governments, Faruq was ousted from power by the 1952 Revolution (q.v.). The army officers who took over the government talked with Nahhas about forming a cabinet, but concluded that the Wafd was more the cause of Egypt's problems than a solution. In January 1953 the officers ordered all political parties to surrender their assets and dissolve themselves. Many Wafdist leaders were tried and some received long prison sentences, notably Fuad Siraj al-Din, who survived to found the New Wafd (q.v.) in 1977. The Wafd was a popular movement as much as a political party. It fared best when it strove to free Egypt from British domination, but poorly when it had to coexist with politicians and policies that were outside its direct control.

WAFD PARTY, NEW. The revived Wafd Party (q.v.), led by Fuad Siraj al-Din (q.v.), with Ibrahim Faraj as its secretary-general. Its basis lay in Sadat's (q.v.) 1976 Party Reforms (q.v.) within the People's Assembly (q.v.). Under the new law, parties needed only 20 members of Parliament to become legal. Muhammad Hilmi Murad was able to form a 25-member Wafdist parliamentary group. The Wafd quickly revived its Central Command with 35 members, soon to become 50. Women's and students' committees followed, as did branch committees in the provinces and the towns. Siraj al-Din made his speech formally proclaiming the new Wafd in August 1977 at the Egyptian Bar Association (q.v.) and appealing especially to landowners and middle-class voters who were disenchanted with Arab socialism (q.v.). Reestablished in February, it was disbanded in June 1978, when Sadat (q.v.) issued a new internal security law that barred anyone who had held a ministerial post before 1952 from taking part in politics. The Egyptian courts invalidated this law in 1983, legalizing the New Wafd in time to contest the 1984 elections. Running in coalition with the Muslim Brothers (q.v.), it won 58 seats with 15 percent of the total popular vote. It ran independently in 1987, winning 35 seats. It boycotted the 1990 elections, protesting the government's unfair electoral laws. Lately, it has identified with secularists against the *jama'at* (q.v.) and with private enterprise capitalists against the Mubarak (q.v.) government's renewed stress on state-owned industries.

WAFDIST BLOC. Small faction formed by Makram Ubayd (q.v.) when he left the Wafd Party (q.v.) in 1942. It joined several anti-Wafdist coalition cabinets.

WAGHORN, THOMAS (1800–50). British promoter of the overland route to India. Born in Rochester, England, he entered the Royal Navy at the age of 12. Unable to find naval employment after the Napoleonic Wars, he became a merchantman and realized that Britain could cut the time and cost of transport between Europe and India by using the Egyptian overland route. In 1827 Waghorn made a test voyage to carry messages from London to Bombay and to return with a reply within three months. Overcoming great hardships, his mission succeeded. After living for some years among the Egyptian bedouin (q.v.), he managed to develop a regular system of caravans, secure from nomadic raids, with eight halting points between Cairo (q.v.) and Suez. By 1840 he provided a service of English carriages, vans, and horses to convey travelers. He wrote several pamphlets, including *Egypt as It Is in 1837*, promoting his enterprise. Waghorn's achievement was a step toward building the first railroad (q.v.) linking Alexandria (q.v.) to Cairo and ultimately the Suez Canal (q.v.).

WAHBA, YUSUF (1859–1934). Leading Copt (q.v.), judge, cabinet minister, and premier from 1919 to 1920. Born in Cairo (q.v.), he was educated at Cyril IV's (q.v.) Coptic college, where he became fluent in French and English. He helped to translate the Code Napoléon into Arabic and to develop the National Courts (q.v.). He also helped to revive the Coptic Council (*majlis milli*) against the wishes of Patriarch Cyril V (q.v.) and was a founder of the Tawfiq Benevolent Society. He later became a chancellor in the Mixed Court (q.v.) of Appeals in Alexandria (q.v.). When Muhammad Sa'id (q.v.) and his successor resigned from the premiership, Wahba became the Coptic member of the cabinet with the portfolio for foreign affairs. He became finance minister in the first Husayn Rushdi (q.v.) ministry in 1914 and continued to serve in the cabinet during the war and the 1919 Revolution (q.v.). He agreed to head the government in November 1919 despite massive protest demonstrations by leading Copts, backed by many Muslims, and narrowly escaped assassination in Midan Sulayman Pasha (now Tal'at Harb). He later served in the Senate, where he generously arranged for his erstwhile assailant to find employment as a clerk.

WAHHABI. Ultraconservative, puritanical Muslim movement founded in Najd by Muhammad ibn Abd al-Wahhab (d. 1787) and now dominant in Saudi Arabia. The Wahhabis, who call themselves *mutawahhidun* ("unitarians"), originally preached that Muslims had abandoned their faith in one God and distorted Islam (q.v.) by their innovations. They based the Shari'a (q.v.) solely on the Quran and on the sayings and acts of the prophets, rejecting all later interpretations in Islamic law and theology. They rejected Sufism (q.v.) and veneration of saints and tombs, prohibited the decoration of mosques, and banned all luxury. At the behest of the Ottoman sultan, Muhammad Ali (q.v.) sent his troops to drive the Wahhabis out of the Hijaz (q.v.) in 1811–19. They regained power under Abd al-Aziz ("Ibn Sa'ud"), who built up the Kingdom of Saudi Arabia in the early twentieth century. Wahhabi ideas influenced the Salafiyya (q.v.) movement in Egypt and in other Muslim countries.

AL-WAQAI' AL-MISRIYYA. Egypt's official newspaper since 1828.

WAQF. Religious endowment of land or other property, usually designated for a pious or beneficent purpose, called a *waqf khayri*, usually by and for Muslims, but in Egypt also by and for Copts (q.v.). Another type of endowment, the *waqf ahli*, was sometimes used in Egypt before the 1952 land reforms (q.v.) to protect estates from excessive division under Muslim inheritance laws. Originally managed by the ulama (q.v.), the Muslim *awqaf* came under Palace control under Muhammad Ali (q.v.). Later, when Abbas Hilmi II (q.v.) abused his control over the *awqaf*, the Egyptian government set up a ministry to administer them. Coptic *awqaf* were controlled by the clergy up to the land reforms.

WINGATE, [FRANCIS] REGINALD (1861–1953), FIRST BARONET. British army general and high commissioner of Egypt. Born in Port Glasgow (Scotland), he was educated at the Royal Military Academy, Woolwich, and was commissioned in 1880 as a second lieutenant in the Royal Artillery. Although posted to India, he was sent to Aden, where he learned Arabic, and joined the Egyptian army in 1883, becoming an aide-de-camp to its commander-in-chief, Sir Evelyn Wood. Wingate took part in the relief expedition for General Charles Gordon (q.v.), but saw no more active service. He was named assistant military secretary, then assistant adjutant general, and in 1889 director of military intelligence, with special responsibility for the Sudan (q.v.), about which he wrote *Mahdiism and the Egyptian Sudan* (1891). He also translated the accounts by Father Ohrwalder and R.C. Slatin of their experiences as prisoners of the Mahdi (q.v.). He accompanied Kitchener (q.v.) during the 1896–98 Sudan campaign and succeeded him as commander-in-chief of the Egyptian army from 1899 to 1916 and concurrently governor-general of the Sudan. Wingate restored order and established British rule in that country, notably expanding cotton (q.v.) production in the Jazira Irrigation Project begun in 1913. He brought Darfur under Anglo-Egyptian control in 1916.

In January 1917 Wingate succeeded Sir Henry McMahon (q.v.) as Egypt's high commissioner. This office proved challenging, because of the large influx of British Empire troops during World War I (q.v.), the shortage of foodstuffs and animals, and rising opposition to British rule among the Egyptian people. Wingate's warnings to the British government were ignored, and in November 1918 he received a formal visit at the Residency (q.v.) from Sa'd Zaghlul (q.v.) and two of his friends, who asked to send a delegation to negotiate with the Foreign Office in London for an end to the Protectorate (q.v.) that Britain had proclaimed in 1914. However, Foreign Secretary Curzon refused to accept Sa'd's demands or even Wingate's advice that the British government should negotiate with the Egyptian ministers. When the 1919 Revolution (q.v.) proved that Wingate had better grasped the situation than the Foreign Office had, the

British government replaced him with General Allenby (q.v.), who was to implement a more conciliatory policy in Cairo. Wingate never again held a responsible government position, although he served on the boards of various local organizations and of Gordon College in Khartum. His services to the British Empire as a military commander and civil administrator have never been adequately recognized. His papers are in the Sudan Archive, Palace Green Library, Durham University.

WISA-WASIF, RAMSES. Noted patron of Egyptian peasant artists, especially young children, whom he encouraged to weave tapestries representing scenes from village life. His studio in Harraniyya, near the Giza Pyramids, remains a center of creativity in the arts (q.v.).

WOLSELEY, SIR GARNET (1833–1913). British army officer, imperial administrator, and leader of the 1882 expedition that occupied Egypt. Born in Dublin to a small landowning family, he eventually attained a commission in the British Infantry, serving in India, the Crimean War, the Indian Mutiny, China, Canada, the Confederate States (during the American Civil War), the Ashanti Wars, Natal, Cyprus, the Zulu Wars, and the War Office in the years prior to 1882. Wolseley was dispatched by the British government to take charge of its forces in Egypt after the bombardment of Alexandria (q.v.) in July and masterminded the successful invasion of the Suez Canal (q.v.) and Ismailia (q.v.) that enabled his troops to defeat the Egyptian army at Tel el-Kebir (q.v.). He was promoted to general, appointed a baronet, and voted a 30,000-pound grant by Parliament, but soon returned to Egypt to organize the 1884 Gordon (q.v.) relief expedition. The operation failed, perhaps due to Wolseley's much-criticized decision to advance up the Nile (q.v.) rather than overland from the Red Sea, but the Mahdi's (q.v.) forces would probably have taken Khartum no matter what the rescue mission did. Wolseley returned to the task of reorganizing Britain's army, preparing for its role in World War I (q.v.), which he did not live to see.

WOMEN. In Egyptian society, the Coptic Church (q.v.) and Islam (q.v.) have set norms for the behavior of both men and women. Although both religions claim to support women's rights, the clerics and ulama (q.v.) who have interpreted their laws have created societal expectations that limited women to essentially domestic activities. Islam in particular has given men authority and power over their wives or female relatives, charging men with supporting women financially, but giving them greater rights to use force against them, to limit their freedom of movement, and to initiate divorce proceedings. Both men and women may inherit property under the Shari'a (q.v.), but male relatives receive twice the portion allotted to women. The legal testimony of two women is considered equal to that of one man, and traditionally women did not appear in the Shari'a Courts (q.v.) or indeed in most other public places. Upper-class women traditionally covered their hair, and often their faces, whenever they left their homes. In Upper Egypt, genital mutilation, often called "female circumcision," is practiced by some Muslims and Copts, even though the practice is illegal. Many of these disabilities diminished during the Westernization of Egypt. Egyptian feminism (q.v.) has challenged surviving patriarchal customs, but the rise of Islamism (q.v.) in Egypt since the 1970s has caused some men and women to revive them.

WORLD WAR I (1914–18). When Britain declared war on Germany in August 1914, it proclaimed Egypt's neutrality but also arranged for the expulsion of German and Austrian nationals from the country. Once Egypt's legitimate suzerain, the Ottoman Empire (q.v.), entered World War I on the German side, Britain had to decide whether to annex Egypt or to devise some legal stratagem to go on stationing its forces in this strategically vital country. The British cabinet decided against annexation, for fear of inflaming Muslim opinion elsewhere in its empire, but severed Egypt from its formal Ottoman connection, declared a Protectorate (q.v.), and replaced Khedive Abbas Hilmi II (qq.v.), with Husayn Kamil (q.v.), giving him the title of "sultan." Egypt was placed under martial law for the duration of the war and soon became the headquarters for most British military operations in the Middle East. Guarding the Suez Canal (q.v.) was their paramount concern, but the British also wanted to drive the Ottomans out of the war by invading the Dardanelles in the 1915 Gallipoli campaign or occupying Alexandretta (Iskenderun); eventually it succeeded in organizing an Arab revolt and sending the Egyptian Expeditionary Force (EEF) (q.v.) to fight against them in the Hijaz (q.v.), Palestine, and Syria. Egyptians had been told that they would not have to contribute to the British war effort, but many in fact did so, sometimes under compulsion, as farm animals were commandeered, young men were conscripted as EEF auxiliaries, and donations in cash and kind were solicited for the Allied cause. Egyptians also suffered from price inflation, government limits on the land area that could be used for raising cotton (q.v.), and the rowdy behavior of Australian soldiers in Cairo (q.v.) and Alexandria (q.v.). German bombing raids on Cairo caused light casualties, and few civilians were affected by Ottoman attempts to capture the Sinai Peninsula (q.v.). Egyptians assumed that the British Protectorate was strictly a wartime measure. When the 1918 Armistice did not lead to immediate troop reductions, popular disillusionment fueled the 1919 Revolution (q.v.).

WORLD WAR II (1939–45). When Britain and France declared war on Germany in September 1939, the Egyptian government upheld the 1936 Anglo-Egyptian Treaty (q.v.) by allowing the British additional base facilities and by expelling German nationals. It did not, however, declare war on Germany and remained officially neutral. The fall of France in June 1940 shocked Egypt's government and people, leading many to think that Britain would be defeated and that Germany and Italy would soon liberate their country. Britain took strong measures to suppress pro-Axis sentiment and to reinforce its control of the Suez Canal (q.v.), airports, radio stations, and other vital facilities. British Empire forces in Egypt numbered 80,000–100,000 when the war began; by November 1941 there were 140,000 just in Cairo and its vicinity. Italian and German forces invaded the Western Desert and seemed likely to reach the Nile (q.v.), but were repulsed in the Battle of al-Alamayn (q.v.). The Axis also bombed Alexandria (q.v.), causing many civilian casualties. Some Egyptians saw military service in World War II, and their army was required to turn over most of its weapons to the Allies. The Egyptian government estimated the country's wartime casualties at 1,278 civilians and 201 soldiers killed. Other problems for Egypt included British interference in its internal politics, notably the 4 February Incident (q.v.), price inflation and urban crowding, restrictions on cotton (q.v.) cultivation, and disorderly behavior by British, Australian, and American soldiers. As a result, popular demand grew for the evacuation (q.v.) of all foreign forces from Egypt after the war, contributing eventually to the 1952 Revolution (q.v.).

- Y -

YAHYA, ABD AL-FATTAH (1885–1951). Politician, cabinet minister, and premier. He was justice minister in 1921 and again in 1930, then held the portfolio for foreign affairs from 1930 to 1934, also serving as premier at the behest of King Fuad (q.v.) after Sidqi's (q.v.) fall from power, and again in several coalition cabinets from 1937 to 1939. He lacked the ability or the personality to lead the government at a time when public opinion was turning against the king and the government, and he was soon replaced by Tawfiq Nasim (q.v.). Elected to the 1926 Chamber of Deputies, Yahya was appointed in 1931 to the Senate. Elected a senator in 1936, he chaired the Senate, a role for which he was better suited than that of premier. He served on the delegation that negotiated the 1936 Anglo-Egyptian Treaty (q.v.) and helped to represent Egypt at the San Francisco Conference that created the United Nations (q.v.).

YAKAN, ADLI (1864–1933). Politician, cabinet minister, and three-time premier. The great-grandson of Muhammad Ali's (q.v.) sister, Adli descended from one of Egypt's main landowning families. Elected to the Legislative Assembly (q.v.) in 1913, he also served as foreign minister in the 1914 Rushdi (q.v.) cabinet up to the declaration of the Protectorate (q.v.), then held the portfolio for public instruction from 1917 to 1919 and for interior in 1919. Adli became prime minister for the first time in 1921 and took part in negotiations with Lord Curzon that were eventually stymied by the Wafd's (q.v.) obstructionism. He was a founder of the Constitutional Liberal Party (q.v.) in 1922. He was interior and prime minister in 1926–27 and 1929–30. His policies served the interests of Egypt's landowners, especially those of King Fuad (q.v.); he could not compete with Sa'd Zaghlul (q.v.) for popular support.

YEMEN CIVIL WAR (1962–67). Struggle between Saudi-backed royalist tribes and Egyptian-supported republican revolutionaries in north Yemen, or what came to be called the Yemen Arab Republic. Neither side emerged as the clear winner. Nasir's (q.v.) decision in September 1962 to commit large numbers of Egyptian troops to the conflict proved costly to Egypt, financially and militarily. Allegations that Egypt used chemical weapons against the Saudi-backed Yemeni tribesmen were often raised, but never proven or refuted. Egypt pulled its forces out after the Khartum summit (q.v.), and a Yemeni coalition cabinet, excluding any member of Yemen's former royal family, was formed in 1970.

YOM KIPPUR WAR, ***see*** **OCTOBER WAR.**

YOUNG EGYPT, ***see*** **MISR AL-FATAT.**

YOUNG EGYPT CONGRESS. Name applied to a series of Egyptian conferences held between 1908 and 1910 in Geneva under the direction of Muhammad Fahmi, a privat-docent at the University of Geneva's Faculty of Law. The best-known of these congresses was the one held in September 1909 and attended by leaders of the National, Umma, and Constitutional Reform Parties (qq.v.), as well as by the leader of Britain's Labour Party, Keir Hardie. The Young Egypt Congress had a permanent organization, quite separate from the National Party, in Geneva.

YOUNG MEN'S MUSLIM ASSOCIATION, ***see*** **AL-SHUBBAN AL-MUSLIMIN.**

YUNUS, MAHMUD (1912-). Engineer, army officer, and first director of the Suez Canal (q.v.) Authority. Born in Cairo (q.v.), he was trained by the Engineering Faculty of Cairo University (q.v.) and the Staff Officers College. He began his career in the mechanical and electrical department of the public works ministry and became an army engineer in 1937. He became director of the general headquarters of the army's Technical Affairs Office in 1952, chairman and managing director of the General Petroleum Authority in 1954, and counselor to the ministry of commerce and industry and mineral wealth. After Nasir (q.v.) nationalized the Suez Canal Company (q.v.) in 1956, Yunus became its first managing director. His efficient operation of the Canal, despite the walkout by most of the foreign pilots, belied predictions by some Western experts that Egypt would never be able to manage the waterway. Yunus chaired the Suez Canal Authority in 1957–65, then served from 1965 to 1967 as deputy minister for transport and communications and in 1967 as minister of oil transport. He also presided over the engineers' syndicate in 1954–65 and was elected in 1964 to the National Assembly (q.v.). He later became a consulting engineer in Beirut.

YUSUF, ALI (1863–1913). Pioneer journalist who founded the influential Arabic daily newspaper *al-Muayyad* (q.v.). Born in Balasfura, a village near Jirja in Upper Egypt, Ali was educated at al-Azhar (q.v.). He began his literary career as a poet, then co-edited a weekly magazine, *al-Adab*. Backed financially and politically by Prime Minister Mustafa Riyad (q.v.), be began editing *al-Muayyad*, the first Muslim paper to challenge and eventually surpass in popularity the dominant Syrian dailies, *al-Ahram* (q.v.) and *al-Muqattam* (q.v.). Under Khedive Abbas Hilmi II (qq.v.), *al-Muayyad* became the Palace organ, often publishing articles by Mustafa Kamil (q.v.) and other Muslim Egyptians hostile to the British occupation (q.v.). He later broke with the National Party (q.v.), as the khedive became reconciled with the British. His marriage in 1904 to the daughter of the Shaykh al-Sadat (q.v.), against the shaykh's wishes, was highly controversial and was opposed by conservative Muslims because of his lowly background. He became estranged from the nationalist movement, and, as Abbas drew closer to Gorst (q.v.), he espoused collaboration with the British occupation.

- Z -

ZAGHLUL, SA'D (1860?-1927). Lawyer, politician, and leader of the Wafd (q.v.). Born to a prosperous peasant family in Ibyana, he was educated at al-Azhar (q.v.). He served as a judge for several years in the National Courts (q.v.) before a wealthy patron financed his legal studies in Cairo (q.v.) and Paris. An intellectual disciple of Muhammad Abduh (q.v.), he later backed the Umma Party (q.v.). In response to the nationalist upsurge following the 1906 Dinshaway Incident (q.v.), Sa'd was named education minister. He clashed openly with his British adviser but won popular support for his insistence on Arabic as the medium of instruction in government elementary schools. He served as justice minister in 1910–12. In 1913 he was elected to the new Legislative Assembly (q.v.), where he became the elected vice president and leader of the opposition. When the Assembly was prorogued during World War I (q.v.), he retired, reportedly to study German, and was considered for a cabinet post when Fuad (q.v.) became sultan in 1917, but was rejected.

After the Armistice, he and two of his colleagues asked the British high commissioner if they could go to London to discuss Egypt's postwar status, but thc Foreign Office refused to see these politicians. Sa'd proposed to lead an Egyptian delegation, or *wafd* (q.v.), to the Paris Peace Conference (q.v.) and circulated petitions throughout the country to gain popular support, but the British blocked that idea as well. The Egyptian ministers resigned, and riots broke out in Cairo and the provinces in March 1919. Sa'd and three of his friends were arrested by the British and interned in Malta, but the disturbances intensified. A new high commissioner, Sir Edmund Allenby (q.v.), suppressed the riots, but let the Wafdist leaders go to Paris, where they stayed for a year without gaining a hearing at the Conference. Sa'd talked with Milner (q.v.) in 1920, but the two men could not agree on Egypt's future status. His return to Egypt caused new disturbances, and he was exiled to Aden, the Seychelles, and Gibraltar. He did not return until the 1923 Constitution (q.v.) had been written, but he converted his delegation into the Wafd Party (q.v.), which won the Parliamentary elections held late in that year.

In January 1924 Fuad invited him to form a Wafdist government. Sa'd's cabinet hoped to reach an agreement on Egypt's status with the new Labour Party government in Britain. He narrowly escaped an attempt on his life in June of that year. His Wafdist ministry fell after the assassination in Cairo of the commander of the Egyptian army, Sir Lee Stack (q.v.), in November. High Commissioner Allenby handed Sa'd an ultimatum with conditions that were viewed as extreme and humiliating. He resigned in protest, and the king named a caretaker government from which the Wafd was excluded. In new elections held in February 1925 the Wafd won a partial victory and Sa'd was elected president of the Chamber of Deputies, but the King ordered Parliament closed. In the 1926 elections Zaghlul led the Wafd again to victory, but declined to form a government and was reelected president of the Chamber. He died in August 1927 and was mourned throughout Egypt. Hailed as the "father of Egypt's political independence," he was popular and patriotic, but often vain and stubborn. He did more to arouse the masses than to remove the British from Egypt.

His memoirs are being published by the Center for the Study and Documentation of Egypt's Contemporary History. By 1991, four volumes, covering up to September 1914, had appeared.

AL-ZAWIYA AL-HAMRA. Mixed, working-class neighborhood in Cairo (q.v.), the site of violent fighting between Muslims and Copts (q.v.) in June 1981. Sadat's (q.v.) loss of legitimacy, hot weather, and cuts in the water supply contributed to the fracas, but its immediate cause is unknown. Egged on by mysterious provocateurs, both sides committed murders, other atrocities, arson, and looting. Leaflets were distributed in other parts of Cairo, urging each community to take up arms. Belatedly, the police sealed off the neighborhood. The disturbances have been cited as portents of rising fundamentalism (q.v.) in Egyptian politics, leading to Sadat's mass arrests of Coptic and Muslim leaders in September, followed by his assassination.

***ZAYNAB*.** Romantic novel glorifying Egyptian village life, written anonymously by Muhammad Husayn Haykal (q.v.) while he was studying law in Paris in 1912 and first published in 1913 without attracting much attention. It was later republished in Haykal's name in 1929 and has generally been considered the first Egyptian novel.

AL-ZAYYAT, AHMAD HASAN (1885–1968). Arabic teacher and scholar, writer, and editor of *al-Risala*, a monthly literary magazine, from 1933 to 1953. Educated at al-Azhar (q.v.) and the University of Cairo (q.v.), he taught at the École des Frères (q.v.), a Muslim school founded by Shaykh Jawish (q.v.), and the American University in Cairo (q.v.). As a writer and editor, he helped to reorient Egyptian public opinion to Arab nationalism (q.v.), influenced by his sojourn in Iraq between 1929 and 1933. In the early Nasir (q.v.) years, Zayyat edited al-Azhar's monthly journal. He was awarded the State Prize for Literature in 1962 and was elected to the Arabic Language Academy (q.v.).

ZIONISM. Movement to create or sustain a Jewish state in Palestine or Israel. Most Egyptian Jews (q.v.) were anti-Zionist, but an Istanbul native, Joseph Marcou Baruch, who came to Egypt in 1896, formed in the following year the Bar Kochba Society. By 1901 it had 300 members, most of whom were Jews of southern or eastern European background who joined for ideological reasons or philanthropic motives. A youth group, B'nai Tzion ("Sons of Zion"), was formed in 1900, and an ephemeral Zionist school, Bet Sefer Tzioni, was set up in Cairo (q.v.). The early Egyptian Zionist movement was hampered by the heterogeneity of Egypt's Jews and by the hostility of the Syrian-dominated Arabic press. The

Jewish influx after the abortive 1905 Russian revolution and from Palestine during World War I (q.v.) stimulated interest in Zionism among Egyptian Jews, as did the Balfour Declaration and the postwar creation of the British mandate in Palestine. In 1921 there were five Zionist groups in Cairo and one each in Alexandria (q.v.), Mansura, Tanta, and Port Said (q.v.). A Zionist weekly, *Israel*, was published from 1920 to 1937 in French, Spanish, Hebrew, and English; another, *La Revue sioniste*, came out in French. Egypt had chapters of Mizrahi, the Women's International Zionist Organization, and Maccabi (the Zionist athletic club). A permanent Zionist committee was formed in Cairo in 1929; it later raised funds for the Jewish National Fund and Keren ha-Yesod ("Palestine Foundation Fund") and established a social center, Bet ha-Am ("The People's House"), in Cairo. In Alexandria a Zionist library was opened in 1932, and a Hebrew Club sponsored weekly debates.

The Arab-Jewish contest for Palestine, combined with the rise of al-Shubban al-Muslimin (q.v.), Misr al-Fatat (q.v.), and the Muslim Brothers (q.v.), turned many Egyptians against Zionism. Although successive Egyptian governments tried to protect the Jewish community from attacks, newspapers, officials, and cabinet ministers became openly anti-Zionist. As Egypt took the lead in creating the Arab League (q.v.), the government spoke out against Jewish immigration to Palestine and plans to form a Jewish state there. Egypt adhered to the Arab boycott of Zionist goods, at times applied indiscriminately against Jewish businesses not involved in Zionism. All Zionist activities were banned when Egypt entered the Palestine War (q.v.). Clandestine efforts to smuggle Jews out of Egypt became the Zionists' main concern from 1948, although some took part in the 1954 bombing attempts in Cairo that led to trials of several Egyptian Jews–two of whom were hanged in 1955–and since have become a part of the Lavon Affair (q.v.). In 1956, after the Suez War (q.v.), the Nasir (q.v.) government enacted Law 329, which deprived all Zionists of Egyptian citizenship. The 1979 Egyptian-Israeli Peace Treaty (q.v.) and consequent establishment of diplomatic ties have led to a small Israeli community in Cairo, but Egyptian Zionism has not been revived.

ZIWAR, AHMAD (1864–1945). Lawyer, cabinet minister, and premier. Born in Alexandria (q.v.) to a family of Circassian (q.v.) origin, he was educated at the Azariyya College there and in the Jesuit College in Beirut and received his law degree at Aix University in France. Ziwar served as a judge and counselor, governor of Alexandria, minister of *awqaf* (q.v.) from 1917 to 1919, education in 1919, communications in 1919–21 and in 1923, foreign affairs in 1924–26, and also interior from 1925 to 1926. The Senate's first president under the 1923 Constitution (q.v.), he succeeded Sa'd Zaghlul (q.v.) as premier following the assassination of Sir Lee Stack (q.v.) in November 1924. After the 1925 elections, in which the Wafd (q.v.) won a majority of the seats in the Chamber of Deputies, he formed a coalition cabinet made up of Constitutional Liberals (q.v.), Ittihad (q.v.) partisans, and Independents. The newly elected Chamber was dissolved when it elected Zaghlul as its speaker. Backed by King Fuad (q.v.), Ziwar's coalition amended the electoral law to prevent the Wafd from returning to power. Ziwar's government increased controls over the Egyptian press (q.v.), passed an associations law to curb the activities of the political parties, ceded the Jaghbub oasis to Italian-ruled Libya (q.v.), passed an electoral law raising the financial requirements and qualifications for both voters and candidates, and muzzled "Bolshevik" propagandists. His government was viewed as Palace dominated and repressive. Its fall in January 1926 was ascribed to the intrigues of High Commissioner Lord Lloyd (q.v.). Ziwar remained in the Chamber of Deputies until 1930 and was an appointed senator from 1931 to 1934. He then became director of King Fuad's office until he resigned in 1935. Tall, stout, lazy, and affable with foreigners, he ignored nationalistic attacks on his policies.

BIBLIOGRAPHY

Writers on modern Egypt have created many useful scholarly and literary works. Any bibliography must, therefore, be selective. Although such works, too, are many, the existing lists, most of which appear under "Bibliographies and Archival Sources," are incomplete. Among those listed, the earlier bibliographies by Ibrahim-Hilmy (1885–86), Maunier (1918), and Pratt (1929) were the best of their time; the most complete modern one is by Makar (1988). On-line bibliographies, such as that of the Research Libraries Information Network (RLIN), now facilitate bibliographical control over Egypt. Even so, scholars using Arabic-language materials may want to consult Harvard's six-volume *Catalog of the Arabic Collection*, edited by Fawzi Abdulrazzaq. A second edition was published in 1983 by G. K. Hall. It may be supplemented by the *Index Islamicus*, which originally covered periodical articles from 1906 to 1955, to which have been added five-year cumulative volumes up to 1985, but for more recent years the researcher must check each quarterly fascicle, without a subject index. See also Wolfgang Behn's *Index Islamicus 1665–1905* (Millersville, PA: Adiyok, 1989) for earlier periodical articles.

Because of the P.L. 480-funded program for purchasing books and periodicals published in Egypt with Egyptian pounds and supplying them to selected U.S. libraries, these institutions now have the world's strongest collections of Arabic-language materials. For modern history, they are the Library of Congress, American University in Cairo, University of Arizona, Boston Public Library, the University of California at Berkeley, Columbia, Georgetown, Illinois, Indiana, Michigan, Minnesota, New York Public Library, Portland State University, Princeton, Texas, Utah, Virginia, and Yale. Other strong collections are in the Bibliothèque Nationale (Paris), Bodleian Library (Oxford), Cairo University, Cambridge University Library, Egyptian National Library (Dar al-Kutub), Harvard's Widener Library, University of Pennsylvania, School of Oriental and African Studies (London), University of California at Los Angeles, and University of Washington (Seattle). Major archives for modern Egypt include Dar al-Mahfuzat, Dar al-Wathaiq, and the Shari'a Court Archives in Cairo; the Public Record Office in London; the French Foreign Ministry Archives in Paris; and the U.S. National Archives in Washington, DC. German Foreign Office archives for the period from 1866 to 1945 are available from University Microfilms in Ann Arbor, Michigan.

Table of Contents

General Histories

Collins, Robert O., and Robert L. Tignor. *Egypt and the Sudan.* Englewood Cliffs, NJ: Prentice-Hall, 1967.

Flower, Raymond. *Napoleon to Nasser: The Story of Modern Egypt.* London: Stacey, 1972.

Goldschmidt, Arthur. *Modern Egypt: The Formation of a Nation-State.* Boulder, CO: Westview Press, 1988.

Hanotaux, Gabriel, ed. *Histoire de la nation égyptienne.* 7 vols. Paris: Société de l'Histoire Nationale, 1931–1940.

Holt, P. M. *Egypt and the Fertile Crescent, 1516–1922: A Political History.* Ithaca, NY: Cornell University Press, 1966.

________, ed. *Political and Social Change in Modern Egypt.* London: Oxford University Press, 1968.

Kedourie, Elie, and Sylvia G. Haim, eds. *Modern Egypt: Studies in Politics and Society.* London: Frank Cass, 1980.

Lacouture, Jean and Simone. *Egypt in Transition.* Translated by Francis Scarfe. London: Methuen; New York: Criterion Books, 1958.

Little, Tom. *Modern Egypt.* 2d ed. London: Benn, 1967.

Marlowe, John. *Anglo-Egyptian Relations, 1800–1956.* 2d ed. London: Frank Cass, 1965.

Petrie, W. M. Flinders, ed. *A History of Egypt.* 6 vols. London: Methuen & Co., 1898–1905.

Sa'id, Amin. *Tarikh Misr al-siyasi* ("Political History of Egypt"). Cairo: Dar Ihya al-Kutub al-Arabiyya, 1959.

Sami, Amin. *Taqwim al-Nil* ("Chronology of the Nile"). 6 vols. Cairo: Royal Press, 1916–36.

al-Sayyid-Marsot, Afaf Lutfi. *A Short History of Modern Egypt.* Cambridge: Cambridge University Press, 1985.

Sharubim, Mikhail. *al-Kafi fi tarikh Misr al-qadim wa al-hadith* ("Complete History of Ancient and Modern Egypt"). 4 vols. Cairo: Royal Press, 1898–1900.

Vatikiotis, P. J. *The History of Modern Egypt from Muhammad Ali to Mubarak.* 4th ed. Baltimore: The Johns Hopkins University Press, 1991.

Warburg, Gabriel R., and Uri M. Kupferschmidt, eds. *Islam, Nationalism, and Radicalism in Egypt and the Sudan.* New York: Praeger, 1983.

Waterfield, Gordon. *Egypt.* London: Thames and Hudson; New York: Walker, 1967.

History and Archaeology to 332 BCE

Aldred, Cyril. *The Egyptians.* London: Thames and Hudson, 1961.

Baines, John, and Jaromir Malek. *Atlas of Ancient Egypt.* New York: Facts on File, 1980.

Breasted, James Henry. *History of Egypt from Ancient Times to the Persian Conquest.* 2d ed. New York: C. Scribner's, 1937.

________. *History of the Ancient Egyptians.* London: Smith, Elder & Co., 1908.

Budge, E. A. Wallis. *A History of Egypt from the End of the Neolithic Period to the Death of Cleopatra VII.* 8 vols. London: Kegan Paul, Trench, Trubner & Co., 1907.

Clayton, Peter A. *The Rediscovery of Ancient Egypt: Artists and Travelers in the 19th Century.* London: Thames and Hudson, 1982.

Emery, Walter Bryan. *Archaic Egypt.* Baltimore: Penguin Books, 1961.

Gardiner, Sir Alan. *Egypt of the Pharaohs: An Introduction.* Oxford: Clarendon Press, 1961.

Grimal, Nicolas Christopher. *A History of Ancient Egypt.* Translated by Ian Shaw. Oxford: Blackwell, 1992.

Harris, John. *The Legacy of Egypt.* 2d ed. Oxford: Clarendon Press, 1971.

James, T. H. H. *Egypt: The Living Past.* London: British Museum Press, 1992.

Johnson, Paul. *The Civilization of Ancient Egypt.* New York: Atheneum, 1978.

Maspero, Gaston. *The Struggle of the Nations: Egypt, Syria, and Assyria.* Edited by A. H. Sayce and translated by M. L. McClure. 2d ed. Reprinted. London: Macmillan, 1925.

Montet, Pierre. *Eternal Egypt.* Translated by Doreen Weightman. London: Weidenfeld and Nicolson, 1964.

Murname, William J. *The Guide to Ancient Egypt.* New York: Facts on File, 1983.

Murray, Margaret Alice. *Social Life in Ancient Egypt.* London: Constable and Co., 1932.

________. *The Splendor That Was Egypt.* 2d ed. New York: Hawthorne Books, 1963.

Rawlinson, George. *Ancient Egypt.* 10th ed. London: T. F. Unwin, 1910.

Trigger, B. G. *Ancient Egypt: A Social History.* New York: Cambridge University Press, 1983.

Wilkinson, John Gardner. *The Manners and Customs of the Ancient Egyptians.* Edited by Samuel Birch. 3 vols. Boston: Cassino, 1883.

Wilson, John A. *The Burden of Egypt: An Interpretation of Ancient Egyptian Culture.* Chicago: University of Chicago Press, 1983.

History, 332 BCE-640 CE

Butler, Alfred J. *The Ancient Coptic Churches of Egypt*. Reprint. Oxford: Clarendon Press, 1970.

________. *The Arab Conquest of Egypt and the Last Thirty Years of Roman Dominion*. Edited by P. M. Fraser. 2d ed. Oxford: Clarendon Press, 1978.

Canfora, Luciano. *The Vanished Library*. Translated by Martin Ryle. London: H. Radius, 1989.

Davis, Harold Thayer. *Alexandria: The Golden City*. 2 vols. Evanston: Principia Press of Illinois, 1957.

Fraser, P. M. *Ptolemaic Alexandria*. 3 vols. Oxford: Clarendon Press, 1972.

Johnson, Allan Chester, and Louis C. West. *Byzantine Egypt: An Economic Study*. Princeton: Princeton University Press, 1949.

Kasher, Aryeh. *The Jews in Hellenistic and Roman Egypt*. Tübingen, West Germany: J. C. B. Mohr, 1985.

Lindsay, Jack. *Daily Life in Roman Egypt*. London: F. Muller, 1963.

Samuel, Alan Edouard. *The Shifting Sands of History: Interpretations of Ptolemaic Egypt*. Lanham, MD: University Press of America, 1989.

Thompson, Dorothy. *Memphis under the Ptolemies*. Princeton: Princeton University Press, 1988.

Van 'T Dack, E., et al., eds. *Egypt and the Hellenistic World*. Lovanni (Louvain), Belgium: Orientaliste, 1983.

History, 640–1517

Ayalon, David. *Studies on the Mamluks of Egypt*. London: Variorum Reprints, 1977.

Devonshire, R. L. [Henriette Caroline]. *Moslem Builders of Cairo.* Cairo: Schindler, 1943.

Glubb, Sir John Bagot. *Soldiers of Fortune: The Story of the Mamlukes.* New York: Stein and Day, 1973.

Imad, Leila S. *The Fatimid Vizirate, 969–1172.* Berlin: Klaus Schwarz, 1990.

Inan, Muhammad Abdallah. *Misr al-islamiyya* ("Islamic Egypt"). 2d ed. Cairo: Maktabat al-Khanji, 1968.

Khafaji, Muhammad Abd al-Mun'im. *Mawakib al-hurriyya fi Misr al-islamiyya* ("Triumphs of Freedom in Islamic Egypt"). Cairo: General Egyptian Book Organization, 1987.

Lane-Poole, Stanley. *Cairo: Sketches of Its History, Monuments, and Social Life.* London: J. S. Virtue & Co., 1893.

________. *History of Egypt in the Middle Ages.* Reprint. New York: Haskell House, 1968.

Lapidus, Ira M. *Muslim Cities in the Later Middle Ages.* Cambridge: Harvard University Press, 1967.

Lev, Yaacov. *State and Society in Fatimid Egypt.* Leiden: E. J. Brill, 1991.

Maqrizi, Ahmad ibn Ali. *A History of the Ayyubid Sultans of Egypt.* Translated by R. J. C. Broadhurst. Boston: Twayne, 1980.

Muir, Sir William. *The Mameluke, or Slave Dynasty of Egypt, 1260-1517, A.D.* London: Smith, Elder & Co., 1898.

O'Leary, De Lacy Evans. *A Short History of the Fatimid Khalifate.* London: Kegan Paul, Trench, Trubner & Co., 1928.

al-Rafi'i, Abd al-Rahman, and Sa'id Abd al-Fattah Ashur. *Misr fi al-usur al-wusta* ("Egypt in the Middle Ages"). Cairo: Maktabat al-Nahda al-Misriyya, 1970.

Wiet, Gaston. *Cairo: City of Art and Commerce.* Translated by Seymour Feiler. Norman: University of Oklahoma Press, 1964.

Yusuf ibn Taghribirdi. *History of Egypt, 1382–1469*. Translated by William Opper. 3 vols. Berkeley: University of California Press, 1954–1958.

History, 1517-1798

Abd al-Rahim, Abd al-Rahim Abd al-Rahman. *al-Rif al-misri fi al-qarn al-thamin ashr* ("The Egyptian Countryside in the Eighteenth Century"). Cairo: Ayn Shams University Press, 1974.

Baer, Gabriel. "Village and City in Egypt and Syria," in *The Islamic Middle East, 700–1900*, edited by Abraham Udovitch. Princeton, NJ: Darwin Press, 1981.

Behrens-Abouseif, Doris. *Egypt's Adjustment to Ottoman Rule: Institutions, Waqfs, and Architecture in Cairo*. Leiden: E. J. Brill, 1994.

Cezzâr Ahmad Pasha. *Ottoman Egypt in the Eighteenth Century.* Edited and translated from Turkish by Stanford J. Shaw. Cambridge: Harvard University Press, 1964.

Crecelius, Daniel. *The Roots of Modern Egypt: A Study of the Reigns of Ali Bey al-Kabir and Muhammad Bey Abu al-Dhahab, 1760–1775*. Minneapolis: Bibliotheca Islamica, 1981.

Gran, Peter. *The Islamic Roots of Capitalism, 1760–1840*. Austin: University of Texas Press, 1979.

Hanna, Nelly. *An Urban History of Bulaq in the Mamluk and Ottoman Periods*. Cairo: Institut Français d'Archéologie Orientale du Caire, 1983.

Hansen, Bent. "An Economic Model for Ottoman Egypt," in *The Islamic Middle East, 700–1900*, edited by Abraham Udovitch. Princeton: Darwin Press, 1981.

Huseyn Efendi. *Ottoman Egypt in the Age of the French Revolution.* Translated from Arabic, introduced, and annotated by Stanford J. Shaw. Cambridge: Harvard University Press, 1964.

Kimche, David. "The Political Superstructure of Egypt in the Late Eighteenth Century," *Middle East Journal* 22 (1968): 448–462.

El-Nahal, Galal H. *The Judicial Administration of Ottoman Egypt in the Seventeenth Century*. Minneapolis and Chicago: Bibliotheca Islamica, 1979.

Raymond, André. *Artisans et commerçants au Caire au XVIIIe siècle*. 2 vols. Damascus: Institut Français de Damas, 1973–1974.

________. "The Economic Crisis of Egypt in the Eighteenth Century," in *The Islamic Middle East, 700–1900*, edited by Abraham L. Udovitch. Princeton: Darwin Press, 1981.

Shaw, Stanford J. *The Financial and Administrative Organization and Development of Ottoman Egypt, 1517–1798*. Princeton: Princeton University Press, 1962.

Volney, Constantin François, Comte de. *Travels through Syria and Egypt in the Years 1783, 1784, and 1785*. London: Robinson, 1787; Farnborough, UK: Gregg International, 1972.

Walz, Terry. *Egypt and "Bilad as-Sudan," 1700–1820*. Cairo: Institut Français d'Archéologie Orientale du Caire, 1978.

Winter, Michael. *Egyptian Society under Ottoman Rule, 1517–1798*. London and New York: Routledge, 1992.

________. *Society and Religion in Early Ottoman Egypt*. New Brunswick, NJ: Transaction Books, 1982.

History, 1798–1882

Abu-Lughod, Ibrahim. *Arab Rediscovery of Europe: A Study in Cultural Encounters*. Princeton: Princeton University Press, 1963.

________, "The Transformation of the Egyptian Élite: Prelude to the Urabi Revolt," *Middle East Journal* 21 (1967): 325–344.

Barakat, Ali. *Tatawwur al-milkiyya al-zira'iyya al-kabira fi Misr, 1813-1914, wa atharuhu ala al-haraka al-siyasiyya* ("The Evolution of

Large Landownership in Egypt, 1813–1914, and Its Effects on the Political Movement"). Cairo: Dar al-Thaqafa al-Jadida, 1977.

Bréhier, Louis. *L'Égypte de 1798 à 1900.* Paris: Combet, 1900.

Broadley, A. M. *How We Defended Arabi and His Friends.* London: Chapman and Hall, 1884; Cairo: Arab Center for Research and Publishing, 1980.

Cameron, D. A. *Egypt in the Nineteenth Century.* London: Smith, Elder & Co., 1898.

Cannon, Byron. *Politics of Law and the Courts in Nineteenth-Century Egypt.* Salt Lake City: University of Utah Press, 1988.

Charles-Roux, François. *Bonaparte: Governor of Egypt.* Translated by E. W. Dickes. London: Methuen, 1937.

Cole, Juan R. I. *Colonialism and Revolution in the Middle East: Social and Cultural Origins of Egypt's Urabi Movement.* Princeton: Princeton University Press, 1993.

Crabitès, Pierre. *Ibrahim of Egypt.* London: George Routledge and Sons, 1935.

________. *Ismail, the Maligned Khedive.* London: George Routledge and Sons, 1933.

Cuno, Kenneth M. *The Pasha's Peasants: Land, Society, and Economy in Lower Egypt, 1740–1858.* Cambridge: Cambridge University Press, 1992.

Delanoue, Gilbert. *Moralistes et politiques musulmans dans l'Égypte du XIXe siècle.* 2 vols. Cairo: Institut Français d'Archéologie Orientale du Caire, 1982.

Dodwell, Henry. *The Founder of Modern Egypt.* Cambridge: Cambridge University Press, 1931.

L'Égypte au XIXe siècle. Paris: Centre National de la Recherche Scientifique, 1982.

Galbraith, John S., and Afaf Lutfi al-Sayyid Marsot. "The British Occupation of Egypt: Another View," *International Journal of Middle East Studies* 9 (1978): 471–488.

Ghorbal, Shafik. *The Beginnings of the Egyptian Question and the Rise of Mehemet Ali*. London: Routledge, 1928; Ann Arbor: University Microfilms International, 1978.

Hanna, Sami A. "The Saint-Simonians and the Application of State Socialism in Egypt," in *Medieval and Middle Eastern Studies in Honor of A. S. Atiya*, edited by S. A. Hanna. Leiden: E. J. Brill, 1972.

Herold, Christopher. *Bonaparte in Egypt*. New York: Harper and Row, 1962.

Hill, Richard L. *Egypt in the Sudan, 1820–1881*. London: Oxford University Press, 1959.

Hopkins, A. G. "The Victorians and Africa: A Reconsideration of the Occupation of Egypt, 1882," *Journal of African History* 27 (1986): 373–374.

Hourani, Albert. "Ottoman Reform and the Politics of Nobles," in *The Beginnings of Modernization in the Middle East*, edited by William R. Polk and Richard L. Chambers. Chicago: University of Chicago Press, 1968.

Hunter, F. Robert. *Egypt under the Khedives, 1805–1879*. Pittsburgh: University of Pittsburgh Press, 1984.

Isa, Salah. *al-Thawra al-urabiyya* ("The Urabi Revolution"). Beirut: al-Muassasa al-arabiyya li al-Dirasat wa al-Nashr, 1972.

al-Jabarti, Abd al-Rahman. *Ajaib al-athar fi al-tarajim wa al-akhbar* ("Amazing Records from Biographies and History"). 4 vols. Cairo: Government Press, 1880.

________. *Al-Jabarti's Chronicle of the First Seven Months of the French Occupation of Egypt*. Edited and translated by S. Moreh. Leiden: E. J. Brill, 1975.

Kinross, Patrick Balfour, Baron. *Between Two Seas: The Creation of the Suez Canal*. London: John Murray, 1968.

Landau, Jacob M. "Prolegomena to a Study of Secret Societies in Modern Egypt," *Middle Eastern Studies* 1 (1965): 135–186.

Landes, David S. *Bankers and Pashas: International Finance and Economic Imperialism in Egypt*. 2d ed. Cambridge: Harvard University Press, 1979.

Lane, Edward William. *Manners and Customs of the Modern Egyptians*. Introduction by Mursi Saad el-Din. London: Dent; New York: E. P. Dutton, 1963.

Lawson, Fred H. *The Social Origins of Egyptian Expansionism during the Muhammad Ali Period*. New York: Columbia University Press, 1992.

Marlowe, John. *Perfidious Albion: The Origins of Anglo-French Rivalry in the Levant*. London: Elek Books, 1971.

________. *Spoiling the Egyptians*. London: André Deutsch, 1974.

Moorehead, Alan. *The Blue Nile*. New York: Harper and Row, 1962.

________. *The White Nile*. New York: Harper and Row, 1960.

Mubarak, Ali. *al-Khitat al-tawfiqiyya* ("Tawfiq's Realm"). 20 vols. Cairo: Royal Press, 1888–89.

Owen, Roger. "Agricultural Production in Nineteenth-Century Egypt," in *The Islamic Middle East, 700–1900*, edited by Abraham Udovitch. Princeton: Darwin Press, 1981.

________. "Egypt and Europe: From French Expedition to British Occupation," in *Studies in the Theory of Imperialism*, edited by R. Owen and B. Sutcliffe. London: Longmans, 1972.

al-Rafi'i, Abd al-Rahman. *Asr Isma'il* ("The Age of Isma'il"). 2 vols. 2d ed. Cairo: Maktabat al-Nahda al-Misriyya, 1948.

________. *Asr Muhammad Ali* ("The Age of Muhammad Ali"). 3d ed. Cairo: Maktabat al-Nahda al-Misriyya, 1951.

________. *Tarikh al-haraka al-qawmiyya wa tatawwur nizam al-hukm fi Misr* ("History of the Nationalist Movement and the Evolution of Egypt's System of Government"). 2 vols. 5th ed. Cairo: Dar al-Ma'arif, 1981.

________. *al-Thawra al-urabiyya wa al-ihtilal al-inglizi* ("The Urabi Revolution and the British Occupation"). 2d ed. Cairo: Maktabat al-Nahda al-Misriyya, 1949.

Ramadan, Ali. *al-Hayat al-ijtima'iyya fi Misr fi asr Isma'il* ("Social Life in Egypt in Isma'il's Era"). Alexandria: Munsha'at al-Ma'arif, 1977.

Robinson, Ronald, and John Gallagher (with Alice Denny). *Africa and the Victorians.* 2d ed. London: Macmillan, 1981.

Sabry, M. *L'Empire égyptien sous Ismaïl et l'ingérence anglo-française, 1863–1879.* Paris: Librairie Orientaliste Paul Geuthner, 1933.

________. *L'Empire égyptien sous Mohamed-Ali et la question d'orient, 1811–1849.* Paris: Librairie Orientaliste Paul Geuthner, 1930.

________. *La Genèse de l'esprit national égyptien, 1863–1882.* Paris: Association Linotypiste, 1924.

Salim, Latifa Muhammad. *al-Quwwa al-ijtima'iyya fi al-thawra al-urabiyya* ("Social Power in the Urabi Revolution"). Cairo: General Egyptian Book Organization, 1981.

al-Sayyid-Marsot, Afaf Lutfi. *Egypt in the Reign of Muhammad Ali.* Cambridge: Cambridge University Press, 1984.

Schölch, Alexander. *Egypt for the Egyptians! The Socio-Political Crisis in Egypt, 1878–82.* London: Ithaca Press, 1981.

________. "The 'Men on the Spot' and the English Occupation of Egypt in 1882," *Historical Journal* 19 (1976): 773–785.

Stephens, John Lloyd. *Incidents of Travel in Egypt, Arabia Petraea, and the Holy Land.* Edited with an introduction by Wolfgang von Hagen. Norman: University of Oklahoma Press, 1970.

Taha, Samir Muhammad. *Ahmad Urabi wa dawruhu fi al-hayat al-siyasiyya al-misriyya* ("Ahmad Urabi and His Role in Egyptian Political Life"). Cairo: General Egyptian Book Organization, 1986.

Toledano, Ehud R. *State and Society in Mid-Nineteenth-Century Egypt.* Cambridge: Cambridge University Press, 1990.

Urabi, Ahmad. *The Defense Statement of Ahmad Urabi.* Translated and edited by Trevor Le Gassick. Cairo: American University in Cairo Press, 1982.

Verdery, Richard. "The Publications of the Bulaq Press under Muhammad Ali of Egypt," *Journal of the American Oriental Society* 91 (1971): 129–132.

Wallace, D. Mackenzie. *Egypt and the Egyptian Question.* London: Macmillan, 1883; New York: Russell and Russell, 1968.

Walz, Terry. "Asyut in the 1260s (1844–1853)," *Journal of the American Research Center in Egypt* 15 (1978): 113–126.

History, 1882–1952

Ahmed, Jamal Mohamed. *The Intellectual Origins of Egyptian Nationalism.* London and New York: Oxford University Press, 1960.

Berque, Jacques. *Egypt: Imperialism and Revolution.* Translated by Jean Stewart. London: Faber and Faber, 1972.

al-Bishri, Tariq. *al-Muslimun wa al-Aqbat fi itar al-jama'a al-wataniyya* ("Muslims and Copts within the Framework of National Collectivity"). Beirut: Dar al-Wahda, 1982.

Botman, Selma. *Egypt from Independence to Revolution, 1919–1952.* Syracuse: Syracuse University Press, 1991.

________. *The Rise of Egyptian Communism, 1939–1970.* Syracuse: Syracuse University Press, 1988.

Colombe, Marcel. *L'Évolution de l'Égypte, 1924–1950.* Paris: G. P. Maisonneuve, 1951.

Cromer, Sir Evelyn Baring, Earl of. *Modern Egypt*. 2 vols. London: Macmillan, 1908.

Deeb, Marius. *Party Politics in Egypt: The Wafd and Its Rivals, 1919-1939*. London: Ithaca Press, 1979.

L'Égypte: aperçu historique et géographique, gouvernement et institutions, vie économique et sociale. Cairo: Institut Français d'Archéologie Orientale, 1926.

Erlich, Haggai. *Students and University in 20th Century Egyptian Politics*. London: Frank Cass, 1989.

Gershoni, Israel. "Egyptian Intellectual History and Egyptian Intellectuals in the Interwar Period," *Asian and African Studies* 19 (1985): 333–364.

________. "Imagining the East: Muhammad Husayn Haykal's Changing Representation of East-West Relations, 1928–1933," *Asian and African Studies* 25 (1991): 209–251.

Gershoni, Israel, and James P. Jankowski. *Egypt, Islam, and the Arabs: The Search for Egyptian Nationhood, 1900–1930*. New York: Oxford University Press, 1986.

Ghali, Ibrahim Amin. *L'Égypte nationaliste et libérale de Moustapha Kamel à Saad Zaghloul (1892–1927)*. The Hague: Martinus Nijhoff, 1969.

Ghurbal, Muhammad Shafiq. *Ta'rikh al-mufawadat al-misriyya al-britaniyya* ("History of Anglo-Egyptian Negotiations"). Cairo: Maktabat al-Nahda al-Misriyya, 1952.

Goldberg, Ellis. *Tinker, Tailor, and Textile Worker: Class and Politics in Egypt, 1930–1952*. Berkeley: University of California Press, 1986.

Ismael, Tareq, and Rifa'at el-Sa'id. *The Communist Movement in Egypt, 1920–1988*. Syracuse: Syracuse University Press, 1990.

Jankowski, James P. "Egypt and Early Arab Nationalism, 1908–1924," in *The Origins of Arab Nationalism*, edited by Rashid Khalidi et al. New York: Columbia University Press, 1991.

________. *Egypt's Young Rebels: "Young Egypt": 1932–1952*. Stanford, CA: Hoover Institution Press, 1975.

________. "The Government of Egypt and the Palestine Question, 1936–1939," *Middle Eastern Studies* 17 (1981): 427–453.

Kazziha, Walid. "The Jaridah-Ummah Group and Middle Eastern Politics," *Middle Eastern Studies* 13 (1977): 373–385.

Kedourie, Elie. "Sa'ad Zaghlul and the British," in *The Chatham House Version and Other Essays*, edited by the author. London: Weidenfeld and Nicolson, 1970; Hanover, NH, and London: New England Universities Press, 1984.

Kelidar, Abbas. "Shaykh Ali Yusuf: Egyptian Journalist and Islamic Nationalist," in *Intellectual Life in the Arab East, 1890–1939*, edited by Marwan R. Buheiry. Beirut: American University of Beirut Press, 1981.

Kilani, Muhammad Sayyid. *Abbas Hilmi al-Thani, aw asr al-taghalghul al-britani fi Misr, 1892–1914* ("Abbas Hilmi II: The Era of British Penetration into Egypt, 1892–1914"). Cairo: Dar al-Firjani, 1991.

Kirk, G. E. *The Middle East in the War*. London: Royal Institute of International Affairs, 1952.

Landau, Jacob M. *Middle Eastern Themes: Papers in History and Politics*. London: Frank Cass, 1973.

________. *Parliaments and Parties in Egypt*. Tel Aviv: Israel Oriental Society, 1954.

________. *The Politics of Pan-Islam*. Oxford: Clarendon Press, 1990.

Lloyd, George Ambrose, Lord. *Egypt since Cromer*. 2 vols. London: Macmillan, 1933–34; New York: Fertig, 1970.

Marlowe, John. *Cromer in Egypt*. London: Elek Books, 1970.

Mayer, Thomas. *Egypt and the Palestine Question, 1936–1945*. Berlin: Klaus Schwarz Verlag, 1983.

McBride, Barrie St. Clair. *Farouk of Egypt: A Biography.* London: Robert Hale, 1967.

McIntyre, John D., Jr. *The Boycott of the Milner Mission: A Study in Egyptian Nationalism.* New York: Peter Lang, 1985.

McLeave, Hugh. *The Last Pharaoh: Farouk of Egypt.* New York: McCall Publishing, 1969.

Milner, Alfred, Viscount. *England in Egypt.* London: Edward Arnold, 1892; New York: Fertig, 1970.

Mitchell, Timothy. *Colonising Egypt.* Cambridge: Cambridge University Press, 1988.

Mohamed, Duse [Ali, Dus Muhammad]. *In the Land of the Pharaohs: A Short History of Egypt from the Fall of Ismail to the Assassination of Boutros Pasha.* Introduced by Khalil Mahmud. London: Frank Cass, 1968.

Mostyn, Trevor. *Egypt's Belle Epoque: Cairo, 1869–1952.* London: Quartet, 1989.

Newman, E. W. Polson. *Great Britain in Egypt.* London: Cassell, 1928.

Owen, E. R. J. "The Attitudes of British Officials to the Development of the Egyptian Economy, 1882–1922," in *Studies in the Economic History of the Middle East,* edited by M. A. Cook. London: Oxford University Press, 1970.

Porath, Yehoshua. *In Search of Arab Unity, 1930–1945.* London: Frank Cass, 1986.

Quraishi, Zaheer Masood. *Liberal Nationalism in Egypt: Rise and Fall of the Wafd Party.* Allahabad, India: Kitab Mahal, 1967.

al-Rafi'i, Abd al-Rahman. *Fi a'qab al-thawra al-misriyya* ("In the Wake of the Egyptian Revolution"). 3 vols. Cairo: Maktabat al-Nahda al-Misriyya, 1947–1951.

________. *Misr wa al-Sudan fi awail ahd al-ihtilal* ("Egypt and the Sudan at the Beginning of the Occupation Era"). Cairo: Matba'at Mustafa al-Babi al-Halabi, 1947.

________. *Muhammad Farid: ramz al-ikhlas wa al-tadhiyya* ("Muhammad Farid: Exemplar of Loyalty and Sacrifice"). 3d ed. Cairo: Maktabat al-Nahda al-Misriyya, 1961.

________. *Mustafa Kamil: ba'ith al-haraka al-wataniyya* ("Mustafa Kamil: Reviver of the Nationalist Movement"). 4th ed. Cairo: Maktabat al-Nahda al-Misriyya, 1962.

________. *Thawrat sanat 1919* ("The Revolution of 1919"). 2 vols. 2d ed. Cairo: Maktabat al-Nahda al-Misriyya, 1955.

Ramadan, Abd al-Azim. *al-Ikhwan al-Muslimun wa al-tanzim al-sirri* ("The Muslim Brothers and the Secret Organization"). Cairo: Matba'at *Ruz al-Yusuf*, 1982.

________. *Tatawwur al-haraka al-wataniyya fi Misr min sanat 1918 ila sanat 1936* ("Development of the Nationalist Movement in Egypt from 1918 to 1936"). 2 vols. 2d ed. Cairo: Madbuli, 1983.

________. *Tatawwur al-haraka al-wataniyya fi Misr min sanat 1937 ila sanat 1948*. 2 vols. Beirut: al-Watan al-Arabi, 1968.

Reid, Donald M. "Political Assassination in Egypt, 1910–1954," *International Journal of African Historical Studies* 15 (1982): 625–649.

Rizq, Labib Yunan. *al-Hayat al-hizbiyya fi Misr fi ahd al-ihtilal al-britani, 1882–1914* ("Party Life in Egypt in the Era of the British Occupation"). Cairo: Anglo-Egyptian Bookshop, 1970.

________. *Tarikh al-wizarat al-misriyya* ("History of the Egyptian Ministries"). Cairo: Muassasat *al-Ahram*, 1975.

________. *al-Wafd wa "al-Kitab al-aswad"* ("The Wafd and *The Black Book*"). Cairo: Muassasat *al-Ahram*, 1978.

Royal Institute of International Affairs. *Great Britain and Egypt, 1914-1951*. Information Papers No. 19. 2d ed. London: RIIA, 1952.

al-Sayyid, Afaf Lutfi. *Egypt and Cromer: A Study in Anglo-Egyptian Relations*. London: John Murray; New York: Praeger, 1968.

al-Sayyid-Marsot, Afaf Lutfi. *Egypt's Liberal Experiment, 1922–1936.* Berkeley, Los Angeles, and London: University of California Press, 1977.

Schonfield, Hugh J. *The Suez Canal in Peace and War, 1869–1969.* London: Vallentine Mitchell; Coral Gables, FL: University of Miami Press, 1969.

al-Shafi'i, Shuhdi Atiyya. *Tatawwur al-haraka al-wataniyya al-misriyya* ("Development of the Egyptian Nationalist Movement"). Cairo: al-Dar al-Misriyya li al-Tiba'a, 1957.

Shilliq, Ahmad Zakariyya. *Hizb al-Umma wa dawruhu fi al-siyasa al-misriyya* ("The Umma Party and Its Role in Egyptian Politics"). Cairo: Dar al-Ma'arif, 1979.

Smith, Charles D. "4 February 1942: Its Causes and Its Influence on Egyptian Politics and on the Future of Anglo-Egyptian Relations, 1937–1945," *International Journal of Middle East Studies* 10 (1979): 453–479.

Stadiem, William. *Too Rich: The High Life and Tragic Death of King Farouk.* New York: Carroll and Graf Publishers, Inc., 1991.

Terry, Janice J. *The Wafd, 1919–1952: Cornerstone of Egyptian Political Power.* London: Third World Centre, 1979.

Tignor, Robert L. *Egyptian Textiles and British Capital, 1930–1956.* Cairo: American University in Cairo Press, 1989.

________. *Modernization and British Colonial Rule in Egypt, 1882–1914.* Princeton: Princeton University Press, 1966.

________. *State, Private Enterprise, and Economic Change in Egypt, 1918–1952.* Princeton: Princeton University Press, 1984.

The Times Book of Egypt. London: *The Times* Publishing Co., 1937.

Warburg, Gabriel. *Egypt and the Sudan: Studies in History and Politics.* London: Frank Cass, 1985.

Wilson, Arnold T. *The Suez Canal: Its Past, Present, and Future.* 2d ed. London: Oxford University Press, 1939.

Wilson, Keith M., ed. *Imperialism and Nationalism in the Middle East.* London: Mansell Publishing, 1983.

Yusuf, Hasan. *al-Qasr wa dawruhu fi al-siyasa al-misriyya, 1922–1952* ("The Palace and Its Role in Egyptian Politics, 1922–1952"). Cairo: Muassasat *al-Ahram*, 1982.

Zayid, Mahmud. *Egypt's Struggle for Independence.* Beirut: Khayat's, 1965.

History and Politics since 1952

Abdalla, Ahmed. *The Student Movement and National Politics in Egypt, 1923–1973.* London: Al Saqi Books, 1985.

Abdel-Malek, Anouar. *Egypt: Military Society.* Translated by Charles Lam Markmann. New York: Random House, 1968.

Ajami, Fouad. *The Arab Predicament: Arabic Political Thought and Practice since 1967.* 2d ed. Cambridge and New York: Cambridge University Press, 1992.

Ansari, Hamied. *Egypt: The Stalled Society.* Albany: State University of New York Press, 1986.

Ayyubi, Nazih. *Bureaucracy and Politics in Contemporary Egypt.* London: Ithaca Press, 1980.

________. *The State and Public Policy in Egypt since Sadat.* Reading, UK: Ithaca Press, 1991.

________. *al-Thawra al-idariyya wa azmat al-islah fi Misr* ("The Administrative Revolution and the Reform Crisis in Egypt"). Cairo: Center for Political and Strategic Studies, 1977.

Baker, Raymond W. *Egypt's Uncertain Revolution under Nasser and Sadat.* Cambridge: Harvard University Press, 1978.

________. *Sadat and After: Struggle for Egypt's Political Soul.* Cambridge: Harvard University Press, 1990.

Bar-Siman-Tov, Yaacov. *The Israeli-Egyptian War of Attrition, 1969-1970.* New York: Columbia University Press, 1980.

Barnett, Michael N. *Confronting the Costs of War: Military Power, State, and Society in Egypt and Israel.* Princeton: Princeton University Press, 1992

Batatu, Hanna. *The Egyptian, Syrian, and Iraqi Revolutions: Some Observations on their Underlying Causes and Social Character.* Washington, DC: Georgetown University Center for Contemporary Arab Studies, 1983.

Beattie, Kirk. *Egypt during the Nasser Years: Ideology, Politics, and Civil Society.* Boulder, CO: Westview Press, 1994.

Beinin, Joel. *Was the Red Flag Flying There? Marxist Politics and the Arab-Israeli Conflict in Egypt and Israel, 1948–1965.* Berkeley and Los Angeles: University of California Press, 1990.

Binder, Leonard. *The Ideological Revolution in the Middle East.* New York: John Wiley and Sons, 1964.

________. *In a Moment of Enthusiasm: Political Power and the Second Stratum in Egypt.* Chicago: University of Chicago Press, 1978.

Brown, L. Carl. "Nasser and the June War: Plan or Improvisation," in *Quest for Understanding: Arabic and Islamic Studies in Memory of Malcolm H. Kerr*, edited by S. Seikaly, R. Baalbaki, and P. Dodd. Beirut: American University of Beirut Press, 1991.

Bulloch, John. *The Making of a War: The Middle East from 1967 to 1973.* London: Longman, 1974.

Cantori, Louis J., and Peter Benedict. "Local Leadership in Urban Egypt: Leader, Family, and Community Perceptions," in *Local Politics and Development in the Middle East*, edited by Louis J. Cantori and Iliya Harik. Boulder, CO: Westview Press, 1984.

Carlton, David. *Britain and the Suez Crisis.* Oxford: Basil Blackwell, 1988.

Cohen, Raymond. *Culture and Conflict in Egyptian-Israeli Relations: A Dialogue of the Deaf.* Bloomington: Indiana University Press, 1990.

Cooper, Mark N. *The Transformation of Egypt.* Baltimore: The Johns Hopkins University Press, 1982.

Cremeans, Charles D. *The Arabs and the World: Nasser's Arab Nationalist Policy.* New York and London: Frederick A. Praeger, 1963.

David, Steven R. "Alignment and Realignment in Sadat's Egypt," in *Choosing Sides: Alignment and Realignment in the Third World.* Baltimore: The Johns Hopkins University Press, 1991.

Dawisha, Adid I. *Egypt in the Arab World: The Elements of Arab Policy.* New York: John Wiley and Sons, 1976.

Dekmejian, R. Hrair. *Egypt under Nasir: A Study in Political Dynamics.* Albany: State University of New York Press, 1971.

Dupuy, Trevor N. *Elusive Victory: The Arab-Israeli Wars, 1947–1974.* New York: Harper and Row, 1978.

Egyptian Society of International Law. *Egypt and the United Nations.* Prepared for the Carnegie Endowment for International Peace. New York: Manhattan Publishing, 1957.

Fahmi, Ismail. *Negotiating for Peace in the Middle East.* Baltimore: The Johns Hopkins University Press, 1983.

Friedlander, Melvin A. *Sadat and Begin: The Domestic Politics of Peacemaking.* Boulder, CO: Westview Press, 1983.

Fullick, Roy, and Geoffrey Powell. *Suez: The Double War.* London: Hamish Hamilton, 1979.

Gordon, Joel. *Nasser's Blessed Movement: Egypt's Free Officers and the July Revolution.* New York and Oxford: Oxford University Press, 1992.

Hamrush, Ahmad. *Qissat thawrat Yulyu* ("The Story of the July Revolution"). 5 vols. Cairo: Madbuli, 1977–84.

________. *Thawrat Yulyu fi aql Misr* ("The July Revolution in the Mind of Egypt"). Cairo: Madbuli, 1985.

Harik, Iliya. "Continuity and Change in Local Development Policies in Egypt: From Nasser to Sadat," in *Local Politics and Development in the Middle East*, edited by Louis J. Cantori and Iliya Harik. Boulder, CO, and London: Westview Press, 1984.

Hasou, Tawfiq Y. *The Struggle for the Arab World: Egypt's Nasser and the Arab League*. London: Kegan Paul International, 1985.

Haykal, Muhammad Hasanayn. *al-Infijar 1967: Harb al-thalathin sana* ("The 1967 Explosion, or the Thirty Years War"). Cairo: Markaz *al-Ahram* li al-Tarjama wa al-Nashr, 1990.

Heikal, Mohamed [Haykal, Muhammad Hasanayn]. *Nasser: The Cairo Documents*. Garden City, NY: Doubleday, 1971.

________. *The Sphinx and the Commissar: The Rise and Fall of Soviet Influence in the Middle East*. New York: Harper and Row, 1978.

Hinnebusch, Raymond A. *Egyptian Politics under Sadat*. 2d ed. Boulder, CO: Lynne Rienner, 1988.

Hirst, David, and Irene Beeson. *Sadat*. London: Faber and Faber, 1982.

Hopkins, Harry. *Egypt–the Crucible: The Unfinished Revolution of the Arab World*. London: Secker and Warburg, 1969.

Hopwood, Derek. *Egypt: Politics and Society, 1945–1990*. 3d ed. London: HarperCollins, 1991.

Ismael, Tareq. *The U.A.R. in Africa: Egypt's Policy under Nasser*. Evanston, IL: Northwestern University Press, 1971.

Karem, Mahmoud. *A Nuclear-Weapons-Free Zone in the Middle East: Problems and Prospects*. Westport, CT: Greenwood Press, 1988.

Kays, Doreen. *Frogs and Scorpions: Egypt, Sadat, and the Media*. London: Muller, 1984.

Kerr, Malcolm H. *The Arab Cold War: Gamal Abd al-Nasir and His Rivals, 1958–1970.* 3d ed. London: Oxford University Press, 1971.

Kimche, David. *The Afro-Asian Movement.* Jerusalem: Israel Universities Press, 1973.

Kyle, Keith. *Suez.* New York: St. Martin's Press, 1991.

Lacouture, Jean. *Nasser: A Biography.* London: Secker and Warburg, 1973.

Lewis, William Roger, and Roger Owen, eds. *Suez 1956: The Crisis and Its Consequences.* Oxford: Clarendon Press, 1989.

Lippman, Thomas W. *Egypt after Nasser: Sadat, Peace, and the Mirage of Prosperity.* New York: Paragon House, 1989.

Love, Kennett. *Suez: The Twice-Fought War.* New York and Toronto: McGraw-Hill, 1969.

Mansfield, Peter. *Nasser's Egypt.* Baltimore: Penguin, 1965.

McDermott, Anthony. *Egypt from Nasser to Mubarak: A Flawed Revolution.* London: Croom Helm, 1988.

Morris, Mary E. *New Political Realities and the Gulf: Egypt, Syria, and Jordan.* Santa Monica, CA: Rand, 1993.

Murad, Mahmud. *Man kana yahkum Misr?* ("Who Was Ruling Egypt?"). Cairo: Madbuli, 1975.

Nour, Salua, and Carl F. Pinkele. "Egypt under Sadat: The Contours of Asymmetrical Interdependence," in *The Contemporary Mediterranean World*, edited by Carl F. Pinkele and Adamantia Pollis. New York: Praeger, 1983.

Nutting, Anthony. *Nasser.* New York: E. P. Dutton, 1972.

O'Ballance, Edgar. *The Electronic War in the Middle East, 1968–70.* London: Faber and Faber; Hamden, CT: Archon Books, 1974.

Palmer, Monte, Ali Leila, and El Sayed Yassin, *The Egyptian Bureaucracy*. Syracuse: Syracuse University Press, 1988.

Perlmutter, Amos. *Egypt: The Praetorian State*. New Brunswick, NJ: Transaction Books, 1974.

Quandt, William B. *The United States and Egypt: An Essay on Policy for the 1990s*. Washington, DC: Brookings Institution, 1990.

al-Rafi'i, Abd al-Rahman. *Thawrat 23 Yulyu* ("The 23 July Revolution"). Cairo: Maktabat al-Nahda al-Arabiyya, 1959.

Ramadan, Abd al-Azim. *Abd al-Nasir wa azmat Mars* ("Abd al-Nasir and the March Crisis"). Cairo: *Ruz al-Yusuf*, 1976.

Rubinstein, Alvin Z. *Red Star on the Nile*. Princeton: Princeton University Press, 1977.

Safran, Nadav. *From War to War: The Arab-Israeli Confrontation, 1948-1967*. New York: Pegasus, 1969.

Shazly, Saad El. *The Crossing of the Suez*. San Francisco: American Mideast Research, 1980.

Shoukri, Ghali. *Egypt: Portrait of a President, 1971–1981*. London: Zed Books, 1981.

Singer, Hanaa Fikri. *The Socialist Labor Party: A Case Study of a Contemporary Egyptian Opposition Party*. Cairo: American University in Cairo Press, 1993.

Springborg, Robert. *Mubarak's Egypt: Fragmentation of the Political Order*. Boulder, CO: Westview Press, 1989.

Stephens, Robert. *Nasser: A Political Biography*. New York: Simon & Schuster, 1971.

Sykes, John. *Down into Egypt: A Revolution Observed*. London: Hutchinson, 1969.

Talhami, Ghada Hashem. *Palestine and Egyptian National Identity*. New York: Praeger Publishers, 1992.

Tripp, Charles, ed. *Contemporary Egypt through Egyptian Eyes: Essays in Honour of Professor P. J. Vatikiotis.* London: Routledge, 1993.

Tripp, Charles, and Roger Owen, eds. *Egypt under Mubarak.* London: Routledge, 1989.

Troen, Selwyn Ilan, and Moshe Shemesh, eds. *The Suez-Sinai Crisis, 1956: Retrospective and Reappraisal.* London and Savage, MD: Frank Cass, 1990.

Vatikiotis, P. J., ed. *Egypt since the Revolution.* New York: Praeger; London: Allen & Unwin, 1968.

________. *The Egyptian Army in Politics.* Bloomington: Indiana University Press, 1961.

________. *Nasser and His Generation.* London: Croom Helm, 1978.

Waterbury, John. *Egypt: Burdens of the Past, Options for the Future.* Bloomington: Indiana University Press, 1978.

Wilber, Donald N. *United Arab Republic, Egypt: Its Peoples, Its Society, Its Culture.* New Haven, CT: Human Relations Area Files Press, 1969.

Woodward, Peter. *Nasir.* London: Longmans, 1992.

Intellectual History

Abdel-Malek, Anouar. *Idéologie et renaissance nationale: l'Égypte moderne.* Paris: Éditions Anthropos, 1969.

Abduh, Ibrahim. *Jaridat "al-Ahram": tarikh wa fann* ("The Newspaper *al-Ahram*: Its History and Technique"). Cairo: Muassasat Sijill al-Arab, 1964.

Awad, Louis. *Tarikh al-fikr al-misri al-hadith min asr Isma'il ila thawrat 1919* ("History of Modern Egyptian Thought from the Age of Isma'il to the 1919 Revolution"). Cairo: General Egyptian Book Organization, 1980.

Booth, Marilyn. "Colloquial Arabic Poetry, Politics, and the Press in Modern Egypt," *International Journal of Middle East Studies* 24 (1992): 419–440.

Boyd, Douglas A. *Broadcasting in the Arab World: A Survey of the Electronic Media and Television in the Middle East.* 2d ed. Ames: Iowa State University Press, 1993.

Crabbs, Jack. *The Writing of History in Nineteenth Century Egypt: A Study in National Transformation.* Detroit: Wayne State University Press, 1984.

Egger, Vernon. *A Fabian in Egypt: Salama Musa and the Rise of the Professional Middle Class in Egypt, 1909–1939.* Lanham, MD: University Press of America, 1986.

Hourani, Albert. *Arabic Thought in the Liberal Age, 1798–1939.* 2d ed. New York and Cambridge: Cambridge University Press, 1983.

Imara, Muhammad. *al-Jami'a al-islamiyya wa al-fikra al-qawmiyya inda Mustafa Kamil* ("Pan-Islam and Nationalism in Mustafa Kamil's Thought"). Damascus: Dar Qutayba, 1989.

Makarius, Raoul. *La Jeunesse intellectuelle d'Égypte au lendemain de la Deuxième Guerre Mondiale.* Paris and The Hague: Mouton, 1960.

Mayer, Thomas. *The Changing Past: Egyptian Historiography of the Urabi Revolt, 1882–1983.* Gainesville: University Presses of Florida, 1988.

Nasir, Munir K. *Press, Politics, and Power: Egypt's Heikal and "al-Ahram."* Ames: Iowa State University Press, 1979.

Reid, Donald Malcolm. "The Egyptian Geographical Society: From Foreign Layman's Society to Indigenous Professional Association," *Poetics Today* 14 (1993): 539–572.

Rejwan, Nissim. *Nasserist Ideology: Its Exponents and Critics.* New York and Toronto: John Wiley and Sons; Jerusalem: Israel Universities Press, 1974.

Ridwan, Abu al-Futuh Ahmad. *Tarikh Matba'at Bulaq* ("History of the Bulaq Press"). Cairo: al-Matba'a al-Amiriyya, 1953.

Rugh, William A. *The Arab Press.* 2d ed. Syracuse: Syracuse University Press, 1987.

Safran, Nadav. *Egypt in Search of Political Community.* Cambridge: Harvard University Press, 1961.

al-Sayyid-Marsot, Afaf Lutfi. "The Cartoon in Egypt," *Comparative Studies in Society and History* 13 (1971).

________. "Egyptian Historical Research and Writing on Egypt in the 20th Century," *Middle East Studies Association Bulletin* 7, 2 (May 1973): 1–15.

Shamir, Shimon, ed. *Self-Views in Historical Perspective in Egypt and Israel.* Tel Aviv: Tel-Aviv University, 1981.

Islam in Modern Egypt

Adams, C. C. *Islam and Modernism in Egypt.* London: Oxford University Press, 1933; New York: Russell and Russell, 1968.

Ajami, Fouad. "In the Pharaoh's Shadow: Religion and Authority in Egypt," in *Islam in the Political Process*, edited by James P. Piscatori. Cambridge: Cambridge University Press, 1983.

Ayyubi, Nazih B.M. *Political Islam: Religion and Politics in the Arab World.* London and New York: Routledge, 1991.

al-Banna, Hasan. *Five Tracts of Hasan al-Banna: A Selection from "Majmu'at Rasa'il Hasan al-Banna."* Translated and annotated by Charles Wendell. Berkeley: University of California Press, 1978.

Berger, Morroe. *Islam in Egypt Today: Social and Political Aspects of Popular Religion.* Cambridge: Cambridge University Press, 1970.

Cantori, Louis J. "Religion and Politics in Egypt," in *Religion and Politics in the Middle East*, edited by Michael Curtis. Boulder, CO: Westview Press, 1981.

Crecelius, Daniel. "Nonideological Responses of the Egyptian Ulama to Modernization," in *Scholars, Saints, and Sufis*, edited by Nikki R. Keddie. Berkeley: University of California Press, 1972.

De Jong, F. "The Sufi Orders in Egypt during the Urabi Insurrection and the British Occupation (1882–1914), *Journal of the American Research Center in Egypt* 21 (1984): 131–139.

________. *Turuq and Turuq-Linked Institutions in Nineteenth Century Egypt*. Leiden: E. J. Brill, 1978.

Dekmejian, R. Hrair. *Islam in Revolution: Fundamentalism in the Arab World*. Syracuse: Syracuse University Press, 1985.

Dessouki, Ali E. Hillal, "The Resurgence of Islamic Organizations in Egypt: An Interpretation," in *Islam and Power*, edited by Alexander S. Cudsi and Ali E. Hillal Dessouki. London: Croom Helm, 1981.

Esposito, John. *Islam and Politics*. 3d ed. Syracuse: Syracuse University Press, 1991.

Farah, Nadia Ramsis. *Religious Strife in Egypt: Crisis and Ideological Conflict in the Seventies*. Montreux, Switzerland: Gordon and Breach Science Publishers, 1986.

Faraj, Muhammad Abd al-Salam. *The Neglected Duty: The Creed of Sadat's Assassins and Islamic Resurgence in the Middle East*. New York: Macmillan, 1986; London: Collier Macmillan Publishers, 1986.

Gibb, H. A. R. *Modern Trends in Islam*. Chicago: University of Chicago Press, 1947.

Gilsenan, Michael. *Saint and Sufi in Modern Egypt: An Essay in the Sociology of Religion*. Oxford: Clarendon Press, 1973.

Haddad, Yvonne Y. "Sayyid Qutb: Ideologue of Islamic Revival," in *Voices of Resurgent Islam*, edited by John L. Esposito. New York: Oxford University Press, 1983.

Harris, Christina Phelps. *Nationalism and Revolution in Egypt: The Role of the Muslim Brotherhood*. The Hague: Mouton, 1964.

Heyworth-Dunne, J. *Religious and Political Trends in Modern Egypt.* Washington, DC: Privately published, 1950.

Ibrahim, Saad Eddin. "Anatomy of Egypt's Militant Islamic Groups," *International Journal of Middle East Studies* 12 (1980): 423–453.

________. "Egypt's Islamic Militants," *MERIP Reports*, no. 103 (February 1982): 5–14.

Kedourie, Elie. *Afghani and Abduh.* London: Frank Cass, 1966.

Kepel, Giles. *Muslim Extremism in Egypt: The Prophet and the Pharaoh.* Translated by Jon Rothschild. 2d ed. Berkeley and Los Angeles: University of California Press, 1993.

Kerr, Malcolm H. *Islamic Reform: The Political and Legal Theories of Muhammad Abduh and Rashid Rida.* London and Berkeley: University of California Press, 1966.

Mitchell, Richard D. *The Society of the Muslim Brothers.* London: Oxford University Press, 1969.

Rubin, Barry. *Fundamentalism in Egyptian Politics.* London: I. B. Tauris, 1990.

al-Sayyid-Marsot, Afaf Lutfi. "The Beginnings of Modernization among the Rectors of al-Azhar, 1798–1879," in *The Beginnings of Modernization in the Middle East*, edited by William R. Polk and Richard L. Chambers. Chicago: University of Chicago Press, 1968.

________. "The Ulama of Cairo in the Eighteenth and Nineteenth Centuries," in *Scholars, Saints, and Sufis*, edited by Nikki R. Keddie. Berkeley: University of California Press, 1971.

Von Grunebaum, Gustave. *Modern Islam: The Search for Cultural Identity.* Berkeley and Los Angeles: University of California Press, 1962.

History of Education

Abd al-Karim, Ahmad Izzat. *Tarikh al-ta'lim fi asr Muhammad Ali* (History of Education in the Muhammad Ali Era). Cairo: Maktabat al-Nahda al-Misriyya, 1938.

________. *Tarikh al-ta'lim fi Misr min nihayat hukm Muhammad Ali ila awail hukm Tawfiq, 1848–1882* (History of Education in Egypt from the End of Muhammad Ali's Rule to the Beginning of Tawfiq's Reign, 1848–1882). Cairo: Matba'at al-Nasr, 1945.

Aroian, Lois A. *The Nationalization of Arabic and Islamic Education in Egypt: Dar al-Ulum and al-Azhar.* Cairo: American University in Cairo Press, 1983.

Ayyubi, Nazih. *Siyasat al-ta'lim fi Misr* ("Education Policy in Egypt"). Cairo: Center for Political and Strategic Studies, 1978.

Cochran, Judith. *Education in Egypt.* London: Croom Helm, 1986.

Dodge, Bayard. *Al-Azhar: A Millennium of Muslim Learning.* Washington, DC: Middle East Institute, 1961.

Eccel, A. Chris. *Egypt, Islam, and Social Change: al-Azhar in Conflict and Accommodation.* Berlin: Klaus Schwarz Verlag, 1984.

Heyworth-Dunne, J. *An Introduction to the History of Education in Modern Egypt.* London: Luzac, 1939; London: Frank Cass, 1968.

Murphy, Lawrence R. *The American University in Cairo, 1919–1987.* Cairo: American University in Cairo Press, 1987.

Radwan, Abu al-Futouh Ahmad. *Old and New Forces in Egyptian Education.* New York: Columbia University Teachers College, 1951.

Reid, Donald M. *Cairo University and the Making of Modern Egypt.* Cambridge: Cambridge University Press, 1990.

________. "Turn-of-the-Century Egyptian School Days," *Comparative Education Review* 27 (1983): 374–393.

Steppat, Fritz. "National Education Projects in Egypt before the British Occupation," in *The Beginnings of Modernization in the Middle East*, edited by William R. Polk and Richard L. Chambers. Chicago: University of Chicago Press, 1968.

Economic and Social History

Abdel-Fadil, Mahmoud. *The Political Economy of Nasserism: A Study in Employment and Income Distribution Policies in Urban Egypt, 1952–72*. Cambridge: Cambridge University Press, 1980.

Abdel-Khalek, Gouda, and Robert Tignor, eds. *The Political Economy of Income Distribution in Egypt*. New York: Holmes and Meier, 1982.

Abu-Lughod, Janet L. *Cairo: 1001 Years of the City Victorious*. Princeton: Princeton University Press, 1971.

Adams, Richard H., Jr. *Development and Social Change in Rural Egypt*. Syracuse: Syracuse University Press, 1986.

Amin, Samir [Hassan Riyad]. *L'Égypte nassérienne*. Paris: Éditions de Minuit, 1964.

Amir, Ibrahim. *al-Ard wa al-fallah: al-Masala al-zira'iyya fi Misr* ("Land and the Peasant: The Agricultural Question in Egypt"). Cairo: Matba'at al-Dar al-Misri, 1958.

Baer, Gabriel. *The Egyptian Guilds in Modern Times*. Jerusalem: Israel Oriental Society, 1964.

________. *Studies in the Social History of Modern Egypt*. Chicago: University of Chicago Press, 1969.

Beinin, Joel, and Zachary Lockman. *Workers on the Nile*. Princeton: Princeton University Press, 1987.

Benedick, Richard Elliot. "The High Dam and the Transformation of the Nile," *Middle East Journal* 33 (1979): 119–144.

Berque, Jacques. "The Establishment of a Colonial Economy," in *The Beginnings of Modernization in the Middle East*, edited by William

R. Polk and Richard L. Chambers. Chicago: University of Chicago Press, 1968.

________. *Histoire sociale d'un village égyptien au XXème siècle*. Paris and The Hague: Mouton, 1957.

Bianchi, Robert. *Unruly Corporatism: Associational Life in Twentieth-Century Egypt*. New York: Oxford University Press, 1989.

Birks, J. S., and C. A. Sinclair. *International Migration and Development in the Arab Region*, Geneva: International Labour Office, 1980.

Blackman, Winifred. *The Fellahin of Upper Egypt*. London: George G. Harrap, 1927.

Brinton, Jasper Yeates. *The Mixed Courts of Egypt*. 2d ed. New Haven and London: Yale University Press, 1968.

Brown, Nathan J. *Peasant Politics in Modern Egypt: The Struggle Against the State*. New Haven and London: Yale University Press, 1990.

________. "The Precarious Life and Slow Death of the Mixed Courts of Egypt," *International Journal of Middle East Studies* 25 (1993): 33–52.

Denoeux, Guilain. *Urban Unrest in the Middle East: A Comparative Study of Informal Networks in Egypt, Iran, and Lebanon*. Albany: State University of New York Press, 1993.

al-Disuqi, Asim. *Kibar mallak al-aradi al-zira'iyya wa dawruhum fi al-mujtama' al-misri (1914–1952)* ("Large Agricultural Landowners and Their Role in Egyptian Society, 1914–1952"). Cairo: Dar al-Thaqafa al-Jadida, 1975.

Dunn, Michael C. "Egypt: From Domestic Needs to Export Market," in *The Implications of Third World Military Industrialization*, edited by James Everett Katz. Lexington, MA: Lexington Books, 1986.

Fakhouri, Hani. *Kafr el-Elow: Continuity and Change in an Egyptian Community*. 2d ed. Prospect Heights, IL: Waveland Press, 1987.

Fakhry, Ahmed. *Siwa Oasis.* 2d ed. Cairo: American University in Cairo Press, 1990.

Fathy, Hassan. *Architecture for the Poor: An Experiment in Rural Egypt.* Chicago: University of Chicago Press, 1973.

Gallagher, Nancy Elizabeth. *Egypt's Other Wars: Epidemics and the Politics of Public Health.* Syracuse: Syracuse University Press, 1990.

al-Gritli, Ali. *Khamsa wa ishrun aman: dirasa tahliliyya li al-siyasat al-iqtisadiyya fi Misr* ("Twenty-five Years: An Analytical Study of Economic Policies in Egypt"). Cairo: General Egyptian Book Organization, 1977.

Harbison, Frederick, and Ibrahim Abdelkader Ibrahim. *Human Resources for Egyptian Enterprise.* New York: McGraw-Hill, 1958.

Harik, Iliya F. *The Political Mobilization of Peasants: A Study of an Egyptian Community.* Bloomington: Indiana University Press, 1974.

Hill, Enid. *Mahkama! Studies in the Egyptian Legal System.* London: Ithaca Press, 1979.

Hopkins, Nicholas S. *Agrarian Transformation in Egypt.* Boulder, CO: Westview Press, 1987.

Howell, P. P., and Allan, J. A., eds. *The Nile: Resource Evaluation, Resource Management, Hydropolitics, and Legal Issues.* London: School of Oriental and African Studies, 1990.

Hurst, H. E. *The Nile.* London: Constable and Co., 1951.

Ikram, Khalid. *Egypt: Economic Management in a Period of Transition.* Baltimore: The Johns Hopkins University Press, 1981.

Issawi, Charles. "Asymmetrical Development and Transport in Egypt," in *The Beginnings of Modernization in the Middle East*, edited by William R. Polk and Richard L. Chambers. Chicago: University of Chicago Press, 1968.

________. *Egypt in Revolution: An Economic Analysis.* London: Oxford University Press, 1963.

Kerr, Malcolm H., and El Sayed Yassin, eds. *Rich and Poor States in the Middle East: Egypt and the New Arab Order.* Boulder, CO: Westview Press, 1982.

Kuhnke, LaVerne. *Lives at Risk: Public Health in Nineteenth Century Egypt.* Berkeley: University of California Press, 1990.

Mabro, Robert. *The Egyptian Economy, 1952–1972.* London: Oxford University Press, 1974.

________. *The Industrialization of Egypt, 1939–1973: Policy and Performance.* Oxford: Clarendon Press, 1976.

Mabro, Robert, and Patrick O'Brien. "Structural Changes in the Egyptian Economy, 1937–1965," in *Studies in the Economic History of the Middle East*, edited by M. A. Cook. London: Oxford University Press, 1970.

el-Mehairy, Theresa. *Medical Doctors: A Study of Role Concept and Job Satisfaction–The Egyptian Case.* Leiden: E. J. Brill, 1984.

Moore, Clement Henry. *Images of Development: Egyptian Engineers in Search of Industry.* Cambridge: Massachusetts Institute of Technology Press, 1980.

Nelson, Nina. *Shepheard's Hotel.* New York: Macmillan Co., 1961.

O'Brien, Patrick. *The Revolution in Egypt's Economic System: From Private Enterprise to Socialism.* London: Oxford University Press, 1966.

Oweiss, Ibrahim M., ed. *The Political Economy of Contemporary Egypt.* Washington, DC: Center for Contemporary Arab Studies, Georgetown University, 1990.

Owen, Roger. *Cotton and the Egyptian Economy, 1820–1914.* Oxford: Clarendon Press, 1969.

Radwan, Samir, and Eddy Lee. *Agrarian Change in Egypt.* London: Croom Helm, 1986.

Reid, Donald M. *Lawyers and Politics in the Arab World, 1880–1960.* Minneapolis: Bibliotheca Islamica, 1981.

Reimer, Michael. "Colonial Bridgehead: Social and Spatial Change in Alexandria, 1850–1882," *International Journal of Middle East Studies* 20 (1988): 531–553.

Richards, Alan. *Egypt's Agricultural Development, 1800–1980.* Boulder, CO: Westview Press, 1982.

Rivlin, Helen A. B. *The Agricultural Policy of Muhammad Ali in Egypt.* Cambridge: Harvard University Press, 1961.

Rivlin, Paul. *The Dynamics of Economic Policy Making in Egypt.* New York: Praeger, 1985.

Saab, Gabriel. *The Egyptian Agrarian Reform, 1952–1962.* London: Oxford University Press, 1967.

Sadowski, Yahya M. *Political Vegetables? Businessman and Bureaucrat in the Development of Egyptian Agriculture.* Washington, DC: Brookings Institution, 1991.

Selim, Mohammad El-Sayed. "Egypt," in *Arms Production in Developing Countries: An Analysis of Decision Making*, edited by James Everett Katz. Lexington, MA: Lexington Books, 1984.

Sonbol, Amira El Azhary. *The Creation of a Medical Profession in Egypt, 1800–1922.* Syracuse: Syracuse University Press, 1991.

Van Nieuwenhuijze, C. A., ed. *Commoners, Climbers, and Notables.* Leiden: E. J. Brill, 1977.

Voll, Sarah P. "Egyptian Land Reclamation since the Revolution," *Middle East Journal* 34 (1980): 127–148.

Waterbury, John. *The Egypt of Nasser and Sadat: The Political Economy of Two Regimes.* Princeton: Princeton University Press, 1983.

________. *Hydropolitics of the Nile Valley.* Syracuse: Syracuse University Press, 1979.

Weinbaum, Marvin G. *Egypt and the Politics of U.S. Economic Aid.* Boulder, CO: Westview Press, 1986.

Wheelock, Keith. *Nasser's New Egypt: A Critical Analysis.* London: Stevens and Sons; New York: Praeger, 1960.

White, Gilbert F. "The Environmental Effects of the High Dam at Aswan," *Environment* 30, no. 7 (1 September 1988): 4–7.

Wikan, Unni. *Life among the Poor in Cairo.* London: Tavistock Publications, 1980.

Winter, Michael. "The *Ashraf* and *Niqabat al-Ashraf* in Egypt in Ottoman and Modern Times," *Asian and African Studies* 19 (1985): 17–41.

Zaalouk, Malak. *Power, Class, and Foreign Capital in Egypt: The Rise of the New Bourgeoisie.* London: Zed Books, 1989.

Women's and Family History

Ahmed, Leila. "Feminism and Feminist Movements in the Middle East," in *Women and Islam*, edited by Azizah al-Hibri. Oxford: Pergamon Press, 1982.

Atiya, Nayra. *Khul-Khaal: Five Egyptian Women Tell Their Stories.* Syracuse: Syracuse University Press, 1984.

Badran, Margot. "Competing Agendas: Feminists, Islam, and the State in 19th and 20th Century Egypt," in *Women, Islam, and the State*, edited by Denis Kandiyoti. Philadelphia: Temple University Press, 1991.

________. "Independent Women: More than a Century of Feminism in Egypt," in *Arab Women: Old Boundaries, New Frontiers*, edited by Judith E. Tucker. Bloomington and Indianapolis: Indiana University Press, 1993.

________. "The Origins of Feminism in Egypt," in *Current Issues in Women's History*, edited by Arina Angerman et al. London: Routledge, 1989.

Badran, Margot, and Miriam Cooke, eds. *Opening the Gates: A Century of Arab Feminist Writing.* Bloomington: Indiana University Press, 1990.

Baron, Beth. "The Making and Breaking of Marital Bonds in Modern Egypt," in *Women in Middle Eastern History*, edited by Nikki R. Keddie and Beth Baron. New Haven: Yale University Press, 1991.

________. "Mothers, Morality, and Nationalism in Pre-1919 Egypt," in *The Origins of Arab Nationalism*, edited by Rashid Khalidi et al. New York: Columbia University Press, 1991.

________. *The Women's Awakening in Egypt: Culture, Society, and the Press.* New Haven and London: Yale University Press, 1994.

Botman, Selma. "Women's Participation in Radical Egyptian Politics, 1939–1952," in *Women in the Middle East*, edited by Selma Botman. London: Zed Books, 1987.

Cannon, Byron D. "Nineteenth Century Arabic Writings on Women and Society: The Interim Role of the Masonic Press in Cairo–(*al-Lataif*, 1885–1895)," *International Journal of Middle East Studies* 17 (1985): 463–484.

Cole, Juan Ricardo. "Feminism, Class, and Islam in Turn-of-the-Century Egypt," *International Journal of Middle East Studies* 13 (1981): 387–407.

Early, Evelyn. *Baladi Women of Cairo: Playing with an Egg and a Stone.* Boulder, CO: Lynne Rienner Publishers, 1993.

Fernea, Elizabeth Warnock, ed. *Women and the Family in the Middle East: New Voices of Change.* Austin: University of Texas Press, 1985.

Haddad, Yvonne Yazbeck. "Islam, Women, and Revolution in Twentieth-Century Arab Thought," in *Women, Religion, and Social Change*, edited by Yvonne Yazbeck Haddad and Ellison Banks Findly. Albany: State University of New York Press, 1985.

Hussein, Aziza. "Recently Approved Amendments to Egypt's Law on Personal Status," in *Religion and Politics in the Middle East*, edited by Michael Curtis. Boulder, CO: Westview Press, 1981.

Ibrahim, Barbara Lethem. "Family Strategies: A Perspective of Women's Entry to the Labor Force of Egypt," in *Arab Society: Social Science Perspectives*, edited by Nicholas S. Hopkins. Cairo: American University in Cairo Press, 1985.

MacLeod, Aelene Elowe. *Accommodating Protest: Working Women, the New Veiling, and Change in Cairo.* New York: Columbia University Press, 1991.

Philipp, Thomas. "Feminism and Nationalist Politics in Egypt," in *Women in the Muslim World*, edited by Lois Beck and Nikki Keddie. Cambridge: Harvard University Press, 1978.

Rugh, Andrea B. *Family in Contemporary Egypt.* Syracuse: Syracuse University Press, 1984.

________. *Reveal and Conceal: Dress in Contemporary Egypt.* Syracuse: Syracuse University Press, 1986.

el-Saadawi, Nawal. *The Hidden Face of Eve: Women in the Arab World.* London: Zed Books, 1980.

al-Sa'id, Aminah. "The Arab Woman and the Challenge of Society," in *Middle Eastern Muslim Women Speak*, edited by Elizabeth Warnock Fernea and Basima Qattan Bezirgan. Austin and London: University of Texas Press, 1977.

al-Sayyid-Marsot, Afaf Lutfi. "The Revolutionary Gentlewoman in Egypt," in *Women in the Muslim World*, edited by Lois Beck and Nikki Keddie. Cambridge: Harvard University Press, 1978.

Springborg, Robert. *Family Power and Politics in Egypt: Sayed Bey Marei–His Clan, Clients, and Cohorts.* Philadelphia: University of Pennsylvania Press, 1982.

Stowasser, Barbara F. "Women's Issues in Modern Islamic Thought," in *Arab Women: Old Boundaries, New Frontiers*, edited by Judith E. Tucker. Bloomington and Indianapolis: Indiana University Press, 1993.

Sullivan, Earl L. *Women in Egyptian Public Life.* Syracuse: Syracuse University Press, 1986.

Toubia, Nahid, ed. *Women of the Arab World, the Coming Challenge: Papers of the Arab Women's Solidarity Association Conference.* Translated by Nahed El Gamal. London: Zed Books, 1988.

Tucker, Judith E. *Women in Nineteenth-Century Egypt.* Cambridge: Cambridge University Press, 1985.

Williams, John A. "Veiling in Egypt as a Political and Social Phenonenon," in *Islam and Development*, edited by John Esposito. Syracuse: Syracuse University Press, 1980.

Zenié-Ziegler, Wédad. *In Search of Shadows: Conversations with Egyptian Women.* London: Zed Books, 1988.

Zuhur, Sherifa. *Revealing Reveiling: Islamist Gender Ideology in Contemporary Egypt.* Albany: State University of New York Press, 1992.

Literature and the Arts

Abdel-Wahab, Farouk. *Modern Egyptian Drama.* Minneapolis and Chicago: Bibliotheca Islamica, 1974.

Allen, Roger M. A. *The Arabic Novel: An Historical and Critical Introduction.* Manchester, UK: University of Manchester, 1982.

Ammoun, Denise. *Crafts of Egypt.* Cairo: American University in Cairo Press, 1991.

Badawi, M. M. *A Critical Introduction to Modern Arabic Poetry.* Cambridge: Cambridge University Press, 1975.

________. *Early Arabic Drama.* Cambridge: Cambridge University Press, 1988.

________. *Modern Arabic Drama in Egypt.* Cambridge: Cambridge University Press, 1987.

Brugman, J. *An Introduction to the History of Modern Arabic Literature in Egypt.* Leiden: E. J. Brill, 1984.

Danielson, Virginia L. "Artists and Entrepreneurs: Female Singers in Cairo during the 1920s," in *Women in Middle Eastern History: Shifting Boundaries in Sex and Gender*, edited by Nikki R. Keddie and Beth Baron. New Haven: Yale University Press, 1991.

Egyptian Museum, Cairo. New York: *Newsweek* Great Museums of the World, 1969.

Forman, W. and B., and Ramses Wissa Wassef. *Tapestries from Egypt, Woven by the Children of Harrania*. Translated by Jean Layton. London: Paul Hamlyn, 1961.

al-Hakim, Tawfiq. *The Maze of Justice*. Translated by A. S. Eban. London: Harvell Press, 1947; Austin: University of Texas Press, 1989.

Karnouk, Liliane. *Modern Egyptian Art: The Emergence of a National Style*. Cairo: American University in Cairo Press, 1988.

Khouri, Mounah A. *Poetry and the Making of Modern Egypt*. Leiden: E. J. Brill, 1971.

Landau, Jacob M. *Studies in the Arab Theater and Cinema*. Philadelphia: University of Pennsylvania Press, 1958.

Mahfouz, Naguib [Mahfuz, Najib]. *Children of Gebelawi*. Translated by Philip Stewart. Washington, DC: Three Continents Press, 1988.

________. *Fountain and Tomb*. Translated by Soad Sobhi, Essam Fattouh, and James Kenneson. Washington, DC: Three Continents Press, 1988.

________. *Midaq Alley*. Translated by Trevor Le Gassick. Beirut: Khayat's, 1966.

________. *Miramar*. Translated by Fatma Moussa-Mahmoud. Washington, DC: Three Continents Press, 1983.

________. *Palace of Desire*. Translated by William Maynard Hutchins, Lorne M. Kenny, and Olive E. Kenny. New York: Doubleday, 1991.

________. *Palace Walk*. Translated by William Maynard Hutchins and Olive E. Kenny. New York: Doubleday, 1990.

________. *Sugar Street*. Translated by William Maynard Hutchins and Angele Botros Samaan. New York: Doubleday, 1992.

Peled, Mattityahu. *Religion, My Own: The Literary Works of Najib Mahfuz*. New Brunswick, NJ: Transaction Books, 1983.

Prisse d'Avennes, Achille Constant Theodore Emile. *Arab Art as Seen through the Monuments from the 7th Century to the 18th*. Translated by J. I. Erythraspis. London: al-Saqi, 1983.

Said, Hamed, ed. *Contemporary Art in Egypt*. Zagreb: Jugoslavija Publishing House (for the U.A.R. Ministry of Culture and National Guidance), 1964.

Sakkut, Hamdi. *The Egyptian Novel, 1913–1952*. Cairo: American University in Cairo Press, 1971.

El-Shamy, Hasan M., ed. *Folktales of Egypt*. Chicago and London: University of Chicago Press, 1980.

Sharkawi, A.R. [al-Sharqawi, Abd al-Rahman]. *Egyptian Earth*. Translated by Desmond Stewart. London: Heinemann, 1962.

Somekh, Sasson. *The Changing Rhythm: A Study of Najib Mahfuz's Novels*. Leiden: E. J. Brill, 1973.

Ethnic Groups, Minorities, and Foreign Communities

Abu-Lughod, Lila. *Veiled Sentiments: Honor and Poetry in a Bedouin Society*. Berkeley: University of California Press, 1986.

Atiya, Aziz S. *A History of Eastern Christianity*. Millwood, NY: Kraus Reprint, 1980.

Behrens-Abouseif, Doris. *Die Kopten in der ägyptischen Gesellschaft von der Mitte 19 Jahrhunderts bis 1923*. Freiburg-im-Breisgau, West Germany: Klaus Schwarz, 1972.

Brugger, Suzanne. *Australians and Egypt, 1914–1919.* Melbourne: Melbourne University Press, 1980.

Carré, Jean Marie. *Voyageurs et écrivains français en Égypte.* 2d ed. 2 vols. Cairo: Institut Français d'Archéologie Orientale du Caire, 1956.

Carter, B. L. *The Copts in Egyptian Politics.* London: Croom Helm, 1986.

Clément, R. *Les Français d'Égypte aux XVIIe et XVIIIe siècles.* Cairo: Institut Français d'Archéologie Orientale du Caire, 1960.

Cooper, Artemis. *Cairo in the War, 1939–1945.* London: Hamish Hamilton, 1989.

Fahim, Hussein M. *Egyptian Nubians: Resettlement and Years of Coping.* Salt Lake City: University of Utah Press, 1983.

Fernea, Robert A. *The Nubians in Egypt: Peaceful People.* Austin: University of Texas Press, 1973.

Geiser, Peter. *The Egyptian Nubians: A Study in Social Symbiosis.* Cairo: American University in Cairo Press, 1980.

Haddad, Robert. *Syrian Christians in Muslim Society: An Interpretation.* Princeton: Princeton University Press, 1970.

Hobbs, Joseph J. *Bedouin Life in the Egyptian Wilderness.* Austin: University of Texas Press, 1989.

Hopwood, Derek. *Tales of Empire: The British in the Middle East.* London: I. B. Tauris, 1989.

Hourani, A. H. *Minorities in the Arab World.* London: Oxford University Press, 1947.

Kitroeff, Alexander. *The Greeks in Egypt, 1919–1937.* London: Ithaca Press, 1988.

Krämer, Gudrun. *The Jews in Modern Egypt, 1914–1952.* Seattle: University of Washington Press, 1989.

Landau, Jacob M. *Jews, Arabs, and Turks: Selected Essays.* Jeruslem: Magnes Press, 1993.

________. *Jews in Nineteenth Century Egypt.* New York: New York University Press, 1969.

Laskier, Michael. *The Jews of Egypt, 1920–1970.* New York: New York University Press, 1991.

Mansfield, Peter. *The British in Egypt.* London: Weidenfeld and Nicolson, 1971.

Meinardus, Otto F. A. *Christian Egypt: Ancient and Modern.* Cairo: Cahiers d'Histoire Égyptienne, 1965.

Mikhail, Kyriakos. *Copts and Moslems under British Control.* London: Smith Elder, 1911; Port Washington, NY: Kennikat Press, 1971.

Philipp, Thomas. *The Syrians in Egypt, 1725–1975.* Stuttgart, West Germany: Steiner, 1985.

Saad el Din, Mursi, and John Cromer. *Under Egypt's Spell: The Influence of Egypt on Writers in English from the 18th Century.* London: Bellew Publishing, 1991.

Sattin, Anthony. *Lifting the Veil: British Society in Egypt, 1768–1956.* London: J. M. Dent & Sons, 1988.

Shamir, Shimon, ed. *The Jews of Egypt: A Mediterranean Society in Modern Times.* Boulder, CO: Westview Press, 1988.

Wakin, Edward. *A Lonely Minority: The Modern Story of Egypt's Copts.* New York: Morrow, 1963.

Biographies, Memoirs, and Diaries

Abbas Hilmi. *Ahdi: mudhakkirat Abbas Hilmi al-Thani, khidiwi Misr al-akhir, 1892–1914* ("My Covenant: The Memoirs of Abbas Hilmi II, Egypt's Last Khedive, 1892–1914"). Translated by Jalal Yahya. Cairo: Dar al-Shuruq, 1993.

Ahmed, Leila. *Edward W. Lane: A Study of his Life and Work and of British Ideas of the Middle East in the Nineteenth Century.* London and New York: Longman, 1978.

Amin, Ahmad. *My Life: The Autobiography of an Egyptian Scholar, Writer, and Intellectual Leader.* Introduced and translated by Issa J. Boullatta. Leiden: E. J. Brill, 1978.

Amin, Osman. *Muhammad 'Abduh.* Translated by Charles Wendell. Washington, DC: American Council of Learned Societies, 1953.

al-Aqqad, Abbas Mahmud. *Sa'd Zaghlul: sira wa tahiyya* ("Sa'd Zaghlul: A Biography and a Tribute"). Cairo: Hijazi, 1936; Beirut: Dar al Shuruq, 1975; Cairo: Dar al-Hilal, 1988.

Badeau, John S. *The Middle East Remembered.* Washington, DC: Middle East Institute, 1983.

al-Baghdadi, Abd al-Latif. *Mudhakkirat* ("Memoirs"). 2 vols. Cairo: al-Maktab al-Misri al-Hadith, 1977.

al-Banna, Hasan. *Memoirs of Hasan al-Banna Shaheed (1906–1949).* Translated by M. N. Shaikh. Karachi: International Islamic Publishers, 1981.

Blunt, Wilfrid Scawen. *My Diaries: Being a Personal Narrative of Events in 1888–1914.* One-volume edition. London: Secker, 1932.

Bowman, Humphrey. *Middle-East Window.* London: Longmans, Green, and Co., 1942.

Charmley, John. *Lord Lloyd and the Decline of the British Empire.* London: Weidenfeld and Nicolson, 1988.

Coles, Pasha. *Recollections and Reflections.* London: Saint Catherine Press, 1918.

Farid, Muhammad. *The Memoirs and Diaries of Muhammad Farid: An Egyptian Nationalist Leader (1868–1919).* Introduced, translated, and annotated by Arthur Goldschmidt, Jr. San Francisco: Mellen Research University Press, 1992.

Fawzi, Mahmoud. *Suez 1956: An Egyptian Perspective.* London: Shorouk International, 1986.

El-Gamasy, Mohamed Abdel Ghany [al-Jamasi, Muhammad Abd al-Ghani]. *The October War: Memoirs of Field Marshall El-Gamasy of Egypt.* Translated by Gillian Potter et al. Cairo: American University in Cairo Press, 1993.

Gendzier, Irene L. *The Practical Visions of Ya'qub Sanu'.* Cambridge: Harvard University Press, 1966.

Grafftey-Smith, Lawrence. *Bright Levant.* London: John Murray, 1970.

Hadidi, Ali. *Abdallah Nadim: khatib al-wataniyya* ("Abdallah Nadim: Orator of Nationalism"). Cairo: al-Muassasa al-Misriyya, 1961(?).

Haykal, Muhammad Husayn. *Mudhakkirati fi al-siyasa al-misriyya* ("My Memories of Egyptian Politics"). 3 vols. Cairo: Maktabat al-Nahda al-Misriyya, 1951–75.

Hourani, Albert. "Wilfrid Scawen Blunt and the Revival of the East," in *Europe and the Middle East*, edited by Albert Hourani. Berkeley and Los Angeles: University of California Press, 1980.

Husayn, Taha. *An Egyptian Childhood.* Translated by E. H. Paxton. London: Routledge, 1932.

________. *A Passage to France.* Translated by Kenneth Cragg. Leiden: E. J. Brill, 1976.

________. *The Stream of Days: A Student at the Azhar.* Translated by Hilary Wayment. 2d ed. London: Longman's, Green and Co., 1948.

al-Jami'i, Abd al-Mun'im. *Abdallah al-Nadim wa dawruhu fi al-haraka al-siyasiyya wa al-ijtima'iyya* ("Abdallah Nadim and His Role in the Political and Social Movement"). Cairo: Matba'at al-Jablawi, 1980.

Keddie, Nikki R. *Sayyid Jamal al-Din "al-Afghani": A Political Biography.* Berkeley: University of California Press, 1972.

Khadduri, Majid. *Arab Contemporaries: The Role of Personalities in Politics.* Baltimore and London: The Johns Hopkins University Press, 1973.

Killearn, Miles Lampson, Baron. *The Killearn Diaries, 1934–1946.* Edited and introduced by Trefor E. Evans. London: Sidgwick and Jackson, 1972.

Lashin, Abd al-Khaliq Muhammad. *Sa'd Zaghlul wa dawruhu fi al-siyasa al-misriyya hatta sanat 1914* ("Sa'd Zaghlul and His Role in Egyptian Politics up to 1914"). Cairo: Dar al-Ma'arif, 1970.

________. *Sa'd Zaghlul wa dawruhu fi al-siyasa al-misriyya* ("Sa'd Zaghlul and His Role in Egyptian Politics from 1914"). Beirut: Dar al-Awda, 1975.

Magnus, Philip. *Kitchener: Portrait of an Imperialist.* London: John Murray; New York: E. P. Dutton and Co., 1959.

Malti-Douglas, Fedwa. *Blindness and Autobiography: "Al-Ayyam" of Taha Husayn.* Princeton: Princeton University Press, 1988.

Mar'i, Sayyid. *Awraq siyasiyya* ("Political Papers"). 3 vols. Cairo: al-Maktab al-Misri al-Hadith, 1978.

McPherson, Joseph. *The Man Who Loved Egypt: Bimbashi McPherson.* Edited by Barry Carman and John McPherson. London: British Broadcasting Corporation, 1983.

Mellini, Peter. *Sir Eldon Gorst: The Overshadowed Proconsul.* Stanford: Hoover Institution Press, 1977.

Mubarak, Ali. *'Ali Mubarak und seine Ĥitat: Kommentierte Übersetzung der Autobiographie und Werkbesprechung.* Translated by Stephen Fliedner. Berlin: Klaus Schwarz Verlag, 1990.

Musa, Salama. *The Education of Salama Musa.* Translated by L. O. Schuman. Leiden: E. J. Brill, 1961.

al-Nadim, Abdallah. *al-Mudhakkirat al-siyasiyya li Abdallah al-Nadim* ("The Political Memoirs of Abdallah Nadim"). Edited by Muhammad Ahmad Khalafallah. Cairo: Anglo-Egyptian Bookshop, 1956.

Najib, Muhammad. *Kuntu raisan li-Misr* ("I Was President of Egypt"). Cairo: al-Maktab al-Misri al-Hadith, 1984.

Nasser, Gamal Abdel [al-Nasir, Jamal Abd]. *Egypt's Liberation: The Philosophy of the Revolution.* Washington, DC: Public Affairs Press, 1955; Buffalo, NY: Smith, Keynes and Marshall, 1979.

________. "Nasser's Memoirs of the First Palestine War," translated and annotated by Walid Khalidi, *Journal of Palestine Studies* II, 2 (Winter 1973): 3–32.

Neguib, Mohammad. *Egypt's Destiny: A Personal Statement.* Garden City, NY: Doubleday, 1955.

Nelson, Cynthia. "Biography and Women's History: On Interpreting Doria Shafik," in *Women in Middle Eastern History*, edited by Nikki R. Keddie and Beth Baron. New Haven: Yale University Press, 1991.

Nightingale, Florence. *Letters from Egypt: A Journey on the Nile, 1849-1850.* Edited by Anthony Sattin. New York: Weidenfeld and Nicolson, 1987.

Nubar. *Les Mémoires de Nubar Pacha.* Annotated by Mirrit Butros Ghali. Beirut: Librairie du Liban, 1983.

Perrault, Giles. *A Man Apart: The Life of Henri Curiel.* London: Zed Books, 1987.

Philipp, Thomas. *Gurgi Zaydan: His Life and Thought.* Wiesbaden, West Germany: Steiner, 1979.

Qunaybir, Salim Abd al-Nabi. *al-Ittijahat al-siyasiyya wa al-fikriyya wa al-ijtima'iyya fi al-adab al-arabi al-mu'asir: Abd al-Aziz Jawish, 1872–1929* ("Political, Intellectual, and Social Trends in Contemporary Arabic Literature: Abd al-Aziz Jawish, 1872–1929"). Benghazi, Libya: Dar Maktabat al-Andalus, 1968.

al-Rafi'i, Abd al-Rahman. *Mudhakkirati* ("My Memoirs"). Cairo: Dar al-Hilal, 1952.

Reid, Donald M. "Fuad Siraj al-Din and the Egyptian Wafd," *Journal of Contemporary History* 15 (1980): 721–744.

Riad, Mahmoud [Riyad, Mahmud]. *The Struggle for Peace in the Middle East.* New York: Quartet Books, 1981.

Richards, J. M. (Sir James Maude). *Hassan Fathy.* Singapore: Concept Media, 1985.

Royle, Trevor. *The Kitchener Enigma.* London: Michael Joseph, 1985.

Russell, Thomas. *Egyptian Service, 1902–1946.* London: John Murray, 1949.

el-Saadawi, Nawal. *Memoirs from the Women's Prison.* Translated by Marilyn Booth. London: Women's Press, 1986.

________. *Memoirs of a Woman Doctor.* Translated by Catherine Cobham. London: Al Saqi Books, 1988.

al-Sadat, Anwar. *In Search of Destiny: An Autobiography.* New York: Harper & Row, 1978.

________. *Revolt on the Nile.* Translated by Thomas Graham. London: Allan Wingate, 1957.

Sadat, Jehan. *A Woman of Egypt.* New York: Simon & Schuster, 1987.

Said, Laila. *A Bridge through Time: A Memoir.* New York: Summit Books, 1985.

Shaarawi, Huda. *Harem Years: The Memoirs of an Egyptian Feminist (1879–1947).* Translated, edited, and introduced by Margot Badran. London: Virago Press, 1986.

Shafiq, Ahmad. *A'mali ba'da mudhakkirati* ("What I Did after My Memoirs"). Cairo: Matba'at Misr, 1941.

________. *Mudhakkirati fi nisf qarn* ("My Memoirs of Half a Century"). 3 vols. Cairo: Matba'at Misr, 1934–1936.

Sidqi, Isma'il. *Mudhakkirati* ("My Memoirs"). Cairo: Dar al-Hilal, 1950.

Smith, Charles D. *Islam and the Search for Social Order in Modern Egypt: A Biography of Muhammad Husayn Haykal.* Albany: State University of New York Press, 1983.

Storrs, Ronald. *Orientations.* London: Ivor Nicholson and Watson, 1937.

Thompson, Jason. *Sir Gardner Wilkinson and His Circle.* Austin: University of Texas Press, 1992.

Tilmisani, Umar. *Dhikrayat la mudhakkirat* ("Recollections, not Memoirs"). Cairo: Dar al-Tiba'a li al-Nashr al-Islamiyya, 1985.

Tugay, Emine Foat. *Three Centuries: Family Chronicles of Turkey and Egypt.* London and New York: Oxford University Press, 1963.

Umm Kulthum. "The Umm Kulthum Nobody Knows," in *Middle Eastern Muslim Women Speak*, edited by Elizabeth Warnock Fernea and Basima Qattan Bezirgan. Austin and London: University of Texas Press, 1977.

Willcocks, William. *Sixty Years in the East.* Edinburgh and London: William Blackwood & Sons, 1935.

Youssef, Amine. *Independent Egypt.* London: John Murray, 1940.

Zaghlul, Sa'd. *Athar al-za'im Sa'd Zaghlul* ("The Papers of the Leader Sa'd Zaghlul"). Edited by Muhammad Ibrahim al-Hariri. Cairo: Maktabat Madbuli, 1991.

________. *Mudhakkirat Sa'd Zaghlul.* 4 vols. to date. Annotated by Abd al-Azim Ramadan. Cairo: General Egyptian Book Organization, 1987–91.

Guidebooks

Baedeker's Egypt 1929. Reprint. Newton Abbot: David and Charles, 1974.

Blue Guide: Egypt. 2d ed. New York: W. W. Norton, 1988.

Egypt and the Sudan. South Yarra, Victoria, Australia: Lonely Planet Publications, 1987.

Forster, E. M. *Alexandria: A History and a Guide.* Garden City, NY: Doubleday Books, 1961.

Harvard Student Agencies. *Let's Go . . . : Budget Guide to Israel and Egypt.* New York: St. Martin's Press, 1993.

Murray, John. *Handbook for Egypt and the Sudan.* Edited by H. R. Hall. 11th ed. London: E. Stanford, 1907.

Nelson, Nina. *Essential Egypt.* Boston: Little, Brown, 1990.

Parker, Richard B., and Robin Sabin. *A Practical Guide to Islamic Monuments in Cairo.* Cairo: American University in Cairo Press, 1974.

Rodenbeck, John, ed. *Insight Guides: Cairo.* Boston: Houghton Mifflin, 1993.

Russell, Dorothea. *Medieval Cairo and the Monasteries of Wadi Natrun.* London: Weidenfeld and Nicolson, 1962.

Showker, Kay. *Fodor's Egypt.* New York: Fodor's Travel Guides, 1992.

Youssef, Hisham, and John Rodenbeck, eds. *Insight Guides: Egypt.* 3d ed. Boston: Houghton Mifflin, 1993.

Ziock, Hermann. *Lehnert & Landrock's Guide to Egypt.* Translated by H. Ritter and D. Harris. Cairo: Lehnert & Landrock, 1965.

Collective Biographies, Dictionaries, and Encyclopedias

Amin, Ahmad. *Zu'ama al-islah fi al-asr al-hadith* ("Reform Leaders in Modern Times"). Cairo: Maktabat al-Nahda al-Misriyya, 1949.

Atiya, Aziz S., ed. *Coptic Encyclopedia.* 8 vols. New York: Macmillan Press, 1991.

Bunson, Margaret. *The Encyclopedia of Ancient Egypt.* New York: Facts on File, 1991.

Daghir, Yusuf As'ad. *Masadir al-dirasa al-adabiyya* ("Sources for Literary Study"). 3 vols. Beirut: al-Maktaba al-Sharqiyya, 1956–72.

Dawson, Warren R., and Eric P. Uphill. *Who Was Who in Egyptology.* 2d ed. London: Egypt Exploration Society, 1972.

Egypt: A Country Study. 5th ed. Washington, DC: U.S. Government Printing Office, 1991.

Encyclopaedia of Islam. 2d ed. 6 vols. to date. Leiden: E. J. Brill, 1954- .

Fahmi, Zaki. *Safwat al-asr fi tarikh wa rusum akabir al-rijal bi-Misr* ("The Purity of the Age in the History and Pictures of Egypt's Greatest Men"). Cairo: Matba'at al-I'timad, 1926.

Haykal, Muhammad Husayn. *Tarajim misriyya wa gharbiyya* ("Egyptian and Foreign Biographies"). Cairo: Matba'at Misr, 1929.

Husayn, Ahmad. *Mawsu'at tarikh Misr* ("Dictionary of Egyptian History"). 3 vols. Cairo: Dar al-Sha'b, 1978–1979.

Karam, Fuad. *al-Nizarat wa al-wizarat al-misriyya* ("Egyptian Cabinets and Ministries"). Cairo: Maktabat Dar al-Kutub, 1969.

The Middle East and North Africa. 40th edition. London: Europa Publications, 1993.

Mostyn, Trevor, and Albert Hourani, eds. *The Cambridge Encyclopedia of the Middle East and North Africa.* Cambridge: Cambridge University Press, 1988.

Mujahid, Zaki Muhammad. *al-A'lam al-sharqiyya* ("Famous Orientals"). 3 vols. Cairo: al-Matba'a al-Tijariyya, 1949–63.

Reich, Bernard, ed. *Political Leaders of the Contemporary Middle East and North Africa: A Biographical Dictionary.* New York: Greenwood Press, 1990.

Shimoni, Yaacov. *Biographical Dictionary of the Middle East.* New York: Facts on File, 1991.

Taymur, Ahmad. *A'lam al-fikr al-islami fi al-asr al-hadith* ("Famous Islamic Thinkers in Modern Times"). Reprint ed. Cairo: Lajnat Nashr al-Muallafat al-Taymuriyya, 1967.

United States. Library of Congress, Federal Research Division. *Egypt: A Country Study*. Edited by Helen Metz. 5th ed. Washington, DC: U.S. Government Printing Office, 1991.

Who's Who in the Arab World, 1993–94. Beirut: Éditions Publitec, 1993.

Wucher King, Joan. *Historical Dictionary of Egypt*. African Historical Dictionaries, No. 36. Metuchen, NJ, and London: Scarecrow Press, 1984.

Zakhura, Ilyas. *Mirat al-asr fi tarikh wa rusum akabir al-rijal bi-Misr* ("Mirror of the Age in the History and Pictures of Egypt's Greatest Men"). 3 vols. Cairo: Privately printed, 1897–1916.

al-Zirikli, Khayr al-Din. *al-A'lam* ("Famous People"). 4th ed. 8 vols. Beirut: Dar al-Ilm li al-Malayin, 1980.

Bibliographies and Archival Sources

Atiya, George N. *The Contemporary Middle East: A Selective and Annotated Bibliography*. Boston: G. K. Hall, 1975.

Awad, Ramsis. *Mawsu'at al-masrah al-misri: al-bibliyujrafiyya, 1900-1930* ("Encyclopedia of the Egyptian Theater: Bibliography, 1900–1930"). Cairo: General Egyptian Book Organization, 1983.

Cattaui, René. *Le Règne de Mohamed Aly d'après les archives russes en Égypte*. 4 vols. Cairo: Société Royale de Géographie d'Égypte, 1931–1936.

Conover, Helen. *Egypt and the Anglo-Egyptian Sudan: A Selective Guide to Background Reading*. Washington, DC: Library of Congress, 1952.

Coult, Lyman H., Jr., with the assistance of Karim Durzi. *Annotated Research Bibliography of Studies in Arabic, English, and French of the "Fellah" of the Egyptian Nile, 1798–1955*. Coral Gables, FL: University of Miami Press, 1958.

Coury, Melissa. "Further Notes on Research Facilities in the U.A.R.," *Middle East Studies Association Bulletin* V, 2 (May 1971): 92–94.

Crecelius, Daniel. "Archival Sources for Demographic Studies of the Middle East," in *The Islamic Middle East, 700–1900*, edited by Abraham Udovitch. Princeton: Darwin Press, 1981.

________. *Eighteenth Century Egypt: The Arabic Manuscript Sources.* Claremont, CA: Regina Books, 1990.

________. "The Organization of Waqf Documents in Cairo," *International Journal of Middle East Studies* 2 (1971): 266–277.

Deny, Jean. *Sommaire des archives turques du Caire.* Cairo: Institut Français d'Archéologie Orientale du Caire, 1930.

Geddes, Charles L. *An Analytical Guide to the Bibliographies on Modern Egypt and the Sudan (1798–1972).* Denver: American Institute of Islamic Studies, 1972.

Heyworth-Dunne, G. *Select Bibliography on Modern Egypt.* Cairo: Anglo-Egyptian Bookshop, 1952.

Hunter, F. Robert. "The Cairo Archives for the Study of Elites in Modern Egypt," *International Journal of Middle East Studies* 4 (1973): 476–488.

Husayn, Muhammad Ahmad. *al-Wathaiq al-tarikhiyya* (Historical Documents). Cairo: Cairo University Press, 1954.

Hussain, Asaf. *Islamic Movements in Egypt, Pakistan, and Iran: An Annotated Bibliography.* London: Mansell Publishing, 1983.

Ibrahim-Hilmy. *The Literature of Egypt and the Soudan from the Earliest Times to the Year 1885* [i.e., 1887] *Inclusive: A Bibliography.* 2 vols. London: Trubner and Co., 1886–87; Nendelin, Liechtenstein: Kraus Reprint, Ltd., 1966.

Makar, Ragai N. *Egypt.* World Bibliographical Series, vol. 86. Oxford: Clio Press, 1988.

Mansur, Ahmad Muhammad, and others. *Dalil al-matbu'at al-misriyya, 1940–1956* ("Guide to Egyptian Publications, 1940–1956"). Cairo: American University in Cairo Press, 1975.

Maunier, Henri. *Bibliographie économique, juridique, et sociale de l'Égypte moderne, 1798–1916.* Cairo: Institut Français d'Archéologie Orientale du Caire, 1918.

Mikdadi, Faysal. *Gamal Abdel Nasser: A Bibliography.* Westport, CT: Greenwood Press, 1991.

Miller, E. Willard and Ruby. *The Third World–Egypt: A Bibliography.* Public Administration Series: Bibliography #P2972. Monticello, IL: Vance Bibliographies, 1990.

Nahoum, Haim. *Receuil de firmans impériaux Ottomans adressés aux valis et aux khédives d'Égypte.* Cairo: Institut Français d'Archéologie Orientale, 1934.

Nusayr, Aida Ibrahim. *al-Kutub al-arabiyya allati nushirat fi Misr bayn 1900–1925* ("Arabic Books Published in Egypt between 1900 and 1925"). Cairo: American University in Cairo Press, 1983.

________. *al-Kutub al-arabiyya allati nushirat fi Misr bayn 1926–1940* ("Arabic Books Published in Egypt between 1926 and 1940"). Cairo: American University in Cairo Press, 1983.

Pratt, Ida A. *Modern Egypt: A List of References to Materials in the New York Public Library.* New York: New York Public Library, 1929 (reprinted 1969).

Raccagni, Michelle. *The Modern Arab Woman: A Bibliography.* Metuchen, NJ, and London: Scarecrow Press, 1978.

Rivlin, Helen Anne B. *The "Dar al-Wathaiq" in Abdin Palace as a Source for the Modernization of Egypt in the Nineteenth Century.* Leiden: E. J. Brill, 1970.

Roemer, H.H. "Über Urkunden zur Geschichte Ägyptens und Persiens in islamischer Zeit," *Zeitschrift der Deutschen Morgenländischen Gesellschafts* 107 (1957): 519–538.

Sarkis, Yusuf Ilyas. *Mu'jam al-matbu'at al-arabiyya wa al-mu'arraba* ("Bibliography of Publications in Arabic and Translated into Arabic"). 2 vols. Cairo: Sarkis, 1928.

al-Sayyid-Marsot, Afaf Lutfi. "Egyptian Historical Research and Writing on Egypt in the 20th Century," *Middle East Studies Association Bulletin*, VII, 2 (May 1973): 1–15.

Shaw, Stanford J. "Cairo's Archives and the History of Ottoman Egypt," *Report on Current Research, Spring, 1956*. Washington, DC: Middle East Institute, 1956.

al-Shurbaji, Muhammad Jamal al-Din. *Qaima bi-awail al-matbu'at al-arabiyya al-mahfuza bi-Dar al-Kutub hatta sanat 1862 M* ("List of the Earliest Arabic Printed Materials Held by the Egyptian National Library, to 1862 CE"). Cairo: Matba'at Dar al-Kutub, 1963.

Silverburg, Sanford R. *Middle East Bibliography*. Scarecrow Area Bibliographies, no. 1. Metuchen, NJ, and London: Scarecrow Press, 1992.

Williams, John A. "Research Facilities in the U.A.R.," *Middle East Studies Association Bulletin* IV, 2 (15 May 1970): 47–54.

Zaki, Abdel Rahman. *A Bibliography of the Literature of the City of Cairo*. Cairo: Société de Géographie d'Égypte, 1964.

Periodicals

American Research Center in Egypt, Newsletter. Princeton and New York, 1950- . Semiannually.

Asian and African Studies. Jerusalem and Haifa, 1967- . Three times per year.

Cahiers d'Histoire Égyptienne. Cairo, 1948- . Irregular.

L'Égypte Contemporaine. Cairo, 1910- . Quarterly.

International Journal of Middle East Studies. New York and Tucson, AZ, 1970- . Quarterly.

Journal of the American Research Center in Egypt. New York, 1962- . Annually.

al-Majalla al-Tarikhiyya al-Misriyya. Cairo, 1950- . Annually.

Middle East Journal. Washington, DC, 1947- . Quarterly.

Middle East Studies Association Bulletin. New York and Tucson, AZ, 1977-. Semiannually.

Middle Eastern Affairs. New York, 1950–63.

Middle Eastern Studies. London, 1964- . Quarterly.

WEIGHTS AND MEASURES

For scientific and most other purposes, the metric system is used in modern Egypt. Some older units of area and weight are still used, however, and may appear in this dictionary. Their English and metric equivalents are as follows:

1 feddan	1.038 acres	4,201 sq meters
1 cantar of cotton	99 lb	45 kg
1 metric cantar of cotton	110 lb	50 kg
1 ardeb of cottonseed	2.7 cantars	
1 ardeb of wheat	330 lb	150 kg*
1 ardeb of maize	305 lb	140 kg*
1 dariba of rice	2,050 lb	935 kg*
1 uqqa	2.75 lb	1.248 kg
1 rotl	0.99 lb	449 grams
1 barrel of oil	42 gallons	158.97 liters

*approximate figure

MILITARY RANKS

Egyptian ranks followed the nineteenth-century Ottoman pattern. The titles, mainly Turkish in origin, were not changed until after the 1952 Revolution.

Turco-Egyptian Ranks	Modern Egyptian Ranks	U.S. Army Equivalents
mushir	*qaid amm*	5-star general
	fariq awwal	4-star general
fariq	*amid*	lieutenant general
mirmiran	*liwa*	major general
miriliva	*amid*	brigadier general
mirilay	*aqid*	colonel
qaimaqam	*muqaddam*	lieutenant colonel
bimbashi	*raid*	major
sagh	*za'im*	captain
yuzbashi	*mulazim awwal*	first lieutenant
	mulazim	second lieutenant
shawish	*raqib*	sergeant
onbashi	*naib arif*	corporal
askari	*jundi*	private

ABOUT THE AUTHOR

Arthur Goldschmidt, Jr. (B.A., Colby College; M.A. and Ph.D., Harvard University), is Professor of Middle East History and Chair of the Middle East Studies Committee at the Pennsylvania State University, where he has taught since 1965. He has held fellowships from the American Research Center in Egypt and the Fulbright Commission to conduct research in the modern history of Egypt.

Dr. Goldschmidt is the author of *A Concise History of the Middle East*, a textbook that has gone through four editions, and of *Modern Egypt: The Formation of a Nation-State*. He has also published an annotated translation of the memoirs and diaries of Muhammad Farid, the Egyptian nationalist leader, and his dissertation on Egyptian nationalism was translated into Arabic and published in Cairo. He has written numerous articles and reviews of books pertaining to the modern Middle East and is currently the editor of the Arab Middle East volume of the *Dictionary of Twentieth Century Culture*, to be published by Gale Research.

As a professor at Penn State, he has received five awards for outstanding teaching and advising, including an honorable mention in the first Professor of the Year contest sponsored by the Council for the Advancement and Support of Education.